Chanting Down Babylon

Chanting

Down Babylon

The Rastafari Reader

Edited by
NATHANIEL SAMUEL MURRELL,
WILLIAM DAVID SPENCER,
and
ADRIAN ANTHONY McFARLANE

CLINTON CHISHOLM,
Consulting Editor

TEMPLE UNIVERSITY PRESS ▉T▉ PHILADELPHIA

Temple University Press, Philadelphia 19122
Copyright © 1998 by Temple University
All rights reserved
Published 1998
Printed in the United States of America

Interior design by Erin Kirk New

♾ The paper used in this publication meets the requirements of American
National Standard for Information Sciences—Permanence of Paper for Printed
Library Materials, ANSI Z39.48–1984

Library of Congress Cataloging-in-Publication Data

Chanting down Babylon : the Rastafari reader / edited by Nathaniel Samuel
    Murrell, William David Spencer, and Adrian Anthony McFarlane.
        p.   cm.
    Includes bibliographical references and index.
    ISBN 1-56639-583-6 (cloth : alk. paper).
    ISBN 1-56639-584-4 (pbk. : alk. paper)
        1. Rastafari movement.   I. Murrell, N. Samuel.   II. Spencer,
    William David, 1947– .   III. McFarlane, Adrian Anthony, 1946– .
    BL2532.R37C43   1998
    299′ .676—dc21   97-25810

Contents

Part III. Back-o-Wall to Hollywood: The Rasta Revolution through the Arts

Part IV. Religion: Livity, Hermeneutics, and Theology

Acknowledgments

The editors owe a special thanks to our consulting editor, Clinton Chisholm, for his resourcefulness in obtaining vital archival material in Jamaica and for serving in a mediatory role between our Jamaican contributors and the U.S.-based editors. Since we began consultation on this project at the University of the West Indies in 1994, the Honorable Rex Nettleford, vice-chancellor of the University and Professor Barry Chevannes, dean of the College of Arts and Sciences, have offered seasoned advice and allowed us access to vital resources, a testimony to their long-standing commitment to educating the world about Caribbean peoples and, especially, Rastafarian culture. We are also indebted to Professor Nettleford, editor of *Caribbean Quarterly,* for granting us permission to revise and reprint Chevannes's very valuable essay. The Jamaica Publishers have been very gracious in permitting us to revise and publish in one chapter two essays from the *Jamaica Journal,* and to publish Professor George E. Simpson's invaluable reflections on his research into Rastafari.

Several other scholars, such as Maureen Rowe, Professor Carole D. Yawney of York University, Toronto, and Professor Leonard Barrett, have offered valuable suggestions that have contributed to this book's success. We will forever be grateful to Janet M. Francendese, executive editor of Temple University Press, for reading the early drafts of the chapters and offering invaluable comments and suggestions on style and format, as well as other technical professional advice that gave the book its present shape. We are also grateful to colleagues in the Department of Philosophy and Religion at The University of North Carolina at Wilmington (Don Habibi, Thomas Schmid, Maurice Stanley, and Carol Thysell) for reading and offering invaluable comments on final drafts of the chapters. The American Academy of Religion and the College of Wooster (Ohio), who provided much of the seed money for Nathaniel Samuel Murrell's research on the Rastafarians, will be proud of their investment in this project, as will Gordon Conwell Theological Seminary for ancillary support.

The following is an incomplete list of persons and organizations to whom we owe credit: David "Ziggy" Marley; Kathy Gillis of Virgin Records; L. McLeary; Tim Erdel, former librarian of the Caribbean Graduate School of Theology (CGST) at Kingston; CGST president Dieumeme Noelliste; Drs. Freeman Barton and Meredith Klein, Jr., of Gordon-Conwell Theological Seminary Library, Boston; Marge Spencer, head librarian of CGST Library; Tony Rebel; Pam Turbov; Pamela J. C. Hart; Julie Michailow and

Rikki Betts of Fast Lane Productions; Dr. Peter Kamakaiwiwoole; Bankie Banks, Marvin Gilmore, and the Western Front (Boston); Dr. Edward Osei-Bonsu (Accra); Andrea Madden (Mali); Kurt and Shirley Decker-Lucke; Majek Fashek; Lucinda Fluerant of Interscope Records; the Prisoners of Conscience; Neil Lifton, Ron Seiko, Gloria Rainwater, and the staff at Loon Mountain Park (New Hampshire); Victor Essiet of the Mandators; Salem (Massachusetts) Record Exchange; Rich and the Record Rack; Maria Hitchens and the Ambiente Art Gallery of Montego Bay; Charlene and Free World Music; Ansel Caridland of the Meditations; Garrett Vandermolen and Heartbeat Records; Barbara Blake Hannah; Andrew Tosh; Samantha Glynne; Derrick Simpson, Don Carlos, and Garth Dennis of Black Uhuru; Nicole and Boonoononos Staff; Angela Lang of Mesa/Blue Moon; Dr. John Aboyeji; Dr. Femi Adeyema; Dr. Billy Graham; Stephanie Wills; Billy Bennight and Frontline/Diamonte; Carolyn Kelly and the Middle East (Boston); Jasmin Sung; Dr. Madhukar Shah; Heidi Hudson; Kenneth Arnold; WERS Radio (Boston); Richard DeBacher; Betty Foster of Chatham Cottages (Montego Bay); Stu Burns of the American School of Music (Peabody, Massachusetts); Marlon Caato of *Bossa* magazine (Boston); Caetano Veloso; the New England Conservatory of Music.

A manuscript is incomplete until the copyeditor goes over it with a fine-tooth comb. We are most grateful for the razor-sharp eyes of copyeditor Joanna Lee Mullins, whose penchant for accuracy, clarity, and consistency of style makes this anthology delightful reading.

A final note of gratitude is owed to the following persons: Dr. Aida Besancon Spencer of Gordon Conwell Theological Seminary, who did consulting editing work on several chapters and painstakingly made the first scoring of the index; Elizabeth Lynn, a student at Gordon Conwell, who completed the scoring of the manuscript and transferred to cards the hundreds of entries for the index; and Shirley Houston, a student, who with the full support of her Dean for Academic Affairs, Dr. Dorothy Chappell of Gordon College, typed the index in record time.

Chanting Down Babylon

Introduction:
The Rastafari Phenomenon

NATHANIEL SAMUEL MURRELL

Seldom has such a relatively small cultural phenomenon as Rastafari attracted so much attention from young people, the media, and scholars in the fields of religion, anthropology, politics, and sociology. The signature long, natty dreads on the heads of Rastafarians, who fearlessly chant down Babylon (Western political and economic domination and cultural imperialism) with the help of reggae music, make Rastafari a highly visible movement and "one of the most powerful cultural forces among youths in Jamaica"[1] and in countries around the world where one least expects to find elements of Afro-Caribbean culture. Between the 1930s and the 1950s, few people bothered to study the significance of the political and ideological concepts in Rastafarian culture. Even Jamaicans who may have understood the philosophy of the movement regarded Rastafari as another passing fad, which would die a natural death once the novelty wore off.[2] Former Rastafarian and practicing psychologist Leahcim Tefani Semaj noted that during this phase of the movement, the dominant public opinion toward the Rastafarians was "The damn Rasta dem, wey de Rasta dem want, we just put dem in a damn boat and put dem out in the sea and sink the boat—say dem want go Africa!"[3]

Prior to the 1970s, images of the unsanitary-looking, marijuana-smoking "Natty Dread" with unkempt dreadlocks, often controlling crime-infested streets of Kingston, New York City, or London were the most common perceptions of Rastafarian culture. These stereotypes still persist today among some people in the Caribbean, the United States, and Great Britain. Since the early 1970s, however, Rastafari (the movement's self-styled name) has been recognized not only as one of the most popular Afro-Caribbean religions of the late twentieth century, gaining even more popularity than Voodoo, but also as one of the leading cultural trends in the world; as such, it demands attention from those who study the religions of people who live at the economic and political margins of Western society. A June 1997 estimate puts the number of practicing Rastafarians worldwide at one million,[4] with more than twice that number of sympathizers and many million more reggae fans. Given its humble beginnings and the unfriendly climate in which Rastafari was born, none of its founders could have dreamed of such international exposure and acceptance.

What is it about this movement—developing in the slums of West Kingston, Jamaica—that makes it so appealing to people of very different nationalities, ethnic backgrounds, socioeconomic standings, and academic interests? Rastafari has invited myriad questions in popular culture and the academy, especially as part of the recent surge of interest in this once "insignificant" twentieth-century phenomenon. Among the issues addressed herein are the basic doctrinal beliefs of Rastafarians and how they differ from Christian beliefs; why Rastafarians are so hostile to Christianity but so dependent on Christian traditions in developing their ideology, teachings, and cultic practices; whether a relationship exists between Rastafari and the Ethiopian Orthodox Church, and how African Rastafari is; what inspired Rastas in the first place to make Haile Selassie such a towering figure and deity in the movement, and whether his divinity and kingship are still central to Rastafarian thought; what the role of women is in this overtly patriarchal and "chauvinist" movement; whether the Rastafarians are a religious group or a political organization, dopers supporting (or running) drug cartels under the guise of religion or authentic religious devotees; whether Rastas are anti-white prophets, preaching a doctrine of reverse racism and hate in society, or social critics; and what it means for Rastas to "chant down Babylon," and who or what Babylon is.

Who or What Is Rastafari?

In *Chanting Down Babylon,* we use the terms *Rastafari,*[5] *Rastafarians,* and *Rastas* synonymously. The nomenclature *Rastafari,* with or without the definite article, describes the movement as a collective whole, and the combined expression "Jah Ras Tafari" refers specifically to Emperor Haile Selassie I, the deity. Rastas often replace the title *Jah* with *Rastafari,* a designation coined by the early founders of the movement (especially Leonard Howell), who recognized Emperor Haile Selassie I—*Ras Tafari,* an imperial title used by Ethiopian emperors—as divine. Rastas often argue that every true black person is "Rasta," a category that suggests unity and connectedness to Africa rather than cultic or religious affiliation. Seretha Rycenssa of Jamaica defined a "true Rasta" as one who "believes in the deity of the Ethiopian monarch . . . , sees black liberationist Marcus Mosiah Garvey as his prophet . . . , sticks to [his] path, does not shave, cut or straighten the hair, rejects the customs of 'Babylon' society," and "looks on his blackness and sees that it is good and struggles to preserve it."[6] Not included among these, of course, are persons whom Rex Nettleford calls "designer dreads"—middle-class youths and yuppies who adopt the dreadlocks hairstyle, carry a "ragamuffin" appearance, and listen to reggae music but have no commitment to the teachings of Rastafari.[7] Nor do the brethren (Rastafarians) regard as true Rastas persons they call "wolves in sheep's clothing" or "rascals" and "impostors"—unsavory characters who hide behind "the locks" (dreadlocks) and "Rasta looks" (Rasta appearance) in order to commit crime and smoke marijuana. Rastas or Rastafarians are, therefore, followers of Ras Ta-fari or persons who believe in the Rastafari ideology.

Notwithstanding these simple explanations, Rastafari defies traditional ways of con-ceiving, being, and knowing. As a result, many researchers and media persons have been unsuccessful in their attempts to pigeonhole the movement into preconceived, stereo-typical categories, such as "religious cult"; "escapist movement"; "reactionary, anachronistic, eccentric Judeo-Christian heresy"; "apocalyptic Christian movement"; "messianic millennial cult"; "African-Caribbean religious myth"; and "West Indian Mafia" in England—or, as Claudia Rogers recorded with approbation, "religious fa-natics," a "nuisance [and] an embarrassment to the Jamaican people, or [even] treach-erous criminals who should be jailed or hung for their traitorous acts against Jamaican society."[8] The hit movie *Marked for Death*, regarded in Jamaica and among Jamaican Americans as anti-Jamaican and anti-Rastafari, "identifies Rasta characters as a brutal segment of the Jamaican 'posse' and links Rastafarians with obeahism." Hollywood has thus "further embedded the stereotype in the American psyche."[9]

To make the task of defining the movement more challenging, a few Rastas have also spoken about Rastafari as though it is a reform movement within Christianity. Rasta-farian *sistren* (the term is always used in the plural) Imani Nyah says, "We are African-centered Christians who proclaim that Ethiopia is Judah, and that Christ was mani-fested in the person of His Imperial Majesty Haile Selassie."[10] In a letter to the Jamaica *Sunday Herald*, another sistren and political activist, Barbara Blake-Hannah, noted quite correctly that "members of the Ethiopian Orthodox Church are Christians" and that "the Church proudly claims to be a strong and founding member of denomina-tional Christianity." But then she added, "Among them are many persons who have come to see Christ through Rastafari. Indeed, the words *Ras (Tafari)* mean head = Christ, and, therefore, any man who claims that he is a Ras, must identity himself with Christ," for "Haile Selassie means: Power of the Trinity, which Trinity is the Father, the Son and the Holy Spirit."[11] Responding to an article by Alex Walker titled "The Other Side of Rasta History," which appeared in the lead section of an earlier issue of the *Sun-day Herald*, Blake-Hannah refuted Walker's claim that Rastas are not Christians and that "the most they can hope for is to be able to function within the communion of Christianity." She rebutted, "That is precisely what Rastafari do, who are members of the Ethiopian Orthodox Church. . . . The dreadlocks of the Rastafarian who feels him-self/herself drawing close to God through the Christ within [them], is a direct link through the unknown of time, to this Ethiopian Orthodox Church priestly habit."[12]

While the Rastafarian ideology contains elements of some of the above characteriza-tions, they are all limiting stereotypes—and in many cases, uninformed misrepresenta-tions—that do not grasp the movement's definitive character and ethos. For example, Rastafarians, whose theology is rooted in Judeo-Christian scriptures, have a very strong millenialist orientation; they believe in the possibility of social, political, and religious reform. As Claudia Rogers says, the movement can be considered "millennial in the sense that brethren constantly refer to a hoped for period of peace, joy and justice." That is, "typical of other groupings . . . which stress the dream of the millennium, Rastafarians stress positive change" in a variety of tenets.[13] The belief in an imminent, this-worldly, total salvation wherein the white world and its oppressive political institutions will fall, after which Blacks will reign in the new millennium, is only one of those tenets. To limit the still-evolving Afro-Caribbean phenomenon only to Christian ideas of an apocalyptic end of the world is, therefore, nearsighted and misinformed.

There is no denying that Rastafari is a legitimate religion for legal purposes (with regard to religious freedom), as recognized in Jamaica, Great Britain, the United States, and other countries. Recently, three federal appellate judges of the U.S. Court of Appeals for the Ninth Circuit in San Francisco reversed a marijuana possession conviction of Rastafarian Cameron Best of Billings, Montana, "citing violations of the 1993 Religious Freedom Restoration Act (RFRA)." More specifically, the judges argued that "Best's use of marijuana as a Rastafarian sacrament was largely and wrongly proscribed by the lower court as an element in his defense." The ruling may imply that as soon as Rastas prove that their marijuana use is part of their religious sacrament, they may not be guilty of criminal activity. But it also establishes that the U.S. government is following an earlier action by the British government—after Rastafarian clashes with the British "Bulldogs" in 1977 in Handsworth, Birmingham, which led ultimately to the Brixton riot of 1981—in recognizing and protecting the religious liberty of Rastafarians.[14]

In spite of Rastafari's religious character and the attempt to make it a reform Christian movement, it is neither a Christian nor an African traditional religion; it is a *tertium quid,* a different kind or religious species among New World (if not New Age)[15] or nontraditional religions, one that is distinctly Caribbean.[16] Like its antecedents within the African diaspora—such as Voodoo (*Voudou*) in Haiti and New Orleans; Santeria in Cuba; Yoruba, Kaballah, and Orisha in Trinidad and Tobago; Shango in Grenada; and Candomble in Brazil—Rastafari is a modern Afro-Caribbean cultural phenomenon that combines concepts from African culture and the "Caribbean experience" (social, historical, religious and economic realities) with Judeo-Christian thought into a new sociopolitical and religious worldview. So while Rastafarian beliefs and practices are influenced by such Africanisms in Jamaican culture as Myalism, convince cult, revivalism (Zion), Bedwardism, Pocomania,[17] and Burru (all Afro-Jamaican religious and cultural traditions), Rastafari's rise and ethos are driven by social, economic, and political forces in the region.

In this regard, Rastafari is more than a religion. It is a cultural movement, "a system of beliefs and a state of consciousness,"[18] that advances a view of economic survival and political organization and structure that challenges the dominant cultural political "narrative" (ideology) in the "politics of Babylon." According to Carole Yawney, Rastafari is "a constellation of ambiguous symbols which today has the power to focalize and even mediate certain socio-cultural tensions that have developed on a global scale."[19]

Rastas regard themselves as members of a legitimate religious movement and a cultural revolution for world peace, racial harmony, and social, economic, and political reform. Two of the Rastas' stated policies of the 1960s were: "To promote educational progress of the African continent, its languages, culture and history," and "To recognize the hurt suffered by the Continent of Africa through colonialism and to devote time and energy towards the development of Africa by all possible contributions."[20] As Semaj noted, the Rastafarians shared other concerns:

> All the brethren wanted local recognition and freedom of movement and speech, which are essential human rights. All wanted an end of persecution by government and police. Some brethren wanted improved material, social and economic conditions until repatriation. Some brethren wanted educational provisions, including adult education and technical training, and employment. Some brethren suggested that a special fund be established. Others asked for a radio program to tell Jamaica about their doctrine, and some asked for press facilities.[21]

Essentially, the Rastafarians are "Africanists" who are engaged in consciousness-raising with regard to African heritage, black religion, black pride, and being in the world. This African-centered ideology is a form of "conscientizing" that draws attention to the distortions of African history in the various forms of literature, which tend to obscure the continent's contribution to the origin of Western civilization. Long before the term *Afrocentricity* came into popular use in the United States, Jamaican Rastafarians had embraced the concept as the most important recipe for naming their reality and reclaiming their black heritage in the African diaspora. Rastas reserve the right to think, know, name, reinterpret, and define their "essence and existence" in nontraditional categories. Their consciousness of who they are determines their "Being" relative to naming and being in the world. (That is, one defines and authenticates one's existence as a matter of primary concern and then names oneself and one's world in relation to that mode of consciousness.)

What Do Rastas Believe?

Prior to the mid-1970s, Rasta believers supported the following major themes and doctrinal tenets: belief in the beauty of black people's African heritage; belief that Ras Tafari Haile Selassie I, emperor of Ethiopia, is the living God and black Messiah; belief in repatriation to Ethiopia, qua Africa, the true home and redemption of black people, as "having been foretold and . . . soon to occur"; the view that "the ways of the white men are evil, especially for the black" race; belief in "the apocalyptic fall of Jamaica as Babylon, the corrupt world of the white man," and that "once the white man's world crumbles, the current master/slave pattern [of existence] will be reversed."[22] Jah Ras Tafari will overthrow or destroy the present order, and Rastafarians and other Blacks will be the benefactors of that destruction; they will reign with Jah in the new kingdom.

In 1973, Joseph Owens published a concise, ten-point summary of Rastafarian theology, which the Guyanese clergyman Michael N. Jagessar rehashed in 1991. These theological themes are: "the humanity of God and, correspondingly, the divinity of man"—that God's divinity is revealed through the humanity of the God-man Haile Selassie I, "God is man and man is God"; "God is to be found in every man," but "there must be one man in whom he exists most eminently and completely, and that is the

supreme man, Rastafari, Selassie I"; the "historicality of the experience of God's workings"—that historical facts must be seen in the light of the judgment and workings of
God; the "terrestriality of salvation"—that salvation is earthly; the "supremacy of
life"—that human beings are called to celebrate and protect life; the "efficacy of the
word"—that the spoken word as a manifestation of the divine presence and power can
create and bring destruction; "the corporate dimension of evil"—that sin is both personal and corporate, so that "corporations and economic powers like the International
Monetary Fund" must be held responsible for Jamaica's fiscal problems; the "immi-
nence of judgment"; the "sacramentality of nature"—that human beings are called to
protect the environment by conserving energy, reducing pollution, and eating natural
foods; and "the priesthood of Rastas"—that the brethren are the chosen people of Jah
to manifest God's power and promote peace in the world.[23]

While Rastafarians, by their very nature, are not a homogeneous group, true believers subscribe to the most important Rasta doctrine, that Haile Selassie I is the living
God. Many Rastas still regard Haile Selassie as Christ, the black Messiah whose
promised return or "second coming" the emperor fulfills; Selassie is seen as a living de-
scendent of King Solomon and the King of Kings, Lord of Lords, Conquering Lion of
the Tribe of Judah, and Elect of God. But since the "disappearance"[24] (according to
Rastas) of Selassie and the popular acceptance of Rastafarian culture in Jamaica in the
mid-1970s, Rastafari has shown modest change in some of its theological and ideological concepts. For example, brethren have reinterpreted the doctrine of repatriation
as voluntary migration to Africa, returning to Africa culturally and symbolically, or rejecting Western values and preserving African roots and black pride. The idea that "the
white man is evil" has also become less prominent in later Rastafarian thought, and
the concept of Babylon has broadened to include all oppressive and corrupt systems of
the world.

Under the influence of some articulate sistren, since the early 1980s many brethren
and Rasta camps have had to reevaluate their patriarchal view of sexuality. Rastafari
sistren are becoming more vocal and active in the movement, especially in the Twelve
Tribes of Israel (one of the recent influential groups in Rastafari), than they were before
1980. Rastas have also shown a greater social and political involvement in Jamaican society than they did before the Michael Manley (former prime minister of Jamaica) era
of the 1970s. Some developments no doubt were influenced by change in the public perception of and attitude toward Rastafari, the "disappearance" of Selassie, the international acceptance of Rastafari via Bob Marley and reggae, and the improved social and
economic status of some of the believers.

Why the International Surge of Rastafari?

Several incidents occurred in the first twenty years of the movement that gave Rastafari
national publicity. In 1930 the would-be founders of Rastafari capitalized on the publicity surrounding the coronation of Ras Tafari as emperor of Ethiopia, broadcast on

the British Broadcasting Corporation (BBC) and national and international television networks. By building its fundamental doctrines around Ethiopianism and the coronation of Ras Tafari Makonnen (Haile Selassie I), Rastafari attracted the attention of many critics throughout Jamaica and Ethiopia. At first the Jamaican public brushed aside as a Christian heresy the theological claims Rastas made about Selassie and saw the idea of repatriation as wishful thinking among the uneducated. But when Leonard Howell and his followers began having encounters with law-enforcement officials in 1933—especially when Howell sold five thousand postcards of Selassie as passports to Ethiopia—the *Daily Gleaner,* the *Sunday Guardian,* Jamaica Broadcasting Corporation (JBC), and other media frequently covered Rastafari in the daily news.

When the Italians invaded Ethiopia in 1936, Blacks in Jamaica, the United States, Britain, and Africa protested against Benito Mussolini's imperialism and raised funds to support the underground resistance fighters. The Jamaican Rastafarians even appealed to the British government to rescind a law that prevented Jamaicans from joining the Ethiopian army to repel the invaders from the "promised land." So strong was the pro-Selassie sentiment among Blacks in the West that it resulted in the Ethiopian World Federation (EWF) organizing chapters in Harlem, New York, in 1937 and in Detroit, Michigan, and Kingston, Jamaica, in 1938. The Rastafarians who were closely associated with the EWF became known for their uncompromising chant against the Italian Babylon in the Ethiopian political struggle. When Selassie successfully drove the Italians out of Ethiopia in 1941,[25] the media publicized the Rastafarians' celebration of the event. That same year Rastas got added attention when the police raided Howell's commune at Pinnacle Hill and arrested many of his followers on charges of marijuana growing and violence.[26] Again, the negative publicity from the media gave the Rastafarians added exposure as they gained strength among Jamaica's dispossessed.

According to Leonard Barrett, at least five significant events brought the Rastafarian movement into national and international prominence during the 1950s and early 1960s: the EWF's increased activity in Jamaica in 1953; the Rastafarians' 1958 convention; Rasta-leader national emergencies in 1959 and 1960; the University of the West Indies' interest in the movement in 1960; and Jamaican delegations to African countries in 1961 and 1962.[27] In 1955 the media brought the Rastafarians into the international spotlight when a delegation from the EWF in Harlem told some Jamaicans that Selassie was building ships that would sail to American and Jamaican ports in order to transport Rastas to Ethiopia, and that His Majesty had decided to set aside a large acreage of land for repatriated black people from the West. In spite of the quixotic nature of the rumor, the enormous cost of transport, and the many obstacles to migrating to Africa, the call "created an atmosphere of great excitement and expectancy"[28] among many who wanted immediate repatriation. In 1956 hundreds of Jamaicans "were seen at the port in Kingston awaiting the arrival of a ship which would transport them to Ethiopia," and "in 1959, thousands of black Jamaicans, following the Rastafarians, sold all they had to obtain a ticket for a passage to Ethiopia from Claudius Henry."[29] The press found these events highly amusing and gave the Rastafarians more publicity than they could have given themselves.

The Rastafarians gained new strength and exposed many aspects of the movement to the public when they attempted to organize their various factions into a united body in 1958. Emboldened by the publicity from the convention and their sense of solidarity and strength, three-hundred bearded Rastas gathered at Victoria Park in Kingston in March 1958 and announced a takeover of Jamaica. Three months later, several Rastas and their families daringly occupied Old King's House, the governor's house, in the name of Negus Negusta.[30] The shedding of Rastafari's benign persona in the sudden appearance of a military front exacerbated the tension and clashes between law enforcement and the Rastas. In 1959, when the police raided Claudius Henry's headquarters and found "2,500 electrical detonators, 1,300 detonators, a shotgun, a caliber .32 revolver, a large quantity of machetes sharpened [on] both sides like swords and laced in sheaths, cartridges, several sticks of dynamite, and other articles,"[31] Rastas were condemned nationally in the Jamaican media. After Henry was convicted of treason and given a six-year prison sentence, his son, Ronald, collaborated with some hard-core Rastas who had military training and mounted an attack against the government of Premier Norman Manley. The rebellion had to be repelled by more than one thousand men, including soldiers from the British regiment stationed in the region and Jamaican police, aircraft, and mortar and rocket crews.[32] The BBC, the *Times,* national television, and other media reported these incidents, and Rastafari became internationally infamous.

The Claudius and Ronald Henry incidents startled many Jamaicans and the academy, which "called for an in-depth inquiry into the beliefs, aims, and aspirations of the movement."[33] The 1960 University College of the West Indies (now UWI) study found that, since the 1940s, the Rastafarians had become popular among large numbers of the disfranchised, poor, unemployed, hopeless, and belligerent youths of the Jamaican underclass—persons who felt they were left behind by the colonial government and its supposed progress toward Jamaican nationalism and independence. The strange image of unkempt clothes and dreadlocks (or natty dreads), "the phenomenon of rudeboy," and the spirit of militant protest[34] made Rastafari rather appealing to the dispossessed. Finally, in 1960, Premier Norman Manley's government took a sympathetic posture toward the Rastafarian cause on the question of repatriation to African countries. Although in 1962, when the Jamaican government changed hands, the repatriation program was shelved,[35] public curiosity and the new understanding that the 1960 UWI study engendered were contributing to the growing popularity of the Rastafarians among the youth. Even the mass arrests of Rastas in 1963 as a result of the Coral Gardens incident in Montego Bay, in which Rasta leader Claudius Henry was again charged with treason (see Chapter 2 by Clinton Hulton and Nathaniel Samuel Murrell and Chapter 3 by Barry Chevannes), did not dissuade inquirers from becoming Rastas or sympathizing with their cause.

The visit of Emperor Haile Selassie to Kingston in 1966 gave the Rastafarians unprecedented publicity and created a sustained national and international interest in the movement. Jamaicans greeted the royal personage with such enthusiasm that devotion to Ethiopia, qua Africa, and to Selassie rivaled, and appeared to threaten, the rising Jamaican nationalism and patriotism. According to Rex Nettleford, such strong feelings were engendered toward Africa that "one month after the Royal visit, a member of the Jamaican Senate gave notice of a Motion that the Jamaican Constitution be amended to make the Emperor of Ethiopia, H.I.M. Haile Selassie, the king of Jamaica in place of the Queen Elizabeth II of the United Kingdom."[36] This catapulted the Rastafari movement into the spotlight and allowed its medals to shine in the light of international publicity.[37]

When Michael Manley's People's National Party (PNP) came to power in 1972, the Rastafari again received support and strong political endorsement from both the new prime minister of Jamaica (1972–1980) and his party. The flamboyant and charismatic British-educated mulatto spared no effort to portray himself as antiestablishment, pro-black, grassroots, or a "roots man" of the suffering Jamaican masses. During the election, Manley used the Rastafarian flag, colors, slogans, signs, and music and quoted the Dreads in his public speeches to win votes. (It is also believed that Rastas helped Manley win a resounding second-term victory at the polls in 1976.)[38] Sometime after the 1972 election, Manley visited a "dunghill" (a Rasta commune) to solicit the help of Rasta leaders in the government's attempt to deal with the problem of youth violence. Manley's government gave such prestige to the Rastafarian movement that dreadlocks became the "in thing" in Jamaica in the 1970s.[39] From the early 1970s, the Rasta persona ceased to be the exclusive domain of the underclass and became, instead, a fashion trend among the youths of the Caribbean middle class and Blacks in Britain, Canada, and the United States.

The Rastafarian movement gained such strength and popularity that the "disappearance" of Haile Selassie I in 1975 only strengthened the element of mythmaking and mystery in its religious cultus and contributed to its broader circulation in the Caribbean media. According to Leonard Barrett, "The large number of representatives from the Eastern Caribbean at the Rastafari Theocratic Assembly (held at the U.W.I., Mona, Jamaica, July 18–25, 1983) was solid evidence that the Rasta movement is now a force throughout the region." Barrett said then, "Rastas from the Eastern Caribbean are a new phenomenon, and they are having serious confrontations with their governments and police." But we should not forget that "several of these movements were established after the death of Haile Selassie," and that "most of those attending the assembly were young, articulate, and revolutionary. . . . There were representatives from Grenada, Dominica, St. Lucia, Guyana, St. Kitts, St. Eustatius, the Grenadines, Barbados, [and] Trinidad and Tobago."[40]

As scholars in this book and elsewhere have demonstrated so accurately, reggae music has been the most powerful force behind the international spread and popularity of Rasta culture. This need not be discussed here—except to mention that in 1978, Nettleford said, "The music has gone beyond fulfilling the universal need for entertainment to attract acute interest in its deep significance for Jamaican and Caribbean cultural search for form and purpose."[41] In many ways, to feel the reggae beat is to think Rasta, as well as to celebrate the life and work of Bob Marley, who made reggae music and Rastafari so internationally accessible. Youths from different parts of the world who understand very little, if any, of Rastafarian culture celebrate its reggae "ridims."

A final reason for the popularity of and international interest in Rastafari—and one that is at the heart of this collaborative work—is that since the mid-1950s, a significant number of scholars from many different countries have increasingly shown interest in this grassroots religious and cultural phenomenon. Although Frank Jan van Dijk is correct in noting, in this anthology and elsewhere, that research on the international dimensions of Rastafari—especially in Europe and the Pacific—is still in its infancy, the literature on the movement in the Americas is most impressive. By November 1996, I had found over 150 substantive publications (books and articles), many unpublished essays read at national and international conferences, and dozens of theses and dissertations on this fascinating movement. Also, there are literally scores of brief commentaries, newspaper editorials, columns, and Web sites on this phenomenon. Important publications are also found in obscure and, sometimes, uncertified sources, several magazines (e.g., *The Beat* and *Reggae Report*), and university and seminary archives; they provide invaluable information to researchers studying Rastafari.

What Is This Book About?

"Come we go chant down Babylon one more time," sang the charismatic Rastafarian reggae musical statesperson Bob Marley in "Chant Down Babylon," a song included on his *Confrontation* album, issued two years after his death.[42] The title of this volume, *Chanting Down Babylon,* did not originate with Marley but is an old Rasta catchword that has come down from the earliest Rasta camps and permeates reggae. It is reflected in such traditional Rasta music as "Rasta Man Chant," recorded by Count Ossie and the Mystic Revelation of Rastafari and popularized by the Wailers. The phrase is echoed in Bunny Wailer's "Ready When You Ready," in which he invites listeners to chant Babylon down in a "rhythm." The Wailers' protégé Freddie MacGregor also fields his own version of "Chant Down Babylon," and Judy Mowatt adapts it as "Sisters' Chant" while Lincoln "Sugar" Minott urges listeners to "Chant Them Down." The list goes on. The title *Chanting Down Babylon* was also given respectability in the academy when Carolyn Cooper published her often-cited essay "Chanting Down Babylon: Bob Marley's Song as Literary Text" in 1986.

How does a marginalized liberation movement from a "little rock"—as the band Third World identified Jamaica in its song "Reggae Ambassador"—beat down Babylon's racism, cultural prejudice, and economic disfranchisement? The Rastas do it by showing political dissonance and cultural resistance; developing a psychology of Blackness and somebodiness; exorcising the demons of racism; rejecting bigotry, classism, and stereotypical ways of being and knowing that are partially encoded in Jamaican folklore; attacking social problems with the creation of a "big, big music," an art that is irresistible and coded with situation-changing messages;[43] and holding onto a messianic hope for the future. Throughout this *Rastafari Reader,* the Rasta mission in society is seen as one of deconstruction and reconstruction, of infusing and thereby replacing society's destructive, negative vibrations with positive ones, and of undermining and altering evil with good.

This book brings together an array of material from the leading scholars in Rastafarian research, whose training is in various fields of the humanities and who cross national boundaries as well as race and gender lines. The book has drawn from both unpublished and published material most of which has not been available to the public, as well as from exclusive interviews and conversations with leading Rastas. *Chanting Down Babylon* therefore provides a full grasp of the Rastafarian ethos: the movement's founding; evolution; successes and failures; belief system; cultic practices; philosophical, psychological, social, and cultural underpinnings; and impact on the society at large.

Part I treats key ideological concepts of the movement to chant down Babylon and the historical, social, and cultural context within which Rastafari arose. Here we show the Rastafarian reasoning, the categories and methodology employed in an attempt to free the African soul in the diaspora from the legacy of colonialism. Sociologist Ennis Edmonds's chapter, "Dread 'I' In-a-Babylon: Ideological Resistance and Cultural Revitalization," provides a concise and easy-to-grasp study of the nature, meaning, and function of the Rastafarian ideology and its mission to chant down Babylon's "economic rapacity, mental slavery, and political trickery." This "Rasta-friendly" interpretation of the Rasta argot and key ideas and concepts sets the tone for the reader-friendly but scholarly nature of the book.

In "Rastas' Psychology of Blackness, Resistance, and Somebodiness," Caribbean scholar Clinton Hutton and Nathaniel Samuel Murrell identify the psychological concepts that enabled Blacks to survive a legacy of oppression in Babylon and that now undergird the Rastafarian ideology. Hutton and Murrell trace the development of the Rasta psychology of resistance, liberation, and redemption through Ethiopianist, Garveyite, and Afro-Caribbean sources. They contend that Rastafarian psychology is Afrocentric and came to birth, over a long period of time, in an oppressive environment in the diaspora that made a black psychology absolutely necessary for the survival of people of African ancestry. This is probably the first publication of its kind on the psychology of Blackness in the Caribbean.

For more than twenty years Barry Chevannes has researched, taught, and written about Rastafari. As Rex Nettleford notes in his chapter, the now leading Caribbean sociologist and premier authority on the Rastafarian phenomenon has published the most definitive work on Rastafarian ethnography to date. Chevannes's engaging "Rastafari and the Exorcism of the Ideology of Racism and Classism in Jamaica" is an invaluable addition to this book. Chevannes analyzes the social, cultural, and political context in which the Rastafarian ideology arose and the impact of the movement on racism in Jamaican culture. He argues that, through its criticism of and cultural resistance to domination and oppression in its myriad forms, Rastafari was very effective in raising racial consciousness, exorcising the demons of creole racism, and forging social and political change in Jamaica during the second half of this century.

The editors of this book are sensitive not only to the issue of gender but also "the insider/outsider controversy" in Rastafarian research and have been careful to listen to voices from within the movement, across gender lines. In addition to the many citations and references to Rastafarian writers in this volume, we are fortunate to present two chapters by the leading Rastafarian "sistren" (sisters) in Jamaica, as well as an interview-essay done by a self-styled Rastafarian, Eleanor Wint, professor at the University of the West Indies, with "brethren."

Maureen Rowe's "Gender and Family Relations in RastafarI: A Personal Perspective" and Imani M. Tafari-Ama's "Rastawoman as Rebel: Case Studies in Jamaica" reflect a growing body of literature on and by women in their attempt to deal with the ideology of patriarchy in Rastafari while collaborating with the brethren in the chant to pull down Babylon. Rowe's beautifully written personal experiences from within the movement and her very articulate and accessible interpretation and analysis of gender issues in Rastafari and the wider Jamaican society, the "rudeboy" phenomenon, the rise of the women's movement in the Caribbean in the 1970s, the impact of women on the Rastafarian movement and new trends among the sistren in the 1990s are unrivaled. Tafari-Ama is another practicing Rastafarian who breaks the unofficial code in Rastafari and "tells it like it is" in the voices of several anonymous informants. With insightful and nuanced critiques and analyses of Rasta ideology, Tafari-Ama exposes several taboo subjects within Rasta patriarchy. She dares to expose the shifting scales of power between brethren and sistren, less-than-savory survival strategies in Rasta families, and issues of sexuality, domestic violence, and classism in Rastafari, which the brethren rarely admit. These two chapters provide a gold mine of ethnographic materials.

Is it appropriate to use hegemonic Western (European) philosophical categories to analyze an anti-European/anti-Western social-cultural movement? Philosopher Adrian Anthony McFarlane, the brother of a practicing Rasta, says yes. McFarlane's "The Epistemological Significance of 'I-an-I' as a Response to Quashie and Anancyism in Jamaican Culture" gives a perceptive analysis of the Rastafarian "I-an-I" locution (Rasta "I" words) in Jamaican speech and demonstrates that one can use European and Greek philosophical categories to analyze issues related to a popular cultural movement in the Caribbean without allowing those categories to determine or control the discourse on Rasta reality. McFarlane provides an insight into Rastafarian philosophy via an epistemological analysis of the attitudinal chant against folklorist Anancy and Quashie stereotypes in the Jamaican culture of Babylon and their attendant biases and challenges to Rastas.

In Part II, Neil J. Savishinsky, Rupert Lewis, and Clinton Chisholm explore vital links between Rastafari, African traditions, Garveyism, and Ethiopia, while Frank Jan van Dijk and Randal L. Hepner take the reader on a tour of the internationalization of Rastafari. "African Dimensions of the Jamaican Rastafarian Movement" is the result of informed ethnographic research in several West African countries by the American sociologist Savishinsky, who has also done substantial work among the Jamaican Rastafarians and whose publications on Rastafari are well known in the field. One is often struck by the family resemblance between the cultural concepts and lexicography in Voodoo, Rastafari, Orisha, and Santeria, on the one hand, and those on the African continent, on the other hand. Savishinsky has found several direct African continuities in the Jamaican Rastafarian chant against Babylon, which demonstrates a vital connection to African cultural traditions that hitherto has not been articulated clearly and accurately.

The extent to which Garveyism influenced Rastafari is the main focus of "Marcus Garvey and the Early Rastafarians: Continuity and Discontinuity." Rupert Lewis, a Marcus Garvey scholar and Jamaican political scientist who also has published several works on the Rastafarians, provides a provocative analysis of the similarities and the not-so-obvious differences between Garveyism and the Rastafarian ideology. Contrary to popular opinion, Lewis argues that the early Rastafarians were not Garveyites and that Marcus Garvey did not embrace the Rastafarian ideology. Yet he admits that Garvey's philosophy had an unmistakable influence on early Rastafarian thought, and that his Universal Negro Improvement Association (UNIA) shares an important part of the historical and cultural genre in which Rastafari arose.

In the English-speaking Caribbean, the Reverend Clinton Chisholm is recognized as the most active and articulate Jamaican apologist in the Rastafarian-Christian dialogue. The British Caribbean–educated clergyman and freelance public speaker conducts workshops throughout the region on Caribbean cultural traditions and Christian thought, in which he applies rigorous critical thinking to the theological debate on Rastafarian and Christian "truth claims." Chisholm's "The Rasta-Selassie Ethiopian Connections," which challenges certain perceptions of the Ethiopian emperor in Rastafarian thought and other issues related to doctrinal beliefs, provides a necessary critical perspective on Rastafari that readers, especially non-Rastas, may find instructive. Chisholm raises critical questions about fundamental beliefs in Rastafari that give a healthy balance to our *Chanting Down Babylon: The Rastafari Reader*.

The Dutch anthropologist Frank Jan van Dijk, who has published a most impressive dissertation on Jamaican Rastafarians, carefully documents the development and spread of the movement in three major corners of the world through the influence of Bob Marley and reggae. In "Chanting Down Babylon Outernational: The Rise of Rastafari in Europe, the Caribbean, and the Pacific," van Dijk argues that even in France, Germany, Portugal, the Netherlands, New Zealand, Australia, and countries in the Far East, where the Rastafari ideology, chant, symbolism, and lifestyle are hardly understood by the fans, white youths fall "head over heels" for the reggae "ridims" and the unorthodox hairstyle and dress. Through immigrants from Suriname and Britain, the Rasta-reggae culture has developed deep roots in the Netherlands and other European countries, either as a lifestyle or as a religion.[44] Van Dijk also provides intriguing historical accounts of the Rastafarian experience in the Caribbean and Britain, where the chant against oppression and marginalization met with vicious and brutal responses from the "Babylon governments."

Since the 1960s, the Rastafarians have formed an important segment of the very large Jamaican population in the United States and are now found in even larger numbers in metropolitan areas. U.S.-born, White Dreadlocks sympathizer Randal Hepner bemoans the fact that, in spite of this growing presence of Rastafarians in the United States, no substantive study hitherto has been done on the movement. Hepner's "Chanting Down Babylon in the Belly of the Beast: The Rastafari Movement in the Metropolitan United States" therefore is essential for studying the internationalization of Rastafari. It provides the first substantive exposure of Americans' perceptions of Rastas; Rastas' encounters with U.S. law-enforcement officials; the movement's organizational structure, practices, and ethos north of Jamaica; and where and how Rastas survive in a less-than-friendly environment.

George Eaton Simpson, professor emeritus at Oberlin College, was the first scholar to conduct serious field research on Rastafari in Jamaica. His chapter "Personal Reflections on Rastafari in West Kingston in the Early 1950s" is therefore an essential contribution to this *Rastafari Reader*. Simpson's eyewitness accounts of activities among the Rastafarians in Trench Town and anecdotes of his experiences corroborate the stories and events retold throughout the book. Another important contribution of this chapter is Simpson's disarming observation that many contemporary Rasta practices, concepts, and phrases—even use of the term *Nyabinghi*—were either not popular among the Rastafari or nonexistent in the early 1950s.

In the spirit of the enigmatic Junior Byles and Delroy Wilson, who call on Rastas to "Chant Down Babylon" and "Beat Down Babylon," Part III examines the Rastafarian mission through the arts to see how Rasta music, art, craft, and film have attempted to hit repressive society with painless change. It provides glimpses of Rastas in the arts so that readers can anticipate the movement's place in the future, as it seeks to follow what it sees as its divine calling: to chant down Babylon's negativity with a positive vibration. Verena Reckord's most informative chapter, "From Burru Drums to Reggae Ridims: The Evolution of Rasta Music," traces the evolution of Rasta music from Burru drums to ska, rock steady, and reggae "ridims." The experienced Jamaican ethnomusicologist notes that early Rastafari had no music of its own, before Count Ossie encountered the Burru people at "Back-o-Wall" in Kingston. But once the brethren learnt the ridims, it was only a matter of time before they hijacked them and made the Burru drums the most important Rasta musical symbol and the heartbeat of reggae for chanting down Babylon worldwide.

This book would not have been complete without a chapter on Mr. Rasta Reggae himself, Bob Marley, who was largely responsible for popularizing Rastafari. We are therefore delighted that leading reggae critic Roger Steffens, the man known as "the honorary member of the Marley family," has written a fine chapter, "Bob Marley: Rasta Warrior," focusing on the "King of Reggae." Digging deep into his vast resources, Steffens shares never-before-published material on this reggae giant and Third World superstar, shedding new light on Marley's mission, context, and self-perception and the growing appreciation of persons who were close to him and those from around the world who cannot get enough of Marley's records.

Most books available on reggae deal primarily with its origins and developments in Jamaica and are usually sketchy on its international impact; they are understandably silent on the place and function of the rest of the Rasta contribution in art. But in this book, William David Spencer expands the existing picture of Rasta in the arts, gathering up primary and secondary source material to trace reggae's global impact while sampling the achievements of Rasta artists in other art forms. Spencer shows that at the same time that Rastas are attempting to destroy Babylon by chanting it down, they also recommend a positive function for the word, sound, power of song; for Rastas' beautiful expressions are more than simple declarations of protest and pride in the form of cultural one-upmanship. His chapter, "Chanting Change around the World through Rasta Ridim and Art," demonstrates that Rastas' chants are also proclamations of beauty, assurances of divine love and justice, and encouragement for self-reliance in the face of the reality of dwelling within Babylon's repressive structures. The Rasta aesthetic is both a response to oppression and a call to freedom incarnated in art. Thus, while Great Britain's Steel Pulse, for example, orders "Chant a Psalm" to combat society's cold disregard, Judy Mowatt urges "Get Up Chant (to the God of creation)," John Holt extols the positive power of "Chanting," and the Twinkle Brothers celebrate "Babylon Falling" with their *Chant Rastafari*.[45]

If technological society has moved from the oral to the written, it is now moving, in the late twentieth and twenty-first centuries to the postliterary—the visual. As Rasta images from a still largely oral Caribbean context are appropriated by the more technological European-American culture, how are they envisioned? Kevin Aylmer, longtime cultural critic, Marcus Garvey expert, reggae concert promoter, and friend and supporter to numerous Rasta artistic enterprises, tackles the Rasta sojourn in Hollywood through an analysis of eight well-known movies. Some questions that Aylmer's chapter, "Towering Babble and Glimpses of Zion: Recent Depictions of Rastafari in Cinema," addresses are: How have the images of Rasta been appropriated and transformed in film? What images have the films made in the Caribbean and in the United States apprehended, interpreted, and then presented to viewers? The Rastafarian voice in audible and visual art, like all voices, will increase as the place of art in our increasingly technological, visual, global culture expands.

Part IV of the *Reader* provides answers to important questions related to the religious beliefs or theology and to the cultic or ritual practices of Rastafari long recognized as central to the movement. But this section also provides a context in which to engage a critical evaluation of the "Christian apologetic" on Jamaican Rastafari. We are delighted to open the critical discussion with the chapter "Discourse on Rastafarian Reality" from the deputy vice-chancellor of the University of the West Indies, the Honorable Rex Nettleford, himself a veteran in the field of Rasta research since 1960 and the "Academic Dean" of the study of Caribbean culture. Nettleford underscores that research and scholarship on the Rastafarian phenomenon in the academy are imperative for better understanding and appreciating the movement. He provides the most current assessment of the discourse, namely, the demarginalization and unfettering of "Rastology" from the hegemonic, Babylon paradigms and methodologies of North Atlantic Eurocentric theology and cultural traditions. In a very timely critique of misconceptions of the Rastafarian ethos in the media, popular culture, and religion, Nettleford defends the Rasta ideology as a legitimate cultural phenomenon in its own right and as entitled to its own system of values, categories, linguistic locutions, beliefs, and practices, in the manner of the classical religions of the world. Nettleford's analysis of the nature of biblical materials, Christian orthodoxy, and Rastas' use of the Bible puts the reader on notice that there are very different perceptions of the Rastafarians, both in the academy and in popular culture. Some of those differences are given a voice in this attempt to spread the knowledge of Rastafari and chant down Babylon in print.

In "The Black Biblical Hermeneutics of Rastafari," Nathaniel Samuel Murrell and Lewin Williams trace the twisted path to a Rastafarian hermeneutics as the movement "hijacked" Judeo-Christian Scriptures and converted them into vehicles for identity, "ideation," and liberation. The chapter analyzes the use of biblical materials in a variety of Rastafarian discourses on issues related to the divinity of Haile Selassie and his alleged connection to the Hebrew king Solomon, as well as the black experience in the Bible. Ennis Edmonds's concise "Structure and Ethos of Rastafari" explains the informal organizational structure that characterizes the movement, its ritual activities— ganja smoking, "Nyabinghi I-ssemblies," and "groundation"—which form the true ethos of Rastafari. Edmonds shows that in spite of its nonhomogeneous character and lack of formal structure, Rastafari is not a movement in total chaos but one that has its own peculiar levels of social organization in "houses," camps, and "yards"; and while it does not have a developed clerical system, its elders are well recognized for their leadership roles and abilities.

A treasured feature of Part IV, and of the *Reader* as a whole, is William David Spencer's extensive commentary on the fourteen-page *The Promised Key,* the earliest writing on Rastafari from Leonard Howell, one of the founders of Rastafari. As Spencer notes, this long-sought-after piece of ephemera and primary source material on early Rastafarian thought has previously been inaccessible to the reading public. We are delighted that we are able to make it available to our readers in the present format. Spencer's carefully arranged chapter takes readers through a variety of theological, religious, cultural, gender, and other issues addressed by Leonard Howell and provides one safe passage through the hermeneutical minefield of Judeo-Christian theological and ecclesiastical thought forms, founded on the Bible, as the Rasta preacher used (or misused) these to degrade women and chastise Christianity.

Nathaniel Samuel Murrell and Burchell Taylor's "Rastafari's Messianic Theology and Carribean Theology of Liberation" brings closure to the discourse on Rastafarian reality in this volume. But the authors raise important theological and methodological questions, about Rastafari which could set the tone for future conversation on a Caribbean theology of liberation that wishes to enter into dialogue with Rastafari and other Afro-Caribbean religious traditions.

The book appropriately ends with a tribute to Leonard Barrett for the pioneering work he has done in Rastafarian research, his commitment to the study of African culture in the diaspora, and the inspiration he has given to all of us who attempt to carry on the mission of educating society at large about the culture and ethos of Rastafari and the Caribbean. We thank the students at Hartwick College for collaborating with Adrian Anthony McFarlane in making available the interview with Leonard Barrett in Appendix A. The contributors to this book were encouraged to document appropriate sources carefully in their notes and, by so doing, make a general bibliography unnecessary. As a substitute for the traditional bibliography, Nathaniel Samuel Murrell's concluding literature review in honor of Leonard Barrett, Appendix B, highlights the most significant works on the Rastafarian movement since the 1960s and the influence Barrett's works have had on younger scholars in this field of research.

Although this anthology gives a substantive treatment of the ethos, development, and mission of Rastafari internationally, the editors were unable to secure scholarly contributions on the state of the movement among the large black populations in Canada, Central America, Venezuela, Brazil, and southern Africa, where, in some cases, the language and the literature proved problematic. It is our hope that this book will inspire further research on the fast-growing Rastafarian presence in these parts and in other regions not mentioned herein. May the *Reader* take Rastafarian research to a new level of academic inquiry and find a busy life in the United States, Canada, England, the Caribbean, and among the more than 100 million Blacks in South America and the 850 million Africans "in the motherland," and around the world.

Notes

1. Peter B. Clarke, *Black Paradise: The Rastafarian Movement in Jamaica and Britain* (Wellingborough, Northamptonshire: Aquarian Press, 1986), 11.

2. Before the 1960s, Christians largely ignored the movement or criticized it privately and occasionally in sermons. See Roger Ringenberg, "Rastafarianism: An Expanding Jamaican Cult" D. Min. thesis (Jamaica Theological Seminary, Kingston, 1978), 1.

3. Leahcim Tufani Semaj, "Inside Rasta: The Future of a Religious Movement," *Caribbean Review* 14, 1 (1986): 8. This is an incendiary Jamaican patois expression, meaning "Those damn Rastas, what do they really want by saying they want to go to Africa? We should drown them in the sea."

4. Kim Leighton, "Doper or Devotee? Smoking Out Rastafarianism," *Liberty: A Question of Compulsion* 91, 6 (November/December 1996): 8. Published by International Religious Liberty Association, 12501 Old Columbia Pike, Silver Springs, Maryland, 20904-6600.

5. Some Rastas reject the term *Rastafarian*ism, used in the media and the academy, because to them, an-"ism" is a false movement or religion. It is not uncommon, however, to find even committed Rastafarian believers using the designation *Rastafarianism*.

6. Seretha Rycenssa, "The Rastafarian Legacy: A Rich Cultural Gift," *Economic Report of Jamaica* 4, 1 (1978): 22, 23.

7. See Rex Nettleford, "Discourse on Rastafarian Reality," Chapter 18 in this book.

8. See editorial by Michael N. Jagessar, "JPIC and Rastafarians," *One World* (February 1991): 1; Claudia Rogers, "What's A Rasta?" *Caribbean Review* 7, 1 (January–March 1978): 9; Ringenberg, "Rastafarianism," 1.

9. Charlene Robinson, "Marked for Death Said Giving Bad Impression of J'cans, Rastas," *Daily Gleaner*, November 3, 1990, 1; Leighton, "Doper or Devotee?" 8.

10. Quoted in Leighton, "Doper or Devotee?" 8.

11. Barbara Blake Hannah, "Misunderstanding Rastafari," *Sunday Herald*, April 4, 1993, 5A.

12. Ibid.

13. Rogers, "What's A Rasta?" 9.

14. Leighton, "Doper or Devotee?" 6. See also John Brown, *Shades of Grey: Police-West Indian Relations in Handsworth* (Birmingham, England: Cranfield Police Studies, 1977); Clarke, *Black Paradise*.

15. Anthropologist Carole D. Yawney of York University, Toronto, who has done ethnographic research on the Rastafarians since the 1960s, says, "Rastafari . . . represents a remarkable picture, not only for Caribbeanists, but also for students of *New Age religion*" ("Rasta Mek a Trod: Symbolic Ambiguity in a Globalizing Religion," in Thomas Bremer and Ulrich Fleisch-

mann, eds., *Alternative Cultures in the Caribbean*, report of the First International Conference of the Society of Caribbean Research, Berlin, 1988. [Berlin: Vervuert Verlag, 1993], 161; emphasis mine). On Rastafari as a New Age religion, see also Neil J. Savishinsky, "Rastafari in the Promised Land: The Spread of a Jamaican Socioreligious Movement among the Youth of West Africa," *African Studies Review* 37, 3 (December 1994): 35–39.

16. The attempt to classify Rastafarians as Christian and to judge them by Judeo-Christian standards and categories only adds to the growing number of misconceptions about the movement.

17. Scholars disagree on the extent to which Pocomania ("Poco") has influenced Rastas, but Nettleford is convinced that Poco must be included among the Afro-Caribbean antecedents of Rastafari.

18. See Barry Chevannes, "Rastafari: A New Approach," *New West Indian Guide* 64, 3 and 4 (1990): 136.

19. Yawney, "Rasta Mek a Trod," 161. In an earlier publication, Yawney argued that Rastafari "is a complex phenomenon which cannot be analyzed easily in terms of strictly traditional models of utopian or millenarian movements" ("Remnants of All Nations: Rastafarian Attitudes to Race and Nationality," in Frances Henry, *Ethnicity in the Americas* [Chicago: Morton Publishers, 1976], 232).

20. Ivor Morris, *Obeah, Christ and Rastaman: Jamaica and Its Religion* (London: James Clarke & Co., 1982), 79.

21. Semaj, "Inside Rasta," 8.

22. Rogers, "What's A Rasta?" 9; Semaj, "Inside Rasta," 8.

23. Joseph Owens, "The Rastafarians of Jamaica," in Idris Hammid, ed., *Troubling of the Waters* (San Fernando, Trinidad: Rahaman Printery, 1973), 167–70; Jagessar, "JPIC and Rastafarians," 15–17. See Chapter 22, "Rastafari's Messianic Ideology, and Caribbean Theology of Liberation," Nathaniel Samuel Murrell and Burchell K. Taylor, below, for a fuller treatment of these doctrinal themes.

24. Some Rastas say Selassie disappeared because, like Christ, his body was not found on the third day after his death.

25. As Rupert Lewis noted, the request to join the Ethiopian army was ridiculed by high-ranking officials in the British government. See Lewis's "Marcus Garvey and the Early Rastafarians," Chapter 8 in this book.

26. Sheila Kitzinger, "The Rastafarian Brethren of Jamaica," in Michael M. Horowitz, ed., *Peoples and Cultures* (New York: Natural History Press, 1971), 580.

27. Leonard Barrett, *Soul-Force: African Heritage in Afro-American Religion* (Garden City, N.Y.: Doubleday Anchor Books, 1974), 164.

28. Clarke, *Black Paradise*, 49.

29. Ibid., 50. Henry was imprisoned for fraud in 1960.

30. *The (Kingston) Star,* 22 March 1958, 1; cited in Barrett, *Soul-Force,* 166.

31. Barrett, *Soul-Force,* 169.

32. Two soldiers were killed, and the revolutionaries were captured and given the death sentence.

33. Clarke, *Black Paradise,* 50.

34. Rex Nettleford, *Identity, Race and Protest in Jamaica* (New York: William Morrow & Co., 1972), 50.

35. Ibid., 68–71.

36. Ibid., 64.

37. Although in 1966, at the World Congress on Evangelism in Berlin, Selassie affirmed his faith as a Christian and, to the day of his death, thought the Rastafarians were misguided in their religious claims, the movement benefited from its association with the name of His Imperial Majesty. See Haile Selassie I, "Building an Enduring Tower," in Carl F. H. Henry and W. Stanley Mooneyham, eds., *World Congress on Evangelism,* Vol. 1: *Berlin 1966* (Minneapolis: World Wide Publications, 1967), 19–21.

38. Clarke, *Black Paradise,* 52.

39. Frank Jan van Dijk, *Jahmaica: Rastafari and Jamaican Society, 1930–1990* (Utrecht: ISOR, 1993), 186–232.

40. Leonard Barrett, *The Rastafarians: The Dreadlocks of Jamaica* (1977; reprint, London: William Heinemann, 1988), 235.

41. Rex Nettleford, *Caribbean Cultural Identity: The Case of Jamaica* (Kingston: Herald, 1978), 22.

42. Bob Marley, "Chant Down Babylon" (Bob Marley Music Ltd./Almo Music Corp., ASCAP), on *Confrontation,* performed by Bob Marley and the Wailers, Island Records 90085, 1983.

43. The delightful song "Reggae Ambassador," by W. Clarke, M. Cooper, S. Coore, R. Daley, and W. Stewart can be found on Third World's album *Serious Business,* Polygram/Mercury 836–952–1, 1989.

44. See Frank Jan van Dijk, "Chanting Down Babylon Outernational," Chapter 11 in this book; and Peter E. J. Buiks, *Surinaamse jongeren op de Kruiskade: Overleven in een etnische randgroep* (Deventer, Neth.: Van Loghum Slaterus, 1983), 153–89.

45. On his melodica, a handheld wind instrument with keyboard—a kind of flute-piano—Augustus Pablo issues a "Chant to King Selassie I," while Freddie MacGregor matches his chanting down Babylon with an uplifting "Zion Chant."

Part I

Ideology and the Cultural Context

I Dread "I" In-a-Babylon: Ideological Resistance and Cultural Revitalization

ENNIS B. EDMONDS

Any interpretation of the significance of Rastafari must begin with the understanding that it is a conscious attempt by the African soul to free itself from the alienating fetters of colonialism and its contemporary legacies. To accomplish this freedom, Rastas have unleashed an ideological assault on the culture and institutions that have dominated the African diaspora since the seventeenth century. In Rastafarian terms, this consists of "beating down Babylon." They have also embarked on an ambitious endeavor of "steppin' outa (out of) Babylon" to create an alternative culture that reflects a sense of their African heritage. This chapter pursues these two themes in order to demonstrate how Rastafari has been self-affirming and empowering for its adherents in the face of "downpression."

Beating Down Babylon: Ideological Delegitimation

Rastas may differ among themselves concerning many of their important beliefs, but all are in accord regarding the Babylonian nature of life in the African diaspora, and all declare their psychological and cultural rejection of the values and institutions of Babylon. That Rastas adopted the term *Babylon* from Christian Scriptures is not surprising. Babylon embodies the cultural ethos of the forces that worked against "the people of God," the Hebrews. It is mentioned in eighteen books of the Bible and not only is portrayed in Revelations as the final earthly city but epitomizes everything that is evil and oppressive in the world. According to this last book in the Christian Bible (also called the Apocalypse of John), there will be an apocalyptic and dramatic collapse of Babylon. This is an idiom and imagery Rastas find most fitting for conceptualizing that which they wish to chant down and destroy.

The Rastafarian choice of the term *Babylon* as the symbolic designation of the forces that seek to "downpress" and dehumanize them is, in effect, an attempt to neutralize those forces. Therefore, Babylon constitutes a symbolic delegitimation of those Western values and institutions that historically have exercised control over the masses of the African diaspora. John Paul Homiak, who researched the role of eldership in the Nyabinghi Order, said: "Babylon is a term of varying levels of concreteness and specificity; historically, the predecessors of the Romans and the entire white European colonial world; presently, the entire post-colonial western power structure and its supporting ideology and political apparatus; the oppressive condition of 'exile' in the Black diaspora; the cosmic domain presided over by the pope of Rome and his Anglo-European political cohorts; the source of death-dealing and destructive spiritual power."[1]

As indicated by Homiak's definition, the term *Babylon* has several levels of significance. The most immediate referents are the gut-wrenching experiences of suffering and estrangement faced by the "underside" of Jamaican society. These people have experienced not only the pain of economic hardship and political marginalization but, even more, a sense of cultural alienation—a feeling of uprootedness and being "out of sync" with one's environment. The Rastafarian intellectual Dennis Forsythe succinctly sums up this aspect of the Babylonian experience: "Babylon is the psychic image sustained by real life experiences, busted hopes, broken dreams, the blues of broken homes and of disjointed tribes of people trapped by history. It is an image of fire and blood, of being on the edge, in limbo, in the wilderness, in concrete jungles. . . . It is a desolation in which man feels disjointed and out of line with the plans of creation."[2] The Rastafarian poet, vocalist, and prophet Bob Marley echoes the same sentiment in graphic personal terms: "I've been down on the rock so long, I seem to wear a permanent screw."[3] It is the experience of suffering and alienation in the African diaspora that makes the term *Babylon* most appropriate; it recalls the experience of the forced deportation and servitude of the ancient Hebrews under the Babylonian world power.

At the sociopolitical level, the term *Babylon* is used in reference to the ideological and structural components of Jamaica's social system, which institutionalizes inequity and exploitation. In this respect, Babylon is the complex of economic, political, religious, and educational institutions and values that evolved from the colonial experiment. Rastas see Jamaica as a part of an international colonial-imperialist complex. Hence, Babylon extends to the British-American alliance, which has been the benefactor of colonialism and international capitalism.[4] These two world powers, through their domination of international politics and their exploitative relationship with the "Two-thirds World," demonstrate that they are the successors of the ancient Babylonians and Romans. Babylon is, therefore, "the whole complex of institutions which conspire to keep the black man enslaved in the Western world and which attempt to subjugate colored people throughout the world."[5]

Globally, Babylon is that worldly state of affairs in which the struggle for power and possessions takes precedence over the cultivation of human freedom and the concern for human dignity. Rastas include in this state of affairs not only the West, led by the Anglo-American alliance, but also the former Soviet bloc and the politically powerful

Roman Catholic Church, presided over by the pope. In fact, most Rastas contend that political leaders of the world get their authority from the pope; they cite the frequent visits of world leaders to the Vatican as evidence for their belief.

At the highest level of generality, Babylon portrays the forces of evil arrayed against God and the righteous (Haile Selassie, Rastas, and the poor). These evil forces, however, are not metaphysical entities; rather, they are human attitudes and activities that are out of touch with the divine-natural order. This imagery is applicable to the proliferation of armaments of mass destruction and the exploitation of natural resources, both of which threaten human existence and the health of the environment. Any human activity that militates against harmonious relationships is a reflection of Babylonian values. Babylon is not a geographic locality or a specific social system. Babylon is any system of ideas and institutions that constitutes a culture in which people are oppressed and alienated from "Jah" and the life-giving, self-affirming reality of Rastafari.

In the Rastas' conception of Babylon, the experience of forced captivity of Africans in the West parallels the Babylonian experience of the ancient Hebrews, and their own constant subjugation and downpression recall the Roman iron rule over its empire. Therefore, Rastas find the spirit of Babylon surviving as an oppressive force in twentieth-century political and economic systems and institutions in the West generally and in Jamaica particularly.

Since Rastas do not have official theologians or social theorists to codify and systematize their beliefs, Rastafari lacks systematic treatment of its point of view on any subject. However, in their limited writings and, especially, in their poetry and reggae lyrics, the Rastas' evocative images address various aspects of Babylon's reality: its historical atrocity, economic rapacity, mental slavery, and political trickery. These are discussed here in introductory form in order to give clarity to the Rasta agenda.

Historical Atrocity

Rastas can recite, almost endlessly, historical atrocities of Babylon, from its days as a Middle Eastern world power to its contemporary Euro-American manifestations. As the conqueror of the ancient world, Babylon wreaked havoc on Jerusalem and deported the ancient Hebrews (whom the Rastafarians believe to have been black people) to Mesopotamia. The Romans, who are later manifestations of the spirit of Babylon, made incursions into Africa, conquering the African queen Dido, fighting Hannibal, and sacking Carthage. Rome, the beast of Revelation, persecuted Christians and executed Jews. With the blessing of the pope, Benito Mussolini (a Roman) invaded Ethiopia and drove Haile Selassie into exile.[6]

Most painful for Rastas is the memory of the Middle Passage—the experience on the slave ships from West Africa to the New World—and their subsequent suffering in modern Babylon. The manner in which Rastas speak of the Middle Passage and the institution of slavery reveals that they still bear the psychic scars of those experiences. They seem to reach back across the years to feel the pain and indignity of everything that befell their foreparents. Thus they are able to speak of such experiences in the first person, as though they underwent them personally. For example, in the song "Slave Driver," Bob Marley speaks of his blood running cold at the sound of the whip used to punish the slaves on the plantations. He also speaks of remembering his soul being brutalized during the miserable trans-Atlantic journey to the New World.[7]

To the Rastafarians, Babylon's propensity for atrocity remains unabated in the twentieth century. The two world wars, the Holocaust, Soviet labor camps, the killing fields of Vietnam, the Persian Gulf War, and the genocidal killings in Bosnia exemplify such atrocities. Furthermore, the evil powers of the world continue to increase their capacity for brutality, especially in the proliferation and perfection of instruments of mass destruction. Marley speaks eloquently of the twentieth century's predilection for violence as "technological inhumanity," which engenders a state of worldwide insecurity.[8] To him, no country in the world escapes this inhumane phenomenon.

At a more immediate level, Babylon continues its atrocity in the brutal treatment of those who threaten or are perceived as threatening to its system. For Rastas, the most hated element of the Babylonian system consists of those who are "dressed in uniforms of brutality,"[9] that is, the police. As British Rasta scholar Ernest Cashmore puts it, "They [the police] were the living proof that Babylon was alive, active and waiting for any opportunity to suppress them [the Rastas]; they constitute the empirical referents to the Babylon conspiracy theory."[10] The equation of law enforcement with Babylon was formed in the crucible of repeated persecution, intimidation, and harassment of Rastas by the Jamaican police. As Babylon's frontline agents, the police officers who defend and protect oppressive social institutions are mere puppets of those who have high stakes in these institutions. Cashmore quotes a young English Rasta as saying, "Them just respond to the needs of Babylon, wearing 'the badge of brutality.'"[11]

Economic Rapacity and Mental Slavery

The Rastafarian critique of the Jamaican economic system, and of capitalism in general, is a response to the country's colonial ethic of profiteering and exploitation. The exploitation began when the Europeans invaded Africa, robbed the continent of its natural resources, and enslaved millions of its people. The economic rapacity continued under colonialism long after the emancipation of the slaves and into the twentieth century. Rastas argue that the International Monetary Fund (IMF) and the multinational corporations that invest in modern Jamaica have their own economic interest at heart; they extract huge profits on their investments from taxpayers and Jamaican companies, thus robbing the country of its wealth. But the colonial ethic has also corrupted local Jamaican investors and entrepreneurs, who imitate Babylon's "dog-eat-dog" ethic—some of them stash huge sums of currency in foreign banks and imperil the Jamaican foreign exchange, thereby strangling the economy.

The Rastafarian view is succinctly expressed in two of Marley's most powerful images. One image refers to the Jamaican and Western capitalist economic state of affairs as "Pimper's Paradise."[12] In other words, ours is an economic system that justifies the profiteering of some at the expense of others. Rastas say the "economic prostitutes" sell themselves not so much for their own profit but for the benefit of their pimps— those who control the economic system. Marley's other image depicts the "Babylon system" as a voracious vampire "sucking the blood of the sufferer,"[13] a depiction that highlights the predatory nature of Babylon's economic system and its deadly effects on the poor. Marley's message is clear: the economic philosophy and institutions of Babylon sanction the exploitation of the poor and justify the avarice and profiteering of the well-to-do.

Rastas' critique of the Babylon system is very much akin to the socialist analysis of the capitalist system, in which those who own the means of production exploit the laborers to maximize their profits. This is eloquently expressed in "Crazy Baldhead," where Marley muses about "I-an-I" constructing the houses and raising the crops, only to have them appropriated by the profiteering capitalist interests.[14] Rastas argue that this profiteering destroys any sense of communality, so that economic activities in Babylon become a struggle for the survival of the fittest—a struggle in which people trample one another to get ahead.

According to Rastas, slavery did not end in Jamaica in 1834; it continues in many forms. The educational and religious institutions of Babylon, for example, specialize in obscuring the truth and teaching the people "misphilosophy." The firm conviction of the Rastafarians is that Babylon's Eurocentric system of education contrives to brainwash black people; it degrades what is African and glorifies what is European. In the words of one Rasta, "What is taught is untrue, immoral and indoctrination."[15] The end result of Babylon education is the "whitewashing" of the African mind, by stripping it of its African vibrations and inculcating in it European values, perspectives, and tastes.[16] Walter Rodney, the late Guyanese historian, Rasta sympathizer, and Black Power activist, claimed that "the brainwashing process was so stupendous that it has convinced . . . many black people of their inferiority."[17]

Rastas have therefore taken a posture of resistance to Babylon's system of education, because of its evil intent and its dehumanizing effects. The Rastafarian poet Bongo Jerry intones against what he calls the "double meaning," "crossword speaking," and "word rearranging" of the English language, the medium of Babylon's education. In his opinion, by means of its negative description of black people's reality and culture, the English language spreads confusion among Africans in the diaspora and makes them ashamed of their African identity and heritage.[18] Marley's expression of resistance to Babylon's education system is even more blunt. In the song "Babylon System," he declares his adamant refusal to embrace the values taught by Babylon's education and expresses his resolve to be what he is—an African: "We refuse to be what you want us to be; we are what we are and that's the way it's gonna be."[19]

Along with the schools, the church is implicated for participating in mentally enslaving the people. In addition to providing legitimation for the values and institutions of Babylon, the church teaches people to bear their suffering bravely because they have "a pie in the sky when they die." Teaching people to be patriotic instead of telling them the truth about the forces that conspire to oppress them, the church fails to prepare the people to take their liberation into their own hands.[20] Therefore, the Rastafarians are not impressed with the aura of respectability that seems to surround the educated in Jamaican society. Instead, they are likely to see, under the facade of respectability, con artists who are "slicker" than Anancy, the scheming trickster of Jamaican folklore.

Political Trickery

Jamaica's political system is based on the Westminster (British) model. Since the coming of universal adult suffrage to Jamaica in 1944, the political landscape has been dominated by two major parties, which compete for political control of the country. Although this has worked well for the democratic process, the system has encouraged electioneering and what Jamaicans call "patro-clientelism" (the practice of using government resources to favor party supporters), which has encouraged violence since the early 1960s. The conflict between the two dominant political parties in Jamaica, the People's National Party and the Jamaica Labour Party, escalated to near civil war in the 1980 general elections; more than eight-hundred people lost their lives that year in political violence.

Although inner-city gang warfare has been associated with political alliances and corruption, changes in political administrations have always come about by means of the ballot. In fact, Jamaicans often pride themselves on having one of the most stable democracies in the developing world. However, despite occasional flirtations with politics—Ras Samuel Brown's candidacy in 1961 and the Rastas' support for Michael Manley in the early 1970s, for example[21]—Rastafarian philosophy has always shunned participation in Babylon's political process.

This posture of nonparticipation grows out of the Rastafarian conviction that politics, as practiced in Jamaica and the West, is really "polytricks," or "politricks." *Politricks* refers to what the Rastafarians regard as the deceptive nature of Babylon's political activity. It is not the art of statecraft but the art of deception, machination, and manipulation. In Babylon, politicians pretend to be government representatives of the people[22] while they engage in unending scheming to maintain their positions of privilege and to keep the populace downpressed. The Rastafarian poet Mikey Smith portrays politicians as using trickery, lies, and secrecy to subdue the poor and make them vulnerable to exploitation.[23] Marley describes them as "con-men" brandishing "conplans" and trying to bribe their way to the top.[24] According to Smith, their politics is "full of complexity and folly formalities like demockroicy" (a mockery of the people).[25] Politicians, pretending to be public servants while seeking personal profit and self-aggrandizement, participate in civil ceremonies that are masquerades and hypocritically claim to govern by democratic principles.

Beyond being deceptive, Babylon's politics is divisive. Part of Babylon's strategy of domination is to sow seeds of discord among the poor and powerless (a form of "divide and rule"), especially in depressed urban communities. By turning powerless people against one another, Babylon creates a situation wherein the dominated lack the unity to undertake any collective action to change their situation and to challenge Babylon's power structure. Because they have seen Jamaican ghetto youths drafted into political factionalism, Rastas have firsthand experience of this divide-and-rule strategy. Instead of uniting to fight their common enemy, the youths fight and gun down each other in the name of allegiance to political parties. Therefore, because of the deceptiveness and divisiveness of Babylon's politics, most Rastas take the position that "politics is not the black man's lot, but the white man's plot."[26] That is, the bitter rivalry existing among politicians and in the broader Jamaican society is caused by Europeans who, through a history of colonialism, taught Blacks to hate and fight one another. The Rastafarians say Babylon does not want Africans to unite because its leaders are afraid of the strength of black people when they work together.

Using Babylon as the "primary symbol for the interpretation and assessment of the colonial establishment,"[27] Rastas have effectively relegated the Jamaican establishment to the realm of evil. Jamaica and the West form the evil empire. But Rastas are not only concerned with analyzing and describing Babylon; they also want to destroy it, or at least to revolutionize it. Marley's "Crazy Baldhead" is therefore not a dispassionate analysis of Babylon institutions but a revolutionary call to "chase those crazy baldheads out of the town."[28] Nor is Marley's "Babylon System" a detached portrayal of Babylon's economic system; it is a call to "rebel, rebel, rebel now."[29]

In one respect, the Rastafarians regard themselves as the agents of Babylon's destruction and reggae music as their primary weapon. As William Spencer and others show in this book, reggae music is seen as a potent instrument for "chanting down" or "beating down Babylon." Hence reggae musicians and lyricists are regarded as the avant-garde in the struggle against Babylon. Reggae is significant because it is the medium through which the people are restored to self-awareness. By telling Blacks the truth about their African roots and African identity, it emphasizes that they do not have to chase after European trappings and lifestyle in order to achieve a sense of dignity. Reggae also teaches the people about the oppressive, deceptive, and divisive nature of the system under which they live. As Linden F. Lewis observes, reggae is the Rastafarian vehicle for "political, cultural, moral and religious purposes and protests."[30] Reggae, therefore, sets the stage for a departure from the Babylon lifestyle and the eventual demolition of its system.

In addition to their faith in the power of reggae to "beat down Babylon," Rastas believe that the demise of Babylon will come about by self-destruction. According to Imani Jabulani Tafari, Babylon will be "destroyed in a predestined apocalyptic judgement of volcanic eruptions, earthquakes . . . plagues, hurricanes, drought, famine, tidal waves, hail and heat waves . . . by what could be described as a supernaturally controlled ecological backlash."[31] Rastas believe that Babylon's predatory and exploitative relationship with the environment will eventually precipitate this ecological backlash. Furthermore, Babylon's refusal to live naturally and its commitment to artificiality are out of sync with the divine principle in nature and hence must ultimately self-destruct. A sign of Babylon's impending doom is its loss of power over Rastas, who have made the mental and cultural break with Babylon and are in the process of re-creating and revitalizing themselves, that is, "steppin' outa Babylon" and "steppin' into Mount Zion" through the reappropriation of their African cultural heritage.

Steppin' Outa Babylon: Cultural Revitalization

Along with their ideological assault on Babylon's institutions, values, and aesthetics, Rastas are engaged in revitalizing their African identity and heritage in order to complete their liberation from the powers of Babylon. Rex Nettleford, a leading authority on Jamaican culture, describes the emergence and evolution of Rastafari as a quest in which Rastas are being "liberated from the obscurity of themselves."[32] Dennis Forsythe rightly describes Rastafari as a movement that is preoccupied with the cultural identity of the African diaspora: "Rastafarianism is the first mass movement among West Indians preoccupied with the task of looking into themselves and asking the fundamental question, *Who Am I?* or *What Am I?* . . . It is a desperate call for an alternative counterculture more suitable to the needs of black people in these times."[33] Rastas find the suitable alternative in the reaffirmation of their African heritage, which they view as a source of self-knowledge and power to be used in the struggle against Babylon.

This reaffirmation of Africa must be viewed against the background of the European assault on African and Afro-Jamaican cultural ways. It was not just the Jamaican folk culture that was denigrated but Africa and all that was associated with it. As Forsythe reminds us, Africa, to the white colonialists, was "the antithesis in terms of which they defined themselves."[34] Forsythe continues, "Africa, in terms of this white-constructed symbolic imagery, was the *dark* continent inhabited by ape-men, and incapable of creating the arts, sciences and other evidences of authentic civilization."[35] In this context of cultural denigration, Afro-Caribbean people became alienated from their African selves and cultural heritage and began to evaluate their goodness in terms of their degree of approximation of the European ideal.

Historically, Caribbean people of African descent were caught between their often-maligned natural African ways and the European culture held out to them as the best of human civilization. The tension produced by being "sandwiched" between those two cultures gave rise to the question of identity that Rastafari seeks to settle by proposing attainable and "healthy answers to the question of WHO AM I."[36] The answers are arrived at mainly through the Rastafarian affirmation of "the African spiritual and cultural presence in the New World,"[37] leading the movement to create its own ethos, with distinct ideas, symbols, and lifestyle.

While Babylon is symbolic of the negative forces of oppression and exploitation, Africa is evocative of the positive vibrations of pride, community, charity, and serenity. As much as Rastas seek to escape from or overcome the negative forces of Babylon, they also seek to imbibe the positive vibrations of Africa. The deification of Haile Selassie, the call for repatriation, and the adoption of the Ethiopian national colors are all indicative of the reappropriation of Africa. The act of deifying Selassie signals a break with, and a rejection of, white European religion and the whole cultural system that it legitimated. Instead of a white "gentle Jesus, meek and mild," Rastas posit an African liberator, Haile Selassie I, "Conquering Lion of the Tribe of Judah." Selassie has become "the nucleating agent for the jelling of the spiritual thoughts, concepts . . . experiences and emotional cravings of Rastas."[38] And despite the death (or, for some Rastas, the disappearance) of Selassie, the emperor is thought to have a continued existence as an ever-living spirit and thus remains a religious and political symbol, inspiring the Rastafarian struggle against the stifling presence of oppression.

Drawing on Marcus Garvey's "Back to Africa" campaign, Rastas have always made repatriation to Africa one of their main tenets. However, there are divergent views concerning its meaning and means of achievement. To some Rastas, repatriation means the literal, physical relocation to Africa/Ethiopia. For others, repatriation means the psychological and cultural reappropriation of their African identity and culture. Still other Rastas expect repatriation by divine intervention, which will occur either through some political action of the Jamaican or British government as a gesture of restitution or by means of Rastas' own rational sociopolitical efforts. While awaiting the full realization of repatriation (however it is understood), all Rastas have adopted the Ethiopian national colors of red, gold, and green as a means of symbolizing their identification with and allegiance to Africa. These colors, displayed on houses, vehicles, clothing, and accessories, have become a Rastafarian trademark; they "clearly and unambiguously" unite members of the movement into a "single social structure,"[39] though not organization, and declare their identity to the world as a means of stepping out of Babylon.

The Rastafarian cultivation of dreadlocks began in the 1940s. It was apparently inspired by the appearance in the Jamaican press of Africans wearing a similar hairstyle. Those whose pictures appeared have been variously identified as Gallas, Somalis, Masais,[40] or Jomo Kenyatta's Freedom Fighters.[41] Along with the implicit justification of the dreadlocks hairstyle that comes from its alleged African origin, Rastas invoke the biblical teaching concerning the nazirites, whom the Levitical laws forbade to trim their hair or shave (Numbers 6:5),[42] to support their practice of growing uncombed and knotted locks.

Two different traditions have emerged concerning who first adopted the dreadlocks hairstyle in Jamaica. The first tradition, and the one more widely circulated, traces the adoption of the dreadlocks hairstyle to Howell's "guardsmen" at his Pinnacle commune.[43] As the security force of the commune, the guardsmen's cultivation of this hairstyle was an attempt to accentuate their fearsomeness. The other tradition traces the dreadlocks trademark to the House of Youth Black Faith, a group of young radical Rastas who exerted considerable influence on the movement from the late 1940s to the 1960s. According to Barry Chevannes, members of the House of Youth Black Faith grew their locks as a direct assault on the Jamaican social norms concerning grooming, with full consciousness that the society would regard them as antisocial, if not outright crazy. However, they were bent on accentuating their sense of alienation through their dreadlocks hairstyle.[44] While the question of which tradition best accounts for the origin of dreadlocks must await further research, that this hairstyle has become the most salient and visible symbol of Rastafarian identity is beyond dispute.

A faction calling itself the Dreadlocks arose also as an element of reform within Rastafari itself. As Chevannes explains, the Dreads emerged among the Rastas during the course of their attempt to overturn the authority of the older generation, who they believed were compromising with Babylon. The Dreadlocks had strong separatist lean-ings and symbolized their ideological position in their peculiar hairstyle. The older generation had regarded the scissors and the razor as taboo. The Dreadlocks added the comb to this list, and they institutionalized other beliefs and practices, such as using ganja as a sacred sacrament, "developing of an argot focused on the concept of the personal pronoun I, symbolic identification of the status quo with Babylon, ritual ascendency over women," and "extension of the concept of God as man to include man as also God."[45]

As with other Rastafarian symbols, dreadlocks have multiple levels of significance. Aesthetically, dreadlocks indicate a rejection of Babylon's definition of beauty, especially as it relates to European features and hair quality. According to Rastas, hair straightening and skin bleaching by black people reflect a yearning for Whiteness and are therefore symptomatic of alienation from a sense of their African beauty. Against this background, dreadlocks signify the reconstitution of a sense of pride in one's African physical characteristics. As Ernest Cashmore explains, dreadlocks are "used to marry blackness to positive attributes and so to upgrade the black man and align him with elite groups—and so render white stigmatic conceptions of blacks impotent."[46]

Ideologically, dreadlocks express the Rastafarian belief in and commitment to naturalness. Since trimming, combing, and straightening one's hair change the natural looks, they are regarded as artificial and are proscribed by most Rastas. Dreadlocks thus bespeak Rastafari's uncompromising posture against the artificiality of Babylon.[47] Dreadlocks also function as a mystical link or "psychic antenna"[48] connecting Rastas with their God and with his mystical power, or "earthforce," which is immanent in the universe. Since they connect Rastas with earthforce, the shaking of the locks is thought to unleash spiritual energy that will eventually bring about the destruction of Babylon. The locks are therefore symbolic of Babylon's unavoidable doom. The very sight of the locks is supposed to generate fear in the hearts of Babylonians, and that is part of the reason for calling them *dread*locks.[49]

The emergence of "dread talk," a distinct Rastafarian argot, is another symbol of Rastas' rejection of one of Babylon's standards of civility. In the Jamaican status quo, the parlance of the poor is regarded as inferior to the staid articulation of the educated. Thus one of the symbols of respectability or of being "cultured" is the ability to "speak properly," which means to show mastery of the intricacies of the English (British) language in both grammatical correctness and impeccable diction. Rastas have repudiated this British symbol of respectability by creating their own linguistic devices, which directly attack the integrity of the English language and which make their speech almost incoherent to the uninitiated.

Beyond its symbolic protest, the Rastafarian argot represents an effort to develop a medium of expression that will convey the depth of Rastafarian experiences and perceptions. As Rex Nettleford notes, "The Rastafarians are inventing a language, using existing elements to be sure, but creating a means of communication that would faithfully reflect the specificities of their experience and perception of self, life and the world."[50] The ingenuity of dread talk is reflected in its ability to encapsulate loaded and sophisticated concepts in simple expressions, which outsiders experience as linguistic crudities but which convey a whole range of meanings to the initiated. "I-an-I" is one such expression.

Since "I" in Rastafarian thought signifies the divine principle that is in all humanity, "I-an-I" is an expression of the oneness between two (or more) persons and between the speaker and God (whether Selassie or the god principle that rules in all creation). "I-an-I" also connotes a rejection of subservience in Babylon culture and an affirmation of self as an active agent in the creation of one's own reality and identity. In Jamaican patois, "me" or "mi" is used as both object and subject. In Rastafarian understanding, this is an indication that people conceive of themselves as objects. In contrast, Rastas use "I-an-I" as subject (even when the sentence calls for an object) to indicate that all people are active, creative agents and not passive objects.

The Rastas have thus encoded their ideology in certain evocative symbols. Abner Cohen defines symbols as "objects, acts, concepts, or linguistic formations that stand *ambiguously* for a multiplicity of disparate meanings, evoke sentiments and emotions, and impel to actions."[51] Both Cashmore and Paget Henry have observed that marginalized peoples, especially minority groups, who lack access to political and economic power, often turn to "symbolic strategies"[52] and "symbolic processes"[53] in an attempt to articulate their grievances and to effect social change. This is particularly true of the Rastafarian movement. To quote Cashmore: "Through symbolic strategies the Rastas were able to exteriorize their implicit critique of society," and their "symbolic activity articulated a concern not purely with incumbents of power positions but with power arrangements themselves."[54]

So, in responding to the Babylonian experience and in attempting to redefine their identity as Africans, Rastas have evoked certain symbols and employed symbolic activities as weapons against Babylon. All of these symbols—dreadlocks, Ethiopian colors, dread talk—are exploding with critical significance, the essence of which is a rejection of the Babylonian character of Jamaican society and a commitment to the struggle for selfhood and dignity through the development of an African cultural identity.

The elements of the Rastafarian ethos that I have recounted here are by no means exhaustive (other elements are dealt with by other contributors to this book), but they suffice to illustrate the Rastas' determination to abandon Babylon's values and create their own. They indicate that the Rastafarian movement constitutes a deliberate undertaking aimed at delegitimating the Jamaican sociopolitical order that has emerged from colonialism. Declaring Jamaica's social institutions and cultural values to be a contemporary expression of ancient Babylon, the Rastas have embarked on the creation of a new order and a new identity.[55] Against the prevailing idea that linked Jamaicans culturally with Britain, the Rastas define themselves in relation to Africa, challenging the hegemonic society's view of what is aesthetically pleasing and culturally acceptable. Against the notion that Black is inferior, Rastas have celebrated their Blackness and have sought to re-create themselves in the image of Africa. Against the notions that African hair is not of good quality and that wearing beards is indecorous, Rastas have cultivated long and knotted locks and have displayed them with the pride of a lion showing off its mane.

Contrary to the notion that to be civilized is to adopt or approximate a British accent and Western aesthetic taste, Rastas create their own argot, their own style of dressing, and their own musical and artistic expressions.

Notes

1. John Paul Homiak, "The 'Ancient of Days' Seated Black: Eldership, Oral Tradition and Ritual in Rastafari Culture" (Ph.D. diss., Brandeis University, 1985), 510.

2. Dennis Forsythe, *Rastafari: For the Healing of the Nation* (Kingston: Zaika Publications, 1983), 96.

3. Bob Marley and the Wailers, "Talkin' Blues," on *Talkin' Blues*, Island Records 848243-4, 1991.

4. Joseph Owens, *Dread: The Rastafarians of Jamaica* (Kingston: Sangster's Book Stores, 1976), 74–80.

5. Ibid., 70.

6. Ibid., 70, 73.

7. Bob Marley and the Wailers, "Slave Driver," on *Talkin' Blues*.

8. Bob Marley and the Wailers, "Survival," on *Survival*, Island Records 90088-4-7, 1979.

9. Bob Marley and the Wailers, "Burnin' and Lootin'," on *Talkin' Blues*.

10. Ernest Cashmore, *Rastaman: The Rastafarian Movement in England* (London: George Allen & Unwin Paperbacks, 1983), 173.

11. Ibid., 177.

12. Bob Marley and the Wailers, "Pimper's Paradise," on *Uprising*, Island Records 422-846211-4, 1980.

13. Bob Marley and the Wailers, "Babylon System," on *Survival*.

14. Bob Marley and the Wailers, "Crazy Baldhead," on *Rastaman Vibration*, Island Records 422-846205-4, 1976.

15. K. M. Williams, *The Rastafarians* (London: Ward Lock Educational, 1981), 27.

16. Klaus de Albuquerque, "The Future of the Rastafarian Movement," *Caribbean Review* 8, 4 (1979): 44; Owens, *Dread*, 75.

17. Walter Rodney, *Groundings with My Brothers* (London: Bogle L'Ouverture/New York: Panther House, 1971), 10. See also Chapter 2, "Rastas' Psychology of Blackness, Resistance, and Somebodiness," by Clinton Hulton and Nathaniel Samuel Murrell.

18. Bongo Jerry, "MABRAK," in *The Penguin Book of Caribbean Verse in English*, Paula Burnett, ed. (Harmondsworth, Middlesex: Penguin Books, 1986), 70–71.

19. Marley and the Wailers, "Babylon System."

20. Owens, *Dread*, 81, 85. This is a criticism that Karl Marx made against Christianity in his famous critique of religion; see Karl Marx and Friedrich Engels, *On Religion* (Moscow: Progress Publishers, 1975).

21. Leonard E. Barrett, *The Rastafarians: Sounds of Cultural Dissonance,* rev. ed. (Boston: Beacon Press, 1988), 148, 150–52, 220–25.

22. Jack Anthony Johnson-Hill, "Elements of an Afro-Caribbean Social Ethic: A Disclosure of the World of Rastafari as a Liminal Process (Jamaica)" (Ph.D. diss., Vanderbilt University, 1988), 360.

23. Mikey Smith, "Tell Me," quoted in ibid., 362.

24. Marley and the Wailers, "Crazy Baldhead."

25. Mikey Smith, "Dread," quoted in Johnson-Hill, "Afro-Caribbean Social Ethic," 364.

26. Rex Nettleford, *Mirror, Mirror: Identity, Race and Protest in Jamaica* (Kingston: W. Collins/Sangster's Book Stores, 1970), 60.

27. Paget Henry, "Indigenous Religions and the Transformation of Peripheral Societies," in Jeffrey K. Hadden and Anson Shupe, eds., *Prophetic Religions and Politics: Religion and the Political Order,* (New York: Paragon House, 1986), 135.

28. Marley and the Wailers, "Crazy Baldhead."

29. Marley and the Wailers, "Babylon System."

30. Linden F. Lewis, "Living in the Heart of Babylon: Rastafari in the USA," *Bulletin of Eastern Caribbean Affairs* 15, 1 (March–April 1989): 22

31. Imani Jabulani Tafari, "The Rastafari—Successors of Marcus Garvey," in Rex Nettleford, ed., *Caribbean Quarterly Monograph: Rastafari* (Kingston: Caribbean Quarterly, University of the West Indies, 1985), 2.

32. Nettleford, *Mirror, Mirror,* 47.

33. Dennis Forsythe, "West Indian Culture through the Prism of Rastafarianism," in Nettleford, ed., *Caribbean Quarterly Monograph,* 62.

34. Ibid.,64.

35. Ibid.

36. Leahcim Semaj, "Race and Identity and the Children of the African Diaspora: The Contributions of Rastafari," *The Caribe* 4, 4 (1980): 17.

37. Lewis, "Living in the Heart of Babylon," 22.

38. Ajai Mansingh and Laxmi Mansingh, "Hindu Influences on Rastafarianism," in Nettleford, ed., *Caribbean Quarterly Monograph,* 112.

39. Cashmore, *Rastaman,*169.

40. M. G. Smith, Roy Augier, and Rex Nettleford, *The Rastafari Movement in Kingston, Jamaica* (Mona, Jamaica: University College of the West Indies, Institute of Social and Economic Research, 1969), 9.

41. Horace Campbell, *Rasta and Resistance: From Marcus Garvey to Walter Rodney* (Trenton, N.J.: Africa World Press, 1987), 96.

42. Williams, *Rastafarians,* 15; Barry Chevannes, "Era of Dreadlocks" (unpublished manuscript, n.d.), 15.

43. Theodore Malloch, "Rastafarianism: A Radical Caribbean Movement/Religion," *Center Journal* 4, 4 (fall 1985): 74.

44. Chevannes, "Era of Dreadlocks," 15.

45. Barry Chevannes, "Healing the Nation: Rastafari Exorcism of the Ideology of Racism in Jamaica," *Caribbean Quarterly* 36, 1–2 (1990): 69.

46. Cashmore, *Rastaman,* 158.

47. Chevannes, "Era of Dreadlocks," 15.

48. Leahcim Semaj, "Rastafari: From Religion to Social Theory," in Nettleford, ed., *Caribbean Quarterly Monograph,* 29.

49. Claudia Rogers, "What's A Rasta?" *Caribbean Review* 7, 1 (January–March 1978): 11–12.

50. Rex Nettleford, introduction to Owens, *Dread,* ix.

51. Abner Cohen, *Two-Dimensional Man* (London: Routledge & Kegan Paul, 1974), quoted in Cashmore, *Rastaman,* 152.

52. Cashmore, *Rastaman,* 152.

53. Henry, "Indigenous Religions," 124.

54. Cashmore, *Rastaman,* 154.

55. Henry, "Indigenous Religions," 131–32.

2

Rastas' Psychology of Blackness, Resistance, and Somebodiness

CLINTON HUTTON AND
NATHANIEL SAMUEL MURRELL

In 1976, Bob Marley released his second solo album, *Rastaman Vibration*. On the title track, he portrays reggae and Rastafari as positive "irations" with dynamic "vibrations," or a self-affirming and dynamic phenomenon. Marley's characterization of the feeling (vibration) and creation (iration) of Rastafari as positive captures essential qualities of Rasta psychology and identity, the underpinnings of which are rooted in the culture of Pan-Africanist resistance that generations of black Jamaicans conducted against British colonialism. In fact, some Rastafarians view the long history of black resistance to colonialism prior to the emergence of Rastafari as "Rasta works." During this process of resistance, the formation of a black social psychology essential to black liberation took shape.

The Nature of Rastafarian Psychology

Essentially, the psychology of Rastafari is an Afro-Caribbean way of feeling, perceiving, defining, affirming, and fighting for human dignity and hope in the African diaspora, and in Jamaica in particular. Rastafarian psychology involves expressions of self-confidence, affirmation of one's Blackness and personhood, a rejection of Eurocentric understandings of black people and their cultures, and a longing for liberation and ultimate redemption of the black peoples of the world (especially the oppressed). Blacks exuding this psychology are characterized by a strong sense of purpose, pride in their African heritage, racial solidarity, racial sovereignty, and self-reliance. Rasta psychology is, therefore, resistance and liberation psychology—the sum total of the organized and spontaneous campaign against racist subjection, fired by the burning desire to be free from all forms of social, economic, and political domination.

Rastafari arose as a movement of dissonance and protest against the British hegemonic oppression and dehumanization of the black masses of Jamaica. The movement came out of the social, political, and religious consciousness of a people who found self-affirmation and cultural identity in Africa and their African disposition, as a means of surviving depersonalization and deprivation. As a consequence, early Rastafari attracted mainly the dispossessed from the urban underclass and the disenchanted youths of Jamaica, the generation who had lost hope of finding a better tomorrow for themselves and their offspring in the Anglo-Jamaican political process and who were looking to Africa for liberation from "downpression" (their oppressed condition). Among these, hope for salvation through migration, African identity, and repatriation to Ethiopia ran high in the 1950s and 1960s. As William Lewis says, "The disfranchised black Jamaican, whether a dispossessed peasant or underemployed factory worker, proved to be a receptive audience for such fundamental Rasta themes as their communitarian economic philosophy and their emphasis on the positive identity of blackness in Africa."[1]

Rastafarian "psychology of redemption" is Afrocentric—an ideology that exemplifies a positive understanding of and commitment to African culture and tradition, which permeate every aspect of Rastafarian life and thought. This emphasis on one's African heritage, black liberation, and repatriation to Ethiopia, qua Africa, is an act of consciousness-raising, which Barry Chevannes calls the "idealization" of Africa—a broad concept in which Africa is given a symbolic character for black identity. Chevannes identifies four periods in the idealization of Africa in Jamaican history: "(a) the pre-Christian period, up to 1784 with the arrival of the Baptist preacher George Lisle; (b) the period of Christian evangelization from 1784 to 1900; (c) the Pan-African years, from the launching of [Trinidadian H. Sylvester Williams's and Jamaican] Robert Love's Pan-African Association in 1901 and Marcus Garvey's Universal Negro Improvement Association (UNIA) in 1914 to 1930; (d) the Rastafari years, from the coronation of Emperor Haile Selassie in 1930" to the present.[2] This idealization of Africa is firmly rooted in African continuities in the Americas as well as in the racial nature of the "black experience."

Without being aware of the existence of black psychology as a field of study—it emerged in the "1920s when African-American researchers began to address some of the biased notions promoted by white researchers about African-American people"[3]— Rastafari brought to light the practical characteristics of this discipline, whose major characteristics are defined by leading African American psychologists as

> a de-emphasis on deficiency based hypotheses about black behavior . . . a concurrent emphasis upon the positive aspects of black behavior which have permitted survival . . . in a racist society . . . a rejection of white normative standards when understanding and assessing black behavior . . . a quest for explanations of black behavior rooted not only in psychological phenomena but also in social and economic factors as well which serves to maintain the system which . . . subjugate[s] blacks.[4]

These themes define the basic premise, task, and focus of the academic study of black psychology and correspond rather closely with Rastas' understanding of themselves, their experiences, and their African heritage. Rastas, for example, reject completely white stereotypes of black people's behavior and redefine their reality in thought forms and cultural traditions that, though influenced by Christian Scriptures, are mainly Africa-centered. The self-confidence, "somebodiness," and hope of redemption so important to Rasta psychology are rooted in the notion of reversals of the roles of the oppressed and the oppressor: the oppressed will unseat and replace the oppressor in the new age through the help of the Almighty (God) in the person of Ras Tafari. Essential to this hope is the certainty that the often-cited biblical prediction "The stone that the builders rejected has become the chief cornerstone" (Psalm 118:22 NRSV; cf. Luke 20:17; Acts 4:11; 1 Peter 2:6–7; Ephesians 2:20) refers to the African race in general and Rastafari in particular.

The characteristic optimism in the psychological and intellectual thinking of Rastafari is traceable, in part, to the genesis of the movement. For some Jamaicans, Ras Tafari's accession to the throne of Ethiopia is the fulfillment of the much-overused biblical prophecy "Princes shall come out of Egypt; Ethiopia shall soon stretch out her hands unto God" (Psalm 68:31 KJV). To these Jamaicans, the coronation of Haile Selassie[5] marks nothing less than the commencement of a new world dispensation or era; it is the beginning of the end of the colonial European-Christian world order, the ascendancy of the black race, and the freedom of humanity in the new order. Past generations of black Jamaicans were emboldened to resist colonialism by force (e.g., the Maroons and fighters in Sam Sharpe's Baptist War and in the Morant Bay Rebellion of 1865), as well as with the help of Obeah priests and other African-influenced spirit mediums in communication with ancestral spirits and deities. However, after 1930, Selassie I, the supreme and living God of Rastafari, was placed at the center of the struggle as the new, ultimate method of fighting oppression and depersonalization. His coronation is the true beginning of redemption in the belief system of Rastafari.

This psychology of redemption thus combines the historical anticolonialism of the black struggle with the return of Christ (expected in Christian theology) in the person of Selassie. According to one police report, Leonard Howell told a meeting at Trinityville in St. Thomas in 1933, "The Lion of Judah has broken the chain, and we of the black race are now free. George the Fifth is no more our King. George the Fifth has sent his third son down to Africa in 1928 to bow down to our new king Ras Tafair [sic]. Ras Tafair is King of Kings and Lord of Lords. The Black people must not look to George the Fifth as their King any more—Ras Tafair is their king."[6]

Howell's teaching that Ras Tafari is the returned Messiah, though amusing and fanciful to many Jamaicans (especially those of the middle class), aroused interest among the poor in depressed and rural communities. As a result of the preaching of Howell and the other founders of Rastafari, some people embraced Ras Tafari as God in a spirit of hope and anticipated liberation. In the folk culture of Jamaican Christianity, the salutation "Greetings in the name of our Lord and soon coming King, Jesus Christ," is often spoken. But among the Rastafarians the salutation is "Greetings in the name of our Lord and Savior, Jesus Christ, who has revealed Himself to us in the Personality of His Imperial Majesty, Emperor Haile Selassie I." Thus the crowning of Selassie I was a critically important psychological foundation of the movement, in an environment where an Ethiopianist ideology and message brought pride and hope to downtrodden Blacks.

Ethiopianist Sources of Rasta Psychology

One of the traditions of resistance on which Rastafari drew is the "Ethiopianist" tendency that existed among Blacks throughout the African diaspora and surfaced most visibly in the fight for liberation, black abolitionism, Pan-Africanism, and Black Nationalism. According to Robert Hill, there existed, "prior to the coronation event in Ethiopia in 1930, a considerable tradition of 'Ethiopianism' that was traceable back over a lengthy period."[7] Broadly speaking, the Ethiopianist tendency in black people's struggle against European domination dates back to the epoch of the antislavery resistance movement, when Ethiopia (Africa) became a symbol of hope for black liberation and return to the homeland.[8]

Historically, expressions of Ethiopianism can be placed into two broadly defined categories. In the first category, the spiritual and or physical repatriation to Africa became an inspiration to the struggle for freedom. As many Pan-Africanist scholars have shown,[9] the yearning among Blacks of the diaspora to identify with the land of their origins began after the first abducted Africans were taken to Hispaniola as slaves, at the turn of the sixteenth century. Even when some slaves were driven to commit suicide on the Middle Passage and on the plantation, they held onto the belief that at death their spirits would be liberated to return to Ethiopia (Africa) and be reunited with their ancestors—a concept that is still cherished in Voodoo and other African traditions in the Americas.

Blacks made numerous attempts to mutiny on slave ships and ignited hundreds of revolts on the plantations to free themselves from slavery and return to Africa. The Maroons of Nanny Town and the Cockpit Country (some of the most rugged, mountainous terrain in Jamaica), for example, repeatedly held the British army at bay in fierce guerrilla warfare that continued for over a century. This and similar acts of resistance boosted the self-confidence and courage of black freedom fighters and kept hope alive for Africans in the diaspora seeking freedom from slavery. When the revolutionary Black Jacobins of Saint-Domingue (Haiti) rose up to end their infamous servitude to Whites (1791–1803) and became the first independent Africanized Caribbean nation, the positive psychological impact on other enslaved Blacks in the Americas was instant. The success of the revolution and the rise of black consciousness, self-determination, and self-government in Haiti were on the lips of multitudes of enslaved Blacks and inspired dozens of revolts in the Caribbean, Latin America, and the United States (e.g., the Nat Turner revolt, the Gabriel Prosser uprising, and the Denmark Vesey rebellion).[10] These revolts, though largely unsuccessful and often bringing more pain and suffering to the slaves themselves than to their masters, instilled morbid fear in the hearts of Whites, who frantically enacted stiffer laws governing slave life, inflicted stiffer punishment for slave infractions, and opposed what was called "western Africanization" or Ethiopianism—the battle for freedom and independence among Blacks in the Caribbean and the southern United States.

The hope of one day being free or returning to Africa that sustained Blacks paid off in 1800 for five hundred Maroons of Jamaica who were shipped to Sierra Leone via Nova Scotia, Canada. Between 1829 and the European scramble for Africa in 1870, early Pan-African Ethiopianists such as John B. Russwurm, the Jamaican-born editor of *Freedom's Journal* in New York City; Edward Wilmot Blyden, a journalist and clergy member from the U.S. Virgin Islands; Robert Campbell, a Jamaican teacher and chemist; and Arthur Barclay, who accompanied 348 Barbadians back to Liberia and later became the president of that country, assisted in the repatriation and liberation of many Africans. Ethiopianism had triumphed for a brief moment in history, and although the victory was small, it would have a powerful psychological impact on the thinking of Blacks through the next century.

In the second category of Ethiopianism, the biblical references to African states and peoples became an important current in black abolitionist thought. Often the mere mention of the word *Ethiopia* or *Africa* inspired hope among the slaves. In their campaign against slavery in the 1700s and 1800s, Blacks developed a tradition of abolitionism in which the Bible became a principal guide to action. They drew on biblical themes and texts, many related to Ethiopia, that lifted the psyche of black people, reinforced their resolve for liberation, and enhanced their self-worth and sense of somebodiness during slavery and under suppression and negation of the African personality. At that time the Bible was in use by slave masters as a tool of oppression and anti-black propaganda, constituting one of the most important colonial guides for the theoretical and practical justification of slavery. Biblical writings, introduced to North Africans by early Christians (100 to 400 C.E.) and later by Portuguese missionaries (since the 1400s), were taught to Caribbean Blacks on the plantation. Soon after the Bible's introduction to the African diaspora, however, Blacks invented their own interpretations of the Scriptures to strengthen their struggle for freedom and develop a psychology for survival under oppression.[11]

That the Bible portrays Blacks, Semites, and Whites as originating from the same bloodline and progenitor became an important argument in support of racial equality, in black abolitionist thought as well as in Rastafari. Furthermore, Blacks who utilized the Bible in the ideological struggle against slavery and colonial domination were able to reject the racist notion that the Blackness of the African is in consequence of a curse that Noah allegedly placed on Ham (a theme discussed fully elsewhere in this volume). More important, the fact that Ethiopia and the Ethiopians figure prominently in the Bible (Psalm 68:31; Numbers 12:1; Jeremiah 38:6–14; Acts 8:26–40) instilled a tremendous sense of somebodiness and self-worth in the minds of oppressed Blacks in the Americas. The beliefs that Moses, the great liberator in biblical history (and an inspiration to some black abolitionists), married an Ethiopian; that the king of Ethiopia is a descendant of Israel's wisest king, Solomon; that an Ethiopian saved the life of the well-known Hebrew prophet Jeremiah; and that the Bible predicted "a prince will come from Ethiopia" to save the human race (especially the black race) were of immense importance psychologically to the survival and aspirations of black people—ideas that later found a permanent place in Rastafarian psychology.

Historically, the words *Ethiopia* and *Ethiopian* designated all of Africa, a specific political-geographical region in Africa, a person who originates from the Ethiopian state, as well as a black person. A biblical parable asked, "Can the Ethiopian change his skin, or the leopard his spots?" (Jeremiah 13:23 KJV). During slavery, the term *Ethiopian* was used by Whites generally as a designation (often negative) for black people—a designation with which Garvey's followers were familiar.[12] At the beginning of the American Civil War, for example, Abraham Lincoln said he did not want any Blacks shedding American (white Americans') blood on the battlefield and that the war was not about freeing Ethiopians from slavery. But in a desperate, last attempt to fortify Union army lines teetering on the brink of defeat to the Confederates, three of Lincoln's "generals stretched out their hands to Ethiopia"[13] and recruited the forbidden Blacks to strengthen Union supply lines. Lincoln was furious and sternly reprimanded two of his generals. But a great psychological victory was won the following year, when dangerous circumstances in the war forced "Honest Abe," the mythic "liberator of black people," to sign the Emancipation Proclamation, "only as a war measure," putting an end to slavery in the rebellious states on January 1, 1863, and allowing Ethiopians (Blacks) to defend the country they regarded as their home. Ethiopia had triumphed psychologically for another brief moment, and the effects of the Black-assisted victory of 1865 on the psyche of black people in the Americas would last throughout the Reconstruction period (1865–1877) and surface again to inspire black ascendancy in the Garvey movement in the early twentieth century.

Regardless of the connotations or subtexts that whites attached to the word *Ethiopian,* many Blacks in the African diaspora saw it as a positive symbol, ingrained in their psyche and bringing them a ray of hope for liberation and redemption. In this way, Ethiopia provided an important sign, context, and source of black identity, black consciousness, and positive self-affirmation of black people. The Ethiopianist tendencies in black anticolonialism and the fight for liberation were later strengthened by Ethiopia's defeat of the Italians at Adwa in 1896; its preservation of its independence during Europe's colonial scramble for Africa in the 1870s and division of the continent after the Berlin Conference of 1884; its ancient Christian roots and tradition, which contrasted with European Roman and Protestant Christianity and linked Blacks to what Rastafari termed "the ancient order"; the coronation of Ras Tafari in 1930;[14] and the interpretation of certain themes in the Bible (e.g., making Selassie the returned Christ), treated elsewhere in this book.

The Garveyite Source of Rasta Psychology

Ethiopianism or the African consciousness in Rastafarian psychology got its strongest support from Garvey's Pan-African movement of the 1920s. As Kenneth King noted, "A number of influences produced a New World black interest in Ethiopia after the

Great War, the most potent of which was Garveyism."[15] Marcus Mosiah Garvey was a committed Afrocentrist who underscored the need for Blacks to interpret their own history and control their own destiny in Africa and the black diaspora. He embraced the idea that Ethiopia, qua Africa, "was the cradle of the black race and that its contributions to the development of civilization were paramount to the realization of racial equality for the black diaspora."[16] Garvey worked as an ardent campaigner for the decolonization of Africa under the slogan "Africa for the Africans at home and abroad; one God, one Aim and one Destiny."[17] He launched the famous "Back to Africa" resettlement movement "to encourage skilled and professional blacks to return and contribute to the development of Africa."[18] Garvey's philosophy of black pride, dignity, self-worth, and "bootstrap" or self-help reform and his Afrocentric view of life represented to millions of Blacks—and in particular, to the founders of Rastafari—who had lived all their lives in the ghetto of racial inferiority and helplessness hope for deliverance from oppression and impoverishment.

Garvey disavowed association with Rastafari when it emerged in 1930, but his interest in the history, politics, and religion of Africa (particularly Egypt and Ethiopia) and his Afrocentric perspective on life provided the foundation and an apocalyptic vision for Rastafarian thought. "Like the many preachers before him, Garvey tirelessly used the biblical references to the name Ethiopia,"[19] which "excited powerful emotions in the hearts of Christian Blacks"[20] and of the members of the Universal Negro Improvement Association (UNIA). With exclamations such as "Wake up Africa!" "Rise up Ethiopia!" "A black prince shall come from Ethiopia!" in his many speeches, Garvey developed a powerful rhetorical and polemic tradition based on the importance of Blackness, without calling for hatred toward Whiteness. As he exhorted Blacks to take pride in themselves and not be ashamed of their color and kinky hair, he exclaimed, "To be a Negro is no disgrace, but an honor, and we of the Universal Negro Improvement Association do not want to become white."[21]

As the world-renowned contemporary theologian James Cone has rightly noted, "Garvey understood the pain of color discrimination because he experienced it personally and observed it in the lives of other blacks in Jamaica and also during his travels in Central America, Europe, and the United States."[22] Garvey gave a descriptive account of his traumatic and sudden encounter with race prejudice as a youth. He said he "grew up with other black and white boys" and made them "respect the strength" of his arms. To him, "at home in my early days, there was no difference between white and black." One of his father's properties adjoined that of a white neighbor who had two boys and three girls. His minister in the local Wesleyan church was a white neighbor whose property also bounded the Garveys. Garvey said the minister had three girls and one boy, and they were his playmates. "We romped and were happy children, playmates together. The little white girl whom I liked most knew no better than I did myself. We were two innocent fools who never dreamed of a race feeling the problem."[23]

Garvey then related the experience that completely changed his attitude toward white people and set him on a course to affirm a psychology of "blackness and somebodiness" as a tool for building an independent black nation:

At fourteen my little white playmate and I parted. Her parents thought the time had come to separate us and draw the color line. They sent her and her sister to Edinburgh, Scotland and told her that she was never to write or get in touch with me for I was a *nigger*. It was then that I found for the first time that there was some difference in humanity, and that there were different races, each having its own separate and distinct social life. . . . After my first lesson in race distinction, I never thought of playing with white girls any more, even if they might be my next-door neighbors. . . . At maturity the black and white boys separated and took different courses in life. I grew then to see the difference in the races more and more. . . . I went traveling to South and Central America and parts of the West Indies to find out if it was so elsewhere, and I found the same situation. I set sail for Europe to find out if was different there, and again I found the stumbling block—"You are black."[24]

Garvey began to ask soul-searching psychological and political questions: "Where is the black man's Government? Where is his King and his kingdom? Where is his President, his country, and his ambassador, his army, his navy, his men of big affairs? I could not find them, and then I declared, *I will help to make them.*"[25] As James Cone says, "In a world where blackness was a badge of degradation and shame, Garvey transformed it into a symbol of honor and distinction."[26] Garvey envisioned the potential for enormous power stemming from black pride and the rule of Africa by and for Africans. To him, Blacks are the superior race, and when Africans develop a true understanding of themselves, they discover they have a world status that is second to none. Garvey urged Blacks, "Let us work towards the one glorious end of a free, redeemed and mighty nation. Let Africa be a bright star among the constellation of nations."[27]

Thus, although scholars have argued correctly that Rastafari is not exactly a child of Garveyism, Garvey's thoughts played a significant role in the origin and evolution of the Rastafarian movement. Next to Haile Selassie I, Garvey, the world's best known Black Nationalist and Pan-Africanist, is the most important figure in the Rastafarian identity. Garvey's birth date, August 17, is one of the most important dates on the Rasta calendar. It is a commonly held belief among Rastafarians that Garvey, a Jamaican, was the forerunner of Haile Selassie I; Rastas regard Garvey as a prophet in the same light as the biblical John the Baptist.[28] They generally hold that Garvey predicted the crowning of a black king who would redeem the black race. The use of Garvey's alleged assertion that "whenever a Black king is crowned in Africa our redemption is near"[29] is typical of the link that Rastas make between Garveyism and the origin and development of the Rastafarian movement. To the Rastafarians, Garveyism *is* prophecy. Ras Negus asserted that "Garvey was a prophet that sparked off the light of some form of reculturing of Black people."[30] In 1974, one Rasta asserted that Marcus Garvey prophesied that power is the only argument that satisfies humans. Unless "the individual and the race or the nation has POWER that is exclusive, it means that individual, race or nation will be bound by the will of the other who possesses this great qualification."[31]

The impact of Garveyism on the psychology and worldview of masses of black Jamaicans is well known. Garvey's pathfinding philosophy of black pride and African consciousness received its highest symbolic note of recognition at his death, when his remains were returned from Britain to Jamaica for a historic burial and the Jamaican government declared him a national hero. That Garvey's legacy became a living folk-lore among the Jamaican masses is due mainly to the efforts of Rastafarians. Their songs, poems, sermons, chants, writings, and "groundings" (expositions, reasonings, and teachings) are replete with the uplifting teachings of Garvey and extol his prophe-cies of hope. Indeed, Rastas who have accessed the works of Marcus Garvey, especially his philosophy and opinions, read and cite them with the same intensity as they do the Bible. Slogans made or popularized by Garvey, such as "Up You Mighty Race, You Can Accomplish What You Will"; "One God, One Aim, One Destiny"; and "Africa for the Africans, at Home and Abroad," have been adopted as essential vocabulary in Rasta-farian psychology and philosophy.

In mapping an ideological path to black sovereignty, nationhood, and development, Garvey was acutely aware that a prerequisite for action and a necessary component of the struggle was for people of African descent to overcome the fettering psychology of the slave mentality and colonial subjection. For Garvey, the greatest and most enduring impact of slavery and colonialism is psychological. It destroys one's sense of person-hood and self-worth and limits the vision and potential of black people. This psycho-logical legacy has also caused Blacks to engender self-hatred, to wallow in the mire of self-pity, and to be dependent on Whites for direction, guidance, and economic support or handouts. "Liberate the minds of men," Garvey asserted, "and ultimately you will liberate the bodies of men."[32] At one meeting, Garvey said to his audience:

> We say with courage to any black [people], do not be despondent, do not even in an instance feel yourself unfit, because if you will but fall back upon the strength and possibilities of your own mind, and the stubbornness of your own character, you can climb, yes climb to the highest mountains of human intellectual reach. . . . The leaders who inspire you to change your colour or complexion, the leaders who influence you to adopt completely the social and other attitudes of alien men, are those who are willing to submerge you; but be inspired by those of your race who think you as good and worthy as others.[33]

Given such powerful words of exhortation, self-affirmation, and inspiration, it is not surprising that early Rastafarians were either ex-Garveyites or Garvey admirers.[34] In the 1920s, several Garveyites—many of them of Caribbean origin—visited Ethiopia and some West African countries, spreading Garvey's philosophy of black pride, self-reliance, and nationhood. Garveyism also had a direct influence on the Ethiopian students in New York City and on Ethiopian delegates who visited Harlem in the late 1920s to solicit trained black colonists for Africa. One delegate, Workneh Martin, when visiting Harlem in 1937, announced to Garveyites that Ras Tafari—Haile Selassie, emperor of Ethiopia—would welcome skilled artisans and other craftspeople to Ethiopia.[35]

The Barbadian-born, black Jewish rabbi Arnold Ford, who taught music in the British navy and, for about three years, served as music director at Garvey's Liberty Hall in New York, did more than any other Garveyite to spread Garvey's philosophy of Black-ness in Africa through hymnody. With a vision for Africa similar to those of Edward Blyden from the Virgin Islands, Benito Sylvan of Haiti, H. Sylvester Williams of Trinidad, and many U.S.-based Black Nationalists, Ford "believed that the awakening of Africa was a major obligation upon the blacks of the diaspora"[36]—an ideology that he effectively conveyed through hymns written specially for Ethiopia, such as "O Africa awaken," "O bright and glorious country," and "O land of our tropic splendor."[37] According to Kenneth King, Ford's imagery and vision for Africa shared with those of other New World Blacks the idea that the experience of the African diaspora parallels "the earlier Jewish exile from Jerusalem." King says, "This was no accident in Ford's case, because by the early twenties he had become the leading spokesman of the various sects of black Jews in Harlem," and he shared with "the sectarians a scrupulous avoidance of the slave-given name of *Negroes*, and a preference for such terms as: *sons of God, Children born of love, Pilgrims, Ethiopian sons and daughters, or Ethiopian children.*"[38]

International travel allowed for the fruitful exchange of Ethiopianist ideas among Jamaican Garveyites and those in the United States on the eve of Rastafari's advent in Jamaica. The Selassie phenomenon gave Garvey admirers political and religious legitimacy and historical connection to Africa as they defined their new self-identity and purpose for living under the banner of Ras Tafari. This African connection was so strong that Black Nationalists of the Harlem Renaissance, who saw in Selassie a black man with the power and capacity to restore respect, rights, and dignity to African peoples, joined in a celebration of Haile Selassie and Ethiopia in New York City in 1935. Members of their faction groups—the Abyssinians of Detroit, Chicago, Washington, D.C., and New York, who had declared themselves citizens of Ethiopia—burned U.S. flags while selling the Abyssinian flag for a dollar. They were joined by Blacks in London and Jamaica in a worldwide demonstration against the Italian invasion of Abyssinia in 1935. Several popular-culture publications, such as *Plain Talk* and *Public Forum Journal,* showed that Blacks rioted in New York against Italian Americans and raised funds to help Ethiopia—a powerful political statement with direct practical psychological implications for black ascendancy and pride.

Psychological Foundations of Rastafari

The Black or Native Revivalist Baptist movement, led by Alexander Bedward in Jamaica during the close of the nineteenth century, was a stream that fed Garveyism in 1914 and Rastafari in the 1930s.[39] Indeed, several Bedwardites, including Robert Hinds, who marched in social protest with Bedward against harsh economic conditions and poverty and preached spiritual reform in Jamaica in 1921, became founding members of the Rastafarian movement. Hinds, a Bedwardite activist, was Howell's deputy and a leading spokesperson of early Rastafari. Like other Bedwardites, Hinds regarded Bedward as the Christ, a belief that preceded Garvey's assertion of a black Christ. Rastafarians such as Bongo Jerry hold that Bedward preached about a black Christ in the 1890s and was thus regarded as a prophet.[40]

Also influencing Rastafari from the Native Baptist tradition is the movement of Paul Bogle, which dates back to the 1860s. Two of the slogans of the Morant Bay Rebellion, which Bogle led against the cane-sugar planters in St. Thomas in 1865, have become

slogans of Rastafari: "Colour for Colour, Skin for Skin" and "Lion." During the rebellion—which was suppressed by the British with a severity unrivaled in the history of
Britain's suppression of black disturbance in the Caribbean—Bogle supporters raised
the slogan "Black Skin, White Heart" to define those Blacks who supported the "plantaclass" and the suppression of black people's aspirations.[41] The concern for Blacks
who appear to have become supporters and psychological clones of the white plantaclass and opponents of black liberation has been an important issue for Rastafari. Along
with other Jamaicans, Rastas coined the term *Roast breadfruit* to mean the same as
"Black Skin, White Heart." These terms are, above all, psychopolitical designations.

The beginnings of the most important group of Rastafarians were sustained in St.
Thomas, the home of the Paul Bogle movement.[42] Indeed, the social core around which
the Howellite tendency evolved, giving Rastafari some of its most important characteristic features, originated in that parish. When Howell was forced by persistent harassment and persecution from the police to leave St. Thomas, the core of people who left
with him to establish the Pinnacle Commune in St. Catherine at about 1940 were persons of Native Baptist/Kumina tradition. According to Kenneth Bilby and Elliot Leib,
"A number of informants state that the original group at Pinnacle was composed primarily of persons originally from St. Thomas, the parish where Kumina is most strongly
represented."[43] Kumina, a Central African cultural and religious tradition especially
linked to the Congo people,[44] became an important source for Rastafari's rituals. Under the colonial government immigration scheme, Central Africans settled as indentured
laborers in their largest concentration in St. Thomas. The scheme to supply the Jamaican
labor force with indentured African labor began in the early 1840s.[45]

A commonly held view among Kuminists and many Jamaicans is that the ancestral
spirits do not eat salt. (See Howell's use of salt in healing and protection in *The
Promised Key,* Chapter 21 in this anthology.) Within Kumina tradition, Africans who
do not consume salt are able to develop the power to "interpret all things," as well as
the ability to "fly from Jamaica back to Africa."[46] The strongly salt-based diet introduced on the estates by the "plantocracy" was thus viewed by some Africans as a European plan to thwart their desire to repatriate to Africa and to corrupt their minds with
colonial thoughts. It is not hard to see why, within the context of communal life at Pinnacle, where Kumina people constituted the core, cooking without salt—now an essential feature of Rasta menu—fit with Howell's ideas of knowledge, repatriation, anticolonialism, and the rejection of European values. While eating unsalted food may not
have any religious value in and of itself, in Rasta communes, psychologically this practice engenders hope, self-preservation, and identity with African roots.

Without a clear understanding of the sources of Rastafarian psychological thinking,
as outlined above, serious errors like that of Ajai Mansingh and Laxmi Mansingh (discussed in Neil J. Savishinsky's "African Dimensions of the Jamaican Rastafarian Movement," Chapter 7, below) are inevitable. Having erroneously posited that Hindu influence constituted the spiritual and intellectual core of Rastafari, the Mansinghs asserted
that "the basic concepts, philosophy, beliefs, rituals and codes of Rastafarianism" are
founded on "parochial Hinduism."[47] But the profoundly liberating qualities of Rasta

psychology and its antecedents are best understood when compared with the acquired racist psychology evident among significant sections of the black Jamaican population. Confronted with a regime of persistent violence, racist propaganda, psychological warfare, and the negation of anything African, many Blacks came to believe the racist stereotypes that Europeans assigned to Africans. Consequently, they developed a psychological condition in which submission, docility, and servility became the accepted or even preferred modes for easing their pain and preserving their lineage and race.

A classic example of this condition was displayed by a young black Jamaican woman toward the close of the nineteenth century. In expressing her opinion on the kind of baby she would like to have, this woman said, "I neber could lub a black little Chile same as I do de white. I worship de little Massa, an' if I lucky, eben I may hab a fair Chile one day. Not, ob course, a real white one, dat asking too much, but still one dat is almost white, an' den I worship it, an' work for it fe true; Dress it nicely too, in clean white clothes, wid shoes an' all, jest like a Buckra baby. . . . I hope I neber hab a black or dark Chile to shame me."[48] This black woman was thinking, psychologically and philosophically, like the white racists who kept her and the black race in colonial bondage. The attitude she exhibited is that identified by nineteenth-century Blacks who supported Paul Bogle as "Black Skin, White Heart." Unable to resist the mental, spiritual, psychological, and physical brutality of colonialism, Blacks who were categorized as having a black skin and a white heart, like the woman above, developed a behavioral condition in conflict with those who responded with defiance and resistance to European subjection. These behavioral traits, along with a sense of cultural ambivalence, became the principal psychological foundations of the Jamaican folk culture.

Rastafari was thus spawned in an environment in which hundreds of thousands of Jamaicans of African descent sustained the culture and tradition of submission, docility, servility, and self-contempt. Many Blacks continued to see their freedom in ideological, cultural, and psychological terms defined by Europeans. They asserted acquired racist (folklorist) stereotypes, such as "Anything tu Blaak nuh gud" (Anything that is too black is not good); "Him Blaak like sin"; and "She Blaak an' ugly." Both black and white Jamaicans thus bought into the notion that beauty and ugliness were related to skin color and ethnicity, and these concepts continued to affect people in all aspects of life: in teachers' fondness for "lighter skin" students; in hiring practices that showed preference for light-skinned Jamaicans over persons of darker complexion; in black Jamaicans being treated with less respect than coloreds (mulattoes) at government offices, commercial banks, and hotels and by police officers on the beat.

The "Jamaican colonials" relished membership in the Church of England (the Anglican or Episcopal Church), at the same time that the small but influential Jamaican intelligentsia scorned Garvey's "Back to Africa" program and his "black is beautiful" philosophy as reactionary and wishful thinking and were deeply offended by the presence of "those damn dirty Rastas all over the place." As the Jamaican-American scholar Marian Miller noted, "Up until the time of independence, and for at least a decade after, Jamaica's emerging cultural identity devalued the African contribution, in spite of the fact that about 93 percent of the population could claim African origin."[49] The wholesale disdain that

Jamaican Creoles had for their own Africanism and the glorifying of the European Christian culture constantly projected a pro-white philosophy in the society on matters of politics, culture, education, and religion. The psychology of white superiority became so pervasive and appeared so natural to the Christian culture that few Jamaican Sunday worshipers ever paused during their singing to think seriously about the words of such popular Christian hymns as "My heart was *black with sin* until the Savior came in," "Christ cleansed my heart from sin and made me *white within*," and "Whiter than snow, yes whiter than snow; Lord wash me and I shall be whiter than snow" (emphases added).

This internalized culture of racism was, of course, not an exclusively Jamaican phenomenon. People in the Caribbean and in the African diaspora as a whole, especially the middle class and the elite, had embraced the Eurocentric idea of white superiority and black inferiority.[50] Throughout the region, the lingering ghost of European prejudice based on notions of African inferiority led Blacks to believe that the Christian God was a white male and that only what was culturally white was right. The anti-African attitude, the all-pervasive Eurocentric values of the Christian Caribbean culture, and the system of education imposed on the Caribbean by fiat of the "metropoles" (Britain, France, Spain, etc.) threatened black consciousness and African culture in the region with total extinction, and at a monstrous price to black dignity and pride.

According to Eric Williams, the middle class in the British Caribbean were European in training, outlook, dress, taste, opinions, religion, and aspirations. With their educations from Oxford, Cambridge, the Sorbonne, and universities in other Eurocentric foreign cities, such as Madrid and Toronto, these Blacks retained hardly any trace of their African origin except the color of their skins.[51] As Fernando Henriques said a decade after Williams, these colored Caribbean individuals became a Euro-Caribbean hybrid, almost completely ignorant of African history and culture. They despised what little they learned of Africa in colonial textbooks that portrayed life on the continent as primitive and characteristic of the undesirable. Rather than confront Eurocentric cultural norms, these people would do anything to identify with the "Englishman."[52]

But this was not the fault of black people in the English-speaking Caribbean. In addition to the pervasive influence of British culture in the region, the educational system was controlled by external examinations—Junior Cambridge, Senior Cambridge, Teachers' Examination, and the General Certificate of Education, or London GCE—which Caribbean students were required to sit (a tool of colonialism). These examination papers originated in Britain and were sent back to the so-called mother country to be graded by "external readers." In this way, the British people defined the colonial "canon of learning," better known as the curriculum or the syllabus, in which the study of black people's history and culture was either nonexistent or marginal and seen through the eyes of Europeans as a history of slaves.

African history was the study of European exploits in Africa, a continent that *The Students Companion,* a textbook used widely in the public school system, called "the Dark Continent." To pass the London GCE in literature or history or the "general paper," for example, students studied British poets and playwrights (William Shakespeare, Geoffrey Chaucer, William Wordsworth, et al.); the British parliamentary system and its history; and the history of seafaring admirals, unscrupulous pirates, thieving bucca-

neers, and the squabbling kings, queens, dukes, and barons of England and their domination of the Caribbean since the 1600s. As one of the great paradoxes created by this
Anglicized view of the world, many Caribbean intellectuals got to do "Caribbean Studies" only after they entered European and North American universities, usually while
researching a topic for a thesis in Caribbean history, sociology, politics, or economics.

The psychological impact of this Eurocentrism on black people was profound; it not
only encouraged the glorifying of things European but showed a reckless distrust of
black people and a flagrant disregard for African-Caribbean cultures. Teachers both
white and black instructed pupils that Africa was "a white man's grave" and a mission
field for converting the heathen to Christianity. When students staged their normal elementary school pranks, teachers told them they were behaving like people "from the
jungles of Africa," meaning they were acting like "uncivilized peoples" or like something less than people—like chimpanzees or another type of ape, or monkey. Some black
children—like young Marcus Garvey—were forced to terminate their friendship with
their white missionary childhood friends as soon as they reached age thirteen. They were
not allowed to date or to establish serious intimate relationships with white teenagers,
who were often sent back to Britain, Canada, and the United States as soon as they
reached puberty. Their parents may have wanted to give them a "superior education"
abroad but also dreaded the idea of their daughters marrying black men.

The Rastafarians brought awareness of this "psychological downpression" to the forefront in the 1960s and 1970s by forcing the Jamaican government and the society at large
to take seriously the African consciousness in the diaspora on issues of race, class, and
political and economic oppression. In a society where lightness of skin color determined
status and the value of persons, Rastas propounded an Africanist psychology which contended that absolutely nothing is wrong with black people and that, contrary to the negative Eurocentric feelings about Africans, everything is right with them.[53] Blacks must
therefore define their reality in the African worldview, look for dignity within themselves, and not be ashamed of their natural hair. Instead of deprecating their dark pigmentation, Blacks need to view themselves as *the* privileged race, who will lead the
world to a higher spiritual, moral, and cultural plane at the time of reversals in the new
millennium, after "Babylon the Great" has fallen. Millenarianism aside, the Rastafarians set out on a deliberate course to deconstruct the dominant Eurocentric social-cul-
tural-political "narrative" (the accepted worldview) of black people, using religious,
musical, and cultural symbols as well as an ideology and psychology of resistance, dissonance, and black consciousness and practices that are pro-Africa in nature.

When compared as a group with other Jamaicans, Rastafarians are tremendously self-
confident, highly motivated, deeply self-assured, very proud, and profoundly hopeful.
They have exhibited a strong divine sense of purpose and are suffused with a deep feeling of personal freedom. "Rasses" have a strong sense of self-reliance and are highly resourceful. This profile applies to both men and women who regard themselves as a chosen people ("Jah people"), prophets and "ever-living" ones who, as Bob Marley sang in
his song "Exodus," "come to break down oppression, rule equality, wipe out transgression and set the captive free." The most profound expression of Rasta psychology is the
notion that Rastas have "ever-living life," that is, the belief in the immortality of their

being.[54] This belief is inspired by Rastafari's interpretation of the Selassie phenomenon and the Rastas' role as a chosen people in defining and implementing "Jah works" in place of the colonial world order. To fight the "devilism" of colonialism, the "downpress" (oppressed) represented in "Jah army" must possess and develop the necessary spiritual, psychological, and godlike qualities to counteract and overcome "satanism."

Psychology in Names and Personal Identity

One important measurement of Rasta psychology is seen in the way Rastas identify themselves. While many black Jamaicans resent being categorized racially as Africans and insist instead on being called Jamaicans, Rastafarians assert their Africanness as central to their being and identity. They often refer to themselves as "Rasses" or add to their names Ras, a title of honor and nobility in Ethiopia (for example, Ras Daniel Hartman and Ras Dizzy).[55] Other Rastas add Jah to their names, as in the case of Jah Lloyd and Jah Neville Bunny "Wailer" Livingstone. Rastafarians have also used the Kumina names Bongo and Kongo to identify themselves (for example, Bongo Herman and Kongo George). Bongo appears to have been a term "by which Central Africans proudly designated themselves."[56]

According to Monica Schuler, Mbongo, which means "wealthy" or "civilized," is the name of a Myal and Kumina (Afro-Caribbean religions) spirit that has survived in the songs and rituals of Kuminists in St. Thomas.[57] Male Rastas frequently refer to themselves as "King," "Kingman," "Lion," "Dread," and "Iya" (Nya) or "Bingi" (Binghi).[58] Rasta women are invariably referred to as "Queen," while female children and young women are called "Princess." Some Rastafarians have changed their names entirely to African names, especially to names in the Ethiopian Amharic language, spoken by King Selassie I. According to Seretha Rycenssa, Rastas believe that the initial step toward bringing about the millennium is realizing their "heritage which was stolen from them when they were uprooted from their native African soil."[59] A major part of that heritage is "the adoption of the Amharic language, and a lifestyle and appearance which distinguishes them from the rest of the populace."[60] What is most important about African names is the psychological identity and black consciousness that they inspire in diaspora Africans, and in Rastafarians in particular, as they identify themselves with African nobility, strength, endurance, deities, and resistance.

In their self-affirmation, Rastas have gone beyond the use of African names and linguistic adaptation to actual language creation. That is, they have created a language with its own vocabulary, much of which was never encountered before in Jamaica: Bongo Nyah and Bongo Natty (Rastaman), jollification (relaxation), groundation (verbal exchange in a learning session), dunza (money), dally (erratic bike riding), iration (creation), to name a few. According to former Rastafarian Leahcim Tufani Semaj, with this new language Rastas answer the question "Who am I?"—the most critical issue for cultural identity of Caribbean people.[61] The preeminent "I-an-I" in Rastas' oral and written communication (discussed elsewhere in this anthology) can be understood as performing a similar function. The psychologically powerful "I" precedes everything and qualifies Rasta speech. Thus words such as *I-man* (Rastaman), *I-frica* (Africa), *I-tals* (food produced from the ground and unspoiled by preservatives), and *I-laloo* and *I-nana* (callaloo and bananas) not only demonstrate Rastas' determination to free themselves completely from the culture of Babylon but also make a statement to the primacy of the black presence and reality in social and cultural discourse that is fundamental to the Rasta psychology of somebodiness.

Rastas' psychology and symbols define their reality and convey their religious and political ideas as ones of difference from and dissonance to the culture of Babylon. The symbolism of their ragged dress and other attire is that of identity with biblical prophets, traditional African dress, and the downtrodden of the world, whom they believe will inherit planet Earth at the time of reversals, when Jah judges this wicked world. Occasionally, standing with a special pose, lifting the hand with a particular movement, and changing vocal intonation contribute to the Rastafarian idea of difference. The "screw face" (contorted face) is used as part of what Barry Chevannes calls the "ritualized aggression"[62] with which a Rasta might begin the process of engaging in an antagonistic discourse with a visitor in an apparently friendly and unprovoked atmosphere.

The Rasta psychology engendered through the process of "Rastification" can thus be regarded as an essential historical manifestation and condition of resistance and freedom. In a real sense, Rastafari has given Jamaica a way to its neglected soul. This movement has engendered the kind of psychology the island needs to deal with important aspects of its colonial legacy and usher in national development. By identifying with African heroes and with folklorist and ancestor stories, by adopting cultural and religious symbols of Africa, by carrying a nonconformist and non-Western persona or physical appearance, and by affirming and reclaiming the beauty and dignity of Africa, Rastas help Blacks fill a cultural and ethnic void in their inner being. By forcing the issue of identity on national consciousness, Rastafari seeks to overturn certain assumptions of the ideology of racism among the middle class in Jamaica and throughout the black diaspora.[63]

Notes

1. William F. Lewis, *Soul Rebels: The Rastafari* (Prospect Heights, Ill.: Waveland Press, 1993), 2.

2. Barry Chevannes, *Rastafari: Roots and Ideology* (Syracuse, N.Y.: Syracuse University Press, 1994), 34.

3. Lisa A. Whitten, "Infusing Black Psychology into the Introductory Psychology Course," *Teaching of Psychology* 20, 1 (February 1993): 15. See also Gerad Jackson, "Black Psychology: An Avenue to the Study of Afro-Americans," *Journal of Black Studies* 12 (1982): 241–60.

4. Whitten, "Infusing Black Psychology," 15; Robert Jones, ed., *Black Psychology* (New York: Harper & Row, 1972), xii. See also James Baldwin, "African (Black) Psychology: Issues and Synthesis," *Journal of Black Studies* 16 (1986): 235–49; Wade W. Nobles, *African Psychology: Toward Its Reclamation, Reascension and Revitalization* (Oakland, Calif.: Black Family Institute, 1986). Nobles, a leading black psychologist, says elsewhere, "Black psychology is rooted in the nature of black culture which is based on particular indigenous African philosophical assumptions" ("Social and Psychological Behavior of African Peoples" [lecture given at the Africana Studies Institute of the W.E.B. DuBois Center for Pan African Culture, Accra, Ghana, August 1993]).

5. This historic event is of such importance to the Rastafarian psyche that every Rastafarian researcher finds referencing it, even in a peripheral way, an absolute necessity.

6. Cited in Robert Hill, "Leonard P. Howell and Millenarian Visions in Early Rastafari," *Jamaica Journal* 16, 1 (February 1983): 32–33.

7. Ibid., 26.

8. From its inception, Rastafari developed a strong identification with Africa. This is seen in its political, religious, social, and cultural life and takes many different forms of expression. One of these forms is the desire for repatriation to Africa, a spirit that was evident throughout the enslaved Americas up to the late 1800s.

9. Immanuel Geiss, *The Pan-Africanism Movement* (London: Nigeria Information Service, 1961); Tony Martin, *The Pan-African Connection* (Dover, Mass.: Majority Press, 1983); George Padmore, *Pan-Africanism or Communism?* (London: Dobson Press, 1956). See also Rupert Lewis, *Marcus Garvey: Anti-Colonial Champion* (London: Karia Press, 1987).

10. C.L.R. James, *The Black Jacobins: Toussaint L'Ouverture and the San Domingue Revolution* (New York: Vintage Books, 1989).

11. Horace Campbell, *Rasta and Resistance: From Marcus Garvey to Walter Rodney* (Trenton, N.J.: Africa World Press, 1987); Leonard E. Barrett, *The Rastafarians: The Dreadlocks of Jamaica* (Kingston: Sangster's Book Stores, 1977).

12. When George Washington took command of the continental American troops in the Revolutionary War, he publicly forbade the enlistment of "Ethiopians" (black patriots such as Barbadian-born Crispus Attucks of Boston) who were already fighting bravely for American independence. But after Washington's humiliating ordeal at Valley Forge in December 1777, brought on in large measure by Blacks fighting for the British army, Washington retracted the prohibition and authorized the enlistment of Ethiopians, who helped secure the decisive defeat of British rule in America. Although Blacks were promised the exercise of certain civil rights if they would fight on the side of the Continental army and help win the war, after the mission was accomplished in the historic defeat of British hegemonic "taxation without representation," slave owner Thomas Jefferson—author of the Declaration of Independence and one of the minds behind the Constitution—argued that Ethiopians did not have the capacity to grasp and appreciate the value of the Constitution and therefore should not benefit from its protection, a major political and psychological setback for aspiring black patriots. After Benjamin Banneker, a black mathematician and astronomer from Maryland, was named to the "commission which made the original survey of Washington D.C." for the capital, an editorial in the Georgetown *Weekly Ledger* (March 12, 1791) said of Banneker that he was "an Ethiopian whose abilities as surveyor and astronomer already proved that Mr. Jefferson's concluding that that race of men were void of mental endowment was without foundation" (cited in Lerone Bennett, Jr., *Before the Mayflower: A History of Black America* [New York: Johnson Publishing Co., 1982], 75; also 55–70; see also Thomas Jefferson, *Notes on Virginia* [1781]).

13. Bennett, *Before the Mayflower* 196.

14. See Campbell, *Rasta and Resistance,* 48; Joseph Owens, *Dread: The Rastafarians of Jamaica* (Kingston: Sangter's Book Stores, 1976); Hill "Leonard P. Howell."

15. Kenneth J. King, "Some Notes on Arnold J. Ford and New World Black Attitudes to Ethiopia," in Ronald K. Burkett, ed., *Black Apostles: Afro-American Clergy Confront the Twentieth Century* (Boston: G. K. Hall, 1978), 49.

16. Wardell J. Payne, ed., "Rastafarianism," in *Dictionary of African American Religious Bodies: A Compendium by Howard University School of Divinity* (Washington, D.C.: Howard University Press, 1991), 133.

17. Ibid.

18. Barry Chevannes, "Healing the Nation: Rastafari Exorcism of the Ideology of Racism in Jamaica," *Caribbean Quarterly* 36, 1–2 (1980): 67.

19. Chevannes, *Rastafari*, 39.

20. Lewis, *Marcus Garvey*, 168.

21. Amy Jacques Garvey, ed., *Philosophy and Opinions of Marcus Garvey* (New York: Arno Press/New York Times, 1969), 2: 326.

22. James Cone, *Martin and Malcolm and America: A Dream or a Nightmare?* (Maryknoll, N.Y.: Orbis Books, 1992), 12–13.

23. Marcus Garvey, "Garvey Tells His Own Story," in Milton C. Sernett, ed., *Afro-American Religious History: A Documentary Witness* (Durham, N.C.: Duke University Press, 1985), 380.

24. Ibid., 380–81.

25. Ibid., 382.

26. Cone, *Martin and Malcolm and America*, 13.

27. Garvey, ed., *Philosophy and Opinions of Marcus Garvey*, 1:2. Cited also in Cone, *Martin and Malcolm and America*, 13.

28. Editorial, *Rasta Voice*, no. 84 (1975): 6; Owens, *Dread*, 45.

29. Editorial, *Rasta Voice*, 6.

30. Ras Negus, in *Abeng* 1, 11 (April 12, 1969): 2.

31. Ibid.; see also *Rasta Voice* (1974). One of Nathaniel Samuel Murrell's colleagues in the philosophy department of The University of North Carolina at Wilmington told him a similar statement was made by Adolf Hitler.

32. Amy Jacques Garvey and E. U. Essien-Udom, eds., *Moral Philosophy and Opinions of Marcus Garvey* (London: Frank Cass, 1977), 3:57.

33. Ibid., 146.

34. Owens, *Dread*, 23.

35. King, "Some Notes on Arnold J. Ford," 50.

36. Ibid., 50–51.

37. Arnold J. Ford, *The Universal Ethiopian Hymnal* (New York: Beth B'nai Abraham Publishing Co., n.d.), 17.

38. King, "Some Notes on Arnold J. Ford," 49, 51.

39. Lewis, *Marcus Garvey*, 38–39; Hill, "Leonard P. Howell," 38; K.W.J. Post, *Arise Ye Starvelings: The Jamaican Labour Rebellion of 1938 and Its Aftermath* (The Hague: Martinus Nijhoff, 1978), 165–66.

40. Bongo Jerry, in *Abeng* 1, 22 (June 27, 1969): 3.

41. Clinton Hutton, "Colour for Colour; Skin for Skin: The Ideological Foundations of Post-Slavery Society, 1838–1865" (Ph.D. diss., University of the West Indies, 1993).

42. Campbell, *Rasta and Resistance*, 71; Post, *Arise Ye Starvelings*, 165; Hill, "Leonard P. Howell," 32, 34–37.

43. Kenneth Bilby and Elliot Leib, "Kumina, the Howellite Church and the Emergence of Rastafarian Traditional Music in Jamaica," *Jamaica Journal* 19, 3 (August–October 1986): 26.

44. Monica Schuler, *"Alas, Alas, Kongo": A Social History of Indentured African Immigration in Jamaica, 1840–1865* (Baltimore: Johns Hopkins University Press, 1980), 95–96.

45. Ibid., 95.

46. Ibid., 67, 93, 95–96.

47. Ajai Mansingh and Laxmi Mansingh, "Hindu Influences on Rastafarianism," in Rex Nettleford, ed., *Caribbean Quarterly Monograph: Rastafari* (Kingston: Caribbean Quarterly, University of the West Indies, 1985), 111.

48. Alice Spinner, *A Study in Colour* (London, 1994), 58.

49. Marian A. L. Miller, "The Rastafarian in Jamaican Political Culture: The Marginalization of a Change Agent," *Western Journal of Black Studies* 17, 2 (summer 1993): 112.

50. See David Hume, "Of National Characters" (1754), cited in Eric Eustace Williams, *From Columbus to Castro: The History of the Caribbean 1492–1969* (New York: Random House, 1984), 208. The eighteenth-century prejudice against black people articulated by Thomas Jefferson and by the celebrated Scottish philosopher, historian, and skeptic David Hume survived well into the twentieth century. Hume contended that Blacks were naturally inferior to Whites. He wrote of the so-called Negroes, "There scarcely ever was a civilized nation of that complexion, not even an individual, eminent either in action or speculation. No ingenious manufactures among them, no arts, no sciences . . . Not one of the Negro slaves dispersed all over Europe" has indicated any "symptoms of ingenuity." Thomas Jefferson's views also gave strong support to the advocates of black inferiority. According to the late distinguished historian, scholar, and prime minister of Trinidad and Tobago Eric Eustace Williams, "Jefferson regarded the Negro in America as inferior not only to the white man but also to the Amerindian, whose drawings, paintings, carving and oratory proved, in his view, the existence of a germ in their minds which only needed cultivation. But he found the Negro incapable of any thought above the level of plain narration, without even an elementary trait of painting or sculpture" (Williams, *From Columbus to Castro,* 208, referring to Thomas Jefferson, *Notes on Virginia* [1781]).

51. Eric Eustace Williams, *The Negro in the Caribbean* (Washington, D.C.: Panaf Publications, 1942).

52. Fernando Henriques, *Family and Colour in Jamaica* (London: Eyre & Spottiswoode, 1952).

53. Barry Chevannes, "Rastafarianism and the Class Struggle: the Search for a Methodology" (paper read at the University of the West Indies Symposium, Mona, Jamaica 1978; unpublished proceedings), 247.

54. Owens, *Dread,* 133–43.

55. *Ras* is also a part of the official name used by Haile Selassie and other emperors.

56. Schuler, *"Alas, Alas, Kongo,"* 67.

57. Furthermore, Kuminists have long called themselves "Bongo" from the "Bkongo nation," an ethnic designation. *Kongo* is derived from the word *Bakongo,* or simply *Kongo* (Congo), the name of the African homeland and probably the most important and influential Central African group to settle in St. Thomas during the colonial government's immigration scheme. Bakongo thinking is at the heart of the Kumina tradition. See Schuler, *"Alas, Alas, Kongo,"* 67, 78–79, 93–96.

58. *Nya* and *Binghi* are derived from the Nyabinghi anticolonial movement in Kigezi, Uganda, which was founded in the early 1920s.

59. Seretha Rycenssa, "The Rastafarian Legacy: A Rich Cultural Gift," *Economic Report of Jamaica* 4, 1 (August 1978): 23.

60. Claudia Rogers, "What's A Rasta?" *Caribbean Review* 7, 1 (January–March 1978): 10. Many Rastas are self-taught in Amharic, which they claim is the only true language of humanity.

61. Leahcim Tufani Semaj, "Race and Identity and Children of the African Diaspora: Contributions of Rastafari," *The Caribe* 4, 4 (1980): 14–18, esp. 17. Rastas have adopted many Ethiopian words and names for the deliberate naming of Rasta reality, self-identity, and solidarity with African culture.

62. Chevannes, *Rastafari,* 208.

63. Ibid.

3 Rastafari and the Exorcism of the Ideology of Racism and Classism in Jamaica

BARRY CHEVANNES

From the point of view of development theory as well as anthropology, this chapter explores Rastafari's contribution to the solution of what must be one of the most debilitating features of colonial underdevelopment, namely, racism. By keeping alive the issue of identity and forcing it on national consciousness, the Rastafari movement helped to expose—and by so doing, to overturn—certain assumptions of the ideology of racism in the 1940s and 1950s, particularly among the middle classes. I illustrate here the varied ways in which the ideology of racism was propounded and, in some measure, internalized so that I may contextualize what I argue constituted the raison d'être of the Rastafari movement. Others in this anthology discuss the racial climate in Jamaica during the 1930s, 1940s, and 1950s—the "before Rastafari" picture—a different aspect of which I address below.

The "after" picture, drawn from quantitative research carried out among middle-class university students in the early 1980s, looks like this:

> Black Jamaicans emerged as the most accepted of all groups on all categories of the social distance Scale, and also as the group towards which the most favourable attitudes were expressed on the Attitudes to Minorities Scale. Such a finding suggests that the low esteem he enjoyed from others is now a thing of the past. . . . Since the largest group in the sample was of mixed origin, it is not only the pure African alone who accepts himself, his blackness, his kinky hair, but the figures strongly suggest that Black is now indeed both beautiful and desirable generally.[1]

Wondering what might have brought about this change, Cultural anthropologist Mary F. Richardson mentions the Black Power movement and the fact of independence. My argument is simply that *the main credit for this change in consciousness belongs to Rastafari.*

Because the movement's membership is still relatively small,[2] its contribution to social change in Jamaica is often overlooked. But the story also has wider relevance. Blacks are lowest on the totem pole in virtually every nonblack country of the world. Thus, while the case of the Rastafari may well enrich our understanding of the role of identity in development, it also has direct implications for black identity in other parts of the world (including Latin America, where religion rather than race seems to be the major issue).

Class, Race, and Morality

A brief reflection on the class structure of Jamaica is necessary for understanding the context of Rastafari. Social theorist Fernando Henriques, whose book *Family and Colour in Jamaica* was the first to show interest in Rastafari, drew a sketch of a three-tiered triangle, representing a lower, a middle, and an upper class, and correlated it with color ranging from black to colored to white, respectively.[3] Caribbean social scientists have never had any doubt that race and skin color figure prominently in the stratification systems of the Caribbean. The question is: What are their relative roles? Is stratification based on class, on race and color, or on both? If on class, then we are dealing with an open system, in which there are broadly shared values; if on race, with a system of ethnic segregation, one prone to ethnic violence.

The divisions over the issue have been mainly between functionalism and pluralism. Adopting the economic model of pluralism developed by J. S. Furnival, M. G. Smith has argued that Caribbean societies are pluralities; they comprise different racial segments within the same polities, with each having its own distinct and separate cultural practices and norms. These segments are brought together only by the marketplace and held together by the political system.[4] Thus, in a country like Jamaica, race is closely identified with culture. (Smith's model of pluralism has triggered considerable debate, which has continued into the present.) From a functionalist perspective, Lloyd Brathwaite argued that Trinidadian society was integrated by a universally shared system of values, among them the ascriptive norms by which skin color was associated with privilege: the closer to white, the more of it; the closer to black, the less.[5]

Most scholars accept the applicability of pluralism to Caribbean society up to the end of slavery but reject it as no longer a useful model for understanding the dynamics of the modern societies of the region. Race and color remain as attitudinal remnants of the colonial past. For example, though 80 percent of Jamaica's population is of African descent, 15 percent of mixed African and European, and the rest of European and other white ethnic minority, the small mixed population dominates the middle class. The fact is, however, that upward social mobility by Blacks is changing the complexion of the middle classes.

In a recent effort aimed at reconciling both paradigms, Charles Mills made use of the Gramscian concept of *hegemony* to argue that while Caribbean societies are structured by class, race nevertheless functions as the ruling ideology. Concerned though he also was to answer widely expressed criticism that Marxism, by its one-sided focus on class, has no comprehensive answer to the realities of the Caribbean, he in fact touched upon the issue that I believe to be central in any explanation of the rise of the Rastafari, namely, racism as an ideology.[6]

The following brief sketch of racism as ideology provides an indication of its scope. I focus on the black population because the ideology was primarily aimed at subordinating Blacks. A racial ideology always presents itself as a cognitive system of binary opposites. All the qualities singled out for devaluation in the racially different group are the opposites of qualities that provide the subject group with a positive self-evaluation. Racism and ethnocentrism are always packaged as "they" and "we." In European culture, white is a symbol of purity and goodness and its opposite, black, a symbol of impurity and evil. By calling Africans "black" and themselves "white,"[7] Europeans set the stage whereupon the enslavement and subsequent subordination of Africans could be elevated to the level of mythology.

One common explanation of the racial difference was that the "darker" races were the children of Ham, that son of the biblical Noah who was allegedly struck with a curse for having looked on his father's nakedness. Both in the United States and throughout the Caribbean, stories of creation may be found that offer explanations as to why some men are white, others black.[8] While the tongue-in-cheek humor of many of them suggests that they are not accorded mythological status, they are nevertheless significant in that the common theme running through them all is that Blackness is a mistake, due either to error on God's part or to weakness and sin on the part of human beings.

The concepts of "white" being pretty and "black" being ugly went effectively unchallenged until the emergence of Marcus Garvey in the 1920s, and these usages are not yet uncommon today. The incongruity of black Christians praying that God wash them "white as snow" has presented not merely an ecological problem but a religious one as well. As the prophet Alexander Bedward saw it, even the skin color of Blacks was to become white after their ascent to heaven.[9] No wonder Jesus and his angels are themselves seen as white. And skin color has represented only one of the phenotypical differences between Whites and Blacks; others are hair quality (fine versus coarse, straight versus spiraled), nose shape (straight versus flat, narrow versus wide), and lip size (thin versus thick). These qualities also contributed to defining who was beautiful, who ugly. A common practice among black Jamaican mothers was the pinching of a child's nose to make it straight and thin.

Character stereotyping of Blacks was very much a part of that Euro-Jamaican tradition. "Kofi," the day name for males born on Friday, and "Bungo," the name of one of the Congo tribes and of a religious cult appearing among the Maroons, were used to characterize Blacks as stupid and uncouth. This was also true of the character Quashie, the Twi day name for males born on Sunday (Twi being the language of an ethnic group in Ghana), used by Whites to personify their stereotype of the African slaves as deceitful, lying, capricious, and lazy. Orlando Patterson contends that the slaves responded "by either appearing to, or actually internalizing" these stereotypes.[10] After slavery, and certainly into the twentieth century, the term *Quashie* shed its connotation of "deceitful" and acquired, instead, that of "stupid" or "foolish." It was more hurtful to call one Quashie than to call one stupid, since an element of race still clung to the usage. No doubt, the Euro-Jamaican misuse of these day names was partly responsible for their gradual disuse and the preference of biblical and Anglo-Saxon names among Blacks.

Another "failing of character" that became ideological was the accusation by Whites that Blacks were sexually irresponsible. Ironically, the proof of irresponsibility was not the large colored population of the island but "illegitimate births." There were two issues here: one was the failure to enter into the legal institution of marriage, and the other was what some sociologists have referred to as "serial polygamy"—a target of theological teaching on holiness by the Protestant missionaries.

The area of sexual irresponsibility relates to the acceptance of certain social institutions as superior to others based on ethnicity, race, and class. During the late 1930s and the 1940s, for example, a group of upper-middle-class women, at one time led by the wife of the colonial governor, used to stage mass marriages. These often encouraged serial polygamy, a series of consensual or common-law unions into which many people entered during their first fifteen years of cohabitation, resulting in a complex system of half brothers and half sisters. Many women therefore bore children for different genitors, while many men sired children of different mothers, often complicating the situation by their failure either to acknowledge or to bear paternal responsibility. These forms of male and female "irresponsibility" have, through the decades, been viewed as a root cause of crime, lawlessness, and immorality in Jamaica. Though the pattern of mating has not changed much since emancipation, according to George Roberts and Sonja Sinclair,[11] the institution of marriage preferred by most Whites—even though they practice what, too, could be called serial polygamy[12]—is one way of acquiring social respectability. Common-law unions, after the spouses pass thirty-five or forty years of age, thus tend to end in marriage at some point.

Culture: Savagery versus Civilization

Racist arguments about the savagery and lack of civilization of Africa are now too well known to need any exposition here.[13] They were very common in Jamaica, where the ideology seemed to have taken root much more among those exposed to the higher levels of the education system; much evidence can be gathered to show that among the uneducated masses, Africa was always cherished as the land of the forebears.[14] As Africa was the land of darkness and savagery, so was Europe generally, and England in particular, the land of light and civilization. England became for every schoolchild, up to the time of independence in 1962, the "mother country."

Not surprisingly, many of the more important aspects of Jamaican folk culture were the objects of ideological deprecation. The folk religion, in all its variants, was described by one of Jamaica's leading intellectuals of the 1920s and 1930s as "the mud," which he contrasted with "the gold." The mud was the tradition of African superstition and savagery, with its wild drumming, dancing, spirit possession, and polytheism, in which the ignorant masses were mired. The gold was the tradition of real religion, with its Easter-morning pealing of bells, preaching the word of the one true God, and studied reflection.[15] To the missionaries and Christian preachers themselves, Afro-Jamaican religion was the work of the Devil; European-defined Christianity, of which they were the bearers, was the work of God. This is doubly ironic considering that Christianity, from the beginning, developed in Africa centuries before it ever reached hopelessly pagan England.

While not all Blacks were "stuck in the mud," all except the relatively few who acquired a certain level of education spoke "bad" English. In rural Jamaica, "good" English was the speech of the local elite: the schoolteachers, the justice of the peace, the sanitary inspector, and so on. Nothing less was expected of them. People using the island dialect were thought to be common and lacking in "ambition." "Good" English was thus the speech of the upwardly mobile, "bad" English the speech of the uneducated and ignorant. Using "culture" in the narrow sense of the fine arts, Whites inflated their own culture to support their ideology of racial superiority over Blacks.

I have spent some time illustrating the ways in which racism entrenched itself in Jamaica in the cognitive life of the people, because my view is that the impact of the Rastafari is to be sought here rather than elsewhere. Naturally, to claim Jamaica as a special case in this scenario not only may be considered absurd but could render questionable the suggestion I make at the end of the chapter that much about Rastafari may have significance for other countries. One could argue, for example, that racist and ethnocentric ideology has been the experience of all colonialism—of Romans over English, English over Irish, Japanese over Chinese. Racism against the Africans, however, is unquestionably the most extreme.

Behind the studied propagation of white racist ideology always lurked the fear of threat to white racist superordination. Jamaica had experienced more slave revolts and plots than any other colony in the hemisphere; hosted the only Maroon settlement, which forced the British into treaty; brought slavery to an end in 1834 with the greatest revolt in its history; witnessed the suppression of a rebellion on the basis of color in which peasants rallied together and fought their oppressors in 1865; and been overawed by a popular religious movement, whose leader agitated for the overthrow of Whites in 1895. On the eve of the appearance of Rastafari, the country was facing the Black Nationalism of Marcus Garvey.

Garvey was not the first Black Nationalist in Jamaican history, but he was the first to fire the imagination of the masses on a grand and dramatic scale. That Blacks in both Africa and the Americas were inspired to become his followers indicates that theirs was a common experience. Garvey had an impact far beyond his own organization, the Universal Negro Improvement Association (UNIA), or his actual teachings, far-reaching though these were; just the fact that he was such a great man did much to change the self-perception of Blacks. Garvey's organization, political achievements, ideological teachings, and impact on Rastafari, as discussed elsewhere in this anthology (see Chapters 2 and 8), showed that he was revolutionary for his time. By his intense concentration on the black man, he was mainly responsible for the attention that increasingly large numbers of Jamaicans began to pay to events in Africa. Before reaching the peak of his career, Garvey was already a hero to the Jamaican masses, in both the common and mythological senses of the word.[16]

Evolution of Rastafarian Thought

Rastafarian thought and practices, discussed elsewhere in this volume, have developed over the years in phases. In the first two decades the movement centered on the identity of God, and propagating the teachings of the faith took the form of street meetings. Each preacher established his own "King of Kings" mission, which was attended by those converted at the public meetings. Ritual practices varied from mission to mission but included baptism, fasting, and celebration of special anniversaries, such as the coronation of Haile Selassie I, and the cultivation of head and facial hair according to the nazirite vow as set out in the Book of Leviticus. The second two decades, the 1950s and 1960s, were marked by agitation for repatriation and by the rise to ascendancy throughout the movement of a radical trend that became known as the Dreadlocks.

Repatriation is viewed as a divinely ordained act, depending on the will and action of God, not on humans. It is different from migration. In the August 1934 episode in which Leonard Howell told his people to prepare and await the ship for their repatriation to Ethiopia, people allegedly expected the sea to part, just as in the time of Moses—but this time only for those with a beard. Mass agitation for repatriation, when it did take place in 1958 and again in 1959–1960, came against the background of increased migration to Britain and renewed attention by old Garveyites to the possibilities of migration to Liberia and other West African countries. Interest in repatriation again heightened, particularly among the Rastafari, when an Ethiopian World Federation official visited Jamaica in 1955 and announced that Haile Selassie was making a small land grant at Shashamane in Ethiopia for the settlement of Blacks, in appreciation for their support during the fight against Fascist invasion of his country.

In spite of this brief 1955 episode, scholars who argue that the movement is essentially millenarian need to exercise caution, for only at three times in its six decades of existence (1934, 1958, and 1959) did the dream of the millennium result in mass millenarian activity. The growth and impact of Rastafari have not been dependent on the dream of the millennium. Many Rastafarian beliefs and practices are the idealization of beliefs and practices already present within the culture of the folk but carried to extremes. Such, for instance, is the God-man concept, which derives from folk beliefs in the immanence of God; such also is the sacred ritualization of female subordination, which has precedence in social and cultural life. But in other instances, deliberately and consciously Rastafarians identified with traditions that were vilified under racist ideology.

The 1970s and 1980s were marked by three far-reaching developments. The first was the use of reggae music as the medium of expression of Rastafari sentiments and the mutual identity of the two. The second was the internationalization of the movement, due to the impact of reggae, to migration, and to racism in the metropoles of both the Northern and Southern Hemispheres. These have been well documented. (See Chapter 16 by William Spencer in this book). Third, but not yet fully studied, is the triumphant entry of Rastafari into the middle classes. With this last we come to the central point of this chapter.

Race and the Jamaican Middle Class

As the "before" picture I presented earlier made clear, the middle classes, made up predominantly of the colored population, were far from immune to the ideology of racism. In his analysis of class consciousness in the period leading up to the 1938 labor rebellion in Jamaica, Ken Post says, "Race was also a very important factor in the consciousness of the lower middle class. Along with their collars and ties a light brown skin and 'good' hair and features were the marks of their superior status, and were among the criteria for getting a job. But race was . . . crucial for the entire middle class."[17] But the symbols of social mobility were not the only concern of the middle class, Post explains. The people "tended to reproduce quite faithfully the ideas of their betters. Indeed, . . . it was the special task of many of them to develop and propagate those ideas, since clergymen, teachers, journalists and others were concerned specifically with cognitive practice."[18] In other words, white colonial society had produced the intellectuals on whom it could rely for its apologia (rational defense).

But to view the middle classes from this point of view alone would be one-sided. As Peter Phillips explains, in the prewar years a nationalist movement split had emerged among the middle classes between those with a "Jamaican" and those with a "Pan-African" tendency that was "focused on a wider set of Pan-Nationalist concerns."[19] The latter clearly were motivated by the racial contradiction and would have been influenced by Garveyite and pre-Garveyite Black Nationalism. For the former—the larger and more influential segment—nationalism derived from other contradictions, such as the control by the colonial government of "education and other matters vital to the middle class."[20]

Middle-class nationalism, led by the "Jamaican" tendency, crystallized in the formation of the People's National Party (PNP) in 1938, whose demand for self-government, strengthened by the labor rebellion and meeting objectives of the British government, led to a process of gradual decolonization that culminated in independence in 1962. According to Trevor Munroe, the main problem facing the upper middle class (which led this process) was how to secure control of the country without the arousal of the masses. Though this thesis overestimates the independent political potential of the working class and underestimates the significance of the Black Nationalist wing in the nationalist movement, it aptly identifies the process as "constitutional decolonization" and explains its results as the "growth and consolidation of middle class dominance" over political life[21] and a constitution patterned on the British system. In effect, the independence movement avoided the issue of race. Thus the nationalism that researcher Katrin Norris found among the educated in Jamaica on the eve of political independence lay "in the confidence that Jamaica can successfully build a miniature Britain, America or a European-type state" rather than build on the rich "cultural traditions or creative spirit of the Jamaican people."[22]

Rastafari Raises Racial Consciousness

Norris found hope for social change relative to Jamaican cultural traditions in the Rastafarian, who openly "expresses his defiance" to "the conformist . . . [who is] over-deferential" to Whiteness. "While the conformist still looks on a white man as a source of financial assistance and few would hesitate to beg from him if the opportunity offered, the Rastafarian prefers to live in appalling squalor" rather than beg. Norris saw in Rastafari "an instinctive kind of nationalism and an instinctive search for dignity and naturalness" that is "as far removed from race hatred as straightforward national consciousness is removed from hatred of other nations," notwithstanding its being a "cranky" philosophy.[23] In other words, by electing to lead a life based on the affirmation of being black, without at the same time being racist, the Rastafari have seized hold of one of the mainsprings of national development, namely, a sense of national identity. In this respect they represented, for Norris, not so much a signpost leading the way to Rastafari as a symbol of the harmony between the reality of being black and the consciousness of and confidence in that reality. This point must not be glossed over. Some commentators accuse Rastafari of being a form of "reverse racism," sometimes comparing it to the Nation of Islam. Nothing could be further from the truth. As Father Joseph Owens observes, this judgment derives from a failure to grasp the essence of a doctrine that not only "effectively negates the white racism pervading the society, but which also strives to overcome the logical premises which make any type of racism possible."[24] Many other Whites who have studied the Rastafari would share that view. This gives the Rastafari a humanism, with potential lessons for other groups and peoples.

The Rastafarian exorcism of the ideology of racism among the middle classes and its inspiring of a more wholesome sense of identity began in the period of the Dreadlocks, with a millenarian episode that, unsurprisingly blown out of all proportion, had the effect of Jamaicans treating the Rastafari seriously for the first time and beginning a process of self-examination. Ken Post describes Jamaica as an open society prone to external influences. Understandably, therefore, the impact on the middle classes was in no small measure facilitated and enhanced by the rapid acquisition of independence and equal status with other sovereign states of the world by African (and other) nations. But while external processes made the middle classes better listeners, the Rastafari forced them to think, and to choose.

On New Year's Day 1959, Fidel Castro entered Havana in triumph, an event that made a great impact throughout the Caribbean and the rest of the hemisphere. Later the same year, the Reverend Claudius Henry, leader of a group of Rastafari, proclaimed October 25 to be "Decision Day," when Israel's scattered children would return to Africa.[25] Undaunted by the failure of this prophecy, but less open to the public, Henry was planning quietly for repatriation when a police raiding party swooped down on his headquarters and seized an arms cache and two letters. The letters, addressed to Castro, informed the Cuban leader that, as the Rastafari were about to depart for Africa, they wished to hand over the country to him. Henry was charged with felony treason, intent to intimidate and overawe Her Majesty's government and to invite in a foreign power. As if that were not enough, weeks later news broke that members of Henry's church were involved in guerrilla activities in the Red Hills area above Kingston, and that two British soldiers had been killed in an operation against them. A massive manhunt soon resulted in the capture of a four-man squad that included Henry's son, Ronald. These men the authorities charged with the murder of a police infiltrator, whom the guerillas had buried near their training ground in the hills.

The effect was electrifying, especially among the middle classes. Not since the Morant Bay Rebellion in 1865 had a group of Jamaicans taken up arms against the state. Further, here was a group of people who wore their contempt of society in their hair and even facial expressions. It was time to put a stop to the lunacy that was Rastafari. The police were not slow to take their cue from the general public, as a wave of intimidation—shaving of locks, arrests, beatings, and imprisonment—descended on all Rastafari in unprecedented scale and scope.

Acting wisely, a small group of Rastafari led by Mortimo Planno approached the University College of the West Indies with the suggestion that a carefully documented and published study of their movement would go a long way toward convincing Jamaican society that Rastafari was essentially peaceful. It was a brilliant move. The university, then an affiliate of the University of London and headed by W. Arthur Lewis, was already making great headway in challenging the pro-British, anti-Jamaican orientation of the middle classes with a reputation for scholarship and excellence, especially in the field of tropical medicine. The sanction of such an institution would not be lost on the real sources of influence and power.

The urgency of the situation led Lewis to assign three of his finest scholars—M. G. Smith, Roy Augier, and Rex Nettleford, all Caribbeans—to carry out the investigation. The result, after two weeks of intense fieldwork, was *The Rastafari Movement in Kingston, Jamaica,* which Lewis presented to the government. Sketching in brief outline the beliefs and the historical course and structure of the movement, the scholars gave an analysis that exposed appallingly bad social conditions and poverty, in the midst of which Rastafari was the only hope to numbers of people. After careful study, the government acted swiftly and seized upon one of the several recommendations: that a mission be sent to Africa to explore the possibilities for migration there. The mission, which included three Dreadlocks, set off early in 1961, and after visits to Sierra Leone, Liberia, Ghana, Nigeria, and Ethiopia, it returned to present a majority and a minority (Rastafari) report, both of which were published and hotly debated in the press.

Predictably, initial middle-class reaction was very hostile. Some felt betrayed by the sympathetic tone of the university study, while many objected to the mission as a waste of taxpayers' money. But coming from the university and backed by a popular government, both report and mission made it quite respectable for middle-class persons to show sympathy toward the Rastafari.

This was something new. The university initiative was to mark the beginning of an entirely new stage in the development of the society. No scholar has understood this better than Nettleford, and no title conveys more the essence of a book's content than does *Mirror, Mirror.* With the issue of national identity confronting Jamaicans at independence in 1962, history was kind to the country by providing it three events in the course of the 1960s, three lessons for those who wished to learn: the Henry crisis and its aftermath (the report and the mission); the visit of Haile Selassie in 1966; and the Black Power movement in 1968–69. These different events were spurred by the same question and the same search. Assuming the "lessons from the sixties," Nettleford noted "trends which are irreversible," notably the fact that "the established order, despite its misgivings about race consciousness, dares no longer to see itself psychologically as an adjunct of Great Britain."[26]

The three-day visit of Emperor Haile Selassie remains unparalleled in Jamaican history for the extraordinary level of popular enthusiasm, the crowd size, and the degree of tolerance toward the Rastas. As Joseph Owens reported, people gathered spontaneously from all parts of Jamaica to see Selassie. They came "on foot, in cars, in drays, in carts, in hired buses, on bicycles and by every means of transport that can be imagined." The crowds created a nightmare for law-enforcement officials. "The police were surrounded by the tide of it all. . . . The result: all the prearranged ceremony went by the way." Selassie wept as he stood on the steps of the Ethiopian airliner that had brought him to Jamaica via Trinidad and Tobago and surveyed the vast throng that had gathered at Palisadoes Airport to greet him. Although the emperor was "hurried in nervous haste to the Governor General's car to make his triumphant entry into Kingston," his motorcade led perhaps the largest traffic jam in the history of the city. People were shouting everywhere. Some said, "The day has come, God is with us. Let we touch the hem of His garment." Others placed themselves in the path of the governor general's car and shouted, "Remember me! Prepare a place for me in thy kingdom."[27]

Later, in the official state receptions, first with government and then with royal guest as hosts, for the first time middle-and upper-middle-class elites actually came face to face with the Dreadlocks as a group. Indeed, it was said to be the "in thing" to be seen on friendly and familiar terms with the Dreads. Police action against them was muted for the three days, and Rastas made no attempt to conceal their smoking of ganja. The treatment of the Dreadlocks during Selassie's state visit amounted to unofficial legitimization of the movement. All of this took place in Jamaica at the height of the Civil Rights struggle and the rise of the Black Power movement in the United States, which spilled over into other parts of the African diaspora.

Rastafari, Black Power, and Cultural Change

The Black Power movement in Jamaica was the work of Walter Rodney, a Guyanese lecturer in African history at the University College of the West Indies in 1968. Rodney formally launched a Black Power group on the campus and, more important, took his expertise *extra muros* among the Rastafari, including the Claudius Henry group, whose leader had just been paroled from a ten-year prison sentence for felony treason. The government, which had Rodney under surveillance, took advantage of his departure abroad to attend a black writers' conference in Canada 1969 to ban his reentry of Jamaica as dangerous and subversive. A protest march by university students against the government's action triggered several hours of rioting and arson by unemployed youths throughout the city. At several roadblocks that the youths set up, the only white and colored people let through without damage to their cars or injury to their persons were those recognized for their work on behalf of black people.

The "Rodney riot," as the event became known, had its causes in grave economic and social conditions. The process of increased industrialization had resulted in a doubling of unemployment, from 13 percent at the beginning to 25 percent at the close of the 1960s, while all around were the signs of growing affluence. The riot did violence to middle-class consciousness by once again raising the question of racial identity. But this time, thought found expression in action as a group of intellectuals formed the Abeng movement, named after the horn used by the Jamaican Maroons, and began the publication of a weekly newspaper by the same name. Abeng ran for only six or seven months in 1969, but its significance, apart from the dissemination of radical Black Nationalist ideas, is to be found in the organic link it sought to establish in the Rodney tradition between the middle and working classes. It was a partisan voice of the poor.

The middle-class university-based intellectuals, learning from Rodney, understood that Rastafari's critique of the society was already creating changes in the consciousness of the masses. Thus, although many individual Rastafari became active participants in the Abeng group and contributors to and distributors of the weekly, the adoption of the linguistic symbolism developed by the Dreadlocks (by then part of urban street culture) more than anything else proved that the country was indeed at a new stage. The use of words such as *grounding, Babylon, beast, men* was a regular feature of the newspaper[28] and of the vocabulary of intellectuals, especially at the university. Rodney, for instance, titled his reflections on the whole experience *Groundings with My Brothers.*[29] By 1971, amid speculation about the date of the upcoming national election, the prime minister reminded an audience, "Only one man can call a general election, and that man is *I man.*"

That election, when it finally came in February 1972, saw the use of other Rastafari symbols. The understanding of the positive symbol that Africa was for Jamaicans became widespread largely through the impact of the Rastafari. Both incumbent prime minister Hugh Shearer and leader of the opposition Michael Manley made widely publicized trips to Africa in 1971. Each visited Ethiopia and received gifts from the emperor. Manley's gift, however, was a rod, which in the traditional folk semiology represented spiritual power, a tradition the Rastafari, with their brightly painted, multicolored rods, had continued. Coincidentally, there were many allegations of corruptions against the government. Manley, popularly known to his followers as "Joshua," exploited this situation by producing the "rod of correction" that Haile Selassie had given him and in so doing set loose powerful emotions: "Thousands of Jamaicans came to believe that the Rod was imbued with supernatural powers, and everywhere he appeared people wanted to touch this potent source of power, a few ascribing to it healing properties."[30]

Understanding quite well the potency of the symbolism, Edward Seaga, a member of Parliament, then claimed to have found the real rod, which was nothing more than a "stick of detention."[31] The PNP, however, did find Seaga's campaign humorous, and many middle-class persons treated it that way. The PNP responded by publishing a full-page ad refuting Seaga's claim, and at a carefully staged moment during a public meeting, Manley dramatically reasserted possession of the rod by producing a box out of which he took it and held it aloft.

Commenting on the episode, Adam Kuper remarks:

One cannot dismiss this sort of thing as merely symbolic or as cynical vote-mongering. The historical depreciation of blackness and Africanness in Jamaica was achieved by manipulation of symbols, and these symbolic gestures helped to liberate people from ingrained feelings of inadequacy and impotence. . . . Symbolic reversals of the traditional value system have helped to undermine the whole traditional structure of deference. It is true that these things are merely symbolic as opposed to the continued inequalities in Jamaica. But this does not mean that the politicians are being cynical. It would take a very cool man to disrupt these attitudes while deliberately calculating to maintain the established system of privilege.[32]

Assessing the Rastafarian Impact

There can be no doubting the role of the Rastafari in this reversal of values in Jamaica, an achievement accomplished without effecting any large-scale conversion of the population to the religious movement itself. Its methodology, if one may call it that, is one of *symbolic* confrontation on many fronts, also seen in hair, language, dress, and several other modes I have been unable to detail in this chapter. Kuper sees it another way: rejecting the class and race models of Jamaican society (including the plural society model) as being too rigid and out of alignment with reality, and substituting the folk model of status used by Jamaicans, with an ambiguity and a variability that he argues correspond more to real life, he diagnoses the Jamaican political system as fairly healthy, impervious to any threat of division based on either race or class. Thus, he argues, Black Nationalism does not provide any basis on which to change the system. Where, then, does Kuper consign the Rastafari? "'Rastas' and 'rich whites' do not make up Jamaica, except for television crews. But they provide useful reference points for the self-definition, by contrast, of the 'ordinary Jamaican'."[33]

That ordinary Jamaican swept Manley into power, in an election in which 60 percent of the new People's National Party voters and 44 percent of Jamaican Labour Party (JLP) voters who switched to the PNP identified positively with the rod. The rod was a symbol rather than the cause of their identification with Manley's vision of correcting the ills of society. Poll figures of the late, highly respected political scientist Carl Stone, of the Department of Government at the University of the West Indies, showed that identification with the Rastafari movement was proportionately greater than with the rod. More new voters (68 percent PNP and 38 percent JLP) expressed sympathy toward the Rastafari than expressed identification with the rod (60 percent PNP and 12 percent JLP). The new voters were mainly the youths who had reached the voting age of twenty-one between the 1967 and the 1972 elections.

Not only working-class youths but the middle classes as well were now defining themselves as closer to the Rasta than to the white reference point. A fascinating development was the appearance and growth of the Twelve Tribes of Israel, a Rastafari organization formed late in the 1960s that, according to Frank Jan van Dijk, has become a haven for middle-class Rastas. The Twelve Tribes allowed them to preserve liberal middle-class values, such as greater equality between the sexes than is found among other Rasta

Responses to the Rastafari Movement and to the Rod of Correction

	% Sympathetic and Supporting Rastafari	% Indifferent to Rastafari	% Hostile
New PNP voters	68	18	14
New JLP voters	38	12	50
JLP voters who switched to PNP	36	31	50
Consistent JLP voters	35	25	40
	Positively Identifying with Rod	% Indifferent and Unaware	% Cynical and Hostile
New PNP voters	60	18	22
New JLP voters	12	29	59
JLP voters who switched to PNP	44	37	19
Consistent JLP voters	21	49	39

Source: Carl Stone, *Electoral Behavior and Public Opinion in Jamaica* (Kingston: Institute of Social and Economic Research, 1974), 26–27.

groups. For example, women "may speak as often and with as much authority as the male representatives" and "are considered to be equal in all respects but the male comes first, just as in the Bible."[34] Also, there is freedom for those who prefer not to grow the beard or wear dreadlocks and freedom for women to wear pants—a license that is taboo among the Dreadlocks. Not all middle-class Rastafari belong to the Twelve Tribes; there are lawyers, journalists, professors, doctors, and other professionals who have been professing the consciousness of Rastafari but are not members. Twelve Tribes, however, is symbolic of the kind of "shift in consciousness" (to borrow a phrase of Ken Post) that has been forced on the Jamaican middle class by the Rastafari movement. This does not mean that the middle class is becoming Rasta; far from it. But it does signify a tendency to identify more with the African reference point than with the European.

As discussed by Verena Reckord (Chapter 14) and others later in this anthology, one of the most important aspects of Jamaican culture to facilitate this change has been popular music. Originating in the ghettos of Kingston, reggae rose to become a national music whose popularity made the political parties use it in their campaigns. Sections of the middle class used to deplore what they considered reggae's artless monotony. But when the music succeeded internationally, worldwide approval silenced all Jamaican middle-class criticism and opened the way for even greater identification. The appropriation of Rastafari argot by the intelligentsia that began with the Abeng movement proved not to have been a mere transient fashion but to have signaled a profound and lasting

change. In a published paper, Rastafari researcher Velma Pollard, professor of English
literature at the University of the West Indies, traces the use of certain Rastafari words
of philosophical import to convey a sense of black identity in the works of two of the
country's major poets, Dennis Scott and Lorna Goodison. "The culture of Rastafari,"
she observes, "has moved like yeast through the Jamaican society infusing all these expressions with its power."[35]

As an ideology, racism was internalized by black Jamaicans at both the folk and
middle-class levels of the society. For the middle class in particular, adherence to tenets
of this ideology seemed important for upward mobility. Their role in society made the
black middle class serve as the reproducers of anti–black African and pro–white European ideas. But Rastafari, emerging in the 1930s among the marginalized urban population, supplied an ideological antidote. By forcing a reexamination of its identity on Jamaican society—especially on its middle class, whose dominance over social and
political life was consolidated during the period leading up to independence—the movement helped achieve a readjustment to the reality of being black. External factors such
as African independence and internal ones such as the short-lived Black Power
movement also helped bring this readjustment about, but there is no denying the major
role played by the Rastas.

To be sure, Rastas remain a small fraction of the population of over two million
people. Rastafari's impact is therefore assessed not by counting the number of adherents
but by discovering its symbolic role. This the late Edna Manley, wife of Norman Manley
(the man most identified with Jamaican nationalism) and mother of two-time prime
minister (the late) Michael Manley, understood very well. In the last dated entry of her
diaries, she revealed that in the 1950s she had yet to understand the Rastafari, but when
she did, what struck her more was not the belief in Haile Selassie but "the identification
with a Black God." She wrote, "All the white imagery that consciously and unconsciously had found its creative expression in the white Christs all over Europe—all over
the world—carried there with the Christian religion, couldn't mean the truth to the black
people of the Caribbean or black America, and this was true not only in the case of the
poor masses but also to the intelligent thinking youth of the middle class."[36]

All this has not meant the end of racism as ideology in Jamaica. In research carried
out in 1983, Derek Gordon found light-skinned persons moving up the social ladder
more quickly than Blacks and remaining there in larger proportion.[37] But whereas this
was accepted reality in the 1940s, it is no longer the inevitable state of things to the Jamaican middle class.

During the incumbency of Prime Minister Seaga in the 1980s, an often-voiced com-
plaint was that the government relied too heavily on foreign and local white consultants
and advisors. When, therefore, the new Manley administration announced the appointment of some local white advisors in March 1989, its action sparked a public controversy. Many Blacks were of the view that these appointments revealed yet again a
lack of confidence in the ability of Blacks, at a time when they manifested equal, if not
greater, work competence and loyalty to the country. So hot was the issue that the *Jamaica Record,* a newspaper run by a black entrepreneur, devoted two Sunday issues to

the debate. In his contribution Rex Nettleford observed, "Some feel that the deliberate and conscious defocusing of social and economic issues away from the reality of the Black imperative in development is not the least among the causes of past failures."[38] As with Latin America, development policies have failed in the Caribbean because governments ignore the issue of identity—in this case, black identity. Such policies will continue to fail as long as they ignore the issue.

This leads me to a final suggestion. Sociologist Norman Girvan of the Consortium Graduate School of Social Sciences at the University of the West Indies, Mona, argues that the integration of European migrant labor into the industrializing economies of Latin America in the nineteenth and twentieth centuries took place on the basis of a racial segmentation of the labor force into "noncompeting" groups. White workers were assigned the role of supplying skilled labor, Indians and Blacks the role of supplying cheap and unskilled manpower. Thus, in the lowland temperate regions where European migrants settled, Blacks were relegated to *minifundios* in the agricultural sector and to the marginalized low-paying occupations of the city; Indians fared similarly.

> This process was both reinforced by an ideology of racism and in turn reinforced it. Since it benefited both white labor and white owners of capital, it was characterized by a powerful alliance of attitudes and actions within the white community as a whole in relation to non-whites. Therefore, it introduced a deep and abiding cleavage along racial lines so far as the development of a true "proletarian" consciousness, from the standpoint of the relations of production, was concerned.[39]

The white proletariat of Latin America is, therefore, itself a carrier of the ideology of racism. Girvan does not say to what extent Blacks and Indians have internalized the sense of inferiority, but it is quite clear that Black Nationalism and *indigenismo* were natural responses to the specific historical and contemporary conditions of the respective peoples of Latin America. This makes the identity question in Latin America somewhat complex. While it is true that religion plays a major role, the fact that "the struggles of white proletarians and other exploited white groups lacked a racial dimension"[40] makes their struggles of a different kind. Blacks in that region, therefore, could learn from the experience of Jamaica and the Rastafari movement, not necessarily in adopting the religion but in learning from its methodology of ideological transformation through symbolic confrontation.

Notes

1. Mary F. Richardson, "Out of Many, One People—Aspiration or Reality? An Examination of the Attitudes of the Various Racial and Ethnic Groups within the Jamaican Society," *Social and Economic Studies* 32, 3 (1983): 158.

2. There are no figures of membership. Rastafari is still not included in census takes. One "guesstimate" was seventy thousand to eighty thousand in the early 1970s.

3. Fernando Henriques, *Family and Colour in Jamaica* (London: Eyre & Spottiswoode, 1952), 52–53.

4. M. G. Smith, *The Plural Society of the British West Indies* (Berkeley: University of California Press, 1965). See, for example, Vera Rubin, ed., *Social and Cultural Pluralism* (Seattle: University of Washington Press, 1962).

5. Lloyd Brathwaite, "Social Stratification in Trinidad: An Analysis," *Social and Economic Studies* 2, 2–3 (1953).

6. Charles Mills, "Race and Class: Conflicting or Reconcilable Paradigms?" *Social and Economic Studies* 36, 2 (1987): 35–48.

7. Journalist Donald Woods, whose awakening to the atrocities of apartheid was depicted in the 1987 movie *Cry Freedom,* had the South African judge ask Black Consciousness activist Steve Biko why South African Blacks called themselves black when they really were brown. Biko retorted, "Why do you call yourselves white when you are really pink?" "Precisely!" said His Honor.

8. See Zora Neale Hurston, *Mules and Men* (Bloomington: Indiana University Press, 1978); and Daryl C. Dance, *Folklore from Contemporary Jamaicans* (Knoxville: University of Tennessee Press, 1985).

9. Martha Beckwith, *Black Roadways: A Study of Jamaican Folk Life* (Chapel Hill: University of North Carolina Press, 1929), 172–73.

10. Orlando H. Patterson, *The Sociology of Slavery* (London: MacGibbon & Kee, 1967), 174–81. See also Chapter 6 by Adrian Anthony McFarlane in this book.

11. George Roberts and Sonja Sinclair, *Women in Jamaica: Patterns of Production and Fertility* (New York: KTO Press, 1978).

12. See Smith, *Plural Society,* who shows that divorce and remarrying constitute a norm among the Jamaican whites.

13. See Melville Herskovits's summary of these arguments in his *Myth of the Negro Past* (New York: Harper & Brothers, 1941).

14. In my own research, I found positive concepts of Africa that survived in the families of orientation of informants born in the early decades of this century.

15. H. G. Dessler, *Twentieth Century Jamaica* (Kingston: Jamaica Times, 1913).

16. See Barry Chevannes, "Garvey Myths among the Jamaican People," in Rupert Lewis and Patrick Bryan, eds., *Garvey: His Work and Impact* (Kingston: University of the West Indies Press, 1988).

17. K.W.J. Post, *Arise Ye Starvelings: The Jamaica Labour Rebellion of 1938 and Its Aftermath* (The Hague: Martinus Nijhoff, 1978), 103.

18. Ibid., 101.

19. Peter Phillips, "Race, Class and Nationalism: A Perspective on Twentieth Century Social Movements in Jamaica," *Social and Economic Studies* 37, 3 (1988): 106.

20. Post, *Arise Ye Starvelings,* 103.

21. Trevor Munroe, *The Politics of Constitutional Decolonization: Jamaica 1944–62* (Kingston: Institute of Social and Economic Research, 1972), 75. In 1948, Jamaica's House of Representatives unanimously passed a resolution calling on the government to aid the "Back to Africa movement; between March and May 1954, the opposition PNP pressed for government to invite Haile Selassie; and in November 1954, government hosted a state visit from President William V. S. Tubman of Liberia.

22. Katrin Norris, *Jamaica: The Search for an Identity, Institute of Race Relations* (London: Oxford University Press, 1962), 72, 88.

23. Ibid., 98, 99.

24. Joseph Owens, *Dread: The Rastafarians of Jamaica* (Kingston: Sangster's Book Stores, 1976), 57.

25. For a fuller presentation of Henry's activities, see Barry Chevannes, "Repairer of the Breach," in Frances Henry, ed., *Ethnicities in the Americas* (The Hague: Mouton Publishers, 1976). See also other chapters in this anthology.

26. Rex Nettleford, *Mirror, Mirror: Identity, Race and Protest in Jamaica* (Kingston: W. Collins/Sangster's Book Stores, 1970), 221.

27. Owens, *Dread,* 250–52.

28. The derivation of *Babylon* and *beast* is biblical, from Revelation; see other chapters in this book. *Man* refers to a person of integrity and authenticity.

29. Walter Rodney, *Groundings with my Brothers* (London: Bogle/L'Overture, 1969).

30. Olive Senior, *The Message Is Change: A Perspective of the 1972 General Election* (Kingston: Kingston Publishers, 1972), quoted in Adam Kuper, *Changing Jamaica* (London: Routledge & Kegan Paul, 1976), 105.

31. Seaga studied folk religion in West Kingston, which district he represented in Parliament.

32. Kuper, *Changing Jamaica,* 106–7.

33. Ibid., 99.

34. Frank Jan van Dijk, "The Twelve Tribes of Israel: Rasta and the Middle-Class," *New West Indian Guide* 62, 1–2 (1988): 11.

35. Velma Pollard, "Dread Talk—The Speech of Rastafari in Modern Jamaican Poetry" (paper presented at the ACLALS Silver Jubilee Conference, University of Kent, Canterbury, England, August 24–31, 1989), 18.

36. See Rachel Manley, ed., *Edna Manley: The Diaries* (London: Andre Deutsch, 1989), 291.

37. Derek Gordon, "Race, Class and Social Mobility in Jamaica," in Lewis and Bryan, eds., *Garvey,* 265–82.

38. Rex Nettleford, "This Matter of Melanin: Calling a Spade a Spade," *Jamaica Record,* 19 March 1989, 4.

39. Norman Girvan, "The Political Economy of Race in the Americas," in Lewis and Bryan, eds., *Garvey,* 17.

40. Ibid., 20.

4 Gender and Family Relations in RastafarI: A Personal Perspective

MAUREEN ROWE

As is noted elsewhere in this anthology, the RastafarI[1] movement is a uniquely Jamaican phenomenon. It is rooted in the history and experience of the primary contributors to Jamaica's development—the African and European experiences and cultures. The synthesis of the two cultures occurred during slavery, when the Jamaican creole society and culture emerged.[2] Later, the African presence was further strengthened by the arrival of Africans as indentured servants during the postemancipation period.[3] However, RastafarI locates its roots in African traditions and the Bible, which, within the movement, is interpreted as a book of and by ancient Africans.[4] No change has occurred in this view, despite a recent theory of East Indian contribution to the movement.[5] As products of the Jamaican society, however, RastafarI cannot negate the presence of European attitudes and belief systems in "our persons" (our Caribbean experience) and in the movement. This study accepts the theory that gender and family relations within RastafarI, as in the wider society, have been shaped by complex attitudes arising out of the synthesis of African and European cultures in Jamaica.

Gender and the Jamaican Society

Gender and family relations in the Jamaican society are largely responsible for the male-female constructs found in RastafarI. In many ways, RastafarI sought to formalize behaviors that existed among the African masses in the Jamaican society, known in common parlance as the "roots." In recent years, scholars have noted that separate beliefs, attitudes, and behaviors exist at several levels in Jamaican society.[6] However, the "roots" have always been aware of these differences and disparities—an awareness that contributed to the shaping of black Jamaican history in the riotous decade of the 1930s. Because the roots insisted that they be considered equal contributors to national development and that they be allowed to share equally in the wealth of the nation (in which a combination of religious and political forces had conspired to keep them as cheap sources of labor), RastafarI emerged in the 1930s as anti-imperialist, anticolonialist and antiecclesiastical. The movement defended all that it perceived to be African, promoted belief in a black and living God, underscored the necessity to redress historical wrongs done to the "Blackman" in the West, while practicing patriarchy as an expression of its understanding of family relations.

Patriarchy in Jamaica is a subject area that begs for research. In a culture identified by researchers as being matrifocal, the male role has been ill defined and probably little understood by those who have examined it. As one intent on understanding her society, I offer some observations based on my own experiences as a woman born and raised in this culture.

Patriarchy appears to have two ways of being and acting in the Jamaican society: one is decidedly European, and the other is African. European patriarchy appears to be based on wealth. In this construct, male authority has a direct relationship to wealth. Thus the male is the family's breadwinner, and in instances where the female works, she functions as a source of financial support to the male, who continues to hold primary financial responsibility for the family. In instances where the male is underemployed or unemployed, the female in a European-style patriarchy provides the income for the household, but the male is seen as emasculated. He is usually depressed by the fact of his being without income and without power. I have seen instances, based on this model, where the male chose to leave the family unit rather than cope with the perceived loss of power.

African patriarchy appears to draw its authority from the fact of maleness. The male person has a peculiar value from which his power and authority flow. I have often thought that African women place such a high value on procreation that they allocate a value to the male based on their own valuing of children. The male in this context would have a value assigned to him by the female. The African male, therefore, expects to exercise power and authority in the family by virtue of being male. The male role in relation to the female appears to be one of empowerment. The woman is facilitated by the male, who also supports the family in a manner similar to that of a male in a traditional polygamous household. He will often facilitate her income, generating activities by providing critical support in some areas of domestic life.

An interesting observation that I have made over the years is that wealth is not the deciding factor in the normal flow of the male-female relationship in Jamaica; but it becomes a problem when the relationship sours and the European legal system is used as an intervening agent on behalf of the women and children. This is particularly true of the African Jamaican women's use of the family court system, where women have brought men to court for lack of child maintenance in instances where the man is known to have been unemployed during the entire course of the relationship. In such cases, the law could do little to make "deadbeat dads pay up."

If the Jamaican cultural space were divided into segments, a fairly large area would be dedicated to the African worldview. In this space, a number of subspaces would be seen to exist. One space would be occupied by African continuities, that is, spaces where

African customs are practiced with reasonably logical explanations and linkages to Africa. Another space would be used up by what I call the "gray area," so named because it appears to be a space where African behaviors exist without the support of theory and cannot, therefore, be explained logically. These I refer to as retentions.[7] Because this gray space is not a racial one, color is of much less significance than culture to the individual. Possibly that space may be characterized overall by a European ideal and theory and a retained African behavior. This is true of relationships in the gray area, particularly as they relate to patriarchy.

My own theory is that RastafarI came into existence in this space and sought to provide a theoretical base for practices that were accepted by the population but could not be explained. I therefore propose that RastafarI male-female relationships in the early years were rooted in a desire to clarify the male role in a manner consistent with the male perception of an intrinsic maleness, and that its repression of women evolved as secondary, fueled by developments in the wider society. To argue this, I accept the following as given:

1. that RastafarI inhabited the gray space in the Jamaican society where creolization created merged cultural behaviors, often without any rational explanation;
2. that the gray space is, in fact, a confusing one for those from outside who seek to theorize about it;
3. that the behaviors in this space imply a logic about which one can only speculate;
4. that the logic is best explained and exposed by an inhabitant of the gray space, or one who is trodding the path of RastafarI.

None of the above is intended to discount the work of researchers in the field. I believe all contributions are important and valuable, but examinations of this gray area from the outside sometimes amount to seeing through a glass darkly.

Because of the flow of development in RastafarI, I have chosen to divide the movement into three phases: the formative years (1930–1950), the early years (1951–1971) and the later years (1972 to the present). During the 1930s, which marked the coronation of His Imperial Majesty Haile Selassie I and saw the beginning of itinerant preachers crossing the island preaching his divinity, the movement gained ground, and its belief system was shaped by those who inhabited the lower echelons of the society, or the gray area. Between 1951 and 1971, the movement saw the development of a significant following, including an urban presence. Several events occurred that brought its existence home forcibly to the rest of the nation. In the later years, the movement was legitimized both nationally and internationally through the efforts of a number of musicians who incorporated their beliefs in their music; the most notable of these was the Honorable Robert Nesta Marley. The movement also evidenced signs of disintegration as it experienced the trauma of His Imperial Majesty's transition and the kind of ostracism RastafarI found at home in the 1980s, from which it only now appears to be recovering, albeit with a "shot in the arm" from the international African community and from young reggae artists such as Buju Banton, Tony Rebel, and Luciano.

Gender and RastafarI

As I said earlier, RastafarI is a patriarchal movement. Having its origins among the roots of the African Jamaican population, RastafarI inherited all of the complexities of race, gender, and family relations common to this stratum of the society. With its emphasis on meditation and discourse as a means of keeping the individual "I" pure, RastafarI had to examine male-female and family relationships in an attempt to define appropriate and culturally correct ways of perceiving and handling these related issues as the movement expanded. I propose that this happened at three points in the evolution of RastafarI: (1) during the widespread acceptance of dreadlocks, (2) at the advent of the Jamaican rude-boy phenomenon, and (3) with the rise of the women's liberation movement.

Early accounts of the history of RastafarI placed little emphasis on the presence of the woman in the movement. However, a number of elderly females have identified themselves as early trodders within the movement, that is, they have been with it from its early years. George Simpson, the earliest pioneer Rastafari researcher, confirms that in 1946 he saw, in Jamaica, both men and women who were identified as Rastafarians, wearing red, gold, and green caps and scarves.[8] This is borne out by newspaper accounts and oral testimonies, as is evidenced in the work of Barry Chevannes.[9] In the now-famous march of 1954 against police brutality and the routing of Pinnacle Hill, females were noted among the marchers, and in the reports of the trial carried by the newspapers of the day, women were very much present in the court. In fact, some of them were arrested along with the brethren and incarcerated.[10] This bears out testimony given by "Granny," a well-known elder, who reports that she was among the first set of Rastafarians who had, as a matter of course, to defend themselves at public meetings when the police attempted to break those up. Granny said, "Me throw stone after police, and have to run from them too, me and the man them, neck and neck when them come after we."[11] According to Granny, no distinctions were made between male and female at that time, and she certainly operated with a lot of freedom, which she says was because she "always had her own," meaning she was of independent means.

In the formative and early years (1930 to the 1960s), the role of women in the movement does not appear to have been an issue. Jah Bones describes the involvement of sisters in ritual fastings, where the males were in control of the gathering, which he calls a "fasting duty." He speaks of having in attendance, in 1958, five brethren and two sistren. Of the sistren he says, "Sister Alice and Sister Etta chant up the room, all the classical and new Rasta songs were paraded in the sweetest of voices, rich in their variety of sounds and stylistic rending. . . . The sisters were good at licking the chalice . . . they were good for the entire day."[12] Here is additional evidence of women's participation in rituals; the sisters were allowed to "eat" or "lick" the chalice at a male gathering. Jah Bone's two-to-five ratio gives support to Simpson's observation that at these meetings, "women were outnumbered and very much in the background."[13] Chevannes, however, records the vision of a woman in which she received the command of the Father to go out and testify about Selassie.[14] This meant the woman did not always stay in the background, and more important, she did not see herself as unable to speak with His Majesty.

In these speculations on the role of woman in the formative and early days of Rasta-farI, women appear to have been present as members of the movement, participating from the floor at male-organized meetings. However, the woman who was given the in-struction to go out and testify about Selassie would have acted on her vision, although I do not think she would have acted alone. Simpson says that in 1956 he did not witness or hear of any male-female controversies because of the greater participation of males in the movement. That is, from the very outset RastafarI was a movement articulated by males, and the role of women with regard to the doctrine would have been secondary to that of the male, who was the movement's primary exponent.[15] Nevertheless, it would appear that there was agreement on the male and female roles in the movement. While the male remained in the leadership role, the woman was a strong supporter and fol-lower. She appears to have had equal status but restricted doctrinal rights.

Simpson is correct about the absence of controversy with regard to women's roles in the 1950s. This may have been because African women had a fair degree of personal freedom. Granny admits freely to trading in herb and having to travel to the country to get it. But she was not alone in the use of the weed; several older women of the roots have indicated to me that they traded this item with other women. Indeed, Chevannes makes reference to a woman who "sets up" a brethren in the trade, as it were. The African Jamaican woman was actively engaged in determining her own financial affairs by relying on her skills and her wits. Male-female relationships in the early years do not appear to have been under the control of the males; rather, filial (sexual or conjugal) partners seem to have determined what would best suit them both. Although it is not clear that she is typical of the period, there seems to have been something of an equal partnership in Granny's relationships.[16] Perhaps the movement was more concerned with laying the foundation for a belief system that it would articulate in later years than with dealing with gender questions.

The Impact of the Dreadlocks

The first major development that impacted on and brought the role of women in the movement to the fore was the widespread acceptance of "dreadness" as a way of life for the RastafarI male.[17] The specific date of the introduction of dread to the movement is still controversial, but that locks were already in the movement by the early 1950s is a certainty.[18] Whatever the point of entry or the origin, an acceptance of dreadness as a way of life had become entrenched by the end of the 1950s.[19] Before then, combed hair and beards identified the Rasta male and head-ties and scarves the RastafarI fe-male.[20] These, along with the colors red, green, and gold, were the means of defining oneself as Rastafarian. After dreadlocks were introduced to the movement, however, they became more than a hairstyle; dreadness was a way of life, a means of separating the militant and committed RastafarI from the weak-hearted. Many who did not em-brace dreadness fell by the wayside, and by the 1970s, RastafarI no longer recognized "combsomes" (i.e., those who combed their hair, depending on circumstances) as authentic members of the movement. Chevannes documents this process as a "purge" initiated by the founders of the Youth Black Faith to denounce superstitions and Obeah "science." The group militantly declared the right of the RastafarI male to witness in a way that he chose, that is, to use herb as part of his ritual and to grow locks.[21]

The introduction of dreadlocks into the movement also began the process of clarifying male and female roles. The male, already in the leadership position, took charge of the development process of RastafarI and, in so doing, defined what it meant to be a RastafarI male. The woman's role, at this point, was relevant only insofar as certain practices with which members of the movement were familiar were activities in which women played critical roles. In clarifying religious precepts and sharply defining the RastafarI male, the Rastaman, by a process of exclusion, had begun to define the role of females. Locks appear to have been allowed for females; I have observed several elder sisters with locks, which speaks to an early dreading. However, women outside the movement were repulsed by locks and not only refused to consider the Rastaman as mate but would not contemplate wearing locks. My sense of the situation is that, at that point, women already committed to the movement followed the logic of locks, while those outside drew away from the movement. I believe, but have not yet been able to substantiate, that the men were forced to make allowances for the women they were able to attract, and this led to a view that only males must wear locks.

The nature of Jamaican culture is such that many of the cultural practices of an African nature are transmitted by the females. In my own experience, women served as "warners" more often than men.[22] Women tend to form the supporting bodies of most Caribbean religions, whether they are Christian or non-Christian. The likelihood that women were introducing aspects of traditional religious practices into the RastafarI movement is high, and if this was the case, the males would have seen the need to restrict the levels of access that the women had to the doctrine. That all of the African religious and cultural practices in Jamaica would have inhabited the same gray space leads one to believe that there was some overlap at the very outset. Simpson has noted that his formal contact with RastafarI was made when he visited a RastafarI camp situated across the street from a Revivalist compound.

The manner of "conversion" to RastafarI contributes to the free flow of ideas and practices into the movement. RastafarI does not have a formal induction process. Information is shared through discussions among adherents. A new convert takes a while to let go of some of the ideas that he or she brings to the movement; this is probably due to the method of disseminating information within the movement. Information in RastafarI is honed through a series of discourses, or "reasoning," taking place in the "camps" or "camp yards."[23] A camp is a residence, usually of several Rastafarians with a leader who defines standards and generally sets the tone of the camp. Ras Boanerges, or Bongo Watto, had one such camp. Jah Bones said, "Bra Watto, who embraced dreadlocks had his camp at 9th Street Trench Town. . . . [He] had a big yard with about four houses and a tabernacle in the middle of the yard with the drums hung in the middle of the ceiling. Discipline and order with Rasta livity is strictly observed and adhered to. Man, woman and children lived in the yard and naturally, Ital dredness carry the swing."[24]

Bongo Watto is credited in the movement with the founding of the Youth Black Faith.[25] The Youth Black Faith must have seen the influences of other religions creeping into the movement when it launched the purge. RastafarI was already into reasoning. Eloquence was admired in the movement, and meetings would see a variety of reasonings from brethren. The gatherings apparently became home-based at some point, probably due to the activities of the police, who harassed those who were gathered at public meetings. With this development, women already in the movement would certainly have become involved in the reasonings, but to say what the nature of their contributions was is difficult. To define the roles of these women and record their perspectives on their contributions to the development of RastafarI is necessary. In clarifying the religious precepts and defining the Rastaman, the male, by a process of exclusion, had begun to define the role of the female.

In my view, the purge placed restrictions on both the male and the female who were most likely to introduce to the movement such practices as spirit possession and speaking in tongues. However, if one accepts the premise that the transmission of culture is a primary function of the female, then any effort to purify the movement would, by necessity, restrict the female as the bearer of outside cultural influences. I have been told of a female visitor to a Nyabinghi I-assembly in recent times who succumbed to the drums. She was chased away by irate brethren on the grounds that she was bringing devil business to the Bingi (celebration of noteworthy events). In just such a manner must the purge have been implemented. This purge was extremely important in that it solidified the militant aspect of RastafarI, placing emphasis on male ownership and control of the movement. The lifestyle of the Dreadlocks was brought sharply into focus as the movement aimed for a higher level of spiritual functioning.

Rudeboy and the Subordination of Women

The second development, the "rudeboy phenomenon," is extremely important to movement. While I am not sure of the extent to which the rudeboy culture was a national phenomenon, it was very common in urban Kingston to see a group of "rudies," on foot or on bicycles, circling a corner (block) or a favorite hangout spot. I do not know of any studies of the origins of the rudeboy phenomenon; much of what we can now know about it is in the lyrics of music that either celebrated or chastised the rudie's behavior. But I am convinced that "rudieism" was influenced by RastafarI and, in turn, had an influence on the movement.

The rudeboy, or rudie, is a part of the memory of every Jamaican who is old enough to have experienced the 1960s. He was defined by a cool, aloof presence that was quietly menacing. He was macho, defiant, and tended to challenge constituted authority at every opportunity. To me it seemed the rudie came out of the gray area of the African space. The open defiance and opposition to the state linked the rudeboy phenomenon to the RastafarI movement, where rudie tended to seek refuge when fleeing from the authorities.

I suspect more than a passing connection here. What happened to the children of the early trodders of Rastafari? I have met and talked with a few, and I have noted a defiance that reminded me of the rudie, but my contacts were insufficient to make a clear link. I do feel, however, that the references to the criminal element that helped to further marginalize Rastafari and of which early writers speak pertain to the rudies. Were they children returning to the homes of their parents? That is an interesting thought.

That the rudies were macho is well known. They are largely responsible for introducing, in the 1960s, terms such as *ting* and *beef* to refer to women. I recall, in my teen years, a group of rudeboys approaching me one Sunday afternoon while I was out walking. The leader indicated to me that I was the first brown-skinned "ting" that he would like to lie down on. I, in true middle-class, high school girl fashion, asked him whether he thought I was a mattress. His friends were outraged and advised him to "box the girl." They harassed me for a while before eventually leaving me alone, but only after I had "posted" their leader; that is, I gave him a wrong home address. It was afterward that an observer advised me that I had been speaking to a well-known East Kingston rudeboy.

For the rudeboy, women were necessary conveniences. They provided food, sexual favors, shelter, and offspring, but they were never an integral part of males' lives. The rudies lived on their own or, interestingly, with their mothers. The rudeboy culture became the youth culture of the mid-1960s and, with the activities of Walter Rodney and Rastafari, became politicized. The outcome was a reformed rudie and the emergence of a youth culture in the society with a strong alliance to Rastafari. That an obvious link existed between rudie and Rastafari is evidenced by the presence of brethren who, when I first began to trod, kept referring to themselves as "cowboys." "Cowboy" was another way of describing the rudie. Eventually, the association must have raised the consciousness of the rudie; for how else could a self-confessed rudeboy/cowboy become a Rastaman? By the latter half of the 1960s, the rudeboys whom I used to see and fear in my neighborhood had begun to call me "daughter" in the very same macho ways; the term *daughter* had been substituted for "ting" or "beef." In East Kingston, Rastafari's presence was certainly strong, due largely to the presence of a camp led by a Rastaman of note, Ras Negus. There was also strong support and appreciation for the activities of Walter Rodney among the youths. At a rally in the area that I attended, I was subjected to the aggressive and unwanted attention of rudeboys who were also in attendance.

By the time middle-class youths had begun to adopt the stance of the rudeboys, the state had stepped up its efforts to detain and incarcerate the ruder elements among the original rudeboys. This softened the manifestation considerably, and the urban middle-class conscious youth emerged looking very much like a rudie, in terms of appearance and mannerisms, but in his outlook and speech he was more Rastafarian than rudie, with a strong African American–influenced racial consciousness. This group of youths demonstrated an element of fascination with the idea of male supremacy and female subordination. The macho behavior of the "youthman" was not unacceptable to the daughter; in fact, it was required, precisely because it was the "in behavior" among the youths at the time. While these rudies flirted with the Rastafari movement from the fringes, it was more at the level of physical presentation of self and political ideology than with issues such as gender roles. The movement, in turn, emphasized its own political ideology, driven, perhaps, by the demand of the youth and the rising tide of black consciousness among diasporan Africans.

RastafarI emerged from this period a changed movement. It now had a significant youth presence to contend with, which was not easily controlled. Some youths praised RastafarI from a Marxist point of view, others from an extreme black supremacist position; still others were into mysticisms of a variety of origins. The movement needed to retain the support of the youth, and once again, it had to clarify its belief system. Around this time, the movement articulated a clear belief system that included a perception of the woman as evil and a potential source of weakness in the male. The general use of the term *daughter* became a common feature of the movement. Not only did the male solidify his control, even ownership, of the movement, but the woman's role became cemented in her childbearing functions. Thus, from a position of equality—and certainly one that paralleled women's roles in the wider society—in the formative years, the woman had been reduced to helpmate to the male. She was allowed status in this new position because the male placed emphasis on family life. This made the home the woman's sphere of influence. Any potential for influence in the movement itself in her own right had been destroyed. The woman who had her "Kingman's" confidence, however, could influence the movement through her influence on him.

The Movements of Women in the 1970s

By the early 1970s, a significant percentage of the new converts to the movement were females, entering primarily as part of a couple. In what may now be termed an expansionist period of the later years of the movement, females entered and appear to have accepted the doctrine with regard to women. This may have been due to the formalization of camps as education centers. Many of the supporting beliefs of RastafarI were conceived of, honed, and disseminated in these camps. Brethren associated with a particular camp would move in and out of others to "sit in" with other brethren. Information was shared among the brethren, each of whom, in turn, shared with and interpreted for his woman, because it was not a common practice for women to visit the camps. Thus the newly converted woman, having no access to the direct sources of information on RastafarI, had to be "grown" or schooled by the male.

Two aspects of the female presence in the movement converge at this point: (1) the female role as it had been defined by the Rastaman, and (2) a younger, less informed group of females who, cut off from the information source, were groomed by their own brethren into the youth culture of RastafarI. These new female converts were also deliberately cut off from access to the elder women within the movement, and several of these younger sistren have recounted their own awareness that the elder and more articulate women—those who operated as if they, too, owned the movement—were not seen as ideal female types within the movement. They were held up by the RastafarI male leadership as females who behaved like males.

Because of this ostracism of the elderly females, gatherings such as the Nyabinghi Groundation that should have served to orient the young sisters entering the movement into acceptable female roles served only to reinforce the male concept of the RastafarI female by separating the young sisters from their elder counterparts. Thus the young female Rastafarian convert of the early 1970s tended to display a remarkable masculinity in her manner of speech, dress, and general deportment. For many, this was a sign of the extreme militancy of the youth movement in RastafarI; for others, it was a travesty of womanhood. At this point, the women's liberation movement came into the international spotlight and to the attention of the male elders within the RastafarI movement.

The most significant development affecting RastafarI in terms of its response to male-female relationships was the global feminist movement of the 1970s. Originating in the "development world," gender concerns received instant worldwide attention. By the middle of the 1970s, women's issues were being debated all over the world, prompting various RastafarI groups to address the problem of gender in the movement, albeit in a manner most relevant to themselves. Some of the sisters and brothers who came into RastafarI at this time were more liberal than their predecessors and took clear positions on what rights and freedoms a woman should have in a relationship. While not overtly challenging the movement's position with regard to their role, the women became more assertive in their behavior.

The male, however, reacted negatively to feminist ideology. Many of the elders began to see women's liberation as the reason for every action that did not appear appropriate. Sisters were rebuked for exercising initiative, for not appearing to observe the given norms, and, more often that not, were accused of being "women liberationists." The brethren, who seem to have become threatened at the prospect of females wanting equality within the movement, marshaled all forces against them. To forestall a resurgence of women's power, the brethren kept the sistren in the movement "under tight wraps"; that is, the sistren were subjected to restrictions and attitudes that reflected varying degrees of animosity.

The fact that many women had suddenly joined the movement must have come as a shock to the elder brethren who had felt that women could not really be RastafarI— perhaps an inversion of the fact that, in general, women did not want to be with dreadlocked Rastafarians.[26] Faced with a growing female presence in the movement, and constantly bombarded with news of the successful challenges and achievements of the global feminist movement, the elder brethren must have felt themselves and their movement under siege. Their collective response was to increase the frequency with which the doctrines were articulated and to use them as a basis for ostracism, particularly with regard to females. The brethren emphasized what was deemed appropriate or inappropriate behavior for females. I have no clear recollection of a similar emphasis on appropriate male behavior in the movement.

The early 1980s was, therefore, a difficult time for the movement, and for females in particular. Several groups intending to uplift the females fell by the wayside because of the overt and covert actions of the RastafarI male.[27] I was active in two groups, and each fell apart during charges of sexually deviant behavior among sisters—a tactic designed and used successfully to scare sistren from attending exclusively female meetings. Despite those aborted efforts, however, the sistren have reshaped the movement. They did so largely by choosing to remain in a movement that, at one point, was hostile to their presence, particularly if they did not come under the guidance of a Kingman. Perhaps the most significant impact on the movement was made by these "unguided" sisters. Many were employed in the "Babylon system" and chose to present themselves as professionals. By the middle of the 1980s, some were choosing to uncover and groom their hair in fashionable ways. Eventually this became a normal behavior for the younger sisters, including those in relationships. Because of this, the locks have lost the element of "dreadness," much to the chagrin of many individuals (male and female) within the movement. Prior to this decision, women had been schooled to keep hair covered at all times. With this one act, however, the women indicated their intent to have an "impart" (contribution and impact) of their own on the movement.

The Impact of Females on the Movement

The presence of sisters in the RastafarI movement has had different and significant levels of impact. With females taking up the roles of wife and mother, family life in the movement was strengthened. The patriarchy that the Rastafarians had begun to articulate in their livity was one that placed importance on the family unit. This unit was never before as visible as it became during the 1970s and 1980s, when couples and single sisters joined the movement. The family was the topic of many a reasoning session, and a distinct family culture emerged and began to make its presence felt. It was focused on the nurturing and education of the youths. This was motivated by a general awareness that RastafarI was not widely understood or accepted in the society, and that Rastafarian youths were therefore being raised in a hostile environment.

In my view, the emphasis on the youth led to a small degree of acceptance of *polygyny* (commonly called *polygamy* in the movement) by some women. RastafarI males had explored the concept of polygyny and many had found it acceptable. But there was a resistance among the sisters to any form of polygyny, despite the presence of several such families in the movement. Some women remained part of polygynous households because of a desire to keep their children under their father's care and protection. As a model for family and community life, polygyny, though the subject of much discussion, was not an established form. Here, too, the woman guided the movement. Had she been totally submissive to the male, polygyny would have had widespread acceptance in the movement.

Despite all the contradictions and difficulties affecting male-female relationships, family life flourished. Children were the unifying factor and much love and attention were given to them. Efforts were made to ensure that the children developed strong reasoning ability, an Afrocentric perspective, and a strong sense of self. In these responsibilities the male and female shared equally, though the male retained much of the authority. What authority the female gained in her relationship came to her through the role of mother.

One informant said, "Everything change up because of the youth. . . . To me, it come in like the youth give me a certain amount of strength 'mongst the brethren."[28]

The model of family unit that emerged was very interesting, and one that directly resulted from the African-style patriarchy among the RastafarI male. The man was the head of the house. He was the representative of His Imperial Majesty and therefore the "Kingman." The woman was his helpmate and, in the ideal family, occupied a place beside the Kingman in much the same way that the empress remained beside His Majesty—silent and supportive in public but active, as we understood it, behind the scenes. This was not always the case in the movement. In some households that I observed, where the children were males, the women appeared to occupy a place below the children. However, this was not the rule. The man related to the woman as the mother of his children, who were princes and princesses or priests and daughters.

The role of wife is a difficult one to discuss, because Jamaicans tend not to be publicly demonstrative. The man accepted the woman's caring in a manner that made the wife's role precious. That a man would choose to allow his woman to prepare him meals regardless of the time of the month was of extreme importance in a movement where there is a taboo concerning menstruation. That he would publicly indicate that he is comfortable doing so would have to rate highly as an indication of affection. These subtle nuances of behavior are clear indicators of the nature of the relationship between the Kingman and his Queen. From my observations, the long-standing relationships between the younger couples fell into this category. I have not been able to observe the elders in this way. This, I think, is due to the formality that surrounds visits to the elders. However, there are elders who speak highly of their partners.

Was the female in the family equal with the male? The obvious answer is no. The woman responded to a man who had a clearly defined role and status. He was the representative of His Imperial Majesty. The woman was not. However, his family life and his place in the movement depended on her as hers were dependent on him; for, as the family culture gained precedence in the movement, the man defined and was, in turn, defined by the woman. Where a woman was initially presented as "Bongo T's daughter, Sula," the man eventually became "Sula's Kingman, Bongo T." If the female was not equal to the male in the family, it was in the area of status. If the man was God's representative in the family, the woman kept the unit together.

The interdependence of the family unit was borne out by the family's economics. In most instances, both the male and the female generated an income. However, the Kingman remained in control of the family unit and determined its expenditures. Where the woman worked in "the system," her strategies, as she maneuvered through Babylon, were often determined by the man. Many of the sisters were engaged in home-based income-generating activities. Here again, the female's moves would be guided by the male, and he would provide advice on how to develop the business, how to market the products, and when to diversify. If the male earned less than the female, it was not allowed to become an issue. In many instances, the combined awareness that the system was against RastafarI, as manifested in any particular family unit, kept the family together.

Despite the hard work of both the male and the female, women were the first to gain legitimacy in the wider society. (This excludes, of course, the Rastafarian musicians, of whom Bob Marley is the most notable.) A possible reason is to be found in the following story: "One day me and a next sister was in the pharmacy in Liguanea. . . . The governor general [not the current one] came in and started to talk to the two of us. Him put his hand in my locks . . . and then him start say how much him love fe see women with locks but him can't take the locks on the man dem."[29] The sentiment expressed by the governor general is supported by the fact that many more dreadlocksed sistren have been able to gain employment in the Babylon system than have brethren.

Perhaps the most critical indicator of the extent of the interdependence of male and female in the RastafarI patriarchal system is to be found in developments that took place during the early 1980s. For Jamaica, the 1980s was a time for re-creating the years before the "democratic socialist experiment" of the 1970s. RastafarI had found itself "out in the cold" after independence. For example, many brethren were unemployed and unable to contribute to the family's finances. Support came from the woman, who was able to find or maintain employment or, alternatively, who developed cottage industries based on craft or culinary skills. The principle of communal living that the movement espoused, coupled with the African patriarchy, allowed many families to survive the period of the 1980s.

Family units responded to this development in several ways: (1) the family regrouped and allowed for greater equality between the male and female, with the male continuing as the accepted head of the household, meaning he was consulted in all major decisions and often had the final say; (2) the woman assumed some of the male authority, leaving the male to function in the unit as he saw fit; or (3) the woman did not change her status, despite her important role as major income earner. Among the families that I observed, those who adopted the second approach eventually disintegrated. The first and third approaches ensured the family's survival, largely because of the acceptance of the interdependence of male and female. As a result, RastafarI came to the middle of the 1980s a much-changed movement with regard to the role of the woman, not having faced any difficult challenges from the sistren. The ritual gatherings remained the same; all sisters observed the dress and behavior code on formal occasions, despite the individual expression in their daily lives.

I have been asked on more than one occasion why the RastafarI sistren have not openly challenged the restrictions of the movement. Why, for example, have not a group of females decided to stand up together and reason in the tabernacle? I can only speculate in answer to these questions. What I have observed of the women in the movement is a protectiveness of the movement itself. Recognizing that Babylon was hostile to everything that RastafarI stood for, the women were unlikely to mount the kind of challenge that could contribute to the destruction of the movement from within. We identified and discussed certain challenges among ourselves, but rarely with outsiders. (In my own case, my private thoughts and feelings were tape-recorded by a friend of mine, unbeknownst to me, and published in a newsletter under a pseudonym.)[30]

Another important point is that one can justifyingly reject only what one understands. The RastafarI movement was a new phenomenon, known and understood only by males who articulated its various positions and beliefs. Women coming into the movement had to understudy with the males before they could effectively take positions of their own. Their resistance to polygyny, however, gave clear indication that they were not completely submissive to the teachings of the males.

In accepting the doctrine about females taught to them by the males, the women achieved a level of legitimacy that open rebellion might have achieved, but at a cost to the movement that might have destroyed it. I do not believe that this was a deliberate strategy employed by the sistren, nor do I think they had a choice. They were schooled by the males, who defined their role in the movement. Females had no alternative but to absorb the teachings.

True learning, in my view, does not happen until the individual reflects on the information, applies it, and critiques the process. This critique began as a result of male attempts to curtail the activities of the first groupings of RastafarI women, who wanted only to organize themselves for welfare work. In almost every case, the groups wanted to feed the hungry and clothe the naked, in keeping with scriptural admonitions. What began as an effort to keep the sisters from coming together, perhaps out of fear that the brethren would not be able to maintain control of the movement, led to a process of reflection by the sistren. This resulted in a general evaluation of their roles, responsibilities, and rights, in discussions with one another. The outcome of these discussions was an increased assertiveness on the part of the sistren.

Trends of the 1990s

The RastafarI movement in the 1990s has evidenced a number of trends that should be studied in depth as they unfold: the destruction of once-stable families, the presence of a growing number of single Rastafarian females, and denuded households.

The destruction of established RastafarI families has been attributed to two major factors: hard drugs in some instances and brethrens' relationships with non-Rastafarian females in others. Both factors center on the failure of the male to maintain the lifestyle that he promotes. Those who fall victim to drugs are unable to guide the family and, of necessity, have had to give up their roles in the family and in the movement. Those who have chosen non-RastafarI women have introduced a level of conflict in the home and in the movement that only the sistren seem willing to acknowledge. Many brethren and sistren have seen the latter disruptions as being caused by selfishness on the part of the affected females. Another point of view, however, is that the male removed the woman from all that she once held dear and introduced her to a different lifestyle, then turned to the kind of woman his mate would have been had he not come into her life. This is seen as rejection of the values that he once taught and, therefore, of the family. To their credit, some males have been able to convert the non-Rastafarian, but this has not always solved the problem. The sistren, for their part, are now secure enough in their persons to take a stand against what outrages them. An interesting element of this discussion is that of color. As color-conscious as Jamaica is, and in a movement as fiercely black-conscious as RastafarI, many of these non-RastafarI women are not black women.

This issue is closely related to that of denuded households, where sisters faced with choosing a family life shared with other women have elected to "set up house" on their own. The males in these cases have not been ostracized from the movement; rather, they are acknowledged as having other partners. The denuded RastafarI household has a committed Rastawoman as the head; the father often maintains a visiting relationship with the children. But some families have been so broken that they do not keep in touch. In a few instances, children born and raised as Rastafarians in the early years are no longer being raised as Rastafarians, as the mother, in rebuilding her life, has totally rejected RastafarI.

By contrast with these trends, the single Rastawoman, is a part of the movement by choice. She may have entered as an individual or as part of a couple. As an individual, she would have "grown" herself, but as part of a couple, she may have been grown by a Kingman before separation. However she entered, she has remained in the movement, choosing to trod RastafarI on her own terms. She reserves to herself all the decision-making rights over her life, including the right to establish relationships with non-Rastafarian males. A few such relationships have come to the attention of the RastafarI males, who generally tend to inveigh against them. However, given their own example in this area, the likelihood of their objections having an impact on this development is slim.

Single RastafarI females range in age from eightteen to fifty. The paths of members of the younger group are of extreme importance to the future course of the movement. They have been raised in RastafarI families but have been socialized in the public school system. Their choice of partners must come from the pool of available males, and not enough males in the movement are of comparable age. How will these Rastawomen establish relationships? How important will RastafarI be in these relationships? Are they sufficiently committed to RastafarI to grow up a Kingman (rare boys)? Will they have the desire to do so? Given what they may have seen or experienced of RastafarI family life, do they feel that RastafarI should predominate in their lives? To track these young females as they enter adulthood and to observe the choices they make with regard to relationships, family life, RastafarI, and the professions in Babylon will be very interesting, as will seeing if they become more vocal and militant in their stride for empowerment—and how the male will respond to their actions.

Notes

1. The upper-case *I* on the ending of the word is deliberate and carries special significance for a Rastafarian writer.

2. Edward Brathwaite, *The Development of Creole Society in Jamaica: 1770–1820* (Oxford: Clarendon Press, 1971).

3. Melvin Alleyne, *Roots of Jamaican Culture* (London: Pluto Press, 1988), 34.

4. See Joseph Owens, *Dread: The Rastafarians of Jamaica* (Kingston: Sangster's Book Stores,

1976); and M.G. Smith, Roy Augier, and Rex Nettleford, *The Rastafari Movement in Kingston, Jamaica* (Mona, Jamaica: University College of the West Indies, Institute of Social and Economic Research, 1969). See also Maureen Rowe, "Rastafari: Native Jamaican Religion" (paper presented at the Conference on Indigenous Religions, Quito, Ecuador, June 1994; in Collection of the African Caribbean Institute of Jamaica/Jamaica Memory Bank).

5. Ajai Mansingh and Laxmi Mansingh, "Hindu Influences on Rastafarianism," in Rex Nettleford, ed., *Caribbean Quarterly Monograph: Rastafari* (Kingston: Caribbean Quarterly, University of the West Indies, 1985).

6. The definitive works on the subject are Phillip Curtain, *Two Jamaicas: The Role of Ideas in a Tropical Colony, 1830–1865* (Westport, Conn.: Greenwood Press, 1955); and Gordon K. Lewis, *The Growth of the Modern West Indies* (New York: Monthly Review Press, 1968).

7. This observation may have some validity for the European space as well, though the fact that European culture has been supported over the years by the literature of the various groups affects this significantly.

8. George Eaton Simpson, "Some Reflections on the Rastafari Movement in Jamaica West Kingston in the Early 1950's," *Jamaica Journal* 25, 2 (December 1994): 1–10.

9. Barry Chevannes, *Rastafari: Roots and Ideology* (Syracuse, N.Y.: Syracuse University Press, 1994).

10. Ibid., 258.

11. "Granny" a very old RastfarI woman, interview with the author, June 1993. Between 1990 and 1993, I had discussions with Granny in Kingston and actually interviewed her on several issues. As her personal history unfolded, it became clear that Granny had been a black activist for much of her life and that this influenced her transition to RastafarI.

12. Jah Bones, *One Love Rastafari: History, Doctrine and Trinity* (London: Voice of Rasta Publishing House, 1985), 25.

13. Simpson, "Some Reflections," 7.

14. Chevannes, *Rastafari,* 138.

15. Maureen Rowe, "The Woman in Rastafari," in Nettleford, ed., *Caribbean Quarterly Monograph,* 13–21.

16. Her behavior in recent years cannot be construed as typical of an elder female of the RastafarI movement.

17. Jah Bones documents the excitement of his discovery of dreadness as a way of life in *One Love Rastafari.* Chevannes has done extensive work on the origin and purpose of Dreadlocks in the RastafarI movement; see the section titled "The Origin of the Dreadlocks" in his *Rastafari.*

18. Chevannes dates dreadlocks to the 1940s, but my informants make reference to the 1950s.

19. Simpson, "Some Reflections," 7.

20. The *Jamaica Journal* has excellent photographs of a street meeting of "nonlocksed" Rastafarians. Cedric 'im Brooks, a popular Rastafarian musician, told me in a discussion in the early 1980s that with the advent of locks, Rastafarians like himself lost their place in the movement.

21. This position remains at the core of discussion within the movement by the group that wishes to legalize RastafarI "livity" (lifestyle) in Jamaica.

22. Warners were a type of prophet in the Jamaican society. Usually inspired by the spirit to warn the nation, in the fashion of Old Testament prophets, warners were a common presence in my youth. I rarely see them today.

23. Reasonings are not exclusive to the camps; any gathering of "ones and ones" is likely to become a reasoning session. Discourse is an important feature of the movement. Each individual

is encouraged to develop the skill of oratory, which has several manifestations—from the individual who places emphasis on puns to the one who offers discourse through puzzling comments. See Owens's *Dread* for a discussion of this.

24. Bones, *One Love Rastafari,* 29.

25. Bongo Watto (Congo Watto, Ras Boanerges) is a well-known (and feared) elder in the movement. For details regarding his reasons for founding of the Youth Black Faith, see Chevannes, *Rastafari,* 152–70.

26. This was particularly true of the period immediately after the ascendancy of dreadness in the movement.

27. To date, no one whom I know of has researched these movements. While their achievements were not in the public eye, these groups were well received both locally and internationally. Recently, I visited with Sista Ina from Salt River, who showed me two letters she had received in the name of the Theocracy Daughters United. They were sent to her all the way from South Africa. Members of King Alpha and Queen Omega Daughters United still occasionally insist that we should come together to do something for the youngsters whom we had wanted to educate and who are now graduating from high schools. Of the Twelve Tribe groupings I have heard nothing in recent years. For an initial reference to these groups, see Rowe, "The Woman in Rastafari."

28. A reasoning between the author and Sister X, a sister in a traditional RastafarI family who did not give me permission to quote her by name, in Kingston in 1990.

29. In the fall of 1990 my sistren Yvonne recounted this incident, at which both of us were present. This incident took place in the mid-1980s, when the sisters were the recipients of the sympathies of the wider population because of the perceived failure of the males to live up to their own beliefs.

30. For a while, a very good friend produced a California-based newsletter called *Yard Roots.* While visiting me in Jamaica in 1978, he taped a conversation between us in which I spoke very frankly about my personal views. Toward the end of our discussions he produced the tape, which brought the reasoning to an abrupt end. He later published it under the pseudonym of Sister Llaloo.

5 Rastawoman as Rebel: Case Studies in Jamaica

IMANI M. TAFARI-AMA

"How do you remain committed to a movement where male domination is so strong? Don't you pose a serious threat to patriarchy within Rastafari?" some cynics ask. My usual retort is that I-an-I remain committed to Rastafari because it is more than having a relationship with a man; it is about having an identity, seeing the Almighty in oneself and experiencing a fusion with that One. It is about sharing a cosmic consciousness, exploring spirituality, and finding my holistic self-realization, which is at once a creative and re-creative process. It is the authentication of myself as a black queen, with no apologies to the norms and ideology of Babylon.

Without a doubt, Rastafari is a patriarchal movement.[1] However, as with all social systems, Rastafari has, over the years, experienced dynamic shifts in gender power relations as a result of females revisiting their own self-definitions, juxtaposed against designations ascribed by males who created the movement. Rastafarian scholars Carole Yawney[2] and Maureen Rowe perceive a possible "conjunct" between gender relations that operate in the wider society and those within Rastafari. Rowe, one of the female intellectuals within Rastafari, further intimates that the close alliance between Rastafari doctrines and the teachings of the Bible, particularly of the Old Testament, guarantees androcentric interpretations of male-female roles within the family and in relation to the wider society. Rowe traces the evolution of the Rastafari woman from the 1960s through the early 1980s and says that "1980 was significant for daughters[3] [because] the issue of daughters and their abilities and place in Rastafari was raised. . . . The Brethren reiterated their love for the daughters and that the man is the head."[4]

The inclusion of my reflections in a reader on Rastafari might be one means of continuing a conversation that actually began, informally, in 1979 with my own realization of Rastafari. Further, the conversations and testimonies that I record in this chapter may be seen as valid in and of themselves. They provide the critical self-analyses and mechanisms for healing and growth at an individual level. But more important, the rebel voices that echo in these pages may provide a catalyst for deeper interaction within the wider Rastafari community. My literary "reasoning"[5] explores the role of woman in Rastafari from a gender perspective. To arrive at a greater "overstanding"[6] of woman, it is necessary for a female to ascertain the perspective of her significant others, who, in the case of the Rastawoman, are the Rastafari man and the "youth" (child/children). The stereotypes of maleness and femaleness that converge and diverge in society are mirrored "close up" in Rastafari's elongated traditional values, which are preparing to give way to the dawn of a new era. This dawn is hastened by the awakening consciousness of the "sistren," the sometimes silent rebels.[7]

The Rebel Woman Tradition

The historical paradigm of the Caribbean women's movement is informed by the living metaphor of a rebel woman tradition[8] in the person of Nanny the Ashanti Maroon queen, Jamaica's only female national hero, who led her guerrilla army against the British marauders, whom she defeated with amazing regularity. So effective were the Maroons under Nanny that the British failed to infiltrate the freedom fighters' camp and were thwarted by the Maroons until they agreed to a treaty in 1739. The Rastafarians regard themselves as inheritors of the Maroons' freedom-fighting tradition, and the Rastafari woman is appropriately characterized as a "lioness," positioning rebel woman against the Babylon system.[9] Of course, for this lionhearted queen to choose to commit herself to an acknowledged patriarchal movement is an apparent contradiction. Such allegiance is absolutely incomprehensible unless one bears in mind the spiritual transformation of one's life through Rastafari and all the other positive impacts that being a part of the Rastafari family entails.

The issue of the brethren's attitude toward women was raised officially in 1981 within the context of a "Bingi,"[10] or celebration. Eight years later, in the research project on "Gender Relations in Rastafari" that I facilitated,[11] the questions from sistren[12] were more clearly defined and deliberate. The sistren demanded more specific responses from brethren regarding the revision of gender relations to reflect the imperative for female autonomy. For brethren and sistren to be meeting at the headquarters of Sistren Theater Collective (STC), the women's organization concerned with the analysis of working women's lives, was unprecedented in the mid- to late 1980s, to say the least. Extending the scope of Rastafari's social considerations, STC supported the attempt by Rasta brethren and sistren to clarify gender issues related to ideology, sexuality, roles, and image. And for Rastafari to be probing these issues within the space of a feminist organization was doubly significant for the impact the process had on confronting stereotypes associated with women's struggles for the realization of personal power.

Due to women's own aggressive response to conventional classifications of female roles and responsibilities, these stereotypes are quickly being eroded. In 1985, Maureen Rowe observed that the 1970s saw evidence of daughters challenging the restrictive dress codes and demonstrating assertive attitudes: "Daughters are speaking out

more and more about their concerns and their hopes. Even more important, daughters
had begun to articulate their own perception of Rastafari. More and more daughters
were beginning to reason together and this created a solid base from which to approach
the society in general and the Rastafari community in particular."[13]

The changes evident in the wider society are also currently being echoed in the voices
of resistance to patriarchal norms in Rastafari. This profile of the Rastafari woman as
rebel is located along a continuum that originates in traditional acceptance of male dominance and moves to a contemporary questioning of male-designated role definitions
and an affirmation of independence. Some theorists hold that within the context of domestic organization, a nexus exists between males' diminishing ability to act as bread-
winners and increasing female autonomy within the faith. This lessening of male control over women has implications for the traditional hierarchy[14] that has informed the
ideology and reinforces a renewed consideration of the Rastafari woman's role as rebel
against Babylon and within the parameters of her faith.

Domestic arrangements are critically important to power relations that exist between
brethren and sistren in Rastafari. The various household formations that encourage the
woman to live independent of male authority inadvertently challenge males' abilities to
enforce the concept of men being the household heads. Recently published figures from
the Statistical Institute of Jamaica reveal that women comprise just over 45 percent of
household heads in Jamaica and 51 percent of the urban population.[15] This social fact
has relevance for the Rastafari community: if the majority of sistren are heads of their
households, less chance exists for a man to be their head.

Most sisters come to a knowledge of Rastafari through a relationship with a Rastafari man. While this relationship is maintained in some cases, "breakdowns" occur that
sometimes result in disenchantment with the "livity" (strict Rastafarian lifestyle). By
contrast, Rastawoman[16] often emerge from such painful experiences stronger in their
faith in Rastafari but conjugally alone, and less accepting of the "humble" role defined
by the brethren as ideal for the Rastafari woman.

The Rastafari woman rejects the status quo that characterizes fundamental institutions of society. For example, the metaphor of self as object is categorically rejected;
it is the subliminal norm pounding out of television, billboards, posters, calendars,
and like media of mass communication, consistently treating women as commodities
or mere stimuli for the commercialization of goods and services. This lionhearted response to the systemic inhibitors of self-actualization in Babylon is not without its internal contradictions. On the one hand, the livity of Rastafari is designed to ensure a
healthier way of living because of the emphasis placed on things natural, or "ital."
On the other hand, encouragement of natural practices in spheres such as that of sexuality raises challenges: procreation may not be desired every time one is fertile, and
as one informant, Nefertiti, suggested, the protection from risks—for example, vene-
real diseases—is critically important to woman. Sistren also pose the question of
whether the Judaic principles from which much of Rastafari's patriarchal ideology derives are currently proving inappropriate for the self-definition and independence of
females.

Patriarchy: Panacea or Painful Pill?

To a great extent, patriarchal emphases in Rastafari are due to the translation into the livity of practices and beliefs derived from Ancient Israel and Christianity. Furthermore, gender relations in the Jamaican society as a whole have historically been hierarchical and informed by the application of values that reinforce social-stratification stereotypes of race, class, and gender. That is, Rastafari does not present a unique example of the manifestation of patriarchy in the Jamaican family or in other social institutions and more; the patriarchal language of the Rasta doctrine may just be more articulate and the community more easily identifiable than those in the general Jamaican society. The sentiments the elder brethren express regarding the roles of females point to a "reification" of the role of woman, as empresses, queens, princesses, and earth mothers—which is not at all offensive. In fact, Rastawoman take pride in being elevated to queens and empresses, as counterparts to the kings and princes, against the Babylon designations "men," "women," and "people." The role of king involves a Rasta ministering to his queen and offspring in domestic affairs.

This male domestic competence and responsibility is one significant way in which Rastafari males counter the general "normlessness" of male irresponsibility to the family in Jamaican society. The Rastaman is then likely to take care of children, cooking, and performing associated family responsibilities. But the man's role as head in Rastafari is described in economic terms, with no value being ascribed to the other domestic contributions that he makes in the household. Without financial independence, men are perceived as incompetent. This contributes to the pitting of the genders against each other with reference to economic issues.

The House of Rastafari is divided into many mansions. While there may be variations across houses, members of the different houses tend to share central beliefs. Patriarchal dogmas are encountered in all realms, and one exists with—or in spite of—them. One mansion that most clearly organizes around differentiation of roles is the Bobo Shanti,[17] which is typecast into the House of Rastafari and where gender differentiations, especially as they relate to sexuality, are pronounced. In an ethnographic study documenting Priest Emmanuel's[18] life history, C. A. Newland, a member of the Bobo Shanti, notes some of the peculiarities of his group. Newland's views are worth examining in order to appreciate communal definitions of gender relationships within what has been aptly described as the most ascetic[19] aspect of Rastafari. Newland notes, "Perhaps one of the most controversial of all the principles of livity of the Bobo Shanti is the operationalization of the ancient Judaic principle governing the separation of man from woman [or, more accurately, woman from the rest of the congregation] at the time of their menstrual flow. The Bobo Shanti have evolved a twenty-one day observance of separation, a tripling of the custom noted in the Bible."[20] The biblical text in Leviticus says, "And if a woman have an issue and her issue in her flesh be blood she shall be put apart seven days: and whosoever toucheth her shall be unclean until the evening" (Leviticus 15:19 KJV). Bobo Shanti princesses and empresses in the age range between puberty and menopause are required to remain "in house" during the separation period, along with young children and other "polluted."

According to Newland, some Bobo priests argue that the biblical injunction also applies to men. They quote Leviticus 15:2, which says, "When any man hath an issue out of his flesh, because of his issue he is unclean. . . . And when he that hath an issue is cleansed of his issue, then he shall number to himself seven days for his cleansing and wash his clothes, and bathe his flesh in running water and be clean" (KJV). Newland witnessed Bobo priests who claimed that they were ineligible to enter the tabernacle because they had bruised a finger from gathering coconuts. He reported that some priests even claimed they could not enter the tabernacle because they had had a wet dream.

Newland thinks that having to spend three weeks in almost complete social isolation is probably designed to discourage the woman from entering the camp or to prove that men are better than women in the worship of Jah. He conjectures, "Apart from being a period of spiritual purification, the twenty-one day principle, in theory, allows the woman time for her own productive activities and her intellectual and spiritual growth. This principle will never, I think, be favorably viewed from within the paradigms of modern gender role differentiation and modern hygiene."[21]

To suggest that because males are penalized for any emissions they might experience, the separation observances might just be coincidental, based on a biblical teaching, is tempting. However, the multiplication of the sistren's in-house period is excessive and smacks of patriarchal control. During this period, the woman simply receives food from her Kingman, passed through a small "aperture" from which she might glimpse him fleetingly. Sistren from this mansion have told me that to compound the situation, older sistren tend to be even more rigid than some males in enforcing the taboos, an example of internalization of or collusion with oppression. One sistren informant, M. Silver, remarked, "I'm remembering other instances where brethren have defined us as inferior and where we've demonstrated how we have internalized this imposed inferiority by our silence."[22] The question is raised of whether this attitude renders women incapable of economic independence.

Self-Definitions: History or Herstory?

An important outcome of the Rastafari woman's conversion is the cultural freedom that she experiences through a deeper understanding of Jah and of the tenets of Rastafari. The liberation from Babylon, expressed in the growth of locks, is one of the principal statements against the abnormal processing standards of Babylon that emerges from the self-realization that the Rastawoman experiences on "sighting up."[23] This is balanced by the Black-centered ideology of the livity. Her self-identification as a lioness is ideally complemented by union with a lion man to produce their young replications. Sistren have also been attracted to the livity of Rastafari for a number of other reasons. Foremost is their intimate association with a Rastafari man, which invariably leads to their "sighting Rastafari." Some of the sisters have taken their teachings so well that they end up performing their own spiritual leadership roles, both outside and within their relationships. This success extends to the material realm, in which the man may be unable to manage domestic affairs.

That women have been able to achieve through self-sacrifice and soul-searching is attested by David, an informant who describes himself as an "independent Rastafari" (not affiliated to any particular house). He reflected on woman's progress through Rastafari, within the context of the paradox presented by the tradition of females' roles being prescribed by the brethren:

> Before the late seventies, to the eighties, I did not meet any Rasta woman who could carry my head any further. In the 1960s it was only the street women who would deal with Rasta. In the seventies a new order of consciousness emerged with the release of the seven spirits of Light, Darkness and Knowledge. In the seventies, there was an influx of middle class women into Rasta, ninety-five percent of whom were involved with a Rasta man. As Rastafari became more socially acceptable, most were attracted to the natural lifestyle.[24]

Bro. Moses, a long-standing participant in the Rastafari livity (of the Nyabinghi House), was lofty in his explanation of the royal role of sistren who were nevertheless restricted by a gender division of responsibility, which he described in terms of the behavioral responses of His Imperial Majesty Haile Selassie I: "His Majesty elevated sisters to the highest level, to the level where him queen was crowned the same day with him, but you would never find the empress chairing a function if His Majesty was there; once he is there, he is the automatic chairman."[25] Informant Esther's responses in the recent research exercise articulate an acceptance of a traditional definition of roles as recommended by Bro. Moses: "Jah is the head of everything; Jah is the head of man. And that can be man or woman as far as I'm concerned. I would love it if in my household the man has the chance to be the head, to carry the load, to take care of things, be a leader and all of that as a man. If he is playing that part I don't mind being the woman under him. But if a man is not playing these roles then you as a woman have to come up front and play the role, under Jah."

Esther's Kingman defaulted on male responsibilities as head of the household, particularly in terms of financial responsibilities, and this galvanized her into a dominant role that she would rather not assume. Her comfort with the possibility of being in a subordinate position in relation to her man, providing he could assume the role of head (which is interpreted chiefly in breadwinning terms), is nevertheless interesting. This speaks to the sentiment many woman express in Rastafari of not necessarily wanting to perform the role of "superwoman." Self-employment alternatives usually do not provide monetary returns viable for maintaining a household that includes spouse and children. The frustration that results is not only for the sistren, who fails to receive the support contained in her prenuptial expectations, but also for the whole family, on whom the classic "domino effect" impacts. The woman is depressed; the youth is materially and socially deprived; and the self-esteem of the male is guaranteed to be vulnerable under such circumstances, unless he manipulates the situation to his advantage.

Bro. Moses' definition of the woman's role demonstrates a decided divide in intellectual and spiritual capabilities that gives the man the advantage: "The dawta[26] have her role within tradition. She as the quiet warrior; she must be that balance. Her mind has to be even more analytical than the king because him always going. But she can slow it down and analyze it and correct him, perk him up sometimes and show him seh maybe if we do that we can get a better result than if we do this. She must be that little brain box that is always working."

But what happens when the woman wants to be the one who is "going"? What is her source of succor, her "balm in Gilead"? The passionate answer to this question came from Sheba, a queen in her mid-fifties who does not, by any means, subscribe to the stereotypical definitions of passivity and fecundity that traditionally have been applied to the Rastafari woman: "I am a person. Not because I am a woman anyone going to think that they can beat me down. More time, lioness more terrible than lion in the jungle. Without a woman a brethren is nowhere. Is woman do the planning and fixing. She come up with ideas and him come up with strength and finance. Some brethren only want to reason up with them brethren and not them queen but dem soon find out dat dem don't reach nowhere." As to the source of her strength, Sheba is uncompromising in her reliance on faith in His Imperial Majesty for spiritual sustenance: "I highlight His Imperial Majesty, Haile Selassie I, and the good that Jah has done for I-an-I. I believe in my Father dat if I don't have any money and I go down on my knees, I get that. I speak with authority! I as his daughter have to stand and defend that I-an-I know HIM never dead."

As an early pioneer in Rastafari and the only woman among the brethren in her group, Sheba's role was to attend to domestic requirements of the brethren—such as washing and cooking—which, she admitted, was hard work. She hastened to add, however, "Being in Ethiopia made me feel so free, so renewed, that I didn't feel it. It was worth it." She would not play that role again "because it was a burden," she said, although she expressed willingness to "help out any needy one." Sheba's experience as "helpmeet" to the pioneering males is a story common to individual sistren, as well as sistren who, traditionally, formed the minority in Rastafari retreat communities in the hills or remote rural areas. Her domestic role was decided by all the twelve brethren who took advantage of her generosity. Her reflection that she would not acquiesce to such subtle coercion in the future represents an incipient consciousness growing among sistren, as male-defined roles for females are challenged on domestic and other fronts.

Sheba's strong spirit of independence and confessed relationship with His Imperial Majesty, Jah Rastafari, render redundant an intercessory role by brethren on her behalf. In other words, Queen Sheba's defiant responses suggest that a sistren does not strictly require a male's intervention for personal or spiritual validation. This position is a direct challenge to the notion of man as head of woman. But manifestations of patriarchy in Rastafari, or indeed, in the society as a whole, should not be analyzed monolithically; the possibility exists of males and females effecting bargains with a system that offers some succor. Women's strategies are always played out in the context of identifiable patriarchal bargains, which act as implicit scripts that define, limit, and inflect their market and domestic options.[27]

Shifting Scales of Power

Is the Rastaman, like males in the wider society, being marginalized as women au-
tonomously advance, as Errol Miller of Jamaica's Teachers College suggested?[28] One
of my informants, Anijah, thinks so. She anticipates that the sistren's inevitable assumption of more egalitarian roles with brethren, whom the sistren may even supersede
in power, will not be happily received by males: "When you start challenging the norm
of the system within Rastafari culture you are in for a tremendous . . . spiritual and emotional battle. When you have a woman speaking out for change, people say, 'You a
gwaan like you are himportant.'[29] But if you are persistent, you will gain respect; the
opposition will give . . . and keep on giving." Anijah continued:

> Rastaman would like Rastawoman to keep thinking along the lines that say Jah is the head
> and after Jah is man and woman supposed to know dem place! I don't think it works like
> that because if you are going to go according to what is written in the Bible, the rib God
> took to make woman came from man's side, so how can a man say that he is the head of
> woman? And you know when you have head, you must have tail, so who is then going to
> be the tail? Man and woman supposed to move together as one force.

Sister Anijah was resolute in her stance that woman in Rastafari are remorselessly set
against manmade strictures, and if this were to mean challenging the existing power
structures, they would, with the determination of undaunted faith in Jah Rastafari. Anijah reflected that an irresistible trend of change is taking place in Rastafari, much as has
occurred in the wider (Babylonian) society: "A lot of women are becoming more aware
and more feel that they should control their lives. [With] the changes [that are] happening with the few instead of the majority, [many] don't know if Rasta women are
struggling, for the most part. Most seem quite happy to be led along and told what to
do and what not to do. The females who say, 'No!' are seen as freaks."

The changes that Anijah recommends seem to be taking place in some areas, but
brethren who participated in the evaluation process in 1988 spoke to me of initial resistance by elders to the advocacy of autonomy for sistren. However, this resistance has
relaxed somewhat, as my own experience of addressing a Bingi in 1991[30] on the subject of reform of gender relations attests. Bro. Moses concurred that the changes are
quite timely. But he adds, "A lot of dawtas have made a vital contribution to the development of the livity. I have no problem with a woman blocking her own sounds. We
shouldn't want to stultify the talent of our very hard working sisters. But I have seen in
a lot of cases sisters go out there and make a name for themselves and get so big that
the man can't speak to her too tough. It's like she a compete with him. It's now a major problem out inna Rome, not even inna Rasta alone."

Due to the insecurities that are bound to plague brethren who recognize sistren's
power, the obvious question is whether sistren's assertiveness is being interpreted as
competing with the Rastaman. Another informant, Sister Meesha, argued that change
is necessary, since "a lot of brethren are arrogant in the home, but when they are on the
street, they go on humble just to preserve their image." Meesha's outspokenness leads

to an astute analysis of the fear that informs the restraint that is traditionally required of the Rastawoman: "I see too often that Rasta women, because they are not well educated and they have a lot of children, they don't have the power that they should have. To be honest, there are a lot of problems in Rasta, it's just that we don't talk about it. And it must stem with the elders, because when you come to Rasta young and fresh with the love of His Majesty burning in you, you come to learn, and that is what has been happening, but the elders don't always have the right answers."

Casting her vision toward the future and onto her own womanhood, Meesha does not see herself following in the "humble" footsteps of her female forerunners. She envisions a more autonomous role for herself than she has at present. A shift in the balance of power between the genders is being precipitated by sistren's challenging of role determinations that are male-constructed and that do not represent woman's current choices. This shift in gender power relations, which is not unique to Rastafari but represents a trend of the past two hundred years,[31] has threatening survival implications, not only for brethren but for sistren as well. An angry male backlash against the female is not impossible under certain circumstances.

Survival Strategies in the Family

On the question of financial survival strategies, one research respondent, Candace, observed that "most Rastaman don't seem to have it [money]. So, if you are an independent woman, you will find that they lean on you financially. Maybe I attract it too because I make no demands in a relationship. In fact, I don't ask for any particular outcome." She confessed, "I just know that I want to experience a deeper side of myself, reflected through a male."

In response to this evidence of manipulation, Meesha, our young advocate for reforms within the livity, suggested that rather than depending on sistren's earning power or focusing on subsistence forms of survival, "brethren should reconsider" avoiding professions such as law and medicine because "the sistren can't really believe in the brethren's authority when he has no money and they have children to look after." Further, she felt that it was contradictory for the brethren to be denying sistren independence while relying on the woman's resources for survival. Meesha added, "I feel the brethren should not be content to have a craft shop or an ital shop. We can't ignore the value of taking advantage of opportunities which exist in the Babylon system."

Bro. Moses had no sympathy for the man who was unable to maintain his role as breadwinner; he was impatient with rationalizations about the impediments to economic independence. "If a man make the woman become the breadwinner, then he is not a king; he is not a man. That man is a weak man; he has conceded his manhood. The man should be creative about dealing with Babylon . . . lick down[32] barriers, go 'round barriers," to find other ways to survive. These views show that, in Rastafari, a divide exists between the ideal of brethren performing in the role of breadwinner/head of the household and the reality that this obligation is the females' responsibility.

Sexuality in Rastafari

In Rastafari the arena of sexuality is fertile ground for the application of normative control of females. Sistren internalize traditional roles of woman as servant. But my own experience with the Bobo Shanti commune convinced me that I would not choose to be subjected to such severe sanctioning of my sexuality. As a Rastafari journalist-researcher, I had my encounter with the Bobo Shanti principles when I visited Bobo Camp in 1986, as part of an entourage of Prince Dawit, grandson of His Imperial Majesty, Emperor Haile Selassie I. Sister M. was there with me for a particular reasoning session but was denied entry into the camp on grounds of ritual impurity. The brethren used a calendar from which they determined the woman's monthly cycle. We were embarrassed and offended when they pried into our personal lives and asked us when was the last time that we had seen our menstrual period. They determined that Sister M. was unclean and not permitted to enter the camp, because of the positioning of her chart that day in relation to her menstrual cycle.[33]

Another informant, Sister Nzinga, was adamant about taking steps to control her own procreation process, in spite of the passionate pleas of her Kingman. She said:

> I don't want to have any more children. Although I don't have any for him, I already have three and he wants me to get pregnant. He objects very strongly to the fact that I have in a coil, but I have to protect myself because the youths always end up to be my responsibility. I really don't want to tie my tubes, but physically and financially I don't want to have any more. He is threatened by my birth control decision because it means no more production especially for his benefit. . . . I have to be strong about this. That's why I hesitate about legalizing the husbandship [marriage], although, at first, I was insisting on it as a requirement of commitment.

Control of sexuality has implications not only for one's material concerns but for one's spiritual endeavors as well. Avoidance of sexual intercourse has been promoted by brethren who saw woman as embodying many taboos and therefore polluting.[34] Interestingly, celibacy is proposed by Queen Sheba as a means of maintaining spiritual clear-sightedness and facilitating esoteric work. By contrast, for Sheba, sex is highly recommended if the two "ones" are attuned. Meesha's views on the control of her sexuality are typically uncompromising. She intones; "I know Rasta men love to go to bed and they don't love to use protection but the woman should think about the responsibility and whether she can manage it because she ends up doing a lot of the work. If a Rastaman is going to tell me that I should have so many children for him without me first agreeing, then he will just have to go."

Sister Abeba, an interviewee, drew a direct correlation between female sexual acquiescence and male application of behaviors of power and control. This moment, she felt, identified the climax of a relationship and was the potential portent of its ultimate demise. This self-styled Ethiopian princess said, "Fom mi see seh dem [males] naw deal wid nutten, mi tell dem pack up and gwaan.[35] Before you had sex with dem, dem sweet, sweet, sweet to yuh, but from the moment dem get dat, dem want to control you, tell you what to do, where to go, and hall of dat."

When someone at the 1988 workshop, mentioned above, suggested that tubal ligation could be explored as an alternative method of birth control,[36] many "ones" were
shocked. On the one hand, the contemplation of birth control use is taboo in Rastafari,
and on the other, the finality of the act of tubal ligation bordered on the sinful, almost
like abortion. The admission from one sistren that she was wearing a coil might be as
shocking ten years later. But there is nothing new under the sun. African women have
always devised means of birth control. On the continent, the common knowledge was
retained through many generations and in many forms, including the use of papaya
seeds as one pro-active, preventative method in slave population control. The knowledge that African women have passed on through generations[37] is culturally reinforc-
ing; in many cases, knowledge about female sexuality is passed on among females to the
exclusion of males, and vice versa. The problem, as Meesha sees it, is that Rastaman
love to go to bed (i.e., have sex) and invariably eschew the use or accept their partner's
use of birth control methods. The underlying agenda "to have a youth" (a baby) is more
rather than less common.

In the final analysis, there is a correspondence between the efforts that sistren are
making to rebel against the restriction caused by her chains and the historical struggles
that the ancestral Africans waged against all forms of oppression. But to rebel against
oppressive structures and values of the Babylon system and, at the same time, to internalize norms within the livity that militate against one's achieving a pragmatic definition of autonomy is contradictory. Sistren's response to this area of conflict has direct
implications for the future of Rastafari.

Domestic Violence

Physical abuse is another taboo issue in Rastafari; it is spoken of in hushed tones, if ever
at all (as is the case in Christianity). I might even be considered irreverent for mentioning it in writing. I am convinced, however, that facing the fact of domestic violence
through discourse is one step on the path to dealing with the symptoms and resolving
the problem.

Without making a precise statistical claim, we can readily acknowledge that the inci-
dence of domestic violence in Jamaican society is extraordinarily high and is on the rise.
Currently, it accounts for almost half the murders committed in the country. Again, we
observe an instance of collusion between the Babylon system and gender relations in
Rastafari. As much as Rastafari would like to separate itself from the exigencies of the
Babylon system, there is no escaping the fact that individuals are products of their history and socialization in Babylon. Someone who is preconditioned to perpetrate violence against another will do so, despite religious or other persuasions.

Informant Nefertiti admitted to having several times endured the painful experience
of physical abuse at the hands of her Kingman, for whom she has mothered many children; she started conceiving from a very early age. She expressed some bitterness at the
fact that she also does not get the financial support she needs for herself and the chil-

dren, who range in age from five to twenty-four. She referred to her experience of being beaten with thinly veiled venom. This creative artist claimed that the abusive treatment meted out to her at the hands of her Kingman distanced her from him to the extent that she had no choice but to engage in another relationship.

Nefertiti had strong views on the soldierlike role that sisters have to play as Rastafari when they are concerned about not abandoning the faith just because of personal relationship disappointments. She observed, moreover, that the abuse of women is not restricted to Rastafari. "It's a Jamaican Caribbean man thing," she thinks. King Shacka, a Ras from the eastern Caribbean, where males are reputedly more gentle than the aggressive Jamaicans (although this myth might defy empirical research), disgustedly denounced domestic violence in general and its manifestations in Rastafari in particular.

The attempt to deny the existence of domestic violence in order to protect the holy image of Rastafari is not likely to contribute meaningfully to the application of effective response management to ensure that sistren and brethren do not perpetuate this insidious form of self-annihilation, which smacks of psychic preprogramming.

Is Childrearing Only for the Female?

Because women bear children, society has automatically deemed them responsible for the rearing of the children as well. Men are perceived to be peripheral to this process; they help out when they can or if they feel like doing so. Not being able to abdicate their responsibilities without jeopardizing the health of the youth, the majority of working-class women[38] bear the lioness's share of this area of domestic work. As informant David noted, the role of socializing the youth is crucial in determining the direction in which the individual and, eventually, the social group advances: "The woman is traditionally to nurse and feed the youths and be humble because they see man as a brighter light than them. It is true though that sometimes the Rasses level off and the sistren rise in awareness and consciousness, and many [sistren] turn out to be more fervent and righteous."

Here David named some of the quintessential elements that determine woman's role in Rastafari and the basis on which a system of gender discrimination is perpetuated. Unless sistren are prepared to break the cycle of internalized oppression, patriarchal precedents will continue to inform social and power relations in Rastafari. Meesha's youthful perspective on the issue of childbearing and childrearing was as potent as it was precise. She felt that her upbringing and the teachings of Rastafari, which informed her home education, put her at a distinct advantage among her peers, whom she saw as easily influenced by material things. When asked about the coping strategies that she had evolved to address the needs of her children, especially when her income was sporadic, Nefertiti responded, "Mi naw tell you no lie, it hard, because you constantly have to be thinking how to manage to raise them. I did not choose to grow their locks as Rasta except the last one who is so strong! It makes me wish that I had been strong enough to grow them with that kind of confidence because they wouldn't have gone the way they did and cream [their hair] and all of that. I am a grandmother too, so me see the effect of upbringing on children."

In addition to child care, the job of caring for the elderly is also, invariably, seen as a female's task. Five years after repatriating to Ethiopia, Queen Sheba was required to return to Jamaica to care for her ailing mother. This responsibility came to dominate many years of her life; it was literally a reversal of roles and status.

Anijah, who is a mother "many times over," acknowledged that women have always been responsible for the discipline, training, and general rearing of the children. She is also keen in her observations of the options available to her progeny and their peers, as they contemplate the viability of replicating the Rastafari livity. She said they do not find poverty attractive and so are contemplating trodding the Babylon road to achieve professional qualifications.

As far as the process of childrearing is concerned, the bottom line seems to be that effective management of this area of social responsibility is predicated on the parents sharing the responsibility involved. This means that fathers should contribute their time and energies, as well as finances, to the upbringing of their offspring. A prerequisite for appropriate parenting has also been identified as financial solvency, which, according to Anijah, is being demanded by the youth. Coping with the dramatic changes in outlook being exhibited by their youth undoubtedly has presented a tremendous challenge to third-generation Rastafari. Both are forced to come to terms with the contradictions that characterize their lives as they grapple with Babylon system and a way of life that is still evolving, but not in their interest.

The best that Rastafari parents can hope to do is "roll with the punches," with strong doses of domestic and financial creativity to ensure the proper care and education of the youth so that they may be equipped to face the challenges presented to them as inheritors of the livity's struggle. The grim alternative to equal parental responsibility is that the youth might abandon the framework of the livity altogether. They may, like Nefertiti's children, come to process their hair (the ultimate act of denial of one's natural, African self and beauty), thus denying everything that their parents stand for.

Classism and Sexuality in Rastafari

My informant Anijah hesitated to put a name to it but eventually admitted that social cleavages exist in Rastafari, as within any other institution of the Jamaican society. She recognized that attitudinal differences are evident among sistren—who should by no means be regarded as a homogeneous entity—with regard to their perceptions of material possessions or the lack thereof:

> Some Rasta women will tell you dat mi naw deal wid Babylon situation none t'all! They look at non-Rasta women in a negative light, almost. Some think you have to be very aggressive. Some think you are not supposed to be neat say in your dressing. Those ones have the view that you are not supposed to look fashionable and, moreover, *modern*. I think, though, that you live in a society and if you can't beat 'em, you have to join 'em to some extent. Rasta is

. . . a serious thing, and in order to command respect, you have to move with some amount of dignity.

An immediate response to this experiential critique is that it is definitely class-based. However, to suggest that without finances, due to unemployment, one cannot afford the self-presentation that will command the respect of which Anijah speaks might be circular reasoning. Juxtaposed against this argument, following the lead of Burning Spear, a leading reggae singer, is the suggestion that ones "who cannot get work should make work, be creative." In other words, failing to represent oneself in appropriately royal attire on the grounds that spiritual pursuit demands forsaking material amenities for a "sackcloth-and-ashes" existence, is incompatible with the impetus to command respect through self-presentation.

A modern perspective on the Rasta livity tends to suggest a "dialectical" shift away from practices that would serve to stigmatize and ghettoize adherents as unworthy of social acceptance. While prejudices against Rastafari engaging the Babylon system are still strong, some "social closures" have become more and more invalid with the evolution in consciousness as well as the increasing acquisition of intellectual and material means by some Rastas. The class divide might very well be the intellectual distance that exists between the haves and the have-nots; educational achievement in the wider society, as in Rastafari, is the salient ingredient that offers the poor a chance to confront the hurdles of poverty with jumping power. Class operates as a divisive factor, both in the wider Jamaican society and within the livity of Rastafari. It functions as a divisive scale of judgment from which "bald-heads," as non-Rasta members of one's family are called, draw the class ascriptions they use to define their Rastafari relatives or associations within the livity.

Informant Nzinga's struggle to find the right mate is an explicit statement about the class distinctions that undoubtedly pervade the lives of ones in the livity of Rastafari. Her testimony is fascinating because of her expression of social expectations, on the one hand, and the dilemma that her choice of a Rastaman poses to her personally and, more painfully, to her family, on the other hand. Nzinga said she is contemplating getting married because she really wants "a man to provide me with security and stability." She is "not going to be the kind of wife he wants," because she needs to preserve the freedom that she now has. The man she knows is "sexually very good," but she worries "about the fact that he's not physically presentable in a way that people would respect him." Jamaican class consciousness echoes again in Nzinga's voice as she continues to reason about her Kingman:

> What compounds the situation is that my family don't want me to be doing this—mainly because of his social, physical, and intellectual presentation. My mother would not like to identify him as her son-in-law. If him was a Rasta with high school standing, my relatives would not object so strongly. . . . He's not rich but I feel secure with him—perhaps because I know he won't go to anyone else. My king has respect for me, yes; but when I'm alone I can't help thinking about the importance of his poverty.

The importance of class, as defined by Anijah, is directly related to engagement with the Babylon system and the bargains that are effected along the lines of self-presentation, in order to bear an impression of grace and dignity. This form of self-presentation communication, as the sistren suggested, acts as a means of exploding the stereotype that would cast Rastafari as social outcasts, dirty and unkempt.

As Anijah and Meesha suggest, easing into traditional professions is being suggested as a strategy that youth in Rastafari should employ to beat the Babylon system down. This privilege will be available only to a few. The socioeconomic status of the majority of Rastafari adherents combined with the scarring prejudices that still haunt members of the livity constitute a self-fulfilling prophecy that militates against the majority accessing quality primary school education. Still, it is inevitable that some will attain a profession and be competent to confront the Babylon system on familiar territory.

Numerous class issues are bound up in Nzinga's dilemma. She is caught at the crossroads between her expectations for a conjugal relationship and for herself, the one whom she has chosen to be. This confusion stems as much from her upbringing as from her vulnerability to her mother's disapproval of her choice of mate. Nzinga's search for a marriage that would offer her stability and security enacts a value that is presented by the churches and the state as a solution to the woman's as well as society's problems. It was, in fact, a solution recommended by the Moyne Commission[39] after the 1938 riots in Jamaica—that an increase in marriages act as a social healer. For African women in Jamaica, marriage has always been viewed as an institution that competes with their independence, and the Moyne Commision's marriage campaign was resisted accordingly. Many marriages are therefore consummated late in the relationship.

Nzinga's self-esteem can be considered low for her to require the status of being married to validate her existence as a woman, and also for her to find it so difficult to extricate herself from a situation that, by her own admission, she should not have chosen. One might also suggest that the intrusion of the mother's values regarding who constitutes a suitable son-in-law is permissible because Nzinga actually shares her mother's class position and perspectives. This response seems to speak to Nzinga's identity as a woman in general, rather than as a Rastafari woman as such. Girls in Jamaica are socialized early to become "marriage material." Home, school, and social values and institutions prepare the way for a girl to be found by a "nice guy." She has to go to great pains to attract his attention and keep him interested. Nzinga's desire for marriage is rooted in personal insecurity and the expectation that marriage will fill her void. The fly in the ointment, however, is that the rescuing knight—or "correction king"—is not made to order. The fact that he could be provider is an asset that is not offset by his ineligibility to be admitted into certain social circles.

One does not quite abandon one's socialization on sighting up; values imprinted from early in one's conscious and unconscious development remain with one for life. Adult Rastafari are, therefore, acting out roles taught from childhood. Everyone has an agenda. the Kingman is relying on his Queen's proven productive capacity to provide him with Rastafari youths in his own image. Nzinga's intelligence guarantees that the children will be exposed to learning that her Kingman was denied. Her presence in his life in a remote rural village greatly enhances his prestige. Nzinga likes his simple gallantry, which is demonstrated in a uniquely "primitive" way (in the primordially positive interpretation of the term).

In this discussion on the Rastafari woman as "rebel with a cause," I-an-I was obliged to employ the concept of gender as an appropriate tool of analysis. This has allowed us to consider some of the various views and roles that are established in the articulation of these elusive, evolutionary definitions. The complex power relations embodied in the enactment of transactions denoting and affecting sexuality are central to the discourse on sistren's transitional rites of passage toward autonomy. The trend toward the realization of female independence in Rastafari is by no means a generalized phenomenon; however, it speaks to the transience of the practice of brethren maintaining control over their queens through the reinforcement of a hierarchy of "man as the head." This headship is usually expressed in financial terms of reference, but the definition is null and void unless it is substantiated by the physical *fulfillment* of this role. In addition, headship suggests an application of authority that, by extension, requires wives to submit to their husbands (Ephesians 5:22). Paradoxically, the social organization of Jamaican households, including those of Rastafari, is heavily biased toward female headship, which militates against the enforcement of certain male ideological norms.

Financial responsibility, or irresponsibility, in the household has implications for the way children are brought up. Role models are mandatory for the development of positive self and other concepts. The nuclear organization that, in spite of the contradictory agenda, informed the definition of an alleged remedy for social ills is referred to as the ideal family order. However, as Bro. Moses, Nefertiti, and Anijah point out, this ideal does not always correlate with reality. The issue of financial capability has even more challenging implications for sexuality. One may have as many children as one can afford. The choice is the sistren's. Given that females bear the brunt of childrearing responsibilities, theirs should be the ultimate decision regarding procreation.

Domestic violence has left scars on Rastafari just as it has left a trail of pain through the wider society. Sistren will have to fight this form of oppression and abuse while they chant down Babylon and procure their full autonomy.

The issue of class differentiation is also important to the study of woman's roles in Rastafari. The voices of the youth have suggested that there be a concerted attempt to beat Babylon at its own game. Accessing the formal professions could be employed as a strategy to elevate Rastafari to a higher realm of respect than it has traditionally occupied. This tactic could be implemented as a form of resistance against the widespread ghettoization of the livity, due to the underdeveloped lifestyle that characterizes those who find themselves among the poor and the powerless.[40] Class has also been observed acting as a divisive impediment to the pursuance of gender relationships. The social values that children internalize inform their attitudes and behaviors as adults.

What is clear is that the contradictions of race, class, and gender distinctions operate as beguilingly in Rastafari as they do in the wider society. Emancipation from this "mental slavery"[41] that serves to cement the codes of "divide and rule" among Rastafari is a foolproof method of maintaining the positive outlook of Rastafari.

Some Rastawoman are determined to point the way to full consciousness, which will eventually lead to the oppressed throwing off the remaining shackles. As a rebel with a cause, these Rastawoman defend woman's autonomy as a vital ingredient for the maintenance of one's family and integrity. Certainly, the debate is ongoing; these reasonings have merely touched the tip of the iceberg of Rastawoman as rebel with a cause. While the sistren are oppressed in society, we must fight to beat down Babylon. As Judy Mowatt sings so sweetly, "I-AN-I struggle through the pressure, dance through the fire but we never get weary yet."[42] The rebel sistren will overcome Babylon and patriarchy with faith in Jah.

Notes

1. See Maureen Rowe, "The Woman in Rastafari," in Rex Nettleford, ed., *Caribbean Quarterly Monograph: Rastafari* (Kingston: Caribbean Quarterly, University of the West Indies,1985), 13–21; N. Samuel Murrell, "Woman as Source of Evil and Contaminant in Rastafarianism: Championing Hebrew Patriarchy and Oppression with Lev 12," *Proceedings of the Eastern Great Lakes and Midwestern Bible Society* (1994): 191–209.

2. Carole D. Yawney, "To Grow a Daughter," in A. Miles and G. Finn, eds., *Feminism in Canada* (Montreal: Black Rose Books, 1983).

3. An appellation for Rastafari females. *Daughters* is used interchangeably with *dawtas,* while *woman* often replaces the plural *women.*

4. Rowe, "The Woman in Rastafari," 19.

5. A concept employed by Rastafari to denote any form of discourse. Reasonings usually meander from subject to subject, at great length and depth.

6. Rastas conclude that if you are standing and grasping a truth, you should be over and not under a subject matter; hence the term *overstanding.*

7. The view of Rastawoman as rebel is a juxtaposition of her relationship with Babylon alongside her role in the family.

8. L. Mathurin, *The Rebel Woman in the British West Indies during Slavery* (Kingston: Afro-Caribbean Institute of Jamaica, 1975).

9. The Babylon system refers to the social-political culture of exploitation and oppression in the West, and in Jamaica in particular.

10. A Bingi is a celebration of noteworthy dates and events, observed by participants of the Nyabinghi Order.

11. See Imani Tafari-Ama, "An Historical Analysis of Grassroots Resistance in Jamaica: A Case Study of Participatory Research on Gender Relations in Rastafari" (M.A. thesis, Institute of Social Studies, The Hague, 1989).

12. The designation for women, to complement *brethren.*

13. Rowe, "The Woman in Rastafari," 19.

14. Jah is the head of man, and man is the head of woman; see Rowe, "The Woman in Rastafari," 15–19.

15. "Statistical Institute of Jamaica Figures," *Jamaican Herald,* June 21, 1995, 10–11.

16. The Rastafari woman eschews the use of the plural in this instance; "woman" as a collective is comparable to the concept of the indivisible "I-an-I" instead of the polar renditions of "you and me."

17. Officially referred to, by Bobo Rases, as the Ethiopia Africa Black International Congress.

18. The spiritual leader Priest Emmanuel was defined as the reincarnation of Melchizedek, operating in tandem with the king (Haile Selassie I) and the prophet (Marcus Mosiah Garvey).

19. Women are deemed to pollute unless they are "free," that is, potentially unproductive. Females have begun to question the restrictions that observances of the menstrual-time separation place on their movements.

20. C. A. Newland, "The Life and Work of King Emanuel Charles Edwards" (unpublished manuscript, 1994; in Newland's files), 26.

21. C. Arthur Newland, interview with Imani Tafari-Ama, Kingston, 1994.

22. Quotations from various informants come from interviews by the author, done over a period ranging from 1980 to 1990, and are not cited in the notes. Identities have been changed to protect respondents' privacy.

23. That is, acquiring Rastafari consciousness in the commune.

24. Tafari-Ama, "Grassroots Resistance in Jamaica," 89.

25. Rastafari take speeches, utterances, and the life history of His Imperial Majesty Haile Selassie I as gospel.

26. The Jamaican patois rendition of a shortened form of "daughter of Zion."

27. See D. Kyandoti, "Bargaining with Patriarchy," *Gender and Society,* ed. Jayawardena (September 1988): 10; quoted in Tafari-Ama, "Grassroots Resistance in Jamaica," 46.

28. Errol Miller, *Men at Risk* (Kingston: Jamaica Publishing House, 1991).

29. Patois meaning "You are pretending to be more impressive than you really are."

30. At the Pitfour Center in Montego Bay, Jamaica, 1991.

31. Miller, *Men at Risk,* 241.

32. Patois meaning "knock down," as in "chant down Babylon."

33. Newland, interview with Tafari-Ama.

34. The phenomenon of the menstrual cycle is a principal taboo issue, in accordance with Judaic principles.

35. Patois meaning "From the time I see that they are not dealing with anything, I tell them to pack up and go."

36. Use of condoms was condoned by some and rejected by others. Some brethren thought their sperm should not be thrown away but should be emitted into the female, the natural receptacle.

37. Examples of such knowledge in African tradition include quilt making, storytelling, hair braiding, food preparation, language, and forms of dress.

38. The designation "working-class" represents the social point of departure of the majority of Rastafari sistren.

39. The colonists instituted the West India Royal Commission, chaired by Lord Moyne, to investigate social and economic conditions in Jamaica. It produced the Moyne Commission Report in 1945. See J. French, "Colonial Policy toward Women after the 1938 Uprising: The Case of Jamaica" (unpublished conference paper, Institute of Social Studies, The Hague, 1985).

40. C. Y. Thomas, *The Poor and the Powerless: Economic Policy and Change in the Caribbean* (London: Latin America Bureau, Research and Action, 1988).

41. Bob Marley and the Wailers, "Redemption Song," on *Uprising,* Island Records 422-846211-4, 1980.

42. Judy Mowatt, "Never Get Weary," on *Look at Love,* Shanachie Records 43087, 1991.

6

The Epistemological Significance of "I-an-I" as a Response to Quashie and Anancyism in Jamaican Culture

ADRIAN ANTHONY MCFARLANE

Anyone who has at least a nodding acquaintance with "Rasta talk" is likely to have heard the expression "I-an-I" (or "I-and-I"). Some Rastafarian detractors have regarded this self-reflexive use of the first-person subject pronoun as "nothing more than babble." In fact, persons who fail to understand the semantic (linguistic) distinctiveness of Rasta "I-words" have labeled Rasta speech unintelligible and the beginning of the demise of the Queen's English among the uneducated Jamaican underclass. But George E. Simpson, one of the earliest researchers of the Rastafari movement, observes that while the I-an-I expression was not evident in the 1950s, its current use is distinctive.[1] The I-an-I expression does not function simply as a protocol for all I-words; it is the means by which Rastas make all informed utterances related to their principles, cultic practices, and self-affirmation. That is, the expression is a means by which Rastas communicate their basic philosophy or concept of themselves, their community, and the world.

This chapter analyzes the Rasta I-an-I locution as a response to what are referred to as Quashie and Anancyism in Jamaican culture. It shows that the I-an-I locution creates a linguistic device that provides a new sense of self-liberation for a people of the African diaspora. The chapter also suggests that parallels exist between Rastas' I-an-I epistemology (or theory of knowledge) and the theory of ideas of classical philosophers such as Plato, which can be useful in analyzing cultural traditions. The I-words provide an avenue through which Rastas show their total rejection of the values of Babylon while demonstrating their ability to create a new language medium for the liberation of "Jah people" within Western Babylon culture. Out of this I-an-I locution and other I-words comes a new sense of self that leads to a new vision of values, inclusive of art and beauty as well as power.

Rasta I-words form a well-knit semantic and lexical family structure. The incarnation of "I" in Jah Selassie I, previously known as Ras Tafari, is seen as an expression of "the

Word made flesh" of early Christian theology (John 1:14). This word of flesh, power, and life provides the context for all significant and definitive Rasta discourse. Thus, in their exaltation of the I made known in Ras Tafari, Jah Selassie I, the early Rastas reconfigured and appropriated that I as Rasta-for-*I*. This appropriation functions both as an ascription of Jah's care of his own and as a statement of faith, namely, that one has decided and is committed to follow Jah's guidance. Thus the "I" that ends Rastafar*i* is also the first principle of Rasta life, which reverses the order of things to make the last first and the first last, so that everything is within the orb of Jah, who is the beginning and the end. This reversal of the order of things is not as trivial as it may seem; it is a conscious effort to transvalue existing patterns and principles in society, as well as to codify the terms of the emerging self-awareness and validation of Rastafari. Only those who have eyes to see and ears to hear will understand—or as Rastas prefer, "*over*stand"—the deep things of Jah in the thought and action of Rastafari.

Given this interpretation, the I-words of Rasta talk, though stated in the indicative mood, are guided by the form and principles of the imperative "I" (first-person singular) or "I-an-I" (first-person plural). The power of the I lies in its ability to command the self; its reflexiveness is its strength, and its purpose is to create a new identity and meaning for the speaker. Rastas take instructions from no one outside of themselves—a profile that often causes confrontation with law-enforcement officials. All commands come from within, unless issued by a Rasta to "an unbeliever." So even though it sounds odd to have the imperative in the first person, it makes "Rasta sense" to be directed by the I, buttressed by I-an-I. Besides, all effective commands that are positively transforming, rather than controlling, must begin on the inside of the I. In addition, whereas the singular denotes the empirical I, which one sees and feels, the plural denotes a harmonious synthesis of the empirical and the metaphysical: I am one with Jah Ras Tafari. Jah is thereby an active force with which to be reckoned, in speech, action, and presence. Jah's presence in nature is gentle to the oppressed, needy, and open-minded but the source of dread to the acquisitive, cruel, and stubborn. When one looks in the eyes of Rastafari, one sees either gentleness or judgment, fellowship or foolishness, a friend or a foe, a prince or a pauper. To a Rasta, one's vision is informed either by the possibilities of Jah's reign or by the psychological limitations occasioned by a false consciousness.

Colonialism and Quashie in Babylon

With sufficient exposure to, or engagement with, the committed adherents of the movement, one begins to discover that the Rastafari way of knowing is *sui generis;* it stands in sharp contrast to the colonial (Babylon) approach to justifying truth claims. The colonial view of the world, in its barest form, implies that truth—metaphysics, logic, epistemology—and right action—ethics and politics—are functions of superior power; that power and might reside in and issue from a superior people; and that those who possess and exercise this power as might must be right. The history of Western imperialism, which bore and guided colonialism, shows further that white is considered not only superior in might but morally superior in what is allegedly right. Subscribing to this way of thinking about the world and human stewardship of its resources would be an act of social strangulation and slow mental death for African peoples; it justifies the shackles on the body while rewiring and inextricably entangling the mind—the one mirrors the other.

The colonial view of the world is not new; it has been a way of justifying thought and actions, as well as power and domination, throughout the history of Western economic, political, intellectual, and cultural engagements.[2] It is a military model, to be precise, but it is exercised with unusual narcissism in relationship to African peoples. The historical records show that the slave trade and plantation servitude catapulted Caucasians into a false consciousness of their worth and role in the world by demonizing Africans. To attribute a sort of "God-given predestination" (ontological significance) to one's social "luck," validated by one's pigmentation, geographic origins, traditions, and class, is the nadir of arrogance and a dementia that is camouflaged as civility. If, however, Africans were to agree with the philosophy of colonialism that "might makes right," then these exaggerated claims might carry some validity. In that case, the fault might lie with our ancestors' *unwillingness* (since I do not believe that they were *unable*) to make counterclaims. As one might guess, however, the few Blacks who rebelled against that philosophy and its devastating impact on Africans paid dearly for their courageous stance. No wonder Plato's Thrasymachus boldly claims that justice is the (orchestrated) interest of the stronger. Thrasymachus's understanding of "stronger" is not limited to physical strength but extends to whatever it takes to get to the top and stay there—a view that Plato refutes in the *Republic*.[3] In other words, the desire for and attainment of power are justified by whatever means prove successful to the powerful, even the death of the powerless.

Rastafari's Response to the Colonial Worldview

Rastafarians strongly oppose what they regard as the Babylonian abuse of power and argue that "Babylon shall fall." Thus the cruelties of the "Brutish" empire, though devastating to Africans in the Americas and at home, could last only for a season. By contrast, Jah's reign endures time and invites us to anticipate the celebration of eternity. Jah's children do not seek to escape the ravages of time; they attempt to make an opening in time for the introduction of eternity. In the face of insurmountable odds, one is likely to hear Rastas utter this familiar refrain: "In the fullness of time!" or, simply, "Time will tell." While this might sound passive to some people, it connotes strength of character and will to the initiated, as well as a new and enlarged (extended) sense of time.

By their rejection of certain stereotypes of the folkloric traditions in Jamaica, Rastas show that they differ strongly with the questionable ethics of Babylon—that is, colonialism and Western imperialism—and remain an antithesis to its so-called good cultural values. Prior to the 1960s, many Jamaicans had adopted a quiescent approach to the colonial establishment and developed "compliant" strategies for surviving the harsh realities of the system. Two such strategies were the designations Quashie (stupid) and

Anancy (a trickster). But Rastafarians found the colonial, Babylonian way of living and behaving to be an affront to their inherent worth.[4] Rastas unequivocally reject docility, emulation, and sycophantic behaviors as responses to the colonial culture and instead symbolically exhibit, for all to see, Rastafari's will to transvalue the false values that pervade the Jamaican culture. Rastas often wear torn and tattered clothing as a symbol of their transvaluation of Babylon values and revalidation of self, free from European culture and costumes. Their attire is not simply a rejection of European sartorial preferences but, even more, a celebratory overcoming of Elizabethan codes of conduct, manners, and psychological orientation. Thus Rastafarians have done to colonial symbols what the Enlightenment is reputed to have done to tradition, authority, and faith.

The brothers and sisters of the movement are iconoclasts (demolishers of oppressive structures), but little violence is associated with their forceful speech and their intimidating, "dread" personae. In spite of the "sounds" of their rhetoric, most Rastafarians evince a warm, caring side in the exercise of their motto "Peace and Love." Rastas are known to chastise their antagonists verbally rather than brutalize people physically. They are even known to reach out, touch, and empower the much-maligned Quashie, who symbolizes docility and complicity, while rejecting its ethic and philosophy. This might not be immediately apparent, given their angry diatribes against Quashie-like behavior; their verbal salvos serve as challenges to an offensive behavior pattern, not as a physical danger to the practitioners themselves.

The Compliance of Quashie

Quashie is a stereotypical characterization of persons who lack the intelligence and ability to know that someone is exploiting them. They do not have the self-confidence or courage to take charge of their own future; they are compliant with existing conditions and are very quiescent and easily pushed around. They are the equivalent of the American "dummies." The compliance of Quashie is usually attributed to a lack of formal education, poverty, and a weakness of will. Although Rastas totally reject this persona, they have a different notion of who is a true Quashie. To them, a stronger Quashie psyche exists in the suburbs, the civil service, and the private sector (including schools, colleges, and churches) than among the "sufferers" in the economically depressed areas. Quashies, as nuanced by the anti-Africa social structure in Jamaica, are the offspring of cultural rape. Blacks in the diaspora are demoralized by brutish assaults, but some of us are either living in denial of this or are on a quixotic journey in search of our self-image in the mirror of our abusers. The abusers' mirror encourages a cosmetic cover-up of centuries of psychic lacerations to the Jamaican personality. Common sense, if nothing else, should reveal that the mirror answers only the question "Who is the *fairest* of them all?"; it does not tell us who are the most talented, wise, courageous, and beautiful among us. Thus every answer to this ill-formed question functions as a deprecation of the African appearance in the world and a celebration of the European, or near-European, aesthetic paradigms and culture.

It took a so-called beauty contest to make public the long-held notion "that in Jamaica whatever is black is not beautiful. . . . Beauty in Jamaica is judged by European standards and seen through European eyes."[5] The compliant, who wear European-prescribed lenses, experience a *circumscribed* aesthetic sense; they see what they are conditioned to see. For the most part, such persons are exiled in Quashie-land—a psychological bog of debilitating compliance that in folklore is a swampland infested with venomous creatures. It is also a land of shadows, born of the cruelties of servitude which conduces to the docile acceptance of slavery and oppression. Quashie-land is a mire precisely because it engenders a fear of honesty, self-discovery, and freedom. Thus Quashie's expectations are circumscribed by the circumstances of colonial cunning and brutishness, which suppress the will to be free. Whatever theological significance George Matheson's hymn may have had to Europeans of the 1890s, Quashie lives it, albeit with a deferment of the freedom and the conquest:

> Make me a captive Lord,
> And then I shall be free;
> Force me to render up my sword,
> And I shall conqueror be.

When one realizes that Quashie-land is a psychic quagmire that is fenced around with colonial barbwire, reinforced by a self-serving Eurocentric religion that promises comfort and goodwill in exchange for obedience, then one will understand why freedom evokes the terror of punishment for Quashies who say, "Massa is good to me, as long as I serve him faithfully, but he and his God will punish me if I fail to obey." European religiosity creates a dark hole in the Quashie quagmire, thereby ensuring that African enslavement continues beyond the historical event of emancipation, the appearance of self-government or independence, and even the grave. For this reason, the Rastafari movement is not only a corrective to servile behavior but a radical uprooting of uncritical acceptance of life as it is in Babylon and cooperation with the oppressive Babylonians.

In this regard, Rastafari is one of the most plausible and sustainable expressions of liberation in the African diaspora. The collective will of the Rastafari brethren and sistren challenges, enlightens, and nurtures those who heretofore were Quashies but are now responding to the sounds of drumming for renewal and freedom in our historical consciousness. Reflecting on the social ethos of his early upbringing in a Quashie environment, Leonard Barrett, one of the leading authorities on Caribbean culture during the 1970s and 1980s, a pioneer in Rastafari research, and its chief exponent in the United States, writes:

> In my youth, the tendency of the mission was radically to de-Africanize all Jamaicans, which meant total rejection of all things African. . . . The fashionable view was to emulate English behavioral traits . . . thus negating one's African linkages. This I could not do, because it was the African ingredients in me that freed my being. I therefore decided to identify myself with my African heritage, setting loose the rhythm that I felt throbbing in me.[6]

Like Barrett, many Blacks have begun to respond to the African rhythm within, and those who have lost their sense of rhythm are either in pursuit of it or in "cultural exile." Rastafari is another voice crying in the wilderness and constantly reminding Blacks of their

African identity. This voice is a viable and powerful alternative to the Quashie paradigm, which functions as a denial of the real, a resistance to inquiry and discovery, and a promoter of make-believe or fantasy. I-an-I is strong and confident, not Quashie and cowardly.

The Anancy Paradigm

Where Quashie is compliant and cooperates with colonialism and Babylon, Anancy is cunning. In a recent newspaper article Jamaican columnist Geof Brown writes, "The silent hero of this nation [Jamaica] is Anancy. Everyone knows it; few proclaim it. That is in itself the very nature of Anancyism. For Anancy must never manifest itself in its appearance what it is, in fact, carrying out in its behavior. What you see is not what you get. The tricks of deception which lead the victim into self-defeating traps constitute the essence of the Anancy syndrome."[7] According to social theorist and Rastafari scholar and devotee Dennis Forsythe, Anancy was the Jamaican response to the strange and awesome world outside of Africa—"a symbol of black survival and of staying power in such a world."[8]

But who or what is Anancy? Forsythe says, "Anancy is the 'smart spider-man' whose popularity is such that he dominates Jamaican folk-tales."[9] In most of the Anancy stories, in Jamaica as well as in Africa (especially in Ghana),[10] the spider is at the mercy of other animals that are its physical superiors. However, it uses its subtle intelligence to outwit them and hence to survive. Culturally, Anancy typifies a trickster and a con artist, who survives by unscrupulous means. To many among the Jamaican underclass, he has become "a kind of lovable rascal, impersonifying [sic] the genius of our race to survive under Babylon conditions."[11] As the Jamaican folklorist and writer Daryl C. Dance puts it, "Anancy is generally a figure of admiration whose cunning and scheming nature reflects the indirection and subtleness necessary for survival and, occasionally, victory in a racist society."[12]

Since his is an ethic of survival, this spider character is so well known that finding a Jamaican who has not heard or told an Anancy story would be difficult. In legendary tales of this creature's craftiness, Anancy's ability to survive seemingly insurmountable odds, to outwit and confound the allegedly clever, and to disorient the strong and influential wins this unscrupulous creature much admiration. This West African folktale of the crafty spider has functioned as a pedagogical tool for teaching children survival skills. In spite of the fact that "it" is a confidence man, Anancy offers hope and relief to a disempowered population; persons who feel powerless can at least fantasize about using their weakness as a strength, albeit surreptitiously.

Barrett rightly notes that, "regardless of his treachery and cunning, Anansi has those components which make him a folk hero *par excellence* for, elusive and nimble of spirit and witty of tongue, he is representative of techniques of survival at their best."[13] Anyone who attempts to understand the Jamaican psyche without some acquaintance with Anancy's practices is likely to confuse appearance with reality. Anancy is especially charming and cunning; it assumes the faces of persons and institutions and can be referred to inclusively as of male, female, or neuter gender. Anancyism has its positive and negative sides: the one garners an indefatigable spirit in gaining success and the upper hand, but the other fosters, certifies, and institutionalizes deception while appearing innocent, or at least neutral. But this is precisely why all Anancy stories end with a refrain of disavowal. What the Anancy paradigm does for one's consciousness is to encourage survival *at any cost*. This translates into a pragmatic way of parrying with the more powerful in society and remaining vibrantly alive to tell the stories afterward, embellishing tales here and there for dramatic effect. In addition, Anancy functions as an invitation to a joust of wits, thereby perceiving opportunities for mental and verbal adroitness where hitherto one heard only insults.

Not only is Anancy the trickster a provocateur, humorist, skillful negotiator, and resourceful champion, but the paradigm also acts as a heuristic device for testing truth claims—Anancy muddies the stream of certainty with the paradoxical and the unusual and exemplifies the embodiment of the morally unacceptable human elements of our personality, which we exhibit but love to hate and attempt to hide. Through the symbol of Anancy "we can be and not be" simultaneously. Like the Hegelian dialectic, this is either a breach of the logical principle of noncontradiction or a revision of it, depending on one's operating paradigm. Anancy does with impunity what most of us would like to do but refrain from doing in fear of being caught—or lack the wit to do. No wonder, then, that Jamaicans romanticize Anancy's exploits, for through them we vicariously break with tradition. From the perspective of psychology, one might say Anancy functions as our alter ego; from an ethical point of view, it functions as an expression of duplicity. Politically, Anancy demonstrates a chameleon-like adaptation under the ruse of pragmatic diplomacy (what Rastas call "polytricks"), and theologically, Anancy is hypocrisy adorned as the synthesis of the social and spiritual ethos of Jamaica. But from the perspective of philosophy, Anancy is much like the "gadfly" and ironist of Socratic vintage; he plays the fool to catch (confound) the putatively wise, thereby "making the weaker argument defeat the stronger."[14] And in a culture where "Brutish" classism and arrogance lead to baseless claims to knowledge, Anancy is a refreshing presence.

The problem with the Anancy culture is that its only consistency is its inconsistency; it is a moving target and consistently unreliable. It contradicts its own ethical aspirations. Since its ethic is one of survival, Anancy has no resolute moral standard but is characterized by deceit, dishonesty, double-talk, and back stabbing. Self-preservation becomes the driving force in all Anancy's social engagements. Truth is relative and situational, and trust is either an expendable commodity or a great liability in one's relationship to Babylon. One does not have to look too far to observe the lack of trust in the Jamaican society. The saying "Nuh trus no body you nuh know" and the double dead bolts and burglar bars on houses throughout the country are sad reminders that there is an undeclared "Anancy state of emergency" in the country.

Inquiring and conscious minds may sincerely wonder whether anything can be known for certain in a context where trust is a major liability. One usually has to choose between becoming engaged in this social Darwinian state of the survival of the most cunning, dressed up as "the fittest," or finding a basis for advocating and pursuing the verities that nurture a salutary social life. Evidently, the "lovable rascality" of

Anancy, as Rex Nettleford colorfully describes Anancy's complexity, has spun a web of falsehood in the society that seriously threatens to remove the truth claims for any and all statements and engagements. Very much like the Riddler character in the series of Batman movies that have appeared over the last fifteen years, Anancy's antics are potentially devastating to the constitution and continuation of civil society. In its early form, Anancy represented a challenge to the old order that excluded Africans from the category of personhood and civility. In its present state, it puts confusion and deception as tools of survival in the hands of the dispossessed and "downpressed." But this attitude often prevaricates the truth and confuses reality with unreality. As a result, whether Anancy is being true or false, right or wrong, reliable or unreliable, is not always clear. This unmanageable uncertainty will inevitably lead to insecurity and social disintegration.

For this reason and others, Rastas reject the Anancy image as a positive representation of the African personality they wish to exemplify. They seek to move beyond the Anancy paradigm to a more wholesome expression of Jah's social order. Also, the depiction of Anancy as "a little bald-headed man with a falsetto voice and a cringing manner in the presence of his superior"[15] is antithetical to the valorization of dreadlocks, which symbolize fearlessness and fearsomeness. In the same context, the visual and verbal engagements of Rastafari function as sentinels against the intrusions of alien cultural values into Jamaican culture, as well as alarms against wolves in sheep's clothing. Rastas are rightly suspicious of persons who smile or talk too much and who offer unsolicited gifts. Of course, some so-called Rastas have taken gifts from foreign "Anancyesque" admirers to their peril. One speaks here of drugs "beyond the ganja fields," as it were, and guns beyond the military range. These instruments of death are the Trojan horse symbols in the psychosocial, political, and economic life of Jamaica.

However, not everyone who stereotypically looks and sounds like a Rastafarian believes and practices the ways of Jah. My brother, Jah Neville, a Rasta for forty-one years, states emphatically, "There are Rastas and impastas [impostors]!" Again, the discerning I functions as the principle for security clearance to Rasta communes as well as a sign of "Rasta truth." This watchful I of the I-and-I lineage is like an alembic to the soul, and Rastafarians have thereby become the catalyst for healing the soul of African peoples, as well as others. Like the proverbial stone that the builder rejected, the Rastas have become the moral strength of Jamaica's cultural infrastructure and the hope for its superstructure, its social, moral, and political reformation and revitalization. In other words, Rastas view knowledge as an activity of conscious self-awareness that grows "like a tree planted by the rivers of water" (Psalm 1:3 KJV), under the shade of I-an-I (Jah's nurture), "which brings forth fruit in its due season" (Jah's expression).

The Lionhearted Response

The compliance of Quashie is not opposed to the cunning of Anancy; both can coexist without any apparent contradiction. Yet the Rastas who are ruled by "the heart" ("the heartical") see a natural evolution from Quashie through Anancy to the *courage* of the lion. Having repudiated Anancy, they now embrace the lion as "a more fitting ideal for a people bent on a march forward towards their own maximum and ultimate self-realization and self-discovery."[16] Symbolically, the lion suggests nobility, self-confidence, strength, pride, and moral fortitude in the face of oppression. To Rastas, the lion symbolizes "power, dignity, beauty, fearlessness, and wholesome integrity that come from self-realization."[17] Forsythe noted that in West African folklore, Anancy and the lion were always in conflict, the lion being the king amongst animals. It is believed, however, that enslaved Africans exchanged their lion consciousness for the quiet, cunning survival strategies of Anancy. According to Forsythe, "Rastas have become the first Caribbean Africans attempting to break away," on such a large scale, "from this Ananc[y] tradition and are attempting to develop an alternative counter-culture and a philosophy which is distinctively its own."[18] Rastas seem to have intentionally set out to reclaim their power and regality, symbolized by the lion within them. A reggae hit by Frankie Wilmot lyricizes the notion of black imprisonment, obstruction of enlightenment, and vilification of the African spirit and character in Babylon and then counters in the refrain that the lion in suffering people will keep them fighting, surviving, going, and overcoming.[19]

Against the background of the thumping reggae beat is an easy, laid-back, rock-steady fusion of lionhearted confidence that translates, at least for this listener, into "Fret not, those whom Jah loves cannot be destroyed." The hardships in Jamaica cannot be understated, but lions, the king of animals, are not bothered by vipers; the deadly venom of the snake is neutralized by the lion's paw. This explains why the lion is preferred to Anancy as a symbol of strength; it is not subject to common frights or "weakhearted," as are others in the animal kingdom. The lion is the king of beasts and king of the jungle. Conscious Jamaicans spurn the image of Anancy, Forsythe claims, particularly the Rastas who "chose the image of the African lion as representative of the alternative Rasta ideal. The Lion is symbolic of a return to Africa—a return to black originality, black creativity."[20] The lion unmistakably symbolizes a forceful self-assertiveness, a roaring sense of personhood seeking justice, and a dreadful challenge to cowardice.

Jamaican Horace Campbell, the well-known Walter Rodney scholar, political activist, and Pan-Africanist who has taught in Dar es Salaam, Tanzania, since 1981, charts the psychosocial path that Rastafarians have traversed "from Quashie to lion." He asserts that Rastas rejected "the shuffling Quashie traits" by which many slaves survived, deciding to *live* rather than merely survive. "Rastas held their heads high as they walked the streets of their communities, and while spreading peace and love combined the confidence and strength of the *lion* among the poor."[21] This lionized status evolved almost ex nihilo—from being weak and fearful to being assertive, strong, and "dread." From a Rasta perspective, this is a transformation that shows the hand of Jah confounding the oppressors and the skeptics. As Campbell notes, Rastas began to repair the psychological damage of centuries of imposed servility, reactionary docility, and duplicity by declaring "their identification with the *lion*—in its roar, its hair, its body strength, intelligence and total movements."[22] Forsythe expresses it rather well, saying that the lion ideal indicates a "return to black originality, black creativity and to the ideal of 'Everliving life'."[23]

This lion metaphor is what has inspired the Rasta movement. Haile Selassie I not only had lions as pets (friends) but was crowned as "the Conquering Lion of the Tribe of Judah." Hence Rastas have "captured" (taken) the lyrics from an old song, popular in Myal and Pocomania (Afro-Caribbean religious traditions) in the 1950s and 1960s, and intone, "The Lion of Judah will break every chain, and give us the victory, again and again." (The origins of such songs are cultural uncertainties.) The lion is, therefore, a symbol of unapologetic strength—moral, psychological, and social—and confidence; it assumes its role of leadership, in spite of popular disdain, as a natural consequence of Jah's presence in the I-consciousness of Rastafari. Forsythe intimates that the contributions of Rastafari to cultural awareness in the African diaspora, though numerous, are symbolized by the mirror of Rastas' challenging presence—a mirror in which we either see ourselves and run away or see ourselves and return "home" to self-consciousness: "It is in this *looking-glass* or cultural, non-partisan and holistic sense that Rastafari is most significant."[24] The dread stare (gaze) of Rastafari functions as a winnowing instrument to discern and distinguish sincerity from superficiality. In other words, the eye (I) of Jah in Rastafari sees clearly and distinctly and, as such, functions as the yardstick for the determination of knowledge, truth, and reality.

A Rasta Epistemology

In spite of the temptation to rhapsodize about the unusual or distinctive nature of Rasta culture, Rastafarian thought is comprised of more than meets the eyes. In fact, it would be an egregious affront to the Rastafarians, as well as to the cultural life of Jamaica, if "Rasta culture" were trivialized and packaged only for tourism. As the late Jacob Miller, one of the leading musicians and Rastafarian brethren during the 1970s, is often quoted to have said, "Rasta no jesta." What is important at this point is whether Rasta ideas, as we have discussed them, can stand up to a searching "Rastalike" inquiry (engaging, critical, analytic analysis)—whether in the movement, the academy, or the society at large.

In the first place, Quashie, Anancy, and the lion in Rasta appear to have at least one thing in common, namely, a strong desire to survive. Their methods are different, to be sure: Quashie survives by a strategy of diffidence (*compliance*), Anancy by duplicity (*cunning*), and the lion by daring and a dread appearance (*courage*). Quashie and Anancy take a noncombative approach, but the lion is uncompromisingly confrontational. Anancy schemes to outwit both the powerful and the powerless—having scruples is a liability for Anancy, unless they are in a context where the exhibition of such brings favorable rewards—whereas the lion vehemently challenges the "downpressors" and vigorously exhorts the "downpressed" and weakhearted to be strong. Anancy gets its way by stealth, the lion by strength; Anancy ensnares and controls, whereas the lion thunders (roars) and controls. However, whereas Quashie is "spooked" into a psychic state of immobility, and Anancy finds back roads and shortcuts to psychological advantage, the lion freely "walks the old while," claiming (capturing) what is in sight as its own. Lions are known to go wherever they choose and claim control. The lion has the ability to chart new paths and validate them, as well as to tread ("trod through the free") old ones and claim or transvalue them. This sets the lion apart from all others. In short, the lion is more than a survivor; one is a Lion because one enjoys *conquest,* particularly in the ego strength that delivers the courage to reconfigure (reinterpret) one's world.

From the perspective of the justification of knowledge claims, one cannot but inquire how Rastas know that they know. In other words, what is the possibility, scope, and general basis of their claims about Jah, Selassie, or lionheartedness? Is it their ego strength? In 1995, I asked recent converts Ras Michael and Ras James, in Ocho Rios, Jamaica, if they were certain of anything. They answered in chorus, "Yes! The living, never dying, presence of Jah." "What makes you so sure?" I inquired. After much thought, James declared that, for him, before the beginning of time and space, Jah was unexpressed knowledge, truth, and power, and since time and space, Jah has come to mean the source of knowledge, truth, and power. Still dissatisfied, I queried whether Jah might not be a psychological prop for "weak hearts" disguised as lionized Rastafarians. Here Ras Michael interjected with much intensity, "Those who don't know speculate, but I know, and what I know cannot be taken away by cunning arguments!"[25] What I deduced from this and previous conversations with other brethren and sistren is that the zealous Rastas see no difference between *being, knowing,* and *doing.* This ontology underpins Rasta theory of knowledge and sense of responsibility. For one to know, one must be; and for one to do anything (efficaciously), one must know. Knowledge therefore is predicated on the *being* of Jah, which is extended into the consciousness of Rastafari. This state of affairs not only changes the individual but also emphasizes the "livity" (wholeness, well-being, joy) of Rastafari, temporally and eternally.

If the Rasta truth claims are based on indwelling, eternal verities, can Rastas be wrong or have substantive disagreements among themselves? I suppose it is not contradictory for two or more persons to claim to have *x* while giving different accounts of *x*. Here one can either subject such claims to the litmus test of orthodoxy (and eliminate the heretics) or expand one's horizon of knowledge to include a phenomenologically diverse spectrum of interpretation. To do the former is to exercise control via an attenuated body of beliefs. But doing the latter expands the field of beliefs to include subjective responses. Maybe the former is no less subjective than the latter, except that it appears to be objective because it is hedged around under the watchful eyes of tradition. Anyhow, outside of a flaming arrogance or insanity, no Rasta would justifiably claim to be the sole keeper of Jah's truth. Besides, there is a good deal of diversity among Rastafarians to encourage disagreements and debates.

Further, anyone who claims that Jah's truth is univocal, rather than equivocal, makes interpretation (including belief and faith) superfluous. Claims to self-evident truths are problematic; that which is self-evident does not need to be stated. However, even if the alleged univocal truth is not held as self-evident, it poses a problem for the diversity of human experiences and expressions. A Rastafarian sister said to me recently, "Rastas can be as dogmatic, divisive, and exclusionary as Christians, Muslims, and the plethora of 'isms' which sire schisms."[26] What this sister drew to my attention was the ease with which one's fervor for the love of Jah can sour into a siblinglike rivalry. This led me to muse on the philosophical epistemic warrant for Rastafari's claim that Jah is the justification for all justifications, including that of *himself*.[27] Is this anything more than the tendency of religious systems to elevate themselves by the self-certification of their primary beliefs? If the answer is anything close to the affirmative, then Sister E.'s observation that Rastas run the risk of becoming what they spurn (agents of Babylonian division rather than of Zion's inclusive love) is accurate—however, there is more to Rasta discourse than self-certification.

Finally, to claim that Jah stands outside the scrutiny of justificatory procedures raises questions about Rastas' ability to offer compelling arguments for their beliefs and Jah's vulnerability to rational inquiry. Most, if not all, religious epistemologies carry the burden of infinite regress, the *petitio principii* fallacy, or a skepticism fueled by fideism. For example, if *a* justifies *b*, and *b* justifies *c* (and so on through *z*), what justifies *a*? Well, if *a* justifies itself, we have a problem regarding the nature of justification itself, such that we might inquire: What is the criterion for the criterion of justification? This would lead us into an infinite regress, unless we stop the process and say that *z* justifies *a* (which is circular and question-begging) or claim that *a* stands outside of the range of categories for justification. The question then arises: How does one know this? For if *a* can be neither verified nor falsified, are we not saying that there is "something" we know about *a* that hinders us from knowing anything about *a*? In short, one has to take a fideistic position with regard to *a*, namely, that nothing can count as a compelling argument for or against the existence of *a*; one either believes or disbelieves.

It does not take long for one to see the Anancyesque smile on the skeptic's face in all of these moves—infinite regress, circularity (*petitio principii* fallacy), and fideism (the claim that the categories of reason are inadequate to validate or invalidate one's belief). However, these positions are only "fatal" to the systems of thought that place epistemology at the center of discourse. It must be noted, in the spirit of the discussion, that epistemology—though useful in clarifying and systematizing thought—is not exempt from the rational scrutiny to which it subjects all disciplines. In his recent book *Philosophical Arguments,* Charles Taylor declares his task to be the destruction of "the Hydra epistemology." His aim is set on the assumption that we have to achieve full clarity about ideas before we can talk intelligently about them. He strongly demurs: "I believe this to be a terrible and fateful illusion. It assumes wrongly that we can get to the bottom of what knowledge is, without drawing on our never-fully-articulate understanding of human life and experience. There is a temptation here to a kind of self-possessing clarity, to which our modern culture has been almost endlessly susceptible."[28] This statement harmonizes with the Rastafarian practice of the equivocality of terms. Rastas seem to be constantly reinterpreting their utterances, aiming at more and more clarity and shifting positions with the artfulness, if not the craft, of Anancy. Both Anancy and the lion in Rasta strive to save face and win arguments; Anancy does it by craft and prevarication, while Rastas do it by a process of reinterpretation in the preemptive idiom of I-an-I.

One must admit that although Rastas have expressed their thoughts in many different ways and in varied literary and artistic forms, few Rastafarians have written an epis temology or philosophy of the movement and its beliefs. One could argue that Rastas do not need the paradigms and methodologies of Western intellectual history to explain their claims and fundamental ideas. Further, technical philosophical discussion imposes a Western structure on Rasta talk and truth claims, removing the discourse from the community of the poor to the ghettos of the privileged. Rastas simply use the I-an-I expression to synthesize what scholars regard as empirical and metaphysical issues, which Rastas then contemplate in practical ways, thereby giving validation to what they say and do in the name of Jah. However, to suggest that Western paradigms are too complex and sophisticated for the interpretation and analysis of Rastafarian thought would be quite patronizing and insulting to Rastas. This view would also imply that Rastas "enjoy" a degrading uniformity of socioeconomic placement, beliefs, awareness or consciousness in the world, specially designed for a so-called inferior people. I argue that Rastafari's beliefs and actions are sufficiently grounded that the Rasta worldview resists co-option, hybridization, or trivialization. While the cautions are well worth remembering, the inferences are naive, if not insulting. This writer's experiences with Rastafari over the last thirty years reveal a level of elenctic, intelligent discourse that would even stimulate Socrates, inter alios.

While I have attempted to guard against comparing Rasta ways of thinking to that of the early Western philosophers, the parallels are striking in many places. The I-an-I locution, though more colorful, resembles Plato's notion that knowledge resides in the soul and is "teased out" in conversation and introspection. Thus we must not only get in touch with our souls (one's true self), as the oracle of Delphi states ("Know thyself!"), but become aware that no one can give us knowledge. In addition, knowledge, for Plato and Rastas, is based not on things, events, or information but on principles (I-deas) discoverable by the conscious self, under the guidance of Reason (Plato) or Jah within (Rastafarians). There are parallels between the Rastas and Plato's theory of ideas, Diogenes' (412–323 B.C.E.) cynicism toward Corinthian/Athenian hypocrisy, and his "recoining of current values," as well as with Baruch Spinoza's (1632–1677) notion that to understand the world in its correct logical structure, we must view it *sub specie aeternitatis* (under the aspect of the eternal). These are interesting, though not particularly instructive. What is instructive, however, is that Rasta I-deas can and do stand on their own; they are *sui generis*, and there is much to learn from them as long as one is in touch with oneself and, correspondingly, with Jah as I-an-I. Thus Rastas reject what they see as the artificial means of knowing, in favor of an emphasis on the stirrings in persons to the truth conditions of Jah's inspiration. Knowledge becomes self-knowledge, and self-knowledge is made possible by the knowledge of Jah.

Notes

1. George E. Simpson, "The Rastafari Movement in the 1950s," *Jamaica Journal* 25, 2 (December 1994): 4.

2. See Thucydides' account of Agamemnon; Plato's *Republic* 1–3; Thomas Hobbes's *Leviathan;* and Niccolò Machiavelli's *The Prince.*

3. Plato's *Republic* bk. 1, 336–47; see *The Republic of Plato,* trans. F. M. Cornford (New York: Oxford University Press, 1945), 3:18.

4. The claim of inherent worth forms the basis of all Rastafari statements about the self and the world.

5. This is an issue which Rex Nettleford treated substantively more than twenty-five years ago; see his *Mirror, Mirror: Identity, Race and Protest in Jamaica,* 2d ed. (Kingston: W. Collins/Sangster's Book Stores, 1972), 215. His comment quoted here originally appeared in "Letter to Septon Johnson," *Daily Gleaner,* August 22, 1967, 2A. See also Rex Nettleford, "This Matter of Malanin: Calling a Spade a Spade," *Jamaica Record,* 19 March 1989, 2B.

6. Leonard Barrett, *The Sun and the Drum: African Roots in Jamaica Folk Tradition* (London: William Heinemann, 1976), 13–14.

7. Geof Brown, "The Legacy of Anancyism," *Daily Gleaner,* July 14, 1995, 4A.

8. Dennis Forsythe, *Rastafari: For the Healing of the Nation* (Kingston: Zaika Publications, 1983), 218.

9. Ibid.

10. *Anancy* originated from the Twi language of Ghana; see Barrett, *The Sun and the Drum,* 34.

11. Ibid., 74.

12. Daryl C. Dance, *Folklore from Contemporary Jamaicans* (Knoxville: University of Tennessee Press, 1985), 12.

13. Barrett, *The Sun and the Drum,* 35.

14. See Plato's *Apology* 18b, as translated by Hugh Tredennick in Edith Hamilton and Huntington Cairns, eds., *Plato: The Collected Dialogues* (Princeton, N.J.: Princeton University Press, 1961; 10th ed., 1980).

15. Dennis Forsythe, "West Indian Culture through the Prism of Rastafarianism," in Rex Nettleford, ed., *Caribbean Quarterly Monograph: Rastafari* (Kingston: Caribbean Quarterly, University of the West Indies, 1985), 73.

16. Ibid.

17. Forsythe, *Rastafari,* 101.

18. Forsythe, "West Indian Culture," 73. It is worth noting that, in addition to this article, Forsythe's treatment of Anancy, the lion, culture, and identity, as they relate to Rastafarians, in his book *Rastafari,* is most insightful. From these sources, along with Barrett's *The Sun and the Drum,* Nettleford's *Mirror, Mirror,* and Horace Campbell's *Rasta and Resistance: From Marcus Garvey to Walter Rodney* (Trenton, N.J.: Africa World Press, 1987), 99, one gets a family of ideas about the extent of African retentions in Jamaican life.

19. Frankie Wilmot, "The Lion in Me" (an X-rated song produced by Carber Music, executive producer Barry O' Hare); heard on IRIE FM, July 15, 1995.

20. Forsythe, "West Indian Culture," 73.

21. Campbell, *Rasta and Resistance,* 99.

22. Ibid.

23. Forsythe, "West Indian Culture," 73.

24. Forsythe, *Rastafari,* 205.

25. The author's conversation with Ras Michael and Ras James in Tower Isle, Ocho Rios, Jamaica, January 11, 1995. Both Rastas have declined to use their surnames in protest to "the two-face," double-name Anancyism, as well as to sever their links with the colonial structures.

26. A conversation between the author and Sister E. in St. Ann's Bay, Jamaica, July 25, 1995.

27. Rastafarian beliefs are strongly patriarchal and theocratic. However, this does not obviate the customary procedures of justifying truth claims. For R to know that j is true, (1) R has to believe that j is true; (2) R has to adduce evidence to the claim that j is true; and (3) j must be true. Thus, no matter how sincerely R believes that j is true, this alone would not make j true. But how does one know that j is true? The whole matter is circular; it suggests that one needs to decide on what appear to be the best judgments while maintaining an openness to modification.

28. Charles Taylor, *Philosophical Arguments* (Cambridge, Mass.: Harvard University Press, 1995), vii–viii.

Part II

Roots and Historical Impact

7 African Dimensions of the Jamaican Rastafarian Movement

NEIL J. SAVISHINSKY

In the late 1980s, I conducted fieldwork on the spread of the Jamaican Rastafarian movement in West Africa, the bulk of which was undertaken in Ghana and Senegambia (Senegal and Gambia held as one under colonial rule)—two areas of the region that harbor long-standing and fairly sizable Rastafarian populations. West African manifestations of Rastafari, as I was quick to discover, largely derive from and mirror their Jamaican counterparts and forebears in both form and function. This is especially true vis-à-vis adherents' ritual and secular use of cannabis (marijuana) and reggae music; the adoption of dreadlocks, Rasta colors, and "iyaric," or "dread talk;" and outspoken commitment to social, political, and religious ideologies promoting Pan-Africanism, "ital" (healthy living), a belief in a black God and his black prophets, and the use of biblical narrative, allusion, and allegory. Many West African Rastas look on these adoptions as proof of their unerring faithfulness to the original and abiding principles of Rastafari, but others tend to take a more critical view of their compatriots' appropriation of what many consider an alien religion, music, and lifestyle. As one Ghanaian journalist whom I interviewed in Accra in winter of 1989 put it:

> Why do we Africans always have to imitate the ways of foreigners? Look at these so-called Rastafarians here in Accra with their dreadlocks, reggae music, "wee" [a local term for cannabis] smoking, and worship of some former Ethiopian dictator who they say is God or Africa's black prophet or some such nonsense. I just don't know why they refuse to look to their own culture for role models instead of trying to imitate these Jamaican Rastas and reggae musicians.

In an attempt to justify, both to themselves and to the wider society, their adoption of what may appear on the surface to be a foreign belief system, set of religious practices, fashion trend, and contemporary pop music genre, West African Rastas frequently refer to the intense physical, cultural, and historical links that have, throughout the centuries, bound the New World African diaspora to Africa. In effect, what these individuals are saying is that this question of foreign appropriation and mimicry is not really relevant or applicable to them. In their adoption of an Afro-Jamaican religion, music, and cultural identity, they are not merely imitating popular Western trends and fashions but are, in fact, expressing their Africanness through the prism of an Afrocentric, Pan-African movement that happened to originate in the African diaspora. And because the very essence of Rastafarianism is African, according to these adherents, it can and does serve as a legitimate religious, social, and political model and form of expression for Africans and all persons of African descent.

The persistence of African cultural elements and continuities among black populations in the New World represents a fairly widespread and well documented phenomenon.[1] These Africanisms—or neo-Africanisms, as they are sometimes called—are most apparent in the language, folklore, religious beliefs and practices, and music, art, and dance that have evolved within Caribbean and African American communities over the course of the last four centuries. As Caribbean social theorist Edward Brathwaite has observed:

> The African, imported from the area of his "great tradition," went about establishing himself in a new environment, using the available tools and memories of his traditional heritage to set going something new, something Caribbean, but something nevertheless recognizably African. . . . It is in the nature of the folk cultures of the ex-African slave, still persisting today in the life of the contemporary "folk," that we can discern that the "middle passage" was not, as is popularly assumed, a traumatic, destructive experience, separating blacks from Africa, disconnecting their sense of history and tradition, but a pathway or channel between this tradition and what is being evolved, on new soil, in the Caribbean.[2]

This chapter attempts to document the existence of such formal and direct continuities as they relate to the development of the Rastafarian movement in Jamaica. It shows that various African-based beliefs and practices contributed to the creation of a distinctive Jamaican folk culture, which, in turn, inspired many of the social, religious, symbolic, and artistic aspects and expressions commonly associated with the Rastafari. It also examines, in some detail, the connections that exist between Africa and the culture of Rastafari in terms of more abstract, underlying principles and indirect links. Given the considerable heterogeneity of the African populations brought to the New World and the conditions under which they arrived and had to survive in their new environment, it comes as no surprise that many of the cultural forms and institutions developed by slave societies bear little resemblance to their African prototypes. They represent, instead, creative responses to the unique needs and conditions of the enslaved and their descendants.

Direct African Continuities

The Music

Reggae, like many other forms of New World music, was created from the blending of African, neo-African,[3] and African American musical styles and elements. Whereas the various strains of black music (e.g., rhythm and blues, gospel, and soul) that came to

Jamaica via American phonograph records and radio broadcasts accounted for the African American side of this equation, the Rastafari were chiefly responsible for introducing the African or neo-African elements into reggae music—elements that serve to underscore the island's strong links to an African musical past. According to Verena Reckord, when the Rastafarian movement surfaced in Jamaica in the early 1930s, the only form of musical expression employed by Rasta adherents consisted of hymns sung to melodies borrowed from local Christian churches and revival groups (e.g., Pocomania and Zion). In their subsequent search for a musical idiom that would better express their intense commitment to Africa and to the revitalization of a lost ancestral heritage and culture, the Rastafari appropriated instruments and drumming techniques from a number of Afro-Jamaican folk traditions, most notably Burru and Kumina.

One of the few African-derived musical forms in Jamaica that managed to survive fairly intact into the twentieth century is that associated with the Burru men, whose drumming was officially sanctioned by the colonial authorities for its use as a rhythmic aid in keeping cadence among field slaves. As Reckord notes, with the demise of slavery, many Burru drummers left their rural homes in search of employment and eventually settled in the slums of West Kingston. It was here that, a century or so later, they first came into contact with the Rastafari. Being poor and sharing a similar status as pariahs and social outcasts, the two groups quickly gravitated toward each other.[4] Shortly thereafter, a new style of Rastafarian "churchical" (religious) music and worship, referred to as *Nyabinghi*,[5] emerged on the scene. This music combined the instruments and rhythmic techniques of the Burru with Rastafarian Christian-based hymn singing and chanting.

The second strain of Afro-Jamaican music and dance that had a direct impact on the evolution of a distinctive Rastafarian music culture is that associated with the Kumina cult, a largely African-derived religious tradition practiced in the eastern part of the island by descendants of indentured laborers brought from Central Africa to Jamaica in the mid-1800s. Major features of this cult's ritual drumming and dance, which center on communication with ancestral spirits through possession, have been traced back to Africa. Kumina is even sometimes referred to by initiates as "the African dance," and there is little doubt that, like Cuban Santería and Haitian Voodoo, Kumina represents "the living fragment of an African religion in the Caribbean."[6] Kenneth Bilby and Elliot Leib, drawing on evidence from a variety of sources (including ethnographic research conducted by Bilby in Jamaica in the 1970s), maintain that Leonard Howell and his followers began incorporating Kumina drums—a two-drum complex consisting of the *bandu* and playing *cyas*—and drumming techniques into their religious ceremonies in the mid-1930s. Bilby also discovered that these and other Kumina-based practices have been retained by present-day Rasta Howellites, many of whom still possess considerable knowledge of Kumina (or, as now referred to, Bongo or Kongo)[7] language, songs, and history. Bilby and Leib provide evidence of a fairly widespread pattern of cross-fertilization that took place between Burru and Kumina drumming styles, which, they claim, eventually contributed to the development of Nyabinghi drumming and, later, ska, rock steady, and reggae rhythms: "Through such interchange, the invigorating rhythms of Kumina, meshed with those of [Burru] and perhaps others, have indirectly been able, via Nyabingi, to enter the Jamaican musical mainstream . . . and as it turns out, the Rastafari insistence on the 'African roots' of Nyabingi may be historically accurate in ways that even many Rastafari brethren themselves, not to mention others, do not realize."[8]

One of the most important links in this chain connecting African and neo-African music to Nyabinghi and reggae was an early Rastafarian musician named Count Ossie. Steeped in both the Burru and Kumina drumming traditions, Ossie eventually teamed up with other like-minded Jamaican musicians and set about creating a new style of African-derived music that catered to the needs of Kingston's growing Rasta population. During the late 1950s and early 1960s, he also influenced some of the island's leading non-Rasta pop musicians, a number of whom went on to form the definitive ska band of the decade, the Skatalites. Since then, the Rasta drumming and rhythmic styles propagated by "roots" Rasta groups such as Count Ossie's Mystic Revelation of Rastafari and Ras Michael and the Sons of Negus have continued to exert an impact on developing forms of Jamaican popular music.[9]

Reggae's strongest links to an African past may perhaps best be seen in the various roles the music plays in contemporary Rastafarian communities. In Africa, music and dance are commonly viewed as inseparable components, functioning as interconnected parts of a greater whole. Rarely does one find music performed on its own, without an accompanying dance. The latter gives visible form to the former while providing non-musicians in the audience an opportunity for direct physical involvement.[10] Reggae, like much of the music played in Africa, represents a distinctive rhythm that is typically performed in a setting where the audience is given the opportunity, and is even expected, to participate through dance.

Furthermore, Yale University Africanist art historian Robert F. Thompson notes that African religions are essentially "danced faiths," in which reverence toward and worship of the spirits, gods, and ancestors are converted into a combination of sound and motion.[11] For many in Africa, religious worship takes the form of verbal, musical, and bodily action. Evidence of this can be found throughout the ethnographic literature on Africa,[12] as well as in the attitudes Africans express about the close relationship that has always existed between religion, music, and dance in their own societies. As one church-going Ghanaian gentleman asserted half a century ago:

> But why, why, why if you danced were you excommunicated from the Church that missionaries brought here? My parents were pagan but they were the most religious people I have ever known. . . . They said dancing was good. The church said it was wrong. We all got confused. We danced for joy, for sorrow, for anger, and for worship. It is a form of art. . . . Much of this culture could have been incorporated into the Church. Certain aspects can be combined. I say to the Church, "seize these. Use them. They are prayer."[13]

Throughout the African continent, music, dance, and religion work in tandem to facilitate communication and mediation between the human and the supernatural, the visible and the invisible, the individual and the community. This is typically accomplished through rituals aimed at inducing trance and possession states in initiates and devotees.[14] Such a symbiotic relationship of music, dance, and religion is also a feature common to numerous black groups in the New World, the Rastafari included. Once again, the links binding Jamaica and the culture of Rastafari to Africa are clearly discernible. Among Jamaican Rastafarians, Nyabinghi ritual—centered on drumming, dancing, and chanting—represents the fullest expression of individual and collective religious experience, the best means available for "praising Jah" and "chanting down Babylon." And, to a certain extent, reggae music and dance function in a similar capacity.

To those who would argue that there is little in reggae that might qualify as "religious"—since the music is typically listened to, danced to, and performed in secular as opposed to religious settings—one could counter that this blurring of the lines between the sacred and the secular represents another important feature linking reggae and the culture of Rastafari to Africa. As numerous researchers have noted, among Africans and their New World descendants, few rigid dichotomies exist between the sacred and the secular, particularly in terms of music and dance.[15] Black religions are, to quote Thompson, essentially "instruments of moral edification and entertainment, excitement and decorum," and hence "African devotees blend the sacred with the profane, night after night, day after day."[16] For Rastafarians on both sides of the Atlantic, listening to, playing, and dancing to reggae music represent essential components in religious worship. These function as a form of ritual, prayer and devotion, a medium of religious instruction, and a means by which Rastas can enter into direct communion with the Divine.[17]

In addition to the above-mentioned religious associations, reggae music and dance provide Jamaicans with an important source of recreation and entertainment. Describing black culture in the southern United States prior to emancipation, Sterling Stuckey could very well have been speaking about present-day Rastas when he mentioned how, "at times, dances conceived for religious purposes were performed in a setting that to Westerners might appear to serve mainly for entertainment but that to the African was suffused with religious spirit." Stuckey added, "The use of sacred dance for entertainment was natural to the ancestors of those whose dances today derive mainly from slave sacred dance."[18] Because of its strong connections to Rastafari and its socially and politically conscious lyrics, reggae represented a return, in Jamaican popular music in the late 1960s, to what the well-known Jamaican linguist Mervyn Alleyne refers to as the "traditional African fusion of the secular and religious and the symbiotic interaction of religion (including music and dance) and politics."[19]

This merging of the sacred with the profane—and more specifically, the religious with the social and political—is also a feature common to a number of contemporary African pop music genres. One notable example is the Zimbabwean chimurenga music, pioneered and popularized by the internationally renowned Thomas Mapfumo, who, in addition to smoking cannabis, sports a head of lengthy dreadlocks and frequently wears ornaments and clothing that highlight the colors red, gold, green, and black.[20] In its blending of the spiritually based Shona (a major ethnic group in Zimbabwe) mbira, or thumb piano, music with the militant and revolutionary lyrics that helped inspire many a Zimbabwean freedom fighter in the decade-long struggle to win independence from

white minority rule, chimurenga, like reggae, functions on a number of important levels. It is a form of entertainment, a means of venting social and political discontent, and
a medium of personal and collective religious expression.

Reggae, along with other forms of African American and Caribbean music, may,
in fact, represent a kind of "re-Africanization" process wherein suppressed neo-
Africanisms—such as the strong emphasis placed on rhythm, the frequent use of "dirty"
or "buzz" tones, and "call-and-response" singing—reemerge in the pop music produced
by black communities in the New World, after generations of disuse. Reggae and soul
music, of course, are decidedly more African than either mento (a Jamaican creole folk-
song genre played on a variety of instruments, e.g., banjo) or jazz, due, in part, to reggae and soul music's more intimate connections to dance. As music writers and journalists Chris Stapleton and Chris May so accurately point out:

> Everywhere there is mixture, collision and collusion. Africa "impacts" on the West; the West
> on Africa . . . . Since the 1930s, the forms that have had the biggest impact in Africa have
> all come from there in the first place: calypso, reggae and, most significantly, rumba. . . . The
> packaging may have changed: syndrums and synthesized bass and drums, horns and guitars
> reflect a predominantly Western technology. . . . [But] the "new look" African pop and its
> functions remain firmly rooted in African rhythms and African society.[21]

And while reggae is, in the final analysis, a musical genre created in the New World by
and for Jamaicans, it draws on African and neo-African influences, giving expression to
what Ken Bilby refers to as a "more universal, Pan-African impulse."

The Drug

The use of cannabis (ganja) represents another feature of Rastafarian culture that has
strong ties to African and Jamaican folk practices. In a study conducted in the early
1970s, Vera Rubin and Lambros Comitas discovered that more than 60 percent of Jamaica's lower-class population (mainly working-class males) smoked ganja on a regular basis. They also found that the substance was frequently consumed in teas and ton-
ics by lower-class men, women, and children. These researchers concluded that the use
of ganja has, for decades, provided an important release valve and adaptive mechanism
for poor Jamaican males—helping them cope with the prospect of "limited choices in a
harsh environment" while functioning as a "benevolent alternative" to their heavy consumption of alcohol.[22]

Like their West African counterparts, Jamaican Rastas insist that it was Africans who
were responsible for introducing the use of cannabis as a psychoactive and medicinal
substance to the West Indies. Since Rubin and Comitas published their study in 1976,
theories pointing to East Indian origins for the multifaceted use of cannabis in Jamaica
have gained wide currency in academic circles. But anthropologist Ken Bilby has put together a very convincing array of evidence that lends support to claims made by the
Rastafari that Jamaicans' use of cannabis originated in Africa.

Bilby argues that the roots of the "Jamaican ganja complex" are just as likely to be found in Africa as in India. Furthermore, since the multifaceted use of cannabis may have reached West Africa no earlier than the Second World War, he suggests that the most likely place to search for African origins is among those groups who came to Jamaica from Central Africa, where traditional patterns of cannabis use date back to the eighteenth century or earlier. Among certain Central African groups, such as the Batetala, the Basakata, and the Bakongo, cannabis has played an important religious role, one very similar to the role it plays among Rastafarians. This can be seen most clearly in the description, provided by the French anthropologist Marcel Soret, of cannabis use in the northwest Congo region:

> Of all the stimulants, only Indian hemp (Cannabis Indica) is regarded with a quasi-religious respect and its cultivation as well as its consumption are surrounded by genuine rites. . . . The one who sows the hemp must, at the time of sowing, strip himself naked and invoke the spirits of the plant to make it powerful and capable of giving a lucid mind. This ceremony, obligatory, must be repeated at the harvesting of the leaves. . . . When one smokes hemp for the first time, it is also necessary to conduct a special ceremony. . . . In fact, the smoker ought, in principle, to seek in hemp lucidity of mind, vigor in work and, above all, permanent communication with the world of spirits. For, under the effect of the stimulant, [the smoker] sees unknown worlds, and hears the voices of the ancestors.[23]

As Bilby notes, the emphasis placed by this African group on communication with supernatural forces ("the world of spirits") and religious meditation ("lucidity of mind"), as well as their great reverence for cannabis, closely parallels features central to the "proper use of herbs" among Rastas.[24]

According to U.S. anthropologist James Fernandez, in certain regions of Africa cannabis is employed by religious groups that are, for the most part, "expressive" in nature—those wherein individuals seek to change themselves or their external environment through processes involving possession, meditation, dance, and the ingestion of psychoactive substances.[25] The !Kung of the Kalahari, to cite but one example, smoke cannabis throughout the course of their nightly healing dances in order to facilitate the onset of *kia,* an enhanced state of consciousness that a person must attain before he or she can acquire the power to heal.[26] Substantial evidence points to cannabis long being used in ritual by various Afro-Jamaican religious groups, most notably the Kongo-derived Kumina cult. According to Monica Schuler, repeated references are made in nineteenth-century colonial correspondences to the cultivation and smoking of cannabis in Jamaica by Central African indentured laborers. Schuler personally observed the substance being smoked during Kumina ceremonies held in the easternmost part of the island in the late 1970s.[27]

While conducting research in St. Thomas Parish in 1978, Bilby also found cannabis smoking to be a common practice among Kumina adherents seeking spiritual guidance and inspiration. Interestingly enough, many of these individuals regularly employed Central African terms when referring to cannabis[28] and the pipes in which it was smoked. Oral traditions passed down by postemancipation Kikongo immigrants to their offspring also bear witness to the Central African origins of cannabis smoking in

Jamaica and the way in which this practice was used to transmit "African knowledge" to succeeding generations. As Bilby suggests, it is quite possible that Leonard Howell and his followers—who were cultivating cannabis as a cash crop at their Pinnacle Hill commune in the 1940s—first became acquainted with the drug as a result of their contacts with Kumina people. And while Rastafarians rarely, if ever, use the Kumina-based word *diamba* (preferring, instead, the generic term *herb*, as well as other designations such as *lamb's bread* and *kali*, which refer to specific strains or potencies of the plant), two terms for cannabis currently in use by Jamaican Rastas do appear to have Central African origins: *makoni* (or *macony*) and *kaya*.[29]

Admittedly, it is the Hindi word for cannabis, *ganja*, that has gained the widest usage throughout the island. But as Bilby points out, this term probably came into popular currency via the British colonial administration, who, when drafting anticannabis legislation in the early part of the century, chose to use the already-familiar Indian designation[30] rather than the African-derived terms more frequently employed by the common folk. Since it is difficult to draw any definite conclusions about the origins of cannabis in Jamaica, due to the lack of documented evidence on its use prior to the 1830s, Bilby's argument in support of a dual model of diffusion may, in fact, prove to be the most plausible one:

> After all is said and done, one thing is certain. The question of the derivation of the "Jamaican ganja complex" cannot be treated as an either/or proposition, a matter of "Indian" versus "African" influences. That syncretism between the two has long been occurring is evident. A number of the St. Thomas "Africans" that I myself interviewed emphasized, as did Schuler's informants, the close connections between the African and Asian indentured laborers who worked alongside one another on the same plantations during the latter part of the last century. . . . The "Jamaican ganja complex," it is apparent, is the product of years of intercultural exchange, and its origins cannot be traced solely on the basis of nomenclature.[31]

Parallels to the Rastas' combined use of music, drugs, and dance in a religious context can be found among numerous groups in sub-Saharan Africa. Adherents of the Ben-Riamba (Sons of Hemp), a cult that arose nearly a century and a half ago among the Bashilange of the present-day Democratic Republic of Congo, formerly Zaire, were said to have smoked cannabis from huge pipes throughout the course of their nocturnal rituals. They apparently did so while sitting naked in a circle playing drums, blowing ivory trumpets, and chanting.[32] A more recent example of this phenomenon can be found among the Tsonga of southern Africa, who employ the hallucinogenic plant *Datura fastuosa*, along with loud drumming and frenzied dance, to achieve altered states of consciousness during their performances of female initiations and exorcism rites. The Fang of Gabon also utilize a set of four different psychotropic substances in conjunction with music, dance,[33] and singing during the night-long sessions of their Bwiti cult. Through communion with the ancestors, Fang cult members seek to establish a state of *nlem mvore,* or "one-heartedness," among their group.

In summary, then, while a fairly good case may be put forward to support an African origins theory for the multifaceted use of cannabis in Jamaica, of equal or greater interest and significance are the various direct parallels that exist between certain groups in Africa and the Rastafari in terms of their similar use of psychoactive substances, along with music and dance, in the context of religious ritual and worship.

Indirect African Influences

Dreadlocks

Although conflicting theories have surfaced over the years for the origins of matted locks among the Rastafari, all point to the fact that by the mid-1950s, the wearing of the matted locks had come to represent a prominent feature and identifying symbol of the movement.[34] And while some researchers claim that, as with ganja, it was the East Indians who provided the model for the Rastafarians' adoption of dreadlocks, the wearing of matted locks by the Rastafari may, in truth, represent another feature of the movement whose roots can be traced back, albeit indirectly, to Africa. According to Horace Campbell, a Jamaican scholar who taught in southern Africa, Rastas in Jamaica first began wearing their hair in "locks" in the 1950s after seeing photos of the dreadlocked Mau Mau of Kenya.[35] This potent image of the African freedom fighter, capable of instilling fear in the hearts of those who would dare oppose him in his struggle against racism and colonial oppression, took physical shape in the Rastas' appropriation of the hairstyles of these "dread" African warriors. During the 1950s, the term *Mau Mau* came to represent the ideal of defiance in Jamaica among the younger generation. One group of Rastas, the Youth Black Faith, proved particularly active in promoting the cause of this anticolonial guerrilla force. These Rastas identified so closely with the Mau Mau that they organized a protest demonstration in support of the Mau Mau leader Jomo Kenyatta in April 1953, adopted the slogan "Mau Mau" throughout the course of their own ongoing battles with the Jamaican authorities and let their hair mat into locks.

The Youth Black Faith's identification with these African freedom fighters was apparently rooted in their deep sense of affinity to a group regarded internationally as criminals, terrorists, and social outcasts. Their growing of dreadlocks no doubt served as the perfect medium through which they could project a similar image and express anticolonial sentiments. As Barry Chevannes notes, members of the Youth Black Faith conceived of themselves as a people "struggling to leave a society to which they felt they did not belong. They took on a more aggressive, non-compromising stance. This they symbolized in adopting a new approach, a new way of presenting themselves: the dreadlocks. The Dreadfuls or Warriors were the first to start the trend, and as their hair grew they became even more dreadful."[36]

A more recent, though equally pertinent, example of indirect African influence on the Rastas' adoption of dreadlocks has its origins in Ethiopia. The photo of two "dreadlocksed" Ethiopian monks that appeared in the December 1970 issue of *National Geographic* is the piece of evidence most frequently cited by Rastas to support the claim that their adoption of matted locks is based on ancient African practices.[37] The sporting of dreadlocks may, in fact, represent a fairly widespread African phenomenon. In Senegambia, for example, the royal soldiers (*tyeddo*) of pre-Islamic Wolof society wore their hair in long, knotted tresses, as do present-day members of the heterodox, Islamic-based Baye Faal sect. Throughout much of West Africa today, matted hair is commonly associated with traditional healers and religious practitioners; for example, in Ghana many of the *okomfo*—traditional Akan fetish priests and priestesses—have worn and continue to wear their hair in such a manner.[38]

Rasta Colors

Although the Rastafarian color motif of red, yellow (or gold), green, and black functions as one of the most conspicuous symbols of the movement globally, surprisingly little has been written about its origins and significance. Posters, caps, badges, bracelets, pendants, scarves, dresses, and T-shirts adorned in varying combinations of these four colors represent just a sampling of the many items worn and displayed by Rastas, Rasta emulators, and sympathizers worldwide. Leonard Barrett does mention that the Rastas combined the original colors of the Garvey movement—red, black, and green[39]—with the gold of Jamaica's national flag to create their "Pan-African" color scheme, but he has little more to add on the subject, except that the red signifies the blood of the Jamaican martyrs (from the Maroons on down to Marcus Garvey), the black depicts the Africans whose descendants form 98 percent of Jamaica's population, and the green represents the color of Jamaica's vegetation and the Rastas' hope of victory over oppression.

Interestingly enough, one theory has it that Garvey, in his attempts to promote Ethiopia as a model of African strength and independence, chose the colors red, black, and green as a symbol for his nascent movement because he mistakenly believed them to be the colors of the Ethiopian flag (which actually were, and still are, red, *yellow,* and green).[40] Garvey, who envisioned the red, black, and green as a future trademark of a newly independent and united Republic of Africa, free from white domination, made various allusions in his speeches to an army of New World Blacks leading an advance on the continent under this Pan-African banner:

> I can see in my mind's eye now twelve million black citizens of America, with those of the islands of the sea and from Central and South America, from all over the world, educated, uplifted, discovered, proud, prideful, loyal, and royal—and I can see the flag of the green and the black and the red floating to the breeze upon the seven seas, and I can see upon yonder hill the beautiful flag waving in the land of Africa, the home of the gods, the place where liberty first sprang for the black men of the earth.[41]

This color symbolism also appears in the official anthem of the Garveyites—"Ethiopia, thou land of our fathers"—which, interestingly enough, also serves as the principal anthem of the Rastafarian movement. As William Crampton, director of the Flag Institute in London, suggests, the origins of the Rastafarian color scheme may be traced to the movement's merging of the black, red, and green of Garvey's Universal Negro Improvement Association (UNIA) and Black Star Line with the green, yellow, and red of the Ethiopian flag.

The land of Ethiopia also proved a potent source of inspiration for African nationalist leaders, many of whom chose the "Pan-African" colors of the Ethiopian flag as a symbol for their emerging political parties and newly independent states. On gaining its independence from Great Britain in 1957, Ghana was the first to incorporate this color motif in its flag (which also contains the black five-pointed star, the "lodestar of African freedom," used earlier by Garvey). This set the stage for the adoption by other African nations of Pan-African symbolism such as a flag of red, yellow, and green (and, in some instances, black). Apparently, the leaders of these nations chose this color scheme in an attempt to foster a sense of solidarity with other independent African states and to inspire feelings of "African consciousness" among a people just emerging from the deracinating experience of decades of colonial rule. Out of a total of forty-nine nations in sub-Saharan Africa today, sixteen (or one-third) have flags designed around the colors red, gold, and green—with seven of these also employing the "Garveyite" color black.

Although reliable and detailed information about the origins of the Rasta color motif is, at present, unavailable, it is apparent that this color scheme, which features so prominently in the clothing, accoutrements, and symbolism of Rastafarians everywhere, does have its origins in Africa. On the one hand, a possible link to Africa can be traced to Garvey's invention of a Pan-African standard based on what he may have believed were the colors of the Ethiopian flag. On the other hand, such connections can be seen in the Rastas' appropriation of the actual colors of this flag. Furthermore, the incorporation of this Pan-African color scheme into the flags of numerous African nations has, no doubt, provided the Rastafari with a more current and equally potent model for their adoption of the red, gold, green, and black.

African Parallels

Pan-Africanism

Although the origins of the Pan-African movement are found in the diaspora among the likes of men such as the Trinidadian Henry Sylvester Williams, the African American W.E.B. Du Bois, and the Jamaican Marcus Garvey, its development was mediated through a complex trans-Atlantic network that drew together the New World, Europe, and Africa. It is, therefore, not surprising to discover that, from the very beginning, Africans played a prominent role in this global crusade for the dignity and rights of black people everywhere. During the second Pan-African Conference, held in Paris in 1919, the Senegalese delegate M. Blaise-Diagne served as a major spokesperson for the French colonies. With the passing years, Africans came to assume more prominent roles at these international Pan-African forums. Included among the representatives at the sixth Pan-African Congress, held in Manchester, England, in 1945, were a group of young African nationalist leaders from the Gold Coast, Nigeria, Togo, Kenya, and South Africa.

By the late 1950s and early 1960s, the Pan-African movement was firmly entrenched on African soil. A large contingent of African delegates attended the first and second Conferences of Independent African States, held in Accra, Ghana, in 1958 and Addis Ababa, Ethiopia, in 1960; the All African Peoples Conventions held in Accra in 1958, Tunis in 1960, and Cairo in 1961; and the Casablanca and Monrovia Conferences, held in January and May 1961. At these meetings, proposals were drafted calling for the total independence of Africa, solidarity with Africans around the world who were struggling to free themselves from the yoke of colonial domination, and the eventual establishment of a union or community of independent African states. Among the eminent twentieth-century African nationalist leaders who served as major figures in the Pan-African movement were Ghana's Kwame Nkrumah, Kenya's Jomo Kenyatta, Tanzania's Julius Nyerere, Guinea's Sekou Toure, and the Congo's Patrice Lumumba.

Important contributions to this movement were also made by African writers, students, and intellectuals, particularly during the 1920s and 1930s, when the centers of Pan-African activity shifted from the New World to the capitals of Europe and Africans finally had the opportunity to meet face-to-face with their African American and Caribbean contemporaries. In Paris, francophone African intellectuals and writers such as Leopold Senghor (Senegal) and Jacques Rabemananjara (Madagascar), along with the Martinican poet Aimé Césaire, helped spawn the Negritude movement. Across the channel, in London, the work of various anglophone Africans—most notably the lawyers J. E. Casely-Hayford (Gold Coast) and Lapido Solanke (Nigeria)—proved instrumental in establishing two major Pan-African organizations, the National Congress of British West Africa and the West African Student's Union, which championed the causes of anticolonialism, African nationalism, and black solidarity. Casely-Hayford actually played a role in helping shape the Pan-African philosophy of Marcus Garvey, who was the primary ideological influence on the Rastafarian movement and the man credited by many as being the most influential of all Pan-Africanists. And though it is unclear whether Casely-Hayford was among the West African writers, intellectuals, and nationalist leaders Garvey came into personal contact with while in England, the influence of his classic work *Ethiopia Unbound* (1911) on the evolution of Garvey's thinking is readily apparent.

Among the other African figures who exerted a considerable influence on Garvey, two in particular stand out—the half-Sudanese, half-Egyptian journalist Duse Mohammed and the nineteenth-century Gold Coast nationalist-scholar James Africanus Horton. While the formation of Garvey's racial consciousness was, in part, inspired by the writings of Horton—most notably the book *West African Countries and Peoples, British and Native . . . and a Vindication of the African Race* (1868), Garvey's associations with Duse Mohammed were of a more direct and personal nature. During Garvey's sojourn in England between the years 1912 and 1914, he worked for and eventually developed a close friendship with Mohammed, whose radical journal *African Times and Orient Review* served as a major vehicle for the propagation of Pan-African consciousness and

African nationalism. Throughout the course of their often stormy relationship, Garvey managed to absorb a great deal of this man's knowledge about African history and culture and was influenced to a large extent by his strident Pan-African outlook and radical political thinking.

The links between Garvey and Africa were by no means unilateral. A number of noted African nationalist leaders—Jomo Kenyatta, Kwame Nkrumah, and Nnamdi Azikiwe (the first governor general of Nigeria), to name but three—were greatly inspired by this man and the organization he created.[42] And Garvey's influence in Africa was not limited to political leaders and the intelligentsia; during the 1920s and 1930s, copies of his newspaper *Negro World* were circulating throughout the continent, and various chapters of the UNIA were functioning in both western and southern Africa. Garvey's movement may have exercised a much more widespread and profound influence on nationalist thought and expression in Africa than has previously been supposed. At any rate, the constant dialogue and interchange that took place between Africans and Blacks in both North America and the Caribbean served to create a bridge linking Africa to the New World African diaspora. Through the examination of such links, one is able not only to observe the extent to which Rastafarian thought and ideology have been influenced by Africans—albeit indirectly, via Garvey—but also to take note of how the movement's overriding concerns with Pan-Africanism have been paralleled on the African continent itself.

Black God, Black Prophet

> Our God is black
> Black of eternal blackness
> With large voluptuous lips
> Matted hair and brown liquid eyes . . .
> For in his image are we made.
> Our God is black.
> —Togolese writer R. A. Armattoe

While Africans have, throughout the millennia, been paying homage to a God or gods fashioned in an image similar to their own, only with the rise of the separatist, independent African Christian churches over the last hundred years did the worship or veneration of a black Judeo-Christian God and his black prophets (both biblical and contemporary) begin to manifest itself on a continent-wide scale. As disillusionment with European churches grew among African converts, many began to search for an indigenized form of Christianity better suited to meet their spiritual, social, and political needs. It was only a matter of time before these individuals would come to reject the Eurocentric concept of a white God in heaven and choose, instead, to worship a black God and follow local prophets recruited from among their own people. As one nineteenth-century South African preacher admitted, "I have a great sorrow. I know that the Lord Jesus Christ was a white man, yet I could not pray to Him and love Him as much as I do if I did not picture Him as black with wool like myself."[43]

Black Christs and native prophets played a leading role in South African society during the first half of the twentieth century. The cornerstone of the South African messianic independent churches was the biblical injunction "A prophet will the Lord Thy God raise up unto thee from the midst of thee, of thy brethren, like unto me; unto him ye shall hearken" (Deuteronomy 18:15).[44] The many Zulu prophets who arose during this period—men such as Isaiah Shembe, George Khambule, and Paulo Nzuza—shared a single goal: to find, like Moses, a promised land for their followers. Furthermore, they all claimed legitimacy on the basis that they could heal and had experienced death and resurrection. Isaiah Shembe (1870–1935), the most charismatic and influential of these prophets, claimed to be "the Servant," "the Promised One," and the Christ and Moses of the Zulus. Although his followers considered him to be both omnipresent and omniscient, many were hesitant to refer openly to Shembe as God, for fear of recriminations from mainstream Christians. "It is this way," one informant told Bengt Sundkler, a South African missionary scholar, "[Shembe] is God, but in Inhlonipho-language we call him prophet."[45]

In Central Africa, the avowed nationalist and anticolonial Congolese prophet Simon Kimbangu (1889–1951), who preached the imminent coming of a golden age in which all foreigners would be expelled and the dead resurrected, claimed to be the black reincarnation of Moses and Christ, while his followers referred to him as both *Ngunza* (prophet or Messiah) and the "God of the black man." In Angola in the early 1950s, Simon Toko, the founder of the Christian-based Red Star cult, prophesied the second coming of the Messiah in the person of an African who would redeem the black race.

In West Africa, the Liberian William Wade Harris, the first of many black Christian prophets to appear in the region during the present century, was viewed by his followers as both a traditional priest and the Son of God, occupying the same position as Christ, albeit as God's prophet to the "African race." A few decades later, the Nigerian journalist-turned-prophet A. E. Beyioku, founder of the Afro-Christian Orunmla movement, regarded Jesus Christ as an African priest of the Yoruba god Ifa and was reported to have made the following statement to his followers: "Let the image of God be African. Let the angels be African as well and paint the devil any color you choose, but never the color of the Negro race."[46]

No doubt, a great many more instances could be mentioned in which the leaders and membership of Christian-based independent churches in Africa chose, like their Rastafarian counterparts in the New World, to view the divine image in the physical person of a black, as opposed to a white, man and took the revolutionary step of worshiping a black God in heaven and his black prophets on earth.

Biblical Allusions, Appropriations, and Adaptations

Another prominent feature shared by the Rastafari and the independent African churches centers on their utilization of biblical images, themes, and narratives, often recast and adapted to meet the specific needs of local African congregations. Like the Rastafari, these churches looked to the Hebrew Bible rather than the New Testament in their search for relevance, spiritual insight, and moral guidance. The plight of the children of Israel depicted in the Hebrew Bible no doubt provided a cogent model for Africans, who often found themselves in similar straits as the pressures wrought by modernity and colonialism continued to impact and encroach on their lives. As Vittorio Lanternari suggests, the various African cults and churches that identified most intimately with the Jews of the Hebrew Bible did so as a result of their yearnings for self-determination and liberation from foreign oppression. Throughout the ages, the Jews have served as the "unparalleled example of a people able to survive all manner of persecution" and, as such, provided the consummate image of a long-suffering and persevering race.[47]

For a number of African Christians, as well as for their black counterparts in the New World (first and foremost the Rastafari), this connection to the ancient Hebrews was seen as something more than purely allegorical; many claimed to be direct descendants of "God's chosen people." This belief found its most intense expression, both within and outside of Africa, in the form of a movement or religious and sociopolitical ideology commonly referred to as "Ethiopianism." Motivated, in part, by the direct references to Ethiopia in the Hebrew Bible;[48] the Abyssinians' victory over the Italians at Adwa, Ethiopia, in 1896; and the crowning of Ras Tafari as the emperor Haile Selassie I in 1930, many Blacks throughout the globe began to look to Ethiopia as a source of racial pride and a model of African strength and independence.[49]

In the Ethiopian and Zionist churches of South Africa, the Hebrew Bible formed the foundation of belief and worship, with Moses—the penultimate leader, liberator, and lawgiver—serving as the central figure and transplanted Hebrew myths as the central focus of these groups. "Biblical personalities," as noted by Sundkler, "became the archetypes of those who fulfill the aspirations of an oppressed people, so that the Bantu prophet became a Moses, a Nazir, a Messiah."[50] Like these Bantu prophets, Rastas conceive of themselves as modern-day nazirites and view their donning of dreadlocks and adherence to the proscriptions outlined in Numbers 6[51] as a revivification and reenactment of this ancient Jewish practice. Members of the Israelite Church, founded by the prophet Enoch Mgijima in Bullboek, South Africa, adhered strictly to the Hebrew Bible, and like the Rastafari, they believed themselves to be the chosen people of Jehovah, observed the Sabbath on Saturday rather than Sunday, and celebrated various Jewish festivals throughout the year. As a matter of fact, a strict adherence to the Hebrew Bible, belief in being the chosen people of God, and diligent observance of the Jewish Sabbath and annual holidays represent features common to many of these independent African churches.

Among the other elements appropriated from the Hebrew Scriptures by Rastas and independent African churches are the observance of biblically based menstrual and food taboos and the use of the term *Jah* when referring to God. For example, many of the *aladura* (praying) churches that surfaced in Nigeria during the 1920s and 1930s held that the success of prayer was conditional upon strict observance of biblical taboos relating to the foods proscribed in Leviticus and to contact with menstruating women. Individuals belonging to the Cherubim and Seraphim Society, one of the earliest of these churches, frequently employed the term *Jah* when addressing God.

In their utilization of New Testament Scripture, many of these African churches place particular emphasis on the eschatological/millenarian visions contained in the Book of Revelation—another feature shared with the Rastafari. Like their parent organization in the United States, the various Watchtower movements active throughout Central Africa between 1907 and World War II were millenarian in nature and relied heavily on the prophecies contained in Revelation. The Lumpa Church of Zambia, founded by Prophet Alice Lenshina in 1953; the Apostolic Sabbath Church of God, led by the Rhodesian "Messiah" John Masowe; and the Kimbanguist churches of Zaire (now the Democratic Republic of Congo) did likewise. Most of these Afrocentric religious views were influenced by the African repudiation of the "white man's Bible" as a bogus work, brought to Africa by the missionaries to cheat and enslave black people. To cite but one example of this fairly widespread phenomenon in Africa: according to Sundkler, individuals affiliated with independent churches in South Africa held in common a belief that the Bible given to them by the Europeans was little more than a distorted and corrupt version of the original and authentic "black Man's Bible" (i.e., the Ethiopian Bible or the *Holy Piby*).

Although no instances can be cited in which any of the beliefs and practices associated with independent African churches had a direct impact on evolving forms of Rastafarian religious ideology and practice, the parallels outlined above nevertheless serve to highlight the common histories shared by Africans and people of African descent living in the New World. These include their very similar encounters with colonialism and European economic and cultural hegemony, on the one hand, and with the religious doctrines promulgated by Christian missionaries, on the other. Furthermore, for many African Rastas, such parallels provide additional weight to their claims that Rastafari represents, in essence, an African-based religion and sociopolitical system of thought.

Conclusion

As some scholars stress, African Christian movements must be seen as part of a "natural process of religious change in Africa," and as such, special attention must be focused on the African as well as the foreign origins of these new institutions and systems of belief.[52] And it is precisely with such an understanding and purpose in mind that I have attempted to identify and trace the African influences on and contributions to the origins and development of the Jamaican Rastafarian movement. I did this in the hope of providing a more comprehensive insight into the extent to which West African manifestations of Rastafari represent a partially African or Africanized, as opposed to a wholly alien, cultural entity. Admittedly, it is impossible to ignore the many non-African elements that played a role in influencing both the evolution and diffusion of Rastafari—such as Judeo-Christian theology, the global impact of Anglo-American popular culture and the transnational pop music industry, the East Indian connections, and the specifically Jamaican character of the movement. But when one considers all the evidence presented above, a fairly clear picture begins to emerge of the complex network of trans-Atlantic dialogue and interchange that served to connect the New World African diaspora in general, and Jamaica and the Jamaican Rastafarian movement in particular, with "Mother Africa."

Notes

1. See, among others, Mervin Alleyne, *Roots of Jamaican Culture* (London: Pluto Press, 1988); Edward K. Brathwaite, "Kumina: The Spirit of African Survival in Jamaica," *Jamaica Journal*, no. 42 (1978): 44–63; Melville J. Herskovits, *The Myth of the Negro Past* (Boston: Beacon Press, 1958); Joseph E. Holloway, *Africanisms in American Culture* (Bloomington: Indiana University Press, 1990); George E. Simpson, *Black Religions in the New World* (New York: Columbia University Press, 1978); M. G. Smith, "The African Heritage in the Caribbean," in Vera Rubin, ed., *Caribbean Studies: A Symposium* (Seattle: University of Washington Press, 1957); and Sterling Stuckey, *Slave Culture* (New York: Oxford University Press, 1987).

2. Edward Brathwaite, *Folk Culture of the Slaves in Jamaica* (London: New Beacon Books, 1970), 4–5.

3. The term *neo-African,* as used here, refers to forms of African-derived music that have no exact equivalents in Africa itself, since they evolved in the New World from the fusion of the musical traditions of different African groups. Cf. J. S. Roberts, *Black Music of Two Worlds* (New York: William Morrow & Co., 1972).

4. Verena Reckord, "Rastafarian Music: An Introductory Study," *Jamaica Journal* 2, 1–2 (1977): 3–13.

5. *Nyabinghi* also refers to a specific type of Rasta gathering or "groundation," as well as a highly orthodox Rastafarian order whose origins can be traced back to the movement's earliest beginnings. The term itself derives from a fiercely anticolonial religious movement that flourished in East and Central Africa around the end of the nineteenth and beginning of the twentieth century. It was first adopted by Jamaican Rastafarians in the mid-1930s, just prior to the Italian invasion of Ethiopia. See Elliott Leib, liner notes to the LP *Churchical Chants of the Nyabingi,* Cambridge, Massachusetts, Heartbeat Records HB20, 1983; and Ken Post, "The Bible as Ideology: Ethiopianism in Jamaica, 1930–1938," in Christopher Allen and R. W. Johnson, eds., *African Perspectives* (Cambridge: Cambridge University Press, 1970).

6. See Monica Schuler, *"Alas, Alas, Kongo": A Social History of Indentured African Immigration into Jamaica, 1841–1865* (Baltimore: Johns Hopkins University Press, 1980); and Brathwaite, "Kumina."

7. Present-day Rastas, both Howellites and non-Howellites, often refer to themselves as *Bongo* or *Kongo* men, terms popularized by Bob Marley in his song "Rastaman Live Up." See Kenneth Bilby and Elliott Leib, "Kumina, the Howellite Church and the Emergence of Rastafarian Traditional Music in Jamaica," *Jamaica Journal* 19, 3 (August–October 1986): 22–29.

8. Ibid., 27.

9. Electronic instruments are often employed by reggae musicians to simulate the rhythms of the Rasta *akete* drums. Also, the influence of the churchical rhythms of Rastafarian drumming on younger pop musicians in Jamaica probably resulted in the switch that occurred, in the late 1960s, from the more up-tempo, choppy beats of ska to the heavier, slower, and more sinuous feel of reggae. See Dick Hebdige, *Subculture: The Meaning of Style* (London and New York: Methuen & Co., 1979), 58.

10. "In African societies," writes the ethnomusicologist Alan P. Merriam, "large numbers of people participate in musical activities. . . . The separation of the 'artist' from the 'audience' is not an African pattern" ("African Music," in W. R. Bascom and M. J. Herskovits, eds., *Continuity and Change in African Cultures* [Chicago: Phoenix Books, 1959], 56). See also J.H.K. Nketia, *The Music of Africa* (New York: W. W. Norton & Co., 1974); Richard Alan Waterman, "African Influences on the Music of the Americas," in Sol Tax, ed., Acculturation in the Americas (Chicago: University of Chicago Press, 1952).

11. Robert F. Thompson, "An Aesthetic of the Cool: West African Dance," *African Forum* 2, 2 (1966):85.

12. For example, Amaury Talbot observed how dance functioned as the primary form of religious worship among the various groups he worked with in southern Nigeria (*The Peoples of Southern Nigeria* [London: Oxford University Press, 1926], 802).

13. Cited in Emory Ross, *Africa Disturbed* (New York: Friendship Press, 1959), 138.

14. See, for example, Gilbert Rouget's classic monograph *Music and Trance* (Chicago: University of Chicago Press, 1985); and J.H.K. Nketia's article "Possession Dances in African Societies," *Journal of the International Folk Music Council* 9 (1957): 4–9.

15. See Alleyne, *Roots of Jamaican Culture*; J.H.K. Nketia, "History and Organization of Music in West Africa," in Klaus P. Wachsmann, ed., *Music and History in Africa* (Evanston, Ill.: Northwestern University Press, 1971); and Waterman, "African Influences."

16. Thompson, "Aesthenic of the Cool," 85–86.

17. The hypnotic drone and intensity of the drums and bass guitar (a dominant feature of reggae music), in combination with dancing and the smoking of cannabis, might, in fact, produce a psychophysiological state akin to possession or trance.

18. Stuckey, *Slave Culture,* 66.

19. Alleyne, *Roots of Jamaican Culture,* 118.

20. While Mapfumo admits to having been influenced by reggae music and the Rastafarian ethos and culture it espouses, he insists that he is not a Rasta and claims indigenous roots for the various Rasta-linked fashions and practices he embraces. He has said, "Some people think that because I wear dreadlocks I am a Rasta [and smoke ganja]. . . . But I am not a Rasta even though I like reggae music. I started smoking the weed before I knew there was anything known as Rastafari. There were also dreadlocks in Zimbabwe before I saw the Jamaicans" (cited in Fred Zindi, *Roots Rocking in Zimbabwe* [Harare: Mambo Press, 1985], 31–32).

21. Chris Stapleton and Chris May, *African All Stars: The Pop Music of a Continent* (London: Paladin/Grafton Books, 1987), 5.

22. Vera Rubin and Lambros Comitas, *Ganja in Jamaica* (New York: Doubleday Anchor Books, 1976), 173.

23. Cited in Kenneth Bilby, "The Holy Herb: Notes on the Background of Cannabis in Jamaica," in Rex Nettleford, ed., *Rastafari* (Kingston: University of the West Indies/United Cooperative Printers, 1985), 89.

24. Ibid.

25. James W. Fernandez, "Tabernanthe Iboga: Narcotic Ecstasies and the Work of the Ancestors," in Peter T. Furst, ed., *Flesh of the Gods: The Ritual Use of Hallucinogens* (New York: Praeger Publishers, 1972).

26. Richard Katz, *Boiling Energy* (Cambridge, Mass.: Harvard University Press, 1982), 180.

27. Schuler, *"Alas, Alas, Kongo,* 78, 152.

28. The terms include *diamba* or *riamba,* a general word used for cannabis in a number of Cen-

tral African languages (Kikongo included), and *makoni,* a term derived from Kikongo, either from the noun *nkoni,* meaning "flower," or the noun *makoni,* meaning "bundle of grass or herbs." See Bilby, "Holy Herb," 85.

29. According to Bilby ("Holy Herb," 87), the etymology of the term *kaya* can be traced back to either the Kikongo nouns *kaya* (leaf) and *nkaya* (nicotine) or the Kikongo verb *kaya* (to gather medicinal plants).

30. The British had a great deal of prior experience with the Indian ganja complex, owing to their centuries-long colonial involvement in South Asia; see *The Indian Hemp Drugs Commission Report, 1893–1894* (Silver Springs, Md.: Thomas Jefferson Publishing Co., 1969).

31. Bilby, "Holy Herb," 90.

32. The smoking of cannabis became so pervasive among the Bashilange that it led to a partial restructuring of their society. For example, after the introduction of the Ben-Riamba cult, this once fierce and aggressive people ceased all warlike activities and, according to Ernest Abel, began pursuing a more peaceful way of life. *Riamba* became "the symbol of peace, camaraderie, magic, and protection." See Ernest Abel, *Marihuana: The First Twelve Thousand Years* (New York: Plenum Press, 1980), 143.

33. That more than a dozen different dances are associated with this cult should come as no surprise, since the general attitude among adherents is best expressed, according to Fernandez, by the old Fang saying "He who knows the power of the dance dwells in God" ("Tabernanthe Iboga," 240).

34. Prior to this time, Rastafarians in Jamaica were generally identified by their profusion of unshaven and untrimmed facial hair and, as such, were referred to as "Bearded Men," "Beardmen," or "Beards"; see Barry Chevannes, "The Origins of the Dreadlocks" (unpublished paper on deposit at the Research Institute for the Study of Man, New York City, 1989), 7.

35. Horace Campbell, *Rasta and Resistance: From Marcus Garvey to Walter Rodney* (Trenton, N.J.: Africa World Press, 1987), 42. Dreadlocks were worn by members of the Land and Freedom Army (the Mau Mau) and served as a symbol of the movement and its intense commitment to Kenyan freedom from colonial rule and exploitation. The Kenyan historian Maina Kinyatti, in a personal communication with the author in winter of 1991, cited claims made by former Mau Mau he interviewed that many grew dreadlocks (as well as beards) because of a vow they had made not to cut their hair until Kenya was entirely free from European control.

36. Chevannes, "Origins of the Dreadlocks," 15.

37. See Stephen Davis and Peter Simon, *Reggae International* (New York: Rogner & Bernard, 1982), 63. Further evidence that Ethiopian monks wear their hair in such a manner is provided by David Buxton in his book *The Abyssinians* (New York: Praeger Publishers, 1970), 78; and anthropologist Bill Bushnell, in a personal communication to the author spring 1990, reported that nine of the eighty monks he interviewed while conducting fieldwork in Ethiopia in 1989 had matted hair.

38. Refer, for example, to the many photographs of dreadlocked *okomfo* included in R. S. Rattray's ethnography *Ashanti* (London: Oxford University Press, 1923) and in Eva L. R. Meyerowitz's *The Akan of Ghana* (London: Faber & Faber, 1958). Throughout the course of my own research in Ghana, I encountered a number of these traditional "locksmen" among the Akan and various other ethnic groups.

39. See Leonard Barrett, *The Rastafarians: Sounds of Cultural Dissonance* (Boston: Beacon Press, 1977), 143. The red, black, and green color scheme was officially adopted at the first international convention of Garvey's Universal Negro Improvement Association (UNIA), held in

Harlem in August 1920; see David E. Cronon, *Black Moses: The Story of Marcus Garvey and the U.N.I.A.* (Madison: University of Wisconsin Press, 1969), 67.

40. See William Crampton, *The Complete Guide to Flags* (New York: Gallery Books, 1989), 11.

41. Excerpt from a speech made by Marcus Garvey at Liberty Hall in New York City, March 1920; cited in Robert Hill, ed., *Marcus Garvey and the Universal Negro Improvement Association Papers,* vol. 2: 27 August 1919–31 August 1920 (Berkeley and Los Angeles: University of California Press, 1983), 250.

42. Nkrumah, for example, attended UNIA meetings while a student in New York, and in his autobiography he cited Garvey's *Philosophy and Opinions* as the book that had the greatest impact on his thinking. See Tony Martin, *The Pan-African Connection: From Slavery to Garvey and Beyond* (Dover, Mass.: Majority Press, 1983), 18.

43. Cited in Everett V. Stonequist, *The Marginal Man* (New York: Russell & Russell, 1961), 21.

44. Biblical translation from *The Holy Scriptures according to the Masoretic Text: A New Translation* (Philadelphia: Jewish Publishing Association, 1965).

45. Cited in Bengt G. M. Sundkler, *Bantu Prophets in South Africa* (London: Oxford University Press, 1961), 279–86.

46. Cited in Vittorio Lanternari, *The Religions of the Oppressed* (New York: Alfred A. Knopf, 1963), 51.

47. Ibid., 35.

48. The most portentous of these being that found at Psalm 68:31: "Princes shall come out of Egypt; Ethiopia shall soon stretch out her hands unto God" (KJV).

49. For a detailed and scholarly analysis of this fascinating development, see Edward Ullendorff's *Ethiopia and the Bible* (London: Oxford University Press, 1989).

50. Sundkler, *Bantu Prophets,* 334.

51. The vow of the nazirite, adopted in biblical times by those wishing to dedicate themselves wholly to the service of God, prohibited the cutting of head and facial hair, the consumption of alcoholic beverages and grapes, and physical contact with the dead (Numbers 6:1–7).

52. George Bond, Walton Johnson, and Sheila Walker, eds., *African Christianity: Patterns of Religious Continuity* (New York: Academic Press, 1979), 168.

8 Marcus Garvey and the Early Rastafarians: Continuity and Discontinuity

RUPERT LEWIS

This chapter examines political aspects of the origins of the Rastafarian movement at a time when the Garvey movement was in decline in the 1930s. Its main intentions are to underscore ways in which Garveyism has affected the evolution of Rastafari and to identify the many similarities and differences that exist between the two anticolonial ideologies. Many interpretations of the origins of Rastafari have focused on two events during this period: the coronation of Ras Tafari as emperor of Ethiopia in 1930 and Marcus Mosiah Garvey's writings on the significance of this coronation for people of African descent.

In his capacity as president general of the Universal Negro Improvement Association (UNIA), Garvey sent a cable to His Majesty Ras Tafari that read "Greetings from Ethiopians of [the] Western World. May your reign be peaceful, prosperous, progressive. Long live your Majesty."[1] That communique was printed in the New York–based *Negro World* newspaper on November 8, 1930. On that same day, Garvey published an article in his Jamaican newspaper, *The Blackman,* that read:

> Last Sunday, a great ceremony took place at Addis Ababa, the capital of Abyssinia. It was the coronation of the new Emperor of Ethiopia—Ras Tafari. From reports and expectations, the scene was one of great splendor, and will long be remembered by those who were present. Several of the leading nations of Europe sent representatives to the coronation, thereby paying their respects to a rising Negro nation that is destined to play a great part in the future history of the world. Abyssinia is the land of the blacks and we are glad to learn that even though Europeans have been trying to impress the Abyssinians that they are not belonging to the Negro Race, they have learned the retort that they are, and they are proud to be so.
>
> Ras Tafari has traveled to Europe and America and is therefore no stranger to European hypocrisy and methods; he, therefore, must be regarded as a kind of a modern Emperor, and from what we understand and know of him, he intends to introduce modern methods and

systems into his country. Already he has started to recruit from different sections of the world competent men in different branches of science to help to develop his country to the position that she should occupy among the other nations of the world.

We do hope that Ras Tafari will live long to carry out his wonderful intentions. From what we have heard and what we do know, he is ready and willing to extend the hand of invitation to any Negro who desires to settle in his kingdom. We know of many who are gone to Abyssinia and who have given good report of the great possibilities there, which they are striving to take advantage of.

The Psalmist prophesied that Princes would come out of Egypt and Ethiopia would stretch forth her hands unto God. We have no doubt that the time is now come. Ethiopia is now really stretching forth her hands. This great kingdom of the East has been hidden for many centuries, but gradually she is rising to take a leading place in the world and it is for us of the Negro race to assist in every way to hold up the hand of Emperor Ras Tafari.[2]

I have quoted the full text of Garvey's article on the coronation because often commentators refer only to the last paragraph and stress the religious, prophetic dimension, that of a prince coming out of Egypt and Ethiopia stretching out its hands to God (Psalm 68:31), at the expense of other aspects of Garvey's thinking.[3] But Garvey addressed many issues: the attempts by Europeans to separate Ethiopia from the rest of Africa, European attendance at the coronation and its impact, the coronation as a symbol of black pride, and, most important, Garvey's expression of hope for a reign based on modernity within the framework of Pan-African solidarity. In Garvey's thinking and work, Ethiopianism functioned in accordance with his strong modernizing Pan-African outlook.

The emphasis placed on the coronation of Haile Selassie I was important in a colony where the British monarchy was the supreme symbol of power. In the UNIA, Garvey always emphasized a counterhegemonic perspective against European domination and exploitation of Africa. Consistent with this approach, he had written and produced a play, in June 1930, titled *The Coronation of an African King,* which had scenes set in several African, European, and West Indian capitals. The play was also a dramatic portrayal of the UNIA's work and the attempts by the U.S. and European governments to stem the tide of the Garvey movement.[4]

Garvey founded the Universal Negro Improvement Association in Jamaica in 1914. It took off in the United States in the period after World War I and became the largest Pan-African movement of the early twentieth century. The Garvey movement saw its heyday in the early 1920s, but by the late 1920s and early 1930s it was already in decline. Nonetheless, Garvey and the leaders of the UNIA represented early twentieth-century Black Nationalist leadership that mobilized the masses around a program of cultural, economic, and political modernity. They advocated an end to colonialism in Africa and the Caribbean and envisioned the eventual development of the African continent into a modern network of nations that would constitute a United States of Africa. The models for this network of nations were the United States of America and western Europe. In this respect, the Garveyites were an "African Westernizing elite." As African descendants, they claimed the heritage of early African civilization, but they also valued the achievements of the world that had enslaved and colonized them (the so-called Babylon), while rejecting its racial assumptions and notions of their subordinate position within that world.

Continuities

That Rastafari and Garveyism share many similarities is well known among their adherents, as well as among scholars who do research on these movements. Both movements are Afrocentric and unapologetically defend the beauty and dignity of Africa and people of African ancestry. While Garvey emphasized Africa's social and political redemption, Rastas include in that agenda a spiritual dimension, which they often clothe in Judeo-Christian thought and African concepts. Both Garveyism and Rastafari show great respect for the Bible and attempt to distance themselves from biased, Eurocentric interpretations of Scripture that contribute to the oppression of black people. Ken Post, whose work on Rastafari is well known, has stressed the importance of the Bible in Jamaican culture and Rastafari, pointing out that "the religious factor which Jamaicans of all classes had in common was the King James Version of the Holy Bible. For the majority of members of the lower and many of the intermediate classes, the contents of this book represented the essential truth. People were accustomed to search the Bible for answers to their problems."[5]

His love for and frequent citations of passages from the Bible notwithstanding, Garvey was less interested in giving a theological or religious interpretation to his Afrocentric political ideology than the Rastafarians have shown themselves to be. Garvey and the Rastafarians, however, both read the Bible with the knowledge that Africa and Africans had been a part of that recorded experience and wisdom; it is not a book that is alien to black people. The most well known Marcus Garvey scholar in the United States, Robert Hill, has argued that the *Holy Piby* and the *Royal Parchment Scroll of Black Supremacy* are the two books that provide "the actual interpretative basis of Rastafari ideology."[6] These were introduced into Jamaica between 1925 and 1927.[7] Along with the Bible and the oral traditions, they are among a variety of sources that have helped to shape Rastafarian beliefs. Other scholars have examined the history of Rastafari in this context, explored its origins[8] in the peasantry, and also emphasized the impact of traditional Afro-Jamaican religions, such as revivalism and Kumina,[9] on the evolution of Rastafari. Maureen Warner-Lewis, an authority on Caribbean culture, has pointed to the wide range of African continuities in the Rastafarian belief system.[10]

Historically, Garveyism and Rastafari were both started by a person who was unknown and rather insignificant, at first, and both movements were later exported from Jamaica to other countries under the harsh economic and political conditions of the early twentieth century. Whereas Garveyism first surfaced in Jamaica during World War I, Rastafari came out of the depression years of the 1930s, which gave birth to the 1938 labor rebellion. As in Garveyism, the Jamaican roots of Rastafari are to be found in the varied cultural, economic, and political struggles of the Jamaican people in the postemancipation years after 1838. Both movements are committed to an ideology of nationalism that supports political and economic independence for Blacks. That is, they both demonstrate a strong anticolonial stance and show interest in national independence, although they have very different interpretations of what a black independent nation should be.

Both movements gained their popularity abroad before they were accepted at home by the Jamaican middle class, from whom they received much hostility. Garveyism got its early support in Harlem before it was endorsed in Jamaica in the 1920s. Leonard Howell, who is regarded as one of the founders of the Rastafarian movement, first gained a following in the rural parish of St. Thomas and later, in the parish of St. Catherine, set up a commune called Pinnacle, which was constantly under pressure from the authorities in the 1940s and 1950s. In 1954 the commune was broken up by the police.[11] Thus Rastafari's acceptance in Jamaica, especially among the middle class, came only after the university study of 1961, Prime Minister Michael Manley's political interest in and sympathy toward the Rastas, and the reggae explosion of the 1970s. Both Garvey and Howell were, over the course of their careers, arrested and imprisoned on charges of conspiracy, the former in the United States and the latter in Jamaica. Yet, despite the hostile attitudes of the Jamaican society to Garveyism and Rastafari, the 1930s ushered in a period of transition between colonialism and the rise of Jamaican nationalism—due in no small measure to the struggles of both the Rastafarians and the Garveyites.

Rastafarian intellectuals construct a lineage going back beyond the plantation to Ethiopia, and many Rastafarian elders emphasize individual spiritual vision to account for the origins of their conversion.[12] Many versions of the 1930s emergence of Rastafari are proffered other than those that have become standard in scholarly works. However, certain basic facts remain undisputed. That several of Garvey's followers were involved in the founding of Rastafari is common knowledge. Leonard Howell, for example, traveled paths similar to Garvey and was a known Garveyite and Africanist. Coming from a poor rural background, Howell joined the thousands of Jamaicans who migrated to Panama and then to the United States, where he worked with the United States Army as a cook and was said to have had a business in New York. Garvey did not work with the army but made Harlem, New York, his headquarters. Hill notes that Howell's return to Jamaica "coincided with the period of marked upsurge in religious revivalism that began during 1930–31."[13] *The Gleaner* of December 1933 alleged that at Howell's meetings, "devilish attacks are made . . . on government, both local and imperial, and the whole conduct of the meeting would tend to provoke an insurrection if taken seriously."[14]

Discontinuities

Although the Garveyite secular-religious interpretation of the coronation of Ras Tafari and the Rastafarian religious view of that event both originated from a similar Africa-centered tradition, they are not identical. Garvey saw in Selassie an African head of state and someone who could be a major player in the Pan-African Black Nationalist movement; but the Rastafarian interpretation of the emperor recognized divinity. To the Rastafarian way of thinking, no contradiction exists between the secular and the religious elements in Garvey's thinking, nor in his emphases regarding the emperor's coronation. They interpret the whole of Garvey's thoughts from a theocratic point of view. In contrast, Garvey privileged a secular approach, with a preference for modernity over theocracy. So when Garvey later criticized Emperor Haile Selassie for his conduct in Ethiopia's war with Italy, he saw the emperor as a ruler, not as God. Rastafarians, by contrast, saw God in the emperor; Haile Selassie is God, King of Kings and Lord of Lords. The coronation therefore inspired the emergence of the Rastafarian movement in ways that Garvey never envisioned. Rastas fused ancient Hebrew prophecy, so common in Garvey's speeches, with Africanist ideas[15] and gave rise to the most influential cultural and spiritual current to have emerged in the Caribbean in this century.[16]

The differences between the Garveyites and the Rastafarians involve not only Garvey's ideological stance but also the social character of the movement he led and the religious outlook of the early Rastafarians. The early Rastas were drawn predominantly from the African Jamaican underclass, and the religious character and cultural and social practices of early Rastafari are characteristic of the Jamaican peasantry.[17] The style, organizational structures, and practices of the Garvey movement had the stamp of the emergent black petite bourgeoisie or middle class. At the same time, the Jamaican government had supporters drawn from the peasantry but did not attract many followers from the UNIA.[18] In the UNIA, one felt the energy of a group of Blacks repressed by colonialism and American racism but determined to resist and take its place in the world through conventional means, rather than by way of a radical break with Western culture, as advocated by Rastafari. Around the black middle-class thinking and leadership, the black masses coalesced.

The anticolonial content of Howell's preaching was clear in his message that black people's only true king was Emperor Haile Selassie.[19] But Garvey did not approve of Howell's teaching and rejected his claims that Selassie was God. As Hill reports, Garvey refused to allow Howell "to sell the Emperor's pictures in Edelweiss Park, the [Jamaican] headquarters of the UNIA."[20] Garvey found many of Howell's doctrines embarrassing to his own Christian thought, especially on the issues of God and the Messiah. There is little evidence that Garvey read Howell's *Promised Key,* but if he had, he would have found this early Rastafari prophet's interpretation of Bible characters and the Christian church (especially the Roman Catholic Church) highly offensive; Garvey's respect for the Bible is unquestioned.

Another Garveyite associated with the early Rastafarians is Robert Hinds, a follower of Alexander Bedward who was among those arrested on Bedward's 1921 march against oppression and his call for spiritual reform. Chevannes calls Hinds "the most successful of all early Rastafari, in terms of membership. . . . Hinds led an organization of over eight hundred members on roll, and turnout at functions of a couple hundred." Hinds's headquarters was called the King of Kings Mission, and "it was organized along the lines of a Revival group."[21] Again, the connection between Bedwardism, revivalism, and early Rastafari is patently clear. Also, like both Bedward and Garvey, Hinds had the ability to attract a large following.

The 1935 Italian war against Ethiopia gave Rastafari one of its most important impulses. Not only were Rastafarians and Garveyites protesting publicly in Kingston, but the wider black community was also opposed to Italy's aggression. The Garvey-oriented newspaper *Plain Talk* reported that "a group of Jamaicans had decided to launch a series of meetings throughout the Island, for the purpose of getting together a battalion of stalwart men to defend the Ethiopian frontier from the Italian invaders," and that the contingent would be assisted by a black organization in Chicago.[22] Amy Jacques Garvey, wife of Marcus Garvey, delivered the main address at a mass meeting in support of Ethiopia at the Kingston Liberty Hall on October 13, 1935. She concluded that the war would result in the "rising up of the people of Africa in one great effort to emancipate themselves."[23] At this rally, "a petition signed by no fewer than 1400 persons was drafted asking the British Government to allow Jamaicans to enlist in the Ethiopian army so as 'to fight to preserve the glories of our ancient and beloved Empire'."[24] This petition was sent to the British colonial secretary, who represented the custodian of Jamaica's national and international defense. However, the British government did not accede to the suggestions of the Jamaica Garveyites; in fact, one British official "wrote contemptuously of the 'bellicose sons of Ham in Jamaica, so anxious to serve two masters'."[25]

The Rastafarians showed their opposition to the Italians in different ways. Several Rasta groups demonstrated in Kingston, while others voiced their defiance through a variety of approaches. According to Randolph Williams, "There were sections that wanted to send a petition to His Majesty the King of England praying that they be allowed to recruit men in Jamaica to be sent to Abyssinia to do service in the Ethiopian ranks, others wished to collect money to send to Ras Tafari to be used for the purchase of arms, some decided upon just praying three times per day for the triumph of Abyssinia."[26] In Montego Bay, on the western end of the island, about two thousand persons demonstrated against Italian aggression. Similar protests took place in Guyana, Barbados, Trinidad, St. Kitts, and other West Indian territories.

The Garveyite newspaper *Plain Talk* was commended by Dr. Malaku Bayen,[27] Haile Selassie's personal representative in the United States, who was in charge of organizing the Ethiopian World Federation. Early Rastafarian leaders Joseph Nathaniel Hibbert, Archibald Dunkley, and many other Rastas were foundation members of the first local branch of the Ethiopian World Federation to be set up in Jamaica. But Garvey himself was very hostile in his criticism of Haile Selassie. As early as October 1935, Garvey had argued that the Italo-Ethiopian war "affords only another example of what unpreparedness means to a people." Less than two years later he stated the following in his main critique of the emperor:

> He kept his country unprepared for modern civilization, whose policy was strictly aggressive. He resorted sentimentally to prayer and to feasting and fasting, not consistent with the policy that secures the existence of present-day freedom for people whilst other nations and rulers are building up armaments of the most destructive kind as the only means of securing peace . . . and protection. . . . The results show that God had nothing to do with the cam-

paign of Italy in Abyssinia, for on the one side we had the Pope of the Catholic Church blessing the Crusade, and the other, the Coptic Church fasting and praying with confidence of
victory. . . . It is logical therefore that God did not take sides, but left the matter to be settled by the strongest human battalion.[28]

At the very beginning of the Rastafarian movement, Garvey challenged Leonard
Howell's claim that Selassie was divine. Garvey respected the emperor only for the important role he saw him playing in African politics at the time; but he criticized Selassie
openly for his political ineptitude and his defense of his Semitic ancestry at the expense
of his African heritage. Not surprisingly, Garvey's attitude toward Haile Selassie was
bitterly criticized by his opponents, as well as by some of his supporters, in correspondence and articles to *Plain Talk*.[29] Some of the opposition to Garvey derived from the
view that the emperor was a descendant of King Solomon and therefore untouchable.
The power of the Hebrew Bible record was often invoked in the interpretation of the
Emperor's ancient lineage. Others felt that Garvey's criticisms were simply unfair.[30] No
doubt exists that Garvey lost support among his followers as a result of his criticisms.
However, his work and his reputation after his death caused him to become a prophet
to Rastafarians and a national hero in Jamaican society.[31]

Although the Garveyites and the early Rastafarians were minority groups in Jamaica
in the 1930s, they were at the forefront of the challenge to Jamaica's colonial mentality. Rastafari therefore represents an important dimension of popular resistance to
British colonialism, the plantation system, as well as the authority of British-oriented
mulatto and black middle-class values. However, to frame the oppositionist posture of
Rastafari in relation to the more privileged classes is to see it conveniently in a one-sided
way, when, in fact, it has challenged the values not only of the privileged but also of the
underprivileged who accept colonial values. The Rastafarian's "chanting down Babylon" is, therefore, directed at all segments of the Jamaican society that cradle and foster the beliefs that sustain black subordination.

Garveyism and Rastafari are the results of distinct social movements that overlap on
certain ideas and personalities and differ in other respects. For example, while Garveyites shared a similar perspective on Africa to that of the Rastafarians, they differed
over Selassie's divinity. For Garvey, Selassie was a secular figure, not a religious one,
and absolutely not God. Garveyism was broader than Rastafari in social appeal and included a strong element of middle-class Blacks of that era, though it also attracted a
strong working-class and rural following. By contrast, Rastafari was definitely rooted
in the lower socioeconomic classes. It was a movement among the Jamaican poor, un-
mediated. The infusion of the middle class into Rastafari came with Black Power in the
1960s. In this regard, the theme of nationhood articulated by Garvey and other nationalists came into conflict with the theme of repatriation that was strongly held by
Rastafarians.

The imperative of repatriation among Rastafarians reflected trends all over the
Americas, as witnessed in both the mythic and the physical return of Brazilian and
Cuban Blacks to West Africa in the late nineteenth and early twentieth centuries,[32] as
well as in the repatriationist efforts in the United States during the same period. This

trend was also strong in Garvey's successful efforts in establishing UNIA branches in Lesotho, Ghana, Nigeria, Liberia, Sierra Leone, Namibia, and South Africa.[33] In 1961 the government of Jamaica appointed a mission to Africa that included Garveyites such as Z. Munroe Scarlett and Rastafarians Mortimo Planno, D. Mack, and Filmore Alvaranga. Their report helped to shape the policy of the Jamaican government in setting up diplomatic relations with independent African states, in providing solidarity in the struggle against colonial rule, and in securing land in Ethiopia, where a Jamaican settlement still exists.

The religious character of Rastafari is partly due to the way Jamaican people have identified with and appropriated the Hebrew Scriptures and have seen themselves as the Israelites. The oppression of the Middle Passage, slavery, and the brutal postemancipation treatment of the peasantry, when linked to Africa-centered traditions of racial consciousness, led some Jamaicans to identify themselves strongly with the suffering ancient Israelites. While sharing in this religious perspective and drawing on it, Garvey was more secular in his program, policy positions, and outlook than that theological tradition. Garveyism was a program of political, economic, social, and cultural modernity. While incorporating basic fundamental Christian principles, it had to admit to more than one belief system because the Pan-African movement that the UNIA represented had believers drawn from different religious and spiritual persuasions. Among the Garveyites were adherents of the many varieties of African Caribbean and African American Christian religions, as well as of orthodox Christian religions and of Islam. Garvey himself was brought up as a Methodist and had some association with Catholicism. During his heyday, Garvey was a Christian,[34] albeit a nondenominational one, who advocated the perception of God in our own image. This contrasts sharply with the Rastafarian belief in the divinity of Haile Selassie.

Another important difference between Garvey and Rastafarians lies in their views on ganja, which is used ritually and socially by Rastafarians.[35] An editorial titled "The Dangerous Weed" that appeared in Garvey's *New Jamaican* on August 13, 1932, leaves the reader in no doubt as to where he stood on this matter:

> Ganja is a dangerous weed. It has been pronounced so by responsible authorities. The smoking of it does a great deal of harm or injury to the smoker; we understand it has the same effect on the subject as opium has. Every day we hear of cases of ganja sellers being brought before the Court—fines, small and heavy, have been inflicted with the object of destroying the trade, but yet it grows. The other day a man was found in possession of ninety pounds of ganja, this was enough deadly weed to destroy a thousand men. That our people are being destroyed by the use of ganja there is absolutely no doubt. We have come in contact with young men and middle aged men who have become a menace to society through the smoking of ganja. Sometimes they perform in such a crazy manner as to frighten us. Aren't we playing with the danger by not more severely putting it down?
>
> Most of the people who smoke ganja do so as a means of getting themselves in such a state or condition as to forget their troubles and worries—troubles and worries brought upon them by the bad conditions that exist in the country. . . . It would be good that more serious steps be taken to suppress this ganja habit. . . . Between ganja and fanatical religion,

we are developing a large population of half-crazy people who may not only injure themselves but injure us. Some will do it in the name of the "Lord" and others may do it under
the influence of the evil weed.[36]

This position brought Garvey into conflict with those who advocated and practiced the
ritual, sacramental use of ganja, as well as with those who traded in it. (Jamaica had
several herbalists who sold many herbs for various maladies and not as drug dealers.)
But while Garveyism inspired the prophetic and Ethiopianist vision of the Rastafarians,
who hail Garvey as a great hero and prophet of Rastafari, the Jamaican Pan-Africanist
stood in strong opposition to the Rastas' fundamental beliefs and practices. He saw their
rituals and livity as un-Christian and degrading to the true African personality.

Another significant difference between the Rastafari and the Garvey movement is that
the latter was institutionalized and centralized through the UNIA, while the Rastafarian movement is not an institutionalized and centralized establishment. Attempts by
Rastafarians to centralize the movement have proven dismal failures, although no doubt
efforts will continue to be made in that direction. There is no central leadership or hierarchy that makes decisions for the movement, and the various groups exercise a
tremendous measure of independence. Perhaps their only uniting principle is the belief
in Selassie and Ethiopianism.

On the one hand, Garvey does have the status of a prophet in the Rastafarian worldview, and in some ways, Garveyism has influenced the Rastafarian ideology. Indeed, Garveyism is said to be one of the ideological foundations of the Rastafari religion,[37] a result of the cross-pollination that occurred between the Garvey movement and those who
have been identified by scholars as the founders of Rastafari. On the other hand, Rastafari was not a product of the Garvey movement. The spread of Garveyism corresponds
with black militancy after World War I—as seen, for example, in the labor movements
among the Oil Fields Workers Trades Union, led by Uriah Buzz Butler and Captain Author Cipriani of Trinidad and Tobago—and depended on the success of Garvey in organizing and channeling that radicalism in Jamaica and parts of the United States. The
spread of Rastafari outside of Jamaica in the late twentieth century has a different vehicle—that of reggae music and the dreadlocks images associated with Bob Marley.

Given Jamaica's class, color, and race structure, some Garveyites from the middle
class held Rastafarians in contempt, and certainly did not subscribe to any notion of the
divinity of Haile Selassie. Garvey further differentiated himself from Bedwardism[38] and
revivalism. Bedwardism took the name of its founder, Alexander Bedward (1859–
1930), a revival preacher who had been a migrant in Panama and whose headquarters
were in August Town (near the Mona sugar estate). The crucial years for Bedwardism
were the 1890s to the 1920s, and its primary supporters were the poor underclass. The
Garvey movement, by contrast, was multiclass in its social composition and drew from
the black petite bourgeoisie or the emergent middle class: teachers, journalists, small
businesspeople, black industrial workers in the United States, and sugar plantation and
banana workers in Cuba and the Caribbean, most of whom were peasants. Each of these
groups brought to the Garvey movement their view of the world, their distinct interests,
and their common experiences of racial oppression.

As with any nationalist movement having a cross-class composition, conflict was inevitable in the Garvey movement and emerged when the early Rastafarians objected to Garvey's criticism of Emperor Haile Selassie's style of leadership in the war with Italy in the 1930s. But even earlier, Garvey had been critical of revivalist practices, Obeah (not in modern Rastafari), and the smoking of ganja. An editorial in the *New Jamaican*, commenting on a woman who died after "catching the spirit" in the spirit possession of revivalism," clearly represented Garvey's views: "There is good and there is bad in religion. Some religions are foolish, and we have a lot of them in Jamaica. We have religion here, that is running the people crazy. . . . In different sections of our city, and for that matter, on the island, scheming and wicked persons are promoting all kinds of fanatical religions, and they are finding fertile fields among the unfortunate and ignorant people."[39]

These elements, as Chevannes and others have pointed out, were all present in early Rastafari. That was a different phase of the movement, and as such, it is necessary to distinguish among the Howellites, the old supporters of Bedwardites, the revivalists who became Rasta and initiated a campaign to recognize Haile Selassie as God, and the latter-day Rastafarian movement that gained international currency with the music of Bob Marley, Peter Tosh, and Bunny Wailer. Garvey knew the Howellites, the Bedwardites, and the anticolonial milieu, and with these Jamaicans he dialogued. It is the latter-day Rastafarians, however, who, through reggae, have canonized Garvey and become the most active force in Jamaica for perpetuating aspects of Garvey's philosophy. Burning Spear was one of the earliest and still is the most persistent of the "Garveyite" reggae-Rasta lyricists.

The Garvey and Rastafarian movements were, of course, not the only trends that were involved in the anticolonial struggle. Rastafari emerged in a decade of intense social struggle in which the middle classes came to the forefront of nationalist anticolonial politics, stirred into action by the labor movement. The social context in which Rastafari emerged was a trying one. In the world of British colonial Jamaica in the 1930s, the racist attitudes of the white landowning and merchant class, the colorist behavior[40] of the brown people, and the hankering of black Jamaicans after a lighter skin color formed a dominant ethos that was not only Britain-centered but also monarchy-oriented. Values such as admiration of and loyalty to the plantation owners and the British king or queen were strong even among black peasants, moments of resistance notwithstanding.

The Jamaican political elite continued to favor the British monarch being recognized—albeit indirectly—as the head of state in the new Jamaican Constitution. In planning constitutional reform in the 1950s both major political parties, the People's National Party and the Jamaica Labour Party, agreed to replace the queen of England with a Jamaican president. However, substantial disagreement remained between the two parties as to whether the final court of appeal should continue to be the British Privy Council. The People's National Party favored dispensing with the British Privy Council and establishing a Caribbean court of appeal. The Jamaica Labour Party favored continuing with the British Privy Council, because it felt that local political interference would affect the due process of law in a

Caribbean court. This legal recognition of, and contention over, the British monarchy is a consequence of the extended period of acceptance of the legitimacy of the British sovereign that has been a central part of Jamaica's colonial political culture. In their advocacy of Ethiopian monarchism over against British monarchism, Jamaican Rastafari challenged the colonial mentality in the national British conception of monarchy, but they were quite at home with the political conception and ideas justifying the Ethiopian monarchy in Africa. Garvey criticized both monarchies and their support in Jamaica.

British cultural institutions transplanted to Jamaica still make up part of Jamaica's way of life and contribute to the shaping of regional and national norms in the anglophone Caribbean. A good case in point is the English game of cricket, which not only has been mastered but has been modified in style and substance by the English-speaking Caribbean. The West Indies cricket team dominated world cricket from the 1970s to the 1990s.

Jamaican middle-class culture was situated at the axis formed by this British cultural-political legacy and its roots in the postemancipation peasantry and working class. The social and economic trajectory of the middle classes for nearly 160 years has, at best, been characterized by considerable ambivalence toward Africa, on the one hand, and cultural certainty about Britain and Europe, on the other. I have corrected many undergraduate essays, at the University of the West Indies, in which students automatically refer to Britain as "the mother country." Rastafari needs to be seen in the context of these social and racial struggles over a Jamaican identity that is heir to both British and African cultures. Rastafari is therefore the continuation of efforts toward black self-determination on the collective as well as the individual level, and in this respect, it parallels the efforts of the Garvey movement. Self-determination, in this context, is not restricted to political nationalism but extends to what Rastafarians have called "livity," which covers the totality of one's being in the world.

Garveyites and Rastafarians were active in the anticolonial and labor struggles, but the outcomes of those struggles were determined by other players: the British government; the landed oligarchy, who had been shaken by the events but not defeated; and the political brokers drawn from the middle classes. Political leadership drawn from the black and brown middle classes negotiated independence from Britain during the 1960s and, in their nation-building efforts, took some elements of Garvey's program but rejected much of his black assertiveness and pride. They substituted other notions with which the light-skinned upper classes and the British would be comfortable, and to which the majority of the black population acquiesced. One example of the negation of Garveyism is frequently referred to in the Jamaican press; some people claim that the color black in the colorful Jamaican flag, which supposedly represents the dominant race in the country, instead symbolizes hardship. This stereotypes black Jamaicans who would like the flag to represent more positive aspects of their reality, aspirations, and dreams as a nation. Jamaican scholars such as Rex Nettleford and Phillip Sherlock have been campaigning for a change in this symbolism, which Nettleford links to the recognition of Emancipation Day as a national holiday. (It is so recognized in such Caribbean countries as Trinidad and Tobago.) Hence, in a letter to the press, Nettleford wrote,

"The people in Jamaica House [office of the Prime Minister] need, however, to act—take the 'hardship' out of the black in the flag (see my *Mirror, Mirror* of 1970) and restore Emancipation Day allowing Independence Day (August 6) to fall where it will!"[41]

Some of the sharpest critiques of the neocolonial conceptions of the nation have come from old Garvey activists and Rastafarians who had articulated varied conceptions of Jamaica as a black nation and of its relationship to Africa. The brown and black middle class, who benefited considerably from the transition to independence—given the expansion of education and the opening up of the civil service as well as of the executive and legislative areas of government—tended to turn its back on Garvey or used his ideas as a means of social control. In this context, from the 1940s to 1960s, Garveyism tended to be equated with Rastafari, since the Rastafarians embraced Garvey as their prophet. In the thinking of the Rastafarians, after Garvey's death in 1940, he assumed mythic proportions, second only to Emperor Haile Selassie. Barry Chevannes has identified four themes in his Rastafarian informants' understanding of Garvey: Africa for the Africans, black unity, self-reliance, and racial pride. He has also exposed the myths that have developed about Garvey, which he groups into the categories "Garvey as divine," "Garvey as John the Baptist," and "Garvey as prophet." These understandings stand in sharp contrast to what are referred to as "Garvey's curses": financial disaster with the purchase of the worthless Black Star Line and his poor management skills as a leader and financial planner.[42]

Pressures from the rest of society against Rastafari, in the years leading up and subsequent to political independence, have created closer bonds between Rastafari and Garveyism while not eroding differences in outlook among their followers. Moreover, while Rastafari as a movement has grown and spread internationally, no Garvey movement exists, in an organic sense,[43] at the end of the twentieth century. But Garvey's ideas and views remain important and are a point of reference at the popular level as well as in Jamaican state and local politics, due to his status as one of Jamaica's national heroes. An appropriate question to raise is: What will be the future of Rastafari? Might it suffer the fate of Garveyism, maintaining a legacy without a movement? Might it become organized into a political force that would cause it to lose its cultural dynamics and forget its roots and ethos? Perhaps its decentralized and less organized (than Garveyism) nature will prove to be Rastafari's own salvation.

Notes

1. Cited in Robert Hill, ed., *Marcus Garvey and the Universal Negro Improvement Association Papers*, vol. 7: *November 1927–August 1940* (Berkeley and Los Angeles: University of California Press, 1990), 442.

2. Ibid., 440–41.

3. The quotation from Psalm 68:31—"Princes shall come out of Egypt; Ethiopia shall soon stretch out her hands unto God" (KJV)—was used by Garvey in developing his Pan-African message. See Robert Hill, "Leonard P. Howell and Millenarian Visions in Early Rastafari," *Jamaica Journal* 16, 1 (1983): 24–39.

4. For a review of *The Coronation of an African King,* see *The Blackman,* June 21, 1930, 3. See also Beverley Hamilton, "Marcus Garvey: Cultural Activist," *Jamaica Journal* 20, 3 (1987): 21–30, for discussion of Garvey's cultural activities in Jamaica.

5. K.W.J. Post, *Arise Ye Starvelings: The Jamaican Labour Rebellion of 1938 and Its Aftermath* (The Hague: Martinus Nijhoff, 1978), 160.

6. According to Robert Hill, the *Holy Piby* was written and published by Robert Athlyi Rogers in 1924, in Newark, New Jersey. *The Royal Parchment Scroll of Black Supremacy* was published by the Reverend Fitz Balintine Pettersburgh. See Hill, "Leonard P. Howell," 27.

7. Leonard Howell is said to have plagiarized the *Holy Piby* in his 1935 text titled *The Promised Key.* See Chapter 21 on *The Promised Key* in this book.

8. Rastafarian writer E.S.P. McPherson argues that Rastafari had pre-Columbian roots in that Ethiopian people came here before the Spaniards. He does not provide any evidence other than the oral tradition of certain Rastafarian elders. See E.S.P. McPherson, *Rastafari and Politics— Sixty Years of a Developing Cultural Ideology: A Sociology of Development Perspective* (Kingston: Black International Iyahbinghi Press Production, 1991), 22.

9. On Kumina, see an interesting article by Kenneth Bilby and Elliott Leib, "Kumina, the Howellite Church and the Emergence of Rastafarian Traditional Music in Jamaica," *Jamaica Journal* 19, 3 (1986): 22–28.

10. Maureen Warner-Lewis, "African Continuities in the Rastafari Belief System," *Caribbean Quarterly* 39, 3–4 (1993): 108–23. Garvey, of course, would have had less respect than most Rastas for revivalism and Kumina.

11. Joseph Owens, *Dread: The Rastafarians of Jamaica* (Kingston: Sangster's Book Stores, 1976), 18–19.

12. Barbara Makeda Lee, *Rastafari: The New Creation* (London: Jamaica Media Productions, 1982), 14–15.

13. In the 1920s, Garveyites in New York described Howell "as being a 'con-man' but also 'a samfie [Obeah] man'" (Hill, "Leonard P. Howell," 30).

14. Cited in Horace Campbell, *Rasta and Resistance: From Marcus Garvey to Walter Rodney* (London: Hansib Publishing, 1985), 71.

15. For an insightful discussion of the Rastafarian use of the Old Testament, see Dennis Forsythe, *Rastafari: For the Healing of the Nation* (Kingston: Zaika Publications, 1983); and Post, *Arise Ye Starvelings.*

16. On the worldwide spread of Rastafari, see Neil Savishinsky, "Transnational Popular Culture and the Global Spread of the Jamaican Rastafarian Movement," *New West Indian Guide* 68, 3–4 (1994): 259–81. See also Chapter 7 by Savishinsky in this anthology.

17. Barry Chevannes, *Rastafari: Roots and Ideology* (Syracuse, N.Y.: Syracuse University Press, 1994); idem, "Introducing the Native Religions of Jamaica," in Barry Chevannes, ed., *Rastafari and Other African-Caribbean Worldviews* (The Hague: Macmillan Publishers/Institute of Social Studies, 1995).

18. The Rastafarian movement developed an urban character with the drift to Kingston in the 1940s–1950s, and only during the 1960s did it gain significant numbers of adherents among the middle class.

19. For more information on Howell and his role in Rastafari, see William David Spencer's commentary on *The Promised Key* in Chapter 21, below.

20. Hill, "Leonard P. Howell," 32.

21. Chevannes, *Rastafari,* 127.

22. Editorial, *Plain Talk,* July 20, 1935.

23. Editorial, *Plain Talk,* October 26, 1935.

24. Robert Weisboard, "British West Indian Reaction to the Italian-Ethiopian War: An Episode in Pan-Africanism," *Caribbean Studies* 10, 1 (1970): 35–36.

25. Ibid.

26. *Jamaica Standard,* January 14, 1939, 24.

27. *Plain Talk,* August 7, 1937, 7.

28. Cited in Rupert Lewis, *Marcus Garvey: Anti-Colonial Champion* (Trenton, N.J.: Africa World Press, 1992), 172.

29. Robert E. Hood, *Must God Remain Greek? Afro Cultures and God-Talk* (Minneapolis: Fortress Press, 1990), 91. See *Plain Talk,* April 10, 1937, 7; May 1, 1937, 10. See also Hill, ed., *Marcus Garvey,* 7:698–703, for correspondence between Garvey and Una Brown of New York City over Garvey's criticisms of Selassie.

30. Una Brown wrote, "I feel like a lot of others that you have been quite unfair in your writing" (in Hill, ed., *Marcus Garvey,* 7:699).

31. Virtually all the scholarly and popular literature on Rastafari accords Garvey this status. See Jabulani I. Tafari, "The Rastafari: Successors of Marcus Garvey," in Rex Nettleford, ed., *Caribbean Quarterly Monograph: Rastafari* (Kingston: Carribean Quarterly, University of the West Indies, 1985), 1–12, for a statement on Rastafari as successors of Marcus Garvey.

32. Rodolfo Sarracino, *Los que volvieron a Africa* (Havana: Editorial de Ciencias Sociales, 1988).

33. Hill, ed., *Marcus Garvey,* 7:997–1000.

34. See Philip Potter, "The Religious Thought of Marcus Garvey," in Rupert Lewis and Patrick Bryan, eds., *Garvey: His Work and Impact* (Trenton, N.J.: Africa World Press, 1991), 145–163.

35. Scholars are divided on whether ganja was brought on the plantations by indentured Indian laborers or by enslaved Africans (see Bilby and Leib, "Kumina," 23). See Neil Savishinsky's "African Dimensions of the Jamaican Rastafarian Movement," Chapter 7 in this book, for details.

36. Marcus Garvey, Editorial, "The Dangerous Weed," *New Jamaican,* 13 August 1932.

37. Chevannes, *Rastafari,* 87.

38. See Chevannes, *Rastafari,* 39, 126–27, 78–80, for the impact of Bedward on early Rastafari. For the political impact of Bedwardism, see Lewis, *Marcus Garvey.*

39. Marcus Garvey, "The Death of a Fanatic," *New Jamaican,* 11 August 1932, 2; The editorial is very critical of "bad religion."

40. Jamaican novelist Erna Brodber used the term *colorist behavior* in her 1995 emancipation commemoration lecture "Emancipation—The Lesson and the Legacy: . . . As We Forgive Those Who Trespass against Us . . ." (lecture presented at the Bethel Baptist Church, Kingston, Jamaica, on Sunday, July 30, 1995; Kingston Emancipation Commemoration Committee).

41. See Rex Nettleford, "Letter to the Editor," *Daily Observer,* August 5, 1995, 8.

42. Chevannes, *Rastafari,* 87–99, 100–110.

43. By "organic sense" I mean that a social movement has to be an expression of a particular moment and has to grow and change in ways corresponding to the interests and agendas of its members. Research on the Rastafarian movement shows an organic change. However, there is no comparable evidence among those who call themselves Garveyites.

9

Who Is Haile Selassie? His Imperial Majesty in Rasta Voices

ELEANOR WINT IN CONSULTATION WITH MEMBERS OF THE NYABINGHI ORDER

The question "Who is Haile Selassie, His Imperial Majesty?" is as important to Rastafari as the question "Who is Muhammad?" to Islam or "Who is Jesus Christ?" to Christianity. Rastafari brethren searching today for a spiritual identity see Haile Selassie's coming as fulfilling biblical prophecy. When Leonard Howell, on his return from reputedly attending the coronation of Ras Tafari, taught Jamaicans that the newly crowned emperor of Ethiopia was the king of black people—literally, the returned Messiah—the new believers saw it fulfilling both Old and New Testament Scriptures. To the "Rasses" (Rasta brethren), the crowning of Haile Selassie on November 2, 1930, as Emperor Haile Selassie (Power of the Trinity) I, the Conquering Lion of the Tribe of Judah, Elect of God, King of Kings, of Ethiopia was the fulfillment of Old Testament prophecy.

All brethren "overstand" Selassie's place in history, his divinity, and the place of the Scriptures in the doctrines of Rastafari, but there is no unanimity on the biblical point of view relative to His Imperial Majesty (H.I.M.) Some brethren know H.I.M. as a great man, others regard him as a prophet. Many brethren experience H.I.M. as the Son of God, who springs from the Root of David, and the righteous branch that shall execute judgment and justice in all the earth. Even Abuna Blackheart, a spiritual leader of the Royal Ethiopian Judah Coptic Church, described Haile Selassie as "the Most High and Almighty Jah, source of all benefits, above all, and possessing all power to direct all things according to his solemn will."

Pertinent to this belief is the biblical text "I will raise unto David a righteous Branch, and a King shall reign and prosper, and shall execute judgment and justice in the earth" (Jeremiah 23:5 KJV). As Ras Boanerges observed in our 1994 conversation in Kingston, almost two thousand years have passed and people are still confused about the missing body of Christ that did not see corruption. "Scientists have put it in many ways that his people who knew him might well have stolen his body out of the sepulcher. [But] in this generation, when people claim that they have H.I.M. in a mud hut, they don't know again where the body has gone." This mystery is "having the world baffled but so far as my belief [goes], I know that in every set generation, the Messiah reincarnates himself for the new world."

Haile Selassie I, the Prophesied Blessing of Israel

On March 25, 1976, the tenth Annual Issemble of Rastafarians of the Haile Selassie I School made a "Devine Announcement" that read:

> This devine spiritual inheritance
> Referred to in the ancient scriptures
> As the Blessing of the children of Israel
> was transferred from the old Hebrews of the Chaldeans
> The sons of Abraham: descended of Adam's fallen race,
> To I and I the Israelites
> The people of the Almighty
> The ancient Ethiopians: the Sons of Jah Rastafari
> In the reign of Solomon
> King of Hebrews: the Son of David
> The Son of Jesse, the Ephastite of Bethlehem Juda
> The same Melchesidec: Dreaded King of Salem
> Prince of Peace
> King of Kings: Lord of Lords
> Wonderful, Counselor
> Haile Selassie I, Jah Rastafari.[1]

"Wonderful, Counselor" is indeed who Ras Tafari is to Rastafarians; Haile Selassie I has fulfilled Hebrew Scripture, thus revealing his present followers as the true descendants of Abraham, the true Israelites. The Tenth Annual Issemble places all discussions of Rastafari soundly in the realm of history as well as of revealed religion, which, according to the Bible, is God's unique province of activity. Further, the reported statement by Marcus Garvey that there will be a time when God will be made present in one person shifted the focus of the Hebrew Bible prophecies for Rastafarians from present-day Israel to Africa. To brethren, this is definitely fulfillment of the Scriptures. By descending from the line of Jesse, Haile Selassie fulfills the requirement of the Solomonic dynasty.

In this context, Haile Selassie is a unique king and ruler who created the union of church and state that remains a model for the world to come. As head of the church and defender of the faith, he kept the rule of the country within the Christian discipline against the mighty surrounding foes of Islam. As Ras General Muntu Lalibela reflects, "I-an-I man know that within the Rastafari penetration is an idea whose time has come to pass and this is something no man can stop for it is the works of I Father. I-an-I man recognize the Father Jah Rastafari and the sovereignty of Africa. That is the rock of all ages for I-an-I know that any other is sinking sand."[2]

Haile Selassie himself encouraged the Jamaican-African connection in his address to Parliament on April 21, 1966, during the tumultuous welcome he received on visiting Jamaica:

> The relations, in a broader sense, between the people of Jamaica and the people of Ethiopia and Africa are deep and abiding. . . . We have all struggled for independence and have achieved it now. . . . The people of Jamaica, by and large, have originated in Africa. . . . I would broadly say wherever there is African blood, there is a basis for greater UNITY. We must also help each other in our endeavors to expand education, to raise the standard of living of our respective peoples.[3]

This visit gave Rastas a legitimacy of purpose and brought back to the fore the promises of the government relative to repatriation, particularly in light of His Majesty's call for unity.

Haile Selassie I as Jesus Christ Returned

To speak of Rastafari without acknowledging the centrality of H.I.M. to the faith is like propounding a Christianity stripped of Christology. Rastas cannot explain human failing without accepting Christian teaching that "Iyesus Christus" came on earth to help humanity recover from its critical fall from grace. This viewpoint springs from a faith which acknowledges that only God—not humans—can forgive human sins. For the Rastafarians after Leonard Howell, Iyesus Christus, the one whom the world calls Jesus Christ, has returned a second time in H.I.M. of Ethiopia, Haile Selassie I. As Ras Bongo Time, high priest in the Nyabinghi Order, explained to me in a conversation in Jamaica in 1994:

> His Majesty is the resurrected personalities of Christ. We can see this from Acts, chapter 2; Timothy, chapter 6; Revelations 5 and 9. Timothy tells us where he is right now as one which no one can see or approach. According to Revelations 5, he is King David's greater son, not grandson or great-grandson, not his greater son [i.e., far removed in lineage and time]. Descendant of Menelik, he was Ras Makonnen's son. Menelik is a direct descendant of Solomon and his closest friend and strength was his cousin Ras Makonnen.

Ras Da Silva concurs with this overstanding of H.I.M.'s lineage and personhood and recalls the words of a favorite hymn sung by his mother:

> Hail to the Lord's anointed, great David's greater Son
> Hail in his time appointed, His days on earth shall run.

Ras Irie Irons, international coordinator of the Rastafari Centralization Committee, contends that H.I.M. must be divine, as Iyesus is, because so many of his words echo the Bible. As he pointed out in our conversation in Kingston in 1994, Haile Selassie's words on his return to Ethiopia in 1940—exactly five years after Italy's entry into Addis

Ababa, during one year's travel assisted by British supporters, seeing and learning of the apparently endless bloody carnage and invasion of his country—were "My people, do not repay evil with evil . . . do not stain your souls by avenging yourselves on your enemies." These words echo Romans 12:17: "Recompense to no man evil for evil. Provide things honest in the sight of all men" (KJV).

The reputed prophecy of Marcus Garvey is combined with the Bible to point to Christus's coming again in Selassie I. Another Rastafarian, Tekle Ab (Carlton) Rose, explained to me in Kingston in 1994 that he came to such belief through divine meditation and the prophecy of Marcus Garvey: "Marcus said, 'When a black king is crowned, you must look to Africa.' The Bible teaches us more than any other source of the personalities of Christ." Reasoning among brethren has also infused a miraculous element into the missing parts of Haile Selassie's biography. According to Christopher Clapham, an authority on Ethiopia,[4] although H.I.M.'s birthday is celebrated as July 23, 1892, his actual date of birth is not known. Brethren, however, tell of his birth being heralded by thunder, lightning, and floods (breaking the prolonged drought), as his mother gave birth to the only surviving child of seven pregnancies. Such reasonings may fall within the category of "mythmaking," but they create doctrine for a fledgling movement.

In this doctrine-making tradition, Tekle Ab (Carlton) Rose tells of overstanding H.I.M.'s truely divine and perfect nature:

> Since we know H.I.M. as the father of anciency, knowing that he is the only one who holds the perfection of manhood, . . . when you look and see how weak the beings that we are, and we can find H.I.M. as the perfect one, according to the ancient script that man is weak . . . if you are dealing with Christ out of the manhood, we would have nothing, but seeing H.I.M. as the perfect man, that is what makes man still have a chance. That he could complete the perfection of the purpose of God.

Rose explains that His Imperial Majesty—who, as a child, was taken care of by his parents, schooled at home, and accomplished his boyhood in full authority—"walked in his manhood to the heights of angelic orders, namely, the archangel, cherubim, and seraphim. These are the seven heights [humans] have to walk. . . . Most people only live the stage of a man and never reach the stage of archangels. . . . His Majesty walked this path." Rose is absolutely convinced that, like Christ, H.I.M. "had to accomplish all these things to be within the perfect order," and that "whosoever would arrive at that title would have to be the *Messiah, King of Kings, Lord of Lords,*" the judge and ruler of the earth.

Another articulate creator of doctrine—one who uses the tools of the Hebrew and Christian Scriptures, history, hearsay, and reasoning in theological discourse—is Ras Boanerges, who helped found the influential House of Youth Black Faith, which, Barry Chevannes reports, eliminated earlier superstitions and established the Dreadlocks tradition.[5] The following is an example of his reasoning as he assembles a doctrine in response to the question "Who is His Majesty, Haile Selassie I?" As Boanerges reasons, "This [question] is . . . very important . . . to those of us that walk in dis covenant, to be a light to de people." Boanerges claims that when Leonard Howell returned to Jamaica in 1930, he spoke only of Emperor Haile Selassie. At no time did he mention Jah Rastafari. But Boanerges feels the issue of Jah Rastafari's relation to the emperor is important in this time in history, "when the scriptures are truly being fulfilled before our eyes every day." He adds, "The King is your creator and the Creator is your king."

Consequently, no one needs to be ashamed or confused to call Haile Selassie by his rightful name, King Rastafari. The king, as the prophets had foretold, is indeed our King and of the same "Ivine" order. Boanerges continues:

> As Iyesus shows us, I and my Father is one, the same is to be said of Haile Selassie. . . . Our King and our Creator is one. If we read Revelations 19, verse 11 to 16, we learn of the second advent. Hebrews 7 [says,] "For this Melchizedek, King of Salem, priest of the Most High God . . . King of Righteousness, and after that also King of Salem, which is King of Peace." . . . The pagan world use the English and defile this word *God* and the word *king*. They turn these into Baal worship. The same Melchizedek who "without father, without mother, without descent, having neither beginning of days nor end of life, but made like unto the Son of God, abideth a priest continually." Melchizedek, the king of Salem . . . His Majesty came with a new name, King of Kings, king over all kings.

To Ras Boanerges, Haile Selassie seems as unique as Iyesus (Jesus) in every way. In a monologue-type reasoning, Boanerges said:

> Sometimes people talk about his being born to natural man and woman. Remember of Iyesus they said, "Is not this man Mary and Joseph's son that was born and grow amongst us?" In John 6 we read that he was before Abraham. Many times when they sought to stone him he could have destroyed them but rather he would run from them. The Scriptures show that when he come again, they shall know him, that is, after his resurrection and ascension there should be no question as every eye shall behold his glory. We can now identify him to the nation. "And the Gentiles shall see thy righteousness, and all kings thy glory, and thou shalt be called by a new name, which the mouth of the Lord shall name" [(Isaiah 62:2 KJV]. The prophet's words [are] "The beast and the dragon shall make war against the Lamb." You no' see Mussolini, the same way, but the Lamb overcame.
>
> Haile Selassie means "Power of the Trinity," Rastafari means "Eternal Power and Godhead." We need to overstand that this same St. [King] James Version is the translation of the great prophets' recordings of their life. It is a translation from Hebrew to English. God is spoken of by different names in the Old Testament. Look at Elohim, Yahweh, Jehovah or Jah, Adonai in Genesis, El Shaddai [Genesis 17], El Gibbor [Isaiah 9]; all these revelations of his names come at different times in response to the different needs of man. As Revelation 18 shows, he will return and overthrow Babylon.

In response to my question on his experience with the movement, Ras Boanerges gave this testimony:

> In 1947, I just tek up my Bible as a youngster and start to preach the word. I meet much suffering, many police brutality. When Sylvia Pankhurst come to Jamaica with her pamphlets and papers about the emperor's secret force, Black International, it gave me great upliftment to know that I have the inspiration to establish the House of Youth Black Faith. We should adore the I in the form and likeness of the King. When the I call Moses, he said, "Tell the

people that I am the I am." The I is the testimony of the individual. And in this time he tells us that he shall rise us up in his name and we will suffer persecution because of his name. We can't withdraw from the thing that is right . . . His Majesty Haile Selassie I, which is the Godhead, the crowning monarch. . . . "Crown him, Crown him Lord of all, Crown him immortal of your race. Blessed is the nation whose creator is the Almighty." We used to sing these hymns. We don't sing them anymore.

Persecuted for Jah's Sake

Ras Boanerges expects opposition to his message from the overriding Babylon culture. He says, "Although we preach the truth, many ones will compass us about and say we a' foolishness. This we expect" (see Luke 6:22 and Matthew 5:11). As he noted, "When we first started in the thirties [people] used to call us Blackheart Man, say we kill people and eat them. Today they call us evildoers telling our children lies. But rejoice you in that day and leap for joy, for, behold, you reward is great in heaven. The same thing they do already they will do again and again." Identifying specific persecutions of Rastas, Boanerges references Michael Manley's rise to power and his treatment of Rastafarians, saying:

> In 1973, the same Michael Manley tear down Trench Town and dash the poor people out into the streets. There were thousands of homeless, destroyed people. I had my Second Tabernacle on Ashenheim Road, to which people from all over the world come and worship. From 1949, April, I work on the University of the West Indies, with Higgs and Hill in construction . . . right up until 1958, when I continue to preach this doctrine at night and work in the day. All over the island two, three, or more of us blow the trumpet. Trench Town was desolate from the bulldozer in 1973, where people buil' up houses, schools, concrete structures from years of work like I. I used to have a factory that did mattress making. I never recover from that desolation. I had to start again eventually up here, where the board house was, for one thousand dollars and the land free. The same Manley government of today now turn around and charging us one thousand dollars for land that we have been living free on for years. So you see this is the burden that I-an-I bear. Despise and hatred. [This] is a faith where if you don't know yuself properly yu' go partway an' turn back. For us it is clear that King Selassie I come and he came to rule the earth in righteousness.

As Ras Bass of the Nyabinghi Order explained to me in Kingston in 1994, being a member of the faith meant exposure on a day-to-day basis to threats on one's life, to ridicule, and to social ostracism—a reality that led to the search for a new music, one that would express the sentiments of the locals; a beat indigenous to the people that would allow the expression of dissent and hope. It was not unlike the blues or jazz but differed in the message, the experience, speaking of the undying and unmitigated optimism of a people born in adversity. This explains why reggae has such a strong philosophical dimension. For a poor Jamaican "sufferer" like Ras Boanerges, looking past the disappointment of a government that does not ease his condition to another, greater earthly ruler, who assures him God cares about him on earth, gives him hope to continue struggling for life and a mission of hope to proclaim to others.

Writing in 1980 on H.I.M., I addressed the question "When the emperor leaves this earth, whom can one ask for justice?" I made the point that only one thing is certain: when the emperor goes, all of Ethiopia's problems will live on.[6] In 1997 the reality is the same. Despite the emperor's current prolonged disappearance, believers such as the Rastafari Centralization Committee from the Ethiopian Orthodox Church still look to H.I.M. as a source of hope, inspiration, and guidance for their struggle for justice and equality, as well as for the freedom to share earth's goodness in a portion at least equal to that of others. We Rastas confess and pray:

I Jah Almighty Haile Selassie I first and forever, faithful witness of all things whose judgment is perfect, guide with faith, strengthen with courage, enlighten with wise council, and bless with lovingkindness, that I-an-I must renew the covenants of I Brethren and Sistren to liberate mankind and Ethiopia-Africa from injustice, to labor humbly to increase I-an-I righteous kingman upon earth as it is in Mount Zion.

Notes

1. "Devine Announcement," report of the tenth Annual Issemble of the Haile Selassie I School, Jamaica, press release, March 25, 1976.

2. Ras General Muntu Lalibela, foreword to *"Rastafari Speaks . . ."* : *Some Reflections on the Rastafari Movement in Jamaica* (1994). Available from Frontline Distribution International, 751 E. 75th St., Chicago, IL 60619.

3. Haile Selassie I, *Selected Speeches of His Imperial Majesty Haile Selassie I 1918 to 1967* (Addis Ababa, Ethiopia: Imperial Ethiopian Ministry of Information, 1967), 141.

4. See Christopher S. Clapham, *Haile Selassie's Government* (New York: Praeger Publishers, 1969).

5. See Barry Chevannes, *Rastafari: Roots and Ideology* (Syracuse, N.Y.: Syracuse University Press, 1994), x, xii, 152–70.

6. Eleanor Wint, "His Imperial Majesty's Departure" (author's upublished paper presented at Rastafari I-ssembly in Kingston, Jamaica, 1980).

IO   The Rasta-Selassie-Ethiopian Connections

CLINTON CHISHOLM

No tenet of the sixty-seven-year-old Ras Tafari movement is more enduring or more important than belief in the prestigious lineage and divinity of His Imperial Majesty Haile Selassie I.[1] Allied to this belief, but taking second place to it, is the view that modern Ethiopia is a significant piece of real estate—indeed, the new Zion. The importance of Ethiopia in Rastafarian thought is based on the fact that it is the birthplace of His Imperial Majesty, and also on the belief that it is the present domicile of the Jewish ark of the covenant,[2] a lost piece of ephemera spoken of in the Hebrew Bible and the subject of much scholarly discussion in the field of biblical archaeology.

Why did the *Jamaican* pioneers of the Ras Tafari movement, who were exposed to the teaching of a fellow Jamaican and black-advocate luminary called Marcus Garvey, regard an Ethiopian monarch as the "black man's God" or "Messiah returned"? What is unique about Selassie that he should be raised to divine status, above all other emperors of Ethiopia?

As is mentioned elsewhere in this anthology, at the beginning the Pan-Africanist (Black Nationalist and Afrocentric) message and mission of Marcus Garvey (1887–1940) were officially rejected in Jamaica, but the seeds were sown in the minds of a few black admirers. Tradition has it that Garvey had prophesied the crowning of a black king in Africa, which would be a sign to Blacks that the day of deliverance is near. Though the prophecy is, as yet, not verified from any of Garvey's writings or recorded speeches, a crowning of worldwide significance did occur in Africa—in Ethiopia, to be exact—that became an epoch-making event in the founding of Rastafari. On November 2, 1930, the diminutive but politically astute Negus Tafari Makonnen, son of Ras Makonnen, was crowned emperor of Ethiopia. His coronation was the culmination of a career marked by political shrewdness, intrigue, and movement through different ranks of the nobility of Ethiopia.[3]

Tafari Makonnen was born on July 23, 1892, and held the court title *Lij,* meaning "child of an important nobleman." While still a teenager he was appointed a provincial governor, after which he held the title *Dejazmach* (General) Tafari up to 1916. From 1916 to 1928 he held another high military title, that of *Ras,* meaning "head of an army," corresponding to a British duke or prince. From 1928 to 1930, Tafari Makonnen was Negus (King) Tafari, and at his coronation he earned the supreme court rank in Ethiopia, that of Negusa Nagast (King of Kings), to which he added his Christian baptismal name, Haile Selassie. He then became known to the world as Emperor Haile Selassie I, King of Kings, Elect of God, Conquering Lion of the Tribe of Judah. As noted by Clinton Hutton, Nathaniel Samuel Murrell, and Barry Chevannes in this book (see Chapters 2 and 3), the coronation of Haile Selassie as emperor of Ethiopia was front-page news in the leading Jamaican newspaper, the *Daily Gleaner,* and what fired the early preachers of the emerging Ras Tafari faith was the list of impressive names and titles of the emperor—titles they regarded as fulfilling certain passages in the Bible, namely, Revelation 19:16 and 5:5.[4]

Over the years, Rastafarians have searched through the biblical materials in quest of additional proof texts that "support" the divinity of His Imperial Majesty as well as the prestige and spiritual significance of his homeland, Ethiopia. Of special importance to Rastas is Psalm 87:4, which, in the King James Version, reads "I will make mention of Rahab and Babylon to them that know me: behold Philistia, and Tyre, with Ethiopia; this man was born there." Rastafarians believe that this verse speaks definitively of Haile Selassie, simply by the mention of the name Ethiopia (*Cush* in the Hebrew Bible, *A'ithiopia* in the Septuagint, the Greek version of the Hebrew Bible translated in the third century B.C.E.) and the nonspecific person "this man." The fact that Cush, or Ethiopia, was geographically imprecise in the Bible does not seem to affect the Rastafarian application of the passage to modern Ethiopia; nor is it a problem that the "this man" mentioned in the verse could be applied to any Ethiopian, not only Selassie. Psalm 87 is in praise of Zion and seems to be contrasting the mention of the odd person ("this man") who was born and lived in such important gentile regions as Philistia, Tyre, and Cush with the mention of several important persons ("this and that man") who were born in the royal Jewish city of Zion.

Because of their interest in the Bible and in Africa (the motherland), the lineage and divinity of Haile Selassie and the cruciality of Ethiopia as the new Zion are the two most enduring tenets of Rastafari. It is worth noting here that Ethiopian sources have also provided support for the Rastafarian belief in the prestigious lineage (though not the divinity) of Haile Selassie and the importance of Ethiopia as the new Zion. Article 2 of the revised Constitution of Ethiopia (1955), a brainchild of His Imperial Majesty and his gift to the people of Ethiopia, states: "The imperial dignity shall remain perpetually attached to the line of Haile Selassie I, descendant of King Sahle Selassie, whose line descends without interruption from the dynasty of Menelik I, son of the Queen of Ethiopia, the Queen of Sheba, and King Solomon of Jerusalem."[5]

Lineage Claims in the *Kebra Nagast*

The principal source of information supporting the lineage of Ethiopian emperors and Ethiopia as the new Zion is the *Kebra Nagast,* the Ethiopian national saga and cycle of legends. Since the Rastafarian claims made about Haile Selassie and Ethiopia hinge on the *Kebra Nagast,* exploring the nature and caliber of this document is crucial for an informed discussion on those claims. The *Kebra Nagast* was compiled during the late thirteenth or early fourteenth century C.E. and conveys two basic themes: the descent of Ethiopian kings from Solomon and the queen of Sheba and the transfer of the Jewish ark of the covenant to Ethiopia by Menelik I. American Bible Scholar David Allan Hubbard has identified three interrelated motives behind the compilation of the *Kebra Nagast:* political, patriotic, and religious. These motives can be identified in a statement from one of the compilers at the end of the work: "For I have laboured much for the glory of the land of Ethiopia [patriotic], for the going out of the heavenly Zion [religious], and for the King of Ethiopia [political]."[6]

The king in question, in the scribe's statement, was Yekuno Amlak (regency: 1270–1285), founder of the so-called Solomonid dynasty. The *Kebra Nagast* was published, seemingly, to justify the claims of the Solomonid dynasty over against those of the Zagwe family or dynasty, which ruled Ethiopia for approximately 150 years, from the twelveth to the late thirteenth century of this era.[7] Interestingly enough, the Zagwe family, which sprang from the Agau people and was perceived by ancient Ethiopians as being of Hamitic (not Semitic) stock, fought long wars of resistance against the kings of Axum. The Agau finally defeated the Axumite kings and ruled Ethiopia as the Zagwe dynasty. The *Kebra Nagast,* written with a pro-Semitic bias, implicitly denounces the Hamitic Zagwe dynasty thus: "for by the will of God every kingdom of the world was given to the seed of Shem [Semites] and slavery to the seed of Ham [Hamites]."[8]

As a literary piece the *Kebra Nagast* is highly rated by scholars, but they raise questions about its accuracy on historical grounds. Germane to our inquiry is the fact that the *Kebra Nagast,* in chapters 21 and 33, views the queen of Sheba as one and the same, as Candace, the queen of the Ethiopians mentioned in the New Testament (Acts 8:27), despite the colossal time period in history that separated the two queens. Further, in chapter 33 the *Kebra Nagast* asserts that Menelik, in his travels, "came into the country of the neighbourhood of Gaza. Now this is the Gaza which Solomon the king gave to the Queen of Ethiopia. And in the Acts of the Apostles Luke the Evangelist wrote, saying, 'He was the governor of the whole country of Gaza, an enunch of Queen Hendake [Candace].'" Unfortunately, the *Kebra Nagast*'s rendition of the passage in Acts is a misreading of the Greek text. What the *Kebra Nagast* renders as "governor of the whole country of Gaza" is supposed to be a translation of the Greek *epi pases tes gazes antes,* which really means "over all her treasure." The mention of Gaza in Acts 8:26 might have been the undoing (redaction) of the scribe when translating Acts 8:27, because of a deep desire to Christianize Ethiopia's history.[9]

Were Candace and the Ethiopian enunch really from modern Ethiopia, and was the queen of Sheba an Ethiopian monarch? The name Ethiopia in ancient literature, including the Bible, is often quite vague, describing the whole continent of Africa or the territories south-southeast of Egypt. Assessing the biblical references to Ethiopia is made very complicated by the fact that the Hebrew word *Cush,* which is translated *A'ithiopia* (Ethiopia) in the Septuagint, lacks a precise meaning. As Bible scholar and archaeologist Edward Ullendorff notes, "The Biblical 'Cush' is a vague term connoting the entire Nile

Valley, south of Egypt, including Nubia and Abyssinia."[10] Apropos of the Ethiopian and, by extension, Candace, the exegete Howard Marshall notes, "The man came from the country now known as Sudan (rather than modern Ethiopia) where he was a eunuch employed in the court service of the queen mother, who was known by the hereditary title of Candace and was the effective ruler of the country."[11] Even though Josephus refers to the queen of Sheba as the "Queen of Egypt and Ethiopia," the prevailing scholarly opinion concerning the queen of Sheba is that she was a monarch in Arabia, the geographical location of Sheba.[12]

The *Kebra Nagast* contends (chapters 48ff.) that the queen of Sheba had a child by Solomon, Menelik I, who abducted the Jewish ark of the covenant and resited it in Ethiopia. This belief is of critical importance to claims made concerning the prestigious lineage of Ethiopian rulers and Ethiopia as the new Zion. But, one might ask, is there evidence elsewhere to support these claims? Scholars, ancient and modern, have raised serious doubts about the historical validity of both contentions. Concerning the abduction of the ark by Menelik, Hubbard writes, "There exists no parallel account of this event in either rabbinical or Islamic literature although the story occurs in various forms on Ethiopian soil." He continues, "The story of the abduction of the ark appears to be of Ethiopian origin, for I have found no parallel to this in other Near Eastern lore."[13]

With reference to the issue of a sexual liaison between Solomon and the queen of Sheba from which Menelik resulted—and, by extension, from which Selassie descended—I contend that the argument is untenable. While one need not gainsay that Solomon *could* have had sexual intercourse with the queen or even have sired a child by her, I argue (as do others in this anthology) that if Solomon and the queen spent some time in bed together and gave birth to a son, the evidence drawn from 1 Kings 10 does not support it convincingly. Consequently, the Rastafarian claim that Haile Selassie descended from royal blood by way of Solomon cannot be proven conclusively from arguments that are based on Judeo-Christian Scriptures.

Do "extrabiblical" and non-Christian literary sources support the claim that Solomon and the queen of Sheba had a son who is an ancestor of Haile Selassie? Hubbard and Ullendorff have examined other literary sources (Jewish, Arabian, and Ethiopian) for corroborative evidence of a sexual union and offspring of Solomon and Sheba.[14] Of the Jewish sources examined,[15] only one, the *Alphabet of Ben Sira,* seems to have circulated the idea of a sexual intimacy between the two monarchs and a resulting offspring. The child, however, is called Nebuchadnezzar.[16] The Qur'an (Sura 27:15–45), which summarizes *Targum Sheni,* makes no mention of sex or offspring resulting from an alleged sexual encounter between the king and the queen, but Muslim commentators (the Al-Baidawi and Zamakhshari commentaries) make mention of traditions known to them that speak of Bilquis (Arabic name for the queen of Sheba) as Solomon's wife, and some also mention that a son, Ebna Hakim, resulted from the union. One commentary suggests that Solomon gave the queen in marriage to a tribal leader but mentions no offspring. Quite likely, the Arabic versions of the Solomon–queen of Sheba story were influenced by older Ethiopian versions of the same texts.[17]

Assessing Rasta Claims about Selassie's Divinity

Despite the somewhat shaky foundation of the *Kebra Nagast*'s support of Haile Selassie's Solomonic claims, Rastas are able to accept his Solomonic lineage without question because they posit a messianic dimension to his bestowed titles that, in turn, sub-
stantiates the lineage claims they make about him. For example, Ras Dread (formerly
Egbert) James of Spanish Town, who became a Rastafarian as a teenager in the 1950s,
regards Haile Selassie ("Power of the Trinity") as the divine answer to confound "alien
religion with [its] distorted and deceiving approach to defeat the black race in every
way." He holds:

> As the course of time unfold itself, time, which is the essence and owner of all things—time
> would use its tools at various times to work for the benefit of a defeated people. . . . It started
> first in 1892 [the birth of Selassie]. It then restarted in 1930 at the coronation of His Majesty.
> And he, as John the Baptist, lead the political and the economic free world for the race ad-
> vance itself. But there was and is something very deeper than the political and the economic
> where the black man is concerned: the spiritual and physiological [*sic*] awakening. . . . So,
> then . . . because of the subjectivity of all people and the length of that subjectivity, this
> Rastafari way of life tends to be very strange to its own people, the black man.[18]

Further, for many Rastas the Solomonic claims must be true since Haile Selassie's titles appear to point to his being no less than his own divine predecessor Jesus Christ,
reincarnated in this new dispensation. Such "overstanding" (understanding) comes
from "looking into the books" (a Rasta expression), such as the *Kebra Nagast* and the
Bible, following received Rastafarian traditions, and also from looking deeply into oneself. As the fifty-three-year-old elder Ras Sim of Negril, an adherent since the 1960s, explains, "By looking into myself I saw footsteps walk before I that's gone through the
history of man upon the earth. By studying books I saw the one who was before I. So,
I take this tradition: the Son of the Most High, His Imperial Majesty Haile Selassie I."
Sim confessed, "The Lord Jesus Christ manifested himself in such manifestation of His
Imperial Majesty Selassie I."[19] When asked, "So you would see His Majesty as the Lord
Jesus Christ?" Ras Elijah, a fifty-eight-year-old adherent since 1960, replied, "Yes, rein-
carnated in the present temple of His Majesty. . . . Same man, different dispensation,
different name."[20]

Ras Sim continued, "Yes, as I said to you, I have gone through the study of books
and of the Bible and I arrived at that conception based on his divinity and character of
His Imperial Majesty Haile Selassie I as the Lord Jesus Christ, who manifested himself
in that personality in this dispensation in Selassie I . . . so, we have studied about the
lineage of His Majesty and we have come to realize through prophecies and history as
living evidence of the Almighty—His Majesty, yes!" So, to fathom the true cosmic significance of being born black, Ras Sim explains, is to recognize oneself as being born
Rasta: "I was born Rasta, based upon my skin tone. I was born black. . . . The name
Rasta is not a locks thing . . . it belongs to a race. The African was named by the mama
and papa and it based upon the royalness of the Father that he have crowned with in

orderly to make us be royal sons and daughters of his. So we are named "Ras" because "Ras" is the head of the Father and it based upon his skin tone."[21]

Why the pioneers of the Ras Tafari movement and Rastafarians of today regard their faith as "Ras Tafari" when Haile Selassie ceased to be Ras from 1928 and became Negus up to his coronation remains a puzzle. Did Howell and his cohorts really understand the meaning and significance of the different titles? If they did, did they choose Ras Tafari because Tafari has a special appeal and rhymes with the letter *I* in "I-an-I"? The Negusa Nagast Tafari (or even the Negus Tafari) movement would have been more consonant with the historical realities pertaining to Haile Selassie's status in Ethiopia as of 1930.[22] That minor detail, however, need not detain us here. What deserves analysis at this point is the basic argument in support of Haile Selassie's divinity, drawn from his names and titles. What is behind the imperial names and titles that the Rastafarians find so appealing and mystifying?

Much can be learned from Ethiopian history concerning imperial titles in general and the titles of Haile Selassie in particular. Haile Selassie had no name or title that was unique to him. Imperial titles were either assumed by a ruler or conferred on the emperor in power by the Abun, head of the Ethiopian Orthodox Church (EOC), the established—and one might even say, national—Christian religious organization in Ethiopia. The popular ending titles used by many emperors were *King of the Kings of Ethiopia* (or the shortened form *King of Kings*) and *Elect of God* (meaning appointed by God). What is not popularly known, even among Rastafarians, is that the imperial title *King of Kings*, used by many emperors, was always territorial in force and indicated simply the most powerful ruler in Ethiopia. Ethiopia was, for centuries, ruled by regional leaders who would fight and scheme for national supremacy and the title *Negusa Nagast*, or King of Kings.

To isolate just one case of a titles dispute between rivals for the throne of Ethiopia, we mention the nineteenth-century rulers Yohannes IV and Menelik II. Yohannes was Ras of Tigre and Menelik, Negus of Shoa. These two rivals kept changing titles in a bid to assume and assert rulership of all Ethiopia, and only after an agreement between them in 1878 was Menelik II forced to drop the title *King of Kings* and to use instead the title *King of Shoa*. Yohannes IV was emperor of Ethiopia from 1872 to 1889, and after his death, Menelik II successfully reclaimed the title *King of Kings* and added to his title *Elect of God*, which had been used by Yohannes IV in his correspondence.

So, then, the imperial titles *King of Kings* and *Elect of God* were common in Ethiopia. Although Rastas hail the emperor as "King of Kings, Lord of Lords, Conquering Lion of the Tribe of Judah," the nomenclature *Lord of Lords* was never an imperial title in Ethiopia; the use of the term is probably influenced by a reading of Revelation 19:16. Abuna Yesehaq of the EOC contends that Haile Selassie's title *Light of the World* has also been of much significance to the Rastafarians. "This is not a traditional Ethiopian title for kings, and Emperor Haile Selassie I was the first Ethiopian king known as Light of the World—in fact, Rastafarians note very carefully that the title belongs to Christ and therefore justifies their argument regarding who the returned Messiah is."[23]

Concerning the adaptation *Conquering Lion of the Tribe of Judah,* the motto "The Lion of the Tribe of Judah hath prevailed," culled from Revelation 5:5, was used by Ethiopian emperors on their seals to indicate the Christian nature of the empire. This tradition goes back to the sixteenth century under Lebna Dengel. The motto would be in Geez (Ethiopic) and would precede the emperor's name and title(s).[24] During the reign of Selassie, the Ethiopic (Geez) motto was used to open all imperial decrees and proclamations, but the opening words of the English text of the 1942 proclamation establishing the *Negarit Gazeta* read "Conquering Lion of the Tribe of Judah, Haile Selassie I, Elect of God, Emperor of Ethiopia,[25] We proclaim as follows . . ."

Commenting on the English text vis-à-vis the Amharic text, Bible scholar Sven Rubenson observes:

> There are two important discrepancies here. The Gi'iz motto from Revelation 5 is incorrectly translated. The statement has become an attribute. And as a consequence, the pronoun . . . "we," which in the Amharic sets the motto clearly apart from the names and titles of the Emperor, has been moved after the titles, thereby permitting "Conquering Lion of the tribe of Judah" to become part of the titles. That this can hardly have been done intentionally is indicated also by the full stop after "Judah" in the Amharic version. This inaccuracy has been repeated in the legislation of the last twenty years . . . only occasionally is the correction made as in the French edition of the Civil Code of 1960, where the Gi'iz and Amharic is translated: "Il a vaincu, le lion de la tribu de Juda! Nous, Haile Selassie I, Elu de Dieu, Empereur d'Ethiopie."[26]

Rubenson also notes that a similar problem of translation affected the correspondence of Menelik II. Menelik would begin his letters "The Lion of the Tribe of Judah has Conquered. Menelik II, Elect of God, King of the Kings of Ethiopia . . ." But, says Rubenson, "whether the translations of Menelik's letters were made immediately in Ethiopia or in Europe, he almost invariably became 'The Conquering Lion of the Tribe of Judah' in English, French, Italian and German alike. Journalists and writers repeated the phrase and abbreviated it, so that by the time Menelik died he was 'the Lion of Judah' to the rest of the world."[27]

Some Rastafarians make much of the meaning of Tafari Makonnen's names and titles, especially the name Haile Selassie (Power of the Trinity) and the title *Ras* (Head); but since the former emperor had no unique name or title, appreciating the cogency of the argument for Selassie's prestige or divinity based on his names and titles is difficult. The words of Haile Selassie's friend and biographer Christine Sandford should prove instructive here. Speaking of the upbringing of the young Tafari Makonnen, she says, "His companions during these years were his cousin *Imeru Haile Selassie,* later to become *Ras,* and *Tafari Belaw.*"[28] So the names or titles *Haile, Selassie, Ras,* and *Tafari* are not unique to him. Further, perhaps a different view of Haile Selassie's lineage prestige would emerge if the record were set straight concerning the lineage and blood relationship of Ethiopian emperors.

The critical question is: Was there, as article 2 of the 1955 Constitution of Ethiopia claims, an unbroken line of blood-related rulers on the throne of Ethiopia, going back to King Solomon? According to Ullendorff, "The historical fiction [that] an uninterrupted line of kings descended from Menelik I, the son of King Solomon and the Queen of Sheba, has very deep roots in Ethiopia and must be one of the most powerful and influential national sagas anywhere in the world."[29] But for any historian to adduce evidence, beyond reasonable doubt, to answer the above question in the affirmative is extremely difficult, even impossible. Apart from the problems surrounding the existence of a Menelik I and the rulership of Ethiopia for approximately 150 years by the non-Solomonic Zagwe dynasty, we should note that imperial rulership in Ethiopia had more to do with power than with primogeniture or strict lineal descent. We should also bear in mind that the monarchy in Ethiopia collapsed about 1753 and was only restored *a century later,* when Tewodros, or Theodore, became emperor. As historian John Markakis observes, "The period known in Ethiopian history as the 'Age of Princes' [or 'Age of Judges'] lasted until the middle of the nineteenth century. During this time, the state dissolved into its provincial components, which in turn became involved in an endless and ultimately inconclusive struggle for supremacy. The eclipse of the monarchy was followed by the rise of numerous provincial dynasties which competed fiercely for national ascendancy."[30]

Emperors Tewodros (Theodore) (1855–1868), Yohannes IV (1872–1889), Menelik II (1889–1913), and Haile Selassie I (1930–1975) reached the throne only after they emerged the most powerful men in the country. They were not blood-related in any close sense, though all claimed to be of the Solomonic dynasty. Since the restoration of the monarchy in 1855, only Lij Yasu (1913–1916) ascended the throne of Ethiopia based on primogeniture; he was the grandson of Menelik II.[31] Ras Makonnen, Haile Selassie's father, was only a first cousin to Menelik II. In 1909, while suffering from a stroke, Menelik II appointed Lij Yasu as his heir and successor.[32] Because of his Muslim profession, Lij Yasu was deposed by the Council of State in 1916. His successor was Zauditu, Menelik's daughter, and Tafari Makonnen became an heir to the throne.

What comes through loud and clear from the above analysis is the discovery that Rastafarian belief in Haile Selassie as divine is based on the belief that the emperor had unique names and titles and shared a prestigious lineage. The point should be made that it is the cogency of a "belief that" argument that lends credibility and plausibility to a "belief in" posture. This is a neglected dimension in the voluminous literature, scholarly and otherwise, on Rastafari—but it is essential to separate historical facts from faith confession, since the verification of a theological confession is not generally a preoccupation of the history of religions (the scientific study of religion).

Relation to Christianity and the EOC

What is the relationship between Haile Selassie and the Ethiopian Orthodox Church (EOC)? How did Haile Selassie himself and the EOC he championed regard the Rastafarian interpretation of the titles and belief in the divinity of the former emperor? In reference to the first question, the 1955 Ethiopian Constitution stated that "the Church has transmitted legitimacy to the Emperor by anointment, and has generally upheld his authority, though in turn it has demanded his support." Article 5 of the 1974 Draft Constitution says, "The Emperor professes the Ethiopian Orthodox faith and all religious denominations in the country shall mention Ethiopia and the name of the Emperor." With regard to the second question, on his visit to Jamaica in 1966, Selassie responded to the publicity and overwhelmingly warm reception he received with gratitude and humility but was distressed by the thought that Rastas were worshiping him as God. The emperor's response to his experience with Rastafarians in Jamaica can be deduced from statements made by him through Abuna Yesehaq, whom Emperor Haile Selassie sent to establish the EOC in Jamaica in 1970.

In an interview with Rastafarian journalist and author Barbara Blake Hannah, Abuna Yesehaq indicated that His Imperial Majesty mandated him to establish the church in Jamaica, and he quotes the emperor as saying, concerning Rastas, "I want you to help these people. My heart is broken because of the situation of these people. Help them to find the True God. Teach them."[33]

In the section of his book *The Ethiopian Tewahedo Church* (1989) that deals with Rastafari, Abuna Yesehaq comments thus: "The emperor was not God to the Ethiopian people and other nations. He was a religious man who was elected king of Ethiopia. While one can appreciate the respect, love, and devotion given to him, as a clergyman, it is my duty to speak the truth and to strongly advise my brethren and sisters, young and old, to be aware of the commandment of God: 'Thou shall have no other gods before me—for I am a jealous God."[34] The Abun correctly pointed out that some Rastas do not see the emperor as God but, rather, see Christ through the emperor's "person." For them, the emperor "is the Bible, the handbook and effective instrument through which they can learn about Christ."[35]

This raises the important question of the relationship between Rastafari and the EOC, for whom belief in the work and person of Christ is central, as it is for all of Christianity. How does the EOC itself relate to the rest of the Christian community in Jamaica while addressing the Rasta's novel interpretation of vitally important church doctrines? As Verena Reckord correctly noted, the Jamaican EOC

> is not an outgrowth of the Rastafarian movement, although it manifests itself predominantly in that area, but does not exclude non-Rastafarians. An attempt was made to have Ethiopian Church music translated for use in Jamaica. But band leader Cedric Brooks, who composed certain works for use in the church, advises that Ethiopian Church music will have to be introduced gradually because the language is not sufficiently understood, for part of the liturgy is in Ge'ez, and some of the customs can only with very great difficulty be translated outside of the language.[36]

The EOC in the Western Hemisphere was embroiled in controversy in the mid-1990s over whether Abuna Yesehaq or Abuna Paulos is the legitimate archbishop of the church in the region. This provoked a split in the ranks of the EOC in Jamaica that is of concern not only to its members but also to the Rastafarians and the Jamaica Council of Churches (JCC), to which the EOC is an observer. After studying the issues involved in the controversy, the JCC ruled that Abuna Paulos is the person it regards as the current archbishop.[37] But the questions remain of how the Rastafarians who regard themselves as members of the EOC view that ruling by the JCC. Did they welcome the verdict as an amicable solution in the spirit of ecumenism, or did they regard it as Babylon's interference in Africa's religous concerns?

In a recent television interview on the Jamaica Broadcasting Corporation, interviewer Ian Boyne put to Abuna Yesehaq the question of the Rastafarian view that Selassie is God, the divine and "reincarnated Christ." To this the Abuna replied, "To the Rastafarian he is God but to the Ethiopian and to the Ethiopian Orthodox Church he is not God. . . . He is, he was, a member of the Ethiopian Orthodox Church and a defender of the Ethiopian Orthodox Church."[38] In the same interview, the Abuna indicated that Bob Marley was baptized into the Ethiopian Orthodox Church in Jamaica about seven months prior to his death. According to the Abun, Rita Marley, Bob Marley's widow, was baptized in 1973, and officials of the Ethiopian Orthodox Church participated in the funeral service for Bob Marley, whom they considered one of their own.

The recorded speeches of His Imperial Majesty reveal a man who was, in profession, simply a Christian, a family man, and a politician—nothing more. In an address he gave at the 1966 World Congress on Evangelism in Berlin, the emperor urged, "The love shown in Christ by our God to mankind should constrain all of us who are followers and disciples of Christ to do all in our power to see to it that the Message of Salvation is carried to those of our fellows for whom Christ our Saviour was sacrificed but who have not had the benefit of hearing the Good News." He urged, "Christians, let us arise and . . . labour to lead our brothers and sisters to our Saviour Jesus Christ who only can give life in its fullest sense."[39]

In the "Religion" section of the emperor's *Selected Speeches,* not only does the compiler describe Haile Selassie as "a devout Christian," but the emperor indicates his Christian orientation and reliance on God. While accepting formally the title *Defender of the Faith,* the emperor said, "Holy Fathers, We have welcomed the title you have given Us, Defender of the Faith, with great honour. May Almighty God grace your name. May God welcome your work. We have received this title given Us by you Holy Fathers, with religious reverence. May your prayers help Us in Our effort to fulfil the task entrusted to Us."[40] Thoroughly cognizant of his own position in political terms, the emperor yet resisted a cosmic dimension to his titles. By adhering to Jesus Christ and rejecting the Rastafarian attribution of deity, Ras Tafari himself remained a Christian and was not, theologically speaking, a Rastafarian.

The Rastafarian movement has leveled many necessary and commendable chants of indictment at Babylon over the years. As the movement continues its trek to Zion, it must examine the evidence undergirding its fundamental tenets, lest its attractive sociocultural edifice begins to reveal the cracks that result from a faulty historical-theological foundation.

Notes

1. Cf. Joseph Owens, *Dread: The Rastafarians of Jamaica* (Kingston: Sangster's Book Stores, 1976), 14–18; Barry Chevannes, *Rastafari: Roots and Ideology* (Syracuse, N.Y.: Syracuse University Press, 1994), 146–48, 152.

2. For a fascinating, if unconvincing, defense of Ethiopia as the location of the ark of the covenant, see Graham Hancock's *The Sign and the Seal* (London: William Heinemann, 1992). See a review of Hancock's book by Ethiopian scholar Ephraim Isaac in *Biblical Archaeology Review* 19, 4 (July–August 1993): 60–63. The focal point of worship in the Ethiopian Orthodox Church is the *Tabot* (ark)—more precisely, two pieces of altar slabs *representing* the Jewish ark of the covenant.

3. Haile Selassie was effectively emperor since April 3, 1930, immediately after the death of Empress Zauditu; see His Majesty's biography by Christine Sandford, *The Lion of Judah Hath Prevailed* (New York: Macmillan Co., 1955), 55. See also Bahru Zewde's insightful essay "Economic Origins of the Absolute State in Ethiopia (1916–1935)," *Journal of Ethiopian Studies* 17 (November 1984): 1–24.

4. "And he hath . . . a name written, KING OF KINGS and LORD OF LORDS" and "The LION OF THE TRIBE OF JUDAH, the root of David, HATH PREVAILED," respectively (KJV).

5. See Sandford *Lion of Judah*, 60.

6. David Allan Hubbard, "The Literary Sources of the *Kebra Nagast*" (Ph.D. diss., University of St. Andrews, Scotland, 1956), 351–54, 359; Edward Ullendorf, *Ethiopia and the Bible* (London: Oxford University Press, 1968), 74–75, 141.

7. David Phillipson, *African Archaeology* (Cambridge: Cambridge University Press, 1985), 194–95.

8. For a discussion on the so-called Hamitic curse, see Nathaniel Samuel Murrell and Lewin Williams, "The Black Biblical Hermeneutics of Rastafari," Chapter 19, below.

9. Ullendorf, *Ethiopia and the Bible,* 9–10; Hubbard, "Literary Sources of the *Kebra Nagast*," 359.

10. Ullendorf, *Ethiopia and the Bible,* 5, 14–15. See also Joseph E. Harris, *Pillars in Ethiopian History: The William Leo Hansberry African History Notebook,* vol. 1, no. 1 (Washington, D.C.: Howard University Press, 1981), 63; Ivan Van Sertima, ed., *Black Women in Antiquity* (New Brunswick, N.J.: Transaction Books, 1984), 12.

11. I. Howard Marshall, *The Acts of the Apostles* (Leicester: Intervarsity Press, 1980), 162. See also F. F. Bruce, *The Acts of the Apostles,* 2d ed. (London: Tyndale Press, 1952), 191–92; and Ullendorf, *Ethiopia and the Bible,* 9.

12. Josephus *Antiquities* 8.6.5; Charles Laymon, ed., *The Interpreter's One-Volume Commentary on the Bible* (Nashville: Abingdon Press, 1971), 189; J. D. Douglas, ed., *The New Bible Dictionary* (Leicester: Intervarsity Press, 1962), 1172; J. A. Montgomery, *Kings,* International Critical Commentary (1951), 215ff. Larry Williams and Charles S. French contend, though, that "southern Arabia and Abyssinia (Ethiopia) were virtually identical in language, religion, and racial composition," and that Sheba "incorporated both Ethiopia and southern Arabia" (in Van Sertima, *Black Women in Antiquity,* 13).

13. Hubbard, "Literary Sources of the *Kebra Nagast*," 284–308.

14. Ibid.; Ullendorf, *Ethiopia and the Bible,* 135–45.

15. These are Josephus, the Talmud (containing oral law and rabbinical comments), the early and later Midrashim (containing didactic, sermonic expositions), *Targum Sheni* (second Aramaic commentary on Esther 1 and 2), and the *Alphabet of Ben Sira.*

16. Ullendorf, *Ethiopia and the Bible,* 139; Hubbard, "Literary Sources of the *Kebra Nagast*," 292.

17. Ullendorf, *Ethiopian and the Bible,* 138; Hubbard, "Literary Sources of the *Kebra Nagast*," 293–95, 307.

18. Ras Dread (Egbert) James, interview with Clinton Chisholm at Montego Bay, 1995.

19. Ras Sim, interview with William D. Spencer, Gloria Noelliste, and Clinton Chisholm, Negril, 1995.

20. Ras Elijah, interview with William D. Spencer, Glorian Noelliste, and Clinton Chisholm, Negril, 1995.

21. Ras Sim, interview with Spencer, Noelliste, and Chisholm.

22. In fact, in the early years, some Rastafarians (Robert Hinds and his followers) did call themselves the more defensible "King of Kings People." See Chevannes, *Rastafari,* 126ff.

23. Abuna (Archbishop) Yesehaq, *The Ethiopian Tewahedo Church: An Integrally African Church* (New York: Vantage Press, 1989), 220.

24. See the excellent article by Sven Rubenson, "The Lion of the Tribe of Judah: Christian and/or Imperial Title," *Journal of Ethiopian Studies* 3, 2 (July 1965): 75–85.

25. The English text of the Civil Code Proclamation of 1960 begins similarly.

26. Rubenson, "Lion of the Tribe of Judah," 85.

27. Ibid., 84.

28. See Owens, *Dread,* 102–24; Sandford, *Lion of Judah,* 28.

29. Edward Ullendorff, *The Ethiopians* (London: Oxford University Press, 1965), 64.

30. John Markakis, *Ethiopia: Anatomy of a Traditional Polity* (London: Oxford University Press, 1974), 18. For a chronology of Ethiopian rulers since the thirteenth century, see Czeslaw Jesman, *The Ethiopian Paradox* (London: Institute of Race Relations, 1963), 77–82.

31. See Christopher Clapham, "Imperial Leadership in Ethiopia," *African Affairs* 68, 271 (April 1969): 112.

32. Sandford, *Lion of Judah,* 13; Harold G. Marcus, "The Last Years of the Reign of the Emperor Menelik, 1906–13," *Journal of Semitic Studies* 9 (1964): 231.

33. See the report in the *Sunday Magazine* of the *Sunday Gleaner,* November 25, 1984, 2, 3, 11.

34. Yesehaq, *Ethiopian Tewahedo Church,* 225.

35. Ibid.

36. Verena Reckord, "Rastafarian Music: An Introductory Study," *Jamaica Journal* 11, 2 (August 1977): 11.

37. For a perspective from Abuna Paulos on aspects of the controversy, see the television program *Profile,* aired on the Jamaica Broadcasting Corporation (JBC TV), Sunday, July 23, 1995.

38. See *Profile,* JBC TV, Sunday, July 9, 1995.

39. See Carl F. H. Henry and W. Stanley Moneyham, eds., *One Race, One Gospel, One Task* (Minneapolis: World Wide Publications, 1967), 1: 21–20.

40. Haile Selassie I, *Selected Speeches of His Imperial Majesty Haile Selassie I 1918–1967* (Addis Ababa, Ethiopia: Imperial Ethiopian Ministry of Information, 1967), 641; also 625, 633–35, 637, 639.

11

Chanting Down Babylon Outernational: The Rise of Rastafari in Europe, the Caribbean, and the Pacific

FRANK JAN VAN DIJK

Few modern-day movements have spread as widely as Rastafari. Born in the ghettos of Kingston, Jamaica, in the 1930s, today the movement of "Jah people" is chanting down Babylon "outernational." In Canada, particularly in Toronto, the Rastafari movement represents a vital force in the West Indian community. As Randal Hepner describes in Chapter 12 of this anthology, Rastafari is also rooted firmly in several, if not most, urban centers in the United States. In many Central and South American countries, principal among them Belize and the northern part of Brazil, Rastafarian beliefs and ideas are said to be making significant inroads. Across the Atlantic, as Neil Savishinsky related in Chapter 7, growing numbers of youths from Ghana, Senegal, Ethiopia, Zimbabwe, and other African countries are adopting the rhetoric and, in other instances, also the deeper meanings of Rastafari. In Europe, particularly in England, the Netherlands, Germany, and France, the dreadlocks and the red, gold, and green have become familiar symbols even among white youth. On the other side of the globe, in the Pacific and most notably in New Zealand, young people of color are discussing their history and identity from a Rastafarian perspective.

The international dissemination of Rastafari occurred along two different but often coinciding routes. Like all cultures, it traveled with those who journeyed around the globe. Through migration and travel, Jamaican Rastafarians personally carried their ideas and beliefs to sometimes unexpected places and created new bridgeheads for the movement's further diffusion. In all of their encounters with other people, not only abroad but also in Jamaica, they consciously or unconsciously communicated something of their thought, style, and behavior to the new culture. Sometimes they inspired others, but often they encountered incomprehension and even hostility.

Rastafari also travels through the worldwide and ever-expanding web of media and communication channels. Stored on vinyl and tape or floating freely on radio and television waves, the message of Jah people, cached in the powerful rhymes and pulsating rhythms of reggae, travels almost without restriction and sweeps "Rastology" into even the remotest corners of the earth.

Yet, despite Rastafari's almost global dispersion, dating back as far as the early 1970s and in some cases before, research on the international dimensions of Rastafari is still in its infancy. With the exception of a handful of authoritative studies based on original research, most of the information on Rasta International is scattered in often unpublished and sometimes obscure sources.[1] Therefore, as one attempts to focus on the movement's rise and the reactions to its emergence in Europe, the Caribbean, and the Pacific during the 1970s and 1980s,[2] it is necessary to glue together some of those bits and pieces of information.

Rastafari in England

Jamaican migrants of Rastafarian faith clearly laid the foundations for the movement's rise in England during the 1950s and 1960s. During that period, well over two hundred thousand Jamaicans, still British subjects with British passports, migrated to the urban centers of England. The majority were of rural origins, poor and scarcely educated but determined to make a better living abroad. "Willing to make sacrifices in order to achieve their original ambitions," they worked long and hard in often undesirable, low-paying jobs. Most identified with the British way of life, however, and hoped to find social acceptance and recognition in a society that had shaped so much—and yet so little—of the world they had left behind.[3] When the economic situation deteriorated during the late 1950s and early 1960s, racial tensions and discrimination gradually intensified. The black migrants unexpectedly encountered an alien and sometimes hostile society in which they increasingly found themselves unwanted and unemployed, socially and geographically isolated in all-black communities, as well as the targets of racist assaults and harassment from Whites. For many, the dream of social acceptance and equal opportunities turned out to be a bitter illusion. It was against the backdrop of these experiences that the rise of Rastafari in England occurred.

Although the movement's presence in England dated back to the first wave of West Indian migration, the Rastafarians were initially very few in numbers. As early as 1955, an attempt to organize a "Rastafarian-oriented" United Afro–West Indian Brotherhood in London[4] failed, and the movement remained unorganized and hardly noticed. During the late 1960s, however, two developments fertilized the soil in which Rastafari was to sprout. Black Power groups such as the Racial Adjustment Action Society, led by Michael X (de Freitas), and the Universal Colored People's Association, led by Obi Egbuna, forcefully began to articulate black people's common interests and their right, if not obligation, to self-fulfillment. As Ernest Cashmore, a Jamaican Rastafari scholar in Britain, points out, despite being small and short-lived,

British Black Power paved the way for the "awareness necessary for the growth of the later Rastafarian movement."[5]

No less essential in raising awareness was music. Since the early 1960s, record companies and local sound systems had actively marketed Jamaican rhythm and blues, ska, and rock steady. With the advent of a new style known as reggae, "oppositional songs began to predominate, with Rasta and African themes increasingly working themselves into the music. The increasing preponderance of this 'roots' music, with its 'harder' rhythms and more 'conscious' lyrics . . . were just some of the signs of a much wider process of politicisation occurring in the black community."[6] Both the message of the Black Power advocates and the Africa-conscious lyrics of Rasta-inspired reggae singers found a receptive ear among a young black audience that was confronted with declining opportunities and increasing discrimination.

Around the same time, the efforts of the few British-based Rastafarians to create an organizational foundation began to bear fruit. In 1968, Jamaican-born migrants in London founded the Universal Black Improvement Organization (UBIO) and its political wing, the People's Democratic Party. The UBIO was primarily an attempt to revive Marcus Garvey's once mighty Universal Negro Improvement Association and its political counterpart, the People's Political Party. But the new organization also included Rasta-oriented members.[7] Through their meetings and other activities, they gradually reinforced an already growing interest in Rastafari among young West Indians drawn to the movement through reggae.

In May 1972 two of UBIO's founding members, Amanuel Foxe and Norman Adams, went on "a fact-finding mission" to Jamaica, where they met with the archimandrite (bishop) of the Ethiopian Orthodox Church (EOC), Laike Mariam Mandefro, to whom they conveyed their wish to be instructed in the faith and to forge bonds with the Ethiopian World Federation (EWF). Founded in the United States in an effort to assist the besieged Ethiopians during their war with Italy (1935–1941), the EWF had always been closely associated with Rastafari. Since it was officially endorsed by Emperor Haile Selassie and also administered the imperial land grant in Ethiopia during the 1950s, many Jamaican Rastas sought affiliation with the New York–based federation and founded numerous formal and informal "Locals." Some of these maintained close ties with the Ethiopian Orthodox Church, the ancient orthodox Christian religion of the empire, which had established a branch in Jamaica in 1970.

As a result of their visit, Foxe and Adams obtained permission to establish the first British branch of the EWF. In August 1972, Yohannes Local 33 Emporer opened its doors on London's Portobello Road, soon to be followed by branches in Birmingham and Leicester.[8] Two years later, at the continual requests of several EWF members, Mandefro (later known as Abuna Yesehaq) visited London to establish formally the Ethiopian Orthodox Church in England.[9] Many Rastafarians, particularly in the EWF, valued the official religion of Ethiopia and the emperor as essential links to African culture and identity. Others, however, found it difficult to accept the EOC's hierarchical organization, liturgy, and ritual, which in many respects closely resembled that of the despised Roman Catholic Church. Most important, as a Christian church, the EOC baptized in the name of "Yesos Christos" instead of "Jah Rastafari." As in Jamaica, therefore, the relationship between the British Rastafarians and the EOC was to become a highly ambivalent one.

Partly as a result of these differences, one of the founders of the EWF in Britain had, at some time during 1972, established a British branch of the Twelve Tribes of Israel, an organization that, back home in Jamaica, was rapidly emerging as one of the most influential groups within the movement. Led by the prophet Gad, the Jamaican Twelve Tribes included in its membership many middle-class adherents, intellectuals, and leading reggae stars. Accepting Jesus Christ as having revealed himself as their Lord and Savior in the personality of His Imperial Majesty Emperor Haile Selassie I, the Tribes represented a vibrant, and above all, "respectable" version of Rastafari in Jamaica. Efficiently organized, yet liberal in its doctrines, the Reggae House of Rastafari (as the British Twelve Tribes organization was known) soon exerted a strong influence over the movement in England also, establishing branches in Brixton, London, and Old Trafford, Birmingham.[10]

The impact of these groups notwithstanding, the organizational structure of Rastafari in England remained diffuse and fragmented. As in Jamaica, many British Rastafarians were highly critical of the strictly organized EWF, EOC, and Twelve Tribes and chose to remain unaffiliated to any of them. Yet, due to its close contacts with Jamaica, the core of the British movement reflected the strong religious orientation of Jamaican Rastafari.

By the mid-1970s, just as the still small but gradually expanding movement began to take shape, two developments drastically changed its outlook. In September 1974, Emperor Haile Selassie I was deposed and the "promised land" brought under the rule of a Marxist-oriented junta. Although the Ethiopian Orthodox Church pressured its members to give up their belief in the divinity of the Lion of Judah, most initially dismissed reports of the emperor's death as Babylonian lies. Eventually, however, they had to acknowledge the "disappearance" of the Messiah, even if many maintained that it was only a temporary withdrawal from the earthly scene.

Around the same time, reggae experienced its definitive breakthrough into mainstream pop culture. One of the many different reasons for its success was Island Records's ingenious marketing of Bob Marley and the Wailers. Their tours of the United States and Europe and the release of their 1975 *Live* album, recorded at the London Lyceum, gave a decisive boost to reggae's conquest of the international hit charts. The music and the militant message of the Rastafarian "soul rebels" made a tremendous impact, not only on an increasingly conscious black audience but also on considerable numbers of white youths.

In a sense, both developments served to secularize the movement. With the disappearance of Haile Selassie, preoccupation with the reverence of Ethiopia and its emperor gradually gave way to broader concerns. The international success of reggae, for its part, prompted numerous youths to adopt elements of the movement's ideology and symbolism. While some subscribed to the religious beliefs, most embraced the political, social, and cultural message of Rastafari. Many others, however, merely adopted the outward trappings, notably the dreadlocks and the red, gold, and green paraphernalia, as fashionable elements of a major new style. As a result, there emerged a highly diverse Rasta-reggae subculture.

The popularity of reggae music was not the only thing that contributed to the growing appeal of Rastafari in Great Britain. During the 1970s, the economic situation in England had steadily deteriorated. This especially affected the second generation of black migrants, who saw themselves deprived of chances. On top of chronic unemployment, inadequate education, poor housing, and meager social benefits, many faced a "crisis of identity." Neither entirely West Indian nor British, they fell—as it were—between two cultures. For quite a few youths, the Rasta-reggae complex, with its unequivocal pride in and passionate assertion of the African heritage and its forceful denunciation of white hypocrisy, provided powerful points of identification.

The sudden appearance of so many young Dreadlocks did not remain unnoticed. As crime and violence in the urban centers increased, the press began to blame the Rastafari. With headlines such as "Lost Tribes on the Warpath" and "A West Indian Mafia Organisation Called Rastafarians," some tabloids effectively branded the Rastas as a new type of street gang, the worst among "the black muggers" terrorizing neighborhoods, dealing drugs, and preying on defenseless, elderly women. The police added fuel to these tensions by heavily patrolling in black areas and authoritatively confirming already widely held prejudices against the Rastafari. After clashes between young Blacks and the police in Handsworth, Birmingham, in 1977, a local police report (published by the "yellow" press) investigating the causes of the riots concluded that the vast majority of the crimes committed in the area could be attributed to "a particular group—some 200 youths of West Indian origin or descent—who have taken on the appearance of followers of the Rastafarian faith by plaiting their hair in locks and wearing green, gold and red woollen hats." The author's distinction between a "criminalised Dreadlock subculture" and "the true Rastafarians" was completely lost in the media coverage.[11]

The report had a devastating effect on the image of the Rastafarians among the general public, which simply considered every Dreadlocks with a knitted "tea-cozy hat" a Rasta and thus, a priori, a suspect. Similar views were held in official circles, and as a result, quite a few Rastas were remanded in jail, where they were treated shamefully and forcibly trimmed and shaven. Despite repeated requests and loud protests, the British authorities refused to acknowledge that, for many, Rasta was more than a fashionable style. Claims of adherence to the officially recognized Ethiopian Orthodox Church were of little use either, since the church stated that "long hair is not a requirement" for membership. Similarly, the Jamaican High Commission in London informed the Home Office that, in Jamaica, dreadlocks and beards were not regarded as valid religious symbols.[12]

The religious core of the movement watched these developments with sorrow. Some, such as the Rastafarian poet Julia Roberts, made no secret of who they thought should be blamed for the crisis:

> Hey you false RASTA out dere!
> Bout seh you ah locks up yu hair,
> You don't know what locks is all about.
> You tink is new fashion jus com' out?
> You don't even deal in the praising of Jah![13]

Others took action. The newly founded Rastafari Universal Zion (RUZ), for example, actively sought to improve relations with and within the community. Based in Tottenham, the group started a government-sponsored training project and Saturday school for the local youth, while its headquarters also served as an art-and-crafts shop and advisory service. Led by the magnetic Jah Bones, RUZ soon became one of the most visible Rastafarian organizations in England.[14]

Unorganized, internally divided, and without access to the media, the Rastafarians initially had little success correcting their negative image. Ironically, it was another riot that eventually helped produce a more positive attitude toward Rasta in England. In April 1981, the police clamped down on the depressed South London neighborhood of Brixton to curb rising crime rates. They stopped and searched some 950 persons and arrested over 100, more than half of whom were black.[15] When rumor spread that a policeman had stabbed a black youngster, Brixton burst into flames. During the weekend of April 10–12, hundreds of youths, among them many Dreadlocks, took to the streets, looted stores, attacked buildings, and injured over 250 law enforcers. It was the most serious "race riot" London had so far experienced. The smoke had barely lifted in July when the riots spread to several other cities.

Although many believed the Rastafarians to be among the prime offenders in these disorders, Lord Scarman, chairing the commission of inquiry into the Brixton uprising, later concluded that "there was no suggestion in argument, nor any indication in evidence, that the Rastafarians, as a group or by their doctrines, were responsible for the outbreak of disorder or the ensuing riots. The Rastafarians, their faith and their aspirations, deserve more understanding and more sympathy than they get from the British people. The true Rastafarian is deeply religious, essentially humble and sad."[16] Scarman warned the Rastafarians of the risk of being "overwhelmed by the wild and the lawless," but his highly publicized report clearly demonstrated that the movement was not the "terror gang" it was commonly portrayed to be.

Within months of Scarman's inquiry, the Catholic Commission for Racial Justice (CCRJ), an advisory body to the Roman Catholic Conference of Bishops, published a report on the Rastafarian movement in which it urged the authorities to recognize Rastafari as a valid religion and to "scrupulously avoid harassment and discrimination against Rastafarians." The commission recommended that the established churches enter into a constructive dialogue with the Rastafarians and make their premises available to the movement.[17] The latter suggestion provoked sharp reactions from conservative newspapers, which accused the CCRJ of defending "a little-known anti-Semitic sect committed to racial division" and propagating marijuana-smoking in churches.[18]

In spite of such conservative condemnations, Scarman's inquiry and the CCRJ's report signaled important steps toward the accommodation of Rastafari in British society. Although relations often remained ambiguous, during the 1980s both the authorities and several Rastafarian groups worked hard to improve their mutual understanding. Harshly criticized by Scarman for its lack of imagination and heavy policing methods, the constabulary devised several projects to foster better relations with the black communities. In turn, many Rastafarians became actively involved in community centers and youth projects. In December 1982, for example, members of the EWF and the Rastafarian Women's Organization established the Rastafarian Advisory Center. Apart from providing legal assistance to Rastas who ran into trouble with the law, the center set up educational programs and workshops and aimed to to provide information about the movement and its faith to the public.[19]

In early 1983, in an effort to improve relations within the still divided movement, several Rastafarian groups and individuals—excluding the always solitary Twelve Tribes of Israel—organized a conference in Brixton. Initially, some groups agreed to work under the umbrella of the EWF; but when disagreements arose, members of Yohannes Local 33 Emporer turned for leadership to Prince Asfa Wossen, Haile Selassie's eldest son and heir to the Ethiopian throne, who had lived in exile in London since the 1974 revolution. The crown prince concluded that both the federation and the Rastafarian movement had become paralyzed by "personality cults," and that their efforts to uplift Ethiopia and the Ethiopians were "ineffective, uncoordinated and haphazard."[20]

On July 1, 1983, Wossen therefore put an end, at least formally, to the existence of the federation—a decision undoubtedly inspired by hopes to strengthen his control over the "royalist" Rastas and others supporting the struggle against the Ethiopian junta. To replace the old Federation, the crown prince established the Imperial Ethiopian World Federation (IEWF) and issued two royal charters: one for the Asfa Wossen Local 1 in England and another for the Zara Yaqob Local 2 in Jamaica. Amanuel Foxe was appointed international president of the IEWF. In 1984, according to his own claim, he led a massive rally against the regime of Haile Mariam Mengistu in Ethiopia. Not long after this event, however, Foxe decided to return to Jamaica because, in his words, "the Emperor told me to use the Federation to strengthen the movement here [in Jamaica]."[21] His departure in a sense symbolized the extent to which the British and the Jamaican movement were still entwined.

Although some estimated the movement to number some twenty-five thousand adherents during the early 1980s, relatively little was heard of the British Rastafarians after 1985. Only the court case of Trevor Dawkins, a Rastafarian who had applied for a government job but was turned down because of his dreadlocks, made headlines. The court not only ruled in favor of Dawkins but also recognized the Rastafarians as "a protected ethnic group" under The Race Relations Act of 1976. In a sense, the ruling formally sealed the Rastafarians' long quest for recognition and acceptance in England.

Rastafari on the European Continent

On the European continent, young black migrants, from both Africa and the Caribbean, also developed a serious interest in Rastafari. By the early 1980s, several major European cities with sizable migrant communities were homes to small, informal groups that, to varying degrees, had adopted elements of the movement. Though, in general, reggae music functioned as the initial source of inspiration, personal contacts with visiting Jamaican or British Rastas and reggae artists undoubtedly served to further disseminate Rastafarian discourse. In the absence of research, however, few details are known about the Rasta communities that are said to flourish in Germany, France, and Portugal, in particular. Only in the Netherlands did the movement attract the attention of researchers.

During his fieldwork among Surinamese youths in Rotterdam, Dutch sociologist Peter E. J. Buiks found that virtually all his informants had turned to Rastafari after they had settled in the Netherlands. Experiences of racism and discrimination, the impact of roots reggae, and personal contacts with Rastafarian musicians from England had drawn them into the movement. Although the majority conceived Rasta as a lifestyle rather than a religion, a small group also subscribed to the religious beliefs and codes of behavior. However, only a few of these religiously oriented Rastas in Rotterdam spoke about repatriation to Ethiopia. Most longed for a return to Suriname, to settle in the interior and start self-sufficient agricultural communes.[22]

Dutch social theorist Livio Sansone reached similar conclusions on the basis of his research in Amsterdam, where, around 1980, there existed three different groups, the main one being an unauthorized branch of the Twelve Tribes of Israel. Due to a lack of meeting places and leadership, however, the organizations soon fell apart.[23] Nevertheless, Amsterdam is still regarded as the major center of Rastafarian activity on the European continent. Smaller, less organized, and far less politicized than its British counterpart, the movement never had a societal impact comparable to that in England; neither has it been associated with criminal behavior. The semilegal status of "soft drugs," the absence of serious riots, and "the vibrant counterculture" of Amsterdam no doubt contributed to Rastafari's relatively low profile in the Netherlands.[24]

While, just as in England, some white youths became seriously involved in Rastafari, even to including its religious aspects, for many who adopted its outward adornment Rasta-reggae was primarily a style, comparable to punk, new wave, disco or heavy metal. Unable to understand many of the lyrics and often hardly aware of Rastafari's ideological and religious contents, many saw the locks, the "reggae colors," and the buttons depicting Selassie, Marley, or marijuana leaves as fashionable expressions of a musical style with "a damn good rhythm." For some of these reggae fans, however, the music raised questions of a deeper concern. As one young reggae lover wrote to the Jamaican Rastafari Movement Association:

> Hello! I am a boy of 17, living in cold Sweden. I do not know why I am writing this letter but I know that I love reggae. It started some years ago, when I was in England and bought my first reggae record. Now I have got several, a lot of Jamaica records are not distributed in Sweden. . . . Since I started listening to Rasta Music, I . . . have changed to the better, and if everybody listened to reggae, . . . the world would have been better. I am not a Rasta, I call him God and you call him Jah, but it's the same thing, isn't it?[25]

Caribbean Rastafari outside Jamaica

In the wider Caribbean, Rastafari entered slightly later and along a somewhat different route from that to Europe. Although migration and travel by Jamaican Rastas contributed to its dissemination, the scale and intensity of these contacts were not comparable to those existing between Jamaica and England. Thus it was reggae music that acted as the main vehicle and catalyst for the movement's diffusion in the Caribbean. The first Rastafarian-inspired group in the eastern Caribbean to gain public attention was the Dreads of Dominica. A small, poor, mountainous, and sparsely populated English-speaking island situated between the French islands of Martinique and Guadeloupe, Dominica's history had been a struggle from one crisis to another.[26]

In the early 1970s, when the island was still a British colony, several groups of youths from the middle and lower classes adopted the "symbols of resistance which had become so well known in Jamaica—the locks, tam, lion, ites, green and gold, and the use of the herb for spiritual and social communication and inspiration."[27] The ideas among these groups, however, varied widely. Some embraced Rastafarian beliefs in the divinity of Haile Selassie and in salvation through repatriation and propagated peace and love. Others repudiated the emperor as the personification of corruption and strove to change the system on their island, rather than exchange it for Africa. They openly, and sometimes aggressively, agitated against the power and influence of foreign investment, notably American capital, and Dominican society's Western orientation, advocating a sober, natural lifestyle and economic self-reliance instead.[28]

Although there was some support for the Dreads among the young and in leftist circles, the Dominican elite held all of them to be subversive elements, "terrorists" responsible for the harassment of the few tourists who visited the island. During carnival in 1974, when an American visitor, Albert John Jirasek, was murdered, the tensions reached a climax. Two Dreads, Desmond "Ras Kabinda" Trotter and Roy Mason, were arrested and charged with the crime. Based on the ambiguous account of the prosecution's main witness, Mason was acquitted and Trotter sentenced to death. It was only because of strong international protests that the Trotter's sentence was later commuted to life imprisonment. After the murder of Jirasek, Deputy Prime Minister Patrick John announced "more effective measures . . . to stamp out the menace that threatens our progress and development."[29] When, a few months later, John succeeded Edward LeBlanc as prime minister, he immediately introduced the Prohibited and Unlawful Societies and Association Act of 1974.

The act, in which the Dreads were the only "society" named, not only outlawed anyone "wearing any uniform, badge or mode of dress or other distinguishing mark or feature or manner of wearing their hair" but, in section 9, also stipulated that "no proceedings either criminal or civil shall be brought or maintained against any person (police included) who kills or injures any member of an association or society designated unlawful, who shall be found any time of day or night inside a dwelling house."[30] As the press and opposition soon concluded, section 9 of the so-called Dread Act was in fact nothing less than an official "license to kill"—a license some of the Dreads' adversaries eagerly accepted: "As soon as the law was enacted . . . one witnessed a reign of terror unleashed against the Dreads. . . . The armed Dreads took to the hills while the police, whose contempt for the group is no secret, began to [give] chase. To date [1976], there have been about 20 killings in confrontations between police and Dreads."[31] Afraid of being mistaken for "terrorists," many youths parted with their locks and disengaged themselves from the movement. Several groups, however, refused to surrender and went in hiding in the interior.

In July 1975, in response to considerable international pressure, the government declared an amnesty for all Dreads who would give up their resistance. To facilitate negotiations, it also appointed a committee of eight "wise men," chaired by a Methodist minister, the Reverend Didier. But the Dreads in the hills had little or no confidence in the government and refused to lay down their arms, despite the fact that the amnesty was extended until late September.[32] Although it failed to secure a dialogue, the Didier Committee concluded that there were three types of Dreads in Dominica: the majority were members of a peaceful counterculture group, others were political activists, and only a small fringe consisted of criminal elements committed to violence. The committee advised that the Dread Act be revoked, but the government considered the report "weak and too conciliatory." Moreover, it regarded the refusal of the Dreads in the hills to accept the amnesty as proof that they were indeed ordinary criminals and terrorists, and thus it declined to lift the act.[33]

The distinction between peaceful and violent Dreads made by the Didier Committee created room for moderate groups to approach the government. When a group of "baldhead" Rastas met with the prime minister, they complained "that they were being wrongly blamed for the bastardly acts committed by other groups and individuals." They nevertheless asked him to maintain a dialogue with the Dreads in the hills, which the prime Minister refused.[34] With the talks at an impasse, the positions hardened and the clashes continued. In December 1976 a group of Dreads, led by a man known as Galloway or Tomba, was suspected of having kidnapped two girls from Portsmouth. The government immediately posted a reward for information leading to the arrest of this "extremely dangerous" convict, who was, not long afterward, shot and killed during a raid on his camp.[35]

On November 3, 1978, four years after the passing of the Dread Act, Dominica achieved independence. Members of the Rastafari Co-operative Community used the opportunity to call on the government to grant them recognition and to acknowledge their "contribution to the development of the country."[36] Within a few months, however, mass protests against the near dictatorial regime of "Colonel" Patrick John led to the fall of the government. During the confusion, Desmond "Ras Kabinda" Trotter— convicted for the murder of Jirasek—managed to escape from jail but later turned himself in. He was released a few months later, however, after Patrick John revealed that Trotter had been falsely accused. The real murderer of Jirasek was a youngster whose father held a high position in government.[37]

After the general elections in July 1980, the conservative Dominica Freedom Party, led by the Iron Lady of the Caribbean, Mary Eugenia Charles, assumed power in the crisis-ridden island. Despite repeated requests, she refused to lift the Dread Act; it took yet another violent confrontation before the controversial act was revoked. In February 1981, after a shoot-out with the police, two Dreadlocks were killed and another seriously injured. The survivors fled, burned down the nearby farm of Edward Honeychurch (father of the government's press secretary), and took him into the hills as their hostage.[38] The Dreadlocks demanded the release of three brethren held in prison, an impartial investigation into the shoot-out, and the immediate withdrawal of the act. Although the government refused to negotiate and proclaimed a state of emergency, it replaced the Unlawful Societies Act with the Prevention of Terrorism Temporary Provisions Act, which—it was argued—allowed for better differentiation between terrorists and the nonviolent Dreads and Rastafarians.[39]

The crisis, however, was not over. The government of Dominica firmly believed that the kidnappers, led by a certain Pokosion, had received support from abroad. In March it ordered the arrest of several immigrants from Guadeloupe and Îles des Saintes, who were accused of having entered Dominica in order "to meet the brothers in the hills."[40] Two months later, the Dreads in the hills set up roadblocks and handed out messages to passing motorists, in which they demanded an end to their continuous persecution. The police immediately carried out a raid in the area and shot and killed three Dreads. Several others, including Pokosion, were reportedly injured but escaped.[41] When, in June, one of the kidnappers, Eric Joseph, was caught, he confessed that Honeychurch had been killed and his body burned one day after he was abducted. Joseph was sentenced to death, but as of 1996, he was still on death row.[42]

In the years after the revocation of the Dread Act the Dreads of Dominica regrouped, but relations with the government remained tense. The Inity of Rastafarian Idren, led by Desmond "Ras Kabinda" Trotter, emerged as the major group. In July 1985, some two hundred Dreads/Rastafarians formed a twelve-member National Assembly, which produced a statement condemning "the continued harassment and denial of Rasta religious rights as enshrined in the United Nation's declaration of human rights." The assembly also protested the "continued refusal of entry into Dominica of Rasta personnel from overseas" and "the denial of formal education rights to Rasta children."[43] But calls such as these were largely in vain. By 1987, the unremitting "hunting of Rastafarians in the hills" led Trotter to leave Dominica and settle in England.

Despite the extreme pressures generated by the Dread Act and the brutal actions of some of those associated with the movement, most of the Dreads in Dominica had always been nonviolent. Yet such distinctions often escaped the attention of both supporters and antagonists. Both found confirmation of their views in the developments in Grenada.

During the 1970s, progressive groups in the eastern Caribbean island of Grenada united in the New JEWEL (Joint Endeavor for Welfare Education and Liberation) Movement or NJM, and actively opposed the autocratic regime of Eric Gairy. According to Horace Campbell, a Jamaican scholar who has studied Rastafari for two decades, when the armed wing of the NJM—the People's Liberation Army—led by the young attorney Maurice Bishop, finally succeeded in toppling the regime in March 1979, "more than 400 Rastas" were involved in the revolt.[44] During Gairy's rule, the Rastafarians had suffered heavily from the persecution by the ferocious "Mongoose Squads," which "took special pride in cutting the locks of the brethren." After the revolt, however, Rastas were integrated into the armed forces, rising to responsible positions; and with the new trust and cooperation offered by the political leadership, the Rastas took their proper place in the community without fear of harassment. Young brethren from St. Lucia, St. Vincent, and Dominica flocked to see this new society where Dreadlocks did not have to shave their locks to hold responsible positions in the government.[45]

But there were also dissenting voices among the Rastafarians in Grenada. Bishop had announced general elections, but some doubted that he would fulfill his promise and hence began to press for action. Members of the local branch of the Twelve Tribes of Israel accused Bishop's Provisional Revolutionary Government (PRG) of being "anti-Rasta." Within a few days, Rastas supporting the Bishop administration organized a large protest march against the Twelve Tribes of Israel.[46] Eighteen members of the Twelve Tribes were arrested on the PRG's claim that they were involved in a CIA-backed plot to overthrow the government.[47] In its bid to restructure Grenada's weak economy along socialist lines, the new government developed close links with Cuba.

Although the New JEWEL Movement's efforts to relieve unemployment and raise the standard of living were not without success, internal rivalries among its leadership eventually resulted in the fall of Maurice Bishop. In October 1983, the radical Marxist minister of finance Bernard Coard took power. Bishop was arrested and detained, but a party of supporters set him free and stormed the army's headquarters. When the army tried to regain control by ruthlessly firing on the crowd, some forty people were killed, including Bishop. Two weeks later, the United States—afraid that Grenada might turn into a second Cuba—invaded the island "to restore order." Little or nothing was heard of the Grenadian Rastas afterward.

The coup of the New JEWEL Movement may have inspired a group of Rastafarian youths in the Grenadines to action. According to Campbell, in December 1979, only a few months after Maurice Bishop had gained control in Grenada, some fifty youths led by Rastas tried to take power on Union Island, a tiny, impoverished island in the Grenadines, administered by St. Vincent. Shortly before this action, Prime Minister Milton Cato's Labour Party had once again won the elections. In the Grenadines, and especially on Union Island and Bequia, there was widespread discontent with Cato's government and the way in which St. Vincent governed the Grenadines. The majority of the population of the two islands had voted for the opposition New Democratic Party.

On December 7, 1979, a group of young Union Islanders led by Lennox "Bumber" Charles and Camilo Adams fired a few shots and seized the police station, the revenue office, and the local airstrip. Prime Minister Cato declared a state of emergency and requested military assistance from the United States, England, and Barbados. Only Barbados responded favorably and dispatched fifty soldiers to assist the St. Vincent police force. Before they arrived, however, the local police had already put down the rebellion. More than thirty rebels were arrested and detained.[48]

Though Rastafarians and Rasta-inspired youths are not known to have been actively involved in revolts or revolutions elsewhere in the Caribbean, the movement's role in Dominica, Grenada, and Union Island no doubt influenced the perceptions of Rastafari in other Caribbean territories. Everywhere local elites loathed the Rastas, if not because of their "heretic" religious beliefs and unequivocal rejection of Babylonian values then at least because of their appearance and use of marijuana. For many, Rastafari repre-

sented everything they despised. In addition, the movement was involved in revolutionary, sometimes violent, action, which positioned it as a direct threat to internal security of some countries. As a result, Rastafarians elsewhere in the Caribbean became
the objects of not only scorn and biting criticism but also of often-harsh repression.

In Antigua, a former British possession at the northern end of the Leeward Islands,
several Rastas were said to have been killed in clashes with the police during the 1970s.
Some of these incidents were related to marijuana use, but the Rastafarians were also
blamed for "acts of terrorism." In the words of a local newspaper reporter, they "ter-
rify members of the community, particularly in the agricultural area where they ravaged
small farmers' crops. . . . It is felt that they withdrew to the hills in order to practice a
form of anarchism."[49] In an effort to contain the growth of the movement, the Antiguan
government forbade Jamaican reggae musicians to enter the island and, in 1978, even
refused Father Joseph Owens, author of a highly acclaimed study on Rastafari, permission to deliver a lecture on the movement.[50]

Two years later, the Antiguan government apparently concluded that its efforts had
borne little fruit and so appointed a committee "to examine ways and means of developing the talents [in art and craft] of Rastafarians," and to seek possibilities for the Rastas "to fully participate in the economic and social life of the state." It promised acceptance of the religious beliefs but also issued a firm warning against the criminal
impostors and "parasites" hiding behind a Rasta mask.[51] The committee had barely
been installed, however, when, on November 17, 1980, a twenty-two-year-old Rastafarian, Bernard Brown, died while in police custody. A witness testified that, both during his arrest and while in jail, the police had beaten and kicked Brown and had pulled
him around by his locks. A pathologist testified that his death "was due to concussion
of the brain resulting from severe blows he received on the head," but police officers
claimed that Brown died after falling and injuring his head.[52]

Further to the south, in the French-speaking territory of Martinique, similarly tragic
incidents were reported. On June 26, 1983, Thiery Locks, a member of the local Rastafarian movement, was shot and killed by a white man for allegedly stealing mangos. According to the Rastas, who subsequently organized themselves into the Movement of
June 26, "the killer was presented before a Tribunal the next day without handcuffs, although when a brother is arrested for a little herbs, he is chained up."[53] Rastas in Martinique also claimed that they were barred from public transport and arbitrarily harassed and provoked by the police.

In the relatively stable and affluent eastern Caribbean island of Barbados, it was a performance by the Jamaican roots musicians Ras Boanerges and the Sons of Thunder in 1975
that gave a major boost to the rise of Rastafari.[54] Two years later, when some of their representatives requested land "so that they could pursue independent agricultural activities,"
a lively debate ensued in the local newspapers.[55] The *Advocate News* "considered the
Rastafarian commitment to peace, lack of greed and malice and their belief in the oneness
of man as commendable."[56] According to *The Nation,* however, the Rastas of Barbados
were "thieves, dope-users and idlers. . . . the Rastafarians, by standards of modern hygiene,
are now exploring all the possibilities of dinginess, dirtiness and squalor."[57]

According to the October 4 issue of the *Bulletin of Eastern Caribbean Affairs*, the Barbadian government seemed to share the latter view and repeatedly expressed serious concerns about "the spate of crimes involving members of the long-haired sect."[58] The commissioner of police, for instance, held the Rastas responsible for two out of every three crimes in the island and "felt the time had come for the police to respond to the calls."[59] Senator Randolph Field, speaking in October 1980, thought that "the estimated 2,000 'Rastas' should either be jailed or beaten."[60] The police effectively brought such advice into practice. By 1983, as the Trinidadian Rastas noted in their periodical *Rastafari Speaks*, many Rastas in Barbados had cut their locks and disengaged themselves from the movement. *Rastafari Speaks*, however, attributed the eclipse of the movement not only to "pressure from Big Business" and the persecution by the police but also to the "inherent weakness in the brotherhood" itself.[61] Under pressure, only the most devoted stood firm. In the late 1980s, social theorists Maxine McClean and Hyacinth Griffith concluded that "the Rastafarian community in Barbados is primarily a religious group," divided into two major organizations: the Nyabinghis and the Twelve Tribes of Israel. Several Rastas had become active and quite successful in producing and selling leathercraft, but attitudes toward the movement in Barbados had apparently remained unchanged. Most Barbadians still "frequently associated [the Rastafarians] with criminal activity and general lawlessness."[62]

As in Barbados, the Rastafarian movement in the twin republic of Trinidad and Tobago, a short distance north of the Venezuelan coast, emerged in the mid-1970s, and in terms of numbers it was to become one of the strongest in the Caribbean outside Jamaica. By the late 1970s, Trinidad-born Ansley Hamid estimated the Rastas in Trinidad's second city, San Fernando, to number at least fifteen hundred.[63] In Port of Spain, the capital, the movement also had a strong presence, including among its main formations the Ras Tafari Brethren Organization (RTBO), led by Muntu Lalibala. During the 1980s, RTBO gained prominence as the publisher of the movement's only Pan-Caribbean magazine, *Rastafari Speaks*, and as co-organizer of the Third International Rastafarian Assembly in 1984.[64] According to Campbell, Trinidad became "one of the few areas outside Jamaica where young blacks still revere Haile Selassie," which he attributes to the fact that "young activists from Jamaica . . . collaborated in staging a Jubilee celebration" on the island.[65] Although this specific event in 1980 may certainly have played a role, it appears that there were, and still are, fairly close contacts between the Jamaican and Trinidadian movements in general. The Twelve Tribes of Israel, for instance, are known to have a strong branch in Trinidad and Tobago. Also, Haile Selassie's state visit in 1966 and the presence of the Ethiopian Orthodox Church on the island may have contributed to the Trinidadian Rastas being "steeped in religion," as Campbell puts it.

The attitudes toward the Rastafarians in Trinidad, despite their religious orientation, hardly differed from those elsewhere in the Caribbean. In the early 1980s the *Trinidad Guardian* noted that "the Rastas . . . may well qualify as the most unloved group of persons in our midst." The editors of the newspaper also thought "the lawlessness associated with the Rasta cult has reached such critical proportions [that] the time has come

for the authorities to regard the members of this long-haired breed as constituting a particular menace to the society."[66] It is hardly surprising, then, that the Rastafarians in
"Trindago" were frequently subject to arrest and harassment by the police. The RTBO
headquarters in Port of Spain was occasionally raided by the police, and some 150 Rastas were jailed during the 1979 carnival celebrations in San Fernando.

In Guyana, on the South American mainland, the reactions to the movement's emergence were little different. In October 1978, when *The Citizen* featured an article on the
recent appearance of the movement, it spoke about "the smelly Rastas who now plague
Guyana." According to a government spokesperson, the local Rastas had "no connection with African culture and the life style of Africans in their own country" and thus
qualified as mere "impostors." In addition to the usual references to the alleged neglect
of "personal hygiene," the newspaper concluded that the Rastas "erode the foundation
of morality." *The Citizen* accused a group of Rastafarians living in the hills in the vicin-
ity of Linden of growing marijuana and selling their produce not only at nightclubs, beer
gardens, and hotels, but also—"the limits of the sadist [*sic*]activities"—at schools.

Ironically, within a month Guyana's government had a much bigger "cult problem"
on its hands, when Jim Jones forced 924 followers of his People's Temple to join him
in committing suicide after they had murdered several people, including the U. S. con-
gressman Leo Ryan. Although the two groups are hardly comparable, it may be that the
tragic death of so many people contributed to the uncompromising stance the Guyana
government was to take against the Rastafarians. In the late 1970s, the government
banned reggae music and actively began to repress the movement, which, according to
Campbell, "was prominent in the urban working class areas."[67] As a result, many Rastas in Guyana retreated inland to live and work as independent farmers. That, however,
proved no guarantee for an untroubled existence, as a group of some fifty Rasta farmers in the Madhia area were to discover. During a raid on their village in early 1981,
the police set several homes on fire, destroyed tools, and beat up several members of the
group. Twenty Rastas were locked up and treated "very harshly," without charges being laid against them. When three of them were released two weeks later, they contacted
the minister of home affairs, who promised an investigation but also warned that the
Rastafarians "would not be allowed to flout the law."[68]

Despite such incidents, two years later Guyana's president Linden Forbes Burnham
flatly denied that any tensions existed between the Rastafarians and his government. In
an interview with *Rastafari Speaks* he declared, "I don't think the Rastafari movement
has a bad profile in Guyana, certainly not as bad as in some of the other islands. We
have Rastafarians in good positions in the country. Some of them are actually working
with the Government, and many of them are involved in agriculture."[69] Indeed, at least
one Rastafarian in Guyana was in a "good position." In early 1986, Enerva Trotman,
a dreadlocked Rastafarian of ten years' standing, was elected Member of Parliament for
the ruling People's National Congress, thereby becoming the first Rastafarian parlia-
mentarian in the Caribbean. Trotman noted that his colleagues had "reservation[s]
about him in politics at that level," but he was determined to show that he could do a
good job.[70]

In some Caribbean territories, governments continued to resist the inevitable by trying to shut their doors to the "undesirable." In the late 1970s, the British Crown Colony of Grand Cayman issued a directive banning Rastafari. In January 1983, when two non-Rastafarian dreadlocked entertainers from Jamaica were refused entry, the government of the Caymans released a statement saying that while

> the Cayman Islands will always extend a hearty welcome to tourists and visitors from Jamaica, with whom we retain a close connection, it is important to reaffirm the Government's intention to keep out undesirable elements from [wherever] they emanate. In recent years, it has been the consistent policy of the Government of the Cayman Islands to prohibit the entry to these islands by those people whose appearance and dress habits resemble those of hippies and the Rastafarian cult. This policy is subscribed to by the present Government and is well known to, and supported in large measures by, the Cayman community.[71]

Although in Jamaica the ban caused a small controversy between those in favor and those against the Rastafari, there was hardly any protest in the Caymans.[72] Only the editors of the *Caymanian Compass* thought that the ban on Rastafari was "distasteful and smack[ed] of racial, religious and civil discrimination."[73]

Unfortunately, the Cayman Islands were not the only state in the Caribbean to bar Rastafarians from entry. As a reminder that many in the Caribbean still have a long way to go before they will come to terms with Rastafari, the British Virgin Islands followed the example and, as late as the 1990s, continued to refuse Rastas entry under the Prohibited Persons Act.[74]

Rastafari in the Pacific

Although little research into its presence in the region has so far been carried out, Rastafari has, since the late 1970s, made various inroads into Australia, New Zealand, and several small islands in the Pacific, including Fiji, Tonga, and Samoa.[75] As in the Caribbean, reggae was the main vehicle for the dissemination of Rastafari in the Pacific, to which Bob Marley and the Wailers' performances in Australia and New Zealand in 1978 especially gave a major boost. Particularly among young, urban, and often unemployed Maori and Samoans in Auckland, New Zealand, Rasta and reggae are extremely popular. According to Gordon Campbell, writing in the *New Zealand Listener*, the majority of the youths began as reggae fans rather than as potential Rastafarians.[76] One of these fans wrote to the Rasta Movement Association in Kingston in 1982, "I want to know what 'Rastafarian' is, I am seriously thinking of becoming a follower." Apparently, reggae had made such an impression on this New Zealander that he was considering becoming a follower before he knew what it was he was following. Just as in Europe, many of these youths had little understanding of "Rastology." To them, Rasta was music, style, and coiffure. "I have dreads, but they don't stay in," the letter continued. "If you could also tell me step by step the process of dread making that would also be appreciated."[77]

For others, however, Rasta was a vibrant and new political message; a successor to Black Power, emphasizing peace, love, and brotherhood; and a call for the unity of subjugated people around the world to fight oppression. These youths perceived clear parallels between the situations of black people in the Caribbean and in the Pacific. Subjugated and stripped of their cultural traditions by European powers, Pacific Blacks, too, are struggling to regain their heritage and identity. Gordon Campbell records: "Jamaica being in the Caribbean relates to New Zealand because this is a Pacific country and the same sun, the same aura is here. . . . When you have people without a culture, who have been robbed of their culture, the next best thing is to pick up on the topmost culture that's around. . . . Right now, we have to delve into our history and find out where it connects."[78]

Though relatively few in numbers, there are nevertheless some who also subscribe to the religious teachings of Rastafari, including belief in the divinity of Emperor Haile Selassie and the return to the promised land. One of Campbell's informants estimated that there was "a solid one hundred" around Auckland.[79] One of the reasons Rastafarian ideas were quite readily accepted in this part of the Pacific probably lies in their similarity to the strongly millenarian traditions in the region. Since the introduction of Christianity in the early nineteenth century, identification with the lost tribes of Israel, for example, has figured prominently in several religious movements emerging among the Maori. Perhaps this also spurred the prophet Gad, leader of the international Twelve Tribes of Israel, to travel to New Zealand in 1986 in order to establish formally the first branch of the Jamaican organization in Pacific, thereby making yet another connection in the rapidly expanding network of Rasta International.

As in Jamaica, the dissemination of Rastafarian ideas and belief to Europe, the Caribbean, and the Pacific gave rise to an extremely heterogeneous counterculture. This complexity and diversity, along with the limited data yet available, make it difficult to draw general conclusions on the nature and character of Rasta International. Yet it appears that most Rastafarians abroad have embraced the social, political, and cultural ideas associated with the movement, including elements of the Rastafarian "livity," rather than the whole body of its religious teachings. It appears that only in those situations in which the movement spread primarily through close contact with the Jamaican Rastafari, as in Trinidad, did it tend to evolve in a more or less religious form. By contrast, where reggae was Rastafari's main carrier, spreading the message without the guidance, instruction, and explication of its Jamaican progenitors, more secular forms usually emerged.

The cultural setting in which Rastafarian ideas and beliefs emerged also must be taken into account. Shaped and molded by the messianic-millenarian traditions of Afro-Jamaican "folk" religions such as Myalism and revivalism, the religious ideas of Rastafari are, in many respects, typically Jamaican.[80] Only where the movement has emerged in a partially Jamaican context, as in England, or where there existed comparable traditions, as seems to have been the case in New Zealand, were people able to relate to the millenarian expectations of Rastafari. In other cultural settings, however, such ideas were probably hard to incorporate.

The religious underpinnings aside, the sociopolitical implications of Rastafari have had a widespread appeal. The Rastas' resistance to white domination and discrimination; their uncompromising rejection of Western materialism; their unequivocal pride in their African heritage and identity; their passionate calls for solidarity among the poor and powerless; and their relentless quest for freedom, justice, and righteousness can be easily translated into the experiences and aspirations of downtrodden people elsewhere.

Notes

1. In addition to the published studies on Great Britain, Africa, and the Caribbean listed in Nathaniel Samuel Murrell's literature review, Appendix B in this anthology, see Dick Hebdige, *Subculture: The Meaning of Style* (London: Methuen, 1979); Paul Gilroy, *There Ain't No Black in the Union Jack: The Cultural Politics of Race and Nation* (London: Hutchinson & Co., 1987); Simon Jones, *Black Culture, White Youth: The Reggae Tradition from JA to UK* (London: Macmillan Publishers, 1988). The only English-language source on Rasta in the Netherlands is Livio Sansone, "Ethnicity and Leisure Time among Surinamese Adolescents and Young Men in Amsterdam," in Paul van Gelder, Peter van der Veer, and Ineke van Wetering, eds., *Bonoeman, Rasta's en andere Surinamers: Onderzoek naar etnische groepen in Nederland* (Amsterdam: Werkgroep AWIC, 1984), 185–218.

2. Much of the information on which this article is based was collected in the course of research into the history of Rastafari and its changing relationship with the wider Jamaican society; see Frank Jan van Dijk, *Jahmaica: Rastafari and Jamaican Society, 1930–1990* (Utrecht: ISOR, 1993).

3. Nancy Foner, *Jamaica Farewell: Jamaican Migrants in London* (Berkeley: University of California Press, 1978).

4. Sheila Patterson, *Dark Strangers: A Study of West Indians in London* (London: Tavistock Publications, 1963), 354, 360.

5. Ernest E. Cashmore, *Rastaman: The Rastafarian Movement in England* (London: George Allen & Unwin Paperback, 1983), 44–49.

6. Jones, *Black Culture, White Youth,* 39.

7. Cashmore, *Rastaman,* 51–52.

8. "A Brief History of the Imperial Ethiopian World Federation Inc.," *Imperial Chronicle* 1 (London: Imperial Ethiopian World Federation, Asfa Wossen Local 1, 1987) 7.

9. *Ethiopian Orthodox Church St. Mary of Zion/The Ethiopian World Federation, Inc. Emperor Yohannes Local 33* (London: Ethiopian World Federation, 1975), 25–31.

10. Frank Jan van Dijk, "The Twelve Tribes of Israel: Rasta and the Middle Class," *New West Indian Guide* 62, 1–2 (1988): 1–26.

11. John Brown, *Shades of Grey: Police–West Indian Relations in Handsworth* (Birmingham: Cranfield Police Studies, 1977); cited in Cashmore, *Rastaman,* 215.

12. Horace Campbell, *Rasta and Resistance: From Marcus Garvey to Walter Rodney* (London: Hansib Publishing, 1985), 196.

13. Julia Roberts, cited in Len Garrison, *Black Youth, Rastafarianism and the Identity Crisis in Britain* (London: Afro-Caribbean Educational Project, 1979), 25.

14. *JAHUG* I (London: C. Gayle and Y. Gayle for Repatriation Productions, 1992), 2.

15. Terry Jones, "Oorlog in Babylon: De onlusten in England," *Sociologische Gids* 82, 5 (1992): 366–85.

16. Lord Scarman, *The Brixton Disorders, 10–12 April 1981: Report of an Inquiry* (London: Her Majesty's Stationary Office, 1981), 44.

17. Catholic Commission for Racial Justice (CCRJ), *Rastafarians in Jamaica and England* (London: CCRJ, 1982).

18. For a discussion of the CCRJ's report and the reactions in England and Jamaica, see van Dijk, *Jahmaica*, 301–6.

19. *West Indian World,* December 10, 1982.

20. "Brief History," *Imperial Chronicle,* 1.

21. *Daily Gleaner,* April 17, 1988, 6.

22. Peter E. J. Buiks, *Surinaamse jongeren op de Kruiskade: Overleven in een etnische rand-groep* (Deventer, Neth.: Van Loghum Slaterus, 1983), 153–89.

23. Hans Vermeulen, *Etnische groepen en grenzen: Surinamers, Chinezen en Turken* (Weesp; Neth.: Het Wereldvenster, 1984), 75–80. See also Livio Sansone, *Schitteren in de schaduw: Over-levingsstrategieën en etniciteit van Creoolse jongeren uit de lagere klasse in Amsterdam, 1981–1990* (Amsterdam: Het Spinhuis, 1992).

24. Neil Savishinsky, "Transnational Popular Culture and the Global Spread of the Jamaican Rastafarian Movement" *New West Indian Guide* 68, 3–4 (1994): 270.

25. "Letter to the editor," *Rasta Voice* 88 (1982): 11.

26. Lennox Honeychurch, *The Dominica Story: A History of the Island* (Roseau: Dominica Institute, 1984).

27. Campbell, *Rasta and Resistance,* 158–59. See also Bert Thomas, "Revolutionary Activity in the Caribbean: Some Notes on the Dreads in Dominica," *Guyana Journal of Sociology* 1, 2 (1976): 75–92, esp. 76.

28. Chandar Gupta Supersad, "Political Protest in a Transitional Society: A Case Study of the Dominica Dreads" (M.A. thesis, University of the West Indies, St. Augustine, 1986).

29. Honeychurch, *The Dominica Story,* 188.

30. Cited in Supersad, "Political Protest in a Transitional Society," n.p.

31. Thomas, "Revolutionary Activity in the Caribbean," 84.

32. "Dreads' Amnesty May Be Extended," *Jamaica Daily News,* September 2, 1975, 4.

33. Honeychurch, *The Dominica Story,* 192.

34. *Jamaica Daily News,* December 19, 1976, 4.

35. "Reward for Dreads," *Jamaica Daily News,* December 16, 1976, 4.

36. "Dominican Rastas Seek Recognition," *Daily Gleaner,* November 26, 1978, 28.

37. *Jamaica Daily News,* July 21, 1979, 4.

38. See accounts in the *Daily Gleaner,* February 14, 15, 17, and 18, 1981.

39. Arthur Kitchen, "The Dreads of Dominica," *Daily Gleaner,* February 28, 1981, 6; and "Dominican Rastas Live Under the Shadow of Death" *Daily Gleaner,* March 7, 1981, 14.

40. *Daily Gleaner,* March 5, 1981.

41. "Dominica: Police Killed Three Terrorists," *Jamaica Daily News,* May 16, 1981: 5, 22.

42. Amnesty International, "Urgent Action" file 223/90, May 31, 1990 (London: Amnesty International, 1990).

43. "Rastafarians Accuse Educational System of Neglect," *Daily Gleaner,* July 27, 1985, 7; "Rastafarians Lash Out against Discrimination," *Daily Gleaner,* December 6, 1990, 2; "Rastas'

Charges Rejected," *Daily Gleaner,* December 7, 1990, 2; "Rastas Harassed in Dominica: Free Up Eric Joseph, Says Leader," *Jamaica Record,* May 5, 1990, 4.

44. Campbell, *Rasta and Resistance,* 163.

45. Ibid.

46. *Jamaica Daily News,* October 14, 1979, 2; and *Jamaica Daily News,* October 18, 1979, 7.

47. *Jamaica Daily News,* October 15, 1979, 1; October 16, 1979, 3; and October 17, 1979, 4.

48. See the accounts in the *Daily Gleaner,* December 8, 1979, 1; December 10, 1979, 9; December 12, 1979, 2; December 14, 1979, 26–27; and December 17, 1979, 9. Although Campbell says, "Rasta youths led the protest" (*Rasta and Resistance,* 160–61), there was no mention in these reports of the rebels being Rastafarians.

49. *Jamaica Daily News,* October 12, 1980, 21.

50. "Owens Barred From Speaking on Rastafari," *Daily Gleaner,* March 19, 1978, 5; and *Jamaica Daily News,* June 2, 1979, 24. Reference here is to Joseph Owens's Study *Dread: The Rastafarians of Jamaica* (Kingston: Sangster's Book Stores, 1976).

51. Lucien Millette-Gomes, "Coming to Grips with Rasta," *Jamaica Daily News,* October 12, 1980, 21.

52. "Rastafarian Dies after Arrest: Witness Evidence against Police," *Jamaica Daily News,* December 13, 1980, 6.

53. "Accusation! Martinican Connection," *Rastafari Speaks* 11 (1983): 20.

54. Maxine McClean and Hyacinth Griffith, "Rastafarians: The Revivors of Leathercraft in Barbados," *Bulletin of Eastern Caribbean Affairs* 15 (1989): 31–36.

55. "Barbados Press Comment on the Local Rastafari Movement," *Bulletin of Eastern Caribbean Affairs* 3, 7–10 (1977): 23–26, esp. 23.

56. Ibid., 24; "Editorial," *Advocate News,* October 9, 1977.

57. "Rastas: Thieves, Dope-Users and Idlers," *The Nation* (Bridgetown, Barbados), October 4, 1977.

58. "Barbados Press Comments," 25; "Editorial," *Daily Gleaner,* December 12, 1979, 8.

59. Eudiene Barriteau, "Recent Developments on the Rastafari Movement in Barbados," *Bulletin of Eastern Caribbean Affairs* 6, 4 (1980): 21–24, esp. 22, 24.

60. Ibid., 22.

61. *Rastafari Speaks* 11 (1983): 12.

62. McClean and Griffith, *Rastafarians,* 31–32.

63. Ansley H. Hamid, "A Pre-Capitalist Mode of Production: Ganja and the Rastafarians in San Fernando, Trinidad" (Ph.D. diss., Columbia University, 1981), 188.

64. Starting in Toronto in 1982, the movement organized several international assemblies throughout the 1980s and 1990s.

65. Campbell, *Rasta and Resistance,* 171.

66. "Editorial," *Trinidad Guardian,* 9 September 1983; reprinted in *Rastafari Speaks* 11 (1983): 30, and in the *Daily Gleaner,* November 1, 1987, 3.

67. Campbell, "Rasta and Resistance," 171–73.

68. "Rastas Complain of Brutality," *Jamaica Daily News,* February 17, 1981, 5.

69. "Accusation! Guyana," *Rastafari Speaks* 11 (1983): 20.

70. "Rastafarian in Parliament," *Rasta Voice* 95 (May 1986) n.p. Retyped from the *Daily Gleaner,* April 28, 1986.

71. "Are Rastas Banned from Cayman,"*Daily Gleaner,* February 1, 1983, 3; "Rastafarian Hippies Banned from Caribbean Island," *Daily Gleaner,* February 12, 1983, 8, 13.

72. Arthur Kitchen, "Ban on Rastafari," *Daily Gleaner,* February 21, 1983, 8.

73. *Caymanian Compass* (Georgetown, Cayman Islands), February 4, 1983; reprinted in Kitchen, "Ban on Rastafari," 8.

74. See Leahcim Semaj, "Inside Rasta: The Future of a Religious Movement," *Caribbean Review* 14, 1 (1986): 8–11, 37–38; Audre Lorde, "A Deadlock over Dreadlocks in BVIs," *Caribbean Week* (October 20–26, 1985): 4–5.

75. Savishinsky ("Transnational Popular Culture," 272) mentions an M.A. thesis by William G. Hawkeswood, "I'N'I Ras Tafari: Identity and the Rasta Movement in Auckland" (Department of Anthropology, University of Auckland, 1983).

76. Gordon Campbell, "Rasta in Aotearoa," *New Zealand Listener,* January 17, 1981, 18–19.

77. Ibid.; *Rasta Voice* 90 (1982): 8.

78. Campbell, "Rasta in Aotearoa," 18–19.

79 Ibid., 18.

80. For discussions of revivalism and Myalism and their impact on Rastafari, see Barry Chevannes, "Revival and the Black Struggle," *Savacou* 5 (1971): 27–39; idem, "Rastafari: Towards a New Approach," *New West Indian Guide* 64, 3–4 (1990): 127–48; Monica Schuler, "Myalism and the African Religious Tradition in Jamaica," in Margaret E. Crahan and Franklin W. Knight, eds., *Africa and the Caribbean: The Legacies of a Link* (Baltimore: Johns Hopkins University Press, 1979) 65–79; William Wedenoja, "The Origins of Revival, a Creole Religion in Jamaica," in George R. Saunders, ed., *Culture and Christianity: The Dialectics of Transformation* (Westport, Conn.: Greenwood Press, 1988), 90–116.

12

Chanting Down Babylon in the Belly of the Beast: The Rastafarian Movement in the Metropolitan United States

RANDAL L. HEPNER

Although the Rastafarian movement has shown steady growth and vitality since its inception in 1930, it appears to have remained largely a Jamaican phenomenon for its first thirty-five years.[1] However, beginning in the late 1960s and early 1970s, the movement burst upon the Caribbean cultural scene as one of the most potent and dynamic forces in the lives of young people involved in the progressive, anticolonial, and nationalist movements of that era. In the 1970s, Rastafari emerged as perhaps the most important cultural referent for young Caribbean immigrants in London, Amsterdam, and New York City.

The growth and presence of the Rastafarians in the United States followed the waves of Caribbean migration to North America in the 1900s, especially since the 1960s and 1970s. The high concentrations of Caribbean Americans in New York City and Miami now make these metropolitan centers the largest "Caribbean" cities in the world to date. In fact, parts of Miami and Brooklyn have so many Jamaicans that the neighborhoods are referred to, colloquially, as "Kingston 21" and "Little Jamaica" respectively.

The 1990 U.S. Census put the number of Jamaican Americans living in New York at 186,430. But some researchers argue that the high "illegal alien" population among Jamaicans in the United States, as well as immigrants' skepticism of the purpose of the government census, allows an estimate that is substantially higher than that given in the census of Jamaicans, legal and undocumented, living in New York State, most of whom live in the metropolitan area.[2] As Philip Kasinitz, an authority on Caribbean immigrants in New York, noted, after the early 1960s these Caribbean immigrants settled in different parts of New York City, with noticeable internal movements. Between the mid-1960s and the 1970s, the new immigrants moved gradually away from East Flat-bush and Flatbush. During the mid- to late 1970s, however, the core of the community shifted from Harlem and Bedford-Stuyvesant to the Crown Heights, East Flatbush, and Flatbush sections of central Brooklyn. By 1987 about eighty thousand Blacks (mostly Caribbean) were competing with about fifteen thousand Hasidic Jews for space in Crown Heights. In 1990 the Flatbush section of Brooklyn was recognized as "New York's most West Indian neighborhood"[3] and the center of a rich array of Caribbean activities and cultural traditions, of which the most visible, and perhaps the most ap-pealing to young people, is the Jamaican-exported Rastafari.

Although some important studies have been done on the diverse Caribbean Ameri-can population in New York City,[4] surprisingly, I could not find a comparable one con-ducted on the Rastafarian movement in the city or in the United States as a whole. A few studies have discussed the Rastafarians in North America, but not with a full in-vestigation of the various facets of the movement.[5] In his 1980 publication on Rasta-fari, William Spencer conjectured that there were as many Rastas in the United States as in Jamaica and made reference to several popular magazines and tabloids that rec-ognized the Marley-reggae phenomenon; but Spencer's discussion is still awaiting fuller treatment.[6] In 1983, Spencer wrote a sequel to his "Rastafari: Poverty and Apos-tasy in Paradise" and used sociologist Ernst Troeltsch to analyze the experiences of Rastas in New York City and Philadelphia. The paper mentions several important characteristics of Rastafari in North America and raises questions about the move-ment's future. The essay remains unpublished, however, at the Jamaica Theological Seminary.[7]

In 1989, Linden Lewis wrote of the hostility experienced by immigrant U.S. Rastas at the hands of law-enforcement agents and the corporate media, and he lamented that "given the history of racism it is presently inconceivable to imagine America embrac-ing the Rastafarian culture. In short, Rastafari in the United States will continue to ex-perience difficult times and may never gain the kind of status it has acquired in the Caribbean."[8] As late as 1994, Neil Savishinsky regretted that in spite of "the visible Rastafarian presence" in North America, "little serious research has yet been under-taken to assess the movement's impact in the United States."[9] Unfortunately, Sav-ishinsky himself devoted only two pages of his essay to discussing this important phe-nomenon.

This chapter is, therefore, an attempt to address a lacuna in the literature on Rasta-fari in the United States. It provides a glimpse into the vibrant, growing, and multieth-nic community of Rastafarians that exists at present in metropolitan centers such as New York—the heart of "Babylon"—and the "movement of Jah people" that links it both spiritually and historically to Jamaica. Beginning with a historical overview based on media and law-enforcement reports, I provide a mapping of Rastafari in both its or-ganized and unorganized sectors, exploring some of its particular institutions and be-liefs. I then conclude with a note on the spread of the Rastafari movement in North America and the kinds of approaches that begin to make sense of the Rastafari experi-ence "chanting down Babylon in the belly of the beast."[10]

The Media, Law Enforcement, and Rastafari

Although dating precisely the formal beginnings of Rastafari in the United States is not possible at present, I contend that the movement, as an observable phenomenon, is co-extensive with both evolving patterns of Jamaican immigration in the 1960s and 1970s and the phenomenal reception and rise of reggae music to international prominence. The first formal Rastafari churches and associations in the United States were organized in the mid-1970s, and the first media accounts of Rastas in New York date back only to 1971. Leonard Barrett, however, claims to have evidence that dates the movement to the early 1960s.[11] While Rastafari became an important visible phenomenon in the United States only after the 1960s and 1970s, good reasons exist to suspect a deeper, less obvious, and earlier connection than is currently understood between events in North America and the emergence of the movement in Jamaica in the 1930s.

The role of New York City itself, as a contributing locale in the formative stages of Rastafari, has been neglected by many Rasta researchers, despite the fact that New York was the most important arena for Marcus Garvey's Universal Negro Improvement Association, from which came strong, early supporters of Rastafari. Indeed, during the height of Garvey's movement, New York City was the principal port of entry for Jamaican and other Caribbean immigrants seeking opportunities in the industrialized North. The Harlem Renaissance was, in part, fueled by the contributions of recently arrived Caribbean emigrants who joined the hundreds of thousands of African Americans fleeing the South during the "Great Black Exodus." Together they made New York City an international center for Afro-American and Caribbean culture in the diaspora.

Garvey scholar Robert Hill has noted that the early synthesis of Garvey's vision of African redemption and a revived Ethiopianism after 1930 was first signaled during a street parade in Harlem, where Garveyites and black Jews marched together carrying banners and pictures of both Garvey and Haile Selassie I.[12] In addition, key figures in the early Rastafari movement, such as Leonard Howell, spent significant years (1918–1930) in New York prior to the emergence of the movement in Jamaica. Furthermore, the formative document written by Robert Athlyi Rogers, *The Holy Piby* (known popularly as the "Black Man's Bible"), which Hill claims provided "the interpretive basis of [early] Rastafari ideology," was first published in 1924 in Newark, New Jersey.

One should also not forget that the Ethiopian World Federation (EWF) was founded in New York City in 1937, by Blacks who were also instrumental in the formation of a Jamaican branch in 1938—an organization that would later influence developments among the Rastafari in Jamaica. Like Howell before him, the enigmatic Rasta preacher Claudius Henry spent thirteen years in the United States before returning to found his Seventh Emmanuel Brethren and African Reform Church in 1957. Some Rastas allegedly involved in the armed confrontation with Jamaican police and soldiers after Henry's 1960 arrest for sedition and conspiracy to commit treason were born in the United States.[13]

Whatever the formal dating of the movement in New York City, its reception in American society was no more friendly or welcoming than its initial reception in Jamaica, the eastern Caribbean, and Britain. Within a few years of the movement's public appearance in such cities as New York, Washington, D.C., Houston, Los Angeles, and Miami, the media was at work portraying its members and enthusiasts as criminals and illegal aliens intent on doing harm to law-abiding citizens. In 1971, for example, a score of shootings in the Bedford-Stuyvesant section of Brooklyn were attributed to "Ras Tafarian cultists" who, police detectives claimed, "shoot whoever they feel like."[14] In 1977 four Rastafarians were found bound and shot to death in an apartment in Brooklyn, an episode that police and media observers dubbed the "Rasta Easter Massacres." Members of a rival sect of Rastafarians were assumed responsible for the killings.[15] For the remainder of the decade, New York's growing Rastafari community would be publicly associated with criminal violence, drug trafficking, gunrunning, and homicide.

By the late 1970s, the New York City Police Department's intelligence division was conducting full-scale intelligence-gathering operations on the nascent movement. In 1983, a report prepared for law-enforcement commanders and specialized units with large West Indian communities in their respective jurisdictions reported, "Many of the 'Rastas' in this country tend to stray from their [religious] tenets and engage in criminal activity, using their religious doctrines as a cover for their criminal activity."[16] The report also suggested a "propensity for violence" inherent in Rastafari and allegedly related to "heavy ingestion of marijuana," as well as an infiltration of the movement by Marxist groups, revolutionary Cuban terrorists, and violent pro–People's National Party forces around the then recently deposed prime minister Michael Manley. "Cult members were being sent to Havana, Cuba, for extensive training in guerilla warfare" and were "graduating above the level of street crimes," the report claimed, and "beginning to develop small cadres within their cult capable of posing a serious problem to law enforcement."

The report concluded with the lamentation that "the absence of available Federal Funds and limited manpower restrict efforts to wage a full-scale campaign against the Ras Tafarians." Law-enforcement agents in New York and elsewhere were warned, "Most of the Ras Tafarians are armed and will kill to avoid detection or apprehension. They believe in reincarnation and do not fear death. They pose a definite threat to any police officer they come in contact with."[17] This report fed into existing fears in the city. People are generally prone to fear or shun difference and, quite naturally, viewed with skepticism, if not disdain, the unique appearance, beliefs, and customs of the Rastafarians. Many North Americans also tended to fear foreigners, or at least to view them with suspicion, and the police action no doubt heightened that fear.

Throughout the 1980s the U.S. public would be inundated with violent and sinister media images of Rastafarians. In 1980, Dan Rather and 60 Minutes portrayed the movement as a multinational drug-smuggling corporation that used religious beliefs to conceal its illicit narcotics-importing activity.[18] In 1983, the noted syndicated journalist Jack Anderson wrote a series of articles for the Washington Post and Philadelphia Daily News in which he advanced claims similar to those in the New York City Police Department report. Anderson warned that "terrorism experts believe that the racist

Marxist-tinged criminal elements of the Rastafarian cult, already armed to the teeth, will begin striking at American political targets in the next few years."[19] Hollywood contributed to the sinister image with films such as *Marked for Death,* which presented Rastafari as a crazed and murderous "black magic–like" cult controlling illicit crack and cocaine distribution around the country.[20]

The combined media and law-enforcement assaults on Jamaican and U.S. Rastafarians were largely responsible for shaping public perceptions of the movement. By the mid-1980s, more than two thousand Rastafarians were behind bars in New York's state correctional facilities, and scores more languished in state and federal prisons around the country. Until the mid-1980s, prison officials refused to accept the Rastafarians as anything but "drug-crazed cultists." There were no cultural or spiritual programs available to Rasta prisoners. All were forced to undergo a humiliating shave and haircut, which typically resulted in physical confrontations and long periods in solitary confinement. The red, gold, and green colors were considered contraband, and no provision was made for Rasta dietary needs.[21] Although some accommodation has since been made for Rasta inmates and noted in recent court cases,[22] the late 1980s and early 1990s witnessed an escalation in the number of Rasta prison inmates across the nation. In New York State, the numbers have tripled in just one decade.[23] Moreover, while Rastafarians in some states have won the right to retain their dreadlocks behind bars, others are still routinely shaved and trimmed—a policy that continues to result in violent confrontations, as evidenced in the recent rebellion involving Rastafarian and Muslim prisoners at the Broad River Correctional Institution in South Carolina.[24]

In retrospect, the cooperative efforts of law-enforcement and the media in the deprecation of U.S. Rastafarians seem to have been part of a larger "War on Drugs" ideology that developed over successive presidential administrations in the 1970s—a trend that would come to fruition during the Reagan-Bush era. A legacy of that era is today's massive prison building and expansion programs. With more than 1.5 million inmates in federal, state, and local penitentiaries, the United States has one of the highest rates of incarceration anywhere in the world. According to recent Justice Department figures, one in three black men in their twenties are imprisoned or on probation or parole. For the first time in U.S. history, the number of black inmates now surpasses the number of Whites.[25] Clearly, the imprisonment of Rastas is part of this general trend.

However, other ideological sources of the hostility directed at North American Rastafarians should also be noted, including Washington's antipathy to the Manley regime during the mid- to late 1970s. Several well-timed intelligence leaks during this period attempted to associate Manley with allegedly violent criminal elements in the U.S. Rastafarian community. These leaks were probably intended to undermine the credibility and destabilize the government of Manley, whom many at the time perceived as the most important spokesperson of the nonaligned movement in the Third World. The close ties between the Manley regime and Cuba, Manley's fondness for democratic socialist welfare and nationalization schemes, and his resistance to International Monetary Fund's (IMF) fiscal impositions bought him opposition both in Washington and on Wall Street. The Manley-Rastafari-Cuba connection had a comical sensibility that was exploited by political pundits and "policy wonks" alike in Washington and on Wall Street, as well as among their counterparts in the Jamaican establishment.

The illustrations above indicate the difficulties associated with a reliance on print and electronic media and law-enforcement sources in constructing a historical overview of the Rastafarian movement in the United States. What they do tell us is something about the power of the corporate-owned mass media and the corrosive influence of American prejudice and xenophobia in shaping public perceptions of new and foreign-born religious movements. Even more, these illustrations allow one to begin assessing the limitations on religious freedoms in a country literally "awash in a sea of faith" but still unable to allow groups such as the Rastafarians their full religious liberties.

In the absence of other literary source materials, we have had to rely on the oral testimonies of movement activists and on personal observation to construct a more adequate picture of North American Rastafari. The problems with Rasta demographics are legion—not the least of which is the reluctance of many Rastas to participate in such surveys. After thirty years of intense scrutiny by researchers, we still have no accurate numerical account of the movement as it exists in Jamaica, let alone the United States. In 1985 the New York City Police Department estimated approximately ten thousand Rastas living in New York City; however, the department did not indicate by what method it had arrived at that calculation. More recently, the 1989–1990 City University of New York–sponsored National Survey of Religious Identification (NSRI) estimated a national population of fourteen thousand Rastafarians.[26] The NSRI projections, however, are woefully low. A conservative estimate of New York City's Rastafari population alone would exceed the NSRI's entire national projection.

Rastafari Goes North

Although it may yet be too early to project accurate demographic figures, Rastafarians, like other Jamaican immigrants, are to be found in every state in the country today. While the largest numbers are found in the eastern seaboard's urban centers, such as New York; Philadelphia; Boston; New Haven, Connecticut; Miami; and Washington, D.C., there are also sizable communities in Los Angeles, the Bay Area (San Francisco), Chicago, and Houston. The movement appeals first and foremost to young Caribbean immigrants, especially those from the anglophone countries. Perhaps the majority are of Jamaican descent, but nearly all Caribbean islands are represented, as well as a growing number of African, African American, Native American, and white American Rastas. The movement has now crossed racial and ethnic lines, as it did class distinctions in Jamaica in the 1970s.

As others argue in this anthology, the spread of Rastafari, especially its symbols and imagery, is partly due to the popular influence of reggae music, which has introduced currently popular rap and hip-hop youth cultures to particular Rastafarian practices, such as ganja smoking and the wearing of dreadlocks. Throughout North America, dreadlocks now represent something of an Afrocentric fashion statement, and disentangling the genuine Rastafarians from their dreadlocked imitators requires extensive ethnographic research. In terms of the movement's social and class rank in the United States, these, too, are no longer simple matters. While the historical bearers of the movement have always been drawn from subordinate classes (the "sufferahs"), the role of middle-class leaders, intellectuals, entertainment figures, and entrepreneurs has complicated a clear analysis of the movement's class composition. Still, the large majority of rank-and-file Rastafarians appear to be drawn from the lower middle and working classes and the under and unemployed—what some are increasingly calling the "black underclass."[27]

Occupational patterns among employed Rastafarians vary: some work in the low-wage service sector; others find employment as skilled and semiskilled laborers, artisans, and artists. A small but growing entrepreneurial layer has emerged to meet some of the needs of these scattered communities. In addition to scores of reggae music stores, there are manufacturers of Rasta health and medicinal products, as well as Rasta-owned health food stores and "ital" restaurants. A handful of small retail stores carrying distinctive Rasta apparel and other accessories are now found throughout West Indian residential and commercial districts. And Rasta street vendors selling incense, oils, and ritual paraphernalia are nearly omnipresent in the big cities.

Many Rastas in North America, like their counterparts throughout the Caribbean, are motivated by the desire to escape "wage enslavement" in Babylon; hence a high premium is placed on self-employment. However, the lack of resources and other opportunities, combined with patterns of internal ritual consumption of ganja, provides the motivation for some U.S. Rastafarians to participate in the ganja trade. While my research to date does not support the imaginative (but popular) conclusion that Rastas play a dominant or disproportionate role in marijuana trafficking, clearly, some Rastas are involved. Although projecting the number of brothers and sisters involved in such activity is probably impossible, my interviews with current and former ganja dealers indicate that, for most, "professional ganja dealing" was not their preferred occupational choice. Moreover, the typical "career" of Rasta dealers is relatively short. Part-time dealing sometimes fills the gaps between casual employments or during long periods of unemployment. For the few able to "make it big" in the ganja trade, resources are frequently turned to the establishment of legitimate businesses and other community-building institutions, and trafficking is ultimately left behind.

Although more research will have to be done in this sensitive area, this author has not found any evidence to suggest that genuine Rastafarians are involved in the trafficking of crack, cocaine, or other, more harmful illicit substances. The propensity of some Rastafarians to use ganja for ritual, medicinal, and casual (recreational) purposes does not typically extend to other substance use. On the contrary, Rastas are adamantly opposed to substance abuse, whether of the alcoholic or the narcotic variety.[28] Some New York Rastafarians have even recently begun speaking out against the abuse of ganja by young people. As Jah Life, a record-shop owner and longtime Rasta voice in the East Flatbush community of Brooklyn, recently explained, "All smoking, including ganja, the holy herb, can be bad for the body. It is better to boil it and drink it as tea. Don't keep a blunt on you all the time, draw it and draw it until you lose the feeling, the enjoyment of it. Whatever you do, don't abuse it."[29]

The role of ganja in the communal and commercial life of North American Rastafarians is a sensitive but legitimate topic for Rasta researchers. Clearly, the Rasta-ganja connection is a source of tension between the movement and law enforcement, as well as a primary source of negative perception by some sectors of the general public. However, I contend that ganja has too frequently been used as a "smoke screen" to conceal larger sources of tension and conflict between the movement and the state. Moreover, a fixation on the highly ritualized practice of ganja smoking tends to eclipse a broader array of positive community activities engaged in by Rastafarians.

Building Communities in Babylon

The North American Rastafari movement both reflects the organizational disarray of the movement in Jamaica and partially reproduces its highly decentralized and "polycephalous" (multileader) character. A score of formally organized "mansions" (churches, congregations, and associations)[30] compete for the allegiance of a larger, institutionally unaffiliated sector of fellow communicants. No single leader or organization can speak for the movement as a whole. Nonetheless, Rasta community building occurs in every location where Rastas have gathered in sufficient numbers. One can observe a pattern in the institutional dynamics of the movement as it spreads and wins new adherents. The first institutions typically erected are the reggae club or dance hall; the "smoking yard" or "weed gate," where ganja is procured and sometimes smoked; and the various storefronts where Rasta apparel and ritual items, as well as ital foods and medicinal products, can be obtained. Informal networks emerge as brothers and sisters "ground" together at the dance hall or smoking yard. "Reasoning" circles form in small groups when a critical number of Rastas amass in a particular location, and then the building of churches, community centers, and political associations follows.

Perhaps only in New York City can one find a community large enough to sponsor the range of institutional and ecclesiastical options available to Rastas in Jamaica. In New York, one can find Twelve Tribes of Israel congregants competing with Ethiopian Orthodox Church members; followers of Prince Emmanuel and the Bobo Ashanti (Ethiopian African International Congress) reasoning with "bredren" from the Nyabinghi Order of Divine Theocracy; or the Ethiopian World Federation sponsoring a public forum with members of the Church of Haile Selassie I. From Morris Heights in the Bronx to Jamaica and Hillside in Queens, and from 125th Street in Harlem and Washington Square Park in Manhattan to Crown Heights and Bedford-Stuyvesant in Brooklyn, the sights and "word sounds" of Rastafari livity have become an indelible part of the fabric of life in New York City. And the presence of Rasta churches and community centers has added a vital dimension to the religious landscape and cultural mix of America's most diverse city.

What all of the organized formations or mansions have in common is an evolving form of congregational worship. While the details of the "cultus" may differ from case to case, all share a form of local, face-to-face religious assembly that, in part, represents an innovative renegotiation of the movement's institutionally anarchic past. A series of calendrical events centered on important dates in the movement's history provides occasions for larger, more traditional community gatherings, sometimes held outdoors between sunset and sunrise and involving the particular Rastafarian practices of drumming and chanting. However, these gatherings, known as Nyabinghis or "groundations," are too infrequent and impersonal to serve the needs of highly active local Rasta networks. The creation of Rasta churches and congregational associations is an attempt to fill a perceived void in the lives of Rastas whose primary form of association has been the dance halls and smoking yards. In addition to worship proper, each congregation provides a number of services to its adherents, such as Sunday school classes, biblical reasonings, band and choir rehearsals, "Rastological counseling," political education, ital cooking workshops, and African history and language instruction. Such institutions help create the context for community involvement and leadership development, essential to both emerging religious movements and new emigrant groups.

Although only a minority of North American Rastas are affiliated with the organized churches, these groups and individuals constitute the most active and involved enthusiasts in the movement. The disciplined character of weekly gatherings and face-to-face discursive exchanges, not to mention the role of leaders, intellectuals, and formal institutional structures, tends to challenge and constrain the organizationally diffuse and doctrinally idiosyncratic nature of much of the larger movement. Moreover, the organized mansions are able to mobilize a larger resource base and, consequently, provide greater services and public recognition for their members. As Brother Foxe, the founder and spiritual head of the Church of Haile Selassie I in Bedford-Stuyvesant, Brooklyn (with sister churches in Jamaica, England, and a half dozen other Caribbean nations), explained to me in the fall of 1994:

> I-an-I bredrin reason and say, for real I-an-I need a church to provide Rastafari people worldwide with a documented way of worship; a church that would legitimize I-an-I belief and give I-an-I offspring and elders security and religious status in the workplace, community, and at school. I-an-I need a church to rise up the youth dem, to big up [strengthen] the family so I-an-I youths not go lick crack, buy gun, shot and dead. I-an-I youths need to know I-an-I faith so dem can defend His Majesty at school and know why dem carry locks upon dem head. At the same time, it was I-an-I intention that by the twenty-first century His Imperial Majesty, Emperor Haile Selassie I, would be praised in temples all over the world. . . . This means Selassie I must be proclaimed and worshiped among all nations and incense burned intinually [continually] in His name. For His Majesty is the God-of-this-Age, Jah come in the flesh. I-an-I must worship HIM [the] same way as the Indian man worship him own Krishna, Rama, Brahma. For this I-an-I create the church in the divine name, the new name, and it terrible and dreadful, 'cause heathen no like Jah name.

According to Brother Foxe, the church was needed to accomplish several goals: to provide a routinized ritual association in a highly active community, to socialize the new generation in order to create strong families, and to carry out Rasta evangelization in all countries. While these needs may appear to be relatively standard features of North American religious communities, they represent a significant departure from traditional forms of Rastafari practice and organization. Traditionally, Rastas were less concerned with church and institution building than they were with personal identity and movement formation. The ritual practices of drumming, chanting, and communal ganja smoking did not require rigorous organizational structure. Formal gatherings were periodic. Informal reasonings provided the primary form of socialization in the organizationally diffuse rural camps and urban yards. Moreover, traditional Rastas placed little emphasis on educating their women and female children; it was enough if their sons began "manifesting" Rasta by the time they came of age. Finally, traditional Rastas knew nothing about preaching Rastafari to all nations, as it was a message and movement directed to the sons and, to a lesser extent, the daughters of Africa—the true lost sheep of Israel. Babylon was falling, and it was the duty of Rastafarians simply to prepare themselves individually for the coming exodus, when they would flee Babylon and return to Zion.

However, the exigencies of life in a foreign country, the delay of repatriation, and the influx of new members of varying ethnic and religious backgrounds have created new conditions and needs, which the churches and congregational formations are attempting to address. In many ways, the new Rasta congregations provide greater opportunities for both individual and family participation. Rasta women, frequently absent from smoking yards and dance halls, are more noticeably active in the churches, where they serve as Sunday school teachers, recording secretaries, social-event coordinators, and leaders in the auxiliary organizations. In addition to providing protected enclaves in a hostile environment, the churches open up space for women's participation that was frequently absent in both the traditional and secular wings of the movement. At the same time, the development of Rasta churches represents a convergence toward or an assimilation of the deep-seated American religious tradition of church building and congregational involvement.[31] The public presence of Rastafari churches serves as a powerful witness that the movement has arrived at a new stage in its development in North America. While reggae music may have been the historical vehicle for the popular dissemination of Rastafari, it is increasingly the organized religious community that is the primary referent for brothers and sisters deepening their faith or socializing a new generation.

In the past decade, U.S. Rastafari has strengthened its ties with communities of "elders" and other institutional bodies in Jamaica, to ensure the movement's integrity and continuity in its transplanted home. Both Barry Chevannes and Carole Yawney have noted the important role of official delegations of elders from the Nyabinghi House in Jamaica.[32] In public ritual performances, lectures, and extended reasonings, the elders have challenged the negative images of Rastafari sponsored by the press and law enforcement. At the same time, the elders have attempted to strengthen and deepen the faith of local communities while extending the influence of the Nyabinghi, which itself is evolving in the direction of a multipurpose congregation. Other Jamaican-based groups have also sponsored the creation of "daughter" churches in the United States, some of which are legally recognized (tax-exempt) bodies. The first Rastafari prison ministry now exists in New York State with its own officially recognized "Rastafarian chaplain," and another community is sponsoring the first Rastafari Advancement Seminary.[33]

The "movement of Jah people," however, is not a unidirectional operation. Inspiration and influence flow in both directions. The maturation of the movement in North America contributes, in turn, to the movement back home. The recent advent of Rastafarian "womanist" voices owes much to the experience of Rastafari "sistren" in the United States and Canada. And the influx of new groups and individuals into the spirit of the movement reinforces the evolving multiethnic and universalist character of Rastafari. Because of its location in the heart of Babylon, the North American Rastafari community may, paradoxically, play a central role in the continued institutionalization of the movement in Jamaica and elsewhere. Of course, like Rastafarians in Jamaica, a majority of North American Rastas remain "unchurched" or institutionally unaffiliated. Some belong to quasi-organized formations, centered on local leaders, that meet in individual homes or "house churches." Others gather somewhat regularly at Rastafarian-owned businesses, restaurants, and smoking yards. Still others frequent the services and gatherings of the larger churches but remain nonmembers or sympathizers only. A minority retain nominal membership or identify with groups in Jamaica that do not have organized counterparts abroad.

As in Jamaica, a central component in the lived experience of North American Rastas is the collective practice of reasonings. In the absence of formal organizations, participation in reasonings functions as the context within which new Rasta "manifests" (converts) are socialized and educated, linguistic practices are codified, and certain individuals are selected as leaders within the movement. The reasoning is also a principal site wherein the ritual consumption of ganja is sacralized and its psychoactive properties are assimilated to the discursive practices and visionary quests of Rastafarians.[34] However, this activity seems to play different roles among various sectors of the North American community. Less emphasis seems to be placed on the collective practice of reasoning where congregational forms are strong. Moreover, congregational involvement sometimes undercuts the ability of brothers and sisters to reason effectively with members of other mansions. A sectarian propensity appears among some congregational enthusiasts who refuse to recognize the legitimacy of other Rasta churches and lament the "underdeveloped spirituality" of the unchurched masses. This may suggest a development away from the looser, decentralized, polycephalous character of the movement in the direction of what, for lack of a better term, might be called "Rasta denominationalism."

In mapping the Rastafari community, it might be useful to think of a continuum, with organized or church-affiliated Rastas representing one end and the organizationally unaffiliated the other. On both ends of the continuum one can find religiously and culturally motivated actors. Clearly, not all Rastafarians identify themselves as explicitly "religious." For some, the practice of Rastafari is primarily cultural and political, whereas for others, the religious and theological affirmations are central. For example, the religiously motivated emphasize the theological and messianic centrality of Selassie and Ethiopia. They variously interpret Selassie as "Jah"—the divine Creator, the God of heaven and earth—or as a messianic personage, a prophetic figure, or the returned black Christ. In each case, these Rastas stress Selassie's divinity and his supernatural power to effect black liberation.

Among what one might term "cultural Rastas," the historical and political significance of Selassie and Ethiopia in the struggle against fascist and colonial aggression tends to be emphasized, as well as the role that Selassie played in the founding of the Organization of African Unity (OAU). However, for these brothers and sisters Selassie remains a strictly "this-worldly" or human figure, sharply differentiated from Jah. Both "kinds" of Rastas draw on a similar set of historical and cultural symbols, but the meanings ascribed to the symbols frequently vary. As already indicated, one can find both types of Rastas at each end of the continuum, but among the organizationally unaffiliated, one tends to find more who define themselves largely in cultural and political terms.

Ras Amlak, a tall, lanky brother with dreadlocks that extend below his knees, is an example of the organizationally unaffiliated. For more than twenty years he has practiced his trade as an incense and oil manufacturer and salesman in Crown Heights, Brooklyn. At the same time, he has been a militant representative of a politically active and oppositional current within Rastafari. He has gathered around himself a small circle of like-minded "souljahs," who refuse to identify with the organized mansions and do not worship or recognize Selassie as divine. In a "reasoning" of fall 1989, Brother Amlak said:

> It's not that I-an-I have contempt for those Rasses who worship His Majesty. At least that turns their attention away from a white sky-god and the white man's ways. Rasta people need to break with Babylon and look inward. That is why I-an-I say, "Rasta-for-I"—because the "I" is divine, and the divine I lies within every man. That means the church is wherever two or more are gathered. I-an-I don't need a church structure and organization for that. "Man free!" That is I-an-I motto. And I-an-I need liberation, a revolution to destroy downpression, not a church to worship Selassie in.

The intention here is not to draw a hard-and-fast line of demarcation between religious and cultural or political Rastas, let alone to differentiate or distinguish "real Rastas" from impostors. As José Casanova has recently argued in his comparative study of church-state relations around the world, under conditions of late modernity, disentangling the religious from the strictly political domain proves increasingly difficult.[35] Nonetheless, the fact that participants within the movement make such a distinction may indicate a simultaneous process of secularization and religious innovation in contemporary North American Rastafari.

While many differences and similarities between Jamaican Rastafari and U.S. Rastafari abound, one theme that remains unchanged in the North American experience is the militant rejection of Babylon—the ensemble of Eurocentric, imperialist, and capitalist structures of power that "downpress" and dehumanize all working people, but especially working people of color. Since the capitalist system, militarism, and racism of the United States toward Blacks epitomize Babylon, Rastas reject many of the nation's cultural and religious values. Until the day that "righteousness covers the earth," symbolized by Zion, Rastas attempt to create "Zionic" conditions within their respective "exodus" communities. This effort takes many forms. In addition to the ritualized practice of "chanting down" Babylon, wherein Rastafarians signify to themselves and others their rejection of a world based on crass, materialistic values, competition, and racial animosities, Rastas also attempt to identify positive spatial and temporal locations where people can come together for worship and play, for entertainment and fellowship. Here new identities can form and communal structures and relationships based on traditional norms of reciprocity, sharing, and collective ownership emerge. Here also one finds the strength and support necessary to live a life that goes against the grain of Babylon's competitive materialism, individualism, and nihilism. As Brother Judah, a longtime member of the Twelve Tribes in New York City, reported in an interview in September 1990:

> We're building up resistance to let the authorities know that I-an-I will resist and refuse to cooperate, to comply with the norm they set up in this society. That's why we refer to one another [other Rastas] as "I-an-I"—we don't make no one a second person. We don't say "I and him" or "us." We just say "I-an-I," because every person is a first person. And the system tries to put you down—that's why we call it "downpression," 'cause it's not "upful" to be downpressed. That's what the "shitstem" [system] is always trying to do: confuse I-an-I with their language. So, Rasta just sprung up to resist, to resist downpression, to resist being controlled. And that's what Rasta is about. I-an-I refuse to comply with the shitstem, 'cause I-an-I know the system is not right. Instead, I-an-I are struggling for a better world, a world where I-an-I control I-an-I own destinies. And I-an-I know that such a world can only be finally realized when Babylon has fallen!

Rasta language is expressive of a newly discovered confidence, born out of suffering and survival, that somehow the apocalyptic drama of universal human liberation has its starting point in the particular liberation of Africans—at home and abroad. Rastas recognize their position in the socioeconomic structure of capitalist societies as something *dreadful*. And in their typical dialectical fashion, Rastas imbue that term and social position with something more than its obvious or apparent meaning. The word *dread* (and *dreadful*), for example, is imbued with dialectical positiveness by Rastas and performs a variety of grammatical and linguistic functions.[36] "Dread," of course, refers to the unique Rastafari style of hair grooming, or dreadlocks, which is probably the most universally recognizable symbol of Rastafarians. Along with a constellation of other potent symbols and practices, dreadlocks visually announce the symbolic separation of Rastas from modern-day Babylon. But dread means something more than simply hair. For Rastas, good reggae is dread. Natural disasters and storms are also dreadful. But what may be positive for the Dread (that is, the Rasta) is frequently negative for the "downpressor." So, for the heathen, the downpressor and despiser of poor people, Rasta is dreadful, but not in its positive sense. As Rastas say, "It'a go dread in Babylon!" meaning "It's going to be terrible for the wicked come judgment day."

The social position that Rastas inhabit in Babylon also represents a nodal point, a central site of concentration, wherein the fundamental contradictions of racist and capitalist society are made manifest. Most Rastas are keenly aware of their downpressed class and status position within the U.S. system of social and economic stratification. They know what it means to live on the margins of respectful society—"It's dread inna America!" However, Rastas derive comfort from their confidence that the day of liberation cannot be forever postponed, that a day of reckoning must soon come, and that the resolution of their own dreadful oppression in Babylon holds the key to the liberation of all humanity.

The Rastafarian vision encompasses judgment and destruction; but it also embraces life and creation. Beyond and in the midst of present society, Rastas envision (in proleptic fashion) the emergence of a new Zionlike society, symbolized by collective memories of an ancient Africa (Ethiopia) before the era of colonialism but increasingly mediated through the emerging notions of "liberation before repatriation" and the "Africanization of diaspora societies." If they cannot be transported (repatriated) to Zion, then Zion must somehow be brought to or created within the societies in which Rastafarians have been forced to dwell.

Ideologically, Rastafari articulates, among other things, the effort and the interest of an oppressed group to affirm itself as an authentic, legitimate cultural agent. At the core of the Rasta experience exists a profound sense of *empowerment*—a discovery of the "divine I" within and its interconnectedness with others. Just as God (Jah) became human in the personality of His Majesty and, indeed, among all Rasta people, so human beings must become God through a process of self-divinization. In Rastafari, a fundamentally ambiguous set of symbols allows for multiple readings and interpretations by those who move within its spirit. In its own unique dialectic, Rastafari becomes *Rasta-for-I*. The realization of the divine I within all human persons makes a facile reconciliation with Babylon, with actually existing capitalist and racist society, impossible, regardless of the immediate benefits that accrue to those capable of such a feat.

The symbolic ambiguity contained in Rastafari practices and beliefs permits its appropriation by many different peoples struggling for a world where, in the prophetic words of Haile Selassie (immortalized in Bob Marley's anthem "War"), there is "no longer first class and second class citizens of any nation," where "the color of a man's skin is of no more significance than the color of his eyes."[37] Until that day, Rastas will remain, as Jahman, another New York City Rasta militant confided, "Soldiers in His Imperial Majesty's army—dreadlocks fighting until Babylon falls!"

Reggae Music in North American Rastafari

Nearly every contemporary student of the Rastafari movement has noted the powerful role of reggae music in the international spread and dissemination of Rastafari. Neil Savishinsky is not alone when he says, "What is perhaps most unique about Rastafari is that it may represent the only contemporary socioreligious movement whose diffusion is directly tied to a medium of popular culture, [namely] reggae music."[38] The decline of the international youth and New Left movements of the 1960s and the perceived commodification of rock music in the 1970s created the conditions for the emergence of new social movements and new musical forms. The rise to international stardom of Bob Marley, perhaps the most culturally influential musician to ever come out of the so-called Third World, certainly assisted the process of reggae's global reception. These factors, in turn, stimulated interest in reggae's underlying ideational impulses, whose bearers were the Rastafari.

I contend that the role of reggae music in the globalization of Rastafari, especially in terms of its growth and development in North America, has too frequently been over-stated, thus neglecting other pertinent factors. Moreover, a fixation on reggae music, like ganja, obscures the role of many important Rasta institutions. Most importantly, much of the scholarly literature has seriously neglected to document and analyze Rasta-farian organizations, such as its churches, political associations, and other community-building projects. Many researchers have been content to note the "acephalous" char-acter of Rastafari and to bemoan its lack of organizational cohesion, before returning to the decidedly more seductive cultural aspects of the movement.

Part of the explanation for the fascination with reggae has to do with the appeal of the music itself. Its complex percussive and bass rhythms combine with a politicized and highly spiritual lyrical content to create a compelling popular—and increasingly inter-national—cultural medium, capable of articulating the needs and interests of struggling peoples in diverse contexts. The point that needs to be underscored here is that how-ever necessary reggae may have been to the initial dissemination of Rastafari through-out the United States, it is not a sufficient condition, by itself, to account for the growth and maturation of the movement. Certainly, emigration from Jamaica must be factored into a larger synchronic explanation, but here, too, something seems missing. The in-creasingly multiethnic and international character of Rastafari suggests the need for an interpretive approach rooted in the analysis of Rastafari beliefs, practices, symbols, and norms, but one also capable of relating movements such as Rasta to global socioeco-nomic processes at work in all sectors of the modern world (dis)order.

Such an approach has been recently advanced by Terisa Turner and Carole Yawney.[39] For example, Turner argues that contemporary Rastafari must be understood as "part of an international social movement of resistance to [neoliberal capitalist strategies of] structural adjustment" and as an "affirmation of a new society" that transcends the con-tradictions of Eurocentric, racist, sexist and class-divided societies.[40] Likewise, Yawney posits "approaching the vision of Rastafari as a constellation of ambiguous symbols, which today has the power to focalize and even mediate certain socio-cultural tensions that have developed on a global scale."[41] Precisely such an approach seems most capa-ble of making sense of the Rastafari experience in the United States.

Rastafari must be understood and analyzed on its own terms, in conjunction with global economic developments, and, comparatively, in relation to other important po-litical, social, and religious movements. In this respect, it might be useful to combine fu-ture study of Rastafari with the examination of other recent developments in popular, oppositional religious cultures, such as the emergence of base Christian community movements and liberation theologies in Latin America and South Africa. By uniting micro-level analysis of Rastafari's cultural practices, meanings, institutions, and organizations with macro-level analytical and comparative study, a comprehensive account of the movement becomes discernible. Researchers and students of Rastafari would do well to look *through and beyond reggae* to the wellsprings of creativity contained within the Rastafari movement in its confrontation with the modern world.

Notes

1. This essay derives from a larger dissertation project titled "'Movement of Jah People': Race, Class, and Religion among the Rastafari of Jamaica and New York City." The author thanks the Research Institute for the Study of Man (RISM) and the New Ethnic and Immigrant Congregations Project (NEICP) for research grants that made possible fieldwork in both Jamaica and New York City.

2. N. Samuel Murrell, "Jamaican Americans," in Judy Galens, Anna Sheets, and Robyn V. Young, eds., *Gale Encyclopedia of Multicultural America*, vol. 2 (Detroit: Gale Research, 1995); John P. Homiak, "Jamaican Project: Final Report" (unpublished report: Washington, D.C.: Smithsonian Institution, Office of Folklife Programs, 1988), 785–86.

3. Philip Kasinitz, *Caribbean New York: Black Immigrants and the Politics of Race* (Ithaca, N.Y.: Cornell University Press, 1992), 55, 57, 64.

4. See the twelve-page bibliography in Kasinitz, *Caribbean New York*.

5. See Leahcim Tufani Semaj, "Inside Rasta: The Future of a Religious Movement," *Caribbean Review* 14, 1 (winter 1985): 8–11, 37–38; Neil J. Savishinsky, "Transnational Popular Culture and the Global Spread of the Jamaican Rastafarian Movement," *New West Indian Guide* 68, 3–4 (1994): 261–79.

6. William D. Spencer, "Rastafari: Poverty and Apostasy in Paradise," *Journal of Pastoral Practice* 4, 1 (1980): 67–68.

7. William David Spencer, "Manchild by the Rivers of Babylon: An Analysis of Rastafari's Churchly versus Sectarian Aspects to Interpret the Present and Predict the Future of the Rastafarian Experience in the United States" (unpublished manuscript, Zenas Gerig Library, Jamaica Theological Seminary, Kingston, 1983).

8. Linden F. Lewis, "Living in the Heart of Babylon: Rastafari in the USA," *Bulletin of Eastern Caribbean Affairs* 15, 1 (March–April 1989): 20–30.

9. Savishinsky, "Transnational Popular Culture," 263.

10. Because of the constant harassment of Rastas and other black minorities by law-enforcement officials in places such as New York City, some Rastas regard the United States and its police as the epitome of Babylon and see themselves as living in the "belly of the beast."

11. See Leonard Barrett, *The Rastafarians of Jamaica: Sounds of Cultural Dissonance* (Boston: Beacon Press, 1977), xxi, 197–201.

12. See Robert Hill, "Leonard P. Howell and Millenarian Visions in Early Rastafari," *Jamaica Journal* 16, 1 (1983): 26.

13. Barry Chevannes, "The Repairer of the Breach: Reverend Claudius Henry and Jamaican Society," in Frances Henry, ed., *Ethnicity in the Americas* (The Hague: Mouton Publishers, 1976), 278.

14. See "Religious Groups Tied to Shooting," *New York Times*, August 13, 1971, 10.

15. See "Four Slain in Brooklyn Tied to Jamaican Cult," *New York Times,* April 11, 1977, 15.

16. New York City Police Department (NYPD), "Rasta Crime: A Confidential Report," *Caribbean Review* 14, 1 (1985): 12–15.

17. Ibid., 39–40.

18. See broadcasts of *60 Minutes* (CBS-TV) from October 28, 1979, and December 7, 1980.

19. Jack Anderson, "Terrorists Infiltrate Rastafari," *Philadelphia Daily News,* June 29, 1983.

20. The demonization of Rastafari in the United States shares some features with the treatment of Haitian Voodoo in the popular press and media. For an interesting discussion on the denigration of Voodoo, see Laennec Hurbon, "American Fantasy and Haitian Vodou," in Donald Cosentino, ed., *Sacred Arts of Vodou* (Los Angeles: University of California, Fowler Museum of Cultural History, 1995).

21. Sister Morri, "Dread Inna Lion's Den: Rasta in Captivity," *Reggae and African Beat* 5, 5–6 (1986): 22–26.

22. Timothy Tailor, "Soul Rebel: The Rastafarians and the Free Exercise Clause," *Georgetown Review* 37, 3 (1984): 19–50. More recently, a federal appeals court in San Francisco has argued that Rastafarians can use their religious belief that marijuana is a sacrament as a defense against drug-possession charges. This recent ruling is significant in that it represents the first time a drug conviction has been overturned based on the 1993 Religious Freedom Restoration Act. See "Religion Ruled Valid Defense in Drug Case," *New York Times,* February 3, 1996.

23. "Pataki Plans to Lay Off Prison Chaplains, Fears Opposition," *New York Times*, February 26, 1995.

24. "Inmates Stab Five Guards at Prison before Bringing Protest to End," *New York Times,* April 18, 1996.

25. "More Blacks in Their Twenties Have Trouble with the Law," *New York Times,* October 5, 1995; *New York Times,* December 4, 1995.

26. Barry Alexander Kosmin, *Research Report: The National Survey of Religious Identification, 1989–1990 (Selected Tabulations)* (New York: City University of New York, Graduate School and University Center, 1991).

27. William Julius Wilson, *The Truly Disadvantaged: The Inner City, the Underclass and Public Policy* (Chicago: University of Chicago Press, 1987); Kasinitz, *Caribbean New York.*

28. Vera Rubin and Lambros Comitas, *Ganja in Jamaica* (New York: Doubleday Anchor Books, 1976).

29. Isaac Ferguson, "Blunt Posse: Why the Hip Hop Nation Is Getting High on 'the Chronic'," *Village Voice* 22 (June 1993): 34ff.

30. The Rastafari practice of referring to their larger churches, political associations, and community centers as "mansions" is proof-texted in John 14:2: "In my Father's house are many mansions" (KJV). Less formal and, typically, smaller associations are referred to as "camps" and "yards."

31. See R. Stephen Warner, "The Place of the Congregation in the Contemporary American Religious Configuration," in James P. Wind and James W. Lewis, eds., *American Congregations* (Chicago: University of Chicago Press, 1994), 2:26.

32. Barry Chevannes, *Rastafari: Roots and Ideology* (Syracuse, N.Y.: Syracuse University Press, 1994); Carole D. Yawney, "Rasta Mek a Trod: Symbolic Ambiguity in a Globalizing Religion," in Terisa Turner, ed., *Arise Ye Mighty People: Gender, Class and Race in Popular Struggles* (Trenton, N.J.: Africa World Press, 1994), 75–83.

33. "A Rastafari Seminary," *New York Times,* February 26, 1995.

34. John Homiak, "The Mystic Revelation of Rasta Far-Eye: Visionary Communication in a Prophetic Movement," in Barbara Tedlock, ed., *Dreaming: Anthropological and Psychological Interpretations* (Cambridge: Cambridge University Press, 1987), 224–25.

35. José Casanova, *Public Religions in the Modern World* (Chicago: University of Chicago Press, 1994).

36. On Rasta linguistic practices, see Velma Pollard, *Dread Talk: The Language of Rastafari* (Kingston: Canoe Press/University of the West Indies, 1994).

37. Bob Marley and the Wailers, "War," on *Rastaman Vibration,* Island Records/ILPS 9383, 1976.

38. Neil J. Savishinsky, "Rastafari in the Promised Land: The Spread of a Jamaican Socioreligious Movement among the Youth of West Africa," *African Studies Review* 37, 3 (1994): 21.

39. Terisa Turner, "Rastafari and the New Society: Caribbean and East African Feminist Roots of a Popular Movement to Reclaim the Earthly Commons," in Turner, ed., *Arise Ye Mighty People,* 9–55.

40. Ibid., 10.

41. Yawney, "Rasta Mek a Trod," 76.

13 Personal Reflections on Rastafari in West Kingston in the Early 1950s

GEORGE EATON SIMPSON

Prior to my research in 1953, no scholarly attention had been paid to the Rastafari. Why there was a hiatus between the beginning of the movement in the early 1930s and the first scholarly investigation of it, I can only speculate. The University of the West Indies was not founded until 1947, and as far as I know, no one from the University of Puerto Rico, the British universities, or universities in the United States had taken an interest in the Rastas. Perhaps conditions during the Great Depression and World War II did not encourage social scientific research in the Caribbean. Television was not yet providing instant reportage on events in regions of the world that were not well known to viewers.

My interest in the Caribbean region and in West Africa goes back to 1930. While a graduate student at the University of Pennsylvania, I heard Professor Melville Herskovits of Northwestern University speak about the fieldwork that he and his wife had done in remote sections of Dutch Guiana (now Suriname) in 1929. I found his account of the persistence of important parts of West African cultures in northern South America impressive and fascinating. I remember that Frank Speck, a professor of anthropology at Pennsylvania, said Herskovits's report was "like finding an American Indian settlement in the heart of Central Africa." I began then to think about doing fieldwork in Subsaharan Africa or the Caribbean. Because of the differential costs of such trips and the fact that we had two small children, then four and two years old, my wife and I decided on the Caribbean. We went initially to Haiti in 1937, where I did fieldwork on peasant life near the village of Plaisance in the northern part of the island. Herskovits, in fact, had suggested this region, pointing out that no researcher had yet worked in the northern part of Haiti. For professional and other reasons, we did not get to West Africa until 1964, when we worked in the Ibadan region of Nigeria. We made a number of trips to Jamaica (1946, 1953, 1957, 1967, 1971), Trinidad (1960), St. Lucia (1972), and other islands of the West Indies.

From the experience in Haiti grew my interest in studying accumulative processes in the region—that is, understanding the process of cultural change that occurs when the representatives of two or more cultures meet. I found the ideas that Herskovits formulated, including the concepts of retentions, reinterpretations, and syncretism, to be useful in trying to understand what has happened culturally in the meeting of Europeans, Africans, American Indians, East Indians, and Asians in the New World, especially on the islands of the Caribbean Sea. These ideas were on my mind during my first visit to Jamaica in 1946, where I became aware of a range of Afro-Jamaican religious cults as well as of the existence of the Rastafari. It was with these same interests that I traveled to Jamaica in 1953 to conduct fieldwork on Revival groups. Thus the study of Rastafari was not my main reason for going to Jamaica in 1953; my purpose then was to do research on syncretistic religious cults, mainly Revival Zion. In the course of doing this fieldwork, I came in contact with the Rastafari, who shared the same West Kingston environs with members of these revivalist groups, and decided to learn more about this movement. The principal Revival group I studied was that of Mallica (Kapo) Reynolds, a well-known Revival Zion leader, whose meeting place was directly across the lane from a Rasta yard.

Unlike the contemporary Rasta movements, Rastas in 1953 were exclusively a Jamaican phenomenon. They belonged to autonomous groups, augmented by persons who attended meetings or sympathized with the sentiments and aims of the movement. At that time, the revivalist movement (Revival, Revival Zion, and Pocomania) had a large following, particularly among low-income workers and the unemployed in severely depressed areas such as Trench Town in West Kingston. In this same social milieu I first encountered the Rastas. Despite similarities in types of organization, holiday celebrations and excursions, and even ritual procedures, there were important differences between the two movements. Although I encountered forceful leaders among both Rasta and revivalist groups, the latter were clearly more leader-dominated. Drumming, "rejoicing," "spiritual" dancing, and possession trance, invariably features of revivalism, were regarded by Rastas as "backward" and never occurred in their gatherings. Even though Rasta music and Revival music shared a common focus on Sankey—a Christian musical style that inherited the name of its composer and lyricist of the 1930s and 1940s—and on other Christian hymns (the latter adapted to suit Rasta ideology), drumming was completely absent from Rasta gatherings at that time.

Similarly, ganja (marijuana) was not smoked during Rasta meetings, nor did I hear Rastas expound on the biblical aspects or spiritual virtues of ganja, referring to it as "the herb" or "the healing of the nations," as is common today. If this was a feature of the Rasta worldview, it apparently was not yet as fully developed or as widespread in the movement as American anthropologist Sheila Kitzinger[1] reported, based on her fieldwork done twelve years later in West Kingston.[2] Perhaps the Rastas with whom I became familiar were reluctant to use ganja publicly or to use it in my presence. Even so, this practice represents a significant difference from what later students of the movement reported, namely, that members openly invited attention to their use of ganja, extolling its virtues, claiming a biblical warrant, and citing spiritual purposes for its use, to distinguish themselves from members of the wider society.

Beards and dreadlocks were a much less prominent feature of the Rastafari in the early days of the movement than they became later. I can recollect seeing only one or two Dreadlocks in a meeting of young Rastas and only infrequently glimpsed them on the street. I did not encounter the distinctive form of "Rasta talk," based on the use of the self-reflective "I" or "I-an-I," that is now a widely noted aspect of Rasta culture. The term *Babylon* was used to refer to the colonial power structure, and there was use of an associated biblical discourse. However, there was nothing of the vocabulary that is now common among the Rastafari, and never a reference to the term *reasoning*, which is now used to cover their distinctive discourse.[3]

What stands out in my memory is that members of the movement were bitter about injustices based on race and social class. At every meeting they denounced "the white man" and "the black traitors"—the politicians, police, clergy, teachers, landholders, business and professional people who were said to have misled and mistreated the people. In response to this treatment, Rastas (like Garveyites before them) preached race consciousness, based on the program of "Africa for the Africans at home and abroad." While revivalists were engrossed mainly in the quest for personal salvation and the satisfaction to be gained from ritual observances, Rastafarians were concerned and very vocal about economic hardships and racial discrimination. Although many Rastas in the 1950s had been involved earlier in some type of revivalism, most subsequently became hostile to these religious groups. Among Rasta groups I encountered, repatriation to Africa was preached as the solution to the hopeless hell of Jamaica.

On my visit to Jamaica in 1946, I saw men and women, who were identified to me as Rastas, wearing red, gold, and green caps and scarves. Friends told me that I should not expect to go to a closed Rastafari meeting. In fact, at that time no scholar, black or white, had attempted to gain entrance to such gatherings. Philip Sherlock, then director of Extramural Studies for Jamaica Welfare and later principal and vice-chancellor of the University of the West Indies, introduced me to Arthur Bethune, a Boys' Club worker in West Kingston. Then and later, Mr. Bethune was extremely helpful in introducing me to residents of Trench Town and other areas of West Kingston and in advising me on what he thought I could and could not do, and should and should not do, in the Kingston and St. Andrew metropolitan area. Bethune said that going to a Rasta meeting would be impossible. He had seen Rastafari street meetings but had never been present at other gatherings.

Bethune parked his car inside a shedlike building near his office. One day, while accompanying him, I noticed a photograph, torn from a magazine, that hung on a nail which protruded from an inside wall of the building. Outside, I asked Bethune if he recognized that picture. It was, he said, a photograph of Haile Selassie. Half a dozen men worked in the empty space inside this garage, making seat covers for automobiles on small sewing machines operated by hand; I asked Bethune to go back and find out if one of the workers belonged to a Rastafari group, and if so, whether Bethune and I could attend one of their meetings. No one could give us such permission, but one man promised to speak to the leader of his group.

Bethune and I were soon invited to Mr. Joseph Myers's home in Trench Town. I explained to Mr. Myers what I had already told Mr. Mallica Reynolds: that I taught in an American university and that my teaching and writing included studies of Caribbean society and race relations in the United States. Both men were of limited formal education, but they knew about the existence of the University of the West Indies.

Like a number of other early Rastafari leaders, Mr. Myers[4] (Brother Myers, as he was called by Rastas) had traveled outside Jamaica and therefore had a somewhat wider view of the world than did most of his contemporaries. Having traveled to Panama in search of wage labor, he had talked to workers there, as well as to Jamaicans, about the plight of black people everywhere. My earlier experiences in Haiti hence were understandably of interest to him during our initial meeting. We got along well on that occasion, and he agreed that Bethune and I could come to a Sunday-night meeting of his group. After that, I went alone to meetings at least once a week, to frequent interviews—usually group sessions—and on marches to the edge of the downtown business district in Kingston, where meetings were held to publicize the movement and attract new members.

A Rasta yard was distinguished, especially at meeting time, by the presence of such insignia as flags, a banner bearing the name of the group, and a figure of a lion, representing Haile Selassie. Another important symbol was a photograph (or photographs), mounted on a stand, of Haile Selassie. Almost always, a Bible was prominently displayed, often on a table set out for the meeting. Red, gold, and green caps and scarves were worn by some members at Sunday-night and street meetings. Paper streamers made with Rastafarian colors were strung across poles on special occasions, such as the celebration of Haile Selassie's coronation.

There was little protocol for entering a Rasta yard; I simply parked my rented car on the street and walked in. I soon became well known to those who stayed in or near the yard, and there were few formalities. (There was even less protocol in entering a revivalist center. Mr. Reynolds always greeted me cordially, saying that he was glad to see me, whether my visit was by appointment, a walk-in, or during a service he was conducting.)

The first Rastafari meeting that Mr. Bethune and I attended was held in an open space between the housing units where Mr. Myers and others had quarters. A tall "living fence" of cactus, as was common throughout much of West Kingston, surrounded this compound, and a single lightbulb, hanging by an electric cord, produced rather dim illumination. Some of those who attended the meeting sat on benches or chairs; some stood in the background. Two men met us at the gate and escorted us to chairs at the front of this outdoor space. Mr. Myers opened the session by shouting, "Death to the white man!" The gathering of some seventy-five or eighty persons, mainly men, shouted in reply, "And to the black traitors!" (I later learned that the phrase "Death to the black and white oppressors" was the call of the Nyabinghi,[5] but I do not recollect ever hearing the term *Nyabinghi* at that time.) I soon learned that they meant the white man in general and the black betrayers.

Despite these violent-sounding phrases, I never felt physically threatened among the Rastas. Some members of Mr. Myers's group never smiled or spoke to me. They may have been far from congenial, but they were never threatening.[6] Nor did those who were congenial to me attempt to proselytize me or ask me to intervene with authorities on their behalf. A few individuals asked if I could help find them a job or get schooling for a child in Jamaica or the United States.

I had told Mr. Myers that I came from Ohio, but when he introduced me he said, "Mr. Simpson is not a real American. Only the American Indians are real American. He says that he is from Ohio, but he is an Englishman. I was born in Jamaica, but I am an Ethiopian." At one of the first meetings I attended, Mr. Myers asked me to speak, and I chose to make an observation about how Rastas characterized the white man. I said, "You say that white people are evil, and there are some white people that are evil, but there are white people who are good just as there are black people who are good and also some who are evil. Isn't that so?" A number of those present immediately replied, "Yes, yes"—much to the dissatisfaction of others, who grumbled and glared. In his reply Mr. Myers said, "Are all white people bad? No. There are a few good white people. A good white person is the reincarnation of a good slave owner, the kind of man who bought a slave who was being beaten and took good care of him." On at least one other occasion, Mr. Myers announced that I must be such a reincarnation.

What I and others have sometimes called an "anti-white attitude" on the part of Rastafarians John P. Homiak, director of the National Anthropological Societies at the Smithsonian Institution in Washington, D.C., who has done substantial field research on Rastafari, more accurately describes in this way: "*Black* and *white* are categorical identities within the historical Rasta worldview, [but] these racial ascriptions do not necessarily reflect attitudes toward specific individuals in their face-to-face relationships where Rastas tend to evaluate persons on the basis of their 'heart-sincerity-actions.'"[7]

At virtually every meeting I attended, Mr. Myers called on me to speak and enjoyed challenging or rebutting what I said. I suspect that he did so as a way of displaying his own oratorical abilities and enhancing his authority among members of the group. After all, this exchange was probably the first opportunity that the Rastas had to debate with a white person. Some of his followers clearly enjoyed our verbal exchanges. My impression of Mr. Myers was that of a forceful leader, one who had great control over his followers. They respected him, and he often seemed to dominate them. Amid the poverty of Trench Town, he occasionally added a touch of humor to his dealings with me and his followers. During our stay in Jamaica, I rented an automobile from faculty members who were on leave or vacation. Occasionally, I gave Mr. Myers a lift when I left Trench Town and he was about to leave on an errand. One day he said that he didn't see why I could travel about in a car while he had to walk long distances to transact his business. That was the only time I recall that he complained about his personal situation compared with mine.

Soon after I began going to Sunday-night meetings, one member announced that he was opposed to any picture taking and recording of speeches or music. He said that he had taken an oath never to help a white person, and he did not intend to violate that pledge. Others agreed with him, and Mr. Myers sustained their objections. (I did not encounter these restrictions among the Rastafari youth group that I knew best.) Note-taking, however, was permitted, and I spent considerable time in follow-up sessions with members, checking notes and getting additional information. I often sought to record the texts of their songs and presented these back to them for correction and verification. A number of those in Myers's group were impressed that I took the time to do this. Like some of my revivalist informants, they may have been pleased that a university professor had chosen to study the movement. Some may have hoped that my work might set straight Jamaican stereotypes about Rastafari. Others may have felt that I would carry my knowledge of Rastafarians back to the United States, where it would be disseminated. (If so, such expectations would have been in contrast to the way in which some later researchers were initially received by the brethren.) At the conclusion of my research, I gave both Mr. Myers and Mr. Reynolds a copy of the book on race relations in the United States that I had coauthored. Later, I sent a copy of my 1955 article in *Social and Economic Studies* to Mr. Myers.[8]

There was no objection to my marching with members of the group from Trench Town to downtown Kingston for a street meeting. I stood at one end of a semicircle the Rastas made as they faced passersby on a busy street corner. With uniformed police in the background, Mr. Myers would say, "You may wonder who this white man is and why he is here. Don't be afraid of him. He is not an Englishman. He is an American." In general, the proceedings at street meetings were similar to the meetings in Trench Town. The main Rastafari doctrines were expounded and validated through the reading and interpretation of passages from the Bible. A member appointed to read a chapter of Scripture was stopped by the leader from time to time for his explanation of a verse. Oratorical abilities varied widely within the group, and this type of public speech making was limited to a few. Speeches by members were then interspersed with the singing of original songs and of modified Sankey and Methodist hymns.

At these meetings, women were outnumbered and very much in the background. They said little during the Rasta meetings that I attended. I did not witness or hear of any controversies because of the greater participation by males in the conduct of business. In contrast, women played important roles in revivalist groups. In two revivalist groups, led by strong and respected "Mothers," women held such titles as *Armour Bearer, Water Mother, Healing Mother, Deaconess,* and *Nurse.* Where men led as *Captains, Shepherds,* or *Leaders,* women officers assisted with baptizing, read passages from the Bible, helped those who were beginning or coming out of a possession trance, or related a marvelous "spiritual journey" (dream or vision) at a "vowing" service, held the night before a baptismal ceremony.

In contrast to meetings in later years, drums were totally absent from Rasta meetings in West Kingston in 1953. Instead of drums, a "rhumba box"—a medium-sized wooden box that had five or six metal strips fastened at the bottom of an opening on one side of the box—was used. This instrument is the same as the marimba of Haiti, and both may be descended from the *sansa* (thumb piano) of West Africa.[9] Rattles, scrapers, tambourines, and, occasionally, a saxophone made up the Rastafari ensemble.[10]

In the yard near his housing unit, Mr. Myers supervised a woodworking shop where a number of craftsmen made small articles and pieces of furniture for sale to tourists and residents of Kingston. In this respect, Mr. Myers appears to have been like other early Rasta leaders who incorporated programs for economic opportunity into the social organization of their groups. Diagonally across the street, Kapo Reynolds lived and presided over a Revival Zion church. He was a good friend, one of my best informants on revivalism, and his followers were the revivalists that I knew best. Occasionally, arguments and scuffles occurred in the street between the two meeting places. One night, several Rastas tried to break up Kapo's service by coming in and shouting about revivalists worshiping "a dead God" instead of following "the living God," Ras Tafari. As far as I know, these rivalries had no effect on my acceptability to the people of this neighborhood, at least not to these two strong leaders. Interestingly, neither Mr. Myers nor Kapo ever questioned me about my interest in the other's group, although they were undoubtedly aware of my movements between the two yards.

Later in my research, a colleague of Mr. Myers introduced me to Mr. Joseph Hibbert, one of the founders of Rastafari. We met only twice. As I recall the first meeting, we talked about the hardships of life in Trench Town, our respective families, Rastafari beliefs, and a little about the United States and the circumstances of black people there. After some time, I asked him if I could take his picture. A family member then suggested that he put on this ritual robe. I photographed him in his red robe as he held a saber, vertically touching the ground. He also wore a white "crown" with red, gold, and green stripes. Behind him was a homemade painting of Haile Selassie and his queen, and to one side, a small table on which was placed a Bible.[11] I also took several photographs of Hibbert with his family.

Although I intended to return and work with him further, I did not have an opportunity to talk at length again with Mr. Hibbert. I have been told that he was regarded as a "scientist," that is, as one of the early leaders who was thought to have formidable powers of an occult nature that enabled him to withstand the forces of the colonial period. I did not find anything striking or idiosyncratic about Mr. Hibbert. He seemed to me to be a man of great dignity, and his demeanor toward me in our brief meetings was one of service.

In 1953 there were from twelve to fifteen Rastafari groups in West Kingston, with additional bands in other parts of the island. Group names included United Ethiopian Body (Myers's group), Ethiopian Coptic League (Hibbert's group), United Afro-West Indian Federation, African Cultural League, and Ethiopian Youth Cosmic Faith. While revivalist churches were predominantly female, males predominated in Rasta groups. Among the Rastafarians, the age distribution tended to be wider than among the revivalists, although a few Rasta organizations were made up entirely of persons under twenty-five.

A Sunday-evening meeting might open with the singing of a song such as "Oh! Africa awaken, the morning is at hand." On one occasion, a speaker followed the opening song with a series of remarks that outlined the Rasta understanding of slavery and repatriation:

SPEAKER: How did we get here?
CHORUS: Slavery.
SPEAKER: Who brought us from Ethiopia?
CHORUS: The white man.
SPEAKER: The white man tells us we are inferior, but we are not inferior. We are su-

perior, and he is inferior. The time has come for us to go back home. In the near future we will go back to Ethiopia and the white man will be our servant. The white
man says we are no good, but David, Solomon, and Queen of Sheba were black. The
English are criminals and the black traitors are just as bad. Ministers are thieves and
vagabonds. The black man who doesn't want to go back to Ethiopia doesn't want
freedom. There is no freedom in Jamaica. Ras Tafari is the Living God, Ras Tafari
started Mau Mau. Ras Tafari says, "Death to the white man!"
CHORUS: And to the black traitors!
SPEAKER: We believe in "One God, One Aim, One Destiny!" We believe in Ethiopia
   for the Ethiopians.
CHORUS: At home and abroad.

Similar speeches followed, alternating with songs, such as the Sankey "Rejoice, rejoice
the Lord is King"; "Let the song go round the earth"; "Jesus [with 'Negus' substituted
for Jesus] shall reign where'er the sun"; or "Hail to the Lord's anointed"; or a Baptist
hymn such as "Jesus [Negus] the King."
   At one evening street meeting, a speaker used as his text an article titled "Modern
Ethiopia" that had appeared in the June 1931 issue of the *National Geographic* magazine. Holding a well-thumbed copy of the magazine, bereft of its cover, the speaker read
at length from the article, quoting more or less verbatim its description of the elaborate
biblical coronation of Haile Selassie as emperor of Ethiopia. The splendor of the coronation was dwelt upon, and emphasis was placed on "the bowing down of kings and
presidents of the earth before Haile Selassie." Haile Selassie's power, the speaker contended, was acknowledged by the mightiest rulers of the world. This speech was followed by several repetitions of a brief song called "The Lion of Judah shall break every
chain!" In closing the meeting, the brethren stood, faced the East, sang the "Ethiopian
National Anthem," and recited the "Ethiopian Prayer," both composed in West
Kingston.[12]
   I also frequently saw members of the youth group called the United Afro-West Indian
Federation. M. G. Smith, Roy Augier, and Rex Nettleford identified Raphael Downer
as the leader of this group,[13] but the member I remember best was Clement Edie (of 8
Potter's View, Browns Town—off Windward Road near Elletson Road). Unlike Mr.
Myers's group, this group placed no restrictions on me with regard to taking pictures
or recording music. My recording of this group's singing was done in a meeting room
in Trench Town and is included in my album *Jamaican Cult Music*.[14] The instruments
included a rhumba box, shakers, and tambourines. One woman played with the group.
I talked with members of this group before and after their street meetings and in the
yards of the housing settlements where I found them. Mr. Edie migrated to London
around 1955, and he and I continued to correspond about Jamaica, Britain, and the
United States for a year or so after he left Kingston.
   On November 15, 1953, Mr. Myers presided over a celebration commemorating
Haile Selassie's coronation day.[15] The orchestra for this occasion consisted of two
rhumba boxes, three guitars, two saxophones, one violin, one banjo, tambourines, and

rattles. In addition to group singing, there were special recitations and singing by individuals and a quartet. Ten babies were dedicated to Haile Selassie by an official who said, "The King [Ras Tafari] bless thee, keep thee, and give thee peace and life everlasting." Ten speeches were delivered during the program, and many guests from other Rasta groups attended the celebration.[16]

In those days, Rastafarians expected to leave for the homeland "in the near future," but there was no agreement on the date of departure. Some expected to leave Jamaica "any day now"; others set the time for repatriation within the next four or five years. One man said that the exodus would be compulsory for all persons of African descent, but most believed that only those who wished to leave would go. According to the myth that had developed, Queen Victoria had allocated £23,000,000 for the repatriation of West Indian black people. Although her plan had not been carried out, it was believed that the money was still available and that it was only a question of time until Queen Elizabeth II and the emperor of Ethiopia would agree on the implementation of the promise. Some Rastafarians planned to fly to the United States and then take ships such as the *Queen Mary* and the *Bremen* to Abyssinia. This fantasy held that planes would leave Jamaica every five minutes to take the black man out of the country.

In the early days of the movement, opposition came from both rank-and-file Jamaicans and the police. Jamaicans of lower social classes stoned speakers, slashed banners, and smashed lamps at street meetings. A leader of the cult was arrested, jailed, and tried seven times but was never convicted of disorderly conduct, ganja smoking, or lunacy. By the early 1950s, open hostility had declined to some extent, due in part to the discipline of members during street meetings. Some middle-class Jamaicans, as well as some foreigners, still feared the Rastas, but the evidence that was available then did not support the widespread belief that they were bearded hoodlums.

The general attitude of middle-class Jamaicans, English citizens, and Americans living in Jamaica in the early 1950s toward Rastafarians was one of contempt and disgust. There seemed to be no fear of a rebellion, but many believed that the Rastas were hooligans, psychopaths, or dangerous criminals. In 1953 there was much talk among middle-class Jamaicans and white foreigners about the conjunction between Rastas and criminal elements. When serious crimes were reported in the press, especially murders, they were often attributed to the brethren. Frequently the Rastas were referred to as "those dreadful people," and that view was shared by some police officers. (It is noteworthy that the police did not patrol West Kingston in those days but were likely to come into the area solely for the purpose of making arrests. Both revivalists and Rastas with whom I was familiar remarked about and were resentful of this procedure.)

Actually, the movement attracted many types from the Jamaican lower and lower middle classes, as well as some students and professional persons. In 1953, I found many Rastafari members, especially the younger people, to be extremely idealistic. One group forbade the use of "indecent language" in meetings and imposed fines on those who failed to obey the orders of the chairman. Some youthful Rastas did not smoke tobacco, and a few of them spent considerable time reading the Bible, always with a view to finding passages that validated Rastafari doctrines. Although most of the members were poor people, they ranged from illiterate or semiliterate to literate and talented, from confused to articulate, and from bitter to hopeful in their outlooks on life. Perhaps the most important thing sociologically about the Rastas during this period was not the actual range of social types within the movement but who and what others thought its membership was.

Some middle-class Jamaicans, as well as Americans and English residents and visitors, were rather surprised at my interest in the revivalist and Rastafari movements. In general, staff members at the University College of the West Indies (now the University of the West Indies) and a number of professional persons in Kingston were interested in the research and very supportive. Dudley Huggins, the first director of the Institute of Social and Economic Research at the university, provided me with an office. I learned later from him that he received a number of criticisms for publishing my article on the Rastafari, "Political Cultism in West Kingston, Jamaica," in the June 1955 issue of *Social and Economic Studies*. These critics felt he should not have given recognition in an academic journal to "those dangerous people."

My perceptions of Rastas on first contact were twofold. First, and sociologically, they impressed me as a striking instance of an oppressed group in a colonial society. Second, as persons, I found most of them to be likable, desperately poor people who had banded together in an attempt to improve their life conditions and realize their dreams. Their aspiration to return to the homeland seemed to me from the first to be a kind of "collective fantasy," and indeed, that has proved to be the case. However, they played a part in the struggle for status of Blacks in Jamaica and throughout the modern world, and in "the struggle within individual blacks to regain the sense of personal worth and dignity which society has denied," both of which have been furthered by the movement.[17]

Attitudes toward the Rastafarians have changed markedly over the past thirty years. Whereas in the 1950s—and for some years after—the movement was regarded as subversive and as a force to be eliminated, Rex Nettleford, writing in 1982, said that the wider society had come to have greater understanding of the Rastafarian vision, resulting in a "tactical accommodation if not widespread acceptance."[18] While this change was occurring, there was some evidence that Rastas themselves were engaged in a process of reluctant accommodation to Jamaican society.

To conclude, I could not have imagined in 1953 that the Rastafari movement would give birth to reggae, embraced by people throughout the world, and would develop a culture that would spread to North America, Europe, and even Africa; nor could I have envisioned that Rastas would travel abroad to represent their culture at places such as the Smithsonian Institution, Howard University, Johns Hopkins University, York University in Toronto, as well as in South Africa and at other international conferences of social scientists and other scholars. Indeed, it is not beyond the realm of possibility that one or more of the contemporary elders whom John Homiak has assisted in bringing to cultural programs at the Smithsonian, were present as young Rastas at the meetings I attended in Mr. Myers's yard or with the United Afro-West Indian Federation in 1953. These more recent tours by Rastafari who were at one time part of the same milieu as Joseph Myers and Joseph Hibbert attest to the incredible transition of the Rastafari, from peasant and proletarian origins to the global cultural order.[19]

Notes

1. Sheila Kitzinger, "Protest and Mysticism: The Ras Tafari Cult in Jamaica," *Journal for the Scientific Study of Religion* 8 (1969): 240–62.

2. That the ideological orientation toward ganja was changing within the movement is suggested by juxtaposing my 1953 research with the 1960 report of M. G. Smith, Roy Augier and Rex Nettleford, *The Rastafari Movement in Kingston, Jamaica* (Mona, Jamaica: University College of the West Indies, Institute of Social and Economic Research, 1969). This report indicates that brethren held widely divergent opinions about ganja use and its effects.

3. Velma Pollard, "Dread Talk: The Speech of the Rastafarian in Jamaica," *Caribbean Quarterly* 26, 4 (1980): 32–41. See also John P. Homiak, personal communication with the author, May 28, 1992, cited more directly at note 7.

4. The group led by Joseph Myers is identified in Smith, Augier, and Nettleford's *The Rastafari Movement* as the United Ethiopian Body. It is said to have been under the direction of both Joseph Myers and Claudius Stewart. Downer's group is identified as the United Afro-West Indian Federation, the other group with which I had close contact. Both bodies shared a common terrain with the group led by Joseph Hibbert, one of the first individuals to preach Rastafari doctrine. All three of these groups, plus others, apparently came into a much closer working relationship after the advent of the Ethiopian World Federation (EWF) in Jamaica. According to Smith, Augier, and Nettleford, these groups became "locals" within the EWF and functioned for a time under its umbrella.

5. The House of Nyabinghi consisted of seventy-five to one hundred elders, of different generations, who were the mainstay for the house's ritual life islandwide; see John P. Homiak, "From Yard to Nation: Rastafari and the Politics of Eldership at Home and Abroad," in Manfred Kremser, ed., *Any Bobo: Afro-Caribbean Cults, Resistance and Identity. Proceedings of the Second Inter-Disciplinary Congress of the Society for Caribbean Research* (Vienna, 1990), 3.

6. I did not hear the Rastas I knew in 1953 explicitly renounce the use of physical violence, but according to research in later years, even when the rhetoric is violent-sounding, Rastas reject physical action or violence. They indicate that either the "power of the word" or the divine agency of Jah will destroy Babylon (Homiak, personal communication).

7. Homiak, personal communication; see also Carole D. Yawney, "Remnants of All Nations: Rastafarian Attitudes toward Ethnicity and Nationality," in Frances Henry, ed., *Ethnicity in the Americas* (The Hague: Mouton Publishers, 1976), 231–62.

8. G. E. Simpson and J. Milton Yinger, *Racial and Cultural Minorities: An Analysis of Prejudice and Discrimination* (New York: Harper & Brothers, 1953; reprint, New York: Plenum, 1985); George Eaton Simpson, "Political Cultism in West Kingston, Jamaica," *Social and Economic Studies* 4, 2 (1955): 133–49.

9. It is also possible that rhumba boxes were carried back to Jamaica from Cuba, by immigrant laborers returning home from work on sugar plantations there.

10. When I was recording Rasta and revivalist music in West Kingston, someone—perhaps a Rasta informant—suggested that I record some Kumina music. Kenneth Bilby confirmed that the Kumina music I recorded is indistinguishable from what the Rastas would later call "Nyabinghi"; see Kenneth M. Bilby and Elliot Leib, "Kumina, the Howellite Church and the Emergence of Rastafarian Traditional Music in Jamaica," *Jamaican Journal* 19, 3 (1986): 22–28. Moreover, a photograph I took, showing three men on drums, reveals that the drums and the manner in which they were played are the same as the *akete,* or burru, drums that would later be adopted by Rastas under the name Nyabinghi.

11. It is interesting to note that Hibbert presented himself in dress of an ornamental character, showing his ritual authority by closely following the attire in which Haile Selassie was photographed at his coronation, that is, the robe, triple crown, and sword held vertically between his feet.

12. Simpson, "Political Cultism."

13. Smith, Augier, and Nettleford, *The Rastafari Movement*.

14. *Jamaican Cult Music,* recordings by George Eaton Simpson, Ethnic Folkways Library, Folkways Records 461, 1954.

15. Haile Selassie's coronation day was November 2. I believe the coronation was being celebrated on November 15 because in 1953 that day, a Sunday, was preferred to November 2, a Monday.

16. Simpson, "Political Cultism."

17. I did not hear Rastas at this time talking about their African or Ethiopian culture. The Jamaican establishment has historically denigrated the predominantly African roots of that society. Most present observers of the movement acknowledge the role that the Rastas have played in legitimating the idea of an African culture and identity in Jamaica. See Rex Nettleford, *Mirror, Mirror: Identity, Race and Protest in Jamaica* (Kingston: W. Collins/Sangster's Book Stores, 1970).

18. Rex Nettleford, introduction, to Joseph Owens, *Dread: The Rastafarians of Jamaica* (London: William Heinemann Educational Books, 1982), xi.

19. The author gratefully acknowledges the many questions, comments, and suggestions given by John P. Homiak and Harold Courtlander and the editorial assistance provided by Nancy S. Alonzo. Some other sources consulted in this chapter are: Leonard Barrett, *The Rastafarians: Sounds of Cultural Dissonance* (Boston: Beacon Press, 1977); Kenneth M. Bilby, "Black Thoughts from the Caribbean Ideology at Home and Abroad," *New West Indian Guide* 57, 3–4 (1983): 201–14; John P. Homiak, "The Mystic Revelations of Rasta Far-Eye," in B. Tedlock, ed., *Dreaming: Anthropological and Psychological Approaches* (Cambridge: Cambridge University Press, 1987), 220–45; idem, *The Half That's Never Been Told: Pa Ashanti and the Development of Nyabinghi Music* (Kingston: Emperor Haile Selassie I Theocracy Government, Serial No. I, 1990). Works by George Eaton Simpson include "The Ras Tafari Movement in Jamaica: A Study of Race and Class Conflict," *Social Forces* 34, 2 (1955): 167–70; "Jamaican Revivalist Cults," *Social and Economic Studies* 5, 4 (1956): 321–442; *Black Religions in the New World* (New York: Columbia University Press, 1978); *Religious Cults of the Caribbean: Trinidad, Jamaica, and Haiti,* 3d ed. (Rio Piedras: University of Puerto Rico, Institute of Caribbean Studies, 1980); "Religion and Justice: Some Reflections on the Rastafari Movement," *Phylon* 46, 4 (1985): 286–91; "Afro-Caribbean Religions," *Encyclopedia of Religion* (New York: Macmillan Publishing Co., 1987), 90–98.

Part III

Back-o-Wall to Hollywood: The
Rasta Revolution through the Arts

14

From Burru Drums to Reggae Ridims: The Evolution of Rasta Music

VERENA RECKORD

Among the first things that people think of at the mention of Jamaican music is reggae, with its Rasta drums and "ridims." Reggae is Jamaica's greatest cultural export, the main force that identifies the country internationally. Since the advent of ska in the late 1950s, Jamaican popular music experienced a phenomenal growth and evolution that took it from being a response to purely parochial needs to more sophisticated commercial and international acceptance. As the music becomes commercialized, accepted and performed by people of varying tastes and cultures, the tendency is to forget its origin and its deeper meaning and function. Here I trace the evolution of Jamaican Rasta music in an effort to show the role it plays in a people's search for identity.[1]

Jamaican music, created by Blacks who have clung steadfastly to their basic African roots as a source of their identity, is music of the majority on the island and has a history that goes back over four hundred years, to the earliest days of slavery. But very little has been chronicled of African music brought to Jamaica. The European slave masters' instinctive efforts to "civilize" (deculturize) the slaves by imposing on them European culture introduced to Africans Euro-Western religious and secular music. These were assimilated by Blacks, who, in their subculture activities, fused what appealed to them of white cultural practices with those they retained from Africa. The slaves, under severely repressive conditions, preserved what they could of their African cultures, including music and dance in extracts from larger ritual forms. Rituals rich in spiritual vitality characterize the cultural expressions of the intensely religious Africans.

The African fusion is evident in many Afro-Jamaican religions. "Borrowed" elements of music can be seen, for instance, in harmonic and melodic patterns in Jamaican music today. For example, African traditional music is usually based on a five-note scale that gives a certain minor tonality to the melodies. Many traditional Jamaican songs are in minor keys, and reggae artists seem to have a natural feel for the minor in their compositions, which can be quite off-putting to the ear conditioned to Euro-Western harmonic and melodic design.[2] Another basic link with Africa evident in Jamaican folk songs and emergent in the popular music is the call-and-response singing style, which has parallels in the wider musical expressions of the black diaspora. With improved communications in the twentieth century, musical influences of the Americas and the Caribbean territories came to color Jamaican music, mainly in terms of instrumentation and style.

African-influenced traditional and folk forms existing today include Kumina, Burru, Etu, Gombay, Pocomania, Revival, jonkunnu, Maroon, and Rasta music. All of these musical forms have dance movements and use the drum, which provides a rich, "polyridimic" (polyrhythmic) base for voice instruments. The importance of the polyridimic structure is reflected in all forms of Jamaican popular music, which has gone through several clearly defined stages of development: mento, blues beat, ska, rudie, rock steady, and reggae.

In Jamaica's folk and traditional music, the drum plays an important role. In Kumina, for instance, special care is taken of the drums (*kbandu* and playing cast), which function in rituals as the media for messages from the spirit world to devotees and vice versa. The drum in African culture is recognized as an instrument of communication. For Africans, the drum talks. For Jamaicans, the "ridim"[3] talks. In Rastafarian ceremonies, in which music is an integral part, there can be no spiritual peaking,[4] as it were, unless the ridim is right. Sometimes virtuosos or group leaders, as in the Kumina situation, may be heard chiding drummers for not getting the right ridim to suit the needs of the moment.[5]

The Source of Rasta Ridims

Rasta's exotic drumming was first introduced to Jamaican pop music by the leading exponent and credited originator of the form as it is known today, the late Oswald "Count Ossie" Williams, a Rastaman. To understand the importance of Rasta music, one needs to take a look at its development through the drums. Used in the Rastafarian community for "eartical"[6] or "churchical" purposes, the drums are three in number: the bass drum, the *fundeh,* and the repeater (*peta*). The bass drum is fashioned somewhat like a regular military bass drum but with heads protruding slightly over the rims. The heads are ideally made out of ram goatskin. According to Count Ossie, master Rasta drummer, the skin of the ram goat is used because it is less vociferous than the ewe goat by nature, and its skin allows for a slower beat and lower tone. Regardless of the scientific merits of this argument, the sound of the skin, when hit, is of a desirably low pitch. In many cases cowhide and sheepskin are also used for bass drums because of the low tonal quality of these skins.

The diameter of the bass drum varies, from about twenty-two inches ordinarily to nearly three feet, as is the case for the "royal drums" at Prince Emmanuel's Rasta commune overlooking Jamaica's Bull Bay.[7] About twenty-two inches deep, the body of the bass drum is made of barrel staves held together by metal bands and pegs.

The *fundeh* is a relatively long, narrow drum. It has one head, made of ram goatskin, that is about nine inches across. The body is made usually of barrel staves or strips of other wood or, in rare cases, of a hollowed tree trunk. The *fundeh* is also held together by metal pegs and braces. The pegs extend over the open end of the drum so that the body is raised while it is being played.

The repeater has the same structure as the *fundeh*, except that the repeater is shorter. Chiefly it is the skin of the female goat that is used for the repeater's head. Count Ossie explains that the ewe bleats in more strident tones than the ram; hence her skin is ideal for the soprano pitch of the repeater. Some Rasta musicians claim that, when available, stretched pelican crop (stomach) is even better than ewe goatskin for the repeater head.

Rasta drums are tuned by tension in the metal brace at the head of the drums. The *fundeh* is tuned to a representative alto pitch, somewhere on the line between the bass and the repeater. Most Rasta drums are painted in the identifying red, green, and gold colors of the Rasta movement, which are also the colors of the Ethiopian flag. While the three drums represent the vital core of Rasta music, it is not unusual to see Rasta bands augmented by other instruments such as horns, guitars, harmonicas, and many percussives—graters, bottles, and so forth.[8]

Playing the Drums

The bass drum is held on the lap and hit with a heavily padded stick. The head of the stick varies in construction, from thick wads of fabric to tennis balls. The *fundeh* stands on the floor and is played with the fingers of both hands in the closed position. The repeater is played usually with the fingertips in the open position and with the outer edges of the hands. The latter two drums are often held between the knees of the seated player. With the exception of the repeater, the centers of the drums are hit at all times. There is no buoyance after contact; rather, the stick or fingers are plunged into the drumhead and disengaged only long enough for the next tone. Rasta musical meter is fairly straightforward, but there are occasions when exact notation is impossible, especially in the case of repeater work.

In the playing of Rasta music, the *fundeh* carries the steady ridim, or "lifeline." The lifeline ridim is played either on the first and third beats of the bar or on the second and fourth. Sometimes during chants, depending on the pitch of the spirit (of Jah, being shared by the brethren), the placing of the beat in any particular order becomes irrelevant. However, in most chants and churchical songs, the accent is on the first and third, and songs of more secular social commentary have the accent on the second and fourth and are played usually up-tempo.

The bass drum plays much the same pattern as the *fundeh* except that it varies in both tone and ridim. The first beat is with the flat of the stick; the second beat is with the point of the stick stabbing the skin and producing a note approximately a tone or a tone and a half higher. The tone variation is also produced by the technique of drawing the nonplaying hand across the head as a mute.

To play the repeater takes great skill and a keen sense of rhythm. As one Rasta brother said to me in Spanish Town in 1976, "A man really have to have music in him to really play that repeater well. As a matter of fact, him mus' really lean fi play the fundeh well-good, before him touch the repeater, so him can know how fi work-in the repeater on the other ridim them." The repeater is the color instrument of the group. It supplies the "melody line" and the embellishments. This drum is responsible for a great deal of excitement in Rasta music. Although at liberty to do anything he—or, since the mid-1980s, she—feels like, the repeater player, the technical acrobat of the family, must keep within the ridmic tempo set by the *fundeh*. Hence, many repeater players, chief among them Count Ossie, hold the *fundeh* ridim with the left hand even at the height of improvising.

What the repeater does is "cut" against the ridim set by the other two drums. Numerous complex counterpatterns are played on the repeater—many of them impossible to illustrate. For example, in the first bar the repeater fills in the second beat with four sixteenth notes. On the fourth beat it changes, playing an eighth and two half notes. In the second bar it varies again by playing an eighth rest and two sixteenth notes on the second beat. The repeater varies again on the last beat by playing an eighth note and an eighth rest. Then again, the repeater may play triplets on the second beat, with an eighth note followed by an eighth rest on the last beat. This behavior heightens the tension and creates more nuances and excitement in Rasta music.

Local Origins: Burru Music

Many Rastafarians, who do not seem to think about it until they are asked, insist that the music of their movement is originally theirs. However, some Rasta musicians willingly admit that their music, with the vital drums and ridims, is an adoption, and that the drums and ridims first belonged to Burru music. Dating back to the days of slavery, the Burru people were known for their virtuoso African drumming on *akete* drums, supported by *sansa* (marimba box) and other instruments. I have found no written account of Burru music but have heard from several informants in and outside of the Rasta movement that Burru was a music popular during slavery. It was one of the few forms of African music allowed by slave masters because of its function as "a work metronome" for the slaves. Burru bands were allowed in the fields to play the music that buoyed the spirits of the slaves and made them work faster and so speed up production.

After slavery was abolished, Burru drummers were without work. They had little experience as field hands and hence could do very little with their postslavery plots of ground in the hinterlands. As a result, they flocked to the townships, gathering mostly in the slum areas of Kingston and Spanish Town. During the first nine months of each year, Burru players eked out some sort of Robin Hood existence. Then, from September on, they met in groups and practiced songs and music for performance at Christmas time (a custom somewhat akin to the jonkunnu practice).

One interesting aspect of Burru music after slavery is that it had a specific community function. Burru songs closely parallel the "praise songs" of original African tradition, which would expose the good or evil aspects of a person or a village. Like calypsonians in the southern Caribbean, the Burru people sang topical songs about current events and especially about "newsmakers" in the community who, during the year, may have been guilty of some misconduct. This reflects another African custom found among Gold Coast tribes, whereby, at the end of the old year, an ordained sect of the community would go from house to house singing derogatory songs (without calling names) about persons who had committed wrongs during the year. The accused were not allowed to retaliate directly but were free, after the musicians were through, to sing songs in their own defense. It was a sort of purification rite that absolved the village of its sins before it entered the new year. It could be more than a coincidence, therefore, that Burru musicians in Jamaica went around "singing on people" during Christmas time.

I remember that as a child in the late 1940s, when I lived in Spanish Town, my grandmother would send me to buy bread every evening. There was a shortcut through a slum lane called Silverwood Alley. All year round my grandmother never objected to my going through the alley to save time. But come September she would constantly warn "Don't yuh go t'ru Silverwood Alley. Ah doan able fi dem damn Burru man." She meant that the Burru men had come together for the last quarter of the year to play their drums and compose their songs, night and day. The town, especially at nights, throbbed with the earth ridims of Burru. I never went the long way to the bread shop, especially not during the last quarter of the year. The time I was supposed to spend avoiding Silverwood Alley I passed peeping through nail holes in the dirty zinc fence at the Burru men playing their drums around a fire, singing and cursing "bad words" all the time.

To my child's soul, Burru music was the sweetest music ever heard. I could not resist it. If the drums were momentarily silent when I was passing by, I would "dally," hoping for them to start again so I could watch the animated faces and bodies as well as the nimble hands of those unkempt Burru men. Interestingly enough, at home, when my grandmother rocked my baby brother to sleep, it was not to the strains of a European lullaby but to Burru ridims, and I couldn't understand why. I knew later that in trying to keep me from Burru, Grandmother was denying me that part of herself that colonization had stamped as evil, primitive, and wrong. In fact, Burru men of earlier times were regarded by the rest of the community, even in their own social strata, as ne'er-do-wells and criminals. Over the years, Burru men have lost that stigma. The few remaining groups are now being sought out and encouraged to keep the music alive.

The following account concerning Burru drums is based on unpublished notes and drawings loaned to me by folk research officer Marjorie Whylie on her first contact with a Burru group at Spring Village, St. Catherine, early in 1977.[9] A session specially arranged for Whylie and her party took place at the Spring Village schoolroom, about one mile from Gutters on the main road between Spanish Town and Old Harbor. Leader and manager of the band was "Mr. Raphael"; musical director, lead singer, and rhumba box player was "Mr. Coburn." These players had no idea of the origin of Burru. Their only account was that, as children, they were taught the music by older men. They did, however, confirm the story of the group's activities near Christmastime. The Spring Village group, seven players in all, rehearsed topical songs about popular characters, village gossip, and other "happenings" for three months before Christmas. According to the players, "At about 5 o' clock on Christmas morning the fun begins. They walk for miles singing and dancing. They have been known to improvise and extemporize on anything amusing that they may encounter along the way."

The bamboo scraper, *shakka*, and rhumba box are used for purely rhythmic effect. Most songs are carried by the voice alone, but sometimes the *saxa* comes into play. The *saxa* sound is reminiscent of the paper and comb, and the principle is much the same. Saran Wrap or cellophane is stretched over the mouth of a bottle, and the actual notes are produced with the human voice. The bottle is held firmly with both hands, allowing the last three fingers of each hand to extend beyond the broken edge. These freestanding fingers are then used to produce legato and vibrato passages.

Mento to Ska: An Early Stage in the Evolution

The mento-ska phenomenon preceded Rasta music by over two decades. Mento is officially considered the first stage in the development of Jamaican popular music, even though, according to one historian,[10] it emerged in the nineteenth century as a figure in the popular quadrille of the time. Outside the quadrille set of dances, mento is a song and dance form that became the métier of the early troubadours, who carried news, gossip, and social commentary in lively songs and dances, which they played on their mostly homemade drums, bamboo fifes, and fiddles. It was then a music of the majority and expressed the people's views and their philosophy of life, a social role not unlike that which reggae plays today.

Early exponents of mento (from the 1930s onward) included Slim and Sam, Lord Flea, Lord Fly, Sugar Belly, and Count Lasher, performing such songs as "The Naughty Flea," "Rukumbine," "Wheel and Tun Me," "Solja Man," "Linstead Market," "Solas Market," "Run Mongoose," and "Yuh No Yerri." As far as the mento expression was concerned, the evocation of African roots dominated. There was simple phraseology, verses based on two main statements repeated, call-and-response styling, emphasis on polyrhythmic patterns, and a pelvic-centered movement and complementary head and shoulder and arm movements that came out of traditional forms such as Kumina.

The early 1930s and the post–World War II period saw an influx of Jamaicans who had left home to fight in Europe or to seek their fortune in foreign places such as Cuba, the United States, and Central America. The returnees brought back songs and other musical influences from those countries. Also, with the advent of radio broadcasting in Jamaica and with easier access to foreign media, new elements were infused into the indigenous music. This period coincided with the development of black American music, particularly ragtime and swing. Jamaican musicians, by listening to records and imported sheet music, took cues from the popular black musicians of America (especially the sounds of Count Basie and Duke Ellington). They adapted the arrangements to suit the available instrumentation in Jamaica. The big band was the rage. Popular Jamaican bandleaders included Eric Deans, Redver Cook, Ivy Graydon, Roy Coburne, Roy

White, Milton McPherson, and Carlisle Demetrius and his Alpha Boys Band. These bands were usually Kingston-based and played mainly for the rich and middle class; at the grassroots level, it was still a mento scene. Yet it was common practice for certain big band stars to do occasional gigs with the mento players in the less affluent areas of Kingston.

In the late 1940s and early 1950s, the music scene in Kingston began to change. The big bands were breaking up, with individuals seeking "greener fields" abroad or in the developing tourist mecca on Jamaica's north coast. This led to the absence of most of the musicians who had jammed at ghetto sessions. Grassroots impresarios such as "Duke" Reid and Clement "Coxsone" Dodd were at the same time emerging with their "sound system" music (now called disco) to fill the musical needs of the majority. It was black American music that the people responded to most. Black soul, an Afro-American mix, threw up such stars as Fats Domino, La Verne Baker, Louis Jordan, Nat Cole, Lloyd Price, the Drifters, the Coasters, and the Platters. In Kingston, society halls, such as Forresters Hall on North Street, and amusement parks were the venues of usually jam-packed events where the underprivileged danced their troubles away to the heavy, thumping, rhythm-and-blues sounds of America.

Rivalry developed among the leading sound-system operators as the public demand for local pop music became more pressing and the North American source began to dry up. Reid and Dodd went into producing their own sounds, using local talent. Out of this early effort emerged popular song stylists such as Keith and Enid, Laurel Aitken, and Jackie Edwards, to name a few. Many of their songs were borrowed North American material. But the people's demand for their own artists doing original music soon saw the emergence of the "blue beat," which the late, great trombonist Don Drummond has been credited with creating. The blue beat was the Jamaican musician's interpretation of American rhythm-and-blues tunes with a mento flavor. The combination worked, but the taste of success quickly erased the blues beat as Jamaicans began composing their own music, which became known as "ska."

Like all popular Jamaican dance music, ska came with its own set of movements—a kind of charade to music, in which the dancers brought into play domestic activity (washing clothes, bathing), recreation (horseracing, cricket), anything that appealed to the ska dancer in the moment. Some really fancy and furious "footworks" came out of the ska period. In those days lyrics came hard to composers, and artists would even sing nursery rhymes—for instance, Eric Morris singing "Humpty Dumpty." Cedric "Im" Brooks, master saxophonist, composer, and bandleader, noted that during this time, Rasta music began to become popular.[11] By the early 1960s the record producers were multiplying. Leading the contingent were Dodd, Reid, Chris Blackwell, and Ken Khouri. One of the first ska records to come out on Coxsone's Studio One label was Laurel Aitken's "Little Sheila." Soon the audience began to demand lyrics that reflected their own lifestyles and experiences—and songs such as Drummond's "Easy Snappin" and "Wings of a Dove" and the Ffolkes Brothers' and "O Carolina" responded.

What gave ska its big boost was Edward Seaga's cultural revival, a project arising out of Jamaican independence in 1962. Seaga, then minister of development and welfare, in strong nationalist terms pushed for the development of "things Jamaican" in all areas of cultural expression, including international exposure of the ska as the popular indigenous music. Seaga, who eventually became prime minister of Jamaica, was also an early record producer and is an authority on Jamaican folk music. He introduced the Jamaica Festival as a vehicle for the annual exposition of Jamaican arts. This gave a great boost to the development of Jamaican popular music, especially by way of the Festival Song Contest, which forced participants to pay better attention to melody, lyrics, arrangement, and performance. Because the songs had to be about Jamaica, the contest also helped foster nationalism in Jamaican music. Festival songs, from "Bam Bam" (early 1960s) to "Noh Weh Noh Betta Dan Yard" (1981), can be seen as highly nationalistic, as the lyrics and musical arrangements come directly from and reflect Jamaican culture.

The Fusion of Musical Elements

In the beginnings of the Rastafarian movement, there was no "Rasta music." The early disciples, including Leonard Howell and Joseph Hibbert, used Euro-Western church music at their street meetings, especially hymns from the Baptist hymnal and "Sankey," a Euro-Western church-music form popular in Jamaica in the 1930s and 1940s. They also sang popular songs supplied by their mainly Afro-Jamaican Christian audience. At that time, the existing grassroots religious music of Revival and Pocomania (Pukkumina) was an Afro-European mixture.[12]

As time passed, the search for an original Rasta music intensified and the late 1930s saw a natural merger between the Rasta and Burru people of "Back-o-Wall"—one of the most notorious slum settlements of West Kingston, home of "Dungle" and Akee-Walk (where squatters, discharged prisoners, and hoodlums compete for survival), then the heart of cultism, musical change, and poverty in Jamaica.[13] The similarities they shared fostered a compatible relationship between the two groups in the slums of West Kingston. The Rastas were antiestablishment and believed in self-help (though to many miscreants who went under the guise of Rasta, self-help meant helping themselves to other people's property). The Burru people were similarly inclined. Rastas believed in sticking to their African roots, as did the Burru people, especially in the preservation of their music. Also, the communal lifestyle of the Rastas appealed to Burru people, who had more or less lived like that ever since slavery. Both groups shunned the Pocomania, Revival, and Kumina groups, which operated in the same social niche of West Kingston.

As years went by, some Jamaicans of Poco and Revival faiths turned to Rastafari. The Burru people had no religion of their own, while Rastas needed a musical form. The Burru people comprised a slowly disappearing group by the beginning of the 1940s, while the Rastas were growing in numbers. The exchange of music for doctrine in the later 1940s resulted in the merger of these groups and the almost total extinction of Burru people as a social group. According to Pamela O'Gorman:

In Kingston the burra drums were used for secular dances on holidays but they also had a more specialized function. It was the custom of slum dwellers in the early 30's to welcome discharged prisoners back to their communities by burra drums and dances on the night of their return. Only those who know the purpose of such a dance would normally join. Throughout this period no drums were used at Ras Tafari meetings, although Ras Tafari members would often attend these burra dances. . . . The old burra dance by which discharged prisoners were integrated with their slum communities was taken over into the Ras Tafari movement by locksmen. The burra became known as 'akete' drums and the old burra dance was replaced by the Niyabingi Dance.[14]

Kumina Influence?

One area of contemporary research sees Rasta music as a decelerated and direct offshoot of Kumina music. There is a popular report that Count Ossie himself was born in the parish of St. Thomas, the birthplace of Kumina, and that he and his teachers were steeped in Kumina tradition. The similarities shared by Rasta, Kumina, and Burru music cannot be denied. In the case of Kumina, however, only two drums are played—the *kbandu* and the playing cast. The sense of three drums is effected by *katta* ridims of sticks played on the open end of one of the drums. Incidental instrumentation in Kumina includes the grater, *shakkas,* and sometimes claves.[15]

Kumina drums are fairly large, deep, single-headed drums that are played with hands and heel while the players sit astride the drums; the *kbandu* performs much in the same way as the bass drum of Burru and the *fundeh* of Rasta music. Yet there is difference in accent, a variation of tone effected on the third beat. The playing cast of Kumina and the repeater of Rasta and Burru music are characteristically the same. However, the playing cast has a far quicker tempo; the ridims are very complex and almost impossible to notate. Burru repeater ridims can be transcribed with comparative ease.

In a conversation at his community center at Glasspole Avenue in Kingston, Count Ossie made the claim to me, and others who live close to him attest, that he was the originator of a relatively young but already traditional Rasta music. Ossie said that it began in the late 1940s, down in the Salt Lane area of what is known as Dungle. He said that he was living at Slip Dock Road, East Kingston, at the time but visited Dungle often to "reason" with a group of Rasta brethren there. Their chief topics were Garveyism, Rastafari, and the whole question of black awareness. "Yuh know," he said, "man was anxious them time to know the answers to puzzles 'bout himself and his race. Is during that time down there at Salt Lane, under a tree where we generally meet and reason, that the idea of the music come to me and I work at it until we have what people call today *Rasta Music*." Ossie continued, "From a child I was always interested in music, especially drums percussions. I used to play rattle drums in a Boys Brigade band every Sunday evening at Nine Miles."[16]

As Ossie matured he became leader of the "reasoning sessions," which lasted late into the night. Among those gathered was master Burru drummer Brother Job, who sometimes played a drum at Dungle meetings held by a Rastaman called Skipper. During those sessions, Ossie put forward the reasoning to the brethren that in the same way that the white and other races had originated and developed their own culture, the black race, whether in exile or at home in Africa, had the historical and cultural background and the ability to develop its own unique art and culture.[17] Further reasonings focused on the African retention in Jamaica and the significance of the drum as a medium of expression in African culture. Burru drumming was reasoned as one of the few undiluted African forms still alive during the late 1940s. Hence Burru was adopted. Almost every night for several months, Ossie says, he "sat at the feet of Bro. Job," learning to play the *fundeh* to Job's Burru ridims on the repeater. During the days, Ossie, who had no drums of his own, practiced avidly on an empty upended paint tin at Slip Dock Road.

Ossie and the group at Salt Lane discovered that after long periods of serious drumming, their reasoning became more intense and answers to many social-political questions became "crystal clear." So more and more emphasis was placed on drumming at meetings. After a while, Ossie mastered the *fundeh* and was becoming an expert on the repeater. When he could afford it, he ordered Watto King, the Burru drummer who taught Job to play and himself a master drum maker, to make a set of drums. Ossie had the drums made to his specifications but styled like the family of three Burru drums, featuring bass, *fundeh,* and repeater. Ossie was then freer to work out his own ridims based on the original Burru ridims, which he then introduced to the brethren. "And that is how Rasta music was born," says Ossie.

The Dispersal of Rasta Music

Soon after, Rasta music became a primary feature, a grounding force, at the mushrooming campsites of West Kingston and in the hills around the city. The routing of Leonard Howell's Pinnacle Hill commune in 1954 and the constant police harassment of Rastas, at Back-o-Wall and elsewhere in Kingston, in the late 1950s meant even greater dispersal of the Rastafarian brethren, with their pulsating music and their message of black awareness. Chief among the campsites was Ossie's camp, first at Adastra Road and later at the present premises, on Glasspole Avenue in East Kingston, where the Mystic Revelations of Rastafari (MRR) Community Center built by Ossie now stands. Ossie's camps attracted the cream of Jamaican jazz and pop musicians, including the Gaynairs, Tommy McCook, Viv Hall, Don Drummond, Ernest Ranglin, as well as musicians from abroad. During these sessions of reasoning and musical exchange, the compatibility of Rasta drumming and voice instruments and the creative possibilities of the music were realized. It is said that out of this experience, the trombone of the great Don D. (Drummond) took wings.

In the late 1940s and early 1950s, the system of Rasta camps and communal living had become quite the thing for many of Jamaica's social outcasts (those forced to be and those who chose to be). In addition to camps in West Kingston were Issie Boat's camp in the reaches of Wareika Hill and Ossie's meeting place at Slip Dock Road. The Rasta camp at the time was a very mobile community. Brethren came and went as the spirit or occasion moved them. There was a great deal of dialogue, and the exchange of ideas was very strong. This was one of the means by which Rasta music spread from camp to camp and parish to parish in Jamaica.

Christmas 1949 saw the first really big congregation of Rastafarians at Issie Boat's camp at Wareika. Singing, drumming, and dancing by Ossie's group and some Burru players; chanting; herb smoking; and feasting went on for days. At that time, Ossie, Brother Philmore Alvaranga, and "Big Bra" Gaynair, saxophone virtuoso, were known as the "Big Three" of the Rasta world. They, along with then-famous Rasta preacher Brother Love from the Mountain View Area, led the brethren in music and scripture reading and exhortations.

Ossie moved from Slip Dock Road after being displaced in 1951 by Charlie, the killer hurricane. Ossie says that he became a watchman on the building site of the Rennock Lodge housing scheme. There he used to beat his drums day and night with Brother Nyah. Later, Ossie set up his famous camp at 32 Adastra Road. This remained his campsite until 1974, when, along with the Mystic Revelations and with the aid of well-wishers, he built a community center on Glasspole Avenue.

Wherever he camped, Ossie's music was followed and observed by other Rasta brethren, potential drummers from other groups. "Man would come and listen," said Count Ossie, "until they could memorize a ridim. Then they would go back to their group or dem yard and practice on drums, or whatever, until they have that ridim under control. Then they would come back to the camp to learn something else."[18] Not only in this way did Ossie's music spread; he and Phil Alvaranga used to go street-preaching the word of Rastafari. Ossie and his group supplied music for the meetings. They also visited out-of-town campsites, spreading the message and the music.

In the early days, among those who accompanied Ossie (repeater) were Eric Tingling (bass), John "Beck" Dale (*fundeh*), and Leighton "Worms" Lawrence, who sang and danced sometimes. As the Count Ossie Drummers became popular, his steady drummers were George "Little Bap" Clarke (first *fundeh*), Winston "Peanut" Smith (second *fundeh*), and Bunny Ruggs (bass). Later, Ossie's son, Time, became second repeater player, displaying something of the virtuosity of his famous father. Ossie has been acclaimed by many of Jamaica's top musicians as having an extremely keen sense of ridim and timing—one of the most creative musicians alive up to the early 1970s. The dispersal of Rasta music continues to occur chiefly by oral tradition, with the "groundation" acting as the principal medium of dispersal.

The Function of Rasta Music

We have seen something of the nature and the origins of Rasta music. This section deals with the function of the music as it affects the Rastafarian brethren collectively and the person in the street. It is said that no real Rastafarian lives far from a drum, because the music is a vital part of the life of the devotee. Not every Rasta owns a set of drums, but in many homes, a single drum—most often repeater or *fundeh*—is to be found. The "true Rastafarian" attaches great religious importance to the drums. To the devotee, the drum is a reminder of "Ones" doctrinal values. More than that, the ridims comfort the believer, as a maternal pulse would a fetus. The Rastafarian seeks refuge in the music from frustration and oppression and in it finds satisfaction without neurosis. The music gives hope because of the spiritual uplift it provides.

This is the feeling among many of the brethren. One man said, "Suppose, for argument sake, I come home one evening and I really feel downpressed—like I don't make no scufflings [money] all day—instead of beating I wife or roughing up I children, I tek out I drum and start a little ridim, yuh know? Before yuh know what happen, the whole yard is wid I. Yuh no see it? Next thing you know I man mind come off the worries so much so, sometimes I get a little insight into how fi tackle me problems next day." Another brethren confirmed the statement: "The drum can work like that, yes. Yuh just feel youself lif outa downpression."[19] Some Rastafarians even suggest that there are healing powers in the music. They claim that after sessions of drumming and chanting, they have been rid of lesser discomforts such as headaches, fever, and "fresh colds."

Rasta music is sometimes played for what the brethren term "heartical" reasons (strictly for pleasure). Most of the time, though, for the individual and the group, the music serves a highly religious purpose. The music is regarded as the most appropriate way of giving "thanks and praises to the Most High Jah, Ras Tafari, Haile Selassie I, Lion of Judah." The most important religious activity of the brethren on the whole is the "Groundation"[20] ritual, which involves very large gatherings. (Groundation is the same as Nyabinghi.) During a 1974 celebration of the Ethiopian Christmas, for example, Dreadlocks[21] from all over Jamaica met in the far reaches of the Bull Head Mountains in Clarendon for a Bingi. I attended on the third night with a group of brethren from Kingston. Dreadlocks of all ages, with their masses of long, thick, chunky hair, swarmed the grounds. A circular booth erected on a patch of bare earth[22] housed four sets of drums, the lead singers, priests, and dancers. The midnight canopy of stars was occasionally obscured by thick layers of "colly" (ganja) smoke. Every Dreadlock was puffing the holy herb.

I learned then that the meaning of Nyabinghi[23] had evolved from the popular negative interpretations of the Rasta expression "Death to the white oppressors and their black allies." Nyabinghi now had a strong, positive meaning among Rastafarians. A Rasta priest who calls himself the Patriarch Bongo Burru said to me at the gathering, "The real meaning, the real overstanding of the kete drums is death to 'deckman.' That is, death to black and white oppression. When we use the Nyabinghi, any part of the earth the wicked is, him have to move." He said that "death to oppression of any sort" was the single thought in the minds of the brethren during the groundation. The Rasta or Nyabinghi dance is regarded as a distinctive and original dance form. Although the function and focus of Nyabinghi dancing and drumming are greatly altered today, the dance movement was a significant part of reggae king Bob Marley's movement on stage, which was often seen by the uninformed as "prancing about."

Brother Edward explained to me at the celebration what takes place at a groundation. "We meet and chant for days sometimes. The Ethiopian Christmas, like now, lasts for seven days. Ethiopian tradition is not as flimsy as Western tradition. . . . Groundation means the nature of man rising. . . . That is what we call the 'irix' . . . a high spiritual feeling. You get that from the dancing and the drumming and the chanting. And the smoking of the herb now free you mind. . . . Groundation is not just for Rasta, but to help everybody to recognize them true self." It is believed among the brethren that during this state of spiritual uplift and heightened consciousness, they are in direct communion with Haile Selassie. This fosters a sense of togetherness, love, and spiritual bonding among those present.

An interesting function of Rasta music was pointed out to me by the leader of the Nameless Ones, Brother Mortimo Planno. He said that Rasta music was also a weapon. There were those in the community who regarded the music as designed to overcome all resistance to Rasta philosophy and progress, and that it was no coincidence that Rasta music was so influential worldwide. Planno said the lyrics and ridims of reggae and even some pop artists were being calculatedly fed into the international pop scene. The move, he said, was a means of spreading the words of Jah and of capturing the interest of others outside the group. This brother sees Rasta music as a positive, nonviolent force that will gain power for Rastafari in Jamaica and abroad and freedom and supremacy for the black man.[24]

Borrowing in Rasta Music

Another aspect of Rasta music is borrowing. Plagiarism does not exist for Rastafarians, who are prone to "capture" the music of Western writers and call it their own. For instance, the brethren will use the melody of a Western hymn, put their own words to it, and call it their own. The words of a hymn might be given a new melody. In other cases, the same words and melody may be used but with the melody somewhat altered, as was done with "The Church's one foundation" in the Rasta church at Bull Bay; the alteration in words and phrasing sounded something like this:

Jah Church's one founda-a-a-a-a-ati-o-on
As only I is Negus Christ our Lo-o-o-rd;
As only I He is our new crea-a-a-a-a-ation
As only I by water and by word.
As only I from Zion He came and sou-ou-ou-ou-ou-ou-out
As only I to be Jah's holy bride;
As only I with Jah's own blood he bou-ou-ou-ou-ou-ou-out
As I only I and for I life he died.

Sung with this phrasing, the hymn drags in a dirgelike meter with dominant monotones. Still, it manages to retain identifying phrases because the first five notes of each of the original lines are retained. Notice the "As only I" line introductions. There is a regular pattern of word substitution in religious songs and utterances: in Rasta lyrics, the Western words *God* and *King* become *Jah* or *I-an-I,* and *Jesus* becomes *Negus.* Sometimes female pronouns are changed to male pronouns or to collective pronouns. A Rasta rendition of the Western religious benediction goes like this:

(Glory) unto the son, unto the holy wise Jah of creation;
As Jah was in the beginning
Jah is now and ever mus' be
I-an-I, Jah Ras Tafari.
Let the words of I mouth
And the meditation of I-an-I heart
Be acceptable to thy sight O Jah.
Jah is I-an-I strength and
I-an-I redeemer,
Who live up and reign up
For I for I, I for I,
Jah, Ras Tafari.

The changing of words and phrases and the swapping of melody in Rasta music are not limited to borrowed material only. Original Rasta pieces suffer the same fate. This is the first verse of a Rasta song "Come Down, White Bwoy," tape-recorded at a 1975 Rasta celebration:

Come down, white bwoy, come down,
Come down offa blackman shoulder.
   (Repeat)
For the unity of blackman a go t'row dem down,
T'row dem offa blackman shoulder.
Watch the Chiney man make him Chiney move,
Watch the Coolie man mek him Coolie move.
Why can't the blackman rise and mek a black move
And dash whiteman outa A-fri-caa.

As the verse is repeated, "blackman" is substituted by "I-an-I Rastaman" or "African." "T'row" becomes "dash," "splash," or "mash." The penultimate line could read "For I for I a go fling dem down."

The rationale behind borrowing in Rasta music varies. Some of the brethren see nothing wrong in altering or using the melody or lyrics of other writers and claiming authorship. As they argue, the new product no longer belongs to the original creator, in either form or function. Another reason is that many of the brethren were conditioned as children in Western religion, and it was understandable and acceptable to them that elements of the old acculturation would show itself in their music, even after years in Rastafari. Although there are several original chants, such as "Holy Mount Zion," written by the Rastafarians, the organized Rasta churches still use the Sankey and hymnal at service.

Total Expression

A great amount of Rastafarians' creative output goes into music. This is the only medium so far that gives the Brethren scope for total expresson.[25] When the drums speak, the pulsing thump of the bass dominates. The heavily padded drumstick effects a caress on the first beat of the bar, as the stick lies horizontal to the center of the drumhead. The third beat is an accented stab with the point of the stick, again into the most vulnerable center of the drum. This is the drum that really symbolizes the beating down of oppression, a principal objective of Rastafari. The method of playing the drum suggests a certain ambivalence that reflects the love-hate attitude of the Rastas to the rest of society. A sexual connotation also is evident in the caress-and-stab action of the drumstick, which could be seen as symbolic of the Rastafarian male's reassertion of lost manhood and dignity.

The repeater drum protests. It continually defies the rigid bass and *fundeh* patterns. This defiance could be regarded as symbolic of the hope to move out of and above oppression through creative application. The *fundeh* could be regarded as the "peace and love" (Rasta password) drum. With its balanced, regular, one-two, one-two pattern, it is the rational "head" that keeps the peace and holds the "lifeline" (the meter). Without changing its form at any time, Rasta music is at once a music of peace and love, protest, and hope, as well as a music of attack. These aspects of Rasta music are even more clearly stated in the lyrics of the form.

Although borrowing is frequent in Rasta music, the brethren do create lyrics and melodies of their own. These are circulated among the community through the oral tradition. The groundation is the chief vehicle for transmitting new material. Individual groups compose songs or chants on the occasion of a groundation. When the Rastas come together, new pieces are done over and over until the assembly learns them. Rastafarians regard everything they do as performed in honor of Haile Selassie. Hence, whether the music be churchical or heartical, whether it be of peace and love, protest, hope, or attack, it is the music of the King.

Peace-and-love songs are chiefly songs of faith, chants, and exhortations. They include "Peace and Love" and "Holy Mount Zion," Rasta tunes that have become the property of the general public. Rasta chants have even been used in religious ceremonies of established churches: For example, "Little Samuel, O Little Samuel" and "Holy Mount Zion, Holy Mount Zion." Songs such as "Come Down, White Bwoy" are songs of protest and attack; so also is the song "Babylon Yuh Holdin' Me."[26]

Rasta Influence on Local Pop Music

During the mid-1950s, the Count Ossie Drummers became popular performers at ghetto blues dances and at amusement parks. The pattern usually was that, come midnight, all recorded music stopped at these places. Ossie and his drummers were then brought on stage, and patrons would "grounds" to their chanting and drumming into the wee hours. The group got its first legitimate stage break in the late 1950s, when the late famous rhumba queen Marguerita (Mahfood) insisted that she would not appear on a Vere Johns variety show (*Opportunity Knocks*) at the Ward Theater unless Ossie's group was on the bill. Johns was wary then about using Rastas on his show, but Marguerita was his star attraction. He had no choice. Ossie and his drummers were hired and were a hit. They soon became the regulars on Vere Johns's show and at other events.

In the early 1960s, three youngsters calling themselves the Ffolkes Brothers asked Count Ossie's aid and advice on a song they were "making." The maestro willingly gave the boys instruction in arrangement and performance. Then his group backed the Ffolkes Brothers for the recording of that song, "O Carolina." (A classic of the ska era in Jamaican popular music "Carolina" was remade as a major hit recently by the New York–based deejay Shaggy.) After his work with the Ffolkes Brothers, Ossie and his group tried further recordings but, according to Ossie, misunderstandings and frustrations involving a certain record producer made the group drop out of the scene. Yet ever since "Carolina," Rasta ridims have been used by other local musicians "to create on." Rasta music continued as a creative force through the rock-steady period and into reggae, where it now flourishes.

The campsite on Adastra Road was the ideal place for struggling young pop musicians in those early days. The communal life—the all-for-one, one-for-all sharing of possessions—appealed to them. So, too, did lengthy "reasonings" with Ossie, whom they regarded as a source of inspiration and a man of peace. The total freedom of expression that pervaded the camp and the almost continuous drumming sessions gave rise to a fantastic output of original music. None of that music was recorded commercially, but the Jamaica School of Music has a tape recording. The sessions were usually spontaneous exchanges of musical ideas between the drums and the voice instruments of visiting musicians. Among these musicians were Bra and Bunny Gaynair, Little G. McNair, Tommy McCook, Roland Alphonso, Cedric "Im" Brooks—all saxophone players—as well as Viv Hall (trumpet), Ernie Ranglin (guitar), and Donald Drummond (trombone).

Those brethren still speak with fondness of the early days when university intellectuals and handcart pushers, musical novices and virtuosos, holy men and charlatans, professionals and people of questionable employment all met and interacted under a banner of mutual respect, peace, and love. Not only music and reasoning provided the activity and excitement at 32 Adastra Road; Ossie says the camp was the scene of numerous raids by police looking for ganja and stolen goods. (One woman was reportedly arrested and charged with the unlawful possession of her kitchen knife.)

In time, the compatibility of Rasta drums and voice instruments brought about the development of the group called Count Ossie and the Mystics. Later, the aggregation of about twenty musicians became known as Court Ossie and the Mystic Revelations of Rastafari (MRR). Instrumentalists who joined with Ossie's drummers to form MRR included Cedric "Im" Brooks (sax), Jenny Terroade (sax and flute), Joe Ruglass (bass), Les Samuel (baritone sax), and Nambo (trombone). The group not only played beautiful music; they dressed colorfully in flashes of Rasta red, gold, and green. The audiovisual impact of Count Ossie and the MRR made the vibrant Rasta music even more impressive to the people of Jamaica in the early 1970s. The group also took Rasta music to the United States, on an invited tour of the American college circuit. The tour featured concerts as well as lecture demonstrations about the music, art, and religion of Rastafari and its role in Jamaican culture.

Although the star of Count Ossie and the MRR waned somewhat, Rasta ridims developed by Ossie have remained the property of the general public—in contrast to the days when Rasta music was just for Rastafarians. Ossie's music of the ghetto became the people's choice. Even those who did not "see Rasta" or who did not wish to "go back to Africa" found that they could forget their troubles and dance. Soon after Ossie became a performer on regular stages and in the recording studios, many others followed and took the music to a global audience. (Among the pioneers was Big Youth, a popular Rasta artist, noted for his deejay style of vocalizing on top of a reggae ridim. In many instances his voice takes on the personality of the repeater drum, syncopating and otherwise exploiting the ridmic possibilities of the driving *fundeh* pattern on the rhythm guitar.)

Rock Steady to Reggae

The beginnings and endings of musical forms have no exact dates. While Rasta music seemed to have been dormant during the rock-steady period that followed the ska era, Rasta influences lay just beneath the surface, waiting for the spring of the "rudie" period and the magnificent florescence of reggae. In the late 1960s the ska sound, which featured many horns on top of a mento ridim, was hit by the dispersal (again, for economic reasons) of many horn men, as well as by the death of culture hero Don Drummond. Record producer Clement Dodd and leading popular musical composer Jackie Mittoo began experimenting with basic Rasta ridims and available voice instruments. The piano and the guitar were given more importance; the simple, repetitive two- or three-chord progression of ska was retained; the formerly walking bass became more flexible; and the whole thing was colored by an overall slow, bluesy beat, as Jamaicans did the new rock steady to the tunes of Hopeton Lewis ("Sound and Pressure," "Take it Easy"), Alton Ellis ("Get Ready Rock Steady"), and others.

At first, rock steady was strictly for enjoyment—as was ska on the whole—but the easy ridim was found suitable for lyrics of social commentary. Soon the artists were coming to grips with the stifling social conditions that pervaded life in the ghettos, from which most of them came. This was so especially in the short period that was part of the transition from ska to rock steady, which preceded the reggae revolution.

Generally speaking, reggae has three basic components: ridim (the polyridmic overlays in the percussive weave), melody, and voice. As in Rasta music, the ridim in a reggae piece remains constant once it is set. But reggae tempo can be fast or slow, and the emphasis is on the ridim instruments. Aficionados will argue endlessly about whether a reggae is "roots rock reggae," "rock steady," "steady rock," "rumbling roots," "roots reggae rockers," or a host of other styles. A reggae piece can also be expressed in several permutations commonly called "versions": ridim minus melody; new melody on old ridim; speaking voice over set ridim. It goes on.

This extremely flexible music lends itself to almost endless musical exploitation. It is sought after by music makers and lovers all over the world. Reggae's lasting qualities parallel those of African-influenced traditional and folk forms in that, like them, reggae features a great deal of enthusiasm, spiritual vitality, and gnomic (aphoristic) function. Most of the leading artists profess to be Rastafarians; and their empathy with Blacks and sufferers internationally points to a certain universal identity of the Jamaican majority. Although the religious element is strongest, the music has also become the vehicle for the transmittal of wider cultural manifestations and for commentary on internal and international political and social affairs.

Many Rasta-oriented reggae bands have come and gone, but the greatest of them was Bob Marley and the Wailers. The Marley group lead reggae exponents in Jamaica from the late 1960s to his death in 1981. Some say that Marley's success was due to the insight of this gifted musician into the value of his training in Rasta music. According to Mortimo Planno (musician-philosopher and an authentic voice of Rastafari), Marley was trained specially by the Rastas of Trench Town to be a pop hero who would spread the message of Rastafari.[27] In any case, it is largely through Marley and his group that Jamaica owes its present impact on the world pop scene.

From the early 1970s, reggae bands began to show signs of the dominant influence of Rasta music. The bass guitar and the traps imitated the patterns of the Rasta bass drum. The lead guitar and the singer then were left to imitate the repeater drum. This pattern took some time in coming, but it ultimately emerged.

Nowadays, not only the lead guitar but keyboards and horns imitate the repeater. An interesting development is that while the bass guitar faithfully kept the Rasta bass ridims for some time, it has now begun to discover a being of its own. There is greater freedom at present in the bass ridims of reggae. While this behavior need not be directly attributed to the tradition of the Rasta bass drum, it brings to mind the fact that on occasion, in the heat of playing Rasta music, the sedate bass drum takes off on its own, playing triplets and other unprecedented patterns according to the emotional dictates of the player. On such occasions, the whole weight of the lifeline is in the hands of the *fundeh* player (e.g., in Black Uhuru's song "Bassline"). Count Ossie felt that the simulation of Rasta ridims on electronic instruments merely served to drown out the real sound of the Rasta drums: "Yuh know I'd like to sell all reggae bands a full set of Rasta drums because the drums are a vital part of the whole make of Jamaican music today. But some people jus' tryin' to push the drums aside by creating all kinds of substitute."[28]

Not only the instrumental and vocal stylings of reggae but the lyrics of most reggae songs and dance movements as well have been directly influenced by Rasta music. Most reggae lyrics reflect Rasta philosophy and religion. They tell of deprivation and the need for peace among brethren. At the same time, they call for the beating down of oppression, and they extol Jah Rastafari. Songs such as "Mount Zion," made popular by the Ethiopians and Cynthia Richards, and "Satta Massa Gana" ("Give Thanks and Praise") were originally religious chants used at Rasta gatherings. The grinding, hip-swiveling dance movements of the Rastafarians at Bingis, along with certain shoulder thrusts, dominate reggae dancing.

Many of Jamaica's jazz musicians have learned from Rasta music. The late Don Drummond, who has almost been raised to sainthood by local musicians, is regarded as the jazz composer and instrumentalist most influenced by Rasta music. A composer ahead of his time, his fame came about after his plunge into Rastafari. Drummond's "Schooling the Duke" and "Addis Ababa," composed during the ska period, are among his works influenced by Rasta music—which has always been of interest to foreign jazz musicians.[29]

Some Rastafarians I interviewed in the late 1970s claimed that it was within their power to direct Jamaican pop music in whichever way they desired. The Rasta beat still is frequently superimposed on the pop beat, and like the colors red, gold, and green, the music remains a symbol of the movement's identity. The basic ridims have not changed over the years, which points to the psychological need of the brethren to have the constant ridims drum home to them the harsh realities of their life "in exile." The repeater expresses the Rastafarians' attitude to the establishment, which is a further reflection of Third World resentment of the West and its need to change the saddle of Western values.

Jamaican popular music has influenced other art forms. It has given birth to the popular "dub poetry" of exponents such as Oku Onuora and the late Michael Smith. The National Dance Theatre Company of Jamaica has also seen fit to make valid social commentary in dance, using the music of the popular culture heroes: *Street People* (music of Desmond Dekker and other pop artists), *Tribute to Cliff* (music of Jimmy Cliff), *Backlash* (music of Toots and the Maytals), *Court of Jah* (music of Bob Marley and the Wailers), *Rockstone Debate* (Bob Marley and traditional music). A significant boost to the popularity of Rasta music in the early 1960s was the phenomenal gravitation of the young from the Jamaican middle class toward the simple peace-and-love and black consciousness philosophy of Rastafari.[30]

Among Jamaican musicians responsible for the creation of reggae music for recreational, critical, and inspirational purposes are the late Nesta Robert Marley, Toots Hibbert and the Maytals, Third World, Ras Michael Henry and the Sons of Negus, Peter Tosh, Pablo Moses, U-Roy, Big Youth, Culture, the Revolutionaries, the late Jacob Miller, Marcia Griffith, Judy Mowatt, and Rita Marley. All these reggae stars and more have professed the faith of Rastafari. Rasta music speaks of an intensely religious, peace-loving people, who are nevertheless defiant of social oppression and Euro-Western cultural despotism and strongly conscious of their black roots. Even though exponents voice their love for Jamaica, in a spiritual sense they sing more of oneness with the black people of the world, which gives the music a strong universal identity.

It is ironic that the mass marketplace has embraced Rasta music with such enthusiasm. Not all reggae fans accept the Rastafarian philosophy and doctrine, but many have identified with the Rastas' symbolic beating down of Babylon with militant chants and Nyabinghi dancing and drumming, which are at once both entertaining and assuring. Today, the roots of Rasta music do not determine only Jamaican music; they have spread universally.

Notes

1. This chapter combines materials from two articles on Rasta ethnomusicology published previously in the *Jamaica Journal*: Verena Reckord, "Rastafarian Music: An Introductory Study," *Jamaica Journal* 11, 1–2 (August 1977): 3–13; and idem, "Reggae, Rastafarianism and Cultural

Identity," *Jamaica Journal*, 15, 46 (March 1982): 70–80. The revised material is published here with the kind courtesy of the *Journal* and the Jamaica Publishers. Other materials consulted in this chapter are: Augustus Brathwaite, "The Cudjoe Minstrels: A Perspective," *Jamaica Journal* 11, 2–3 (1978); Shirley M. Burke, "Interview with Cedric 'Im' Brooks," *Jamaica Journal* 11, 1–2 (1978); Mackie Burnette, "Pan and Caribbean Drum Rhythms," *Jamaica Journal* 11, 3, 4 (1978); James Carnegie, "Jazz," *Jamaica Journal* 4, 1 (March 1970); Astley Clarke, "The Music and Musical Instruments of Jamaica," *Jamaica Journal* 9, 2–3 (1975); Ruth H. Finnegan, *Oral Literature in Africa* (Oxford: Clarendon Press, 1970); Errol Hill, "Calypso," *Jamaica Journal* 5, 1 (March 1970); John B. Hopkins, "Music in the Jamaican Pentecostal Churches," *Jamaica Journal* 11, 1–2 (1978); *Jamaican Folk Music*, special issue (with record), *Jamaica Journal* 10, 1 (March 1970); Olive Lewin, "Cult Music," *Jamaica Journal* 3, 2 (June 1969); idem, "Jamaican Folk Music," *Jamaica Journal* 4, 2 (June 1976); idem, "The Musical Instruments of the Arawaks," *Jamaica Journal* 11, 3–4 (1978); J. H. Kwabena Nketia, "African Roots of Music in the Americas," *Jamaica Journal* 12 (1979); idem, "Tradition and Innovation in African Music," *Jamaica Journal* 11, 3–4 (1978); Pamela O'Gorman, "Let Folk Song Live," *Jamaica Journal* 2, 2 (June 1968); idem, "Introduction of Jamaican Music into the Established Churches," *Jamaica Journal* 9, 1 (March 1975); idem, "An Approach to the Study of Jamaican Popular Music," *Jamaica Journal* 6, 4 (December 1972); Cheryl Ryman, "The Jamaican Heritage in Dance," *Jamaica Journal* 13 (1980); Lileth Sewell, "Music in the Jamaican Labour Movement," *Jamaica Journal* 12 (1979); Garth White, "Master Drummer" [Count Ossie], *Jamaica Journal* 11, 1–2 (1977).

2. As is frequently claimed, many popular Jamaican artists are untrained musicians. Some of the late Bob Marley's critics mistakenly contended that he could not sing, that his songs were not melodious, and that he spoke rather than sang. One should note that many of Marley's songs were written in minor keys, which may not have been expected from a star on the international stage and may have contributed to the critics' response.

3. Rastafarians are noted for creating new words for use among themselves. These words soon become part of slang usage even for the general society. *Ridim* refers to the polyrhythmic relationship among the three drums in Rasta music. It has now also come to describe the behavior of the rhythm in reggae music. What is popularly called "dub" is also ridim; i.e., the melody is taken from popular music, leaving the percussion only. In short, in Jamaican music *ridim* refers to the drum and percussion patterns and tempo.

4. Referred to by some Rastas as the "rising of the irix."

5. In reggae, the quality of the drum-inspired polyridimic structure of the music is extremely important for the meaning of the song, to artists and aficionados alike. People will say a certain ridim is "macca" or "gummy" or "crabbit," meaning that the percussive intent of the music has touched the emotional center of the listener, causing that person to respond favorably to it.

6. *Eartical,* used synonymously with *heartical,* refers to emotions (for secular purposes), as an attachment to the Rasta culture or aspect of it. Here it refers to the drums.

7. Prince Emmanuel, an aging holy man who, up to the early 1980s, held court over his flock in Bull Bay, where he gave spiritual guidance, was treated like royalty. Diviner-kings are familiar figures in African society.

8. Following the practices of Hebraic psalmists, the Rastafarians believe in praising the Lord with musical instruments, "with harps and cymbals" or anything they may invent.

9. Marjorie Whylie, unpublished notes (Cultural Training Center, Kingston, Jamaica, 1977).

10. Ranny Williams, conversation with the author, Kingston, Jamaica, 1978. According to the late actor, social historian, and folk hero Ranny Williams, the Blacks in Jamaica added the in-

digenous mento to the European quadrille to "liven up" the dance, as well as to insert their own identity.

11. Burke, "Interview with Cedric 'Im' Brooks."

12. Count Ossie said Burru, Rastafari, and Pocomania (Poco) were respected "because they are of African traditions; their roots can be traced to the practices of some tribes in Africa. They have their rightful function still, but through [because] Poco deal in the dead, and spirits and things like that; which really is contrary to Rastafari and the community and the consciousness we're trying to develop. We just didn't find their music appealing enough" ("Conversation with Ossie and Friends," Community Center, Glasspole Avenue, Kingston, Jamaica, 1976).

13. In the late 1950s, Back-o-Wall, and West Kingston in general, was the melting pot of African retentions and indigenous Afro-European forms—Kumina, Burru, Myal, revivalism, Pocomania, and a host of church mutations

14. O'Gorman, "Jamaica Popular Music."

15. For photographs of Kumina drums and *kattas,* see *Jamaican Folk Music,* special issue (with record), *Jamaica Journal* 10, 1 (March 1970). Kumina music can also be heard on the album mentioned in that issue.

16. "Conversation with Ossie and Friends."

17. The brethren reasoned that just as Europe had gone to great lengths to develop and preserve its cultural identity, so, too, should the black man, whether in Africa or in exile, seek to preserve his African identity. Since a dominant feature of African culture is music, and the chief instrument of communication is the drum, Ossie decided he was on the right track to developing a significant black music that suited the Rastafarian expression. In time, he gave Rastas a music of protest that expresses Rastafarian hopes and aspirations—a music that helps indoctrinate those interested in the philosophy of Rastafari. ("Conversation with Ossie and Friends.")

18. "Conversation with Ossie and Friends."

19. Ibid.

20. Throughout the year, there are several days of observance when groundation is possible: the Ethiopian Christmas and New Year, Haile Selassie's birthday and coronation day, the anniversary of Selassie's visit to Jamaica, and several religious days of observation.

21. These are Rastafarians who wear their hair long, matted, and exposed. There are also "turban-men" who wrap their "head backs" (i.e., the backs of their heads) and "comb-cuts" who keep their hair combed.

22. Rastas dance on bare earth so as "not to trample on any living thing."

23. The origin of this word is uncertain. It is believed to have originally referred to those committed to violence. The popular derivative, *Bingi,* now refers to a symbolic death—death to evil forces.

24. Mortimo Planno, conversation with the author, Kingston, Jamaica, 1976. This view is expressed by many Rasta musicians.

25. Rastafarians on the whole are an artistic group. Many are involved in visual arts and cottage industries, by which they make a living.

26. In Rastafarian lingo, the word *Babylon* symbolizes any form of oppression to Rastas in particular and to black people in general. The word is associated with ancient Babylon, where the Israelites of old suffered under great oppression; Rastafarians regard themselves as descendants of ancient Israelites.

27. Mortimo Planno, conversation with the author.

28. "Conversation with Ossie and Friends."

29. Out of the jazz voices of the day came another conscious musician, Carlos Malcolm, a Panamanian trombonist-composer-arranger of Jamaican parentage. From the late 1950s to early 1960s, Malcolm enjoyed great popularity with his Afro-Jamaican Rhythms Orchestra, which featured Latin, jazz, and Caribbean music; this identified Malcolm and his music not only with Jamaica but with the wider black diaspora. The feeling was strong that Jamaica could produce its own exportable jazz. Malcolm, Bertie King, Lennie Hibbert, and other leading musicians, formed a short-lived school of jazz, which arose out of the founders' strong nationalist feelings. The school went under for several reasons, including a lack of instruments and too many students who were too poor to pay even the minimal fees asked.

30. This was a social phenomenon that Rex Nettleford of Jamaica's National Dance Theatre Company saw fit to chronicle in the company's repertoire as *Two Drums for Babylon* in 1964.

15 Bob Marley: Rasta Warrior

ROGER STEFFENS

> I hear the words of the Rastaman say
> Babylon your throne gone down, gone down
> Babylon your throne gone down
>   "Rastaman Chant" (traditional)

Bob Marley is the most famous Rastaman who ever lived.[1] On stage, with his Medusa locks spiraling outward from his head in wild abandon, he was a wraith from out of time, preaching timeless truths of a God that was black and incarnate in living flesh. His songs, as noted by his art director Neville Garrick, were indeed "the true, new psalms," messages of divine inspiration set to music. Bunny Wailer, cofounder with Bob and Peter Tosh of the seminal group The Wailers, quotes Psalm 68:25, noting that "the Bible says that the singers went before, and the players of instruments followed after. . . . So it's a whole spiritual order, where angels sing, and then we carry out that message, so it's something more than just Bob Marley or Bunny Wailer or Peter Tosh or the Wailers. It's the Most High, Ras Tafari."[2]

This sense of God-inspired manifestation was present throughout most of Bob Marley's career—the idea that he was an appointed messenger. In an allusion to Psalm 78:39, Marley said, "I don't make music just to be making it. Nothing I do will ever pass away in the wind." But he never attached any arrogance to portentous statements such as these. A man who made tens of millions of dollars during his brief lifetime, Marley was nevertheless uninterested in the external trappings of success and, in fact, gave away much, if not most, of his earnings. "He returned them to his community," says Colin Leslie, director of several of Marley's companies in the late 1970s. When asked if the claims that the singer was responsible for the direct support of four thousand people were true, Leslie laughed and said, "No, no, it was much more than that!"

In every way, Marley knew and acted on the knowledge that he had been chosen for a purpose and that his time on earth would be almost as short as that of Jesus. Says Ibis Pitts, a friend from Bob's days in Delaware in the late 1960s, "Bob told me that he was going to die at the age of thirty-six,"—just one of the many prophecies he made that, all too sadly, came true. And although his work was brief, the lasting effects of it shall be felt throughout the rest of time, as his philosophy spreads from the bottom of the Grand Canyon to the jagged peaks of the Himalayas, chanting down Babylon in all its insidious incarnations.

Bob's Early Years

Bob Marley was born on February 6, 1945, to a nineteen-year-old black woman in the remote hills of northern Jamaica. His father was a white Jamaican, born in the parish of Clarendon, who had been enlisted by the British army as an overseer of rural lands during World War II. "Captain" Norval Marley was in his early fifties when his son, Nesta Robert Marley, was born. Although he and Bob's mother, Cedella, were married, the couple never really lived together, so violent was the reaction of Marley's family to their union. Bob's grandfather Omeriah Malcolm was a monumental figure in the region around his village of Nine Miles, fathering dozens of children and buying up pieces of land whenever they came available. He was especially fond of his new grandson: "Omeriah was the only person I ever heard Bob speak about who seemed to have genuine love for him," claims Bunny Wailer. As a half-caste, Marley was ignored by Whites and denigrated as "the little yellow boy" by many of his black companions. These reactions set him on a self-sustaining loner's path from his earliest years.

The church figured greatly in his early childhood. Sundays would find him singing hymns such as "Precious Lord, Take My Hand" and "Let the Lord Be Seen in You." Around the house, says his mother, Cedella Marley Booker, "he would always sing along with me, hymns, popular songs, whatever." His grandfather's cache of instruments was made available too, so Bob could explore the sounds of the organ, fiddle, banjo, and guitar. At age three and a half, Bob developed a reputation as a psychic, reading people's palms and accurately informing them of intimate details of their lives that he could not possibly have been aware of through ordinary means.

Then, at age five, his whole world collapsed. Captain Marley, long since returned to Kingston, wrote to Bob's mother and asked her to send the child to him so that he could educate him in the good schools of the island's capital and give him a better shot at life. Reluctantly, Cedella agreed, and she sent the tiny youth off alone on a minibus to Kingston. On Bob's arrival, his father met him and dropped him off at the house of an elderly, infirm woman. Bob never saw his father again and spent the next eighteen months or so fending for himself on the mean streets of the city and caring for the old woman as well. Not until Bob was seven did friends from Nine Miles discover him and his mother rush to bring him home.

An experience such as this can scar a person permanently, turn him cynical and angry and bad. But in Marley's case, the opposite seemed to happen, and it marked his life forever after. He had a keen sense of compassion for those whose lives were shattered by forces over which they had no control: the "Babylon" of many of his most famous songs. In "Babylon System," Bob asserts:

Babylon System is the vampire
Sucking the blood of the sufferers
Building church and university
Deceiving the people continually.
Me say them graduating thieves and murderers . . .
Tell the children the truth.[3]

"Babylon," explained Peter Tosh, "is where they tell you that everything that is wrong is right, and everything that is right is wrong. Everywhere," he said, pausing for effect, "is Babylon."

Babylon was everywhere for Marley as a youth. As he entered his teens, he found himself living once again in Kingston, with his mother and her paramour, "Toddy" (Thaddeus) Livingstone, and his eldest son, Bunny (Neville O'Riley)—this time in a home in Trench Town, one of the city's tumultuous ghettos. When Bob finished school at fifteen, Cedella sent him to work in a welding shop, despite Bob's repeated pleas that he wanted to be a singer. But after an accident that almost blinded him, Bob was allowed to pursue his destiny. His teacher was Joe Higgs, an older Trench Town artist who had great success as a singer and was willing to share his knowledge with youngsters who could demonstrate their own seriousness. Higgs's yard became a kind of unofficial college for budding slum talent. By the end of 1963, Higgs decided that Marley and his pals Bunny (Wailer) and Peter Tosh (along with two others who dropped out not long after) were ready to audition for the island's "rootsiest" producer, Clement "Sir Coxson" Dodd, who ran the Studio One label. The name they chose was "the Wailers,"in part because of all the people they had read about in the Bible (particularly in Jeremiah 9) who were "wailing for their freedom."

The group passed its audition and, "in two quick takes, after rehearsing in the studio all morning,"[4] cut their first record, "Simmer Down" (a single). It became an immediate hit, topping the charts for several weeks, and set the Wailers on course for the career they had sought for so long. During the next two and a half years they cut cover songs of tunes by the Beatles, the Impressions, the Moonglows, Dion and the Belmonts, and even Tom Jones's "What's New, Pussycat?" But mixed in with these were spirituals such as "(I left my sins), Down by the Riverside," "Let the Lord Be Seen in You," and "Amen." Later on they began writing songs about the "rude boys" in their area, young "radics" who would not let the system determine their fate. The local radio would not play these songs, claiming that they glorified crime and criminals, but the records became huge underground hits and helped establish the Wailers' reputation as rebels and spokespersons for the common people.

Despite recording over one hundred songs for Coxson, and having five of the top ten songs on the Jamaican charts at the same time, the Wailers were not seeing any financial rewards for their efforts. Coxson kept them on a short leash, buying them suits whenever they did a stage show and giving them only three pounds a week, no matter how many thousands of records they were selling at the time. In disgust, Bob left in February 1966 for Wilmington, Delaware, where his mother had gone to live a few years earlier. He stayed there until October, and in the process of earning money to start his own record label, he missed one of Jamaica's signal events, the arrival of Haile Selassie I on April 21.

Selassie's visit had been arranged by the Jamaican government in the hope that the emperor would publicly eschew the belief, propounded by the local Rasta sect, that he was in any way a godhead. Unfortunately for the Jamaica Labour Party, he did no such thing, and the massive throngs of matted-haired Rastafarian adherents who turned out at the airport to greet him indicated that Babylon had met its match—and, in fact, led to the greatest increase in believers since the Rastafari creed was first preached in the 1930s. Bob's new wife, Rita, whom he had married the day before leaving (without her) for the United States, was among those who witnessed His Imperial Majesty's procession through the city of Kingston, and she has spoken many times since about how he turned as he passed her, looking directly into her eyes and waving a hand in which she clearly saw the imprint of the stigmata of Jesus. This was a sign, she said, that Selassie was indeed God, and she wrote eagerly to Bob and told him about what she had witnessed. [5]

At any rate, when Bob finally returned to Jamaica, Bunny, Peter, and Rita were all sporting the beginning sprouts of dreadlocks and urging Bob to join them in their newfound faith. Bob was eager to learn everything he could and found solace in the grounations held on the beach at Bull Bay—Rasta religious gatherings at which drums were beaten; hymns were chanted; "reasonings" were engaged in regarding the Bible, Babylon, the Almighty; and ganja was shared in a huge pipe called a "chalice." "Herb is the healing of the nation," said Bob, who defended marijuana use as a way of instant mediation with his Creator. "It bring I-an-I closer together."

Bob learned that to the Rasta, "I-an-I" means "you and I" or "I and the Creator who lives within I," indicating that there is no separation, that disunity is an illusion fostered and imposed on the people by Babylon. Thus Rasta language is evocative and holds the very power of creation in its syllables. Hence it is of critical importance that everything spoken be positive and constructive. "Weakheart conception have fe drop" says a frequently repeated aphorism, meaning that whatever is conceived in a "weak heart," a heart that does not truly believe, is doomed to death; it cannot endure. But that which is created from a "true heart," grounded in wisdom, knowledge, and "overstanding," will live "for I-ver." The belief is based on the trinity of word, sound, and power. The word is conceived, and the sounding of it is the power of ever-living creation. "You" is a division, a falsehood; we are all one, manifestations of the true and living God. Thus one does not attend a university but rather an "I-niversity" in this "I-niverse." One does not study in the library but rather in the "true-brary"—not in the place where lies lie buried. Language has an effect, and nowhere was this better understood than in the encampments of the Rasta elders in the backwaters of Jamaica.

As Bob came increasingly under the sway of Rasta, he began to spend time with a controversial man named Mortimo Planno. He played a key role in reducing public animosity toward Rastas, after Claudius Henry's revolutionary debacle of 1959, by proposing that the University of the West Indies do a study of Rastafari. (See Chapter 3 by Barry Chevannes in this anthology.) In the pictures of Selassie exiting his plane on landing in Kingston, Planno is clearly visible at the emperor's side, dressed in a plain white robe, ropey locks hanging below his waist, and carrying a tall walking stick. He had already been to Ethiopia, and his yard was a magnet for religious seekers—and other, less noble folk as well. Planno kept a large library of books on African history, the Bible, and Black Power. In Planno's yard, one was as likely to "buk up on" (encounter) ghetto sufferers as on uptown Ph.D. candidates from the University of the West Indies. And it was Planno who gave Bob the song that marked his "coming out" as a Rasta, "Selassie Is the Chapel." The tune had recently been a worldwide hit for Elvis Presley, but Planno cunningly changed the words. Over a molasses-slow Nyabinghi drum track, Bob chanted "Haile Selassie is the Chapel, power of the trinity, conquering lion of Judah, He's the only King of Kings." The record was pressed in a limited edition of only twenty-six copies and remains a valuable collector's item in Marley's catalog, commanding prices today that reach thousands of dollars.

Lyrical Prophet

During this crucial period, Bob realized that his music was not just for entertainment but had a more elevated purpose: to tell the world of the presence of the Divinity who lived among us here and now. "Coming from the root of King David, through the line of Solomon, His Imperial Majesty is the Power of Authority" ("Blackman Redemption"). Planno and others urged Bob to incorporate the messages he was learning into his songs, and from the late 1960s onward, Rasta livity was the central facet of the majority of Bob's compositions.

> Music you're the key,
> Talk to who, please talk to me.
> Bring the voice of the Rastaman
> Communicating to everyone . . .
> Come we go chant down Babylon one more time,
> For them soft, yes them soft,
> Them soft, me say them soft.[6]

Curiously enough, at that very time Bob was under the pay of American soul singer Johnny Nash, who had hired Bob as a songwriter and performer. For five years, Nash and his associates groomed Marley as a "soul" singer, based on Marley's own wishes to penetrate the American rhythm-and-blues market and charts. But the experiment failed, and in 1972, Nash sold Bob's contract to Chris Blackwell of Island Records—and the rest is history.

Taking advantage of Nash's rigorous training, Bob produced an international debut album of extraordinary power called *Catch a Fire*. In it were lines of pure poetic inventiveness, haiku-like in their ability to pare down elaborate concepts to their bare essentials, as in this couplet from "Slave Driver" about capitalism: "Good God this illiteracy / is only machine to make money." In other words, keep the masses uneducated, and you can continue to get away with paying them seventeen cents an hour for their labor. The album was notable for its spare rhythms, being heard for the first time in places such as America, and for its bold, provocative, postpolitical take "on the system." In America, the hippie-driven movement to combine politics with pop music had been co-opted by the major record companies, interred in a dither of witless disco. Bob's voice was a cry for liberation from the smothering of capitalist divisionism.

Catch a Fire received rave reviews but sold little. Its follow-up, *Burnin'*, garnered similar notices and likewise meager sales. *Burnin'* would prove to be the final statement of the original Wailers. Told by Chris Blackwell that the Wailers were "nobodies" and that they were going to play only in "freak clubs," Bunny Wailer promptly quit the group in the spring of 1973, just when it looked as if the ten years of work the group had accomplished were finally coming to rewarding fruition. Not long after, the militant Peter Tosh, informed that he "owed" the record label more than forty-thousand pounds, quit too.

Marley spent most of the next year regrouping. He added a backup trio composed of three of the most successful female singers in Jamaica: his wife, Rita Marley; Judy Mowatt; and Marcia Griffiths. *Natty Dread,* the first solo album of his career, emerged at the end of 1974, and if anyone had any doubts about Bob's commitment to the revolution, they were erased by such lines as "I feel like bombing a church / Now that you know that the preacher is lying" ("Talkin' Blues") and

> Revelation reveals the truth . . .
> It takes a revolution to make a solution . . .
> Never make a politician grant you a favor,
> They will always want to control you forever,
> So if a fire make it burn,
> And if a blood make it run . . .
> We got lightning, thunder, brimstone and fire . . .
> Kill, cramp, and paralyze all weakheart conception,
> Wipe them out of creation . . .
> Let righteousness cover the earth
> Like the water cover the sea.[7]

Marley had already recorded a Jamaican single called "Fire Fire" in which he had spoken of the final judgment, a theme that would recur throughout his life. He also spoke of the approaching Armageddon, in "Ride Natty Ride," on his 1979 masterpiece *Survival:*

> Jah says this judgment
> Could never be with water,
> So no water could put out this fire . . .
> Now the fire is burning
> Out of control, panic in the city,
> Wicked weeping for their gold.[8]

Not by coincidence did rock critics, unnerved by the appearance and demeanor of this Third World rabble-rouser, begin to refer to Marley as "an Old Testament prophet."

With the help of a new manager, Don Taylor, Marley was on the verge of becoming a superstar as he headed for England in the summer of 1975. The shrewd Taylor had a policy of underbooking Marley, placing him in halls too small to hold the expected multitudes of new fans who flocked to see the wiry singer, and the result was the expected pandemonium, making headlines wherever Marley appeared. During his tours, Marley was often asked by the press about his music and his motives. He took every chance he got to turn such questions to his metasubject, Rastafari. "Religion is just a word, like politics," he told interviewers, "Religion is just war. It's a warfield. . . . The only good sign I see is Rastafari. Rasta mean head. Fari mean creator. Rastafari is head creator. Head creator is God. What does God mean? Rastafari! Haile Selassie is the Christ who them speak of, Him come again."[9]

He was particularly fierce in his condemnation of the Roman Catholic Church, an attitude fostered in Rastafari by the Italian invasion of Ethiopia in the 1930s. In those days, the Jamaican *Daily Gleaner* newspaper published photographs on its front pages of the pope blessing Italian planes before they flew to Africa to murder innocent people with their cargo of guns and poison gas. This, to the Rasta in Jamaica, was inconceivable: How could an alleged man of God countenance such immoral behavior? The pope, they reasoned, must therefore be the Antichrist, the leader of Babylon. Of this Bob was convinced, telling journalist Chris Boyle, "Babylon is a man-made power, evil, put together to rule the people by force. Keep them killing one another. . . . So where did all the power come from? Rome. The Vatican. That's where they get white power. Pope is white power, represent the Devil. What he is defending is what he is. Show me your company and I'll tell you who you are. By their food you shall know them. . . . For me, God is living and life. That mean I have to live with God. God create you to be free. Free up yourselves, otherwise you worthless."[10]

Marley's uncensored words moved the hearts of people throughout the world. As Jamaican economist Michael Witter has written, Marley's "Rastafarian world view included faith that justice would eventually, inevitably and necessarily triumph over injustice. And this was so central a process to the unfolding universe, creation, that the natural forces in their biblical forms, 'fire, brimstone, lightning, [thunder],' would be part of the arsenal of the just. . . . Only reggae seems to embody this peculiar synthesis of the subversive and the seductive."[11] Indeed, it is sometimes impossible to tell whether Bob is singing "Jah" or "joy."

Marley's outspokenness was sure to make enemies, a result he foresaw in a note on the cover of his 1976 *Rastaman Vibration* album. He had long thought of himself as Joseph, the biblical figure who kept the children of Israel fed through their seven years in the desert. Judy Mowatt says, "Bob was Joseph in these times, bringing us spiritual food during the seven years he toured the world." "Joseph is a fruitful bough," announced *Rastaman Vibration*'s cover. "The archers have sorely grieved him, and shot at him, and hated him." Six months later, assassins burst into Marley's compound in Kingston and shot him in the arm and chest, shot his wife in the head, and shot his manager five times in the groin. Miraculously, all survived, and Marley went on two nights later to perform at the scheduled "Smile Jamaica" concert before eighty thousand people, revealing his wounds to them, then stepping offstage into a fourteen-month off-island exile. "T'ings a come to bump," as the sufferers say.

Exodus appeared in the late spring of 1977, and Bob embarked on what was to have been the largest reggae tour in history. But an old soccer injury, exacerbated by a French player spiking Bob's foot in a Paris match, was found to be infected with melanoma cancer, and the tour was canceled after its initial European leg. Bob spent the rest of the year recuperating. He underwent a skin graft onto the big toe of his right foot, despite doctors' admonitions that he should go further and have his foot amputated as a precaution against the disease's spread.

One Love

In January 1978, Bob was approached by rival gunmen from the two main political factions in Jamaica, who came to his temporary headquarters in England with a special request. A spontaneous peace truce had broken out in the ghettos of West Kingston, and to cement this momentous occurrence, a giant musical event called the "One Love Peace Concert" was to be held in Kingston on April 21, the twelfth anniversary of Selassie's visit. The gunmen begged Marley to return to headline the event. He did, and on that evening, under a full moon in a jammed National Stadium, he implored "the two leading people in this land to come on stage and shake hands, to show the people that you love them right, show the people that you're gonna unite!"[12] Leaping in a frenzy, Bob forced right-wing opposition leader Edward Seaga to shake hands in public with the socialist prime minister Michael Manley, a moment that has become immortalized in Jamaican mythology.

The event was not without its international consequences either. A few months later, Bob was summoned by the United Nations to New York, where he was awarded the UN Peace Medal "on behalf of 500 million Africans" for his work toward peace and brotherhood, with particular mention of his achievements at the peace concert. Africa was much on Marley's mind. *Exodus* was meant literally—the "movement of Jah people" forward home to the motherland. "Our duty," Marley told an assistant, Desi Smith, "is to build a studio in Africa, have hit after hit, and then we laugh!" To others he revealed plans to build a town for repatriated Rastafarian brethren and sistren, with all the proper infrastructure for them to survive. "But Africa must first be united," he cautioned, a theme that revealed itself prophetically in his most militant and unembellished collection, *Survival*. The album was initially to be titled *Black Survival,* a name that was rejected by the record company as "too political." Ultimately, the title appeared above a drawing of the hold of a slave ship, so there was little doubt as to what it referred. *Survival* also contained an anthem called "Zimbabwe" to buoy the spirits of the freedom fighters in what was then Rhodesia.

In "Ride Natty Ride," Bob cautioned:

All and all you see wa gwaan
Is to fight against the Rastaman,

So they build their world in great confusion
To force on us the devil's illusion.
But the stone that the builder refuse
Shall be the head cornerstone.[13]

In "Top Rankin" (referring to the top-ranked officials of the government), Bob sang:

They don't want to see us unite
'Cause all they want us to do is
Keep on fussing and fighting . . .
Keep on killing one another . . .

—the antidote to which comes from an ancient "iwah" (time): "Brotherly love, sisterly love."[14]

But in these waning years of his life, Bob was feeling the pressure from all sides—political, professional, financial, and familial. He was constantly surrounded by petitioners. Whenever he was at his uptown Kingston headquarters at Tuff Gong, lines of the needy would stretch out into the street, long into the night. Embodying the hopes of his people was a heavy strain. He felt that he was a representative of his community, and that the songs he was singing were an amalgam of all he had learned from them; therefore, the money he made from those songs was truly his people's. There has probably never been a popular musical figure as generous as Bob Marley. Nor has there been one more concerned with philosophical and religious questions. Because he was so often called on to explain and defend his faith, Bob was seen as a Rastafarian leader, at times much to his chagrin.

Back home in Jamaica, Bob would call the leaders of the various sects of Rastafari to Tuff Gong, attempting to get them involved in a dialogue with one another to bridge divisions that were becoming apparent. Bob's best friend, soccer star Alan "Skill" Cole, had brought the singer into the fold of the Twelve Tribes, a rather "uptown" organization that had fundamental Christian overtones. But Bob was also baptized in the last year of his life into the Ethiopian Orthodox Church (EOC), at the request of his mother. He often took solace with the roots Nyabinghi elders, who felt that their faith existed essentially in their hearts and not in any organization. What should I be telling people overseas about the doctrine? he asked the assembled elders. If you can't agree among yourselves on basic matters of faith, how am I supposed to represent Rasta to the rest of the world? In his own way, Bob tried to be all things to all people, embracing all of the different segments of the faith, to underscore the unity to which he felt they should be giving witness. Of course, when he passed away, these gatherings were not continued.

Religion not lived was false religion, Bob reasoned. Therefore, given the opportunity to forgive, Bob responded with typical humility and love. At a concert in England in 1978, one of the gunmen who had come to kill Bob in 1976 showed up backstage and confessed his part in the plot. Not only did Bob forgive him, but he invited the man to travel with him for the remainder of the tour. Friends and fellow band members, themselves the objects of that brutal attack, were astonished. But Bob admonished them that the man was being used by other, more powerful Babylonian forces and deserved to be given another chance.

Late in 1978, Bob made his first visit to Ethiopia. Disturbed by the political events following the overthrow of Selassie, Bob sought out the Rasta community in Shashamane, an area in southern Ethiopia that had been given to repatriated Rastas by His Majesty himself during his visit to Jamaica. Marley saw that an enormous amount remained to be done before large numbers of Rasta could make a new life there, and he began to think in larger terms than ever before about what he could contribute to the movement. Had he lived, no doubt by now he would have built the schools, hospitals, community centers, and housing that he saw as necessary. But Bob sensed his short life was coming to an end. In one of the saddest songs he ever wrote, shortly after being told he had cancer in 1977, Bob sang:

> When the whole world lets you down
> And there's nowhere for you to turn
> And all of your best friends let you down
> And you try to accumulate
> But the world is so full of hate
> And all of your best friends let you down,
> I know a place where we can carry on.[15]

On a similarly titled twelve-inch record called "I Know," released posthumously in 1981, Bob identified the place as Zion, because, he said, "Jah will be waiting there."

In April 1980, Bob Marley received one of the greatest honors of his life when he was invited to headline the independence celebrations in Zimbabwe. He was the only performer on the main stage that night, as squadrons of jets screamed overhead, twenty-one cannons were fired, and a thoroughly "discomfitted" Prince Charles furled Britain's Union Jack for the final time. Thousands of freedom fighters broke down the gates to enter the national stadium in Harare, as Bob sang "Zimbabwe" to an ecstatic crowd estimated at one-hundred thousand people. Here was the African returned home to his own people, and Bob was actively recruited by the new revolutionary government of Robert Mugabe to take up residence in Zimbabwe. That summer, Bob released what would be his final album, the haunting and bittersweet *Uprising,* which contained "Redemption Song," a poignant acoustic ballad, as its closing track. In a voice rich with emotion, Bob asks:

> How long shall they kill our prophets
> While we stand aside and look?
> Some say it's just a part of it,
> We've got to fulfill the book.[16]

He was probably aware that something much bigger was being played out in his life, something cosmic and final and fierce.

The *Uprising* tour of Europe brought Marley his biggest audiences ever. In Milan, one-hundred thousand Italians jammed a soccer stadium in which the pope had appeared the week before—and Marley outdrew the pope! A similar throng greeted him in Ireland. Massive crowds thrilled to sold-out spectacles in Germany, France, and England, breaking longtime records held by the Beatles and the Rolling Stones. Bob was truly the "Reggae King of the World."

As the American part of the world tour began in September, Bob was visibly weakened. After two nights at Madison Square Garden, he went jogging on a Sunday afternoon in Central Park. In the middle of his run, he collapsed with what appeared to be an epileptic seizure. Doctors diagnosed a resurgence of the melanoma, telling him that it had metastasized and entered his brain and his lungs, and gave him but a few weeks to live. Nevertheless, Bob flew to Pittsburgh where he performed a vibrant, final concert on the night of Tuesday, September 23, 1980.

Several weeks of outpatient treatment followed for Marley in New York's Sloan Kettering Cancer Center, but doctors ultimately gave up. As a last hope, Bob flew to Germany to a controversial cancer clinic run by a former Nazi SS doctor named Josef Issels, who managed to keep Bob alive until the next May. Bob flew to Miami, where he had bought a home for his mother, and died in a hospital there on the morning of May 11, 1981. It is reported that at the very moment of his death, Judy Mowatt was in her home in Kingston when suddenly a bolt of lightning flashed through her window and struck the metal frame of a picture of Bob that sat on her mantle—a signal she said, "that one of the earth's great spirits had left, transcended to the celestial plane."

Bob's funeral, conducted in Kingston by Ethiopian Orthodox priests, was the biggest in the history of the Caribbean. Most of the roughly two million people in the country lined the route of his cortege back to the gentle, verdant hills of Nine Miles, where he was laid to rest in a mausoleum adjacent to the shack in which he had been born. On his finger he wore a ring that Asfa Wossen, son of Selassie, had given Bob. The ring, the prince had told Bob, had belonged to his father.

The Chant Goes On

In the end, Bob's music is what has triumphed over death. His hour came around at last, and Bob reminded all who cared to listen that what goes around, comes around, and the rhythm remains the same:

Love to see when you move to the rhythm . . .
It remind I of the days in Jericho
When we trodding down Jericho walls.
These are the days when we'll trod through Babylon,
Gonna trod until Babylon falls.[17]

That rhythm is the heartbeat pulse of one love, one heart, one destiny. "One Love," says partner Bunny Wailer,

is the motto that the Nazarene, Jesse, the Christ, said: "Love ye, one to another," which is the same as saying, "One love, ye to another." The Wailers are the Wailing Walls of Jerusalem, and the Nazarene was a part of the foundation of the Wailing Walls of Jerusalem, being connected because he was a Jew from such time. He also had the vein running through him that spells out into his messages that it has come to be fulfilled in the Wailers' message within our times: to be correct, to clear whatever the mist was as it concerns the Rastaman and the Nazarene in this dispensation of time. So it was in the beginning, so shall it be henceforth and forever.[18]

Bob expressed his eschatological views with the use of biblical materials saying, "[God] say within 2,000 years Him gonna come [in a new name]. And when Him come Him shall be dreadful and terrible among the heathen" (cf. Malachi 1:14). Bob continued: "That's where you get the vibration from Rastafari. Anyhow, the man dem get the spirit inna Jamaica and start deal with it till I-an-I get the full knowledge of it, and Him come. But most preacher run from dem t'ing, you know. Because the thing is . . . is just money dem a deal with, collect money. Dem nuh deal with the reality."[19] And as he wrote in "Forever Loving Jah," "What has been hidden from the wise and the prudent / Been revealed to the babe and the suckling" (Matthew 11:25 and Luke 10:21). The Truth is not simply for the black race; although, as Bob noted to poet Wanda Coleman, "it's very hard for white man to say them black and His Imperial Majesty is God. But it's very easy for the black man to say he's black and He's God, and it's true, you know. Black man have to realize that He is the greatest, He the King of Kings."[20] But as Bob said to musician Ras John Bullock, "It's not the color of a man's skin, it's the color of a man's heart that is most important."

Today, the Havasupai Indians who live at the bottom of the Grand Canyon regard Bob as one of their own, a man of the soil who revered Mother Earth and Father Sky as they do. In Nepal, Bob is worshiped by many people who regard him as an incarnation of the Hindu deity, Vishnu. In Addis Ababa he is thought of as a modern reincarnation of the ancient Ethiopian church composer the Holy Yared. On a mountainside above Lima, Peru, carved in huge letters, is the legend "Bob Marley is King." Maori, Tongan, and Samoan islanders join together in a band called Herbs to sing Bob's "songs of freedom." Rebels of every stripe march to battle singing Marley's anthems.[21] Says Jack Healy, head of Amnesty International, "Everywhere I go in the world today, Bob Marley is the symbol of freedom." Thus the music and lyrics continue in the hearts of Jah's people as they chant down Babylon on their way to freedom.

Notes

1. Quotations in the text from Bob Marley, his coworkers, and his family that are not cited in the notes are taken from personal conversations and recollections. My thanks to William Spencer for his helpful editing and for guiding me to the proper biblical citations.

2. Bruce Talamon and Roger Steffens, *Bob Marley: Spirit Dancer* (New York: W. W. Norton & Co., 1994), 30.

3. Bob Marley, "Babylon System," on *Survival,* Tuff Gong 422–846 202-2, 1979, compact disk.

4. Stephen Davis, *Bob Marley: Conquering Lion of Reggae* (London: Plexus, 1993), 43.

5. As occurs with the birth of a religious tradition, this incident belongs to the mythmaking reality in Rastafari. Bob's wife was probably enraptured in the ecstasy of Selassie's visit and inserted the "imprint of the stigmata of Jesus" redaction as she retold the story several times.

6. Bob Marley and the Wailers, "Chant Down Babylon," on *Confrontation,* Tuff Gong 422-846 207-2, 1983, compact disk.

7. Bob Marley, "Revolution," on *Natty Dread,* Tuff Gong 422-846 204-2, 1974, compact disk.

8. Bob Marley, "Ride Natty Ride," on *Survival*.

9. Chris Boyle, "Interview with Bob Marley," *The Beat* 5, 3 (1986): 21.

10. Ibid.

11. Michael Witter, "Bob Marley and the Caribbean Revolution," *The Beat* 11, 3 (1992): 37.

12. Transcript from the soundboard tape of the April 21–22, 1978, One Love Peace Concert, Kingston, Jamaica, in Roger Steffens Reggae Archives.

13. Marley, "Ride Natty Ride."

14. Bob Marley, "Top Ranking," on *Survival*.

15. From an unreleased tape produced by Lee Perry and Bob Marley in 1978, after Marley discovered that he had melanoma cancer; in the Roger Steffens Reggae Archives. This is not to be confused with "I Know," a posthumously released twelve-inch record (1981) and cut on 1983's *Confrontation* album. The song was also covered by Rita Marley on the album *We Must Carry On,* Shanachie Records 43082, 1991.

16. Bob Marley, "Redemption Song," on *Uprising,* Tuff Gong 422-846, 211-2, 1980, compact disk.

17. Bob Marley, "Jump Nyabinghi," on *Confrontation*.

18. From liner notes by Roger Steffens for the *Hall of Fame* compact disk by Bunny Wailer, RAS 3502, 1995, 42.

19. Wanda Coleman, "Interview with Bob Marley," *The Beat* 13, 3 (1994): 45

20. Ibid.

21. See the annual Bob Marley collectors edition of *The Beat* 14, 3 (May 1995). This issue contains several stories by international readers of the magazine concerning Bob's impact on native cultures and how Marley's image mythologies and religious belief.

16

Chanting Change around the World through Rasta Ridim and Art

WILLIAM DAVID SPENCER

Through reggae rhythms, the Rastafarians have attempted to bring about change in society by chanting down their metaphorical Babylon. But what does it mean to "chant down Babylon in a ridim"? How can music and art combat the oppressive economic systems under which the world's poor and often oppressed languish? David "Ziggy" Marley, heir of Bob Marley's musical vision, explained the significance of the ideological expression to me in a telephone conversation on October 27, 1993:

> Babylon causes the system, you know? It's a devil system—that is what it is to us—who cause so much problems on the face of the earth. . . . And by "chanting down" I mean by putting positive messages out there. That is the way we'll fight a negative with a positive, in regard if Babylon system press and push negative things, but we push positive things . . . the thing is: action is under the words. It's how you live your life that is the important thing. So, as now you or me live a life according to the laws of life, which is the Father's law. Now, to me, I believe that there need not be anything written down for man to know how to live. There did not have to be anything written. There the law of God is in man's heart. There's written laws and there's unwritten laws. Each man know what our lives should live. And what are laws of life inside him tell him without having to read anything. Before there were books and before there were writings, man did know the Father and know how to live life according to the law of life, you know?

So chanting down Babylon for Ziggy Marley is "speaking to the people" about the "law of God," about how to live justly together and promote life, as he understands the Rasta tradition he received. Combating the negative with the positive has been the overriding creed of the Marley musical family.[1] And it has been the preferred means of bringing about change for most Rastas since the ferocious battles with the police during the early confrontations at Leonard Howell's Pinnacle Hill commune; in the Ronald (or Julius) Henry revolt of 1960, where the younger Henry reportedly enlisted Rastas in his guerrilla skirmishes after his father, Claudius, was arrested for sedition; and at the various camp and yard raids that occurred sporadically between the 1940s and the

1960s. Since those clashes, which resulted in the Rasta elders' appeal for understanding and tolerance that provided the impetus for the University of the West Indies (UWI) report of 1960, Rastas have chosen the nonviolent over the violent approach to bring down Babylon. The arts have become key "weapons" in that strategy. Rastafarian music has become a worldwide phenomenon. Through music, visual art, drama, poetry, and celebrating new heroes, Rastas have promoted, globally, their message against "Babylon," the oppressive sociopolitical system.

Such a perspective has passed as well into positive dancehall music and stands in sharp contrast to current gangster lyrics by those espousing "Rasta chic." Though Rastas, of course, are not philosophically nonviolent, the majority of Rastas I have met decry the gratuitous celebration of gang violence in lyrics and film. They resort to violence only in self-defense. Chanting down Babylon is their preferred response to oppression, explained one premier dancehall star, the perceptive Tony Rebel, in our conversation in Boston on November 8, 1993. He sees being a musician as a religious act:

> Well, I see myself as an instrument of the Most High and definitely it's not for me alone to chant down Babylon. I'm like a link in the chain. So, I got to just play my part. If a chain is as strong as the weakest link, so all the links got to be strong. And I'm one of that links, so I'm just doing my thing what I'm supposed to do. And we hope to achieve the awareness of people, so that people might understand that there is two force that rule this earth. And then the one you work for is the one who's gonna pay you. It's like God told you what is sin and what is the consequence of sin, but He doesn't determine who sin. But, if you don't know, then it's like you're a lamb to the slaughter. So, the message have to reach to the four corners. So, letting the people aware of what is happening around them, it's OK. And letting them understand also that good is over evil and they must be confident in that picture. So, we're trying also to spread love, which is one of the first commandment.

For Tony Rebel, the music changes people as they study it. He explained further, "Well, we know that the music is very influential. The word is power. They chant around Jericho wall and it fell down. So, therefore, we can use music to chant down Babylon walls also. That is not a literal wall. Is like emancipating the people from those kind of mentality that is negative." When Tony Rebel was told, "This book goes mainly to college professors and their students. Is there any last thing that you'd like to have me put in? A message that you'd like to give to the teachers who teach the students?" he replied:

> To the teachers who teach: well, just be careful what you teach the little children. Make sure it's not anything to hurt them. Because what you teach little children is like a seed and it will germinate, grow, and bear fruit. And if it's the wrong fruit, you might just have to end up eating that fruit. And which it was sown by your hands. So, whatsoever you do, you must be very careful. Make sure that it is accepted by the Creator.

Seeing themselves as instruments of the Most High, spreading love to encourage people to serve good, not evil, Rastas such as Tony Rebel and Ziggy Marley regard their task of chanting down Babylon as having implications for "leavening" the perspectives of future generations. This refreshing attitude of fighting oppression with a positive message in music has propelled Rasta reggae around the world and, as the astute critic Roger Steffens has observed, made reggae the "preferred rhythm of protest worldwide."[2]

Reggae as a Global Rhythm of Protest

After its introduction to Great Britain, reggae[3] became a vehicle to assail economic and class inequities, particularly in regard to the diasporan Caribbean population that has emigrated to the British Isles seeking opportunity. Since Great Britain already had a post–World War II immigrant-oriented West Indian music industry (see Frank Jan van Dijk's "Chanting Down Babylon Outernational," chapter 11), Britain was one of the first places outside the Caribbean to be taken by Jamaica's musical storm. Caribbean music was promoted particularly when Millie Small introduced ska (especially the strain called "blue beat") to the masses while on tour with the Beatles in 1964. Other Jamaican performers, such as Desmond Dekker, Jimmy Cliff, the Kingstonians, Byron Lee, Alton Ellis, Laurel Aitken, Errol Dunkley, and Max Romeo, kept the British public updated on the musical changes occurring from the late 1960s through early 1970s, until the rise of British-grown roots groups such as Matumbi, Aswad, and Steel Pulse in the mid-1970s. When the Anglo band Mungo Jerry reached the popular music charts with "In the Summertime" in 1970, and Eric Clapton scored with his cover of Bob Marley's "I Shot the Sheriff" in 1974, Great Britain had a reggae eruption. Everyone, including aspiring part-time lounge singers such as Johnny Wakelin (with "Reggae, Soul, and Rock 'n' Roll"); the highly successful Sting and his group, the Police; crossover performers such as Dandy Livingstone; and traveling bands comprised of Jamaican expatriates, second-generation Britons of Jamaican extraction, and purely British Jamaican wannabes, burst forth with the reggae sound.

Steel Pulse, comprised of children of West Indian immigrants, began their career with a "Tribute to the Martyrs," looking back across the ocean to celebrate the lives of Jamaican revolutionary Paul Bogle and reformer Marcus Garvey. Then they swept their vision around the world to extol Dominique Toussaint L'Ouverture (who drove "all oppressor man" out of Haiti), Steve Biko of South Africa, the Black Panthers, Martin Luther King, Jr., and Malcolm X. In that context, they assailed racism in Great Britain ("Jah Pickney [Rock against Racism]"), deplored the oppressive class system on behalf of the "lowest of the low" ("Babylon Makes the Rules"), and called for a "Handsworth Revolution" among the poor, black, and dispossessed. Many other diasporan bands have joined them.

In fact, so potent is reggae's identification as a vehicle of protest that even non-Rastas in Britain, such as Linton Kwesi Johnson, an expatriate from Jamaica's rural Clarendon Parish, have employed it to address England's social conditions. Having come to England at the age of eleven, Johnson was schooled, awarded a writing fellowship, employed as a library resources and education officer, then radicalized through Britain's expression of the Black Panther movement, organizing its poetry workshop. Seeking to reach a wider audience, he set his poetry to reggae ridims, achieving great influence with such collections as *Dread Beat an' Blood* (1978), Forces of Victory (1979), and *Making History* (1984). The scope of his cultural critique ranges from decrying the catchall Suspicion of Loitering with Intent to Commit a Felony law, under which minority youth are hauled to jail without specific evidence, to promoting working-class political movements from South London to Gdansk, Poland. Through the hypnotic setting of dub[4] ridim, Johnson has kept news of social inequities in England and abroad pulsing in the ears of the commonwealth.

In North America, reggae was broadcast almost from its beginnings,[5] but for a while, most bands remained underground or alternative. Some, such as Texas's the Pool, were hardly known, while others, such as Columbus, Ohio's Identity on Island Records, and the New York–based Jah Malla on Atco's Modern Records, enjoyed reggae label status. But most artists, including New York City's Abeng; the Boston ska and reggae stalwarts Bim Skala Bim, Bosstones, ITones, the Mighty Charge, Right Time, Danny Tucker, and BARRI; and the plethora of California and Heartland bands, were self-produced or on small local labels until recently. When a band such as Native—Ocho Rios, Jamaica, born but California based—finally got a promotional boost on a label such as A&M, it was still treated like an alternative band. And alternative groups such as Fishbone felt compelled to add a reggae song (e.g., "Iration") to their offerings. Then Maxi Priest with lovers' rock and Shabba Ranks with dancehall hit the United States with force. New York–based performers such as Sister Carol and Shelly Thunder, anchoring on the powerful reggae-oriented labels Island, RAS, and Shanachie (which had used the ensuing years to build a following), started a serious onslaught. Reggae has had its most successful expression in the dancehall/hip-hop mixture emanating from New York City.

The musical action had begun much earlier when Jamaican mento[6] mixed with the calypso (the music of Trinidad) of Irving Burgie and Harry Belafonte, and songs such as Lou Christie's ska-ish "Two Faces Have I" (March 1963) and Millie Small's "My Boy Lollipop" (1964) achieved subsequent chart action. They set the United States on watch. By the autumn of 1968, the rumor of Caribbean musical muscle flexing sent Arthur Godfrey's protégé Johnny Nash to test the U.S. charts with the rock-steady song "Hold Me Tight." The success of Desmond Dekker's "Israelites" and Jimmy Cliff's "Wonderful World, Beautiful People" in 1969, along with Aretha Franklin's "Rock Steady," Bobby Bloom's "Montego Bay," and Paul Simon's "Mother and Child Reunion," opened the door for a sporadic but noticeable interest in reggae.

As a vehicle of protest, some of the most interesting U.S. reggae has originated with groups such as the Havasupai Indians (see Roger Steffens's "Bob Marley: Rasta Warrior," Chapter 15) and anticommercial collections of protest reggae such as those by Resistance Records or Clappers (the "anticorporate record company" whose product is "a weapon without compromise" not "entertainment"). Hawaiians' Jawaiian music has blended reggae into an updated mixture of traditional music with jazz and rock. The Hawaiian Kauihimalaihi "Butch" Helemano has used reggae to push higher education (in a song with that title) and to reintroduce traditional religion ("Hui O Hee Nalu"), while the band Simplisity, keying off Bob Marley's "Waiting in Vain," utilizes reggae's protest orientation to plead that "Hawaiian lands" be put totally in "Hawaiian hands."

The Canadian dub poet Lillian Allen has employed reggae ridims as her vehicle to champion women's causes, encouraging women to struggle for equality ("Sister Hold On"), celebrating childbirth ("Birth Poem"), and protesting the abuse of adolescent girls ("Nellie Bellie Swellie"). Her "Ridim an' Hardtimes" is a quintessential statement of how music springs up as a reaction to oppression and can sustain one's spirit in the struggle to survive that "downpression."

In Mexico and throughout Central and South America, reggae has been warmly embraced. Mexico not only has supported the Hispanic American reggae group Maná but has enjoyed reggae songs regularly adopted by such performers as the great Ana Gabriel ("Baila el Reggae," "Quiero Yo Saber") and the late Selena ("Como la Flor"). Critics who think Hispanic reggae began and ended with Bob Marley's protégé Martha Velez will discover Manuel Jiménez, a leading popular composer of the Dominican República, using reggae in "Son del Sol" and Miriam Cruz y las Chicas blending reggae with merengue in Rento Arias' beautiful "Tómalo Tú." They can also witness a dancehall boom with a plethora of Latin performers, such as Vico C., El General, Nando Boom, La Atrevida (Rude Girl), Brewley MC, DJ Negro, La Diva, Psycho Unity, Transfusion, Kid J., Ranking Stone, Mejicano, Guayo Man, Yaviah, "Gatitó," Shar-I-Mark, Gummy Man, Ledesma, Baron Lopez, Microhouse, Ellie D., Lisa M. (with her "Ja-Rican Jive"), La Banda Show ("Reggae, Reggae"), Shakira ("Un Poco de Amor"), and many others.

For the Afro-Nicaraguan group Soul Vibrations, roots reggae is employed to chant down the Babylon of postcolonial culture. Its *Black History/Black Culture* collection is replete with chants about El Salvador, Mozambique, and freedom in Central America (as well as throughout the world). "A black, English-speaking reggae group from Nicaragua?" asks guitarist Gregorio Landau. "For many of us it is difficult to imagine Nicaragua as the home-base for a reggae group of this calibre. Most people associate Nicaragua with Mestizo culture and are surprised to hear a black group singing about the revolution from a *costeno* [coastal] perspective." Why reggae? The band cites its "'African' identity"; "Afro-Caribbean emphasis"; the influence of Bob Marley and Marcus Garvey; and its general "revolutionary" flavor, so that a Nicaraguan reggae band "could provide a voice for young Afro-Nicaraguans who were in the throes of a cultural renaissance." To them, "music coming from Jamaica and other parts of the Caribbean spoke to their experience" and assisted in the band's aim "to promote the culture of the Coast" as it participates in "political activities."[7]

Similarly, when the Suriname band P-I Man and Memre Buku composed a four-part epic piece, *Masannah,* to push for racial accord, they chose to set their "highly intellectual Surinam [sic] poetry," "historical information" about their country, and their record of black struggle in Suriname against colonialism to a "very rhythmical swinging Afro Caribbean music": reggae, the music of international protest.[8] Reggae's flexibility extends to neighboring Guyana, producing creole-reggae groups such as I-an-I, Krucial Age, and Universal Youth, some of whose members are Maroon descendants. Farther down the coast, in Portuguese-speaking Brazil, many performers have adapted reggae, the most internationally famous being Margareth Menezes and Daniela Mercury. World-renowned composer Caetano Veloso, who has written songs blending

samba and reggae both for his own release ("Meia Lua Inteira") and for others' (e.g.,
Daniela Mercury's "Você Não Entende Nada"), explained to me in an interview at the
New England Conservatory of Music in Boston on June 23, 1997, that samba reggae

> just happened in Bahia. . . . It was invented mostly by people in Olodum [a renowned *bloco-
> afro,* or neighborhood drum ensemble, from Salvador]. They mixed samba and reggae in
> their percussion and they started composing what they themselves called samba-reggae. And
> so, I liked it. I love Bahian carnival. I think Olodum is incredibly creative. They are incred-
> ibly creative people, and so I recorded some of the stuff that was related to what they did.

While some pioneering reggae bands have existed in Brazil, such as Rio Reggae Band,
Kilimanjaro, and their successors the Bantus, as well as Cidade Negra and its now-
independent lead singer Ras Bernardo, still most dreadlocked musicians (such as
Carlinhos Brown, who identifies himself as a syncretist) are not Rastafarian in belief.
Caetano Veloso explains, "Some people in Brazil . . . behave in a Rastafarian way. I mean,
they look like Rastafarians and they kind of dance like Rastafarians. But I don't know if
there are real Rastafarians in Brazil. I mean, with all the religious implications and all of
the fantasies that belong to that belief." Popular music is more likely to promote Brazil's
own pervasive Afro-Brazilian faiths (gathered under the catchall term *Macumba*). Groups
have also blended reggae with other Brazilian rhythms, as Kaoma attempted with lam-
bada in its song "Lambareggae." This acquisition is toasted, in return, in tributes by reggae performers such as Jimmy Cliff (who has enjoyed immense popularity in Brazil and
has himself recorded with Olodum). On Brazil's far side, Uruguay has bands such as Ru-
ina de Moda. In this way, throughout nation after nation, reggae proliferates in Central
and South America, often blending its beat with the local rhythms.

In the English-speaking Caribbean, Anguillan poet Clement "Bankie" Banx sets his
poignant poetry to reggae rhythms. Part of the appeal to him is reggae's identification
with Rastafari. He told me in a telephone interview on November 15, 1992, "Rastafari
is the only thing that holds the Caribbean, the only binding force in the Caribbean, as
far as I'm concerned, and means a lot to the world in general too, you know? Because
people in the Caribbean, a lot of those people, are lost. They have nothing to hold onto."
As a person who does "not like violence," he expresses his rage and protest through music. He continued:

> Personally, I'm a very emotional person. A lot of things make me angry. But if I get angry,
> then you'll get angry too, and that's not going to help the situation. Sometimes I get to the
> point where I say, "What's he talking about?" But then I say to myself, "What's the object
> of this? Are you trying to help the situation? Or are you trying to impress people or what?"
> When you come up with a song, you have to come up with something that allows us to hold
> life, you know? We may be unable to find the solution, but we've got to say something.

Reggae becomes a political vehicle through which this Anguillan political poet can send
positive and life-affirming messages as he critiques oppression.

Like Anguilla, most islands (e.g., Barbados, Trinidad and Tobago) have a burgeoning Rasta community that "salts" reggae in with nationally popular rhythms. French-
speaking Martinique, for example, has fielded such bands as Zion Train Imperial, Black

Star Liner, Meditation, Paradise, Pawol, and a host of others. And, as we saw in Brazil, not all purveyors of reggae have a Rastafarian orientation. Poets Kevin and Robin of Barbados preach a Christian message through dub, while nontheological, experimental bands like Barbados's Spice mix reggae in with their techno-soca. Further, assigning a performer to a specific place is sometimes difficult. Eddy Grant, for example, roars back and forth between London, Barbados, California, and Trinidad and Tobago, where he currently has his recording enterprises set up. In the same way, as the music continues to globalize, even identifying a song as belonging to one genre becomes difficult. "Dancing Mood" by the Tams, a classic U.S. R & B group, transforms to soca (soul calypso) for Montserrat's superstar Arrow, but in the hands of the New York Band, from the Dominican Republic and the United States, it becomes merengue, and in the songbook of Big Youth, it transforms to reggae. As the music reverberates from country to country, reggae songs and rhythms blend into fascinating hybrids.

Hawaii's thriving Jawaiian reggae is not the only adaptation of reggae in the Pacific. Australia has sported not only Men at Work, No Fixed Address, and US Mob as reggae groups but also the Aboriginal Mixed Relations, which mixes a healthy dose of eclectic reggae with its indigenous rhythms. New Zealand, as well, has produced the Aborigine bands Aotearoa and Herbs, which are excellent examples of Maori South Pacific reggae. Reggae, as an art form of protest, lends itself well to expressing the concerns of Aboriginal people (exemplified by Aotearoa's "Maoritanga"), their plea for self-determination and for the preservation of Maori language and culture against increasing "Anglification."

Throughout Europe and even into Asia, one constantly finds bands using reggae as a means to protest injustice and call for change. The former USSR reggae group Kino did this, as did Poland's Gideon Jahrubal (Gedeon Jerubbaal), Daab, and Kultura. Algerian "pop-rai" rebel Cheb Khaled, at odds with the conservative Islamic socialist establishment, journeyed to Paris and from there to Jamaica, recruiting such reggae giants as the I-Three (Rita Marley, Judy Mowatt, Marcia Griffiths), saxophonist Dean Fraser, and Stephen "Cat" Coore of Third World to forge a number of reggae-rai tracks on his boldly innovative 1996 *Sahra* Island album.[9] Meanwhile, after producing roots reggae star Avi Matos, Israel is currently in the grip of dancehall fever. Japan has embraced reggae and fielded its own bands, from Zound Zystem to Sandii and the Sunsetz to deejays such as PJ and other hot child performers. And Japan's other pop bands regularly mix in reggae ridims (as Shonen Knife did in "Oh, Singapore"). Scandinavia has given birth to the roots group the Reggae Team, as well as the commercially successful electro-pop reggae of Ace of Base. Particularly popular has been a form of reggae mixing called "Swemix," out of Stockholm. Italy has produced Different Stylee, among many others; and the list goes on.

But perhaps the greatest adaptation of reggae for the purpose of chanting down Babylon around the world has occurred in Africa. Ghana is the home of such reggae performers as Kojo Antwi and Classique Vibes, Okasa Lamptey, the Classic Handels, Felix Bell, K. K. Kabowo, and Roots Anabo, as well as groups such as the African Brothers, the City Boys, and the "Expensive Boy" Daniel Amakye Dede and his Apollo High Kings, who fuse the reggae beat in with Ghanaian rhythms. These artists see reggae, soca, and other Caribbean rhythms as largely New World adaptations of African rhythms. When Jamaican performers such as Bob Marley spoke of coming home to live in Africa, and others such as Safi Abdullah actually did it, Africans simply saw them as following the reggae rhythm home. To Ghanaian intellectual and Alkan tribal prince Edward Osei-Bonsu of Accra, for example, reggae ridim sounds like the indigenous rhythm of countries such as Ghana and soca like the music of Nigeria, as he explained to me in an interview in Massachusetts in May 1993. Therefore, Africans have welcomed reggae and wedded it to their own national concerns. Of all continents, Africa has explored reggae the most as a means to chant down colonial oppression. (See Neil J. Savishinsky's "African Dimensions of the Jamaican Rastafarian Movement," Chapter 7.)

In Zimbabwe, Bob Marley's song of tribute, "Zimbabwe," inspired the freedom fighters, and it was soon matched by reggae from chimurenga performers such as the great Thomas Mapfumo, with his protest against graft ("Corruption"). When Habib Koité of Mali was asked to spearhead a campaign against smoking and lung cancer, he chose reggae and added his song "Cigarette Abana" to the socially conscious reggae of such stars as Koko Dembélé and Askia Modibo. Kone Seydou, returning to the Ivory Coast from study in the United States, turned to reggae to protest conditions in his country, adopting for himself the name Alpha Blondy ("First Bandit"). As one of West Africa's reggae giants, his platform is now global, and he has inspired a host of other African reggae stylists at home (such as Solo Jah Gunt, Ismael Isaac et les Freres Keita—both of the Sume Dioula people, as is Alpha Blondy—as well as Tangara Speed Ghoda, Serges Kassy, Lystrone Kouame, and P. I. Ray, each representing one of Ivory Coast's other populations). Les Amazones du Guinea have now added reggae to their repertoire.

Sierra Leone has boasted reggae bands such as Sabanoh 75, the Afro-National Band, and the We Yone Band. In Liberia, the great Miatta Fahnbulleh has recorded reggae. From Senegal, the renowned Touré Kunda—whose "Em'ma," recorded and distributed worldwide in both live and studio versions, has been a phenomenal hit—has spread Afro-reggae songs such as "Em'ma" and the ska-ish "Baounane" around the world. Kenya's Mombasa Roots, while celebrating Mombasa island in "Msa-Mombasa," has delivered such winning reggae as the infectious song of greeting "Jambo Bwana" and the rock-steadyish "Reggae Sound of Africa." Cameroon has enjoyed the scat/rap/dub of Ice T. Cool. And the Zion of Rastafari, Ethiopia, has produced a premier reggae band, Dallol. Conscious of the unique authority mandated by its place of origin in Rasta cosmology, Dallol has used its recordings positively. The band has called for peace with the song "Salem," encouraged global cooperation in "Love Is Coming," and promoted "(Africa, Land of the) Genesis."

The two countries that have employed reggae the most as a rhythm of protest are Nigeria and South Africa. Languishing under a strong-arm government that has wielded a heavy hand on such musical protestors as the acerbic Fela Anikulapo Kuti, Nigeria's musicians have embraced reggae's proclivity to use coded language. After Millie Small's two successful tours and an increase in the importation of Caribbean music, one of the first indigenous tributes to the Caribbean that many Africans heard in the mid-1970s was the Afro rock band Black Blood singing their reggae-ish, Latin-ish, Afro-pop-ish rock song "Rastiferia." Currently across Africa—from South Africa's Lucky Dube and his Slaves band to Nigeria's Majek Fashek and his Prisoners of Conscience—Afro-reggae groups use this musical form in a kind of transoceanic call and response to reach out to, and identify with, the descendants of those Africans who were stolen from their shores.

Majek Fashek even appears in concert with his wrists chained to show that all are imprisoned by corrupt politics, so that freeing unjustly held victims symbolically frees everyone. His song "So Long" is a powerful call to Africa and America to achieve that greatness through freedom and unity that was envisioned by such heroes as "King Selassie I," "Marcus Garvey," and "Lord Jesus Christ."[10] Identifying himself to me as a Christian, rather than a Rasta, he called the mixing of these religions in Africa "Rastafarianity." He sees his musical message as applying the ideals of the two faiths to protesting oppressive human conditions. As he explained in our conversation on August 22, 1992, at Loon Mountain, New Hampshire:

> After Rastafarianity is prisoner of conscience. I'll give an example. See? You look at my first record I did: Majek Fashek, *Prisoner* [*Prisoner of Conscience,* Mango 539870-2, 1989]—I was a prisoner—I'm a prisoner of conscience. Good. So right now, "prisoner of conscience," the message, has expanded. You see the message is not for to force people to follow it. The message is in the house among the brethren. It's among the brethren in the house, as a prisoner of conscience. So, see, now we don't have "prisoner of conscience." Print now, it's now Majek Fashek and the Prisoners of Conscience. Before it was just "prisoner."

So reggae spreads his message and creates a community of protest, linked by its ridim.

Another Christian, Victor Essiet of the Nigerian band the Mandators, also uses reggae powerfully to revive the "Power of the People" and call for justice and a return to Christ's righteousness in his song "Thanks and Praises" (a message E. J. Agbonayinma and his EJ's have also brought to America). Like all the African reggae musicians I have interviewed, Essiet sees Haile Selassie as an African emperor, not God. Despite dreadlocks and a deep respect for Haile Selassie, he explained to me in a telephone interview on September 17, 1995, "Haile Selassie was a man saved by grace like either one of us. He was a man who has seen and also come short of the glory of God, and he was fully saved by grace and the mercy of God Almighty through the sacrifice of Jesus Christ, the Lord of love and the Savior of all mankind." Despite this disavowal of Rasta claims to the Ethiopian emperor's divinity, like Majek Fashek, Essiet finds himself resonating with the diasporan African rhythms in reggae and employs them to send a positive message to people searching for hope:

> What I think is that a lot of people have been listening to my songs and a lot of people have been drawing near, and most people thought it was all about ganja and [violence]. And [they] start to look at it like—yes—it's not all about this. And they want to listen to it. And I think they [the songs] have a future for the younger ones and even those who have lost their faith and they have something to offer to the generation to come. They have a hope.[11]

Reggae definitely has the ability to protest—and not simply to protest but also to offer solutions. On the ridim of reggae, the spiritual and socially oppressed can find hope riding on "upfull" words.

Beside these artists stand many other Nigerian reggae singers and groups: Victor Uwaifo has recorded reggae, as have Bongos Ikwue and his Groovies, the great Ras Kimono, leading reggae songstress Evi Edna Ogholi-Ogosi, Rasman Maxwell Udoh and his Masses Militia Band, Musical Power and the Roots Vibrators, Universal Love, and a host of others. Sonny Okosuns, who, with Chief Commander Ebenezer Obey and King Sunny Ade, stands among the giants of Nigerian music, has mixed in reggae elements powerfully in such songs as "Babylon," "Wind of Change," and "Fire in Soweto," which protests the plight of South Africa. This is a message listeners know includes a call for improving social and economic conditions in all of Africa.

The struggle of South Africa to eliminate apartheid in the 1980s enlisted reggae performers around the world. Musicians as diverse as Sugar Minott ("Mandela"), Brigadier Jerry ("Mandela for President"), Carlene Davis ("Welcome Home Mr. Mandela" and "Winnie Mandela"), Daddy Matthew ("Free Mandela"), and Sister Carol ("Mandela's Release") joined their voices with those of expatriates such as Hugh Masakela (in his "Bring Him Back") in calling for Nelson Mandela's release. Further establishing reggae's reputation as a potent rhythm of protest, a multitude of groups arose in South Africa itself to protest apartheid. Lucky Dube promoted "The Hand That Giveth" while lamenting the system's "War and Crime" and begging people to live "Together as One." O'Yaba interceded for Africans everywhere in "Fly Away." Johnny Clegg and Sipho Mchunu's Juluka dipped into reggae for their protest "Bullets for Bafazane." Harley and the Rasta Family attacked religious hypocrisy in "Lion in a Sheep Skin," while, in counterbalance, Senzo Mthethwa, in a beautiful gospel-reggae anthem, looked past the hypocrisy to extol "Nothing but Prayer" in order to point people in the correct way and direct them to live worthwhile lives. So pervasive has reggae culture become that Mahlathini and the Mahotella Queens hit with the light-hearted mbaqanga (township jive) tribute "I'm in Love with a Rasta Man." Meanwhile, the Malopoets' "Bayeza" has adopted reggae beautifully. Dan Nkosi has paused to salute "The Reggae Prince." The Sons of Selassie have employed reggae to plead for "Changes," for "Freedom in Africa," and for all those of the African diaspora to "Come on Home."

Thus, through a new song, musicians of many political, religious, and philosophical persuasions choose reggae as a means of drowning out the messages of Babylon's "Tin Pan Alley." Through the talents of each of these global performers, and in the works of so many more, the call for change is given by musical notes, not bullets. This positive revolution, staged through the means of artistic creativity, is the key appeal that seems to pervade all Rastafarian art.

Chanting Down Babylon through the Arts

While reggae musicians are attempting to effect change through music, Rasta artists strive to replace Babylon's visions of the world with a new, Rasta depiction of reality—a new art. Since many Rastas are also craftspeople, the first attention that most outsiders paid to this positive side of Rastafari (even before drumming and long before reggae and dancehall became worldwide phenomena) was generated through Rasta crafts, paintings, and carvings. In the 1960s, when Ivy Baxter was compiling her classic *The Arts of an Island: The Development of the Culture and of the Folk and Creative Arts in Jamaica, 1494–1962 (Independence)*, for example, she noted that Rasta art could "demonstrate a rudimentary symbolism" and "an interesting use of color," and she praised the use of colorful regalia, singing, and the drumming that Rastas had adopted from the Burru people. She saw the task of Rasta art as largely one of "reorientation" by the dispossessed, who had failed "to cope with life in the face of apparent and very real twentieth century limitation."[12] Rasta art functioned as a means to assist persons who had opted out of society and were awaiting repatriation to Africa, the ultimate rejection of the Western Hemisphere.

Today, galleries worldwide and the streets of Jamaica, as well as neighborhoods in metropolitan areas around the globe, are filled with Rasta handicraft aimed at promoting societal change. Among the most interesting of these Rasta paintings is the *Last Supper* by Ras-Tebah, which depicts a black, dreadlocked Jesus surrounded by equally bearded and dreadlocked disciples. The table is spread with "Ital" (natural) food. This Caribbean Jesus and his disciples laugh and joke with one another while the bright island sun shines warmly into the upper room. The "chanting" in such a depiction is to protest a Jesus co-opted by blond-haired, blue-eyed Europe and to find an image of a Savior who represents the Two-Thirds world.

Perhaps the most visible vehicle for spreading the Rasta message in art is the album cover. Distributed widely and often interpreting the social change–oriented lyrics of musicians whose impact is global, these covers are sometimes exquisitely beautiful, transcending the category "program art." Remarkably striking, for example, is Paul Smykle's cover for the British band Aswad's *A New Chapter of Dub*, which depicts a black Savior, cross-topped staff in hand, returning across the clouds of heaven on a chariot pulled by four roaring lions to judge "the quick and the dead."

Sometimes album art promotes other media besides music, as in the case of the pop art painting of an awakening Rasta, fists clenched, stretching up from the roots of the earth. While Neville Garrick (who created the breathtaking backdrops of Haile Selassie, the Lion of Judah emblem, the Black Star Liner, etc., for Bob Marley's concerts) used one rendition of this work on the Bob Marley and the Wailers album *Uprising*, another was released as a poster, which included the logo "Rasta Is Reality." This complementary poster art also gave a wide audience to Ras Tesfa, a poet who has succeeded in several fields. He is also an actor who appeared with Calvin Lockhart in the Broadway production *Reggae*, a musical play that brought Rasta theatrical themes to the U.S. stage. Such themes are treated in Jamaica by Rastafarian playwrights such as Janet Enright and Madge Hilton, as well as by theater troops such as the Sistren Theatre Collective, the National Dance Theatre Company (in pieces such as *Court of Jah* and *Two Drums for Babylon*), and the Little Theatre Movement's pantomime "Johnny Reggae." Further, Ras Tesfa released his own album, *The Voice of the Rastaman*, on Shanachie's Meadowlark label, as well as a book, *The Living Testament of Rasta-for-I*. In the visions that conclude this liberalized Rastafarian theology, a psalmist chants, "I shall sing praises unto Thy Divine Name, in the heights and depths of earth's social structure, wherever Thou leadeth I-man."[13] Here again, in Ras Tesfa's work, is the chanting within Earth's social structures that attempts to bring about positive change.

As Basil Wilson of the John Jay College of Criminal Justice observed when introducing Ras Tesfa's book, "In this *Living Testament of Rasta-For-I,* we see the decrepit nature of bourgeois society and the tribulation by the Rasta man trying to balance on the tightrope of Babylon. . . . It is the new poetry, the new art, the new music that will have a marked impact in the present decade and, hopefully, that will produce the new politics." The goal as Wilson sees it is addressing the black "identity crisis," wherein "race must be resolved concomitantly with the class question." For him, Rasta, promulgated through its artistic voices, is a "black nationalist institution" that will "culturally enrich the ghetto . . . transforming powerless fragmented communities into consciously, cohesive forces with lasting clout that could serve as a catalyst for the destruction of the prevailing economic system responsible for the perpetuation of racism and mass impoverishment"[14]—or, in Rasta terminology, a voice to chant down Babylon system.

Clearly, the new music, visual art, drama, and poetry of Rastafari are engaged in changing existing social structures outside—and these days, also inside—Rastafari. And no more evident example can be cited than the *Lamentation* of poet Margarett E. Groves. This collection of poetry is remarkable for its introspective look at Rastafari. While much Rastafarian communication seems to be externally oriented, focused on pointing out the evils of the larger society, poet Groves's work focuses as well on the Rasta community. In her foreword, she questions those who "abuse their sisters, so that the sisters are afraid to love their blood brothers. There are wolves among our Rastafari brothers, as wild weeds."[15] This bold challenge assists the swelling women's consciousness movement within traditionally male-dominated Rastafari. Her poems "Rastafari Voice," "Up Full Woman," "Beloved Brothers," "Carnality," "Rejection," and "Convenient Love" all deal with the problems associated with being a woman in Rastafari.

Other social concerns are expressed in the writings of Fay Kemp and other Rasta novelists; in the poetry of Brother Miguel (see his volume *Rastaman Chant*), Tekla Mekfet, and many others; and in the eloquent dub poetry (lines spoken over roots reggae that has been stripped down to bass and drum) of such poets as Mutabaruka, Benjamin Zephaniah, Jean "Binta" Breeze, the late Prince Far-I, U-Roy, Lillian Allen, and others. Mutabaruka once described the origin and task of his poetry to Shivaun Hearne of the *Jamaica Journal* in this way:

> Marcus Garvey Junior used to teach me in school and he had his organization and we used to join the organization. Everyone was interested in Black Power; Malcolm X, Stokely Carmichael, the Black Panthers, yu know. So the enthusiasm fi express mi blackness was there from that time, so the way that I choose to express it was through the poetry, so that is really what inspired the poetry: the need to express mi consciousness, mi black awareness, and to awaken then the conscience and consciousness of other people, yu know, trying to motivate people to do things.[16]

Why add "the Rastafari Connection"? Mutabaruka explains, "The Black Power move-ment, it never had that the spirituality, it only had that, socio-political thing." Rastafari helped Mutabaruka become both a "conscious social political man" and "a conscious spiritual man."[17] All Rasta poetry reveals these two dimensions: the spiritual that changes individuals and the political that changes society.

Rastafarian Arts Celebrate and Promote New Cultural Heroes

With Rastafari's "new politics" come new, nonviolent heroes to replace the violent ones of Babylon. And these are celebrated in Rasta art. One such tribute in folk-art style is the wraparound painting by Tyrone Whyte, which illustrates the fine recording of V. Buckley's "Boat to Zion" by the excellent but lesser-known Channel One recording company group the Mighty Maytones. On the front half of the album cover, resplen-dent in his Universal Negro Improvement Association (UNIA) military uniform, the na-tional hero Marcus Garvey sits at a small wooden ticket table on a tropical shore. Palm trees stretch in partial canopy above him. To his left bends a ragged Jamaican, holding out in both hands a fistful of green paper (dollars) that he has obviously scraped and saved for his journey home to Africa. Garvey, always a benefactor and never an astute businessman, is looking at the money with what appears to be gentle, bemused com-passion, waving the man on to join the throng at his right, who are walking to the wa-ter's edge. Around Garvey is all the currency of barter: eggs, fruits, a chicken, a puppy, a steer. Out on the blue-and-white ocean a vessel draws near, a steamship on whose hull is emblazoned in giant letters: "Zion Boat." It speeds to the shore, leaving a foaming wake behind it, while around the Jamaican suppliant courses a stream of people, some short-haired and others dreadlocked Rastas with cloth crowns. One woman has her hand raised in thanks to God; on the reverse side, another of the Dreadlocks sits propped against a tree, looking squarely at us in apparent invitation to join the exodus of Jah People. A rowboat sits on the shore, its crew waiting patiently to take the pil-grims back to Africa. The vinyl disk within the album cover is as blue and clear as the inviting sea itself. The song and cover art convey the image and message of Garvey to those who may never have read his speeches. The art serves as an ambassador, intro-ducing him to them.

For artists returning to an Afrocentric perspective, celebrating a hero such as Garvey in craft, chant, music, drama, drumming, and dance provides most appropriate means for disseminating their new political aspirations and models. This was also the conclu-sion of the great dancer Patsy Ricketts, who, after becoming Rastafarian and dropping out of the National Dance Theatre, returned to performing in more modest Rasta garb. Marcus Garvey himself was a great champion of indigenous Jamaican art in the late 1920s, a movement brought to fruition by artists such as Edna Manley and Alvin Mar-riott, whom Garvey called the "Michelangelo of the West Indies."[18] As independence approached and was achieved, a swelling interest in Jamaican art produced the Jamaica School of Art (1950), the National Gallery (1974), and the Cultural Training Centre

(1976). These created a hospitable climate in which Rastafarian artists could emerge. For example, Trevor Roache Burrowes, descendant of the printer who once employed Garvey, is noteworthy for having painted (among other works) *The Living Marcus Garvey* (1971).

Art historian Veerle Poupeye-Rammelaere classifies a number of Rastafarians within the postindependence Intuitive Art movement. She includes Rasta patriarch Sam Brown, statesman, spokesman, and releaser of the 1991 Ras Records collection *Teacher,* as well as Everald Brown of the Ethiopian Orthodox Church, the celebrated Ras Dizzy, and Albert Artwell. A helpful compendium of art and commentary is Tekla Mekfet's intriguing little volume *Christopher Columbus and Rastafari,* which interprets art depicting Rastafarian themes by Osmond Watson, Christopher Gonzales, Bono Swaby, and others.[19]

Though he encouraged a "nationalization" of culture that ultimately has provided a platform for Rasta artistic expression, Marcus Garvey himself was neither a Rastafarian nor an admirer of Haile Selassie, and he predated the reggae revolution by at least a quarter of a century. What he would have said about reggae therefore is a matter of speculation. That it might not have been complimentary may be indicated by this charge:

> You men of the Negro race have the same political and intellectual power as other races, but you have not used that power. I want you to challenge the Columbuses and the Washingtons and the Wolfes. The job is mine, and when we have done it completely, even though we do not care about it, they will build their monuments to us as they did to Nelson and others. Isn't that better than to be found playing dice, playing jazz and dancing your life away, so that everybody will remember you for discovering something?[20]

If performing reggae struck Garvey as "playing jazz," he may have disapproved. But had he heard Sky High and the Mau Mau's tribute to him (in conjunction with Yammi Bolo and other artists), taking his speeches and, in dancehall ridims and deejay style, introducing them to a new global generation in the "Marcus Garvey Chant" compilation, Garvey may have paused to reconsider this "jazz." Certainly, he had the astuteness to acknowledge that the metronome is as mighty as the lectern. Garvey once told an audience at the Royal Albert Hall that he was representative of the new Negro in finance, economics, science, art, literature, and music; perhaps he would have stretched his definition from the traditional and classical in music to the responsibly popular. While in jail in the United States from 1923 to 1927, he penned the lyrics for a song called "Keep Cool," which was set to music by Alexander Seymour and copyrighted by his publishing company in 1927. As the music stands now, whether it is the child of "jazz and dancing" or not, Garvey has found a shrine in contemporary reggae. Reggae keeps the memory and vision of Marcus Garvey alive before the listening and watching world.

Winston Rodney, known as Burning Spear, has perhaps done more than any other Rasta to keep the legacy of Marcus Garvey alive in Rasta consciousness through music. On his 1976 debut Island album, he began side one with the tribute "Marcus Garvey" and side two with "Old Marcus Garvey." The dub follow-up collection, *Garvey's Ghost,* featured a "duppy-like" (ghostlike) sketch of Garvey's face—the eyes solid and searing— with the inset African warriors from the first LP looking on. Spear has brought that legacy down through his music over his twenty-year recording history, in song after song: "Follow Marcus Garvey," "Old Boy Garvey," "Love Garvey." "Them Never Love Poor Marcus," sing the Mighty Diamonds on their *Right Time* album, and again, on *Never Get Weary,* "Marcus, We Miss You." "Where is Garvey?" they ask on *If You Looking for Trouble;* and that question echoes not only through all of the Mighty Diamonds' work but through all of Rastafarian reggae.

Further, Michael "Mikey Dread" Campbell salutes Garvey and keeps his memory alive, along with those of Bob Marley, Jacob Miller of the Inner Circle band, and other fallen Rasta heroes, in "In Memory." In addition, Third World, Carlene Davis, Mutabaruka, Spear, Freddie McGregor, the Mystic Revelation(s) of Rastafari, Rita Marley, and Foundation all have songs in honor of Garvey gathered on Rave Music/V.P. Records' 1987 *A Tribute to Marcus Garvey.* These all join Joe Higgs, vocal trainer of the Wailers, when he calls on the "Sons of Garvey" to follow in the patriarch's footprints, for as Joseph Hill and Culture prophesied on their apocalyptic *Two Sevens Clash* album, the "Black Star Liner Must Come" (a sentiment also echoed by Carlene Davis on "Black Starliner" and by so many others). This feeling that Garvey's dream for a diasporan African repatriation can begin mentally, if not physically, pervades hundreds of reggae songs. Marcus Garvey's name, that of his Black Star shipping line, his teachings, and his rallying cry "One God, One Aim, One Destiny" reverberate around the globe, where groups such as Africa's Sons of Selassie extol "Marcus Garvey," his memory at least repatriated in honor.

Reggae: A Positive Agent for Change

In oral cultures, music, poetry, drama, painting, sculpture, and dance become part of the means of educating and disseminating information. When these are infused with themes that call for social change that is beneficial to many, they can transcend cultures and work powerfully to alter attitudes toward injustice and prejudice. Reggae has proved itself to be such a vehicle, one through which its purveyors put out positive messages to combat negative ones. In this chapter we have seen reggae, along with other arts, used to call for laws that promote the welfare of all and to decry child abuse, religious hypocrisy, and economic, social class, and racial oppression, particularly apartheid. It has combated violence and governmental corruption and even campaigned against tobacco. We have also seen reggae used positively to call for political empowerment of the working class, self-rule by national majorities, and self-determination for indigenous minorities. It has championed education, women's causes, the value of indigenous cultures, and a variety of religious stances, primarily (though not exclusively) Rastafari in Jamaica, as well as Christianity in Africa and elsewhere and traditional religions in several localities. It has been employed to inspire freedom fighters, to awaken black identity and pride, to lift up new cultural heroes, to inspire repatriation, to publicize various locales, and to promote peace among all people and hope for all for the future. Particularly open to change are the minds of the young, who do not yet have an irrevocable stake in oppressive social and economic systems. Compelling music like reggae, art, literature, and performance command the attention of all.

In 1993 the United Nations declared Ziggy Marley and the Melody Makers "Goodwill Youth Ambassadors" for their positive messages to youth around the world. In such distinction they follow their illustrious father, Bob Marley, who in 1978 won the UN Medal of Peace, an award given also in 1987 to Third World.[21] The United Nations recognizes the potency of reggae as a force that can be used to promote great good among all people. As symbolized by Bob Marley's anthem "One Love," the Rasta art agenda can align itself with that of all caring, creative people. With a positive, painless message that works to change people's views, reggae can help make the world better for all who live in it without bloodshed. The negative oppressive values represented by the term *Babylon* can be chanted down and replaced with something more pleasing to the Creator and hospitable to all people.

Notes

1. With a few notable exceptions, such as Bob Marley's "Talkin' Blues," which reveals that sometimes he feels like dynamiting a church; see the album *Natty Dread,* Island Records: ILPS 9281, 1974, and *Talkin' Blues,* Tuff Gong 422–848 243–1, 1991.

2. Roger Steffens, "Reggae: The Deliverance of Nigeria," *The Beat* 10, 5 (1991): 34.

3. Some artists such as the Specials, the Selector, the Beat, and other groups of the rock/reggae/ska-ish 2 Tone movement (named for the iridescent "Two Tone" mohair suits that skinheads used to wear to ska nights at clubs in the 1960s) were British punk alternatives. (According to Dick Hebdige, "Ska Tissue: The Rise and Fall of 2 Tone," in Stephen Davis and Peter Simon, *Reggae International* [New York: Rogner & Bernhard GMBH, 1982], Jerry Dammers of the Specials masterminded the 2 Tone movement [159].) Others, such as Cymande, blended jazz with Afro-Caribbean rhythms, while Cedric Myton and Congo experimented with Central African rhythms. Many British and American groups made unity statements by including Whites and Blacks together in the same group—Amazulu, for instance—and some of these, such as UB40, became highly successful, mixing pop in with their conscious lyrics. Devout British-based Rastafarian groups such as Aswad, Steel Pulse, and the Twinkle Brothers became superstars to the Jamaican public as well, and the most enduring of the groups used reggae as a vehicle for protest.

4. Dub is the scaled-down reggae pulse rhythm with kicks on the second and fourth beats, emphasizing drum and bass, with highhats punctuating the "ands": one and *two* and three and *four.*

5. Despite the early interest, chart success, until very recently, was generally limited to one-shot performances, and most reggae bands remained alternative. Superstars such as Stevie Wonder succeeded with singles like "Master Blaster (Jammin')," and bands such as the Fine Young Cannibals, the Hooters, and Living Colour all scored with one-shot reggae hits on the U.S. charts. Crossover disco groups such as Boney M mixed in reggae, and even country and western received a reggae overture through the Bellamy Brothers' "Almost Jamaica" and "Get into Reggae Cowboy." But nobody could successfully launch a roots reggae chart revolution, as Johnny Nash discovered with the declining popularity of his reggae releases after "I Can See Clearly Now" and "Stir It Up." "Roots reggae" is the opposite of the rhythm-and-blues rock beat. In reggae, the

kick is on the second and fourth beats; the clap is on the first and third. This shift derailed rock as it hit the Caribbean and fused with mento. To many, it sounds like an inverted heartbeat. The musical revolution ultimately was left to dancehall. Built out of the religious dance rhythms of Pukumina (also called Pocomania, the revivalist, Afro-Christian cultic development of Christianizing Kumina), secularized "dancehall" has an almost frenetic hybrid waltzing flavor because of its three beats inside and alternately syncopating straight or pulsating kick on the fourth beat.

As in England, North Americans of Jamaican extraction and musical fans of the Caribbean had been regularly releasing albums. Some performers, such as Pancho Alphonso and HR, had garnered respect. But when dub met rap music and blended into New York hip-hop, producing the dancehall mixes of KRS-1, Boogie Down Productions, Monie Love, Queen Latifah in her work with Naughty by Nature, Daddy-O, etc., the rest of the rappers began to join in. Then Shaggy hit the financial jackpot with his updated rendition of "Oh Carolina," an old Ffolkes Brothers Caribbean standard. The resulting dancehall deluge did what roots had not succeeded in doing: the music inundated the U.S. charts. It boosted the status of some U.S. roots reggae acts, such as Texas's Killer Bees' Michael E. Johnson, but buried others. Further, innovative groups such as Nashville's Christafari and Hawaii's Butch Helemano, championing a roots Christianity and an indigenous traditional religion respectively, were able to win a hearing. Christafari enabled North Americans to discover the respected world of Christian reggae (of the Grace Thrillers, Lester Lewis and the Singing Rose, Birthright, the Love Singers, and David Kean) that had been thriving in the Caribbean. Butch Helemano and the band the Players of Instruments spearheaded an entire burgeoning movement of "Jawaiian" reggae (including Marty Dread, Titus Kinimaka and the Kauai Boys, Ho'aikane, Bruddah Waltah, Kapena, Bob Riley and the Fishers). Each had its message to share.

6. Mento is the folk music of Jamaica, a four-beat-to-the-measure rhythm with an upbeat feel, the guitar carrying the rhythm with an upbeat stroke on the "ands": one *and* two *and* three *and* four *and* . . . Kettle floor drums and hand drums underscore and enhance the beat. By the time reggae emerged, much of Jamaican popular music had been cross-fertilized by powerful radio stations in Miami, various coastal cities in Texas, and in New Orleans; Jamaica's new music now returned the effect. It rebounded its impact on zydeco, from Jean Knight's "Mr. Big Stuff" in 1971, through the Wild Tchoupitoulas' "Meet de Boys on de Battlefront" (1976) to Queen Ida's "Dancing on the Bayou" (1989). Jazz performer Earl Grant nodded to reggae as early as 1970 in his posthumously released song "Elizabethan Reggae."

7. Gregorio Landau, liner notes for Soul Vibrations, *Black History/Black Culture: Afro-Nicaraguan Music,* Redwood Records RR9104, 1991, compact disk.

8. Guilly Koster, liner notes for P-I Man and Memre Buku, *Masannah,* S.M.A. (Surinam Music Association) Records 006, n.d.

9. Rai (meaning "opinion" in Arabic) is popular western Algerian music that developed around the port of Oran. Its Bedouin base blends in eastern Moroccan, Spanish, French, and black North African (Gnaoui) influences. Fused with rock and roll, it becomes a "pop-rai." (Definition and information from Philip Sweeney's liner notes to *Rai Rebels,* Earthworks [Virgin] LP 7 91000-1, 1988.)

10. On Majek Fashek and the Prisoners of Conscience, *Spirit of Love,* Interscope Records 7 91742 2, 1991.

11. See also the Mandators, *Power of the People: Nigerian Reggae,* Heartbeat 156, 1994.

12. Ivy Baxter, *The Arts of an Island: The Development of the Culture and of the Folk and Creative Arts in Jamaica, 1494–1962 (Independence)* (Metuchen, N.J.: Scarecrow Press, 1970), 153.

13. Ras-J-Tesfa, *The Living Testament of Rasta-for-I* (New York: Ras-J-Tesfa, 1980), 60.

14. Basil Wilson, introduction to ibid., vii, vi.

15. Margarett E. Groves, *Lamentation: The Voice of a New Poet* (Kingston: Margarett E. Groves, 1989), 5.

16. Shivaun Hearne, "Mutabaruka Talks to Shivaun Hearne," *Jamaica Journal* 24, 2 (March 1992): 49.

17. Ibid., 48.

18. Veerle Poupeye-Rammelaere, "Garveyism and Garvey Iconography in the Visual Arts of Jamaica II," *Jamaica Journal* 24, 2 (March 1992): 25.

19. Ibid., 32. See also Tekla Mekfet, *Christopher Columbus and Rastafari: Ironies of History . . . and Other Reflections on the Symbol of Rastafari* (St. Ann, Jamaica: Jambasa Productions, 1993).

20. Marcus Garvey, *More Philosophy and Opinions of Marcus Garvey*, ed. E. U. Essien-Udom and Amy Jacques Garvey (Totowa, N.J.: Frank Cass, 1977), 3: 26–27.

21. "The United Nations and Jamaican Music Makers," *Jamaica Journal* 25, 3 (October 1995): 66. Those wishing to see reggae set in its Caribbean context as one among many musics (such as Cuban rumba, Dominican merengue, Puerto Rican plena, Trinidadian calypso, etc.) may consult Peter Manuel, with Kenneth Bilby and Michael Largey, *Caribbean Currents: Caribbean Music from Rumba to Reggae* (Philadelphia: Temple University Press, 1995).

17 Towering Babble and Glimpses of Zion: Recent Depictions of Rastafari in Cinema

KEVIN J. AYLMER

The Jamaican-born, Rasta "Babylon" metaphor has provided lyrical grist for the social consciousness of singer-songwriters and "roots" musicians, as well as a fascination in Hollywood for exploring perceptions and aspects of Rastafarian culture. Babylon crops up in hundreds of reggae songs and many movies.[1] Within the last two decades, several films have explored this Rasta conception of the Babylon system as an integral part of a worldview and cultural perceptions. Often Babylon suggests a visceral, explicit menace, as in *The Harder They Come;* sometimes it refers to an alien, corrupting materialism run rampant, as in *Club Paradise;* and at other times it shows the subtly implicit nuances of institutional racism, as in the comedy *Cool Runnings.* But in all of these films, songs about Babylon are being sung while the viewer is engaged in a predominantly passive observation of a primarily visual phenomenon.

This chapter explores, thematically, the depiction of Rastafari vis-à-vis the Babylon system in eight films: *The Harder They Come* (1972), *Heartland Reggae* (1982), *Countryman* (1982), *Club Paradise* (1986), *Cool Runnings* (1993), *Stepping Razor—Red X* (1992), *Marked for Death* (1990), and *New Jack City* (1991). To restore a sense of proportion between the visual and original aural mode, my reflections are punctuated by lyrics from Bunny Wailer's "Ready When You Ready." Included in his landmark *Liberation* album (1988), this hit is a fine example of the Rasta singer-songwriter-griot-preacher conveying the word from the street, "inna ridim":

> Hey, mi ready when you ready fi go chant down Babylon,
> dutty system, Mi ready, you ready fi go lick
> down Babylon in a rhythm . . .
> Mi ready when you ready fi go tear down Babylon
> Mi ready when you ready fi go mash down Babylon[2]

The Harder They Come

Self-reliance and a sunny rural optimism pervade Jimmy Cliff's signature song "You Can Get It if You Really Want"; and with the soundtrack bubbling and a bus careening, one witnesses a youthful Jimmy Cliff (called, alternately, Ivan, Ivanhoe, Rhyging, and Rhygin) headed to town in the opening frames of the classic film *The Harder They Come* (1972). But the idyllic buoyancy of the film's beginning is abruptly shattered by a bus-truck confrontation at a stone bridge, in a characteristically Jamaican highway dispute. It is brief and opinionated, with a hint of banter and repartee that foreshadows significantly more lethal duels to come.

The tragic story of Jimmy Cliff's character Ivan, is an updated Homeric odyssey, tracing our picturesque hero's literal and metaphorical travels—from country to city, innocence to outlaw—in a cinematic tour de force that is part allegory, part Third World documentary. In exploring the legend of a post–World War II era Jamaican gunslinger, *The Harder They Come* is eerily reminiscent of American westerns and the "spaghetti westerns" of Sergio Leone, for instance, *Once upon a Time in the West* and the "Dollars" trilogy (*Hang 'Em High, A Fistful of Dollars,* and *For a Few Dollars More*). Rather than being shot in Spain, however, *The Harder They Come* is set in the suffocating crucible of West Kingston, Jamaica.[3]

In retrospect, *The Harder They Come* was a milestone. It was the first film produced, directed, and shot in Jamaica by Jamaicans. After such releases as *Dr. No* of the James Bond series, *A High Wind in Jamaica,* and *Father Goose,* feeling grew, during the island's postindependence fervor, that cinematic self-expression was in order. Perry Henzell, a veteran of the British Broadcasting Corporation (BBC) Drama Department and film aficionado, conducted interviews and began research for a feature film that would update the story of Rhygin, a celebrated "badman" from the 1940s. Henzell pored over the island landscape, finally deciding to focus on West Kingston. He hired playwright and theatrical producer Trevor Rhone to coproduce a screenplay. As time progressed, the story of Rhygin's ill-fated exploits in late 1940s Kingston began to take on larger-than-life (read "cinematic") possibilities.

Rhyging is Jamaican slang for *raging.* For a few brief weeks, this little gunman-desperado astonished Kingstonians with a flurry of robberies and shootings and a Robin Hood–style bravado. The island's premier newspaper, the *Daily Gleaner,* followed his exploits for six weeks during the autumn of 1948. It reported on the "two-gun" killer of one Detective Lewis and of Lucille Tibby Young; on a spree of shoplifting and larceny in and around West Kingston; on a stint in prison; and his aliases, "Alan Ladd" and "Captain Midnight." Born Vincent Martin in Linstead, St. Catherine, he was variously known as "Ivan Martin," "Ivanhoe Martin," "Ivan Brown," and "Rhyging" or "Rhygin." He eventually escaped from the general penitentiary and became something of a folk hero, taunting the authorities with photos of himself brandishing a brace of pistols. Eventually cornered by the police about seven miles from the old pirate haunt of Port Royal on Lime Cay, he came to an ignominious end on October 9, 1948. A flavor of the sensational, tabloid-style news coverage that Rhyging (and his imitators) elicited can be gleaned from the front-page headlines of that Saturday morning's edition of the *Daily Gleaner*:

'RHYGING' KILLED BY POLICE

GUN BATTLE ON LIME CAY THIS MORNING

KILLER TRAPPED AFTER FLIGHT FROM CITY

KINGSTON'S SIX WEEKS TERROR IS ENDED! 'RHYGING' IS DEAD!!

Related stories and photograph titles trumpeted "I Saw Him Shot," "Down the Crooked Road to Doom," and "Who Was This Man with a Price on His Head?" His funeral was attended by thousands. Most important, this young tough's identification with Hollywood "oat operas" and his masculine swagger, allied with an uncanny ability to seemingly disappear and resurface at will, created a mythic invincibility. He became a cultural icon of the Jamaican working class, whose lives were undergoing dramatic transformations in the years after Jamaica's independence (1962).

West Kingston, the scene of Rhyging's legerdemain, underwent a series of wrenching urban renewals in the early 1960s. Once a fishing village, it was rapidly redeveloped and the shoreline was extended by the creation of a mammoth garbage dump. The poor and homeless were soon joined by squatters and new arrivals in an area that quickly earned notoriety as one of Kingston's foremost slums—a home for the unemployed, transients, criminals, and the brethren of Rastafari. Under the postcolonial social and political pressures of an economy subject to severe periodic fluctuations in commodities markets for bauxite and sugar, a surging movement of semiskilled, temporary workers from rural areas to the city became evident. In addition to these demographic shifts, the area harbored considerable postcolonial suspicion of foreign corporations and institutions. Such conditions made this environment ripe for an artistic response to the potentially explosive mixture of popular discontents. In 1967, bulldozers began clearing the fishing village adjacent to Kingston's harbor, sparking violent demonstrations and rioting— a scene later memorialized in Desmond Dekker's song "Shanty Town." At the same time, the introduction and increased accessibility of transistor radios suddenly made music more available than ever before.

The island's traveling bands and ubiquitous mobile sound systems soon exhibited another development, which would ultimately contribute to the birth of *The Harder They Come*. By the late 1960s, significant elements of the Jamaican music industry had begun to tire of imitating American rhythm and blues and Motown soul artists. In 1968 a singer named Toots Hibbert recorded a single "Do the Reggay," destined to spearhead a movement toward a new, distinctly Jamaican hybrid. Part soul, part ska, part calypso, this recording melded together an irresistible Jamaican-African *akete* backbeat—the beginning of the genre that would be called "reggae." In the hands of Perry Henzell and Trevor Rhone, this raw music form would provide a vehicle to underscore the saga of an updated Rhyging. Cast in this role was Jimmy Chambers, a youth from Somerton, St. James, who was supported by a host of rising musical artists ranging from Toots and the Maytals to Desmond Dekker.

In literary terms, the tragic tale of Rhygin in *The Harder They Come* is the eighteenth-century picaresque novel updated—a sort of "Rake's Progress" through a Hobbesian world—that is "nasty, brutish, and short." With a formidable array of reggae artists contributing in a manner similar to that of the chorus in ancient Greek tragedy, Ivan (or Rhygin) becomes a study in profound cultural dislocation. He is a human outcast from a rural-based sugar monoculture economy, who tries to make it in an environment dominated by a neocolonialist extractive industry and a tourism culture. Struggling to survive, he encounters a host of characters who force him to confront a series of contradictions: national ideals versus a rapacious oligarchy, an emphasis on self versus the value of a community, and simultaneous impulses to destroy "the system" and to emulate. Ivan is torn between the roles of star and outlaw; he pines to be number one on both the radio and the law's "most wanted" list.

In this modern "Gullible's Travels" in super 16 mm, the *dramatis personae* is composed of swaggering rudeboys, venerable old-time hill folk, devout Christians, Rasta brethren, corrupt police, and the "waiflike" manchild pop star. All coexist rather uneasily in a tropical Babylon. A host of powerful images, filmed in *cinema verité* fashion, conjure up a seamy world of opportunists and "sufferahs." There is Babylon in the guise of Mr. Hilton, head of the Hilton recording empire, an impatient, pharaonic presence in a white Mercedes who dismisses several would-be singing stars: "Ah, I can't use it. Too slow." There is Ivan, tripping through the light fantastic of a pinball arcade. Here, in Bunyanesque fashion, Pilgrim is on the way to the Celestial City, blinded by the psychedelic velveteen night in Vanity Fair. A sense of impending doom is heightened by Toots and the Maytals as they intone, "I say pressure drop / Oh, pressure, oh yeh, pressure gonna drop on you / I say pressure drop, oh, pressure drop / Oh yeh, pressure will drop on you / I say when it drops, you gonna feel it / Know that you were doing wrong."[4] In another scene (which originally served as a screen test for Cliff), Ivan, having just arrived from the country virtually penniless, slightly penitent, and ever wary, encounters his mother. Mendacity lurks behind a facade of filial piety as Ivan fends off his mother's inquiries, for Ivan never notified his city-bound relatives of his grandmother's demise. As Psalm 137 ("Rivers of Babylon") drones in the distance, his mother's uneasiness quickly turns to incredulous alarm:

> Ivan? Aw right. Come inside . . .
> Grandma dead!
> Dead! Dead! How she can dead and I never know?
> And when she goin' to bury? . . .
> Bury already?
> Bury already and I never get to go to the funeral?[5]

Panoramic shots of West Kingston as "Paradise Lost" reveal a side of Jamaica unfamiliar to many tourists. Amid these dumps, scavengers and human detritus struggle to maintain a modicum of dignity while Cliff sings (moanfully), off camera, "Many Rivers to Cross."[6] Another sequence contrasts the claustrophobia of poverty and invisibility that envelops Ivan with the fleeting euphoria he and his girlfriend, Miss Elsa, share on a bicycle ride. Beneath Ivan's sunny, romantic disposition, however, is a simmering, mercurial rage, as he powerfully illustrates one morning in Preacher's bicycle shop. With "Johnny Too Bad" playing on the radio, Ivan, sporting some natty head-gear, is accosted by his boss, Longah, whose manner of dismissive annoyance becomes highly inflammatory: "Hey pretty boy! Pretty hat. Johnny Too Bad . . . You have on pretty hat this morning. You really look like Johnny Too Bad. Ya gwan hav a gun to look like Johnny. But before you get a gun, get the broom and come sweep out the shop!"[7]

The film's benign Rasta presence is Pedro, whom we first see heading home with his son, ambling down railroad tracks, beckoning, "Rupert, com mek we go home!" Un-like rudeboy Ivan, Pedro is a Rasta who lives simply, upright, eats fresh foods with no salt or preservatives, eschews violence, reads the Scriptures, and besides daily praising Jah Rastafari, tends to his family. Unfortunately, he fails as a role model for Ivan, serv-ing as a convenient, virtuous counterpoint to the corrupt, self-serving, self-destructive, and narcissistic self-idolatry of Ivan. Another glimpse of the Rastafari community re-veals Ras Pedro and the brethren smoking the "chillum" pipe.[8] Between heady drafts, Pedro discusses the subject of violence and admonishes Ivan to forgo the purchase of pistols: "Are you ready to kill somebody? Leave it, mon, leave it!" Of course, Ivan buys the pair of revolvers and becomes further enmeshed in the ganja trade, attaining celebrity status as a notorious freebooter. Eventually, Ivan recklessly challenges au-thority; shoot-outs ensue, and ultimately, he is extinguished on a lonely stretch of Lime Cay in this melodic chronicle of a death foretold.

As the tale of Rhygin passed into legend and the oral tradition of Jamaica, folk em-bellishments imbued the sordid odyssey of Ivanhoe Martin with a sheen barely tarnished by the passage of time. Indeed, the legend was burnished by *The Harder They Come*. Nearly two decades after the release of the film, Jimmy Cliff is still identified with the 1940s gunman. On the street, for example, he is often still hailed as "Ivan" or "Johnny Too Bad." Sitting in his Montego Bay office in January 1990, the diminutive singer-actor shared some reflections on images of Rastafari and the Rhygin mystique, from the vantage point of almost twenty years of experience with the character:

> There's still a problem with the "Johnny Too Bad" image in Jamaica. . . . Before the Rasta-farian movement there was the rudeboy era, which was knife and guns and that, you know. Society created that because of poverty and those things. . . . If there was equal opportunity and everybody could get a job, a decent job, you don't feel that if you're a farmer you're less than a man who works in a bank. These mentality exist, this class mentality, which is the aftermath of the British slavery system. . . .
>
> . . . Ivan was a country boy, very innocent, and him turn out to be bad. Society like twists him. He tried to make a living. Anyway, while there are people like him, there's also people who are very positive and know that there's another way outside of taking up a gun. . . . In a lot of ways, *The Harder They Come* did influence a lot of the gun situation. I think nega-tively. Because, actually, we grew up going [to the movies] and watching John Wayne and Humphrey Bogart and all of those gangster guys. They were glorified on the big screen. And you come out of the movie, subconsciously you think, well that's the way to do it. That's what happened to Rhygin. So, here comes Jimmy Cliff playing a Rhygin on the screen for them with a gun and trying to get his rights through the gun, the bullet.[9]

Despite the crowd-pleasing defiance of the gun-wielding stage Johnny Too Bad, Cliff's live performance demeanor has shifted significantly since he made *The Harder They Come*. Nowadays he's the "Bongo man," one in touch with an ancestral sensibility and his African homeland, a proponent of a roots consciousness ("Bongo culture") as incisive and uncompromising as any espoused by Ras Pedro in the film. In chanting down Babylon from the concert stage, Cliff accents the positive images of Rastafari: an ancestral sensibility, cultural revitalization, and a recognition of "equal rights and justice" as indispensable ingredients in the formation of a healthy identity.

For Michael Thelwell, a professor of Afro-American studies at the University of Massachusetts at Amherst, the movie *The Harder They Come* was an inspiring introduction to understanding the tragedy of Rhygin. But Thelwell, a writer, decided that the inherent limitations of cinema meant that the movie could only be a prologue. Hence he embarked on the project of writing a novel that would, in painstaking detail, clarify the immensity of context, nature, and nurture, which were formative influences on Rhygin's sorrowful odyssey.[10] Thelwell's novel, *The Harder They Come*, thus commences with a lyrical evocation of the Jamaican countryside, a section he has titled "The Hills Were Joyful." In the first one-third of the novel, Ivan is relegated to the background. Meanwhile, Ivan's kin and neighbors stand in stark relief, resplendent in a life-affirming network of folk custom, patois, religion, and ritual.

Thelwell demonstrates considerable sensitivity—first, to his readers, by including a glossary of Jamaican terms and idiomatic expressions; second, by sharing old-time people's sayings and wisdom culled from folk traditions. His true craftsmanship is manifested in a vital portraiture of a web of interdependent threads of cause and effect, in discerning the bloodlines of an ecological-cultural context. Moreover, the soft-spoken novelist delineates several crucial components of the Rasta ethos: the lingering effects of migration from country to city; the resultant sense of "psychic displacement, dislocation and alienation"; the breakdown of generational continuity; and the adaptive rise of a new vocabulary based on "language deconstruction."

Although Rhygin was an ephemeral figure in Jamaican history, he became "the first media-created 'superstar' in our cultural history," according to Thelwell. As a symbol of the urban rudeboy subculture, he became a legendary figure, a prototype for a later generation, and the antithesis of the Rasta brethren's insistence on complete separation from Babylon.[11] Foreshadowing the rise of "gangsta rap" films such as *Marked for Death* and *New Jack City*, the character of Rhygin/Johnny Too Bad became the basis for commercially attractive, popular images of the rudeboy, often supplanting the more revolutionary, antimaterialist Rastafari in the public eye. Disparity between these romanticized images of rudeboys ("the Rhygin mystique," in the words of Jimmy Cliff) and positive images of Rastafari is a recurring theme in depictions of Jamaicans in particular and West Indians in general, as we shall see further in this chapter. A generation later, Rhygin's political offspring, one could argue, were the groups of gunmen recruited by Jamaica's two main political parties, the Jamaica Labour Party and the People's National Party. These gangs enforced territorial boundaries with an almost medieval malevolence, propping up the patronage system and enforcing party discipline with a ruthless efficiency that often resembled an outright civil war in Kingston's shantytowns and ghettos. By the spring of 1978, both sides were exhausted from the bloodletting, the poisoned atmosphere having made a mockery of the national slogan "Out of Many, One People." Talks began gradually, finally leading to the suggestion of a "peace concert" to restore some semblance of amity.

Heartland Reggae

In this context *Heartland Reggae* (1982) was filmed, a combination documentary of an island in ferment and archival concert compilation. Central to the creation of what was later to be termed the "One Love Peace Concert" (April 21–22, 1978) was the involvement of two gunmen and the reggae community. When two notorious rival political gang leaders, Claude Mossop and Bucky Marshall, were herded off to jail, both were locked in a single cell. These gunmen and their followers eventually decided to support and promote an islandwide peace concert to be held at Kingston's National Stadium.

Heartland Reggae is a slow, languid travelogue that almost immediately reveals its Third World origins. It shows exotic customs and patois interspersed with exceedingly picturesque Dreadlocks producing a torrent of invective against Babylon. The human vitriol is a sharp contrast to the benign, sun-drenched verdancy of the landscape, superimposed on a sparkling Caribbean. Off camera, Prime Minister Michael Manley concedes that "reggae music is a people's language," while on camera, the late Jacob Miller, a well-known Rasta leader and reggae disciple, twists and gyrates his way through "Peace Treaty," a reggae broadside celebrating a document, signed some three months earlier, that had brought a tenuous cease-fire between political strongholds. With Miller striding along the stage admonishing, "Camera mon take no picture," we glimpse one of the most outspoken of reggae's disciples.

In "Whip Them, Jah Jah," reggae's crown prince, Dennis Brown, acts out his perennial role of avuncular sage as he observes the oppressors of Babylon "weeping and a moaning, Lawd."[12] "Babylon," he croons, "dem a weeping and a moaning, only Dread can come over, Babylon can't come over. Mek we chant them down to the foundation." More images of Rastafari chanting down Babylon come in quick succession. Peter Tosh, on rhythm guitar, sings "African" ("As long as you're a black man, you're an African . . . ").[13] A reprise of Jacob "Killer" Miller captures the gargantuan leader of the band Inner Circle leading the assembled congregation in "I'm a Natty," predicting the eventual triumph of Rasta with a body language suggestive of Joe Cocker in a Woodstock mode. Here, too, are Bob Marley and the I-Threes, revisiting the Trench Town domain of "Natty Dread."[14] All these performers accent Rasta themes: Rastafari as a way of life, as millennial expectation, as non-violence and separation. Their embrace of Rastafari is a psychic sanctuary in a tropical maelstrom of daily struggles to survive.

For those less inclined toward the printed word, *Heartland Reggae* provides several provocative tableaux of Rasta consciousness. A luminescent Judy Mowatt describes the travails of the sisterhood in "Black Woman." Simultaneously, a succession of images depicts the plight of cane workers, frozen in an island landscape—a touch of artist Jean François Millet in the land of Marleymania, the cane workers suggesting the equivalent of Millet's painting *The Gleaners*. Rasta militancy flourishes in the truculence of Peter Tosh's Word, Sound and Power band; "the architect of the Wailers" beckons onlookers to "Get Up, Stand Up." He later excoriates the status quo as "four hundred years and it's the same old-time Columbus philosophy."[15] Preceded by film clips of Haile Selassie I visiting Jamaica in 1966, Bob Marley and the I-Threes perform the anthemic "War," in which Earl "Chinna" Smith fills in on rhythm guitar. The use of ganja is ably demonstrated here as "Jamaica's Bushdoctor," Peter Tosh, intones his "Legalize It" amid a profusion of smoke, chillum pipe, sno-cones, blunts, and croissant-sized spliffs. Tosh is followed in another sequence by Jacob Miller, who, not to be outdone, denounces the Babylon system for sacramental persecution ("Them get up and big stripe go fe lock up Rastafari").[16]

Miller's litany of oppression and his pipe dream of liberation in late-1970s Jamaica commence with a rollicking paean to pot: "Tired fe lick weed in a bush, tired fe lick weed in a gully . . . " It culminates with a wish: "We want to come out in the open, so the breeze can take it so far away, from the North to the South, from the East to Weh, Weh, Weh, West!" The climax is a remake of the children's song "London Bridge," here adapted to "Babylon, Babylon, falling down, Babylon, Babylon falling down."[17] Maintaining a discreet camera distance throughout this film, the producers (from Canada Offshore Cinema, in association with Tuff Gong) conclude with the peace concert's finale: Bob Marley, Michael Manley, and Edward Seaga embrace on stage, and an ecstatic Bob proclaims, "The moon is high over my head," as David "Ziggy" Marley and his brother, Stephen, dance in the foreground. Metaphorically speaking, it was a Jamaican version of Edward Hicks's *The Peaceable Kingdom* come to life in the Kingston of 1978.

Countryman

Like *Heartland Reggae* and *The Harder They Come, Countryman* (1982) was shot entirely on location in Jamaica. More than in any other film studied in this chapter, here an almost palpable ambience is created through setting, place, and Marley's "Natural Mystic" pervading a political allegory. *Countryman* is a tale of betrayal, duplicity, and good triumphing over evil. Rasta is central to this drama; it is a positive force that is energetic and redemptive. The soundtrack features a cavalcade of reggae talent, ranging from Bob Marley and the Wailers to Dennis Brown and to Toots and the Maytals; it includes session men and producers such as Rico, Lee Perry, and Wally Badarou, as well as the British heavyweights Aswad and Steel Pulse.[18] The plot is fairly simple. Against a backdrop of an upcoming election in an unidentified Caribbean island nation, a small passenger airplane crashes into a remote hillside. Subsequent media reports indicate that the pilot and cargo belong to a Central Intelligence Agency (CIA) destabilization plot, in which foreign provocateurs and elements of the opposition are conspiring to disrupt the election. A state of emergency is declared, and rumors run amok.

Into this political tempest floats Countryman, introduced as a moonlit net fisherman, paddling his dugout canoe to the strains of Marley's "Natural Mystic." He is a humble figure, making a subsistence living along the mangrove-studded shoreline of the Hellshire Swamps, near modern civilization yet apart. He now becomes ensnared in a race to find the missing pilot before the arrival of search parties organized by patrols that suspiciously resemble the Jamaican Defense Forces (JDF). Outracing a military helicopter to the crash site, Countryman rescues the unwitting pilot, Bobby, and his girlfriend, Beau, escorting them to safety deep in the recesses of the Jamaican littoral. In a series of short takes and brief, humorous monologues, the forces of good (Countryman, Bobby, and Beau, among others) are quickly drawn into a political quagmire. Babylonian connivance is embodied in several characters: the menacing Colonel Sinclair and his lackey Captain Benchley, certain governmental ciphers, an unscrupulous hit man (Mosman), and the obligatory Obeahman, whose cultivation of the occult upsets the elemental lifestyles of "the suffer-ahs," who are attuned to the rhythms of nature, reggae, custom, and community.

The character Countryman, in word and deed, consistently reinforces both Thelwell's and Cliff's depictions of Rasta. For Thelwell, Countryman displays a consciousness sensitive to the ecological interdependence of humans and nature. But the character also dramatizes Jimmy Cliff's perspective of Rasta as a way of life—positive, spiritual, and attuned to an ancestral sensibility in the eternal conflict between good and evil. Instead of rudeboys, two powerful Rasta presences dominate this exquisitely atmospheric saga.

One is Countryman, an adept fisherman, naturalist, cook, healer, and forager, festooned with shark's teeth and given to aphorisms and one-liners. Climatologist, clairvoyant and meteorologist rolled into one, his holistic, machete-wielding, self-reliant lifestyle is punctuated with a terse commentary of preindustrial vintage. His self-sufficiency in the kitchen is revealed early in the film as this fisherman becomes the galloping gourmet, whipping up a tasty combination of jelly coconuts, red snapper, and various island delicacies cooked over a blazing driftwood fire. Moreover, he is skilled enough in the healing arts to set a broken leg.

The second formidable Rastaman is called Jah Man, a saintly teacher of children—or, more precisely, "I-dren"—patiently instructing and leading by example ("not my teachings, but teaching those of the higher force"). The beloved, patriarchal, psalm-spouting mentor is captured ("Jah Man gwan a jail!") and led away for interrogation. He is subsequently battered, eventually expiring while in police custody.

Countryman, meanwhile, is a blur in a fragmentary landscape, evoking the loneliness—and mission—of the long-distance runner. Despite the depredations of thugs and the timely intercession of a spectral Obeahman (complete with the Gothic flourishes of a sacrificial shrine), the renegades Bobby and Beau remain safely sequestered. Finally surrounded by government henchmen, Countryman displays kick-boxing and martial arts prowess rivaling that of the late Bruce Lee. With characteristic humbleness, he intones such Rasta sentiments as "Guidance, Sister, I live through guidance. I just live in I life. . . . Me hand clean, my heart pure, nothing can harm me. . . . The wind, the sea, even the earth defend I."

Attuned to the sun, the moon and stars, the birds (and one owl in particular), the character of Countryman is the embodiment of Rasta's interconnectedness with the seamless fabric of life, a lifestyle that confers on a select few glimpses of Zion. This is the Edenic, life-supporting habitat that Ivan left in *The Harder They Come*. Here it is both refuge and preserve. Not a Dreadlock but a survivalist with jerhi curls, paddling his canoe by the fixity of moonlight, Countryman implicitly praises Jah, Head Creator and Preserver, with every action. In one memorable scene, Lee Perry voices his own praise poem: "How you gonna feel when the knife is at your throat? / For sowing brings reaping and reaping is harvest, the seed that you sow, that's what you shall reap. . . . Jah is I light and salvation, whom shall I fear?"[19]

Club Paradise

While *Countryman* dealt with human foibles, *Club Paradise* (1986) works in a comic vein. On one level, it is a sophisticated Hollywood satire of the tourist industry, with a special emphasis on the lures of travel advertising and marketing, where promised glimpses of paradise in actuality become a sojourn in purgatory. Actor Robin Williams is the center of *Club Paradise*. Williams portrays Jack Monica, a Chicago firefighter retired on a disability pension. Monica is a whirling vortex of comic asides, quips, and entirely credible antics spinning around the verities and variables of managing a tropical nightclub fallen on hard times. Jimmy Cliff resurfaces as Ernest Reed, bandleader of an island ensemble, Ernest Reed and the Flamboyants. Ernest Reed and the local Rasta community sense the economic doldrums but are favorably disposed toward Monica. Their rapport is distilled into several telling scenes variously set in live band performances at the club, ganja deals, kitchen antics, and a "groundation" ceremony.

Nonetheless, some of the dialogue also captures an implicit tension on this mythic island of St. Nicholas. Peter O'Toole, as the very British governor general, Anthony Croyden Hayes, reflects in his Edwardian demeanor the fading world of the late empire. Adolph Caesar, playing the part of Prime Minister Solomon Gundy, is the incarnation of wheeling and dealing. His various cronies include an Arab sheikh attempting a hostile takeover of Club Paradise. Gundy and his associates conspire to replace the funky ambiance of Club Paradise with a multimillion-dollar resort complex. All of this occurs on an island where the wildly disheveled Rastafari are inclined toward late-night revels and chanting down Babylon with such sentiments as "Fire burn in Babylon" while crowding around bonfires or milling about dance halls, thereby adding requisite coolness.

Many years after *The Harder They Come*, the Cliff character of Ernest Reed now displays the more positive influences of Jamaica's Bongo culture. In the shadows, however, he still glowers with indignation and Rhygin-flavored militancy. When a joke is cracked about slavery days, for instance, as part of some ancient past barely recalled, Cliff is quick to retort, "Gone but not forgotten!" Nonetheless, as the situation demands, he maintains a tuneful mode as well. Johnny Too Bad is resurrected as the Bongo man entrepreneur in this comedy, shot largely in Port Antonio, Jamaica. Although his band looks a bit stiff on film, Cliff evokes a sense of reggae solidarity with his bouncy "Club Paradise" theme song, the militant-style "The Lion Awakes," and the effervescent "Third World People."

The plotters having been thwarted, they respond by declaring a national state of emergency. The edict is delivered in the style, if not the exactitude, of Franklin Roosevelt or Winston Churchill: "This is a day that will live in infamosity." The unlikely triumvirate of Monica, Hayes, and Reed marshals the islanders to resistance—including the cook Porta, played by famed Jamaican scholar and performer Louise Bennett. Unruffled by events swirling around her, Porta the cook dispenses country-style common sense as a paragon of feminine resilience. In her kitchen, moreover, she presides with a Solomonic authority. When a lanky Rasta cook is about to be discharged for his five-foot-long dreadlocks, Porta is the one who devises a solution. "Very boogooyaga," she initially declares, mixing mirth, patois, and body language in a timeless evocation of country mannerisms. She then procures for the extra-tall Dreadlock a five-foot-high bonnet.

Conversely, the island community is depicted in a more clichéd fashion—as an assortment of slightly zany natives, rent-a-dreads, or high and low elements shuffling at the dance, "nicin' up the area." Inevitably, two rather gauche male tourists from New York decide to score some ganja. This leads to a late-night rendezvous with a dealer and the local Africa-oriented community. Their Nyabinghi ceremony borders on parody, its participants caught in the throes of a mysterious Orientalism that speaks in tongues, chants, and shouts jeremiads with blood-curdling ferocity. Submerged just beneath the comic exterior, however, is a Rasta-like indignation over the schemes and connivance of the Babylonian authorities, especially the excessive and corrupting money-flooding Paradise, bringing to mind Bob Dylan's observation that "Money doesn't talk, it swears!" Before long we are hearing the singer–disk jockey Yellowman (Winston Foster) off camera singing, "Soldier Take Over." This hint of coup menace nicely anesthetizing with comedy any parallels with recent events in such countries as Suriname, Chile, Guatemala, Egypt, or Liberia, *Club Paradise* quickly descends into Gilbert and Sullivan theatrics, becoming a comic operetta with a calypso/reggae soundtrack.

Full of hilarious scenes depicting questionable advertising techniques and culminating in some rocky landings and midflight turbulence, the film strikes a highly resonant chord with travelers of all ages. This chucklefest concludes with a subtlety that might elude the casual observer. Even though this is St. Nicholas, home of Club Paradise, the Rasta community still feels trapped in Babylon and prays daily for deliverance. In the film's final scene, Rastas are depicted in rapture, chanting, "So free our souls from Babylon." Suddenly, a contraband sack of ganja comes crashing down at their feet, jettisoned by the long-suffering, homeward-bound tourists. The Rasta astonishment at this celestial package triggers ringing shouts of affirmation: "Jah Rastafari, Selassie I!"

Cool Runnings

Cool Runnings (1993) is a retelling of the surprising successes of the first Jamaican bobsled team. Once the subject of innumerable one-liners, the team ultimately proved they were no bunch of jokers. Instead of a tale of musicians miraculously winding up at Carnegie Hall, this production of Walt Disney Pictures recounts how these bobsledders made it to the fifteenth Winter Olympiad in Calgary, Canada (1988). The film has been hailed as another *Rocky* on ice, exploring pride, power, and dignity. On closer examination of the film, however, the classic Rastafarian themes of racial pride, self-reliance, self-assertion, and cooperation have been co-opted and transformed into a sports success story, where commercialism is the subtext and competition is an indispensable means to a decidedly Babylonian end—Olympic glory. The discerning viewer will quickly note, for instance, that this is not the Jamaica of Trench Town tinderboxes, ghetto alienation, and urban anomie. Instead, we view cameos of country life and folk patois, shot with all the ringing clarity of a Hallmark card or the telegenic gloss of a Jamaican Tourist Board commercial.

Billboard's Timothy White, a lauded Marley biographer,[20] was quick to jump on the celebratory bandwagon of publicity hype. He lauded a film "whose pan-stylistic uplift earmarks it as the '90s screen-reggae equivalent of 'The Harder They Come'[21] Another critic, Janet Maslin of the *New York Times,* noted that the Disney production "unfolds with humor and ease. . . . Reggae rhythms give it another big boost."[22] Few theatergoers or reviewers, though, actually deciphered the soundtrack at the cinema (with the exception of the "Jamaican Bobsledding Chant"). The soundtrack was usually relegated to a minimal volume level, thus obscuring a tasty mélange of artists including Jimmy Cliff, Wailing Souls, Tiger, Supercat, Diana King, and Tony Rebel. Most important, the majority of viewers missed the real drama behind this fictionalized account of Jamaica's first bobsled team.

Among the ingredients of that drama are the true successes and embarrassing failures of the Jamaican bobsledders in 1988.[23] "Can lightning run on ice?" is the weighty metaphysical question posed at the film's beginning, the inspiration behind the unlikely collaboration of a motley crew. For starters, there is a pushcart driver, Sanka Coffie (Doug E. Doug), who has named his cart "Rasta Rocket." He is assisted by Junior Bevil (Rawle D. Lewis), a Jamaican of the middle-class, boarding-school variety. Adding a glowering attitude is the shaven, ill-dispositioned sprinter Yul Brenner (Malik Yoba), still chafing over having been tripped in a qualifying bobsled final, at which time star sprinter Derice Bannock (Leon) also lost his bid to join the national sprinting team and represent Jamaica in the upcoming Olympics. Redemption comes in the figure of a dispirited former Olympic coach, Irving Blitzer (John Candy). So it is easy, initially, to see the film as another tale of victory against insurmountable odds—of pride and power reaffirmed against a backdrop of polar extremities and temperaments: "We have no snow, just wood and water, the temperature ranges from hot to hotter, / No spring, no fall, much less no winter at all. Yet we have a bobsled team holding onto an Olympic dream!" ("Based on a true story . . . ")[24]

Thus the audience cheers these spandex-clad argonauts as the comedy engulfs them like an avalanche. There is the repetition of a one-liner for every mishap: "Sanka, you dead?" "Yeh, mon!" There are the sight gags of a superstitious Sanka with his lucky egg and an empty auditorium after one showing of Olympic bobsledding archival footage to an audience of aspirants. The Stephin' Fetchit slapstick continues with the sight of frozen dreadlocks and the five-member Jamaican delegation being buffeted by arctic blasts on arrival at Calgary airport ("Temp. −25" reads a digital thermometer). Later, one witnesses an ignominious debacle at the starting gate: the crew is chasing a runaway sled. Consistently formulaic, the story includes one touching moment when these outsiders feel the pangs of singularity, a brightly colored frieze of Caribbean cool marooned in Canadian whiteness, which leads to the observation "We're different. People are always afraid of what's different."

Even this team's prayer is subject to some Hollywood irreverence, wherein the rehabilitated coach, Irv Blitzer, intones a patriotic homily, guaranteeing laughs at the expense of religious piety:

> Our Father who art in Calgary, Bobsled be thy name.
> Thy kingdom come, gold medals won on Earth as it is in Turn Seven;
> With liberty and justice for Jamaica and Haile Selassie, Amen.[25]

Considering that the Ethiopian emperor had been ousted from the throne in a 1974 coup, the team's refrain of "Jah Rastafari" suggests, perhaps, a good deal more irony than simple comic relief for Western suburban audiences. This is history transformed into commodity, with the screen as a theme park, in a process one might term the "Disneyfication of reggae" a decade after the passing of Bob Marley. It should be noted that Marley, back in the 1970s, had sung, "We're coming in from the cold." In at least three instances, the reality depicted on the screen is skating on some pretty thin ice, camera angles notwithstanding. The screenplay for *Cool Runnings* is clever scriptwriting, a reimagining of the Jamaican bobsled team's trials in visceral dramatic terms. Yet, despite claims of being "based on a true story," this is fiction; history revised, and not without precedent in the Disney empire. But for observers of Jamaican culture, it might spark some lively future debates: on the pitfalls in recapturing history or on ethics and propaganda in cinema, where "virtual reality" has come to the fore and Clio, the Greek Muse of history, has been relegated to a backseat in the visitor's gallery.

In *Cool Runnings,* the Jamaicans placed last in their first run; in reality, they fared poorly, barely qualifying. In the film's dramatic second qualifying run, these ninjas in Lycra finished in eighth place. Actually, the 1988 Olympic records reveal that they finished in the twenty-fourth position, out of twenty-six teams competing. On that climactic last day of competition, Disney's foursome have a magnificent initial start, only to experience mechanical malfunction; the Jamaican quartet finally carries their sled over the finish line, icons of Olympian detachment. In truth, however, driver error caused the crash, precipitating a mishap wherein their overturned sled slid to the finish line and had to be hauled off by race officials. Although the film highlights the Jamaican sprinters' much-vaunted push-start capability, this, in fact, was never a competitive advantage. Indeed, in no aspect of their run did the Jamaicans ever place among the top half of the teams entered—not at the push start and not at the split times for four hundred, eight hundred, or twelve hundred meters.[26]

Tellingly, the epic's finale features the services of composer Hans Zimmer, whose lush score in "The Walk Home" resounds with a timpani-driven panache. The score's Teutonic martial passages recall the orchestral theme from CBS's coverage of "War in the

Gulf" and the theme song of ABC's *Wide World of Sports*. While the strings swell and then subside, the voices of authentic Trench Town survivors such as the Wailing Souls, Tony Rebel, Tiger, and Jimmy Cliff are co-opted by the symphonic strains of synthesizer calypso (or "Enya does Jamaica"):

> If I had to fight for emancipation,
> Then I shall resist for my liberation,
> And with truth and right I shall win my liberty.
> We shall unite to secure the victory,
> Cujoe and Nanny, their courage and their bravery,
> Cuffy and Quashy, delivered their race from slavery.[27]

Stepping Razor—Red X

Stepping Razor—Red X (1992) is a landmark documentary exploring the Rastaman *in extremis*. This milestone in Jamaican cultural documentation focuses on Westmoreland Parish's messenger of "roots and culture," the iconoclastic Peter Tosh. Tosh was a Jamaican country lad whose career followed the classic trajectory of a rock star. After obscure beginnings in the western parish of Westmoreland, he resettled during the turbulent 1960s in the capital, Kingston. He soon blossomed as a musician, songwriter, and vocalist par excellence. Tosh achieved a meteoric rise to fame as one-third of the reggae trinity known as the Wailers, along with Bob Marley and Bunny Wailer Livingston. Internal controversy plagued the trio, and in the early 1970s, Peter launched a solo career, fronting a band called Word, Sound and Power. It was an incendiary ensemble, with the outspoken Tosh articulating a philosophy of black pride, "equal rights and justice for all," and liberal use of ganja-herb as a sacrament "for the healing of the nation." World tours, critical acclaim, and an unsettling militancy characterized the last years of Tosh's life, during which he recorded audiotapes intended to provide raw material for an autobiography.[28]

Stepping Razor—Red X is a highly subjective look at the life of Jamaica's Bushdoctor, Tosh. It is a Canadian documentary that utilizes concert footage, interviews, reenactments, and Tosh's so-called Red X tapes. These are incorporated into a fast-paced, choppily edited, *cinema verité* style, part montage and part collage, at best a mélange that presents an alternative to the officially accepted robbery motive behind Tosh's assassination on September 11, 1987. This film marks the debut for director Nicholas Campbell (a Canadian film actor, whose credits include appearances in David Cronenberg's *Naked Lunch, Hoover vs. the Kennedys,* and *The Dead Zone*). Campbell is to be applauded for his sensitive portrayal of Rastafarian groundation ceremonies as a formative influence on young Tosh, especially as later transmitted with percussive passion in drumming solos during concert performances of "Rastafari Is." He illuminates the ancient folk customs associated with the medicinal uses of ganja and other herbs. His superimpositions of images of Tosh and Marley during the 1973 BBC sessions in London are almost hallucinatory. In terms of archival footage, the 1978 *Saturday Night*

Live segment is the film's masterstroke, wherein Tosh performs with the preening peacock Mick Jagger in a juxtaposition of devastating clarity: Jumping Jack Flash with Judge Dread on guitar, singing "(Walk and) Don't Look Back."

The Austrian producer and cinematographer Edgar Egger is also to be commended for his candid cinematic dispatches from a Third World crucible. He depicts scenes of the human slag amid rubbish dumps; of Kingston's market area (Parade); of abject squalor in squatter camps and tenement yards; of the detritus of five hundred years of colonial domination and what Tosh called "four hundred years of the slavish mentality." Egger's images of solitary citizens shuffling along rain-spattered city streets capture a tropical torpor equal to volumes of sociological reports or International Monetary Fund (IMF) annual statements.[29] Campbell, Egger, and co-executive producer Wayne Jobson have created a tantalizing trailer to the controversial life and career of the lanky, outspoken, querulous, and charismatic Tosh. Avoiding linear development and narration, they employ hyperactive film editing, crosscuts rivaling MTV's, reenactment, and effects to probe the mysteries behind the man known as "Stepping Razor."

Stepping Razor—Red X is beset by several problems and omissions that require clarification. As someone who knew Peter Tosh personally, who visited his New York City apartment and Kingston home, and who interviewed the loquacious equal rights advocate on numerous occasions, I would like to correct several misunderstandings, which I hope will clarify both the public and the private image of the wailing rudie known to colleagues as "Peter Touch." The most serious of these problems is the sensationalism of, and overdependence on, the idea of ghosts (duppies) and vampires surrounding Tosh. Although Tosh himself commented vociferously on the presence of such spectral visitors, the sensationalizing effect is to subordinate his real enemies, the "corruption in high and low places" that he observed around him daily.[30]

"My job," Peter once explained to Jamaican radio personality Basil "Bagga" Brown, "is to be the constructive awakener of the black masses of the world so them know themself and others know what black people suppose to be, and where. I deh pon earth to preach, I am a walking speech."[31] Most fans recall Tosh as either a stepping razor or a ranting Wailer, enshrouded like an Arab Bedouin or clad in khaki with a black beret, denouncing Babylon and "the colonial imperialistic shituation" with sulphuric intensity.[32] Yet in conversation, Tosh was often slyly gentle, accommodating, brief, and succinct. "I enjoy watching the karate practitioners because of their high spiritual level," he once confided in his languorous, sloe-eyed delivery. "I like football [soccer] also, but why I prefer karate is that in karate if a man kick me I can kick him back; in football that is a penalty."[33] Describing his weapon as music, he would often declare, "Is word, sound and powa dat break down de barriers of oppression an drive away transgression an rule equality."[34] Lambasting Babylon to reggae archivists Roger Steffens and Hank Holmes in September 1979, Tosh noted, "I love to watch television in Babylon, especially the news because it's so full of corruption. I-man know there is so much corruption, there is bound to be an e-ruption!"[35]

Chanting down Babylon was synonymous with Tosh's sense of Rasta. Indeed, his self-image was a virtual glossary of Rasta themes: militancy, resourcefulness, racial pride, spiritual upliftment, life as a struggle for redemption. Having numerous enemies and detractors, he often employed a caustic wit with devastating effect. Although he frequently appeared quarrelsome, in conversation he might suddenly reveal a linguistic flexibility not only endearing but revelatory of an entirely different cultural outlook—reverberations of Rasta in speech. "People go to school and get educated," he once pontificated in Los Angeles in 1979. "But most people who go to school and become a graduate in education still don't know what the word 'education' means. . . . 'Educo' means to bring out. Seen? So if I go to school to be educated, it is to extract my concept of creativity, to brainwash me in bullshit, seen? And makes me a gradu-hate."[36]

On another occasion, in New York City (which he referred to as "New York Shitty"), Peter shared his philosophy about a popular American holiday: "Thanksgiving? Every year I hear about Thanksgiving. Who do one give thanks to? . . . And who is giving thanks? What are they giving thanks for? For lots of poverty that's on the earth, and lots of war that is a-rumoring, all over the earth. For lots of people who die daily and the crime that multiply?" Peter laughed a long, slow, sardonic chuckle. "So I'll make a joyful noise unto Jah," he intoned, a flurry of blues notes providing an acoustic requiem for the forgotten, the vanquished throughout history. "It's not the one-half that's never been told," he patiently corrected this author late one evening, "it's the three-quarters."[37]

Tosh, a consummate singer-songwriter, never sings a complete song in the biography *Stepping Razor–Red X*. For a film focusing on an artist who could galvanize stadiums full of concertgoers, this is an egregious oversight (which could have been avoided by using 70 mm Dolby Sensurround). Instead, we hear choruses, fading soundtracks, sound bites, and annoyingly muffled commentary. Perhaps the organic approach of allowing the Bushdoctor to emerge from his recorded works would have produced a far more moving, naturalistic portraiture, especially for such an inspired devotee of farming and the herbal botanical agent known locally as "ganja." (One of the seemingly inexplicable mysteries behind Tosh's demise was the role of Marlene Brown, his common-law wife and Queen. Peter Tosh acquiesced to Marlene's assumption of managerial control of his career on recognition of their mutual birthday, October 19. In the film this mystery is referred to as "the enigma of Marlene Brown.")

Campbell, Egger, and Jobson missed an opportunity for a telling insight into Tosh's militancy with the song "Fight Apartheid." In their production, a crosscutting technique is employed while the track plays, showing newsreel footage of demonstrators battling South African security forces in what was then a beleaguered country; it was an effect also employed in the recent MTV video of Ziggy Marley and the Melody Makers' "Brothers and Sisters." But in 1968, Tosh was in fact arrested and severely beaten at an anti-apartheid march in front of the British consulate in Kingston. Nearly two decades later, observing a television news report of South Africa's racial turmoil, he declared to this author, "It brings tears to my eyes."[38]

Prophecy and coincidences abound in the "Mystic Man's" life and career, but these are largely absent in *Stepping Razor*. We never hear some of the more quixotic riddles from this reggae meteorologist: the prophecies of "wars and rumors of war" and "the day the dollar die." Looking into a "Crystal Ball," he predicted some rough weather ahead for the world: "churches lock down, schools close down, teachers striking, gas shortening, and the dollar devaluing, youths rising, and fire burning."[39] On what would have been his forty-third birthday (October 19, 1987), the U.S. stock market plummeted to its lowest point in history. On the day of his murder—September 11, 1987—heavy winds, torrential rains, lightning, and thunder suddenly brought to a premature close a papal mass in Miami. It was the first time in history that the pope was forced to leave a public mass unfinished. A year later, to the day, Hurricane Gilbert whipped through Jamaica. Old-time people and hill folk still speak of Peter Tosh in terms of prophecy, but many of his messages seem to have been forgotten in the excesses of contemporary dancehall and jungle mixes. Yet his presence lingers, for in one of the Mystic Man's most dramatic compositions, the disco-driven "Buk-in-Hamm Palace," Tosh's baritone conjured up a scenario of fire and smoke driving out the vampires from the London royal residence of the House of Windsor. On November 20 1992, fire severely damaged Windsor Castle.[40] Also in 1992, the retrial of Los Angeles police officer Laurence Powell—the lone policeman not acquitted in the beating of black motorist Rodney King—was scheduled to begin on Peter Tosh's birthday, October 19. Although the trial actually began somewhat later, after procedural delays, nevertheless the first announced date was for Peter Tosh's birthday.[41]

Behind every political tirade Tosh voiced from the concert stage was a memory of police brutality personally endured. This Jamaican Job was severely beaten on at least three occasions: but the film *Stepping Razor* seems to telescope these tribulations into one retelling, thereby reducing their radicalizing effect on his songwriting and herbal advocacy: "Hmm, legalize it, don't criticize it, legalize it, yeah ahh, I will advertise it."[42] Nor does the film explore the irony of black militancy betrayed by Black-on-Black violence, a maddening, Faulknerian cycle of tragedy that has engulfed the likes of Malcolm X, Marvin Gaye, and, more recently, rap artist Tupac Shakur.

Tosh strove to rise above the confusion, petty jealousies, and backbiting in Babylon, as well as the real enemies to progress: from notoriously mythic figures like "the pirates Christopher Columbus and Henry Morgan" to latter-day pirates masquerading, Tosh maintained, as "preachers, managers, advisors, police, record company executives and bookkeepers."[43] For all his maneuvering and verbal sallies, however, Tosh never escaped the Babylonian ensnarements of the ghetto—the contract, endless litigation, and recurring bouts of financial embarrassment. In a lifetime spent avoiding checkmate, Jamaica's Bushdoctor understood virtually every nuance of the game but one: the graceful exit. Moving from the autobiographical story of Jamaica's Malcolm X to recent Hollywood depictions of Rastafari, one looks in vain for what Tosh termed "spiritual upliftment" in depictions of Rasta after this cautionary tale. Unfortunately, in cinema Jamaicans and West Indians have been getting a bad rap, a scapegoating and stereotypical treatment analogous, perhaps, to the old *Amos and Andy* radio programs or Hollywood's treatment of hippies and counterculture fringe elements in the television series *Hawaii Five-O*.

Marked for Death and New Jack City

Two films, *Marked for Death* (1990) and *New Jack City* (1991), survey an American urban abyss: the "hood" and hoodlums of a fictional African American experience, in place of Rhygin's Kingston or Marley's Trench Town. In Walt Whitman's Mannahatta (*Leaves of Grass,* 1888) nearing the millennium, the Jamaican "bredren" and "suffer-ahs" are not so much victims of a plague as its bearers, while reggae and rap join forces. Marketing caricatures of rudeboys, Hollywood has almost completely ignored the positive images of the Rastafarian way of life, one nurtured within a Caribbean environment, a product of the African diaspora. In the 1990s, Caribbean exoticism becomes image exploitation and commodification, a recycling of "the Rhygin mystique," while xenophobia replaces any semblance of Rasta's emphasis on community and Pan-Africanism. And the antithesis of Rasta, a moral bankruptcy, pervades the screen within the coded slang of urban street thug chic.

The flashy urban exteriors of *Marked for Death* and *New Jack City* could be from the streets of Roxbury (Boston), Bedford-Stuyvesant (New York), South Central (Los Angeles), Watts (Los Angeles), Miami, or Detroit—a uniform grittiness rules. In these crime melodrama-action movies, urban primitivism is hip, gangsta rap is cool, and murder and misogyny are merely further elaborations of the film noir genre. Meanwhile, in reality, young black men are being murdered at five times the U.S. national average, with eight hundred gang-related deaths in Los Angeles County in 1992 alone.[44] Concurrent with calls for a congressional review of gangsta rap and the raising of related First Amendment issues, these films were a box office success, provoking criticism from some quarters that "the black exploitation" genre of the 1970s was reemerging. As Paul Delaney noted in a recent opinion piece in the *New York Times,* titled "Amos 'n Andy in Nikes," "When I witness these comedians' and rappers' routines, I can only recall the old Amos 'n Andy show: George (Kingfish) Stevens, the scheming, bumbling buffoon, declaring 'I denies the allegation and I resents the alligator.' A generation later, the image of blacks as scheming, bumbling buffoons is still prevalent in television, movies and, most dangerously, the crotch-holding rap artists."[45]

In *Marked for Death,* a drive-by shooting propels a Drug Enforcement Agency (DEA) undercover troubleshooter, John Hatcher (Steven Seagal), out of premature retirement. In a crucial scene, a television news reporter files a story on camera from the scene of a gang shoot-out; spin doctor and talking head, she crisply announces, "Although less than one percent of Jamaican immigrants are involved, Jamaican gangs known as posses are now dominating the American drug trade."[46] Enter Steven Seagal, claiming, "I've had enough"—champion of the oppressed, dressed to kill. Resplendent in a Gianni Versace wardrobe, forever squinting and scowling, his ponytail flopping, Seagal is the quintessential American good guy pushed too far. An expert in the martial arts, he is a master of mayhem awaiting "high noon," utilizing techno-glitz weaponry and night-vision optics with a vengeance in pursuit of Jamaican drug kingpins, Monkey and Screwface.

Seagal's adversaries resemble what are known in Negril as "rent-a-dreads." Invariably fashion-conscious, these West Indians are the scourge of school yards, surreptitiously selling spliffs and bags to the more adventurous of high school students (right beside the varsity training field, in one instance). True to Hollywood clichés, these menacing Dreads are mere ciphers, communicating in stage patois ("Wait here for de mon!" "Everybody want to go to heaven, but nobody want dead") and even engaging in the occult. There is one memorably nightmarish sequence suggestive of both a seance and Santeria, replete with an ideogram and Voodoo fowl, an altar, glowing candles, and a rum spray. Heightening the atmosphere of malicious cunning, the adder-tongued Dread dabbles in scarification. His cronies make up an incompetent, wild bunch more inclined toward macho posturing than effectiveness.

One of the film's unintentional ironies is casting our erstwhile Rhygin, Jimmy Cliff, as a reggae singer, although this time he is an urban griot counterpoint to the "badness," singing of "No Justice," "Rebel in Me," and "John Crow." In *Marked for Death*, Rhygin has become righteous, warbling, "Dibby, dibby wicked boy, your time has come, / You don't live right, you'll have no more fun. . . . General wha go yam Rudeboy, someday, / General wha you go lead the children astray, / General gonna meet your retribution." Although Babylon is omnipresent in the film, additional suggestions of Rastafari are basically limited to the subliminal, as in the red, green, and gold lights that bathe the lair of these Jamaican mobsters, the soon come O.K. Corral. In the film's finale, "truth, justice, and the American way" triumph, as Seagal dispatches a seemingly endless supply of baddies in a plaster-busting display of physical prowess that concludes with the obligatory gory flourish. Perhaps unwittingly, *Marked For Death*'s finale echoes the cowboy shoot-out scene in *The Harder They Come*—in both instances, West Indians are in thrall to the romance of violence come full circle.

Hollywood's occasionally surreal casting reached new depths with the character of Scotty Appleton (Ice T) in *New Jack City*. As a camera pans over scenes of degradation and urban decay, we first view a fragment of 1 Corinthians 6:9—"Don't be deceived by the fornicators"—as graffiti scrawled on a tenement wall; then Ice T appears, as an undercover cop. This is the same Ice T notorious for a song that justified the killing of police officers ("Cop Killer"). In *New Jack City* he is in pursuit of a gangster, Nino Brown (Wesley Snipes). Nino Brown and his henchmen have embarked on fantasy power trips of violence, sexism, and greed. Depicted as almost inevitable by-products of 1980s America, their disdain for any sense of individual moral culpability is reflected in one climactic conference: in their boardroom they agree unanimously, "You got to rob and get rich during the Reagan era. Change the product, change the market strategy." Brown and his cohorts then agree to take over an apartment complex and turn it into a crack house. In a sense, we bear silent witness to the excesses of a retro cowboy frontier capitalism, fueled by an urban crack epidemic. With a soundtrack consisting of songs by such contemporary artists as Color Me Badd, 2 Live Crew, Grandmaster Flash, and N.W.A., American urban music is in our ears as camera work underscores the Dickensian gloom of New Jack City. "Am I my brother's keeper?" sneers Nino Brown, reputed drug trafficker, murderer, tax evader and racketeer.

The Jamaican singer-deejay Eek-a-Mouse (Ripton Hilton), "six-foot-six above sea level," is the film's Rastaman. As the character Fat Smitty, he is cast as a preacher in a wilderness of unspeakable horrors. His fate is sealed early in the film at the aforementioned conference. Referring to Fat Smitty, one implacable gang girlfriend snarls, "This Dreadlock, bumba Rass. Even blinks wrong, you lullaby his ass." Smitty is soon history, suddenly annihilated with a gunshot to the head in broad daylight, as horrified onlookers scatter. Much murder and mayhem later, Nino Brown and company are also eliminated in this predictable tale of greed gone awry. As in most of the films explored in this survey, a formulaic leitmotiv is evident: a cycle of betrayal, murder, patois, violence, guns and confrontation, where a towering babble of rhetoric and rationalization is portrayed as equivalent to getting and maintaining respect.

Jamaican deejay Sister Carol recently addressed these issues in her 1994 release *Call Mi Sister Carol* (Heartbeat Records). Having seen these films and endured the dancehall antics and macho posturing of deejays with names like General Nuisance, Major Worries, Captain Mackerel, and Private Parts, she voices her concern about ethnic stereotyping in a selection titled "Jamaican People." Surveying the celluloid landscape of Hollywood crime-action films, she observes:

> Dem claim seh we come a make too much money
> Dem claim seh we import too much sensi
> Dem make wi look bad inna some idiot movie
> "Marked for Death," "Predator 2," and di "New Jack City."[47]

In most of the films surveyed here, there is a subtext supporting the notion that Jamaicans (and black men in general), at home and abroad, have been facing a holocaust. Peter Tosh articulated his concern for the youth, quite vehemently using the word *holocaust,* many times in the last months of his life. Bob Marley, too, saw this future, singing, "Many more will have to suffer, many more will have to die, don't ask me why."[48] Escaping the clichés of Babylon in cinema will entail some very real sacrifices, not the least of which are illusion and fantasy on the part of filmmakers, American ethnocentrism, and a myopic preoccupation with "boys in the hood." The directors of the future could begin with the international African experience as one alternative; in fact, they could begin with the island of Jamaica, home of such role models as the Maroons, Cudjoe and Sister Nanny, George William Gordon, Paul Bogle, Sam Sharpe, Marcus Garvey, Peter Tosh, and Nesta Robert Marley.

Conclusion

Jimmy Cliff, surveying a thirty-year career on stage and in film, has articulated the continued need for positive images of Rasta to supplant the popular preoccupation with rudeboys and criminal elements. A quarter century after the release of *The Harder They Come,* Cliff is preparing a sequel. "After eighteen to twenty years in prison, Rhygin gets spiritual," reggae's grand master predicted in a conversation with the author. Cliff continued, "He's still very angry at what society did. He was pushed to guns by society"[49] The sequel will undoubtedly resonate with Cliff's personal metamorphosis: from semiangelic rudeboy to the African ambassador of the Rasta-Muslim sensibility.

On his "Higher and Higher" tour (1996), the Grammy Award winner still concluded his concerts with the ancestral sensibility and homage of "Bongo Man/Rivers of Babylon." Just after an August show in Massachusetts, Cliff explained to the author, "Rasta is consciousness, a positive image. Rasta is about the interrelatedness of nature, about man being interdependent. The greatest problem for man today is that man is removed from nature. It is a world problem."[50] The challenge for cinema devotees of the future is to achieve an organic wholeness of images, weaving ancestral voices toward a new synthesis of culture, community, and cosmopolitanism: a future started in the eight films reviewed above, and where the militancy of a dub poet such as Mutabaruka meets the stamina of Sugar Minott's "Sprinter Stayer."[51]

Notes

1. Bunny Wailer clarified the subtle distinction between biblical Babylon and the Rasta metaphorical Babylon in numerous references to the "shitstem" (Babylon system) in reggae songs. He said, "People get the impression that we're talking about people or a place; it's a system. It's the system that keeps people divided, people hating each other, where you see wars when there aren't any reasons to create wars. . . . So that's the system of Babylon that's been for some time now" (Bunny Wailer, interview with the author, Kingston, Jamaica, March 13, 1989). See also Cynthia Ozick, "The Moral Necessity of Metaphor," *Harper's*, May 1986, 62–68. Film sources worth exploring include the movies *Rockers* (1979) and *The Mighty Quinn* (1989), as well as the documentary *Time Will Tell* (1992) and the largely anthropological travelogue *Land of Look Behind* (1982).

2. Bunny Wailer, "Ready When You Ready," on *Liberation*, Shanachie 43059, 1988. Copyright by Solomonic Music 1987–1988; copyright owner: Bunny Livingston.

3. Along with Cliff, reggae artists such as Toots Hibbert and the Maytals, Desmond Dekker, the Melodians, and the Slickers take the listener over the rivers of Babylon and through a modern inferno haunted by a bittersweet nostalgia evocative of Thomas Wolfe's novels *You Can't Go Home Again* (1940) and *Of Time and the River* (1935).

4. Toots Hibbert and the Maytals, "Pressure Drop," on *The Harder They Come: Original Soundtrack Recording*, Mango MLP 9202, 1973. The allusions to Pilgrim, the Celestial City, and Vanity Fair are from John Bunyan's prose allegory *The Pilgrim's Progress from This World, to That Which Is to Come, Delivered under the Similitude of a Dream* (1678; New York: Signet, 1964).

5. Dialogue transcribed from *The Harder They Come* soundtrack. The Melodians, "Rivers of Babylon," on *The Harder They Come: Original Soundtrack Recording*.

6. Referring to "Many Rivers to Cross," Cliff has located its origin in his 1965 trip from Jamaica to England: "I wrote it one day when I found myself lost in the English countryside. I'd been doing a lot of drugs, I was in a very confused state, with no money, no food, and no shelter, just my guitar" (Jennifer French, "Jimmy Cliff: Still Crossing Rivers," *RAPS* 1, 3 [November–December 1987]: 12). The festering sense of exploitation Rhygin emotes has an analogue in the real life experiences of the actor who would portray the doomed gunman in *The Harder*

They Come: Jimmy Cliff. Cliff relates in his press materials that after recording his first single, "Daisy Got Me Crazy," "It was never released and I got no money for it. All they [the producers] offered me was a shilling [twelve cents] for my bus fare to school, which I refused. I thought it was an insult."

7. Dialogue transcribed from *The Harder They Come* soundtrack. The Slickers, "Johnny Too Bad," on *The Harder They Come: Original Soundtrack Recording*.

8. A chillum is a smoking vessel, usually fashioned out of a gourd or calabash, utilizing water as a cooling agent. It is always passed in a counterclockwise direction, with symbolic rebellious and communal significance.

9. Jimmy Cliff, interview with the author, Montego Bay, Jamaica, January 16, 1990.

10. Michael Thelwell, "The Harder They Come: From Film to Novel," *Grand Street* no. 37 (1992): 135–65. Special thanks to Thelwell for the photocopy of the *Daily Gleaner,* October 9, 1948.

11. Ibid., 141.

12. Dennis Brown, "Whip Them Jah Jah," from the soundtrack of *Heartland Reggae* (Canada Offshore Cinema, 1982).

13. Peter Tosh, "African," from the soundtrack of *Heartland Reggae*.

14. Bob Marley and the Wailers, "Natty Dread," from the soundtrack of *Heartland Reggae*.

15. Peter Tosh, "Get Up, Stand Up," from the soundtrack of *Heartland Reggae*.

16. In addition to the documentary evidence of the "One Love Peace Concert," *Heartland Reggae* utilizes footage shot in Jamaica during the spring of 1978, including performances by Dennis Brown, Judy Mowatt, U-Roy, Junior Tucker, Jacob Miller and the Inner Circle, and Althea and Donna, recorded in Savanna-la-Mar and the Trelawny Beach Club.

17. Jacob Miller, "Tired Fe Lick Weed in a Bush," from the soundtrack of *Heartland Reggae*.

18. The result is a cinematic adventure with the sinister overtones of Graham Greene or Oliver Stone.

19. Lee Perry, "Dreadlocks in Moonlight," on *Countryman,* Island Records MSTDA, 1982.

20. Timothy White, *Catch a Fire: The Life of Bob Marley* (New York: Holt, Rinehart & Winston, 1983).

21. Timothy White, "'Stayin' Cool': Wailing Souls' Story," *Billboard,* September 25, 1993, 5.

22. Janet Maslin, review of *Cool Runnings, New York Times,* October 1, 1993, C8.

23. Critically examined, *Cool Runnings* represents history sanitized and homogenized, bleached and glossed over in a welter of high-tech masculinity, a polar version of the Mighty Morphin Power Rangers or *The Three Musketeers* updated.

24. WORL-A-GIRL, "Jamaican Bobsledding Chant," on *Cool Runnings, Music from the Motion Picture,* Chaos Records OK 57553, 1993.

25. Monologue transcribed from the *Cool Runnings* soundtrack. Although lovable and laughable, the character of the bobsled team's coach, Irv, is another example of Hollywood scriptwriting taking liberty with the facts. That the bobsled team's coach was a washed-up former Olympian, stripped of his medal for cheating, is pure fabrication. See "Sled Team Likes 'Cool,' despite Factual Detours," *USA Today,* October 8, 1993, 5D.

26. Amateur Athletic Foundation of Los Angeles, *Sports Letter* (October 1993): 2–3.

27. Bunny Wailer, "Ready When You Ready."

28. In September 1987, while preparing for a tour to support his *No Nuclear War* (EMI) release, Tosh was murdered in his Barbican (Kingston) home, allegedly by three gunmen with robbery as the motive.

29. Co-executive producer Wayne Jobson has rendered invaluable service in assembling the musical segments; in gathering quotations from Tosh, family, friends, and colleagues; and in providing some telling anecdotes that illuminate this often testy mystic man, Jamaica's Malcolm X.

30. Peter Tosh, interview with the author, New York City, May 11, 1987.

31. Basil "Bagga" Brown, "Interview: Peter Tosh and Bunny Wailer," *High Times* (April 1983): 33.

32. See Jah Ugliman, "The One Love Peace Concert," *Jah Ugliman* (October 1978): 31.

33. Basil (Bagga) Brown, "Better to Be Peter D. Fighter Than Johnny B. Good till Africa and All Africans Are Free," *Rockers* 3, 1 (Spring 1984): 21.

34. Ugliman, "One Love Peace Concert," 30.

35. Hank Holmes and Roger Steffens, "Reasoning with Tosh," *Reggae News* 2, 3, and 4 (December 1979): 1.

36. Ibid.

37. Tosh interview, New York City, November 25, 1986; interview, New York City, June 10, 1987.

38. Tosh interview, New York City, May 11, 1987.

39. Peter Tosh, "Crystal Ball," on *Mystic Man,* Rolling Stones Records, 1979.

40. Peter Tosh, "Buk-in-Hamm Palace," on *Mystic Man.* The late Peter Tosh's "Babylon Burning" provides an alternative to the euphoria surrounding the hollow victory of Operation Desert Storm, especially in light of the controversy surrounding veterans' complaints of Persian Gulf War ailments. Huddled over an acoustic guitar, the reflective Tosh often sang of "mystery Babylon" for guests. With a few introductory bass runs and several strummed chords, he was then a solitary muse in a humming meditation, enveloped in clouds of myrrh and frankincense. One recalls his voice rising and falling softly, a griot suspended in time, performing the song as part dirge, part lament, sharing a vision: "Babylon burning, Babylon burning." See Kevin J. Aylmer, "War inna Babylon: Prophecy and the Gulf War," *The Beat* 10, 6 (1991): 33–41. Also check the radio broadcast recording "Peter Tosh '88 Fund Drive," KCRW-FM, Los Angeles, California, January 26, 1988, for an extempore rendition of "Babylon Burning."

41. Peter Tosh's murder date also suggests some strange congruences and a lesson in Rasta numerology or chronology. On September 11, the following occurrences are historical fact: 1973, a coup in Chile results in the death of the freely elected president Salvador Allende Gossens; 1974, in a coup in Ethiopia, Haile Selassie is overthrown; 1977, anti-apartheid activist Steve Biko dies while in police custody near Pretoria, South Africa; 1987, on the same day that Peter Tosh is murdered in Kingston, a papal mass is brought to a premature close in Miami; 1988, Hurricane Gilbert devastates Jamaica. See Kevin J. Aylmer, "In Touch with Tosh," *Reggae Report* 10, 8 (1992): 21.

42. Peter Tosh, "Legalize It," on *Legalize It,* Columbia Records, CBS PC 34253, 1976.

43. Peter Tosh, interview with the author, New York City, November 25, 1986.

44. Carl Upchurch, "I Still Have a Dream," *New York Times,* August 27, 1993, A29.

45. Paul Delaney, "Amos 'n Andy in Nikes," *New York Times,* October 11, 1993, A17.

46. Monologue transcribed from *Marked for Death* (1990), as are subsequent quotes. After the closing credits, the producers add a disclaimer in fine print to the effect that only a very small percentage of Jamaicans are actually engaged in illegal activity.

47. Sister Carol, "Jamaican People," on *Call Mi Sister Carol,* Heartbeat Records, CD HB 93, 1994.

48. Bob Marley and the Wailers, "Natural Mystic," on *Exodus,* Island Records, 90034-1, 1977. Recall that Marley himself survived an assassination attempt on December 3, 1976. Mar-

ley updates the Shadrach, Meshach, and Abednego saga of the Book of Daniel in his composition "Survival," on *Survival,* Island Records, 90088-4-7, 1979. See also Marley's reference to Babylon during his 1979 tour, in the selection "Africa Unite"; on a tour stop in Santa Barbara, California, November 25, 1979, he would sing, "To see the unification of all Africans, Marcus Garvey said it, so let it be done. . . . Because we're moving out of Babylon . . . moving to our Father's land."

49. Jimmy Cliff, interview with the author, Montego Bay, Jamaica, January 16, 1990.

50. Jimmy Cliff, interview with the author, Cohasset, Massachusetts, August 31, 1996.

51. Mutabaraka, *The Ultimate Collection,* Shanachie 45026, 1996; Sugar Minot, *Breaking Free,* Ras 3176, 1994.

Part IV

*Religion: Livity, Hermeneutics,
and Theology*

18 Discourse on Rastafarian Reality

REX NETTLEFORD

Jamaica, as part of the Caribbean, remains a source of energy and a laboratory for exploration of fundamental issues of cultural import in the development of humankind. The Rastafarian *phenomenon* or *movement* is a major issue among these. Ever since George Eaton Simpson of Oberlin College[1] did his field study of the *cult* of Rastafari in the mid-1950s—followed by the public policy survey by three scholars of the University of the West Indies, at the request of members of the Rastafarian movement, in 1960[2]—debates over Rastafari have proceeded apace, resulting in the publication of a rich body of literature in books and scholarly journals, as well as in what may be described as informed opinion pieces and investigative journalism in the print and electronic media, on both sides of the Atlantic.[3] To those must be added the expansive and insightful analyses, comments, and examinations that are to be found in the oral utterances and written expositions by actual members of the movement, providing valuable primary material for further study and understanding.[4]

The conversion to the Rastafarian faith of many educated middle-stratum Jamaicans in the late 1960s and throughout the 1970s has produced the Twelve Tribes of Israel[5] wing of the movement, which is structured, orderly, and formal in its institutionalization, a feature that was unknown to the fissiparous movement that had developed by the late 1950s and early 1960s. But it has also introduced into the formal discourse many professed adherents who write and speak in response to arguments that appear to them to perpetuate the marginalization and trivialization of the movement, as well as to deprecate the belief system in its religious orientation. These undisguised detractors deem Rastafarian religious practices to be a violation of Christian orthodoxy, which has been, for a long time, the rock on which the intense religiosity of Jamaica firmly stands.

The 1995 Christmas Eve issue of Jamaica's leading daily newspaper[6] carried an article by Ika Tafari, a Rastafarian, in response to an earlier article in the *Sunday Gleaner* titled "Rastafarians Need a Systematic Theology," by Ian Boyne, listed as "a specialist writer on religion" and himself the Jamaican representative of Garner Ted Armstrong's Church of God International (a religious sect founded by Herbert W. Armstrong).[7] This gave the debate a special edge when seen in the context of the cultural discourse that has, for five centuries, involved Christendom and "the rest" throughout the Americas. "The rest" can be taken to include, as major contenders/disputants, diasporic Africans, the formerly enslaved and their *emancipated* descendants, and the formerly colonized. All three categories of souls embrace those who have made the Rastafarian commitment a means of defense and of self-actualization.

Ika Tafari was driven to his rebuttal by Boyne's seemingly harmless and *objective* call for the Rastafarians "to move into the 21st century [by] learning the tools of hermeneutics and exegesis . . . to develop a rigorous epistemology and cut the anti-intellectual rubbish," and to stop holding back the Rastafarian movement by "glorifying of ignorance which is at the heart of Rastafari as religion."[8] Ika Tafari's ire is understandable, for while the claim that Christian exegesis and hermeneutics have the pedigree of genealogical legitimacy is one thing, to assert further that they are the only ones capable of finding the Holy Grail (or the Holy) is quite another. Moreover, true Rastafarian believers would not number themselves among the anti-intellectuals in Jamaica. They certainly can boast a record of spirited, energetic discourse about racism, identity, black dignity, and equality in numerous "groundings" among themselves as well as with discussants willing to engage in such reasoning. Christian orthodoxy and heterodoxy may find it incomprehensible, but the Rastafarian's creed is not short on exposition and interpretation— exegesis and hermeneutics, to the scriptural scholar. The richness of the content of the "conscious" lyrics to the widely acclaimed songs of Rastafarian composers—from ska to reggae—further attests to this.

Boyne's call prompts the question of whether he genuinely means to take the debate into the realm of detached scholarship, thereby fostering a dialogue that demonstrates "reciprocal anti-defamation [with one] religious tradition explaining itself to others, [and] with the aim of increasing mutual understanding and tolerance"—in other words, "open-minded encounter with other religious possibilities on the level of their truth claims."[9] But Boyne's liberal use of such words as *ignorance* and *rubbish* in reference to the Rastafarian creed tempts one to wonder if the discourse he advocates does not reflect a common approach in Christian theology today that "goes on as if the Judaeo-Christian tradition were *alone* in the world— with modern secularity as its only external conversation partner."[10] Ironically, Ian Boyne offers to defend orthodox Christianity against Rastafari, but he himself professes faith in a branch of Armstrongism, which departs from orthodox Christianity in perhaps as many ways as Rastafari and is itself little more than half a century old, having arisen about the 1930s. Did Herbert W. Armstrong or his son, who succeeded him, develop a "new systematic theology"?

Surely the twenty-first century into which the Rastafarians are being invited to enter will not be the one-dimensional, all-powerful, slave-owning, and imperialistic Christendom that the fifteenth to twentieth centuries were to millions of persons, including many of those "civilized" through conversion to Christianity. Southeast Asia—indeed, all of Asia—with its native Confucianism, Taoism, Buddhism, and Islam (in all their variations), along with its increasing economic productive power, must be taken into account. Ika Tafari is saying, in effect, that the shift of paradigms and of centers of gravity is also manifested in the Rastafarian *overstanding* of self and society, of Being and non-Being, and must be seen as a viable alternative to received religious dispensations.

Admittedly, in his article Ika Tafari all too frequently makes claims that rest on the untenable epistemological fallacy that if one has not actually experienced something, one cannot really know or comprehend it. "It must be noted," he begins his rebuttal, "that many of those who are studying, analyzing and writing about the Rastafarian culture are not of the faith." However, his further claims of impositions of Eurocentric forms of discourse, rooted in European experience and preferences, seem to be justified, especially when he asserts that "there are aspects of cultural expression that are systematic within the life of the majority of those who adhere to the knowledge and understanding of being Rastafari." "There is," he continues, "no established religion that has not taken a considerable amount of time, sometimes many centuries, to establish itself, especially if it opposes the basic fabric of the established religion which dominates and governs the masses."[11] Such an assertion—as evidenced in history, ancient and modern—is impatient of debate.

Ika Tafari is here reminding his readers that Rastafari is more than religion; for the struggle for intellectual and psychic space in the defining, or redefining, of self and the world which that *self* inhabits and must function in is still a struggle between Christendom (the secular manifestation of which is Western civilization) and those who used to be called "infidels" or "heathens"—between Europe as colonizer and Africa as colonized. Boyne's article, Ika Tafari stresses, was "in most part a reflection of outright prejudice [since] it reflects a shallow intellectual criticism" of a group of people who, over a short period of time, have contributed to and also challenged the establishment's authenticity as it relates to black cultural values for the masses of African descendants—persons who have found themselves victims of white supremacy and other institutionalized methods to keep them enslaved to a foreign-based theology and self-image.[12]

This brings to mind the injunction of Marcus Garvey, in a speech he delivered in Menelik Hall, Nova Scotia, in 1937, when he called on black people to emancipate themselves from mental slavery, this being a major responsibility for themselves and themselves alone.[13] This exhortation was later echoed by the Rastafarian reggae superstar Bob Marley, in what has become a much-sung and oft-repeated couplet from one of his classic compositions:

Emancipate yourself from mental slavery,
None but ourselves can free our minds.[14]

This is what Rastafarian "theology" is about: taking the discourse into intellectual landscapes beyond narrow theological hermeneutics and exegesis, whose methods of argumentation are considered Christian-specific and predetermined in that tradition. This is so despite Rastafari's own sense of *divine reality*, rooted in large measure in the Hebrew Bible but also in the historical experience of a sustained period of severance and suffering, followed by continuing psychic exile, alienation, and anomie. This allows for rank shoots of dialogue and colloquies, of reasonings and groundings, involving journalists such as Boyne and clergy such as the Reverend Clinton Chisholm (whom Boyne credits with having "done the most exhaustive research on Rastafarianism"), as well as scholars such as "Rex Nettleford, Barry Chevannes, Rupert Lewis and others" (who, Boyne insists, "must now do more than just give an historical analysis and sociological function").

The idea that such efforts do nothing for hermeneutics and exegesis betrays a lack of sense of process and appreciation that Rastafari may well be working its purpose out in this exegetical fashion, just as Judaism, Islam, and Christianity did over time and through changing encounters in human history. Exegesis may, after all, have something to do with evolution, growth, and development. Scholars are further called on to "assess how potent the Rastafari ideology has been against the all-pervasive nationalist and consumerist North American culture which has, for the first time, decisively shaped a One-World culture."[15] Here, Boyne seems to fall in that category of orthodox Christian *debaters* who lack ecumenical sensitivity, and, as sociologist of religion Peter Berger puts it, behave as if the "Judeo-Christian tradition were alone in the world with modern secularity . . . as its only exernal conversation partner."[16] As the situation stands, Rastafari is a conversation partner as well and on its own terms with Christian orthodoxy, the umbrella theology that shelters the very secularity that is seen as its nemesis.

That the continuing discourse, in all its multifaceted complexity, is a form of action against the prevailing materialism even in the face of surrender by Rastafarian superstars to worldly goods should be of little surprise to those who know anything about the history of Christianity in the world. In one discourse, is Christianity not deemed to have been central to the rise of capitalism,[17] even as it advocated values of temperance, equity, and honesty, standing side by side with the glorifying of inequalities said to be of divine preordination? In one Christian praise song (hymn), "All things bright and beautiful," believers lustily wail:

> The rich man in his castle,
> The poor man at his gate;
> God made them high or lowly
> And ordered their estate.[18]

The Rastaman finds it hard to believe that Yahweh/Jehovah/Jah (his God) would sanction any such inequality; and he is tempted to ask for whom are "all things bright and beautiful." Nor is he willing to do penance, for he does not buy into the notion of original sin, since any original sin committed would have been committed against him, sentencing him to exile in Babylon and all the vile consequences of this. The idea of a black African holocaust, complete with notions of reparation, is therefore not as quaint or unfounded as it may seem to people nowadays.

The present anthology may well turn out to be a significant contribution to the continuing discourse, for its contents reinforce the argument that the Rastafarian movement or phenomenon and its reality do not constitute an irrational indulgence that is incapable of explanation and theory, having suddenly catapulted itself into human consciousness. Rather, Rastafari has a genealogical pedigree and is an integral part of a discourse that turns on the age-old resistance to forms of oppression. These experiences of oppression have their origins in the expansionist zeal of European nations and in the barracoons of West Africa, which preceded that sustained *downpression* of humans by humans in the Americas and continued long after slavery was abolished, with more than vestigial traces languishing in tarnished splendor to this day.

That ancestral pedigree, rooted in a long-standing dialogue with the history of diasporic Africa, is the greatest and most powerful theme of one of the recent publications on Rastafari, authored by the West Indian sociologist Barry Chevannes (the book that prompted Boyne's original article).[19] Chevannes's *Rastafari: Roots and Ideology* is supported by the ethnographic accounts of informants, themselves the authentic avatars of that hallowed tradition of resistance that has been manifested, in turn, by what Chevannes refers to as "revivalism." The revivalist tradition is itself an act of re-creation, continuity of life, and living through some cycle of death, resurrection, and ascension—ascension into areas of inviolability that afford not only survival but acres of space beyond survival (through the dialectic of scattering, exile, and return).

The centrality of the religious experience to this process of ontological assertion is, therefore, on target; and Chevannes illustrates this brilliantly in his analysis and clear and engaging historical-contextual account. Slavery, emancipation, and the rise of the free peasantry as signifiers of fundamental change are critical to any such analysis. But no less so are the persistent elements of race, color, and class designations as effective determinants of ranking and status in a social structure akin to that of the Middle Ages. Such a structure has given to the dynamics of social change a vaulting ascent of the entire Jamaican complex, leaving those at the base to stagnate there even if the levitation offered by statutory freedom (heralding equality under the law) has spelt upward social mobility for some: that phenomenon of persistent marginalization (of which persistent poverty is only one aspect) and of dictated persistent resistance, or, as I have said elsewhere, of deep-structured "strategies of demarginalization."[20]

The Rastafarians have tuned into a major strategy of demarginalization: religion. Having one's own God in one's own image was a grand flowering in Rastafari of what had earlier begun in Myal and developed in Zion revivalism and Pocomania, with the hijacking of the oppressor's God in a move that served to discommode the oppressor. The slave forebears of Rastafarians understood fully that there are areas of inviolability beyond the reach of oppressors, and that these are what guarantee survival and beyond. Such exercise of the creative imagination and intellect remains, then, the most powerful weapon against all acts of inhumanity; and the Rastafarians have drawn on the tradition, which was nurtured since the eighteenth century, to cope with and defy the harshness of twentieth-century indulgences. Wresting *the Christian message from the Messenger* as a strategy of demarginalization helped bring slaves and the free peasantry nearer a perceived mainstream as "children of God." Rastafari were to extend this by proclaiming selves as "pieces of God."

The divinity of all black people—in fact, of all human beings—here becomes the basis for the equality, liberty, dignity, mutual respect, and equity in terms of access to economic resources, and all the values claimed by civil or democratic society but yet to be achieved in what, to exiles from Africa, is Babylon. That the advocacy first made its presence felt with millenarian intensity under the invocation of "Jah" is no reason to deny its importance to Jamaican and human development, any more than one would dismiss the claim that certain Christian virtues gave rise to the capitalism of Christendom or that the myth of a kingdom of necessity gave rise to communism. In this, the originality and seminal nature of Rastafari have been greatly underestimated in many studies since the publishing of the 1960 University of the West Indies report, which triggered public and widening academic interest.

In this respect, Barry Chevannes has offered a welcome corrective, speaking to ideas as well as forms of actions—for that is the lineage to which Rastafari belongs. The central tenets of pan-divinity and repatriation indeed belong to that lineage, as earlier studies had discovered. The idea of "lineage," indeed, suggests "continuity rather than break," to quote Chevannes again.[21] This idea of continuity gives primacy to culture over politics and confirms the increasing relevance of the study of Rastafari to the burgeoning body of literature that has at last found form and purpose in the academy. This has come long after the Rastafarians tried to get Jamaicans and the world to understand the centrality of their concerns to the reality of human development (or underdevelopment) over the past five hundred years, as well as in the daily scheme of things. In desperation, some of them have wanted to "leave earth," but most have stayed the course and maintained a dialogue with both their history and existential reality. By so doing, they have attracted to their cause, their ideas, and their actions not only now great reggae composers[22] but also young scholars from North America and Europe who have helped to expand the literature on "Rastafarian Studies" in its myriad aspects.[23]

A number of those scholars bring to the discourse a certain authenticity that the literature needs in addition to the ethnographic collections of evidence "from the horses' mouths". Within that discourse are several pillars of debate. Prominent among these are what some scholars refer to as the dynamics of culture and power in a newly "global" world, since "globalized processes" are repeatedly transforming the composition and spatial arrangements of power and culture. The specificity of the Jamaican Rastafari phenomenon has itself been integral to a process of transforming the composition and spatial arrangements of power and culture in Jamaica and the wider Caribbean.

The engagement of Rastafari in this process has brought to the agenda conflicts between classes of persons on many issues: (1) aesthetics and artistic manifestations (classical music versus ska, rock steady, and reggae; fine arts versus intuitives; classical ballet versus African-derived "creative" barefoot dance; and so on); (2) religion (New Testament Christianity versus Hebrew Bible–driven Jah worship; nineteenth-century missionaries found the indigenous Myal to be evil, one will recall); (3) language legitimacy (Standard English versus the Rastafarian "I-an-I" locution and other innovative uses of "the Master's" tongue to discommode in the assertion of powers of autochthonous communication); (4) economic development strategy ("eating what one grows" and being self-reliant versus importing to satisfy a North Atlantic consumption pattern; living within one's means versus the wanton overconsumption of the ostentatious *nouveaux riches*; diligence in application of energy on the job (if a job can be found) versus laid-back indolence; and (5) governance (democratic cooperation, comprising individuals coordinating for social action, in defiance of autocratic, self-indulgent rule).

The culture of resistance echoes in the tension now evident in a world that is threatened with homogenization under the name of economic globalization. This threat finds a counterthreat in the retreat to areas of specificity that would enable discrete groups of people to be firmly enough rooted so as to withstand the raging "global" whirlwind. Such areas of specificity take different forms—ethnicity, religion (fundamentalist or otherwise), metaphysical authenticity (as in the case of Native Americans), and even dietary peculiarities. The Rastafari and their slave and free-peasant forebears were "ahead of the game" in coping with earlier forms of globalization fueled by mercantilist greed. This suggests a paradigm of universal application out of the realities of specific experience and is bound to inspire scholarship in the finest tradition.

In line with such a tradition, Chevannes wisely indulges a "bias" and, better still, acknowledges it: he calls it the "Barnes bias," and it guarantees his study a certain reliability and authenticity through the recorded accounts of the true believer as informant. He has no time for "designer Dreads,"[24] which the Rastafari movement by the 1970s had certainly begun to attract. He targeted instead the vintage devotee, who could lead him nearer to the truth about a number of "facts" about the movement, thus allowing him to see it from a better perspective. He need not have apologized for the dangers of oral evidence, for his method is an answer to Ika Tafari's concern that "outsiders" speak with little authority about Rastafari, not having the firsthand experience of "believing."

Much of what historians consult as primary material, scribally documented, are oral accounts put into writing. The biases in these have to be balanced by other biases. The oral tradition among an oppressed people who may have distrusted writing down anything need not be without its own integrity and internal consistency. The art of the griot is not always an atavistic indulgence; it can be an invaluable source of facts, interpretations of those facts, exaggerations admittedly for emphasis (we who write put "in italics," "my emphasis"), and so on. It is for the scholar to decode, decipher, and make sense of it all. Any work on the Rastafari— a still-evolving reality—is bound to benefit from the vitality of Chevannes's "Barnes bias," as well as from a network of informants who can push the investigators into firsthand discoveries that are of universal appeal and relevance.

Such are the challenges for any work that wishes to stand as a significant contribution to the "sharpening of the reader's insights into the provenance and stubborn tenacity of this most complex, irritating phenomenon which has distorted, even while shaping, human history through out the half a millennium since 1492."[25] I speak here of the hijacking of power, aided and abetted by peculiar notions of class, race, and color superiority with the added claim that these are sanctioned by a divine force fashioned in the image of the oppressor. To the persistence of the oppressor's theology of exclusive claims to that divine force, underpinning an exclusive cosmology and ontology, Ika Tafari and other brethren of the Rastafarian faith take exception. By the same token, the Rastafarian claim to an incontestable belief in the divinity of Haile Selassie, "Conquering Lion of the Tribe of Judah and King of Kings," is an anathema to many such as the Reverend Clinton Chisholm, who finds the claim theologically unsound and historically false, as does the journalist-churchman Ian Boyne, to whom the claim is the result of "ignorance."

Rastafari may well be the type of religious experience characterized by what Peter Berger, in his book *The Heretical Imperative,* refers to as the "interiority of the divine," as opposed to experience by "confrontation with the divine." As such, it receives an on-slaught of criticism by Christian believers who share with other monotheistic religious adherents "a strong built-in bias against mysticism"[26]—the characteristic par excellence of "the interiority type." Thus, God, having revealed himself in Christ, goes the Christian argument, could not possibly be found "within the interiority of mystical consciousness." The Rastafarians are hence considered blasphemous, for being in cognitive conflict with Christianity. Their truth claims are therefore summarily neutralized and targeted for annihilation.

The position taken by the Reverend Clinton Chisholm in revealing the "crack" in Rastafarian beliefs resulting from "a faulty historico-theological foundation"[27] may indeed have on its side the logic of scholarship (in terms of the rigorous analysis of secondary texts) but fall short of the *faith* that undergirds all religions—as Mutabaruka, the Rastafarian dub poet, was quick to point out in a televised debate between himself and Chisholm on a program moderated by none other than Ian Boyne.[28] Both debaters invoked the *Kebra Nagast*—the principal source, according to Chisholm, of "the two notions pertaining to the lineage of Ethiopian emperors and to Ethiopia as the new Zion"[29]—and disagreed on interpretation, just as debaters on passages of the Bible have done.

To the Rastaman, Jah, the divine Selassie, lives in much the same way as Christ lives: that is, within one's heart and one's spirit, instead of beyond the clouds to which the Son of Man ascended (according to the "myths" entertained by some Christian fundamentalists). The Rastafarian response to Jamaicans who ridiculed the faith's position on Haile Selassie's divinity when the emperor suffered a humiliating arrest on September 12, 1974, and an undignified death in August 1975 at the hands of political enemies was understandably the ready reference to what happened to Christianity after the judicial murder by crucifixion of Jesus almost two millennia ago. Bob Marley, for instance, triumphantly wrote his song "Jah Lives."[30] The belief in the divine Selassie was reinforced in spirit and in truth among the devout. The creed has spread ever since, much the way Christianity did after the departure of the mortal Jesus and in the wake of oppression and sustained persecution. Why, indeed, should the historical process be restricted to Christian evolution? In any case, goes the Rastafarian argument, the lineage and divinity of the Christian deity and his final abode in heaven are matters of faith to believers, not of historical verity or incontestable empirical evidence. The accuracy of the synoptic Gospels, the inspired historical accounts of the life of Christ, is even now under scrutiny and is the subject of scholarly debate.[31]

An immaculate conception, a resurrection, and an ascension may be challenges to historical investigation, but not to faith. Faith has a unique approach to facts. Archaeological digs are suggesting the recent discovery of an ossuary containing the bones of one "Jesus son of Joseph," casting doubts on the Resurrection itself.[32] But faith conquers all: belief is here meant to cure, not to kill—at least in the eyes of true and faithful Christians. So the very claims to an empirical historicity—Christianity's strength—become a legend. The legend becomes the "truth" and is printed. In the absence of a holy book, the Rastafarian faith continues to depend largely on an oral tradition, though with a scribal literature in the making. The previously "neglected dimension [of proof of the divinity and iconic lineage of Haile Selassie] in the voluminous literature, scholarly and otherwise,"[33] may be so only because these are early days yet. Religions, like Rome, are not built in a day, as Ika Tafari, the Rastafarian, reminds Boyne, the Armstrongite Christian. The Rastaman's "livity" may inhere in the lived reality of his experience in Babylon and be celebrated or rued in the lyrics and music of the internationally acclaimed art form of reggae, as well as in the "reasonings" and the groundings of the brethren and in the history and sociology of the movement as so far recorded, analyzed, and argued, as these will continue to be.

Belief that took time to become *belief in* in all religious expressions that have endured—and this is equally applicable to the Immaculate Conception, the Crucifixion, the Resurrection, and the Ascension as defining moments in the evolution of the Christian tradition. One may well be tempted to assert that Christ was not a Christian any more than Marx was a Marxist; "Our Lord" was careful, according to the Scriptures, to make no exaggerated claims for himself,[34] although John portrays him as claiming equality with God (John 8). Nor could Selassie see himself as a Rastafarian, despite the fact of his pre-imperial name Ras Tafari. If, indeed, the "teachings" and "sayings" are what serve as evidence for a founder's allegiance to the movement named after him/her, then there are plenty of examples from Selassie's own utterances that can pass muster, and this is not lost on Rastafarian adherents. The emperor's famous speech against racism and people's inhumanity to other humans, delivered in San Francisco on February 28, 1968, has been appropriately immortalized in Bob Marley's song "War":

> Until the philosophy which holds one race superior and another inferior is finally and
>   permanently discredited and abandoned;
> Until there are no longer first class and second class citizens of any nation . . .
> Until the colour of a man's skin is of no more significance than the colour of his eyes . . .
> Until the basic human rights are equally guaranteed to all without regard to race . . .
> Until that day, the dreams of lasting peace, world citizenship and the rule of international
>   morality will remain but a fleeting illusion to be pursued but never attained!
> Until the ignoble and unhappy regimes that now hold our brothers in Angola, in
> Mozambique, South Africa, in subhuman bondage have been toppled and utterly
>   destroyed . . .
> Until that day, the African Continent will not know peace.
> We Africans will fight, if necessary. And we know we will win as we are confident in
>   the victory of Good over Evil.

To many a Rasta believer who sees himself or herself as the targeted victim of the obscenities of the ages, the words of this song[35] carry the inspiration for battle against the "devil," as is the will of Jah, and for artistic celebration through a brilliant musical setting, in much the same way that Christian scriptural writings have inspired grand oratorios, cantatas, and settings to a whole range of psalms of the Hebrew Bible for Christian worship. Selassie's plea for decency and humanity may well have the impact on Rastafarian believers that the Sermon on the Mount and other sayings of Christ have had on Christians. Difficult as this may be for contemporary orthodox Christians to swallow, it is a fact of life that needs to be understood in a discourse where all ideas are allowed to contend, over against a tradition of scholarship that indulges the binary syndrome expressed as left or right, true believers or infidels, Christians or others.

The Rastafarian creed is considered by the brethren to be no less true or theologically legitimate than those of Christianity, whose historicity, by implication, allows for the manifestation of God on earth in a form appropriate to the felt needs of a people. Most Jews, lest we forget, are yet to be convinced that the Jesus of Christian theology is the Messiah; and their persistence in such (dis)belief has outlived Roman Catholicism's "righteous" denunciation of the Israelites for the "betrayal" that is linked to the Crucifixion. Rome and Tel Aviv have at least declared peace on this score, in celebration of ecumenism and twenty-first-century realities. God is in heaven, indeed, but all is not necessarily right with the world—not for the "black Israelites," as Rastafarians designate themselves. This designation draws on the Judaic dialectic of scattering, exile, and return—scattering via the trans-Atlantic slave trade, exile in plantation slavery (hence Babylon), and return to a promised land, seen as black Africa in general and Ethiopia in particular.

The Hebrew Bible remains an indispensable source of inspiration for Rastafarians (as for Jews), in the same way that the New Testament does for Christians. The Rastaman does make a compromise: at least one wing has long regarded Haile Selassie as the Christ reincarnate, signifying the Second Coming. This explains the prominence of Jesus in the Twelve Tribes of Israel's pantheon of divine icons and the seeming contradiction of Selassie worshipers seeking formal membership in the Ethiopian Orthodox Church (EOC)—which, of course, does not recognize the divinity of Haile Selassie but sees him as merely the earthly defender of the faith and head of the Coptic Church, in the same way that the British monarch is head of the Church of England. Many EOC adherents will remind others that Queen Elizabeth II (who also happens to be the most recent queen of Jamaica), is not divine.

Such contradictions may well prompt the call for scriptural exposition, which is certainly in the making for Rastafarians. They are not short of griots who may well become, in time, the "apostles" of their creed, which is finding interpretation from several points of departure. The parallels with the process that resulted in the continuing confrontation with the dominant religion—which, after all, served to *enslave* (as justification for greedy Christians wanting to civilize the pagans through the exploitation of labor) as well as *liberate* (as advocacy against inhumane practices) exiled Africans—are as provocative as they are challenging to Christian theological discourse and forays into its "hermeneutics and exegesis."

Chisholm bravely tries to meet the Rastafarians on one of the strongest grounds of their existence: the theological edifice of a divine Haile Selassie, King of Kings, Conquering Lion of Judah, and His Imperial Majesty—all titles of power, authority, recognition, and status. In fact, Chisholm raises several questions relative to the historical traditions behind the Ethiopian titles that are not unimportant for a work of this caliber. (See Chapter 10.) Such titles carry great sociocultural significance for a people long de-

prived of self-esteem and a sense of self-worth. The history of this deprecation, dehumanization (even of Christians by Christians, as it turned out), and deracination is what
gives the creed its point of power, its sense of urgency, and its persistence in its defiance
of certain received "truths"; for these truths manifest falsehoods in their application, re-
inforcing the Rastafarian quest for a sense of Being while in, and of, a world that for
half a millennium indulged in obscenities, depriving hosts of humanity of first-person
existence, including many who would wish to be the creators and determiners of their
own destiny.

The appeal to an authority beyond the reach of the perpetrators of such transgres-
sions was a necessary and handy strategy for survival and beyond. One authority had
to be God, the irreducible kernel of religious faith here seen as more than Sunday worship—indeed, as a sociocultural edifice and the essence of liberation and redemption. It
had to be more than the religion of the oppressor. It had to take form in the context of
the creolizing imperatives of a history of encounters between civilizations in superordinate-
subordinate relationships. It makes sense that the creolized form would wish to find
its own logic and consistency, to be sufficiently distinct from that of the superordinate
entity that it might make a difference.

Rastafari has indeed made a difference—not simply as religious expression (narrowly
defined), however compelling may be this mode of representation on the part of its adherents, but as an ontological and cosmological phenomenon of equally secular proportions, as Christianity was once claimed to be. Rastafari can claim to be the only major indigenous Caribbean-creole phenomenon of its kind (apart from Garveyism). All
other such "total systems" that have served Jamaica and the wider Caribbean in its
resistance-driven process of "becoming" have been imported, whether they be Christianity, political nationalism, militant trade unionism, socialism (in all its myriad
forms—from Fabian socialism through democratic socialism to Marxism-Leninism), or
latter-day market-forces liberalism. To argue from this that Rastafari cannot solve the
wide-ranging problems of Jamaica and is therefore useless is to ignore the fact that none
of the above importations, all of "pedigreed stature," has been able to do so either. The
case for tolerant, open, and frank discourse on a belief system such as Rastafari here
recommends itself.

The creed/movement/phenomenon of Rastafari has, in fact, drawn on all indexes of
culture known to humankind—language, religion, kinship patterns, artistic manifestations, political organization, and systems of production, distribution, and exchange.
This gives it inordinate inner strength and accounts for its worldwide impact among diasporic Africans as well as others. The refraction of all such phenomena through the
prism of Rastafari results in colors of different intensities, some stronger than others. It
cannot claim with any certainty that it has all the answers for human development, but
to deny the positive energy it brings to the quest is to perpetuate notions about the in-
ability of African peoples to create anything or to think through their destiny on their
own terms.

This book describes, evaluates, analyzes, and draws conclusions regarding the impact
of Rastafari on Jamaican, Caribbean, and global existence in the short period since its

formal appearance on the scene in the 1930s as a genuine twentieth-century liberation movement. That Rastafari—the people and the movement—should wish to assert a claim for inclusion in the dialogue, discourse, and determination of what happens to humankind over the next five hundred years is of great import to all of humanity engaged in the quest for civil society, democratic governance, and spiritual well-being. The proffered return of exiles, psychological or physical, may not be simply to Zion or Africa (real or imagined) but to all that constitutes planet Earth, which was meant for all of humankind to tenant in any case.[36]

Notes

1. George Eaton Simpson, "Political Cultism in West Kingston," *Social and Economic Studies* 4, 2 (1955): 133–49; also idem, "Culture Change and Reintegration Found in the Cults of West Kingston," *Proceedings of the American Philosophical Society* 99, 2 (1955): 89–92

2. Michael G. Smith, F. Roy Augier, and Rex Nettleford, *The Rastafari Movement in Kingston, Jamaica* (Kingston: Institute of Social and Economic Research, University College of the West Indies, 1960).

3. See Leonard Barrett, *The Rastafarians: A Study in Messianic Cultism in Jamaica* (Rio Piedras: Institute of Caribbean Studies, University of Puerto Rico, 1968); Wolfgang Bender, "Liberation from Babylon: Rasta Painters in Jamaica," in Jurgen Martini, ed., *Missile and Capsule* (Bremen, W. Ger.: Universitat, 1983), 129–34; Horace Campbell, *Rasta and Resistance: From Marcus Garvey to Walter Rodney* (London: Hansib, 1985); Robert A Hill, "Leonard P. Howell and Millenarian Visions in Early Rastafari," *Jamaica Journal* 16, 1 (1983): 24–39; John P. Homiak, "The Mystic Revelation of Rasta Far-Eye: Visionary Communication in a Prophetic Movement," in Barbara Tedlock, ed., *Dreaming: Anthropological and Psychological Approaches* (Cambridge: Cambridge University Press, 1985), 220–45; idem, "The Ancient of Days Seated Black: Eldership, Oral Tradition and Rituals in Rastafari Culture" (Ph.D. diss., Brandeis University, 1985); Sheila Kitzinger, "Protest and Mysticism: The Rastafari Cult of Jamaica," *Journal for the Scientific Study of Religion* 8, 2 (1969): 240–62; Peter M. Michaels, *Rastafari* (Munich: Trikont Verlag, 1980); Rex Nettleford, *Identity, Race and Protest* (New York: William Morrow & Co., 1972); Joseph Owens, *Dread: The Rastafarians of Jamaica*, with introduction by Rex Nettleford (Kingston: Sangster's Book Stores, 1976); Karl Erich Weiss, "Die Rastafari-bewegung auf Jamaica: Entwicklungsphasen und Ausdrucksformen einer Gegenkultur" (M.A. thesis, Münster: Philosophischen Fakultät, Westfalischen Wihelmus, 1981); Carole D. Yawney, "Lions in Babylon: The Rastafarians of Jamaica as a Visionary Movement" (Ph.D. diss., Department of Anthropology, McGill University, Montreal, 1978).

4. Among Rastafarians who have written about Rastafarian beliefs, with expositions and interpretations (exegesis and hermeneutics) of the creed and its application to lived reality, are I. Ras Dizzy, "The Rastas Speak," *Caribbean Quarterly* 13, 4 (1967): 41–42; idem, *Vision of Black Slaves* (Kingston: I. Ras Dizzy, 1971); E.S.P. Mcpherson and Leachim Semaj, "Rasta Chronology," in Rex Nettleford, ed., *Caribbean Quarterly Monograph: Rastafari* (Kingston: Caribbean Quarterly, University of the West Indies, 1985): 116–19; Leachim Semaj, "Rastafari: From Religion to Social Theory," *Caribbean Quarterly* 26, 4 (1980): 22–23; Maureen Rowe, "The Woman in Rastafari," *Caribbean Quarterly* 26, 4 (1980): 13–24; Jabulani I. Tafari, "The Rastafari—Suc-

cessors of Marcus Garvey," *Caribbean Quarterly* 26, 4 (1980): 191–205; Garth White, "Rudie O Rudie!" *Caribbean Quarterly* 13, 3 (1967): 39–44.

5. See Frank Jan van Dijk, "The Twelve Tribes of Israel: Rasta and the Middle Class," *New West Indian Guide* 62, 1–2 (1980): 1–26: also idem, *Jahmaica: Rastafari and Jamaican Society, 1930–1990* (Utrecht: ISOR, 1993).

6. Ika Tafari, "Rastafari: A Divine Reality," *Sunday Gleaner,* December 24, 1995, 8C.

7. Ian Boyne, "Rastafarians Need Systematic Theology," *Sunday Gleaner,* December 10, 1995, 1D–2D.

8. Ibid.

9. Peter L. Berger, *The Heretical Imperative: Contemporary Possibilities of Religious Affirmation* (New York: Doubleday Anchor Books, 1979), 165.

10. Ibid., 166.

11. Ika Tafari, "Rastafari," 8C.

12. Ibid.

13. Marcus Mosiah Garvey, speech at Menelik Hall, Nova Scotia, 1937, quoted by Ken Jones, "The Black in the Flag," *Daily Gleaner,* April 4, 1996. Garvey remains a major "prophet" to adherents of the Rastafarian faith, providing inspiration for beliefs and utterances by believers. In his "Image of God" (1922) speech, Garvey said, "We, as Negroes, have found a new ideal. Whilst our God has no color, yet it is human to see everything through one's own spectacles. We have only now started out (late though it be) to see our God through our own spectacles. The God of Isaac and the God of Jacob let Him exist for the race that believes in the God of Isaac and the God of Jacob. We Negroes believe in the God of Ethiopia, the everlasting God—God the Father, God the Son, and God the Holy Ghost, the One God of all ages. That is the God in whom we believe, but we shall worship Him *through the spectacles of Ethiopia*" (*The Philosophy and Opinions of Marcus Garvey,* comp. Amy Jacques Garvey [London: Frank Cass & Co., 1967], 34). The doctrinal tension between Ethiopianism and Christian orthodoxy is manifested in this statement by Garvey.

14. Bob Marley, "Redemption Songs," on *Uprising,* Island Records ILPS 9596, 1980. See also Ken Jones, "Celebrating These August Occasions," *Daily Gleaner,* July 12, 1996.

15. Boyne, "Rastafarians Need Systematic Theology," 1D–2D.

16. Berger, *Heretical Imperative,* 166.

17. R. H. Tawney, *Religion and the Rise of Capitalism* (London: John Murray, 1926).

18. See the hymn "All things bright and beautiful," words by Cecil F. Frances Alexander (1818–1895), tune by W. H. Monk (1923–1989), in *African Methodist Episcopal Church Hymnal* (Nashville: A.M.E. Church, 1984), hymn 434. The Presbyterian hymnal *The Hymnbook* (Atlanta: The Presbyterian Church in the United States, 1952), interestingly enough, omits the stanza cited. Church of England hymnals also no longer carry that stanza.

19. Barry Chevannes, *Rastafari: Roots and Ideology* (Syracuse: N.Y.: Syracuse University Press, 1994).

20. Rex Nettleford, *Inward Stretch, Outward Reach: A Voice from the Caribbean* (London: Macmillan, 1993), esp. the chapter "The Battle for Space," 80–89.

21. Chevannes, *Rastafari,* 18.

22. The best known among these are Bob Marley (the don of reggae music), Jimmy Cliff (a highly influential forerunner), Peter Tosh (the integrity of whose rage against downpression is legendary), Bunny Wailer, Dennis Brown, Gregory Isaacs, Bob Andy (the talented lyricist and songwriter), and their "dancehall" successors, such as Buju Banton and Garnet Silk. Among the well-

known female reggae artists of the Rastafarian faith are Rita Marley and Judy Mowatt of the I-Threes, who were the backup singers to Bob Marley. Marley's international success identified reggae with the Rastafarian movement, whose message of resistance to oppression and injustice inspired the fight to bring down the Berlin Wall, the struggle for the liberation of Zimbabwe, and the release of South Africa from the jaws of apartheid.

23. See the works listed in note 3 and note 5, above, especially van Dijk, *Jahmaica,* 453–68.

24. This is a reference to the practice, widespread among middle-class youth, of adopting the dreadlocks hairstyle and "ragamuffin" styles of dress, but without commitment to the religious tenets of the movement. A "bourgeois lifestyle" is no longer regarded as a contradiction to the dread look, and knitted caps and woolen belts form part of "Rasta chic" wear, to be found in upscale boutiques both in the Caribbean and outside the region.

25. See Vera Lawrence Hyatt and Rex Nettleford, eds., *Race Discourse and the Origin of the Americas* (Washington, D.C.: Smithsonian Institution Press, 1995), 3.

26. Berger, *Heretical Imperative,* 168–69.

27. See Clinton Chisholm's "The Rasta-Selassie-Ethiopian Connections," Chapter 10 in this book. See also idem, "Rastas' Claim about Selassie Is Fiction," (Barbados) *Sunday Advocate,* July 2, 1988, D3; idem, "The Lineage of Haile Selassie," *Jamaica Record,* July 29, 1989, 11); idem, "Emperor Haile Selassie: God or Godfearer? Rastafarianism Evaluated," audiotape recording (Spanish Town, Jamaica, 1990).

28. *Profile,* weekly television program hosted by Ian Boyne, Jamaica Broadcasting Corporation (JBC), Sunday (1996). The program involving Mutabaruka and Chisholm aired also on radio in June 1996.

29. See Chapter 10.

30. Within a few days of the news of Selassie's passing (August 27, 1975), Bob Marley recorded the single "Jah Lives." The lyrics read:

Selassie lives! Jah, Jah lives, children!

Jah lives! Jah Jah lives!

Fools saying in their hearts

"Rasta your God is dead."

But I-an-I know evermore

Dreaded it shall be, dreaded and dread.

31. See *Time,* December 18, 1995, 62–69, 70, for informative and controversial discussions of the fact-versus-faith debate. In the article "Are the Bible's Stories True?" Michael D. Lenonick writes, "A host of scholars suspect that Abraham, Isaac and Jacob, Judaism's traditional founders, never existed; many doubt the tales of slavery in Egypt and the Exodus; and relatively few modern historians belive in Joshua's conquest of Jericho and the rest of the Promised Land. In the most extreme view, all of the above are complete fabrications, invented centuries after the supposed fact." He goes on to explain that William Foxwell Albright's attempts in the 1920s "to confirm Old Testament stories with independent and archaeological evidence" made biblical archaeology into "a disciplined and scientific enterprise"; but as Dead Sea Scrolls curator emeritus M. Broshi reportedly said, while archaeology throws light on the Bible, "it has no business trying to prove it." John Elson, in his article "The New Testament Unsolved Mysteries," repeats the queries on the agenda as follows: "Was Jesus of Nazareth a real person who trod the dusty roads of Palestine in the first century? Or were his life, death and resurrection, as recorded in the four Gospels, events that belong entirely to the realm of faith?" Many devout Christian believers do not care, since "for them, the divinely inspired testimony of the Gospels is infinitely

more reliable than any evidence unearthed by the hammers of archaeology." See also Carsten Peter Thiede and Matthew D'Ancona, *Jesus Papyrus* (London: Orion Publishing Group, 1996).

32. See Joan Blackwell, "The Tomb That Dare Not Speak Its Name," *Sunday Times News Review*, March 31, 1996, 14.

33. See Chapter 10.

34. See Matthew 16:16–20, where Jesus, who understood he lived in a real world, warned Peter, his disciple, not to tell anyone that he was the Christ (the so-called messianic secret).

35. See also liner notes to Bob Marley's *Rastaman Vibrations*, Island Record RSL-PS-BM-3066-A.

36. Written from the Elmina Castle, Central Region of Ghana, August 1996.

19 The Black Biblical Hermeneutics of Rastafari

NATHANIEL SAMUEL MURRELL AND
LEWIN WILLIAMS

Rastafarians take the study of the Bible seriously, cite lengthy passages in their oral and written discourse as well as in casual conversations, and "spend long hours discussing the meaning of various passages."[1] Biblical texts are cited with predictable frequency throughout the *Rastafari Manifesto*, in support of the proposed Rastafarian theocratic government policy,[2] as well as in *The Promised Key* and *The Living Testament of Ras Tafari*. As Joseph Owens observed, the Bible has a preeminent place in Rastafarian life and thought because, for them, it is a book written by and about Blacks. As a result, the biblical materials pervade almost every form of Rastafarian discourse. For this reason, it is almost impossible to discuss any Rastafarian doctrine without reference to Scripture.

Rastas' excessive use of the Bible forces one to raise several questions: Is there a Rastafarian hermeneutic or hermeneutics? What are the primary characteristics of Rastas' interpretation of the Bible? How does the Rastafarian hermeneutics differ from traditional Christian approaches to biblical materials? Of what significance is Rasta hermeneutics to Caribbean theological reflection? We examine these questions in the sections that follow.

How Do Rastas View and Use the Bible?

Rastafarians do not approach the Bible with a disinterested *tabula rasa*, or blank slate, or with an unbiased mind, hoping to receive objective theological truths from the Divine. Instead, they make known their biases and prejudices in favor of biblical materials that advance a hermeneutics of Blackness. Rastas are not schooled in Western theology or equipped with great commentaries for biblical expositions. They have little or no knowledge of the original languages of the Bible (although many Rastas study Amharic) or of the Western tradition of biblical criticism. Like many among the poor

Jamaican masses, some Rastas are barely literate. Yet they bring intriguing creativity to bear upon the Scriptures simply because of who they are and the position from which they interact with the stories and situations represented in the Bible.

To Rastas, the biblical personalities, writers, and common people were all black, and the books were all "written to give a lesson to the black people of all ages about the proper way to live and worship Jah [God]."[3] But "the Europeans, after enslaving the black man, took his scriptures and attempted to translate them, even though they hardly understood the language in which they were writen"—the Amharic language.[4] In so doing, Whites twisted the Scriptures to favor their race at the expense of black people. White translators and interpreters used the Bible to support their ideology of white superiority and to justify slavery in "Babylon" (Jamaica and the West). "King James the I of Britain, a white man, translated the Bible," from Amharic, "distorting and confusing its message"; but to those who, through Ras Tafari, are given inspiration and prophetic insights, "the false passages put in by the white man for his own purposes are easily detected."[5]

But Rastas would have none of this; they have no use for what they regard as the anti-black or European (white) interpretation of the Bible, which sanctioned the enslavement and oppression of black people for over three hundred years. In the words of Psalm 137:1–4, "By the rivers of Babylon there we sat down, yea, we wept, when we remembered Zion" (KJV)—lyricized, modified somewhat, and used as a theme song—the Rastafarians voice their anger against the evils that slavery and colonialism created for their victims. With their "hermeneutic of suspicion," they are selective in their use of biblical materials, so as not to propagate "white distortions" of the Bible[6] and continue the ideology of Babylon. Rastafari's hermeneutics creates something new. As Leonard Howell puts it in *The Promised Key,* one of the earliest Rastafarian documents, "All that Ethiopians have to do now, is build anew. Get out a new dictionary and a new Bible, and new Board of Education and Money mint. The outfit shall be called Black Supremacy; signed by His and Her Majesty Ras Tafari and Queen Omega the King of Kings, head of this world."[7]

Of course, as Frank Jan van Dijk noted, not all Rastas hold to the view that Europeans distorted the Scriptures. The Twelve Tribes of Israel, for example, accept the Bible from Genesis to Revelation without any restrictions or qualifications; even the Scofield Version of the Bible (1967) is regarded as a favorite. To them, "the Bible is everything. . . . Members of the Twelve Tribes often call themselves Bible-students. Every word, every sentence is carefully studied, a chapter a day. It takes about three and a half years to finish the Bible that way."[8] Says van Dijk, the view that "the white man corrupted the Bible when he translated it from the original Amharic is nonsense, according to the Twelve Tribes. Every word of the book is true and only by studying it over and over again can one come to the wisdom and knowledge of Rastafari."[9] Contrary to Owens's view that, "in contrast to the fundamentalists, the Rastafarians shy away from any strictly literal interpretation of the scriptures,"[10] Rastas have not completely freed themselves from a literal reading of Scripture; many Rastas also have a strict fundamentalist view of the Bible. There is also no unified Rastafarian hermeneutic, but different approaches to the Scriptures.

While for some Rastas the Bible has its own inherent authority, for others the authority derives not from the Bible intrinsically (though it points one to God) but from the validation that comes from His Imperial Majesty and his "depiction" in Scripture—what is seen as the relevance of biblical text to local situations—and Rastas' own sense of inspiration derived from many sources, especially the Hebrew Bible. Interpretation, to a large extent, is left to the individual, and the Bible is understood as "a history and a prophecy" rather than "a religious text." Essentially, Rastas operate a canon within the biblical canon: "the Bible contains the Word of God, but Scripture shows that half of this has not been written save in your hearts."[11] The Scripture is like an open canon, in which Rastas' new insights are as inspired as the written text. For this reason, the books that most Christians consider apocryphal are very important to Rastas, since, as Owens says, they "reveal a certain portion of what has been hidden by the white man up to now, but that there is still much more to be revealed."[12]

In spite of the Rastas' claims of white distortions within the Bible and in European interpretation of it ("Western theology"), the Scriptures still provide "instruction and inspiration for the true sons of Rastafari."[13] Rastafarians use the Bible to address their specific historical, economic, political, and social situation while seeking ways to express and interpret the epoch-making rise of Selassie as a salvific event for black people.[14] Rastas move freely between the figurative and literal senses of the Bible and search for texts that they believe speak to specific contemporary events and issues. They "see clear parallels between ancient biblical and modern times" and place both past and current events "within the biblical context."[15] Different personalities and events portrayed in the Scriptures are seen as present in Rastas' own concrete historical situation.[16]

Essentially, Rastas have adopted an Africa-centered and "free-style" reading of biblical materials; but they are not united on matters of biblical interpretation, and except for the practice of "citing-up" the Bible, they have not defined or developed a consistent methodology for interpreting biblical texts. The art of citing-up places less emphasis on syntax, context, and literary genre of the text and more on the speaker, the setting, and the scene. This citing-up involves a combination of proof text, running oral and written commentaries (in somewhat of a rabbinic style), associations of traditional myths and stories with contemporary parallels, double-intentional (i.e., having double layers of meaning) symbols, and very loose, free-style interpretations of biblical materials. An example of this kind of approach to biblical texts is the discourse in the *Rastafari Manifesto* (*EATUP*) on the word *herb*, as found in the Bible, in defense of the use of ganja. The authors of *EATUP* wrote, "JAH causeth the grass to grow for the cattle, AND HERB FOR THE SERVICE OF MAN" (Psalm 104:14). They continue, "Behold I have given you *every green herb bearing seed*" and "*every green herb for meat*" (Genesis 1:29–30).[17] Under the subtitle "Biblical Herbal Declaration Quotes 1–10," the authors of *EATUP* cite a number of texts (Deuteronomy 32:2; Genesis 9:3–5; Psalm 104:14; Isaiah 1:18; Job 38:25–27; Genesis 2:4–5; Revelation 22:2; Proverbs 15:17; and many others) in which the word *Herb* appears and is given a dual or double-intentional meaning by Rastafarians, of both providing food and supplying biblical warrant or sanction for the smoking of the "chillum pipe."[18]

Such free-style practice often yields a novel and creative use of the Bible in narrative form. According to Rasta author John M. Moodie, for example, "Africa is the birth-place of civilization. The Bible shows her to be the Garden of Eden. . . . Adam and Eve must have been citizens of Africa." Moodie continues: "Traveling through Africa, we find Abraham," who "had two sons, Ismael and Isaac. It was from Isaac that this great Nation was to be formed. Jah told him go to the land of Canaan and he will make him a great nation."[19] This free-style adaptation of biblical text and the different ways of understanding the Bible make outlining a definitive Rastafarian hermeneutics quite a challenge. In this chapter, we have chosen to discuss Rastas' use of the Bible in their doctrinal discourse in the context of the black biblical hermeneutics.

The Hermeneutics of Black Superiority

> The Black Supremacy on triumphant soil of the world's capital.
> The new Bible Land, the Isles of Spring. The same country that the Anarchy
> called Jamaica British West Indies.
> —*The Promised Key*

As Owens says, "Many statements of the brethren . . . indicate a belief in the essential superiority of the black race." For example, he cites statements such as: "Black men were civilized when the white man was living in the caves of northern Europe. The throne of Ethiopia is older than the throne of St. George."[20] Before they became ac-commodating of Whites, Rastas found defending this thesis both psychologically and theologically necessary.[21] At a time when Jamaica was seeing many of its sons and daughters searching for light-skinned mates, students returning from abroad with white life partners, and black women shamelessly bleaching their skin for a lighter complex-ion, Rastafarians not only proclaimed pride in their Blackness but hailed it as superior to Whiteness. This black pride is derived from two historical traditions, namely, Mar-cus Garvey's Ethiopianist Black Nationalism and biblical interpretation.

Garvey's Influence on Rasta Hermeneutics

Although Marcus Garvey detested Rastafarian doctrines, his Afrocentric or Ethiopianist ideas—which, as Clinton Hutton and Nathaniel Samuel Murrell noted in Chapter 2, above, had a powerful impact on Rastafari's political thought and psychological con-sciousness—had a direct influence on Rastafarian hermeneutics. Garvey grew up in a Jamaican Christian environment where the Bible was held in very high regard. As a Black Nationalist leader, he loved the Bible and was very fond of quoting and interpreting biblical passages in light of his African consciousness and Pan-Africanist vision. He denied that black people are portrayed in the Bible as a cursed race (as a result of Noah's notorious curse of Canaan, Ham's son) or that they were predestined to be slaves of Whites as the slave master claimed. Garvey spoke constantly about the "black man's God" (in contrast to the God of the white slave master) and defended the idea that Christ is a black man.

The Black Nationalist was heard popularizing the biblical statement, echoed again and again in the works of African American church leaders of the late 1700s and 1800s (Daniel Coker, Martin Delany, Bishop James W. Hood, and others), "But the promise is that princes shall come out of Egypt, Ethiopia shall stretch out her hands unto God."[22] This promise, for example, inspired courage in Martin Delany when he wrote, "'Princes shall come out of Egypt; Ethiopia shall soon stretch out her hands unto God.' With the fullest reliance upon this blessed promise, I humbly go forward—I may repeat—the grandest prospect for the regeneration of a people that ever was presented in the history of the world. . . . With faith in the promise, and hope from this vision, surely there is nothing to doubt or fear."[23] The black theological tradition thus originated not with Garvey but with Pan-Africanist Dr. Love of Jamaica and U.S. Black Nationalists David Walker, Martin Delany, Alexander Crummel, Bishop Henry McNeal Turner, and others. Turner was the first theologian to declare that God is black[24] and thereby indirectly laid the foundation for Garvey's thinking of a black Christ (the 1920s), Countee Cullen's poem "The Black Christ" (1929), Albert Cleage's black Messiah, and James Cone's black Christ and black theology.[25]

Garvey was an admirer and protégé of Dr. Love, but whether the Jamaican-born Pan-Africanist was aware of the writings or theological thinking of the American Black Nationalists noted above is questionable. Garvey, however, used effectively the black perspective on the Bible to address the problem of racism and segregation, both in the United States and Jamaica. The black presence in the Bible was at the heart of Garvey's belief that being black is not an evil thing or punishment. Garvey's Afrocentric interpretation of the Bible and his Ethiopianist vision and philosophy of Blackness, which had a powerful impact on Garveyites both in Jamaica and the United States, also influenced the Rastafarians.[26] Tennyson Smyth (Ras-J-Tesfa), for example, portrays Garvey as the greatest contemporary prophet of Jah: "Now it came to pass that in the third century, fifth and seventh years of Black Enslavement (B.E.), there came from among the people of color, a man of JAH, whose name was Marcus Mosiah Garvey. He came a witness bearing witness of the Light, that all people of color may see the path to Ire Ites [Jah Rastafari or God]."[27] In his free-style citing-up of Scripture, Smyth further eulogizes Garvey: "He was not the Light, but was sent to bear witness of the Light which lighteth every man that cometh into the world of darkness, for he was like a voice calling out in the west; prepare ye the way of the Lord." Smyth concludes, "He was a man of destiny, the silent will of JAH, whose time had come to fulfill himself and purpose. His was the task of restoring that which was taken from his people at birth, as was that of another before him, spoken unto by He who was The Sender, in such a manner: 'Son of man I will send thee to my children to a rebellious nation that hath rebelled against me.'"[28]

Biblical Narratives and Black Superiority

As Rex Nettleford noted in Chapter 18, Rastas hijacked Christian theology and Scripture and imbued them with new exegetical interpretation for their own self-definition and identity. Most Rastafarians employ a polemic biblical interpretation in defense of black superiority against centuries of extensive use of Scripture in support of racism and white oppression. The most well known (if not notorious) portion of the Bible used to support racism and slavery is the alleged curse of Ham, narrated in Genesis 9:18–27. Ham was the father of Cush, who is seen as representing black people of the world.[29] The traditional interpretation of the story is that while Noah was intoxicated, Ham gazed on his father's nakedness and enjoyed the spectacle of nudity at his father's expense.[30] His older brothers, who apparently knew what the appropriate response was in that culture, graciously covered their father without repeating Ham's mistake. Because of Shem and Japheth's action, Noah blessed them; but Ham, whom some scholars believe was the father of the black race, was cursed with perpetual servitude. (Of course, Canaan was cursed rather than Ham.) As a consequence, black people were heartlessly plunged into the anguish of whips, chains, impoverishment, alienation, segregation, and discrimination. Rastafari will have none of this but, instead, reverses the categories relative to the "cursed race."

Rastafarians do not attempt to discredit the story with a plea for its nonhistorical value or advance theories about its inappropriateness to the African experience.[31] Immediately after the so-called curse of Ham in the biblical text is the appearance, in chapter 10 in Genesis, of a genealogy in which Cush, the son of Ham, fathers the world's first mighty man, Nimrod. A rejection of one story would mean the rejection of the next, but the Nimrod story is far too important for Rastas to lose. Several years ago, Nimrod became a sex symbol in Jamaica: the male with a large genital organ, who showed skillful wantonness in its sexual use, was spoken of as Nimrod. Although some Rastas were regarded as sexually macho, especially under the "rudeboy culture," Rastafarians may not glorify sexual powers (or regard their males as "black studs") more than others do, but they are impressed with the power that Nimrod adds to the argument for black superiority.

Rastafarians also show no interest in repositioning the cursed son in Western theology, so that Canaan becomes the proper object of the curse. While some Rastas believe that Canaan was cursed, others hold that Ham was cursed. Moodie turns the metaphor around and says, "Canaan, son of Ham, enslaved Shem in Egypt and . . . Canaan was enslaved by Shem in Jerusalem, being the 'servants of servants'." Then, "Japhet enslaved Shem and Ham in the modern world in the Western Hemisphere."[32] On whomever Rastas place Noah's curse, they believe it was imposed upon black people, except that divine liberation from the curse took place long ago; it was not meant to last forever because it is not like Jah to punish forever. As for the protracted period in which black people were held captive in slavery, Rastafarians hold the white establishment responsible for prolonging the condition, contrary to the divine charter and will. In a conversation on the campus of the University of the West Indies in 1994, a Rasta brethren told Murrell, "Jah's design is that the black man should live in freedom and not bondage. He should be first and not last, the head and not the tail."

What Rastas see Scripture doing for black ascendancy is only a part of the story; how they treat the claim to white supremacy is another. Leonard Howell, for example, believed that Blacks who were cursed in the Noah-Ham story were afflicted with a disease that turned them white, thus giving birth to the white race. (See *The Promised Key*, also discussed and presented in Chapter 21). In a rather bizarre, sexist, and racist way of thinking, Howell views Eve as the mother of all white Europeans and the mother of all evil; as a result of her sin, the alleged white curse affects the entire human race. But an "interesting" Rasta logic somehow manages to shield the black race from inheriting that curse—even though they are seen as the true descendants of the people of the Hebrew Bible—a clear contradiction in terms and an attempt to "eat one's cake and still have it." That *The Promised Key* is the source of this reverse racism and discrimination is not in doubt. Howell said, "The Adamic apple tree, my dear leper your name is Adam-Abraham Anglo Saxon apple tree, that looks pretty and respectable to your eyes don't it? Yes indeed gross beauty are all white people if you please." So Whiteness is a European curse that dates back to creation and the eating of the forbidden fruit. According to this hermeneutic, Adam, Abraham, and Moses, from whom the Europeans allegedly descended, are all cursed Whites. But in another breath, Abraham and Moses are black and fathers of the black race. So although Blacks are the true Israelite descendants of Abraham, they are not inheritors of the "white Abrahamic curse." What a hermeneutical scandal![33]

While some traditional interpretations of the Bible saw Blackness as a curse (Noah's curse), Rastas reverse the racial epithet so that Whiteness becomes the world's curse. Human life began in the Horn of Africa, the world's first people were all black, and human beings were meant to remain one color, black. As Rasta John Moodie theorizes, "The advent of white skin came as a result of another divine curse, the curse of Miriam" (Numbers 12:1–10).[34] According to the biblical narrative, Miriam and Aaron spoke disparagingly about their brother Moses. God then called the three of them together and, after rebuking Miriam and Aaron, smote Miriam with leprosy and her skin beame white. For some Rastas, the case takes on its own feasibility and character when the reason for Miriam's "deceitfulness" is observed: Moses' brother and sister criticized him for marrying a black Ethiopian woman. In Rastas' view, not only does the punishment for that criticism suit the crime, but it also shows that God is on the side of black people.[35] So, in spite of the scandalous indictment of biblical traditions, the Hebrew ancestors, and white people, Howell and other Rastafarians make suspect their own racist thesis by regarding the early Israelites as black people and relying heavily on biblical materials to develop their messianism and other basic doctrines in support of their idea of black biblical connections.

The attempt to identify and give contemporary relevance to the black presence in the Bible is not the private domain of Rastafarians. Within the last decade, several Bible scholars[36] have given this subject much attention. Howard University Bible scholar Cain Hope Felder says:

> There is an impressive array of Black people found in the Old Testament, beginning with those in Gen. 9 and 10, or I Chron. 1; Hagar's Egyptian origin in Gen. 16; the Cushite wife of Moses in Num. 12, Jer. 38–39, Isa. 37; perhaps even Zephaniah the son of Cushi (Zeph. 1:1; q.v. 2:12; 3:10) and Queen of Sheba (I Kings 10; I Chron. 9); Aaron's grandson, regarded as ancestor of the Zadokite priesthood (Exod. 6:25, Num. 25:6, Ps. 106:30); one of the sons of Eli (I Sam. 1:3; 2:34); and the Egyptian named Phienehas, literally meaning the Nubian.[37]

But Rastafarians go beyond the identification of Blacks in the biblical text and the association of the black experience with those of the ancient Israelites; Rastas go on to "blacken" biblical peoples and biblical theology. That is, Rastafarians believe that they are the very Israelites depicted in the Bible. According to Mikael Kezehemohonenow, a Rasta brethren, "The people of Jah spoken of in the Bible are Africans and black people everywhere." Mikael continues, "Rastafarians look very much to their I-frican identity and [who pronounces] themselves 'reborn Israelites' (with proof) that they are [the] 144,000 who, in Revelation 7:4, Jah has said he would [raise] up in the last days. He [the Rastaman] identifies himself with the Ethiopian Orthodox Church and is a firm upholder of the church."[38] Owens recorded a group of Rasta followers of Prince Emmanuel Edwards as saying, "The black Africans of today are seen to be the sole representatives of that chosen people whose history is recounted in the Bible."[39] Rasta author John Moodie attempts to trace the historical movement of black people (Israelites) in the Hebrew Bible with an embellished and fictitious story that ends with Solomon, the queen of Sheba, so-called Makeda, and Menelik, all of whom are supposed to be black.[40] The main purpose of the story is to show that the ancient Israelites were all black, that Solomon was black, and that through Solomon descended black people, especially Haile Selassie. As Owens noted, Rastas find this theme of Blackness in the Song of Songs 1; Lamentations 4:8; Joel 2:8; Habakkuk 2:10; Job 30:30; Psalm 119:83; Jeremiah 14:2; Revelation 1:4;[41] and other places in the Bible.

Rastas believe not only that the people of the Bible were black but that God is also black and that the name and worship of JAH (God) originated with the black race. Biblical support for the blackness of God is found in Jeremiah 8:21: "For the hurt of the daughter of my people am I hurt; I am black; astonishment hath taken hold of me" (KJV). Rastas refer to God as "Jah," which is the abbreviated form of Jahweh (Yahweh) a name derived from the "tetragrammaton" (four-letter word) YHWH of the Hebrew Bible. They lift the "Jah" directly out of the King James Version of the Bible, which reads "Sing unto God, sing praises to his name: extol him that rideth upon the heavens by his name JAH, and rejoice before him" (Psalm 68:4). This three-letter word is then applied to all occurrences of the word *God* in the Bible. For example, without giving Bible references, *EATUP* opens with an adaptation of the biblical text: "JAH has spoken Once; Twice have I heard this; Power belongeth Unto the Most High. Shall a man rob JAH? Yet have ye robbed I . . . Saith the Most High." This is repeated in the *Rastafari Manifesto*'s "Prayer of Investiture of Office" for head of state.[42] Under its "National Ministerial Portfolio" the *Manifesto* reads: "JAH causeth the grass to grow for the cattle, AND HERB FOR THE SERVICE OF MAN" (Psalm 104:14).[43] Immediately after citing John 1:1, "In the beginning was JAH Word, and the Word was with JAH, and the Word was JAH," the *Manifesto* devotes several pages of citing-up to the occurrences of *Jah* in the Bible, especially in the Psalms. This *Jah*, according to Rastas, is the "Blackman's God."

Rastas as Black Jews, or Falashas

By virtue of what they understand Ethiopia to mean in relation to Israel and the Rastas' relation to Jah Ras Tafari Selassie I, not only do Rastas share a religious association with the ancient Israelites but, a Kingston Rasta informant told Lewin Williams in

1994, they believe they become one with the suffering people of Israel, share in the lineage of Solomon through Selassie, and partake of the Divine, who indwells "I-an-I." Of course, for the Jewish experience to be adopted by other groups of people using the same Hebrew Scriptures is not unusual. Christians have done it for more than nineteen hundred years. Since the days of apostolic preaching in the first century, Christians adopted (or claimed) the Hebrew Scriptures as their own biblical tradition. From the large corpus of sacred Hebrew writings, Christian theologians such as Paul, Peter, John, James, Origen, Jerome, Augustine, and those who succeeded them developed and interpreted their theology, which charters the relationships of humans to one another and to the Divine, through a hermeneutic of common association. As the Scriptures describe and address situations that resemble contemporary conditions, Christian readers see the references in concrete terms and make general applications according to their needs. To a certain extent, the Christian church even speaks of itself as the new, spiritual Israel. So Rastafarians are following a long Christian tradition, but with a difference.

In their theological thinking, Rastafarians were influenced by different Christian and non-Christian groups that share conflicting views about the Bible and the origin of black people. One such group is the Royal Order of Ethiopian Hebrews, or Black Jews—an Afrocentric organization of black Jews that was born in the 1920s (but became incorporated in 1930) and rose out of the flames of the Garvey Black Nationalist movement in Harlem. As George Eaton Simpson noted, a controversial prophet, F. S. Cherry, was the first leader of the Black Jews: "He regarded white Jews as frauds and interlopers and maintained that his followers were the true Israelites of the Bible." Simpson adds, "In the period 1919–1930, at least eight Black Jewish cults arose in Harlem. . . . The rabbis differentiated themselves from one another largely by their interpretations of orthodox Jewish law and custom."[44]

To complete the circle of Hebraic connection, Black Jews claim to be Ethiopian Hebrews, or Falashas, who were robbed of their real names and religion during their European enslavement in the Americas. For this reason, Barbadian-born rabbi Arnold J. Ford and other black Jewish leaders often recommended a name change for their followers and a rejection of the white Christian religion. According to Simpson, their interests centered on their cultic rituals and the "belief that they had recovered their true name, identity, and language." In fact, "rejecting what they called the white man's religion and asserting their independence of his moral principles gave Black Jews a feeling of superiority in a world where black people had long been subjected to scorn and discriminatory treatment by whites."[45]

The founders of Rastafari and other Caribbean Garveyites had direct contact with Black Jews in Harlem. In fact, the cross-fertilization between these U.S.-based Garveyites and Jamaicans has been underestimated. Ford converted to Judaism before he joined the Universal Negro Improvement Association (UNIA), and "most of his Beth B'nai congregation came to the Garvey movement with him," since "he had hoped that Judaism would become the official religion of the UNIA."[46] The black consciousness teachings of Garvey and the Falashas and their dialogue with Ethiopians later made it easy for the founders of Rastafari to make a vital connection to Haile Selassie and the Hebrew Scriptures. As a leader of the Black Jewish Order, one of the many black Jewish groups in New York City, Rabbi Wentworth A. Matthews claimed, "[Blacks] are in truth Ethiopian Hebrews; Jacob was a Black man; Blacks are descendants of the union between King Solomon and the Queen of Sheba, which established the royal line down to the present Haile Selassie; and Judaism is their own and the one true religion."[47]

The Falashas' Connection to Selassie

The Falashas, defined as black Jews, have, in recent times, become the ward of Israel. But a controversy exists regarding their class structure. For years, scholars have studied and speculated on the origin of the Falashas. Interestingly enough, despite their skin color, Falashas are often confused with Oriental Jews. In addition, Falashas are noted for a way of life that is quite proto-Jewish,[48] and which influenced Rastafarian cultic observances.

There are many facets to their beliefs and practices. For example, Falashas are more Jewish in their observances of dietary laws than are many modern Jews. Not only do they not eat the foods forbidden in the Jewish Scripture, but they also perform a ceremonial washing before meals. Their wedding ceremonies, which resemble the ancient Palestinian custom, last for a whole week. Following the ancient practice in the Hebrew Bible, Falashic women are isolated during their period of menstruation—the Rastafarians follow the same practice, as written in the book of Leviticus, in prohibiting their women from attending the "I-ssembly" during menstruation. Falashas have a high regard for the family unit, and as a result, scarcely any infidelity exists among them. By the same token, the divorce rate is very low, since adultery is the primary cause for divorce. As with Jewish people, education is a high priority for the Falashas, and most local teaching is done by a priest whose origin they trace back to Aaron. They have strict forms of worship and observe the Sabbath and Jewish feasts such as the Passover (with the paschal lamb and unleavened bread) and also the new moons. The Falashas are monotheistic in their beliefs, hoping, like Israel, that in time God will send the Messiah.[49] Perhaps most significant of the available information on the Falashas is the claim that their roots lie in Israel.[50]

Some Ethiopian experiences have been more pleasant than others, but Ethiopia's close association with Ancient Israel dates back to the earliest times and cannot be denied. Ethiopians served in the Jewish military (2 Samuel 18:21); Moses married an Ethiopian (Numbers 12:1); an Ethiopian, Ebed-melech, served as king's counsel in Israel and saved the life of Jeremiah the prophet when he intervened in his behalf to Zedekiah, the king of Judah (Jeremiah 38:4–14); the prophet Zephaniah was obviously from an Ethiopian background (Zephaniah 1:1); and Jeremiah was quite aware of the color of the skin of the Ethiopians (Jeremiah 13:23). That both Isaiah (11:11) and Zephaniah (3:10) seem to have known and prophesied about a Jewish diaspora in Ethiopia is also significant. That people known as the Falashas exist in Ethiopia, and that they claim their roots in the Jewish stock, is very important for Rastafari who claim they are Falashas or black Jews.

Falashas ardently believe that their ancestors were the people who followed Menelik I, a founder of the Ethiopian empire, back to Ethiopia when he returned to rule his country. They claim that Menelik was the the son of Queen Sheba of Ethiopia and King Solomon of Israel. The Falashas have held to this belief so tenaciously that Christian missionaries have made very little progress in Christianizing them. Even the violence that Christians and Muslims sporadically meted out against the Falashas in the medieval period has not seriously daunted their faith. Ancient Near Eastern scholar Edward Ullendorff argues that the Falashas are a type of Semitic mixture called Agaus, who were converted to Judaism.[51] A counterargument to this theory is that the Falashas' observances are much more strict and intense than is usually the case with the Judaism that has filtered abroad.

How the Rastafarians make the connection between themselves and the Falashas is not very clear, but the knowledge of the Falashas' existence adds validity to the Rastafarian claim to an Ethiopian Jewish heritage, one that provides the historical-theological tradition for the doctrine of Selassie's divinity. Against this background the Rastafarians could say, "The spirit of David jumps in Solomon, the spirit of Solomon jumps . . . into Rastafari"[52]—or into Haile Selassie, who is the Spirit and God incarnate. Though unintelligible to the outsider and what might be called the "mother of all hermeneutical jumps" of the century, it is a critically important leap for Rastafari.

The leading Marcus Garvey scholar in the United States, Robert Hill, an authority on Leonard Howell and other founders of Rastafari, says that in determining Rastafari's origin, "the underlying identification made with Ethiopia by virtue of Biblical symbolism" is crucial. "Practically all forms of black redemptive ideology have been suffused with this Ethiopianism, so that its compass was historically much broader than Garveyism." Hill continues, "What the Ethiopian emperor's coronation in 1930 did was to stir into being a new phase of Ethiopianism among blacks." The coronation "allowed Garvey's doctrine of racial redemption to fuse inside this broad renewal of faith."[53] Leonard Howell's book *The Promised Key* followed in this literary and cultural tradition and "provides the actual interpretative basis of Rastafari ideology,"[54] one that is baptized in Christian theology, Scripture, Afro-centric thinking, and anti-white rhetoric.

The Solomon-Sheba-Selassie Saga

According to M. G. Smith, Roy Augier, and Rex Nettleford, "All brethren agree that the Emperor Haile Selassie is the living God, the Returned Messiah and the representative of God the Father . . . Proverbs 22, Isaiah 43 and John 16 . . . show that Ras Tafari is the living God, Old Alpha, the lion of Judah."[55] As Barry Chevannes puts it, "The most important belief of the Rastafari is that Haile Selassie, the late Emperor of Ethiopia, is God."[56] But what inspired Leonard Howell, in 1933, to announce that Haile Selassie I is divine? Where did Howell and Archibald Dunkley (another founder of Rastafari) get the idea of advancing the theological viewpoint that Selassie was the Son or the Second Person in the Holy Trinity and King of Kings?[57] Did the Rastafarians' idea that Selassie is divine come from themselves? From black, Afrocentric consciousness? Ethiopianism? Garveyism? Or even Judeo-Christian thought? Apparently, all these elements merged to give Rastafarian theology its distinct character. The Judeo-Christian tradition provided the literary and theological imagination for Rastafarian thought; black consciousness supplied the movement with black pride and a hermeneutic of suspicion of "white" Christian readings of biblical texts; Garveyism created the ideological, political, and religious frame of reference in which to interpret and canonize Ethiopianism and African traditional religions, thus making it possible to conceive of a black Messiah and God in Haile Selassie I.

The Selassie–Solomon–Queen of Sheba connection is a hallmark of Rastafarian theology. As Clinton Chisholm has observed, the "connection is crucial for Rastas because it is that which certifies for them that Selassie, by his ancestry, was on the throne of David"[58] and is qualified to function in the role of black Messiah and God.[59] By a rather intriguing interpretation of the pericope (biblical account) in 1 Kings 10 and 2 Chronicles 9, the Rastafarians trace Selassie's lineage to an alleged sexual encounter of Solomon with the queen of Sheba, which reportedly resulted in the birth of Menelik I and, consequently, a long line of Solomonic kingly descendants pointing to Selassie as the black king, a coming foretold in the Hebrew Bible. Rastaman John Moodie, who fictitiously Ethiopianized the biblical text, writes, "The Queen came to the Palace to see Solomon at work. She was very impressed. After the members of the Court had left, they were alone together. Solomon asked her to spend the night in the Palace. She accepted his request" only on the grounds that he would swear to God that "he would not take her by force." But, according to Moodie, that did not prevent a sexual affair between the two royalties. Moodie summarizes the *Kebra Nagast* by saying that, after the night of sexual pleasure, "Makeda mothered a son from Solomon, whom she named Menelik, 'Son of a Wise Man.' When Menelik came of age, he went to his father for teaching. He was so fascinated by his father's wisdom in ruling his kingdom that he stole the Arc of the Covenant which contained the Ten Commandments and took them to Ethiopia. Menelik the First became the first Judean line of Kings to rule Ethiopia."[60]

The "redacted" (theologically expanded) and mythmaking Ethiopian version of the story is much more elaborate than the biblical account found in 1 Kings 10:1–13 and 2 Chronicles 9:1–12. According to the biblical version, having heard of Solomon's wisdom, the queen came to visit him. Being impressed with his wisdom, she offered to him an impressive array of gifts. He, in turn, extended kingly courtesies, after which the queen took her leave and returned to Ethiopia—in the classic Shakespearian romantic ending, she "exit." What a beautiful comedy! But alas, what in this story is true?

Just as the story of the great flood in Genesis 6:14–8:19 appears in many other Ancient Near Eastern accounts, the story of Sheba's visit to Jerusalem and her encounter with Solomon likewise appears in many ancient texts, with varying shades of emphasis. In Ethiopia this story is treated as fact. The Ethiopian version of the myth states that the virgin queen, on her visit to Jerusalem, was sexually seduced by Solomon. She became pregnant and gave birth to a son, whom they named Menelik. Menelik grew up in Jerusalem at his father's side but later arrived in Ethiopia—having taken the ark of the covenant with him—to form the great Ethiopian dynasty.[61] From Menelik to the emperor Haile Selassie I has extended an unbroken succession of Solomon's descendants upon the throne, as is indicated in Article 2 of the 1955 constitution.[62]

Obviously, the revolution that dethroned Selassie and brought about his death (or, as most Rastas believe, his disappearance) forced some adjustments to the idea of an unbroken tradition in Ethiopia's dynasty. In their radical revolutionary pursuit of justice for the poor, the young anti-imperialist Marxists were in no mood to deal favorably with mythmaking stories from the Jewish Scripture on which the constitution supporting imperialism was based. Some Rastas have made adjustments in their views about Ethiopia's political situation since Selassie's disappearance and the persecution of Rastas loyal to the emperor, but the divinity of His Imperial Majesty is still accepted as a given by many Rastafarians and is the hallmark of their biblical interpretation.

Polemical Questions on the Saga

Biblical and historical evidence does not support the theory that Solomon had a sexual encounter with the queen of Sheba, who then bore him a son named Menelik I. The belief seems to hang essentially on two very different issues: (1) the nature and reliability of the Solomon-Queen of Sheba saga and its relation to Selassie and (2) the meaning of the biblical passages in question. Any attempt to verify the alleged romantic saga between Solomon and the queen of Sheba is immediately confronted with a number of questions for which no clear-cut answers exist: Who is this queen of Sheba mentioned in the genealogical materials? Is she African or is she Arabian, and if she is a black woman, is she Ethiopian or Egyptian? What is the relationship between Sheba and Seba (Genesis 10:7) in the biblical materials? What evidence exists that the queen of Sheba, as a black woman, had a sexual encounter with Solomon? And if she did share her sexuality with Israel's greatest womanizer, what happened to her offspring? And the real question is whether anyone could, with absolute certainty, trace lineage to a biblical personality after thousands of years of wars, holocausts, dislocation, displacement of communities, and interminglings of peoples and races—not to mention intermarriage, dysfunctional family intrigues, and migration.

With regard to the Sheba/Seba controversy, many scholars observe that the nomenclatures denote places, as well as different persons, in biblical materials.[63] Cain Hope Felder, who did a thorough study of the names in the Genesis narrative, says, "In fact, the conflation of different traditions in Genesis 10 doubtlessly accounts for matters such as the discrepancies in identifying the land of Cush, discrepancies in determining the relationship between Cush and Sheba, and the difference between Seba and Sheba." He continues, "Genesis 10:7 mentions Seba as a son of Cush, whereas Sheba is a grandson of Cush according to Genesis 10:8."[64] Randall Bailey says, "The location of Sheba is much in dispute." Since it is mentioned in the records of Tiglath-Pileser IV and shows similarities between the names Sheba and Sabeans, "most geographers place it in the Arabian Peninsula."[65] Many scholars argue forcibly that Sheba is not in Ethiopia and that Josephus confused Sheba with Seba. Those who locate the obscure ancient city in southern Arabia as part of the Sabean kingdom argue that the queen of Sheba lived among a people who were steeped in the tradition of *mashal,* or wisdom, and had a delightful hobby of posing and interpreting riddles; hence her interest in Solomon's wisdom.[66]

Even if we accept the conclusion that Sheba is associated with the Hamites and was located in Africa, we have dealt only with the question of geography and not that of theology. That is, operating on the premise that Sheba was in Ethiopia and that its queen was a black woman, an even greater hermeneutical hurdle is the alleged Solomon–Queen of Sheba romantic extramarital affair, which results in the birth of Menelik I.[67] Rastas read 1 Kings 10:2 and 13 as saying that the queen of Sheba went *in to* Solomon and communed with him intimately and sexually, and that the king met all of her sexual desires. As the Jamaican Bible scholar and Christian apologist (on Caribbean cults and Rastafari) Clinton Chisholm has noted from his personal debates with Rastas, the brethren argue that "Solomon gave the queen of Sheba such coital satisfaction that she was beside herself and conceived a son," Menelik. As proof of this, the brethren contend to Chisholm that the Hebrew expression "to come to, or enter," is a technical term for sexual intimacy. In Genesis 16:2, Sarai had said to Abram, "I pray thee, go in onto my maid; it may be that I may obtain children by her" (KJV).[68]

But the argument is specious. Although Sarai initiates a sexual encounter for Abram with Hagar in Genesis 16:2, the verbs have little correlation to those in 1 Kings 10:2. In fact, the same verb is used throughout the Hebrew Bible to mean "come" in the ordinary sense.[69] Further, the Hebrew imperative *boa nah,* "enter," in Genesis 16:2 has no relationship to *yit-daber,* "conversed," in 1 Kings 10. In Genesis 16 the focus is on reproduction for the saving of progeny; in 1 Kings 10, it is intellectual inquiry that seems to satisfy the queen's curiosity. According to C. Friedrich Keil and Franz Delitzsch, this brilliant woman went to try Solomon, "to put his wisdom to the test by carrying on a conversation with him in riddles."[70]

While 1 Kings 10:2 shows that the two royal personages had an encounter, the context and literary genre of the text do not imply sexuality. Sexual language is pervasive in the Hebrew Bible, and it is not at all clear why the biblical writer would want to conceal this information from the reader if, in fact, coital intimacy did occur. In biblical narratives and Jewish prose, we do find references to women initiating intimacy with men—as in the case of the sexual harassment of Joseph by Potiphar's wife (Genesis 39)—but it was done with a negative commentary in the context of disapprobation. Even if we grant that the queen of Sheba sexually desired Solomon, biblical literature is strangely silent on any offspring they may have had. Solomon's children, however, are always mentioned in the Hebrew Bible. As Ullendorff points out, nonbiblical sources are also either completely silent on this issue or contradictory and apocryphal. As Chisholm has observed, Josephus makes no mention of a sexual encounter or a son. The Jewish Talmud and early midrashim tell of no sexual overture or offspring. A later midrash records the meeting of Solomon and the queen but speaks only about the dialogue between them.[71] And the apocryphal stories are probably self-serving and very unreliable as source material.

"But," asked a Rasta brethren in conversation with Murrell, "wat about the man dem call Jesus of Nazareth? You nuh read wah im say bout King Solomon and the Queen ah Ethiopia in ah de Bible?" Indeed, according to Matthew, in addressing the people of his day who did not accept his message of repentance and baptism, Jesus said "the queen of the south shall rise up in the judgment with this generation and shall condemn it: because she came from the uttermost parts of the earth to hear the wisdom of Solomon; and, behold, a greater than Solomon is here" (Matthew 12:42 KJV). Without question, this text endorses the historicity of the king and the queen, as well as the fact of Solomon's wisdom. It also served as a stern rebuke to the unrepentant of the first century who were undervaluing the importance of Jesus in their midst. What the text does not do, however, is endorse the view that Solomon and the queen had a son from a sexual relation. Even though Jesus authenticated the historical existence of Solomon and Sheba, the evidence for the Solomon–Queen of Sheba sexual liaison is probably as quixotic as the Solomon–Queen of Sheba–Selassie messianic connection to Rastafari.[72]

The questions raised above about the claims concerning Solomon and Sheba are intended as an exercise for the academy rather than a criticism of Rastafari and should not imply that the Rastafarians are not entitled to own Selassie as their Messiah, God, and King. After all, religion is a matter of faith in an ultimate reality, be it real or imaginary, human or divine. All religious groups and communities make claims about their God or gods, and Rastafarians do not have to justify their beliefs and truth claims to the world any more than the Native Americans or the Torajas of Indonesia must defend their ancestral religious practices. The black biblical hermeneutic of Rastafari that is at work here is a hermeneutic of faith rather than a rationalistic, academic discipline. It is a hermeneutic designed to aid a "downpressed" people in their self-definition and in the procuring of liberation in Babylon. The doctrines or theological truths which that hermeneutic supports fall within the category of the confession of faith or of a religious mythmaking that carries its own internal validity; it is true and valid to the devotee.

Apocalyptic Lion of the Tribe of Judah/Messiah

To develop their apocalyptic vision and establish the Selassie ancestry, Rastas make very literal and direct links between the Hebrew Bible, the New Testament (e.g., Matthew 12:42; Revelation 5:5), and contemporary events in the African or black world. The Rastafarians believe that they are divinely endowed, authentic interpreters of the Revelation to John because their God, Messiah and King, Selassie, the Lion of the Tribe of Judah, was the only one found worthy in heaven and on earth to open the book and break the seven seals of the apocalypse (spoken of in Revelation 5), so that his followers could examine their contents and reveal them to the world. Also, Rastas name themselves gods, a view they derived from a rather curious, literal interpretation of the words of the King James Version: "I said ye are gods" (Psalm 82:6).

Not surprisingly, Rastas see in the book of Revelation a number of predictions indirectly and directly related to them—all set in cryptic, codified language. Two important ones are the Italian invasion of Ethiopia and the return of Selassie to his country in 1941.

Another interpretation sees a prediction that Selassie will be the only one capable to unseal the mysteries of God hidden in the Revelation to John. And yet another predicts the history and triumph of black people over Babylon and its oppression, when Jah effects a time of reversals and the first becomes last and the last first.

Rastas' undefined key of "hinspiration" (inspiration) and "hinsight" (insight) of Ras Tafari is used to unlock the hidden mysteries of all Hebrew prophecies and the eschatological visions in the formation of a theology of liberation, repatriation, and life in the new Jerusalem. To this end, Rastafarians regard Revelation 5:3–5 as the most important text in the New Testament—with special emphasis on the King James Version's rendering of verse 5: "Then one of the elders said to me, 'Weep not; lo, the Lion of the tribe of Judah, the Root of David, has conquered, so that he can open the scroll and its seven seals.'" As this text is made applicable to Selassie's life, so it applies in his disappearance; for to Rastas, Selassie is not dead.

The difference between the prerevolution and postrevolution perspectives is how this text is applied to the royal house of Ethiopia and the changes in the political agenda. Rastas view the political situation in Ethiopia as a theocracy: "God made the decree and the people obeyed." Haile Selassie is God's representative, the Anointed One through whom the will of God is expressed for the people. Rastafarian author John Moodie states prophetically, "Haile Selassie I, being of the line of Judah, root of David and on the throne of David, crowned King of Kings, Lord of Lords, conquering Lion of the Tribe of Judah, Elect of God, Light of the World, King of Zion, fulfills many prophecies of the scriptures."[73] Selassie thus becomes the fulfillment of Revelation 5:3–5. He is the King of Kings, Conquering Lion of the Tribe of Judah—the title he assumed at his coronation—and faith in him is expressed both politically and spiritually.[74] As Clinton Chisholm observes, Rastafari's use of the biblical titles *King of Kings, Lord of Lords, Conquering Lion of the Tribe of Judah,* and *Elect of God* is taken directly from the imperial titles in Ethiopia.[75] It is not inconceivable that an Ethiopic writer with interest in the Bible interpolated Revelation 5:5 into his Ethiopian text. The original Ge'ez (Ethiopic) imperial motto used the Revelation passage as an imperial attribute, and it has remained official ever since.[76]

For obvious reasons, then, the Rastafarians claim a special relationship to the tribe of Judah. The *Living Testament of Rasta-For-I* says, "Judah, thou art he whom thy brethren shall praise: thy hand shall be in the neck of thine enemies; thy father's children shall bow down before thee." And again, because of Judah's association with the image of the lion, the *Testament* exclaims, "Judah is a lion's whelp: from the prey, my son, thou art gone up: he stooped down, he couched as an old lion; who shall rouse him up?"[77] After its years of captivity, "the house of Judah was once more restored in the order of JAH-Rastafari, and the lion, his rightful seat upon the throne of the kingdom, bringing with H.I.M. a most fruitful reign for all the land."[78] The 1930 Ethiopian Penal Code reads, "The Lion of the Tribe of Judah hath prevailed. Haile Selassie 1st, the Appointed of God, King of Kings, of Ethiopia, herein rules . . . "[79] This usage was seen as consistent with earlier traditions and the use of Revelation 5:5 and not averse to the Ethiopian territorial understanding of the title *King of Kings.* The 1960 Civil Code

Proclamation, which carries the title "Conquering Lion of the Tribe of Judah, Haile Selassie I, Elect of God, Emperor of Ethiopia," seems to have been affected by loose translations of a Ge'ez motto from Revelation 5:5 and still reflects the territorial force of imperial titles. But this looseness in the use of biblical materials is what allows Rastafari to make a quantum leap from the Solomon-Sheba saga of the Hebrew Bible into the New Testament apocalypse.

Coupled with the belief that Selassie is the apocalyptic "Lion of the Tribe of Judah of the Root of David" is the view that he is the Messiah foretold in the Hebrew Bible— "the Messiah returned, the dead Jah Rastafari, come to judge creation." Owens has quoted an anonymous Rasta as saying, "Just as Jesus was Messiah by virtue of being in King David's line, so also is the Emperor. In Haile Selassie, in fact, we see a definitive manifestation of the same Messiah that the earth saw two thousand years ago."[80] For some Rastas, this Messiah merely disappeared but returned and lives in a holy place called Mount Zion in Ethiopia. From there, a Rasta brethren told Murrell in Kingston in 1994, he will come to judge the world of Babylon, and "hevery knees will bow and hevery tongues confess dat him is King of Kings and Lord of Lords, has the book says." Indeed, Rastas believe that Jesus, in the old dispensation, died for sins so that Selassie I, in the new dispensation, may reign supreme—a lamb to the slaughter versus the lamb to reign. So the Rastafarians use the messianic language and imagery in the New Testament Scriptures to teach that their Messiah, Haile Selassie, lives. Comments on Selassie exist in the present tense because Selassie is alive for the Rastafarians in the same sense that Christ is alive for Christians.[81] However, the imagery of the Messiah is not part of a vague eschatology; the Messiah actually occupies not only the throne of the Ethiopian dynasty but also the promised and established throne of David—the Messiah himself being a true descendant of David.

It is not by chance that Rastafarians "chant down Babylon" while affirming the divinity and kingship of Selassie. They believe that the political and economic systems of Jamaica and the entire Western world are going to collapse, and that Rastas will reign with Jah, Haile Selassie, with power and authority. In one of his early Jamaican hits, "Fire Fire," Bob Marley spoke of the final judgment to come, a theme that would echo again and again throughout his career. In "Ride Natty Ride," on Marley's 1979 masterpiece album *Survival,* the Rasta "rebel prophet" preached about the impending Armageddon and the doom of the Babylon system. Revelation 17:1-5 provides the language, theology, and apocalyptic imagery for that final drama in which Babylon, the "great harlot of harlots," shall come crashing down in the presence of Jah. The author of the biblical apocalyptic book says that upon the harlot's "forehead was a name written, Mystery, Babylon the Great, the Mother of Harlots and Abominations of the Earth" (Revelation 17:5 KJV). To this Tennyson Smyth (Ras-J-Tesfa) adds, "Reward her even as she rewarded you, and double unto her according to her works in the cup which she hath filled, fill to her double." He continues, "How much she hath glorified herself, and lived deliciously, so much torment and sorrow give her; for she saith in her heart, I sit a queen and am no widow, and shall see no sorrow."[82]

To understand the biblical interpretation and theology of the Rastafarians, it is important that we grasp their spiritual perception of the world. For them, two systems exist: Zion and Babylon, the good and the evil. Babylon is the embodiment of evil in biblical literature. On the one hand, few cities apart from Jerusalem embody the cultural significance of Babylon in the Bible. Over five thousand years old, Babylon is the first city mentioned in Genesis and occurs again in eighteen books of the Scriptures. In Revelation, Babylon is the final earthly city. It is a city of magnificence and glory, success, wealth, and fame, whose power is matched only by God and the conquering Lion of the Tribe of Judah, Christ. On the other hand, Rastas see Babylon as a symbol of bondage, not only for ancient Israelites but for all people held in slavery and oppression, especially black people.

The "*Zion system* is Africa or Ethiopia. . . . Africa is the mother of all nations";[83] there human life originated, the ancient Israelites lived, the Bible was written, and the idea of God, or Yahweh (Jah), was revealed. Since Rastas claim a close association with Solomon by way of Selassie, and see themselves as direct descendants of the Israelites,[84] they believe, as Mikael Kezehemohonerow has said, that they are Jah's true 144,000 remnant, spoken of in Revelation 7:4. This free-style approach to the cryptic and mysterious symbolism in Revelation highlights one of the most important aspects of Rasta hermeneutics: hijack biblical materials and concepts and relate them to any situation or problem when their language and imagery fit the categories and ideology of the interpreter or movement. The context of the interpreter takes precedence over the original context of the text and the intent of its author.

The Value of Rasta Hermeneutics

The Rastafarians should be complimented for their keen interest in and devotion to the study and use of biblical materials. Also noteworthy is the creativity that they bring to bear on the Scriptures in their attempt to establish and affirm the black presence in the Bible. We have noted above the direct identifications that the Rastafarians make in the transference of biblical symbols to their situation and perspective on the world and in the appropriation of hope in their understanding of the Scripture. They bring the Bible nearer to the experience of the reader than has been done before. Prior to the advent of Rastafari, meaning and understanding of Scripture in Jamaica were predetermined by those who applied the Bible to people's lives without due regard to their historical experience or social and economic condition. Rastafari challenged this and established a new basis for approaching the Scriptures by making use of their own creative *hermeneutical privilege* as a once oppressed group. The Rastafarians' own ethnic experience, historical and cultural background, and social and economic reality are not divorced from their reading of and meditation on the Bible. The questions, issues, and challenges that surface from their social existence, which are of a most comprehensive nature, are lived through and in relation to the Scriptures. Reading the Bible from where they are, seeing what is redeemable there for their own reality, they detect convergence, correspondence, and continuities between the story of the people in the Bible and their own story in Jamaica.

The Rastafarians read the Bible with what young Jamaican biblical scholar Althea Spencer-Miller calls the eyes of "apocalyptic activism"—an attitude generated by certain conditions when a group perceives that the role it plays in society and "the treatment it receives are not commensurate with the group's understanding of its capacities and abilities." This condition is exacerbated by "an experience of oppression and restriction of self-determination in opposition to that group's quest for autonomy."[85] Spencer-Miller concludes that this situation results in a kind of dissonance and tension that give birth to apocalyptic activism, "an ideology and discourse that are sufficiently compelling to arouse the will to endure, survive and act." The oppressed places "faith in a God who honors the endurance of the disempowered with survival,"[86] in a nontraditional mode.

At the same time, the Rastafarians' "citing-up" and free-style use of biblical text raise new questions for the discipline of biblical interpretation: Should there be a standard method or set of methods for interpreting the Bible? Whose method should it be—that of the dominant, hegemonic class or one designed by and for the underclass? How much should historical, archaeological, and linguistic studies attempt to uncover the original meaning of a text, and to what extent should that meaning affect interpretation today? These questions all concern the nature and purpose of biblical interpretation for people in oppressed societies such as modern Jamaica and point to a need to consider the usefulness of Rasta or Rasta-style hermeneutics to liberation theology in underdeveloped countries; and they highlight the need to consider what hurdles (in addition to those mentioned above) scholars must cross before they can enhance Caribbean theology with nuggets of truths from Rastafari's messianic ideology.

Ultimately, scholars may have to judge "Rastafarian hermeneutics" on its own merit—as a *tertium quid* (a different kind)—rather than by criteria that the academy sanctions but which are rejected by Jah people, "the sufferers." Clearly, the Rastas' hijacking of the Judeo-Christian Scriptures as a vehicle through which to articulate their faith and theology as well as define their reality is not unprecedented in history; many pseudo-Christian and pseudo-Jewish groups have done and continue to do this with biblical materials. What is difficult for most Caribbean Christians to accept is the novelty and strange nature of the Rasta hermeneutics. But even that will pass, as more Caribbean scholars contemplate the possibility of a dialogue between Caribbean theology of liberation and the Messianic hope of Rastafari.

Notes

1. Joseph Owens, *Dread: The Rastafarians of Jamaica* (Kingston: Sangster's Book Stores, 1976), 34.

2. See Issembly of Elders, *The Ethiopian-African Theocracy Union Policy: EATUP, True Genuine Authentic Fundamental Indigenous Original Comprehensive Alternative Policy: FIOCAP* (Kingston: Jahrastafari Royal Ethiopian Judah-Coptic Church, n.d.), 12, 16, 20, 25, 26, 53, 63, 83.

3. Owens, *Dread*, 31.

4. Ibid. See also G. G. Maragh [Leonard Howell?], *The Promised Key* (Accra, Ghana: The African Morning Post, Head Office, n.d.), 13.

5. M. G. Smith, Roy Augier, and Rex Nettleford, *Report on the Rastafari Movement in Kingston, Jamaica* (Mona, Jamaica: Department of Extra Mural Studies, University College of the West Indies, 1960), 19; Owens, *Dread*, 31; K. M. Williams, *The Rastafarians* (London: Williamson Printing, 1981), 13. See also Maragh [Howell?], *The Promised Key* (and Chapter 21 in this book).

6. Williams, *The Rastafarians*, 13.

7. "The Ethiopian Question," in Maragh [Howell?], *The Promised Key*, paragraph 5.

8. Frank Jan van Dijk, "The Twelve Tribes of Israel: Rasta and the Middle Class," *New West Indian Guide* 62, 1–2 (1988): 3.

9. Ibid., 3.

10. Owens, *Dread*, 34.

11. Smith, Augier, and Nettleford, *Report on the Rastafari Movement*, 19.

12. Owens, *Dread*, 36.

13. Ibid., 32. See also Smith, Augier, and Nettleford, *Report on the Rastafari Movement*, 19; Roger Ringenberg, "Rastafarianism: An Expanding Jamaican Cult" (Doctor of Ministry thesis, the Zenas Gerig Library, Jamaica Theological Seminary, 1978), 7.

14. Horace Campbell, *Rasta and Resistance: From Marcus Garvey to Walter Rodney* (Trenton, N.J.: Africa World Press, 1966), 78.

15. van Dijk, "Twelve Tribes of Israel," 2.

16. Owens, *Dread*, 36.

17. Issembly of Elders, *EATUP*, 12.

18. Ibid., 25–26.

19. John M. Moodie, *Hath . . . the Lion Prevailed . . . ?* (Boynton Beach, Fla.: Future Printing and Publishing, 1992), 7, 9. See also the loose use of Scripture throughout the Issembly of Elders' *EATUP*. The same kind of association is made in establishing a connection between the Twelve Tribes of Israel (see van Dijk, "Twelve Tribes of Israel," 3) and Babylon in biblical times and those of Rasta times.

20. Owens, *Dread*, 57, 58. Prior to the 1960s, racism and anti-African sentiments had caused black middle-class Jamaicans to despise their own kinky hair and dark skin and to sacrifice their African ancestral heritage on the altar of British colonial culture.

21. Robert Hill says the influence of Fitz Balintine Pettersburgh's *The Royal Parchment Scroll of Black Supremacy* (Jamaica, 1926) and Leonard Howell's "plagiarized" version of *The Holy Piby* in 1935 (the material in Howell's *Piby* was pulled from other sources) allowed the *Daily Gleaner* to spread the notion that Rastafarians "indoctrinated the people of Jamaica with some seditious ideas on Black Supremacy" ("Leonard P. Howell and Millenarian Visions in Early Rastafari," *Jamaica Journal* 16, 1, [February 1983]: 27).

22. "Daniel Coker to Jeremiah Watts," April 3, 1820, *Journal of Daniel Coker* (Baltimore: Press of Edward J. Cote, 1820); Martin R. Delany, *The Condition, Elevation, Emigration and Destiny of the Colored People of the United States, Politically Considered* (Philadelphia, 1852), 38; James W. Hood, *One Hundred Years of the African Methodist Episcopal Zion Church* (New York: A.M.E. Zion Book Concern, 1895), 55; Edward W. Blyden, *Liberia's Offering* (New York: John A. Gray, 1862), 71–72. Cited in Gayraud Wilmore, *Black Religion and Black Radicalism*, (Maryknoll, N.Y.: Orbis Books, 1984), 103–22.

23. Delany, *The Condition*, 61–62. Cited in Wilmore, *Black Religion*, 112–13.

24. Henry McNeal Turner, "God Is a Negro" (1898), in Edwin S. Redkey, ed., *Respect Black:*

The Writings and Speeches of Henry McNeal Turner (New York: Arno Press/New York Times, 1971), 176–77. Cited also in Wilmore, *Black Religion,* 122–29.

25. Albert B. Cleage, Jr., *The Black Messiah* (New York and London: Sheed and Ward, 1968); James H. Cone, *Black Theology and Black Power* (New York: Seabury Press, 1969).

26. See Issembly of Elders, *EATUP,* 20–21; Tennyson Smyth [Ras-J-Tesfa], *The Living Testament of Rasta-For-I* (Kingston: Ras-J-Tesfa, 1980), 6–7.

27. Smyth [Ras-J-Tesfa], *Living Testament,* 6; *EATUP,* 6–7

28. Smyth [Ras-J-Tesfa], *Living Testament,* 6–7.

29. Edward Ullendorff, *Ethiopia and the Bible* (London: British Academy, 1968).

30. The view that Ham committed a homosexual act with his father is speculation. Gerhard Von Rad seems to imply that in his *Genesis: A Commentary,* trans. John H. Marks (1956; translation, Philadelphia: Westminster Press, 1961), 133.

31. But some scholars do discredit this text on the grounds of its nonhistorical value, arguing that it applies to a specific people in ancient times, with only interpretive relevance to modern culture or to African peoples in particular. Furthermore, biblical scholars have cautioned that identifying a particular modern race using the ancient Genesis narrative is very difficult. See Gene Rice, "The Curse That Never Was," *Journal of Religious Thought* 29, 1 (spring–summer 1972): 13.

32. Moodie, *Hath . . . the Lion Prevailed . . .?* 7.

33. See Maragh [Howell?], *The Promised Key,* 10. See also William David Spencer's commentary on *The Promised Key* in Chapter 21.

34. Moodie, *Hath . . . the Lion Prevailed . . .?* 7; Biblical feminists who regard Numbers 12:1–10 as a patriarchal commentary on women would see the Rastafarian interpretation of the curse of Miriam as sexism, if not reverse racism.

35. Maragh [Howell?], *The Promised Key,* 9–11.

36. See important essays in Cain Hope Felder, ed., *Stony the Road We Trod* (Minneapolis: Fortress Press, 1991); Cain Hope Felder, *Troubling Biblical Waters: Race, Class, and Family* (Maryknoll, N.Y.: Orbis Books, 1989); Ullendorff, *Ethiopia and the Bible.*

37. Cain Hope Felder, "The Bible, Re-Contextualization and the Black Religious Experience," in Gayraud S. Wilmore, ed., *African American Religious Studies* (Durham, N.C.: Duke University Press, 1992), 162.

38. Haile Mikael Yenge Flagot Kezehemohonenow, "The Role of Rastafarianism in the Caribbean" (paper delivered to the Ecumenical Symposium of the Carribean Council of Churches, Chaguaramas, Trinidad, November 1971), 1. See also Kenneth J. King, "Some Notes on Arnold J. Ford and New Black Attitudes to Ethiopia," in Ronald K. Burkett, ed., *Black Apostles: Afro-American Clergy Confront the Twenthieth Century* (Boston: G.K. Hall, 1978), 51–52.

39. Owens, *Dread,* 39.

40. Moodie, *Hath . . . the Lion Prevailed . . .?* 17.

41. Owens, *Dread,* 39.

42. Issembly of Elders, *EATUP,* xxxiv (1), 63.

43. Ibid., paragraph X: 12; See also XI (hiii) and 15 (11) on Genesis 1:11; 2:4–5.

44. George Eaton Simpson, *Black Religions in the New World* (New York: Columbia University Press, 1978), 268, 288–89.

45. Ibid., 270.

46. Ibid., 125.

47. Joseph R. Washington, Jr., *Black Sects and Cults* (Garden City, N.Y.: Doubleday & Co., 1972), 134. Cited in Felder, *Troubling Biblical Waters,* 35; Simpson, *Black Religions,* 269.

48. Simpson, *Black Religions,* 269.

49. Rastas are not disturbed by the fact that the Falashas did not accept Selassie I as that longed-for Messiah.

50. King, "Some Notes on Arnold J. Ford," 52–53; Edward Ullendorff, "Falashas," *Encyclopaedia Judaica* (1971), 1146; Simpson, *Black Religions,* 269–70; Washington, *Black Sects and Cults,* 134–35; Felder, *Troubling Biblical Waters,* 35.

51. Ullendorff, "Falashas," 1146.

52. Simpson, *Black Religions,* 125–26.

53. Hill, "Leonard P. Howell," 26. Hill notes that "Ethiopianism was also manifested in the series of eight essays written by James M. Lowe of Jamaica and published in the *Crusader* in New York City in 1919–1920 under the title, "A Revealed Secret of the Hamitic Race.' "

54. Ibid., 27.

55. Smith, Augier, and Nettleford, *Report on the Rastafari Movement,* 18.

56. Barry Chevannes, "Rastafari: Towards a New Approach," *New West Indian Guide* 64, 3–4 (1990): 127–48.

57. Hill, "Leonard P. Howell," 33.

58. Clinton Chisholm, "The Lineage of Haile Selassie," in Commentaries, *Jamaica Record,* July 29, 1989, 2.

59. Of course, neither the linkage of Selassie to Solomon's lineage nor the notion that Ethiopia is the new Zion is a foreign idea to Ethiopians. The view was "held by Ethiopians as well, and definitely believed by Selassie," that the emperor "is no less than the 225th sovereign in an unbroken line dating from the time of Solomon" (ibid.; Owens, *Dread,* 95). The story even made its way into the revised Constitution of Ethiopia (Article 2).

60. Moodie, *Hath . . . the Lion Prevailed . . . ?* 17–18. This free-style, fictional way of narrating biblical stories is widespread in Rastafarian written and oral discourse.

61. Ullendorff, *Ehiopia and the Bible,* 74–75.

62. "The Imperial dignity shall remain perpetually attached to the line of Haile Selassie I descendant of King Shale Selassie, whose line descends without interruption from the dynasty of Menelik I, Son of the Queen of Ethiopia, the Queen of Sheba, and King Solomon of Jerusalem" (Ullendorff, "Ethiopian Constitution of 1955," in *Ethiopia and the Bible,* 139). See ibid. for further philological discussion on the Kebra Nagast and the Qur'an.

63. John Gray, *I and II Kings: A Commentary* (Old Testament Library; Philadelphia: Westminster Press, 1970), 259.

64. Cain Hope Felder, "Race, Racism, and the Biblical Narratives," in Felder, ed., *Stony the Road We Trod,* 132; idem, *Troubling Biblical Waters,* 22–35.

65. Randall C. Bailey, "Africans in Old Testament Narratives," in Felder, ed., *Stony the Road We Trod,* 171.

66. John Gray says that although the queen of Sheba's visit "has been much elaborated to enhance the glory and wisdom of Solomon, it was probably . . . a trade mission rendered necessary by the Hebrew occupation of the head of the Gulf of Aqaba and their control of Damascus" (*I and II Kings,* 259–60).

67. E. A. Wallis Budge, *The Queen of Sheba and Her Only Son Menelik* (London, 1932).

68. Clinton Chisholm, "Is Selassie Divine?" (lecture delivered at the Jamiaca Theological Seminary, Kingston, fall 1979; copy in the Caribbean Collection of the Zenas Gerig Library, Jamaica Theological Seminary, Kingston). See also Chisholm's "The Rasta-Selassie-Ethiopian Connection," Chapter 10 in this anthology.

69. The text also said the queen of Sheba "came to" or "entered into" the city. She certainly could not have had sexual intercourse with the city, unless "Jerusalem" is taken to be a euphemism for the people or its leaders, which is unlikely here.

70. C. F. Keil and Franz Delitzsch, *I Kings—Esther* (Commentary on the Old Testament; Grand Rapids: Wm. B. Eerdmans Publishing Co., 1985), 1:158.

71. Ullendorff, *Ethiopia and the Bible,* passim; Chisholm's "Rasta-Selassie-Ethiopian Connection," Chapter 10 in this anthology.

72. Was it possible that a sexual liaison could have taken place between the king and the queen without a reliable extant record, or could the information have been suppressed by scribes and redactors? Speculation is fair game in this story.

73. Moodie, *Hath . . . the Lion Prevailed . . . ?* 28.

74. Ibid., 28–36. Rasta letter to the editor, "Haile Selassie the Messiah," *Daily Gleaner,* March 21, 1987; Clive S. Reid, "Haile Selassie and the Rasta Doctrine," Commentary, *Daily Gleaner,* July 20, 1975.

75. See Chapter 10. The titles *King of Kings* and *Elect of God* were used in ancient times and have been conferred in more modern times by the *Abuna,* spiritual head of the Ethiopian Orthodox Church, as popular ending titles. But they are usually related to a special territory and designate a powerful authority.

76. Clinton Chisholm, "Rastas' Claim about Selassie Is Fiction," Commentary, *Sunday (Barbados) Advocate,* July 2, 1988. See also Chapter 10 in this anthology.

77. Smyth [Ras-J-Tesfa], *Living Testament,* book 2, 22.

78. Ibid., 28.

79. Ullendorff, *Ethiopia and the Bible,* 140.

80. Owens, *Dread,* 90, 102.

81. Susann Dodd, "Haile Selassie the Messiah," *Daily Gleaner,* March 21, 1987; Reid, "Haile Selassie."

82. Smyth, *Living Testament,* 34.

83. van Dijk, "Twelve Tribes of Israel," 2.

84. Owens, *Dread,* 96.

85. Althea Spencer-Miller, "Reading the Bible in the Caribbean: The Case of Jamaica," in *Society of Biblical Literature 1995 Annual Meeting, Bible in Africa, Asia and Latin America Group,* SBL Seminar Papers, Philadelphia, November 18–21, 1995, 13.

86. Ibid.

20 The Structure and Ethos of Rastafari

ENNIS B. EDMONDS

Students have raised several questions with regard to the organizational structure of Rastafari: How do Rastafarians function as a group or groups? Are they an actual organization, a lodge, an association, or an ecclesiastical body? Do they have a president, leaders, bishops, priests, moderators (persons who conduct their regular meetings and Nyabinghi), or pastors? Is there an official governing body that clarifies doctrinal beliefs or sets rules and regulations governing Rastafarian life and conduct? Essentially, what kind of movement is Rastafari?

Rastafari has never been a homogeneous movement. No formal organization unites all elements of the movement; no leadership hierarchy exercises control; and no established creed prescribes and ensures orthodoxy.

Many researchers regard the lack of formal organizational links in Rastafari[1] as a very positive characteristic of the movement. It allows the various Rasta groups and camps to enjoy a kind of freedom not always encouraged in many organized religious and secular movements. Each group defines its own ethos within the broader Rastafarian culture. Other scholars view the phenomenon as evidence that the Rastafarian movement is amorphous, acephalous (having no organizational head), polycephalous (having many heads or centers of authority), or fissiparous (having or breaking into many parts). But if such terms apply to the nature of the movement as a whole, they fail to discern the structure or pattern in the activities and relationships of Rastafari. As I will demonstrate, the Rastafarian movement has developed its own complex and enduring forms of social organization[2] and exhibits distinctive features in comparison to other groups in the Jamaican society. For example, Christianity in Jamaica is every bit as polycephalous and fissiparous as Rastafari. It is my contention that the Rastafarian movement is "reticulate" (weblike) but not amorphous. It constitutes a cohesive movement with identifiable structures and a shared ideological-symbolic-ritual ethos.

Reticulate is the word that comes closest to describing the structure of the Rastafarian movement. As Carole Yawney indicates, the Rastafarian movement consists of a loose aggregation of groups connected to one another by personal networks. Yawney further points out that these kind of "decentralized multi-group formations" are prevalent in the Caribbean, Latin America, and Africa.[3] Barry Chevannes's research confirms this point. The Rastafarian movement, he argues, is characterized by the same multigroup formations seen in other Jamaican folk religions, especially in revivalism, Pocomania, and the Native Revivalist Baptist movement. The unifying element in each of these religious traditions is a "fairly uniform system of beliefs."[4]

Informal Organizational Structures

The Rastafarian movement has distinct social structures. At the most basic level are those Rastas whom Velma Pollard, a Jamaican scholar at the University of the West Indies who has done a study on Rasta talk, describes as " 'own-built' Rastas following the philosophy at an individual level."[5] These are individuals who share the foundational beliefs and attitudes of the movement as a whole but who do not belong to any particular Rastafarian group or organization. For these adherents, Rastafari is a way of life. Belonging to an organized group of Rastas is irrelevant. What is important is that one comes to the "I-an-I" consciousness[6] and fashions one's lifestyle according to the precepts of Rastafari. At this individual level, Rastafarian religiousness appropriates the well-known European sociologist Ernst Troeltsch's description of mysticism: it is a radical individualism that de-emphasizes dogma, sacrament, and social organization.[7] It focuses instead on the individual's mystical links with Jah (God, the Creator, or Haile Selassie) and with the cosmic energy that Rastas call "earthforce."

"Houses" and "yards" describe another level of Rastafarian social organization. Houses and yards are small, informal groups of Rastas whose members sustain an ongoing relationship. The term *houses* expresses the idea that each gathering of Rastas is to be guided by the spirit of fraternity and freedom of participation.[8] A Rastafarian house may emerge wherever several Rastas (usually males) attach themselves to a "leading brethren" and frequently gather at his house or in his yard to partake of the sacramental herb (marijuana) and to engage in the dialectical discourse called "reasoning." This discourse is usually about their faith and current or historical events impinging on their understanding of their place in the world.

Within the house leading brethren are often regarded as elders. However, eldership is not a formal position, attained through election, but rather an "inspirational position" that is informally conferred on those who meet at least two criteria. Elders must have a record of uncompromising commitment to and defense of the principles of Rastafari—a commitment that often leads to confronting the establishment and even suffering imprisonment as a result. Elders must also have the ability to "speechify," that is, to expound the philosophy of Rastafari, to interpret historical and contemporary events through the Rastafarian prism, and thus to inspire the brethren to greater understanding and fortitude.[9] Eldership is therefore not an ecclesiastical office with binding authority. In Rastafari, the authority of the elders lies in their ability to exercise the power of persuasion through words. That is why John Paul Homiak, a U.S. researcher in Rastafari at the Smithsonian Institution, describes the Rastafarian elder as "principally a man of words."[10] Membership, like eldership, has no formal requirements. By virtue of their Rastafarian consciousness, Rastas attach themselves to one or more houses of their choice, which they are free to leave at any time.[11] More formal groups of Rastas are organized around particular leaders or groups of elders. These are either communes led by charismatic leaders or voluntary organizations (sometimes legally registered) dedicated to the accomplishment of particular goals. Some Rastas refer to these as "mansions," because compared to the houses which comprise maybe ten to fifteen Rastas, these groups often have hundreds of members. These more formal groups fall into two categories: "churchical" and "statical."

The churchical are so designated because of their emphasis on the development of Rastafarian religious culture and behavior and on the cultivation of African cultural consciousness and lifestyle. Prince Edward's Ethiopian National Congress, Claudius Henry's Peacemakers Association, the Twelve Tribes of Israel, the Rastafarian Theocratic Government, and the Sons of Negus are examples of churchical Rastafarian organizations. The statical groups gain this designation from their commitment to more political and social goals. For example, the goal of the Rastafarian Movement Association is to organize all Rastas to seize power in Jamaica through the political process. In a personal conversation in Kingston in 1993, Ras Historian, the leader of this organization, told me, "Politics is wha wi a deal wid" (Politics is what we are dealing with).

In the 1970s, the Rastafarian Movement Association was very active in organizing mass meetings, marches, and cultural events. In addition, it published a newsletter with information of interest to or concerning Rastas.[12] The Mystic Revelation(s) of Rastafari, founded by the famous Rastafarian drummer Count Ossie, provides another example of a statical organization. This group seeks to organize Rastas to effect repatriation through rational means, rather than waiting for the mysterious arrival of ships. It also has a commitment to the development of the creative arts and to the creation of educational opportunities for young people in the inner city.[13] In the early 1970s, Count Ossie, with the assistance of the Jamaican government, established a community center at the Mystic Revelations' Adastra Road headquarters in an East Kingston ghetto in order to accomplish its goals.

Establishing the group "membership" of Rastas can be quite a complicated exercise. Rastas often belong to more than one Rastafarian organization, and membership in a commune is marked by fluidity. A member of the Rastafarian Theocratic Government may also belong to the Rastafarian Movement Association and vice versa. In the case of Rastafarian communes, various patterns of participation have emerged. Some make their domicile in the commune on a permanent basis. Others alternate between the commune and some other place of residence. Still others belong to a certain commune for a short period, then move to another or abandon communal life. Furthermore, a commune is often frequented by brethren who may stay for a brief or an extended period. Rastas also hold membership in organizations that are not necessarily Rastafarian in nature but that prove attractive to Rastas because of their relationship with Africa and commitment to African causes. For example, many Rastas belong to the Ethiopian Orthodox Church, and others hold membership in the Ethiopian World Federation. When I visited the Ethiopian Orthodox Church in Kingston in May 1991, about one-fourth of the congregants were Rastas.

The decentralized nature of the movement is probably a logical outcome of what Rastafarian scholar Ernest Cashmore calls the "epistemological individualism" or of what sociologist Laurence A. Breiner terms the "authoritative individuality"[14] that pervades Rastafari. Epistemological individualism or authoritative individualism is rooted in the philosophic concept of "I-an-I," which leads to the Rastafarian insistence on radical freedom and democracy that is very resistant to centralization.[15] A Rasta is one who has consciousness of the god within, and thus the adherent is directly linked with the source of truth and life. The common sense of identity and solidarity is powerfully expressed in the concept of "I-an-I," an assertion of the godlike nature and dignity of every individual, notwithstanding the inferiority that Babylonian brainwashing seeks to foist on people of African heritage. Since the basic notion of "I-an-I" is that the principle of divinity inheres in each individual, truth is equally accessible to all.

Therefore, Rastas feel no need for teachers to impart God's truths or for priests to mediate between God and human beings. To know what is right and how to live and act, Rastas just need to get in touch with the God within. This epistemological individualism leads to "a highly democratic process of interrelationships" or the "rule of democratic and charismatic fluidity in Rastafarian groupings."[16] The locus of authority is therefore in each individual. Any agreement among Rastas must be arrived at "intersubjectively" through the process of reasoning (discussed below). Interestingly, the issue of centralization has repeatedly come up for discussion among Rastas. But even in these instances, the emphasis seems to fall on "greater cooperation and communication" rather than on the development of hierarchical structures.

An organization called Rastafari International Theocracy Assembly emerged in the early 1980s, the purpose of which is to bring a united front to the diverse "houses and ranks" of Rastafari, so that coherent unity "might manifest" as a result of this coming together. The Rastafari International Theocracy Assembly seeks to meet annually to discuss issues and problems facing the movement and to devise strategies to address those problems. Though this assembly has the potential to become a formal organization encompassing all Rastas, and though there have been talks of establishing an international secretariat, so far it seems to be nothing more than a forum for intellectual Rastas. It has very little significance for those at the grass roots.

Some researchers have been surprised to discover that, despite the decentralized nature of the movement, Rastafari is not in organizational chaos. It possesses the essential unity and identity necessary for it to be recognized as a single social group. Yawney points out that one of the unifying elements of the movement is the vast network that connects various groups of Rastas, which is maintained through "intervisiting."[17] Thus many Rastas who are scattered throughout the island do, in fact, know one another and are in frequent informal contact. This network functions to disseminate information concerning Rastafarian activities and particularly to announce the time and place of Nyabinghi I-ssemblies.[18] Through this informal network, Rastas are able not only to share information but also to maintain a sense of belonging to a larger collectivity. In addition to networking, Rastafarian unity and identity are established and perpetuated through sharing the same "system of beliefs and a state of consciousness"[19] and through participating in the ritual activities referred to collectively as "grounding."

Noting the heterogeneity of Rastafarian beliefs, Yawney nevertheless identifies four orientations that she believes characterize the Rastafarian movement as a whole: Ethiopianism, Biblicism, anticolonialism, and "I-an-I" consciousness. I argue that the core of the Rastafarian worldview, to which all Rastas give assent, is twofold: a common sense of evil and a common sense of identity/solidarity. The sense of evil is summed up in the term *Babylon*. The common sense of identity/solidarity is expressed in the Rastafarian embrace of their African past, their recognition of the historical suffering of Africans at the hands of the colonial masters, their shared sense of acute pain that comes from living in the underside of the Jamaican society, and their common struggle for liberation from oppression and injustice.

Thus, despite its heterogeneity, the Rastafarian movement has developed an ideological-symbolic matrix that provides its members with what Yawney calls a "rich complex of meaning and symbols," one through which they can filter the world they experience and by which they can shape their response to the pressures they feel. Yawney further says, "The Rastas seem to have evolved a dynamic model of the universe in terms of which members of the lower class, the dispossessed and oppressed, often illiterate, have been able both to construct a more satisfying and meaningful lifestyle for themselves, and to enrich their understanding of what is happening to them and why."[20] This ideological-symbolic matrix functions as a lens through which Rastas experience and interpret the world. In the words of one Rasta, "We were just blinded by European thought—but *Ras Tafari brought us new sight*."[21]

Beyond functioning as a lens through which the world is perceived and as an instrument in the struggle for change, the Rastafarian ideological-symbolic matrix operates as the unifying element in the Rastafarian movement. Cashmore is right on target when he says, "Bonds were expressed through symbolic procedures and such expressions served to consolidate and reinforce the feeling of belongingness and unity. It was these bonds which held the Rastas together as a movement and not as an aggregation of individuals sharing similar social positions."[22] In place of membership cards or confessed commitment to a creedal statement, evocative and provocative symbols that express a common sense of evil and of identity/solidarity became the badge of membership in the Rastafarian movement. These symbols unify and solidify the movement into a potent force in the Jamaican society.

Ritual Activities

In addition to the informal network and the ideological-symbolic matrix, certain rituals serve to shape and perpetuate Rastafarian religion and sociality. These rituals fall under the general rubric of what Rastas call "grounding." Homiak defines grounding as "informal instruction in Rasta precepts and ideology; the ritual process [reasoning] by which circles of like-minded brethren are formed and maintained."[23] This definition places grounding within the context of the yards that I described earlier. However, while these "circles of like-minded brethren" provide the day-to-day context in which Rastafarian religious life is formed and sustained, the periodic gathering called the "Nyabinghi I-ssembly" or "groundation" is another ritual event in which grounding takes place.

Ital Livity and Herbal Healing

An important reality that all Rastas share is their commitment to "ital livity." *Ital* means "springing from the earth, earthy, natural," or organic. *Livity* is living according to the strict principles of Rastafari. Ital livity is therefore a commitment to using things in their natural or organic states. One of the ills of Babylon, according to Rastas, is its departure from naturalness and its commitment to artificiality. Rastas want to escape this artificiality and return to nature. Thus the Rastafarian ideal proscribes the use of synthetic materials and chemically treated foods. I say "ideal" because the economic reality of life for most Rastas makes strict ital living very difficult, if not impossible. This proscription applies to tobacco, alcohol, and most manufactured products, especially canned foods. Rastas proscribe alcohol and other drugs (Rastas do not regard marijuana as a drug) because they view these as part of Babylon's plan to destroy the minds of black people. Ital living also means that Rastas are basically vegetarian, rarely using meat and strictly prohibiting the use of pork, shellfish, and scaleless fish, especially those that are predators. The strong disapproval of fish that are predators coincides with the belief that eating them would be an implicit approval of their "human predator" counterparts.[24]

Central to the ideal of ital living is the belief in herbal healing. Rastas believe that the entire universe is organically related and that the key to health, both physical and social, is to live in accordance with organic principles, as opposed to the artificiality that characterizes modern technological society. In addition to the Rastafarian commitment to a virtual vegetarian diet, there is a commitment to the use of various herbs that the Rastas believe promote human well-being. Foremost among the herbs that Rastas treasure is *ganja* (marijuana), which they often refer to as the "holy herb" or "wisdom weed." Ganja is used in a variety of ways: it is brewed as tea, soaked in rum for medicinal purposes, smoked ritually and socially, and used as seasoning in a variety of dishes.[25]

Vera Rubin and Lambros Comitas, well-known Caribbean scholars now residing in the United States, have argued convincingly that these uses of ganja are fairly widespread in Jamaican society. Kenneth Bilby's research has also uncovered evidence that ganja smoking has long been a ritual exercise in Kumina ceremonies.[26] However, the Rastas, more than any other group, have elevated the plant to a central place in their personal and religious life. Among the Rastas, ganja is highly valued for its physical, psychological, and social therapeutic powers. In accordance with their belief in herbal healing, Rastas regard the use of ganja as a source of physical healing. They contend that their use of ganja, particularly its ritual smoking, ensures perpetual health. Reggae-superstar Bob Marley's initial refusal to seek medical treatment upon discovery of his cancer was due in part to his belief in herbal healing, and particularly in the curative powers of smoking ganja.

Psychologically, ganja smoking is a source of illumination that gives one access to "inner and worldly knowledge."[27] In the words of the Canadian ethnographer Carole Yawney, it provides "inspiration enough to penetrate to the core of whatever is currently occupying their attention" and is "the key to the lock of understanding; God chooses to reveal himself through herbs."[28] Ganja smoking is also a means of creating and celebrating communality. In this respect, the Rastafarian perspective on ganja smoking is opposite to the generally held view (in Jamaican society) that ganja smoking predisposes the smoker to violence. The incidents of violence associated with the Rastas in the late 1950s and early 1960s were thought to have been triggered by ganja intoxication. Rastas, however, contend that in a society ridden with political factions, economic disparities, and racial prejudices, the smoking of holy wisdom weed is "for the healing of the nation."[29]

Rastas say ganja "dispels gloom and fear, induces visions, and heightens the feelings, creating a sensation of fellow love and peace."[30] More specifically, ganja smoking facilitates the transcending of Babylon's boundaries and the apprehending of new perspectives and possibilities. While the pressures and distortions of Babylon separate one from the real source of life and knowledge, ganja smoking aids in dissolving the barriers and in hastening the return home to the reality of Jah. In the visionary state induced by ganja smoking, Rastas come to the "I-an-I" consciousness: "the merging of the individual with all life forces, the realization that all life flows from the same source, and the collapse of the distance between internal and external, subject and object."[31]

Grounding and Reasoning

Grounding, in the context of the yards, takes place when a few Rastas gather to smoke ganja spliffs or to "draw the chalice"[32] and to reflect on their faith or on any current or historical event that impinges on their lives. This is the most informal level of grounding; it can take place anywhere and anytime, without any prearrangement. However, for many, grounding is a daily activity that takes place in the yards of leading brethren or elders. In addition to these daily gatherings, some circles of Rastas hold periodic all-night gatherings, some as often as once a week, others once a month or "as the spirit moves."[33] Rastas who "ground" in other yards on a daily basis may also visit these all-night gatherings, which are somewhat more formal than daily groundings. In addition to ritual smoking and reasoning, drumming, chanting, and sometimes "speechifying" and feasting mark the all-night groundings. In these Rastafarian gatherings, ganja is smoked as a sacrament and is believed to be the source of social and spiritual healing and insights.

As Homiak indicates, an open-ended and informal discussion, known as "reasoning," is an essential part of grounding. Yawney describes reasoning as an open-ended, dialogical discourse between two or more brethren. It has as its aim the exploration of their intersubjectivity, that is gaining "access to *one visionary stream,* to the condition of I and I consciousness."[34] The idea of intersubjectivity, as it relates to Rasta reasoning, speaks to the Rastafarian conviction that truth resides in each individual because the divine "I" is in each person. Therefore reasoning, assisted by the inspiration of ganja, stimulates the intersubjective exploration of truth. Stated another way, in the process of reasoning, all the "I's" present are able to explore the same truth, which inheres in each of them.

Reasoning is a very intense activity that can go on for hours in a dialogical manner until those involved arrive at a consensus. To quote Yawney again, "Two brethren may reason together, each prompting the other to *higher and higher I-ghts* [heights], accreting layer upon layer of meaning until a satisfactory view of reality is reached." Despite the Rastafarian insistence on *knowing* in contrast to *believing* (which implies doubt, in their estimation) and their elevation of the conclusions arrived at during reasoning sessions to the status of knowing, no conclusion or consensus is ever elevated to the status of a binding creed. Each conclusion is subjected to modification or further elaboration at future sessions.[35]

What is most important about these reasoning sessions, from a sociological point of view, is that they function in very much the same manner as catechism or Bible study in a Christian church. The sessions induct the initiates into the movement and confirm old adherents in the principles and precepts of Rastafari. In fact, it is noteworthy that new members of the movement are usually recruited in the context of the yards, through their involvement in ganja smoking and reasoning. The outcome of these collective activities, therefore, is the inculcation in Rastas of a common orientation toward the world.[36] Obviously, reasoning provides the balance that tempers the individualism of the movement. It allows Rastas to pursue common understanding or to reach consensus on particular issues.[37] According to ethnomusicologist Yoshiko S. Nagashima, through this ritual process " 'communitas' can be actualized." Hence the purpose of grounding is to "ground-the-nation" of Rastafari to the "essential foundation." It is the process by which Rastas become steeped in the principles of "Rastology."[38]

The Nyabinghi

Grounding also takes place at a periodic movement-wide convention variously called "Nyabinghi" (or "Bingi" for short), "I-ssembly" (assembly), "Rasta convention," "Nyabinghi convention," and "Nyabinghi I-ssembly." The term *Nyabinghi* was adopted from an East African group of the same name that was reported to be a secret society led by Haile Selassie. The motto of this group is said to have been "Death to the white oppressors." By calling this gathering "Nyabinghi," Rastas are expressing their conviction that the activities at this gathering serve to unleash "earthforce," the cosmic energy that pervades the universe, against those who have historically oppressed African people.[39]

When and where the Nyabinghi I-ssembly has its origin is a matter of some debate. The Rasta convention called by Prince Emmanuel Edwards in 1958 and the one convened by Claudius Henry in 1959 are often cited as the inception of the Nyabinghi I-ssembly. However, Verena Reckord cites a 1949 gathering at a Rastafarian camp in

Wareika Hills (part of the mountain range overlooking Kingston) as the "first really big congregation of Rastafarians." Homiak's research seems to support Reckord's findings. Though he gives no specific dates, he indicates that Rastafarian "grounation" (or "groundation") took place in Rastafarians' camps and yards prior to Edwards's convention in 1958.[40]

The discrepancy may be due to differences in the kind of publicity these events drew. The 1949 Nyabinghi was held in the relative seclusion of Wareika Hills, without press coverage. Reckord apparently came to the knowledge of this gathering during her fieldwork among those who participated, especially Count Ossie, whose drummers provided music for the occasion. In contrast, the 1958 and 1959 conventions were held with much fanfare in the city of Kingston and drew much media attention.[41] So though the 1958 and 1959 conventions came to be regarded as the beginning of the Nyabinghi I-ssembly, they appear to have been the culmination of something started earlier. Their significance comes from the fact that they brought to public awareness a Rastafarian activity that developed in the relative seclusion of the Rastafarian "cloister."

Nyabinghi I-ssemblies are held according to the Rastafarian calendar of "holy days." These are the Ethiopian Christmas on January 7; the anniversary of Haile Selassie's visit to Jamaica on April 21; African Liberation Day (founding of the Organization of African Unity) on May 26; Haile Selassie's birthday on July 23; Ethiopian New Year on September 11; and the anniversary of Haile Selassie's coronation on November 2. At these times, Nyabinghi I-ssemblies are convened. Who convenes an I-ssembly and where it is held are determined in the give-and-take decision-making process within the movement. However, the conveners always seem to have to meet two conditions: they must have a reputation as exemplars of Rastafarian livity, that is, they must be known to live a strict, uncompromising Rasta lifestyle; they must also have the economic means to make a substantial contribution as the sponsors of I-ssemblies. An elder wishing to convene an I-ssembly usually announces his intention at one of the meetings of Rastafarian elders. If he secures the support of the other elders, information concerning planning for the I-ssembly is then disseminated through the personal network that exists in the movement.

The early Nyabinghi I-ssemblies were usually held in and around Kingston. However, since 1970, Nyabinghi I-ssemblies have become a rural event. As Homiak indicates, the shift is related to demographic changes affecting the movement, specifically the dislocation of Rastas from West Kingston by the demolition of Back-o-Wall. Many of the dislocated settled on the periphery of the city or moved to deep rural areas, taking the I-ssembly with them.[42] Nowadays, an I-ssembly can last anywhere from three to seven days and is marked by a festive atmosphere, intense activities, and ecstatic emotions. Large numbers of Rastas from all over the island descend on the site of the I-ssembly, sometimes in a colorful motorcade. During the day, the attendees participate in feasting, ganja smoking, and reasoning in informal groups. At night, everything gets into high gear. The congregants gather around huge bonfires or in booths covered by leaves or thatch and all night engage in drumming, chanting, dancing, and "speechifying," all accompanied by the ritual smoking of ganja. These all-night sessions are very intense, with many participants displaying an array of ecstatic emotions.[43]

While the early Nyabinghi I-ssemblies were regarded as a preparation for repatriation to Africa, and while present-day participants are frequently reminded that they are "sons and daughters of Zion," called out of Babylon, immediate departure to Africa is no longer the central focus. The Nyabinghi I-ssemblies, along with their ritual activities, have become a significant means of facilitating solidarity in the Rastafarian movement as a whole.[44] The I-ssembly is a celebration and reenforcement of the oneness among Rastas and the oneness of Rastas with Jah. This mass gathering, with everyone participating in the same activities, generates a feeling of oneness akin to Emile Durkheim's *conscience collectif* (group consciousness). The I-ssembly is an occasion for the revitalization of Rastas' African roots. A Nyabinghi I-ssembly is therefore a "source of cultural and spiritual upliftment."[45] The I-ssembly is also an occasion for the reenforcement of the value of the strict ital livity and precepts of Rastafari and for the purgation of Babylon's influence from one another's life.

The I-ssembly gains further significance from the role it is assigned in the destruction of Babylon. According to Rastas, the ritual activities of the I-ssembly are means of channeling earthforce against the oppressive agents of Babylon. The drumming, chanting, ritual stamping, and wild tossing of dreadlocks in the I-ssembly sessions are designed to tap into and release this energy. Therefore, these symbolic acts are often aimed at directing earthforce toward the destruction of Babylon.

Finally, the I-ssembly provides an arena for the dramatization of contending claims for leadership within the movement. Since leadership is based on reputation and on facility with words, at these mass gatherings various elders seek to enhance their status and authority. They do so by giving lengthy accounts of their history of uncompromising opposition to Babylon and by demonstrating their ability to interpret historical and contemporary events from the perspective of Rastafari. Daily and periodic participation in Rastafarian ritual activities gives adherents of the movement a sense of belonging to a group of like-minded people. It also facilitates the creation and inculcation of a common ethos. The common worldview and attitude toward life that constitute this ethos repudiate the values and institutions of Jamaican society.

The foregoing discussion is intended to demonstrate that, with all its plurality, Rastafari is a cohesive movement. It is characterized by structured relationships, a distinctive ideological-symbolic ethos, and routine ritual activities, all of which serve to solidify and perpetuate the movement.

Notes

1. Barry Chevannes, "Rastafari: Towards a New Approach," *New West Indian Guide* 64, 3–4 (1990): 137; Carole D. Yawney, "Lions in Babylon: The Rastafarians of Jamaica as a Visionary Movement" (Ph.D. diss., McGill University, 1978), 102.

2. Carole D. Yawney, "Dread Wasteland: Rastafarian Ritual in West Kingston, Jamaica," in N. Ross Crumrine, ed., *Ritual Symbolism and Ceremonialism in the Americas: Studies in Sym-*

bolic Anthropology (Occasional Publications in Anthropology, Ethnology Series 33; Greeley: Museum of Anthropology, University of Northern Colorado, 1978), 156.

3. Yawney, "Lions in Babylon," 107.

4. These are religious groups indigenous to Jamaica. They blend African and Christian elements and are therefore referred to as "Afro-Christian religions." See Chevannes, "Rastafari," 138.

5. Velma Pollard, "The Social History of Dread Talk," *Caribbean Quarterly* 28, 2 (December 1982): 17.

6. In Rastafarian philosophy, "I" connotes the divine essence that is inherent in all persons. "I-an-I" consciousness is an awareness of one's divine essence and therefore of one's links to God and all humanity.

7. See Ernst Troeltsch, *The Social Teaching of the Christian Churches*, trans. Olive Wyon, introduced by Charles Gore (New York: Macmillan Co., 1931), 377–78, 745, 993.

8. Barry Chevannes, "Era of Dreadlocks" (unpublished manuscript, Kingston, Jamaica, n.d.), 13.

9. Ibid., 13; Chevannes, "Rastafari," 138.

10. John Paul Homiak, "The 'Ancient of Days' Seated Black: Eldership, Oral Tradition and Ritual in Rastafari Culture" (Ph.D. diss., Brandeis University, 1985), 355.

11. Chevannes, "Rastafari," 138. While there are no formal rules governing a house, Rastas, and especially the elders, are very desirous of projecting a positive image to the community in which they live. Consequently, there are times when individuals are expelled from and forbidden to visit a yard because of "bad behavior" or "lack of livity."

12. Yawney, "Lions in Babylon," 58.

13. Ibid., 108–10.

14. Ernest Cashmore, *The Rastafarian Movement in England* (London: George Allen & Unwin Paperbacks, 1983), 126; Laurence A. Breiner, "The English Bible in Jamaican Rastafarianism," *Journal of Religious Thought* 42, 2 (fall–winter 1985–1986): 37.

15. Chevannes, "Rastafari," 137. There are only a few instances in which there is any semblance of hierarchical organization: the Twelve Tribes of Israel, Prince Emmanuel Edward's Bobo Dreads, and Claudius Henry's Peacemakers Association are some examples. And even in these cases, the group is dominated more by the personality of the leaders than by rational principles.

16. Sebastian Clarke, *Jah Music: The Evolution of the Popular Jamaican Song* (London: William Heinemann, 1980), 5; Breiner, "The English Bible," 37, respectively. The "democracy" is mainly among men. For discussion on the traditional and changing roles of women in the Rastafarian movement, see Maureen Rowe, "Gender and Family Relations in Rastafari," and Imani Tafari-Ama "Rastawoman as Rebel," Chapters 4 and 5 in this anthology. See also Maureen Rowe, "The Woman in Rastafari," in Rex Nettleford, ed., *Caribbean Quarterly Monograph: Rastafari* (Kingston: Caribbean Quarterly, University of the West Indies, 1985), 13–21.

17. Yawney, "Lions in Babylon," 110, 301–2.

18. Homiak, " 'Ancient of Days' Seated Black," 407.

19. Chevannes, "Rastafari," 143.

20. Yawney, "Lions in Babylon," 9, 258–60, 343; Carole D. Yawney, "Remnant of All Nations: Rastafarian Attitudes to Race and Nationality," in Francis Henry, ed., *Ethnicity in the Americas* (The Hague: Mouton Publishers, 1976), 232.

21. Cashmore, *Rastafarian Movement in England*, 137. The emphasis is mine.

22. Ibid., 151.

23. Homiak, " 'Ancient of Days' Seated Black," 512. In the context of the yard, ganja smoking and reasoning are traditionally male activities. Women are mostly excluded from the circle in

which "the chalice is passed" and in which reasoning takes place. Males are expected to "educate" the "sistren." Women, however, take active parts in Nyabinghi I-ssemblies, though the males dominate. See Rowe, "The Women in Rastafari," 15–16.

24. Claudia Rogers, "What Is Rasta?" *Caribbean Review* 7, 1 (January–March 1977): 10–11; K. M. Williams, *The Rastafarians* (London: Ward Lock Educational, 1981), 23–25.

25. Rogers, "What Is Rasta?" 12. Rastas seldom use the word *ganja*. They regard it as Babylon's derogatory label for the "holy herb."

26. Vera Rubin and Lambros Comitas, *Ganja in Jamaica* (The Hague: Mouton Publishers, 1975); Kenneth Bilby, "The Holy Herb: Notes on the Background of Cannabis in Jamaica," in Rex Nettleford, ed., *Caribbean Quarterly Monograph: Rastafari* (Kingston: Caribbean Quarterly, University of the West Indies, 1985), 85.

27. Rogers, "What Is Rasta?" 12.

28. Yawney, "Dread Wasteland," 165, 169.

29. Dennis Forsythe, *Rastafari: For the Healing of the Nation* (Kingston: Zarka Publications 1983), 118–20.

30. Williams, *The Rastafarians*, 20.

31. Yawney, "Lions in Babylon," 201.

32. Spliffs are huge, conical marijuana cigars. *Chalice* is the ritual name for either of the two pipes used in the ritual smoking of ganja. One is called the *kochi* (also *cutchie*), a kind of water pipe with a bowl on the top to hold the ganja; this pipe is of African origin. The other is called the *chillum*, a conical or cylindrical pipe of East Indian origin. See Bilby, "The Holy Herb," 87.

33. Yoshiko S. Nagashima, *Rastafarian Music in Contemporary Jamaica: A Study of the Socioreligious Music of the Rastafarian Movement in Jamaica* (Tokyo: Institute for the Study of Languages and Cultures of Asia and Africa, 1984), 115.

34. Yawney, "Lions in Babylon," 216. The emphasis is mine.

35. Ibid.; Yawney, "Remnant of All Nations," 239, 243.

36. Cashmore, *Rastafarian Movement in England*, 64.

37. Yawney, "Lions in Babylon," 102.

38. Nagashima, *Rastafarian Music*, 116; Homiak, " 'Ancient of Days' Seated Black," 512, respectively. *Rastology* is a tern used sometimes to refer to the Rastafarian worldview, ideology, or theology.

39. Williams, *The Rastafarians*, 18.

40. Verena Reckord, "Rastafarian Music: An Introductory Study," *Jamaica Journal* 11, 1–2 (1977): 9; Homiak, " 'Ancient of Days' Seated Black," 361.

41. For a discussion of the conventions and their publicity, see M. G. Smith, Roy Augier, and Rex Nettleford, *The Rastafarian Movement in Kingston, Jamaica* (Mona, Jamaica: Institute of Social and Economic Studies, University College of the West Indies, 1960), 14–15; and Clarke, *Jah Music*, 47.

42. Homiak, " 'Ancient of Days' Seated Black," 36, 367, 401.

43. Williams, *The Rastafarians*, 18, 20.

44. Yawney, "Lions in Babylon," 54.

45. Homiak, " 'Ancient of Days' Seated Black," 362–72.

21 The First Chant: Leonard Howell's *The Promised Key*

WITH COMMENTARY BY
WILLIAM DAVID SPENCER

Leonard Percival Howell was a charismatic and enigmatic Jamaican adventurer who is usually credited with being the first person to preach the divinity of Haile Selassie.[1] Rumors had Howell serving in the war against King Prempeh of Ashanti in 1896,[2] though Robert Hill, prominent Marcus Garvey scholar and Rastafari researcher, records that he was born June 16, 1898.[3] Other reports have Howell taking sojourns in Panama, the United States, Africa, and perhaps even attending the coronation of Emperor Haile Selassie I in Addis Ababa on November 2, 1930. What is clear is that Howell started to build a following and by 1933 was attracting police attention because of the size and fervency of his open-air meetings; shortly afterward, the first of his several arrests occurred. With the burgeoning of his movement, Howell was able to purchase a plantation great house called Pinnacle Hill, which was raided by police and from which Howell and his followers were eventually evicted for a variety of provocations, including cultivation of ganja (cannabis), stockpiling of weapons, and the reported harrassment of neighbors.

Incarcerated twice again, Howell kept picking up the pieces of his movement until 1960, when he was committed to an asylum reportedly for claiming divinity for himself. As early as 1941, court depositions quoted him as threatening, "I will beat you and let you know to pay no taxes. I am Haile Sellassie [sic], neither you nor the Government have any lands here."[4] After 1960, Howell's power was all but spent, and the movement was swept up by other commanding figures such as the revolutionary Claudius Henry, the diplomat Mortimo Planno, and the spiritual artist Count Ossie.

In obscurity and reclusive among a remnant of his followers, Howell died in 1981. By that time, the movement he had done so much to foster was entrenched in Jamaica and had achieved international impact through reggae. Few of the worldwide admirers of reggae and Rastafari, however, had heard of Howell outside passing references in books. Only scholars and adherents of Rastafari knew the magnitude of the contribution of this pioneer of the movement.

That Howell had written a pamphlet (whose title page claimed publication in Ghana) called *The Promised Key,* and that it was "a basic Ras Tafari text," according to the 1960 University of the West Indies (UWI) report on Rastafari by M. G. Smith, Roy Augier and Rex Nettleford, was common knowledge.[5] As the literature developed on Rastafari, scholarly articles and books generally ignored the pamphlet until the year of Howell's death. That year, in an important article first published in *Epoché: Journal of the History of Religions* University of California, Los Angeles and later reprinted in the *Jamaica Journal* (1983), Robert Hill reminded readers of the existence of *The Promised Key.* Written under a pseudonym by Howell at the beginning of his preaching, the overlooked volume had become, for many, a nearly mythical and certainly ultrascarce text, regarded much like the original autographs of the New Testament (NT). Scholars knew this seminal work existed, but acquiring a copy of this long-disappeared historical ephemera seemed hopeless. Therefore, many have settled for citing Hill's article and *Gleaner* reports on *The Promised Key.*[6] However, graciously searching in Jamaica at my request, the consulting editor to this volume, Clinton Chisholm, located a copy of *The Promised Key.*

In his treatment, Hill, the editor of the Marcus Garvey papers, seemed particularly concerned with how much Howell's slim volume owed to earlier works such as *The Holy Piby,* the "black man's Bible" published by the Anguillan Robert Athlyi Rogers in Newark, New Jersey, in 1924 and *The Royal Parchment Scroll of Black Supremacy,* a 1926 Jamaican publication by the Reverand Fitz Balintine Pettersburgh.[7] Intrigued by the precise content of Howell's finished product, however, scholars who focus on Rastafari have frequently raised questions such as: How much current Rastafarian thought can be traced directly to Howell's teaching? Which doctrines and practices presented in *The Promised Key* have been retained over the years and developed by Rastas so that they are present today, and which have been transformed or generally discarded? How Howellite is the present Rastafari? What has come down from the beginning from the one who "is generally regarded as being the first to preach the divinity of Ras Tafari in Kingston,"[8] and what has been added to his teaching along the way?

This commentary on *The Promised Key* is intended to shed light on some of these questions and to make Howell's thoughts more accessible to readers. Long since fallen into the public domain, the work is brief enough to reproduce in its entirety in this present volume and share with the scholarly community. After each section, my comments explore the roots of what have become cardinal Rasta tenets while comparing Howell's early recorded vision with today's global adaptation of Rastafari. In making available this long "lost," provocative document, the editors' intent is to put another piece of the fascinating Rastafarian picture into place and to display it for all to consider.

The Promised Key

The Promised Key is a fourteen-page volume credited to one G. G. Maragh and alleging to have been printed by Nnamdi Azikiwe, editor of the *African Morning Post,* a newspaper with its head office in Accra, Ghana. Scholars, however, universally accept that Howell is the author of this document.[9] Edward J. Osei-Bonsu of Accra, a Ghanaian scholar, pastor of Calvary Baptist Church in Accra, and an Akan tribal prince, graciously "digging into the archives of some libraries" for me, has been able to verify in an October 11, 1995 letter, "Yes, *The African Morning Post,* edited by Dr. Nnamdi Azikiwe (who is a Nigerian) existed. . . . It was published by City Press, Ltd, Accra, Ghana (or Gold Coast)." Osei-Bonsu agrees, "It may be that, if they published *The African Morning Post,* they are the publishers of the booklet," yet he was unable to locate proof, by the date of publication of this commentary, "whether the book was printed in Ghana."

The version of *The Promised Key* we located in Jamaica has a redaction in the text by a later hand. On page 8, under the heading "How to Fast," a ritual washing with *salt* and water has been altered to *herb* and water. At the back of the book are two addenda. The first, printed in a type font very close to that of the book, has a title reminiscent of the Ugandan Nyabinghi war cry: "I Yah Bingi Ioder Death To Black And White Wicked." Comprised of two articles (numbered 2 and 4), an adaptation of Joel 3:16 in the King James Version of the Bible ("Jah" is substituted for "the Lord"), and two questions, the document appears to be a response to reports of the death of Haile Selassie I, the emperor of Ethiopia. That would date the addition to no earlier than August 27, 1975. The first paragraph (Article 2) affirms Selassie's claim to Solomonic lineage. The second (Article 4) reaffirms the sacredness, dignity, inviolability, indisputable power, and traditional honor of Selassie's person, threatening punishment to anyone seeking to injure the emperor. It also exhibits the Rasta fondness for wordplay (e.g., "onointing"). Two ideological questions are asked: "How can they say that the King of Kings die and buried same day in utter secrecy?" and "Why do the heathen rage and the people imagine vain things?"—the latter adapting Acts 4:25's rendering of Psalm 2:1 (KJV) to the present situation.

The second document is a two-page manifesto titled "His Grace Diliever Our Divine Theocracry Temple of Rastafari Selassie I Says." A number of rules of holy living follow. The first rules are dietary: no eating of meat, fish, salt (interestingly, as we will see, salt is used in Howell's ritual to remove evil), rum; nothing out of tins or bottles; and so forth. The next set of rules deals with monogamy, mainly being regulations for women and their treatment. It contains prohibitions against physical or verbal abuse of faithful "daughters" but declares that female adulterers are "guilty of death." Women are forbidden to wear dresses above the knee or "eat their Holy Chalice in the congregation." Further, "combs, scissors and Razors," along with congregational admission to alcoholics, "sadamite thief," and practicers of birth control, among others, are forbidden. Gambling is not allowed, nor is attending "cinimas," "dance hall" (so much for today's dancehall reggae), or "whore houses." Respect is urged in all verbal interactions.

On the second page, headed "Exterminate the Pope," marvelous claims are made that "anyone belong to this Theocracey Temple of Sellassie such person can't drown in any water nor burn in any fire and no injues verdict will never rendered against him." A divine-human trinity is envisioned of "Rastafari the Creator," "Rastafari the Almighty Infinite Selassie I," and "Selassie I the Holiest Temple of Heaven and Earth." A challenge is issued: "Whosoever is stronger and mightier than these three men he may bitter assault if he cannot or forever keep his peace with I and I"—at which the document closes with the Psalmic pause word *Selah*.

THE PROMISED KEY

The Mystery Country

I wish to state to you my dear Readers, that Ethiopia is a Country of great contrasts largely unexplored and is populated by Black People whose attitude towards this so called Western civilization has not changed within the last six thousand years.

The people are Christians while retain Primitive customs The result is that the Black People of Ethiopia are extraordinarily blended into a refined fashion that cannot be met with in any other part of the world.

In 1930 the Duke of Gloucester undertook one of the most interesting duties he had been called upon to execute up to this date. The occasion was the Coronation of His Majesty Ras Tafari the King of Kings and Lord of Lords the conquering Lion of Judah, the Elect of God and the Light of the world.

The Duke was to represent his father The Anglo Saxon King. The Duke handed to His Majesty Rastafari the King of Kings and Lord of Lords a Sceptre of solid gold twenty seven inches long of which had been taken from the hands of Ethiopia some thousand years ago.

The Duke fell down bending knees before His Majesty Ras Tafari the King of Kings and Lord of Lords and spoke in a loud tone of voice and said, "Master, Master my father has sent me to represent him sir. He is unable to come and he said that he will serve you to the end Master" See Psalm 72:9 to 11 verses, also see Gen. 49 chap. 10 verse

On one side of the Sceptre was inscribed Ethiopia shall make her hands reach unto God, and on the other side the King of Kings of Ethiopia, the top of the shaft was finished with a seal and above was a clen cross in which a single carbuncle was set.

The sceptre was a magnificent piece of workmanship and had besigned from an historic piece in which the special ceremonies of His Royal Highness of Ethiopia, Earth's Rightful Ruler.

The Duke also handed to Queen Omega the Empress of Ethiopia a sceptre of gold and ivory. The shaft being in the form of a spray of lilies and at the top a spray of lilies in bloom.

It was a brilliant ceremony, the church began to fill. The Ethiopians were brilliant in special robes having discarded their precious white robes, and wore Jewels of great value.

The men's swords being heavily ornamented with gems. On their heads they wore gold braided hats, in which the covered lion's manes were to be seen. In contraction then were the solar note struck by the women who were heavily veiled, and wore heavy cloaks.

His and Her Majesty King Alpha and Queen Omega the King of Kings drove to the Cathedral in a Coach drawn by six white Arab horses.

Queen Omega in a Robe of Silver and the escort on mules wearing lion's skin over their shoulders, forming into procession outside the Cathedral.

King Ras Tafari and Queen Omega the Royal pair, the escort and a line of Bishops and Priests entered, the guests rank obeisance.

King Alpha sitting on his Throne homage was done to him by the Bishops and Priests fulfilling the 21 st. Psalm. The ceremony took 10 days from the second day to the eleventh day of November 1930.

King Alpha was presented with the orb spurs, and spears and many other mighty emblems of His High Office, Dignitaries of the world power presented King Alpha with the wealth of oceans.

The Emperor attended to most of his preparations for the reception of his thousands of guests himself, and day after day could be seen rushing about in his scarlet car seeing how the white labourers were getting on with the new road he had ordered that the lawns he had laid down be attended to and that the extention of the electric lights throughout the city were being hurried on.

Commentary

When George Eaton Simpson began to attend Rasta street meetings in Jamaica in 1953, he witnessed preachers using an article titled "Modern Ethiopia" from *National Geographic* (June 1931). According to Simpson:

> This article deals with the coronation of Haile Selassie as Emperor of Abyssinia, and it is often quoted almost sentence by sentence with appropriate interpretations by the speaker. The splendour of the coronation is dwelt upon, and emphasis is placed on the alleged bowing down of the kings and presidents of the earth before Haile Selassie. Haile Selassie's power, the speaker contends, is acknowledged by the mightiest rulers of the world.[10]

That Howell did not rely on the *National Geographic*'s (1931) articles "Modern Ethiopia" and "Coronation Days in Addis Ababa" is fairly conclusive. Neither phrasing nor details are the same. Further, the article "Modern Ethiopia" observes, "The Ethiopians list their Kings from Ori, of 4478 B.C., to Haile Selassie the First, of A.D. 1930."[11] Howell, however, begins his dating at 4004 B.C.E., some 474 years after Ethiopia's monarchy list begins (though perhaps Howell is adopting the Ethiopian practice of taking time out from the date of the Noahic flood until the fall of the tower of Babel and beginning his dating after the Deluge). Further, all Howell's glowing accounts of obeisance are not in the "Modern Ethiopia" article. The entry of the royal couple is chronicled differently, and in place of Howell's list of gifts, *National Geographic* author Addison Southard merely notes:

> Bestowals of the imperial scepter of ivory and gold and a golden globe of the earth follow.
>
> The diamond-incrusted ring, the two traditional lances filigreed in gold, and the imperial vestments are all bestowed in turn with appropriate and lengthy ceremony. Seventh and last comes the magnificent crown.
>
> Seven differently scented ointments of ancient prescription are received on the imperial head, brow, and shoulders—one with each of these seven ornaments of the coronation.[12]

After this brief description, eyewitness Southard (the U.S. ambassador to Ethiopia) describes the "less elaborate but always impressive rites" that crowned the empress. Finally,

Howell's "Sceptre . . . which had been taken from the hands of Ethiopia some thousand years ago" is nowhere mentioned. What is recorded, however, is that "a gracious British gesture of recent years was the return to Ethiopia of Theodore's throne and crown," seized by Lord Napier of Magdala during an Ethiopian-supported invasion to free imprisoned British diplomats. These items had been housed in the intervening time in the British Museum.[13] Perhaps the returned scepter account grew from that returning of royal items.

Though it drew neither data nor phrasing from that report, the opening of Howell's book has a *National Geographic* flavor with its first bold-type title and its particular attention to the rulers in attendance at Selassie I's coronation. Fascinating variations on the story of the duke of Gloucester bowing before Selassie abound.[14] Of even greater significance to Rastas is the reported pledge by England's representative, in Howell's version, that King George V would "serve" Haile Selassie I "to the end." The list of divine titles bestowed on the Ethiopian emperor and the imparting of ruling scepters underscore Howell's central message in these early years: Haile Selassie is "Earth's Rightful Ruler" (a title celebrated today in hymns such as the melodica piece by Augustus Pablo). His queen, Her Imperial Majesty Itegue Menen, is identified here by a code name, Queen Omega. Alpha and Omega are the first and last letters, respectively, of the alphabet in Greek, the language in which the NT was written, suggesting here a divine totality; it echoes Jesus' words in the King James Version of Revelation 1:8, 11; 21:6; 22:13: "I am Alpha and Omega, the beginning and the ending." Selassie himself compared his queen to Sarah of the Hebrew Bible and lamented at her passing, noting that "she was overtaken by the fate of Adam" at the will of the "Almighty," whom he thanked for "having vouchsafed to us that long and uninterrupted union."[15] *The Promised Key*, however, presents the queen robed in silver splendor, borne on a mule, as in a depiction of Mary entering Bethlehem or of Christ at the triumphal entry. That Howell's perspective took precedence over the emperor's view among ensuing Rastas can be seen in such articles as Queen Omega Communications's "Who Is Queen Omega?" where she is called "the Rastafari Queen Mother of the Creation symbolized by the moon" and where "Mary, the mother of Christ," is called the "Queen Omega within that dispensation."[16]

The claim is made that "homage" given to Selassie fulfilled the messianic Twenty-first Psalm. Verses 3b–4 of Psalm 21 read "Thou settest a crown of pure gold on his head. He asked life of thee, and thou gavest it him, even length of days for ever and ever" (KJV). Perhaps Howell's application of this verse helped inspire the pervasive idea among Rastas that Selassie is immortal and is not dead but has simply disappeared.

The section ends with a provocative image for oppressed black Jamaican toilers, as Howell paints a picture of the black overlord tooling around in his roadster, checking how the "white laborers" are getting on with his many projects.[17] Howell's description of the "precious white robes" being discarded for "brilliant . . . special robes" and of the "Jewels of great value" presents Ethiopia as the heaven of the black spirituals, made this-worldly, with Whites serving black warrior overlords—much like the Black Muslims' depiction of the divine reversal of social power. Also interesting is the opening paragraph's "six thousand years" of unchanged attitude by Ethiopians. Why six thousand years? Rasta biblical literalism may be echoing here the traditional view of Archbishop James Usher, whose *Annales Veteris et Novi Testamenti* (1650–1654) posited that the world was created in 4004 B.C.E.

The False Religion

All the Churches Religious system of today, claims to represent the Lord God of Israel; but the Pope who is satan the devil, false organization, it is a hypocritical religious system that has three elements, first commercial political and ecclesiastical, to keep the people in ignorance of their wicked course.

Money powers is the great bulwarks of their organization and they use the Religious elements as a smoke screen to keep the people in ignorance of the truth.

The false teachers under the supervision of the Pope of Rome who is satan the devil. The agents of his speaking lies, in the churches, and let the people walk in darkness.

My dear Readers you can see that all their foundation of the earth are out of course. Allow me to say that there is no throne for the Anglo Saxon white people, they must come down and sit in the dust on the ground there is no throne for them. See Isiah 47th chapter.

King Alpha was wroth with us the Black People and had polluted our inheritance for 2520 years and had given us into the hands of the Anglo-Saxon white people, they showed us no mercy therefore evil shall come upon them suddenly

Now let the Astrologers and Star-gazers stand up and save the Anglo-Saxon Kingdom from the vengance that shall come upon them suddenly

Commentary

Attempting to set out a new "Christianity," Howell takes issue with Roman Catholicism. Why he attacks the Roman Catholic Church is not at first clear. After 1655 the Church of England, not Rome, had been dominant in Jamaica's political life and culture. Furthermore, no overt conflict was then occurring between Ethiopia's Orthodox Church (an Egyptian church planting) and Roman Catholicism. However, if the publication date of the *Key* was indeed 1935, some light may be shed on Howell's animosity. Mounting hostilities by Italy threatened during the first five years of Selassie's reign, and within a year of Howell's writing, the emperor was forced to flee Ethiopia. Scathing international criticism raked Italy. In Jamaica, such publications as *Plain Talk,* where Ianthe Robinson quoted the Honorable Mr. Wade as charging "Mussolini's God is his Gun," called on Jamaicans "to be true-hearted Ethiopians." Robinson clearly demonstrates the transition being made between a Garvey-informed republican idealism and a Selassie-oriented theocratic idealism:

> Let us try to achieve our aims and try to follow the path that the Hon. Marcus Garvey has made for us, let us teach even our very babes and sucklings of what was being hidden from us is being revealed to them today that we might soon worship under our own vine and fig-tree, and put on our Armour of Courage and our breast plate engraved "One God, One Aim, One Destiny," and print in our Minds that if there should be a battle, the Conquering Lion of Judah, The Mighty King of Kings must win for he is the Lord's Anointed.[18]

L.F.C. Mantle added, "What you have taught us about Jesus, is fulfilling in the land of Ethiopia right now: with the said same Romans or so called Italian or Fascist. These are the said people who crucified Jesus 2,000 years ago, and as we read that after 2,000 years, Satan's kingdom or organizations shall fall."[19] In a series of articles Mantle developed these themes, charging the pope with complicity. According to Mantle, "I have heard that 'Father' said that his followers must fast and pray that Mussolini wins the war." Mantle himself calls for a fast, empowered by Haile Selassie, who "means the 'Power of the Trinity,'" proclaiming, "Through fasting and praying we have Satan's kingdom to subdue."[20]

Justified or not, this identification of the pope with the plunderers of Ethiopia forged a satanic tag for the papacy in the rhetorical furnaces of those 1935 articles and Howell's book of the same period, which passed on into Rastafarian doctrine. A view of the pope as "Satan" is still held by many Rastas today. In Rastafarian reggae, antipapal references abound—from the subtle query in Black Uhuru's "Give My Love" to the overt challenge in the Meditations' "Rome," a song which declares bluntly that Rome is a wicked place. Further, Ansel Cridland of the Meditations (a roots-harmony singing group) explained to me in telephone conversations in May 1993 and February 1996 a Rasta point of view which states that the pope might even have been jealous of Bob Marley:

> When Bob went there, the pope was there before Bob about them two in conference. And was 80,000 people gathered to see him. And was 150,000 people gathered to see Bob. And Bob was there. So, you tell me nobody's saying to the pope now, which is the heart of Babylon, you know? And you have 80,000 people come out to him which is supposed to be a great leader. And a little man now, him have more than 150,000. You think them like those things? And with the world at him was saying and telling the people them how to live. You think this class isn't really making plans for people in this world?

For Howell, however, the main concern seems to be an "Anglo-Saxon" like the pope sitting on a "throne" as God's representative, instead of someone of darker complexion. Howell's citation of Isaiah 47 also introduced "Babylon" as a code name for Rome, a practice still followed today: "Come down, and sit in the dust, O virgin daughter of Babylon, sit on the ground: there is no throne" (Isaiah 47:1a KJV). The second to last paragraph claims that Selassie, as King Alpha, was responsible for allowing the enslavement of Blacks to be used as punishment and has now returned to rule, liberate, and avenge. Howell's vision of Selassie I apparently contained a ferocious left hand of punishment. The allusion to the astrologers of ancient Babylon (see Daniel 2:2) paints biblical detail into the identification.

The Promised Key

The glory that was Solomon greater still reigns in Ethiopia

We can see all the Kings of earth surrendering their crowns to His Majesty Ras Tafari the King of Kings and Lord of Lords Earth's Rightful Ruler to reign for ever and ever.

Upon His Majesty Ras Tafari's head are many diadems and on His garment a name written King of Kings and Lord of Lords oh come let us adore him for he is King of Kings and Lord of Lords. The Conquering Lion of Judah, The Elect of God and the Light of the world.

His Majesty Ras Tafari is the head over all man for he is the Supreme God. His body is the fullnes of him that filleth all in all. Now my dear people let this be our goal, forward to the King of Kings must be the cry of our social hope. Forward to the King of Kings to purify our social standards and our way of living, and rebuild and inspire our character. Forward to the King of Kings to learn the worth of manhood and womanhood. Forward to the King of Kings to learn His code of Law from the mount demanding obsolute Love, Purity, Honesty Truthfulness. Forward to the King of Kings to learn His Laws and social order, so that virtue will eventually gain the victory over our body and soul and that truth will drive away falsehood and fraud. Members of the King of Kings, arise for God's sake and put your armour on.

Dear inhabitants of this Western Hemisphere, the King of Kings warriors can never be defeated, the Pope of Rome and his agents shall not prevail against the King of Kings host warriors you all must stand up, stand up, for the King of Kings.

All ye warriors of the King of Kings lift high King Alpha's Royal Banner, from victory to victory King Alpha shall lead his army till every enemy is vanquished.

Commentary

Now Howell moves to the heart of his work, to what is labeled "The Promised Key." What was somewhat covert in the opening chapter is now overt. This part of *The Promised Key* functions as a commentary on the opening section, interpreting it so as to arrive at the conclusion that Haile Selassie is "the Supreme God." This chapter also contextualizes the reference to the war between "the King of Kings" and "the Pope of Rome and his agents," thereby making what was implicit unmistakably explicit. Most striking is Howell's bold statement that "His Majesty Ras Tafari" is "the Supreme God."

To support his claims, Howell troops out a number of allusions to Scripture passages and hymns that his audience would know. His opening picture of someone "greater" than Solomon may echo Matthew 12:42 and Luke 11:31, where Jesus summons the marveling of the queen of Sheba to claim that "a greater than Solomon is here" (KJV). Variations of that phrase may have provided popular hyperbolic comparisons in Israel. Jesus used a similar phrasing when citing God's care of flowers as proof of God's ability to provide for people's needs, observing, "Solomon in all his glory was not arrayed like one of these" (Matthew 6:29; Luke 12:27 KJV). Most pointed is the lifting out of Ephesians 1:23 and its application to Selassie. In context, that scripture comes as the culmination of the apostle Paul's discussion of hope in the power and glory of Christ. Christ is described as the "head over all things to the church, which is his body, the fulness of him that filleth all in all" (KJV). In Howell, that headship is ascribed to Selassie, whose body allegedly contains the divine fullness that calls all people into it.

Parallel to the scriptures cited are Howell's allusions to hymns. The Latin Christmas hymn "Adeste Fideles," translated by Frederick Oakeley (and others) in 1841 as "O come, all ye faithful," crops up in the second paragraph, "Oh come let us adore him." From the last line of the penultimate paragraph through the final paragraph is a close paraphrase of the 1858 rouser "Stand up, stand up for Jesus." Compare lyricist George Duffield's original with Howell's adaptation:

Stand up, stand up for Jesus, Ye soldiers of the cross,
Lift high His royal banner, It must not suffer loss:
From victory unto victory His army shall He lead,
Till every foe is vanquished and Christ is Lord indeed.

All of this section in Howell is couched in this hymnic and apocalyptic language—for example, for the combination of "diadem" and "a name written," see Revelation 19:12, 16, and compare the hymn "All hail the power of Jesus' name"; or see the Scripture passage Revelation 14:1, for the name's ability to be transferred to the faithful. These biblical and hymnic allusions were intended to cushion what, for Christians, would be a monstrous claim: that Selassie, not simply Jesus, is "the Supreme God."

Today, Howell's view is in much debate among Rastafarians. The best discussion I have seen has been done by the Rastafarian stateswoman Barbara Blake Hannah. She confronts Marcus Garvey's hope and disappointment in Selassie I: "This time Garvey looked to Ethiopia, where the Emperor Haile Selassie I had recently been crowned. But when Ethiopia was invaded by Italy, and Selassie I fled to England, Garvey's dream was finally shattered. In a bitter attack against Selassie I, Garvey called him 'a cowardly lion' for not staying to fight the Italian fascists."[21] Further, Hannah courageously confronts "rumours of Governmental corruption" that blocked "enormous amounts of international aid" from reaching the starving when "Ethiopia suffered a disastrous famine." She writes, "The Emperor was accused of ignoring the suffering of the people, while living in luxury and wealth, and of turning a blind eye to the corruption which kept the aid from reaching the starving." Freeing herself from other Rastas' adherence to Howell's view, Hannah points out that "such an attitude is very selective" with regard to the Bible: "They will use Biblical passages to support their claims and theories, such as the use of Revelations 5:1–5, to support the thesis that Haile Selassie is the Christ and returned Messiah—ignoring the rest of Revelations which specifically refers to Jésus Christ, the Lamb that was Slain for the sins of the World." Finally, Hannah acknowledges Selassie's own denial of claims such as Howell's, noting, "Despite the hero-worship accorded him on his visit [to Jamaica], the Emperor continually repeated, 'Do not worship me: I am not God.' "[22]

Hannah would like to adjust Rastafari to meet these challenges and fit Selassie's self-identification as a follower of Jesus, a defender of the Christian church:

> The worship of Selassie I as the returned Messiah, is held as a basic tenet of Rastafari faith, especially among dreadlocks Rastafari. Though information about Selassie's life is coming to light which shows that he was a man with human weaknesses and faults, it is not unrealistic to perceive HIM as a Christ example, especially because of how racially liberating it has been for Black people to focus on a Black Christ-figure. . . . Even if the question of his divinity remains unverified until Kingdom come, it must be acknowledged that by his inspiration and in his name, Black brothers and sisters awakened and established a new and unique interest in God and Christ.[23]

Hannah's contribution serves to move Rastafari back to Marcus Garvey's focus, "to see God and Christ as black," since "Rastafari have eventually had to acknowledge that

Christ is the only name in which Salvation is given. Selassie cannot replace the supremacy of Christ."[24] As she explained to me during a national prayer breakfast in Kingston in 1989, God manifested the divine self powerfully through Selassie I, as God has done through Martin Luther King, Jr., Mahatma Gandhi, and many others. Although Howell's bold assertion that "the King of Kings warriors can never be defeated . . . till every enemy is vanquished" did not prove true when the emperor's own people revolted, still Hannah's reinterpretation of Selassie as a black spiritual leader and follower of Christ (whom one follows *to* Christ) is a potent corrective for Rastafari's future.

Ethiopia's Kingdom

Dear inhabitants of this world King Ras Tafari and Queen Omega are the foundation stones of the resurrection of the Kingdom of Ethiopia.

Their prayer and labour for our resurrection is past finding out; no library in this world is able to contain the work of their hands for us, for they work both day and night for our deliverance.

As for this generation of the 20th century you and I have no knowledge how worlds are build and upon what trigger Kingdoms are set.

In King Alpha's Encyclopedia he will explain to us all, how worlds are being built and upon what trigger Kingdoms are set on. He will also explain to us the capacities of generations.

Speaking for the Universe and the womanhood of man Queen Omega the Ethiopian woman is the crown woman of this world. She hands us Her Rule Book from the poles of supreme authority she is the Cannon Mistress of creation.

King Alpha and Queen Omega are the paymasters of the world, Bible owner and money mint. Do not forget they are Black People if you please.

Owing to the universal rend of our ancient and modern Kingdoms we are at this junction of our history scattered over the Globe into little sectional groups

All our local bands throughout the globe are bent towards King Alpha's Royal Repository, the Royal Authority is to admit all Bands, Mission Camps, Denominations into this supreme Royal Repository.

Queen Omega being the balming mistress of many worlds she charges the powerhouse right now.

Ethiopia is the succeeding Kingdom of the Anglo-Saxon Kingdom. A man of greater learning and a better Christian soul, than King Alpha is not to be found on the face of the Globe. He makes the nations hearts rejoice with raging joy, we give him the glory. Ethiopia rule book leads us into different departments of the Kingdom, the records of the Kingdom are with us unto this day. The Regulations points us to the basis of the Kingdom.

Many will not see the truth, because they are spiritually blind. See Matthew 3:13. The woman of Samaria first re[f]used to obey the request of our Lord because she was spiritually blind. But when the great Physician opened up her eyes and healed her of her infirmities concerning her many husbands in the city of Samaria, she found out that her first teachers of denominations throughout the state or country of Samaria were false. Then she cried aloud unto the inhabitants of the city and said "Come see a man that told me all that I ever did" and is not a native of Samaria but an Hebrew, is not this man the very Christ. Our cities of today are inhabited with the same qualities of people as it was in the days of Jesus and the woman of Samaria.

Commentary

Biblical language is replete throughout this section. Paul's picture of Christ as the "foundation" of faith in 1 Corinthians 3:11 is applied now to King Ras Tafari and Queen Omega, as is the term *resurrection,* which, in Christian theology, is inseparably tied to Jesus' return from death. The claim that no library is able to contain the record of all their works is taken directly from the last verse of the Gospel of John (21:25), where the disciple supposes the world itself would not be large enough to hold all the books required to account for all that Jesus did. The reference to not knowing how worlds are built is an echo of God's challenge to Job's ignorance (Job 38:4). Howell intentionally invoked Bible knowledge in his readers to suggest they acknowledge that Selassie and his queen are the "Bible owners."

"Paymasters of the world" is an interesting phrase. The 1960 UWI report paints a picture of Howell himself living at Pinnacle mansion, calling himself "God," surrounded by thirteen wives and concubines, acquiring increasing amounts of land, and presiding over a large estate worked by his devoted followers. Howell would not have had a problem with the allegations that Selassie put large sums of money in Swiss banks; he would feel that the wealth of the earth naturally belongs to "God."[25]

The Healing

The healing plough of the repository transplanted and rebuild our very soul and body without fail. The misery of the land is healed by fasting. King Alpha picks us up from out of the midst of the raging misery of the land and hide us from the raging wolves of the land into our Balm Yard. What is a Balm Yard? A Balm Yard is a Holy place that is wholly consecrated to God Almighty for the cleansing and healing of the nations. Where only the holy spirit of God alone is allowed to do the Royal work of healing. Who does the balming work? Consecrated men and women that the holy spirit moves upon the blazing altar of their soul and endowed them with power that they command and handle the infirmities of the nations.

Have we any authority from King Alpha? Yes we are vessels of the divine honour. Have we any authority from the world? Assuredly yes indeed, King Alpha signs for our destiny and gave us His Supreme Affidavit for a trillion centuries after the end of etern[a]l life.

Balm Yard

First and last every soul for admission must be believers in the power of King Ras Tafari the living God.

An admission fee must be paid in advance from four shillings up according to the power and duration of the miserable infirmities whereof one is afflicted. (Special Notice)

Sometimes King Alpha has to perform special medical attention.

Royal Notice

King Alpha said Bands are not runned by Ministers, they are runned by the Priesthood not after the order of Aaron but strictly after the Royal Order of King Ras Tafari the King of Kings of Ethiopia.

Revivalists are not common people, if some individuals of the lower order in the dung heap happen to get into the world by mistake he or she will soon get out and hang him or herself The reason why revivalists world have not been lightened up with radiance before now, King Alpha was awaiting for the Delegates of the Resurrection of the Kingdom of Ethiopia and King Alpha's work is strictly perfect and He and Queen Omega do not business with Anglo Militant white people nakedness.

King Alpha said that a Balm Yard is not a Hospital neither is it a obeah shop. People that are guilty of obeah must not visit balm yards nor in the Assembly of Black Supremacy. No admittance for Fortune tellers witch and old hige. No admittance for obeah dogs none whatever, no admittance for ghost witch lizards, no admittance for Alligators, Snakes, Puss, Crabs Flies, Ants, Rats, and Mice, and Lodestones, Pin, and Needles. John Crows, the Ravens and Candles, fast Cups and Rum Bottles and Grave Yards are not required.

People's clothes a beast hair and fowls and grave dirt not wanted. The Woman's baby will strive in her belly, and your Snake and Lizards; will not be able to hurt her. For your ghosts will come right back to you. For this is Ethiopia balm yard and we do not have leprosy. For ghost only visit the lepers home.

This poison is for all bad spirit it is No. 666 it is good for the Pope of Rome and the Monarch of hell bottom you will not be here to grudge, or obeah, or rob, the people nor breed up the young girls and treat them like dogs.

You will not plant your obeah self with no man or woman so that we who are King Alpha's children cannot get rid of you until the obeah rotten. Science my dear King your black and white heart obeah factory is upside down. Take this ramkin dose of fatal deadly poison and leave for God's sake do it quickly. Supreme law of King Alpha the King of Kings, you will not blind give big foot or sore, or turn any more children across the woman's belly and kill her baby when it is born, nor any time after Every good looking man's wife you see you want to cohabit with her, you rotten gut snake, and anywhere a man put a business you go there to kill and drive him away, you dead cold horse.

This pole is black Supremacy owned by King Alpha the King of Kings, now Ethiopia knew the perfect value of Holy Baptism under water, for King Alpha taught us how to appreciate the power of holy baptism.

Now we the Black People have no pardon to beg white supremacy no favours to ask her for she is an acknowledged deceiver. From B.C. 4004 to A.D. second score, she faked all Christianity

Black Supremacy the Church Triumph have denounced her openly for baptism is a very important subject to Black Supremacy.

Commentary

Modern Rastas distance themselves from Obeah, the West African form of sorcery, the underside of traditional religion.[26] For some, "the Obeah man" has become a symbol of oppression, paralleled with the "rich man," for example, in the musical group Culture's song "Them A Payaka," which pleads for allowing children to get nourishment, not having it stolen away. "Put down the Obeah book," calls the band the Ethiopians in the song "Obeah Book," for it is "iniquity." "Iniquity" is what Andrew Tosh termed it in conversation with me on March 31, 1993, in Cambridge, Massachusetts. He snorted at any literal interpretation of the symbolism of demons in the film *Stepping Razor—Red X* and any suggestion that his father, reggae star Peter Tosh, consulted an African sorcerer for protection (which would mean that Peter Tosh dabbled in Obeah).

When I asked, "Might your father have looked into Obeah himself, or Ouija boards, for protection?" Andrew Tosh replied firmly, "No, man! It's iniquity! My father didn't say nothing like that." Still, he agreed that his father had been plagued by Obeah spells: "It's more than possible. It happened all the time, but it didn't have no effect!" That casting spells is part of "African science" Rastas are ready to admit, but for the group Black Uhuru, whom I interviewed on March 31, 1993, in Cambridge, Massachusetts, it is still a "con." In a telephone conversation on October 27, 1993, Ziggy Marley recognized, "What some of you call 'Obeah' is also part of our heritage, a part of our culture dating way back," but he, too, separated his father from the idea of dabbling in magic, calling Bob's power "natural."

The Myal country remedies preserved by the Maroons are often thought of as a "white witchcraft" that combats the effects of Kumina's Obeah component, and perhaps this is what Howell is recommending in *The Promised Key*. Femi Adeyema, an Evangelical Churches of West Africa (ECWA) pastor in the Niger state, told me in a telephone interview around the spring of 1993, that in Nigeria's syncretistic Cherubim and Seraphim Society churches (which draw from both Christianity and traditional religion), "the priest will give African traditional medicine for counselees. If they feel the witchcraft is strong of satanic forces they might have some other satanic forces to combat this. They encourage the use of candles, prayer vigils, holy waters; a priest himself can use satanic forces. . . . I know ministers who use satanic forces." John Aboyeji of Lagos, a religious leader in Nigeria, amplified this point for me further during an interview around the summer of 1993 in South Hamilton, Massachusetts, in his analysis of the Jehovah Jiri church movement: "These churches believe that God wants you to make an attempt to ward evil away. This is called *ajo*. So, they preach the Bible—and give you a charm." When George Eaton Simpson first analyzed the Rastafari, he observed this balance between Obeah and Myal: "Trances and witchcraft have no place in the Ras Tafari movement itself. While they denounce Revivalist healers and conjurers, Ras Tafarians utilize any knowledge they or their relatives and friends may have concerning bush teas and other traditional remedies for the treatment of illnesses."[27]

Howell may well have been drawing from the Myal tradition in these three adjacent sections, "The Healing," "Balm Yard," and "Royal Notice," reintroducing the healing yard of African traditional religion, where sufferers take up residence until they are healed, in order to combat the destructive effects of Obeah. In the "Royal Notice" section he says explicitly of the healing yard that "neither is it a obeah shop," and Obeah's paraphernalia are not admitted. With acerbity, Howell suggests more than the Ethiopians do in their song "Obeah Book," when they tell the Obeah worker to jump into his own pot; Howell curses these practitioners vehemently, suggesting they take "fatal deadly poison." However, despite his apparent intentions, Howell himself reportedly ran into misunderstanding with the Garveyites in New York City. Eyewitnesses told Robert Hill that Howell was a "con–man" and "samfie (obeah) man," doing "nefarious practices," although Howell's brother defended him as having "excellent hands with sickness" and thereby helping many.[28] Perhaps the difficulty lay with his charging for his services, a provision seen here in the "Balm Yard" section.

One puzzle left hanging in Howell's use of biblical language and imagery in this section (e.g., the "Priesthood not after the order of Aaron," "the Resurrection," "666," etc.) is the intriguing reference to the "perfect value" and "power" of baptism as a "very important subject to Black Supremacy." While present-day Rastas inside and some outside the Ethiopian Orthodox Church practice baptism, others, such as the members of Black Uhuru in our 1993 interview, dismiss it along with Obeah as a "con":

GARTH DENNIS: Yeah, a bottle of water, you know, that maybe take a boat up off the river and say, "God bless you guys . . . "

DON CARLOS: And put up on the shore and say, "It's real vital!"

DERRICK SIMPSON: You know, same as the baptism you guys do in church, and someone be there then, that don't mean nothing too tough. It's just a routine.

Howell, however, seems to have practiced baptism.

How To Fast

The King of Kings of creation the first and last said "Blessed are they that searcheth the deep things on the tree of life for His wisdom is deep and is past all finding out". Thus said the living God owner of life, to overcome white bondage and filth and black hypocrisy amongst your own black skin you have to fast hard for the white man is very filthy and the black man is an hyprocrite and hyprocrite means a crook, a filthy man is that class of white folks who cuts with the crook they are called Black White.

Always have a basin of fine or coarse salt on your fast table as long as God is your ruler. When you break your fast do not throw the water over your heads the trouble will fall on you. When you are all ready with your cup in hand the Elder will ask is it all well with thee, everybody shall say together all is well with me. Then the Elder shall ask again "Who will bear a true witness for the Tree of life?" All shall say by the living God I will God help me for life, and the leader shall say follow me with your cup of troubles to the burying place of sin and shame.

Then everybody walk quietly and respectfully throw away the water, then come in and wash your hands and face in a basin of salt and water Then break your real fast and be happy feeling satisfied and revived and lovely. House to house fasting is very powerful, it lifts the work and remov[e]s devils from homes of those in distress. Once a week for the general assembly is all right A love feast every three or six months is needed.

Commentary

Rastas seek to honor the strict lifestyle of the Nazarite, which is described in Numbers 6 and includes abstinence from alcohol and anything unclean (see also Judges 13:4,7). If, in 1935, L.F.C. Mantle was calling for a fast in support of Selassie, Howell was ordering one to achieve purification and holiness. Involved in his prescription is an elaborate ritual to make sure troubles do not return and sin and shame are buried. The exercise ends with a love feast (if an extra "e" has not crept in on "love fast"), a title taken from the love or agape feast practiced by the early Christian church (1 Corinthians 11:17–34;

and also Justin Martyr's *First Apology* 65, 67, to see how it continued in the early church). Before the time of the Roman emperor Trajan (C.E. 98–117), Holy Communion—also called the Eucharist or the Lord's Supper—was a part of the agape feast, although later it was separated. Today, Rastas in the Ethiopian Orthodox Church celebrate the Eucharist. Perhaps Howell also included Holy Communion in his "love feast."

Also puzzling is Howell's departure from Jesus' teaching that when Christ, the church's "bridegroom," is present, one does not fast (Mark 2:19). For Howell, though Selassie was visibly present on earth, "hard" fasting was still necessary. Also, in the version of *The Promised Key* we found, a later hand has expunged what appears to be a recommendation for washing in a basin of *salt* and water and has substituted the handwritten word *herb*, indicating that the emphasis on ganja (now called by some "the chalice") came later.

Department

Mount Africa the world's capital, the new Bible land, the triumphant lot is for King Alpha own lot until this day. Slave Traders called the world's capital, Jamaica British West Indies. Before the Adamic deadly diseases poisoned the human family with fallen Angels, blue murder, there has been only one perfect language on the face of the globe. Therefore the Anglo Militant fallen Angels tongues are not appreciated by His Majesty King Alpha the Monarch of life. Thus said Ras Tafari the living God to creation; vast Rome has deceived the race of man, and has killed the mortal supreme monarch Ethiopia's glory is no guessor long before this world was Ethiopia's glory has been running Cotrillions of centuries ago.

Ethiopia's Repository will charge and qualify the fallen Angels deadly poisonous indomitable lying tongue. Stupidity is the most they get out of the various tongues spoken by the majority. Ninety five out of every one hundred do not know what they do or say any ghost can fool them at any corner.

Government

Black Supremacy has taken charge of white supremacy by King Alpha and Queen Omega the King of Kings. Instead of saying Civilization hereafter we all shall say Black Supremacy. Just take this drench of indomitable fury and move for the Church triumphant right from the bridge of supreme authority.

Black Supremacy will promote the mortals of every shade according to our power to go. The Black Museum will be opened day and night for life. Education will be free and compulsory to all mortal beings, if you are not an enemy of Black Supremacy.

Men and women can marry right in School if you are of a respectable proportion of dignity. Black must not marry white nor white black, race enmity.

Always be a respectful diplomat, always give an intelligent reply to every person that approach or write you on any subject always ask for the full value inside nature of any written subject Do not put your quick judgment on any person confidence is quick to move, just what the people are that is just the state of your government. Do not follow the Court House and Doctors they will fake you to death. Do not marry any divorced person it is a curse, stick to your own wife and husband.

Do not watch and peep your wife or husband, you are only digging a grave for yourself. Do not try to make your wife or husband or family feel small because you have got more college filth in your head, hold them up, they are the cause of you being what you are. I know thousands of college hogs and dogs, professional swines; also some very fine people.

Eternal Law Office

His and Her Majesty King Alpha and Queen Omega said that they do not call ministers to Black Supremacy banquets for ministers are not working for him they are following Adam Abraham Anglo Saxon the leper. Legislators said one man cannot serve two masters.

Adam Abraham the leper is boss for ministers and lawyers because all they teach and preach about is Adam-Eve and Abraham the leper. For they do not see even one book in the Bible written by Adam and Eve or the book of Abraham or book of Isaac. According to the clearness of this case there is nobody named Adam Eve and Abraham.

If you ever touch the slave papers they catch you sure as His Majesty Ras Tafari lives. The officers and soldiers at camp that have power and influence are well posted by King Alpha the King of Kings, their names you will not know. Legislators said one man cannot serve two masters. Ministers say they can't work with Adam and Eve, and work for King Alpha and Queen Omega the same time. Abraham the historian said despise the both of them; lawyers said you have got to find fault with them, the judge said leave the Alpha and Omega out, because they are black and skin for skin.

Commentary

One rumor that circulated in early Rastafari was that Selassie had become head of a militant organization called Nyabinghi (Niyabinghi), meaning "Death to the white and black oppressors." This is very strange since, in reality, Selassie was a statesman attempting to work peacefully with everyone and a close friend of North American evangelist Billy Graham. At Graham's invitation, Selassie opened the World Congress on Evangelism in Berlin (1966), announcing a "wish to recall here the spirit of tolerance shown by our Lord Jesus Christ when he offered forgiveness to all including those that crucified him."[29] The Selassie of Howell's vision seems much more pugnacious than Graham's friend. While, at the evangelism congress, the emperor simply pledged "not to fail to resist with courage . . . incursions" on his "Christian" nation,[30] the Selassie of Howell's presentation is at war as well with the English language ("Anglo Militant fallen Angels tongues"), Rome, racial intermarriage, legislators, and ministers and would regard Anglo-Saxons (as Graham would be) as cursed lepers.

The distance between Howell's exclusivistic Ras Tafari and the real Haile Selassie's inclusivism is irreconcilable. The emperor himself proclaimed to the Berlin evangelism gathering:

Our Ethiopian Orthodox church, which was cut off for centuries from her fellow Christian churches, has joined the World Council of Churches and cooperates in the task of strengthening the faith and bringing about church unity. We have helped and will continue to help the missionaries who are sent from other lands to preach the Gospel to those of our people who have not come to the knowledge of God's saving grace. As the unity of the church is of great concern to us and, God willing, we are hopeful that this sacred objective might be achieved in our day and age, we were happy to have convened two years ago a meeting of

the Heads of the Oriental Orthodox churches in our capital city of Addis Ababa to deliberate on ways and means of bringing about harmony and unity in the church.

We refer to all this only to indicate that this age above all ages is a period in history when
it should be our prime duty to preach the Gospel of Grace to all our fellow men and women.
The love shown in Christ by our God to mankind should constrain all of us who are followers and disciples of Christ to do all in our power to see to it that the Message of Salvation is carried to those of our fellows for whom Christ our Savior was sacrificed but who
have not had the benefit of hearing the Good News.[31]

In addition, rather than bringing to Jamaica in 1966 the militant "pay master" curses
promised in Howell's cadenced prose, Selassie brought to the parliament a message of
global reconciliation: "I also believe that the peoples of Jamaica and Ethiopia have another important cause in common, that is the cause of international peace."[32]

Against the real personage, Howell's version of Selassie is ferociously exclusivistic.
Howell's personal platform, as we will see in "Eve the Mother of Evil" and "The Rapers,"[33] is an inverse racism to the racist horrors inflicted on black slaves by slavehold-
ers and post-slavery white supremacy movements such as the Ku Klux Klan. The puzzle of why, today, the United States is lumped in with Great Britain and plantocratic
Jamaica as "Babylon" is answered here: the United States is Babylon because of the rape
of black women and the lynching of black men in North America. One irony in Howell's segregationist views with regard to intermarriage is that, one day, the most successful proponent of the Rastafari he helped set in motion would be one of "the third
class," the son of a black woman and a white man: Bob Marley. And further, Marley's
Rastafarian chants would be purchased (and treasured) by millions of ardent Anglo-
Saxon fans. For Howell, however, "King Alpha" is "not any family" to "Anglo Saxon
Slave Owners," who "are to be shot."

Finally, even if Howell was ignorant of Selassie's warm sentiments toward the United
States, the Rastas whom Simpson observed, who often quoted almost verbatim from
Southard's "Modern Ethiopia" article, must have continually read Southard's words:
"An outstanding impression which I have of this country during the 14 years I have
known it first hand is the feeling of friendship and admiration for the United States and
its citizens. . . . A very frequent remark of His Imperial Majesty to me is, 'We want closer
relations with America; we want more Americans to visit us; we want American assistance in the development of our country.' "[34]

Rastas' first clashes with Christian leaders are also evident in Howell's report that
ministers say they "can't work with Adam and Eve, and work for King Alpha and
Queen Omega at the same time" (a section built on Christ's warning that no one can
serve two masters, God and money; Matthew 6:24; Luke 16:13).[35] Also, Howell appears to attack the Hebrew patriarchs as "lepers." Why "lepers?" The Rastafarian author John Moodie explains, "Leprosy is disease that changes the black skin from its natural state to white."[36] In this view, the white race began when "Japhet, last son of Noah,
migrated to the Caucasian mountains where he was struck with leprosy."[37] To be white,
then, is to be cursed with disease. "Adam Abraham," if appropriated by Whites as
white, must, by this view, be cursed with leprosy.

Eve the Mother of Evil

The Adamic tree of knowledge and Eve the mother of Evil, see Genises 2nd. chapter. The Adamic apple tree, my dear leper your name is Adam-Abraham Anglo Saxon apple tree, that looks pretty and respectable to your eyes don't it? Yes indeed gross beauty is the Queen in hell, and Royal leper Adam and Eve and Abraham and Anglo Saxon are all white people if you please.

King Alpha and Queen Omega said that they are Black Arch Sovreign of most Holy Times, and perfect Virginity, and Supreme Crown Head of Holy Times. The Pay Master and keeper of the Perfect Tree of Life and are Creators of Creation, Dynasties and Kingdoms, Holy Genealogy and Holy Theocracy, and Celestial in Terrestial Mediator if you wish to know their profession.

The Eternal Come Back King Alpha the Monarch Sovreign Pay Master, and Owner of this world. Just make one Eternal come back at His Pay Office. King Alpha and his wife Queen Omega, were here on earth before if you please. Old Alpha the Lion of Creation, said to Queen Omega please hand me the Pay Roll and the Militant and Balance Sheet. And your Majesty will mount His Excellency's Great Circle Throne, and throw Old Theocracy above the Wheel of Holy Time, right into Holy Eternity to the Lion of Alpha and Omega the King of Kings of forevermore.

King Alpha and Queen Omega are Black People if you please. They are commonly called the Exodus if you please, the book of Exodus is theirs if you please. Notice if you see Moses and Aaron and Abraham gave any strong report of King Alpha and Queen Omega in their fake Bible if you please.

King Ras Tafari said personally that he is His Majesty King Alpha, the King of Kings the world's pay master if you please. Well since a man has right to pay without work, this world can also work with pay.

There is no book in the Bible for the Anglo Saxon Creation, there is no book of Isaac or his father Abraham in the New Testament.

King Alpha the Most Sacred and Everliving God, Heaven and Earth's creator, said that Adam Abraham-Anglo Saxon white people are not entitled to any eternal reward according to his schedule.

My dear Ethiopians, Ethiopia is the crown head of this earth field since heaven has been built by His Majesty Ras Tafari the living God. Thanks and praise the ever living God as long as eternal ages roll.

King Alpha and Queen Omega said that they are our parents, and the keeper of the Tree of Life. He and his wife are not any family at all to Adam and Eve and Abraham and Isaac and the Anglo Saxon Slave Owners; for that is exactly how His Majesty King Noah the Black Monarch was drowned at Antediluvia by Adam Abraham, the Anarchy.

Judge Samson lost his tribunal and life by marrying the Philistine white woman. See Judges 14, 15, and 16th chapters. See how the Philistine Judges plotting out riddles with the woman how to get him.

The Rapers

The AMERICAN rapers Klu-Klux Klan and Mob Lynching policy! "These unfortunate ones, are the outcome of the advance Rate" on the Anglo Saxon slave train. The Advance Rate means—in the time of slavery, the white slave masters committed boisterous fornication with the black women that were taken for slaves.

In those days the black men had no opportunity to (Rate) that is, to lie with white woman. Therefore, while the black men's blood was burning up in their bodies for the sexual support of their own women the white slave masters took away all the best black women and committed biosterous fornication with them and called it Advance Rate that is how the third class people came into the human vein.

In those days this act was called the Advance Rate of white supremacy; it is the universal spirit of abuse that manifests itself that the common class black man are now raping the common class white women.

Both rapers and mob lynchers and Klu-Klux Klan are to be shot down from off the face of God Almighty's beautiful earth.

Commentary

At this point, Howell uses the vehicle of biblical commentary to wage race war against Anglo-Saxons. His suspicion that the Bible was perverted by Whites is still held by many Rastas (consider, e.g., Steel Pulse's "Not King James Version" or Junior Delgado's "King James"), along with his assection that, in the true Bible, "there is no book . . . for the Anglo Saxon Creation." That the true biblical characters were black (or "citizens of Africa," as Ras Moodie puts it) is universally held by Rastas and endemic throughout Rasta oratory, poetry, lyrics, and discourse. In this context, "Eve" represents a multi-image: the Anglo-Saxon White ("Anglo Saxon apple tree," "all white people if you please"); the whore of Babylon in Revelation 17, which is traditionally understood as pagan Rome ("gross beauty is the Queen in hell"); and perhaps forces as diverse as the Christian church and Jamaican government that Howell saw as opposing him.

What the biblical Noah being "drowned at Antediluvia" by Whites means is enigmatic. That the Samson story is used to indicate Blacks (male) emasculated by white (female) culture is clear enough. The sexual themes in such earlier sections as "Government" here sublimate into highly charged imagery. The phallic "tree of knowledge" planted in Eve makes her "mother of Evil," in contrast to Selassie and his empress's sovereignty and "perfect Virginity." While blame is shared between the two progenitors, the use of the specific noun *Eve* against the adjective *Adamic,* along with "Eve the Mother of Evil" being the sole member of the pair to comprise the title, clearly places more emphasis on Eve than on Adam as the source of evil. Did Howell attempt to salvage this section from a completely pernicious misogyny by putting Queen Omega on a pedestal? Whatever his reasons, Howell's patriarchal message at the dawn of the formulation of Rastafarian doctrine has plagued women within the movement ever since.

Recent attempts to correct this patriarchy in Rastafari have come from the speeches of Barbara Blake Hannah; from a number of new books and articles focusing on women in Rastafari (see Chapter 4 and 5 by Maureen Rowe and Imani Tafari-Ama in this volume); from songs such as Judy Mowatt's "Black Woman," "Slave Queen," "Sisters' Chant" (*Black Woman,* LP, Shanachie 43011, 1983), Carlene Davis's "She Is Not for Sale" and "Taking Control" (*Songs of Freedom,* Lagoon LG2-1076, 1993), Ranking Ann's "Liberated Woman" (*A Slice of English Toast,* Ras Arico 002, 1991), Lillian

Allen's "Sister Hold On" (*Conditions Critical*, Verse to Vinyl 102, 1988), and collections such as *Womantalk: Caribbean Dub Poetry* (Heartbeat 25, 1986) and *Roots Daughters* (Ras Ari 039, 1988), as well as Sister Carol's "Black Cinderella" (*Black Cinderella* Heartbeat 193, 1984) and Mutabaruka's "Great Queens of Africa" (*Blakk Wi Blak . . . K . . . K . . .* Shanachie 43083, 1991); and through a number of films where everyday Rasta women are allowed to speak for themselves. Films such as those by Jasmin Sung (*Rasta Women: Daughters of Zion*), Renee Romano and Eye in I Filmworks (*Rastafari: Conversations Concerning Women*), and Bianca Nyavingi Brynda (*Roots Daughters*) serve as vehicles for the Rasta female voice. In addition, *Roots Daughters* contains a radical reinterpretation of Rastafari as a matriarchal cult, whose Nyabinghi component is named after an African warrior queen Nyabinghi. In various ways, Rastawomen are now seeking to remove from their shoulders the burden of being considered evil and the cause of society's ills that was placed on them by sources such as *The Promised Key*.

Ethiopian Question

The Ethiopia Question is this. The continent of Ethiopia is that national. She is that rich national woman that has charmed the men of nations to lie with her.

After a time when they all have lived and cohabited with her they all broke her down and left her and persecuted her.

That is just how all nations manage to soak through the Ethiopian woman of prosperity. She had too much sympathy for the perishing nations, whose lives are riotously lived until this day.

Slave traders went into Ethiopia and damaged her seeds, beyond any earthly cure. Because she had too much sympathy for wilfull idlers of various nations. So they went into her and robbed her lands, money and took her seeds to be slaves.

Today she and her children have no power in her own land, nor abroad. All that Ethiopians have to do now, is build anew. Get out a new dictionary and a new Bible, and new Board of Education, and Money Mint. The outfit shall be called Black Supremacy; signed by His and Her Majesty Ras Tafari and Queen Omega the King of Kings, head of this world.

The lesson learnt by slave traders through Black Histories is well preserved. We have given our blood, souls, bodies and spirits to redeem Adam Abraham Anglo Saxon the white man from his dreadful downfall and leprosy, but from 4004 B.C. to A.D. second score at his astonishing stop. He is still infested with the indomitable, incurable, accursed, deadly disease. We have given him access to the tree of life, we gave him the Garden of Eden, we gave him Egypt, we gave them Daniel and the body of the Black Virgin, the mother of Jesus and they took Joseph also.

We gave ourselves to be slaves for hundreds of years. We gave up King Alpha and Queen Omega the first and the last Now we are digusted with them, we wash our hands of them for life.

Commentary

Now Howell moves directly to the major concern for Ethiopianist diasporan blacks of 1935: the question of Ethiopia's fate. His approach is to mimic Hebrew prophets' imagery of Israel as a harlot, whoring after other gods. For Howell, however, the concern is economic. Ethiopia is depicted as a "rich national woman" robbed and betrayed by other nations. Since most slaves in Jamaica came from West Africa, the reference to Ethiopia no doubt encompasses all of Africa. Howell's cosmological tableau is certainly all-encompassing—from his beginning of time ("4004 B.C.") to the present ("A.D. second score"), the cursed and therefore leprously white slave trader has been kidnapping Africans. Why Africans? Whites picked Africans because of their generosity: "We have given him access to the tree of life, we gave him the Garden of Eden, we gave him Egypt. . . . We gave ourselves to be slaves for hundreds of years."

Today, this view of Whites taking advantage of black generosity as a reason for the instigation of black slavery continues among Rastas.[38] That Muslims, Arabs, and Blacks enslaved Blacks in Africa centuries before the advent of white European slavers does not figure into Howell's polemic. What is significant for Howell is the archetypal symbol of Whites (Italians) enslaving Blacks (Ethiopians); but this time, the day of deliverance from all oppression has arrived in the figures of royal black deliverers: King Alpha and Queen Omega. These will "build anew" all things—"a new dictionary," "Bible," "Board of Education," and "Money Mint"—creating a new society supportive of Blacks both at home in Ethiopia and abroad in places such as diasporan Jamaica.

The First and the Last

His Majesty Ras Tafari alone with his own bona-fide Lion hearted wife, Queen Omega King of Kings, most Living and Eternal, and Ever Living Sovreign owner of Life, the Biblical Sovreign of this world.

His Majesty Ras Tafari the Bible Owner of Holy Times, denounced the Bible Militant also the Militant Dictionary. And take off the Black man his posterities from off the Anglo Militant Slave Train at Nationality and planted the Church Triumphant.

The Black Supremacy on triumphant soil of the world's capital. The new Bible Land, the Isles of Springs. The same country that the Anarchy called Jamaica British West Indies. Black Supremacy's greatest men and women are sub-ways and air masters of every shade, they sleep in bed and eat with you, and you do not know what triggers your life and destiny is on the Gods of laws are my students said the King of Kings the air you are breathing this minute is for King Ras Tafari. The barbed wire eternity is his; the brimstone and fire, volcanos is his; every thunder and lightning is his. I want you to know that the firmament is his. When He speaks to her she obeys His Royal Voice, His and Her Majesty Ras Tafari and Queen Omega the King of Kings. Races and Nations, languages and tongues and other people will come and go from off the face of this earth. But King Alpha and Queen Omega and we the Black People that is King Alpha and Queen Omega seeds will be here in in gross prosperity as soon as the Anglo Saxon white peoples all die out if you please.

King Alpha and Queen Omega are the type setters for time and eternity if you please. His appointment is an eternal appointment if you please. The keeper of the tree of life, owner of the Zodiac, owner of this earth; they are the Ethiopian Kingdom owner if you please, they are the Register General of Black Supremacy, if you please. Adam Abraham Anglo Saxon the leper has no place in this earth if you please.

Commentary

Jesus' words in Matthew 19:30, "But many that are first shall be last; and the last shall be first" (KJV), provide the section heading. The allusion seems quite appropriate in Howell's schema. Jesus' reply is to Peter's questioning what will happen to Jesus' disciples, who have given up all to follow him (Matthew 19:27). "Ye also shall sit upon twelve thrones, judging the twelve tribes of Israel" (KJV), Jesus assures them in 19:28.

Howell begins the section with the image of the ruling Lion of Judah and his "Lion hearted wife" as "the Biblical Sovreign of this world." This "Bible Owner of Holy Times" will bring about a liberation whose power will affect the "new Bible Land, the Isles of Springs" (the Taino-Arawak meaning of "Xaymaca" from which the name Jamaica was derived). The apocalyptic imagery ("the brimstone and fire, volcanos is his; every thunder and lightning is his") proclaims a divinity whose reign transcends one particular locale (Africa's Ethiopia) and can effect universal change. Appropriating the imagery of Jesus' commanding nature (see Mark 4:35–41) gives Selassie, too, the force of the Genesis, Job, and Psalms pictures of God who creates and therefore commands the "firmament" (e.g. Genesis 1:6-8). Those resisting earth's newly revealed rightful ruler Howell labels "Anarchy" and prophesies their "Jamaica British West Indies" will revert anew to its original status, as their faith ("Bible Militant"), language ("Militant Dictionary"), and oppression ("Anglo Militant Slave Train") will also be replaced. What differs in Howell from the biblical picture is the imagery of divine sexual union, producing "seeds" that will continue and reproduce black Eden when the cursed leprous "Anglo Saxon white peoples all die out."[39]

Matrimonial Affidavit

His Majesty Ras Tafari said: now sweet heart my dear wonder, just take this drench of perfect wonders and live with me for life. His Majesty King Alpha and Queen Omega being the keepers of the tree of life, Dear heart before we take charge of the Guest Chamber of Creation. He said that they had to clear God's perfect reputation and the tree of life. They are requested to call up the medical powerhouse of this world, and have their best physicians to (loose) the Virgin matrix and gave them a crown diploma of our dignity.

The Royal name of this Ethiopian dignity is called Black Supremacy, by the Sacred Order of His Majesty Ras Tafari the living Creator, the living God, and Earth Superior, the master builder of Creation, the perfect Royal Head of this World.

King Ras Tafari and Queen Omega the King of Kings, and Lord of Lords, the conquering Lion of Judah, the Elect of God and the Light of the World, the First and Last, the beginning and ending.

Black People Black People Arise and Shine

Black People Black People arise and shine for the light has come and the glory of the King of Kings is now risen upon thee. Let not the preachers of the white man's doctrine persuade you to turn your back against H. M. Ras Tafari the Lord God of Israel. Every man was created for the earth in order that he might have and enjoy the fullness of the riches on the Earth.

The white man's doctrine has forced the black man to forsake silver and gold and seek Heaven after death. It has brought us to live in disgrace and die in dishonour. Now we the black man have found out that their doctrine was only a trick, and all their intention was to make themselves strong and to fool the black man.

As I G.G. Maragh speak unto you, this is a very serous affair and must not be forsaken The wise black man woman and children gaining knowledge diligently toward the truth of H. M. Ras Tafari Kingdom, but fools despiseth wisdom and instruction. The knowledge of H. M. Ras Tafari Kingdom must be had before one could possibly receive the truth, for he is King of Kings and Lord of Lords, therefore he is earth's rightful ruler in this name alone will the black people receive happines. His throne is forever and ever and a sceptre of righteousness is the sceptre of his Kingdom.

Woe be unto the preacher of the white man's doctrine a hypocrisy or devil worship. There are millions of persons of good will who see the cruel, unjust, and wicked things done in the Church organisations in the name of God.

It is the will of H.M. Ras Tafari that such perons of good will may have an opportunity to get knowledge of truth. May I state that all reasonable persons who hear the truth should readily see that the Pope of Rome and his preachers are H.M. Ras Tafari who is the Lord God of Israel's great opposer and greatest enemy. Persons of good will to the Kingdom of H.M. Ras Tafari will be forever. The other will remain dead forever.

Woe be unto them that forsaketh H.M. Ras Tafari as being God Almighty they shall be cast into hell both body and soul.

PEACE BE UNTO YOU, PEACE BE UNTO YOU.

Commentary

Now, in the final sections, Howell the evangelist pleads and then roars for a decision. He begins with a gentle Song of Solomon–type plea, placed on the lips of this reputed heir of Solomon and Sheba. The phallic and womblike imagery, cast in biblical-sounding language ("tree of life," "Guest Chamber of Creation"), reinforces the reproductive imagery of forging the "new Bible Land" in the previous section. (Consider also "now sweet heart my dear wonder, just take this drench of perfect wonders and live with me for life" as ejaculatory and conjugal references.) Resummoned, too, is the healing component, "the medical powerhouse," which was apparently a hallmark of Howell's proclamation. Whether the "Virgin matrix" refers to replacing Roman Catholic Maryolatry—often the object of appeals for healing—or is meant as a parallel image to the "crown diploma of our dignity," showing a new, pure (virgin) healing available through the power of King Alpha and Queen Omega, is a point of speculation. Another point to ponder is whether the occasional words in parentheses—(loose) here and (Rate) in "The Rapers"—show the presence of an editorial hand, perhaps at publication. The closing titles of the "Matrimonial Affidavit" section seem nearly Masonic in sound (particularly the "master builder of creation"), which is a distinct possibility, since many have postulated a connection between Masonic-type secret societies and the beginnings of Rastafari as a secret, sacred society. The final paragraphs in "Matrimonial Affidavit" blend Ethiopian regal titles with biblical ones to round out the supreme identification being attributed to Selassie: "the living Creator, the living God."

Following that disarming, softer appeal, Howell goes into a direct, hard-line challenge in "Black People Black People Arise and Shine". His message is the same one echoed in Bob Marley and Peter Tosh's "Get Up Stand Up," Toots Hibbert's "Careless Ethiopians," Jimmy Cliff's "The Harder They Come," and many other Rasta and Rasta-influenced reggae pieces: Whites have offered only a "pie in the sky" eternal reward to Blacks while commandeering for themselves this earth's riches. By paraphrasing the language of Proverbs 1:7 in the third paragraph, Howell equates "the knowledge of the Lord" in Proverbs with the "knowledge of H.[His] M. [Majesty] Ras Tafari." If he is "earth's rightful ruler," what follows, albeit intuitively, is that his followers inherit the earth.

Howell shows that one reason Rastafari rose as a reaction to oppressive white interpretations of Christianity is that the church failed to practice what it preached in regard to loving and caring for the "weaker" (that is, "persecuted") among the family of God. Howell's attack on "the cruel, unjust, and wicked things done in the Church organisations in the name of God" continues the indictment of the earliest of post-NT Christian sermons—for example, 2 *Clement,* which charges, "Our deeds are unworthy of the words we utter." Christian images of hell and destruction await those, such as the pope and his preachers, who are blamed for the evil; but "such per[s]ons of good will" are offered salvific "knowledge of the truth" in the kingdom being instituted by Selassie I.

The most dramatic effect of Howell's call resulted in Rastas traveling to Ethiopia and establishing the Shashamane Community. The emperor's feelings toward it were reportedly mixed. He resisted the attempt at deification but appreciated the devoted personal loyalty. Sadly, this repatriated Rasta community suffered persecution when the emperor was removed from office in 1974.[40] The horrifying image of Ethiopian Blacks persecuting faithful Ethiopianistic Rastafarians in the heaven, or Zion, of Ethiopia itself is the sobering reality that challenges the prophetic vision of Leonard Howell. The Ethiopia he extols is one that, despite all its this-worldly hope in a black ruler of earth who will eliminate white overlordship and restore a mythical, pure, primal black Edenic state, is ultimately otherworldly. Against the reality of the emperor's own humanity and inclusive views, his people's growing anti-imperial Marxism, Ethiopia's ties of friendship and cooperation with predominately white nations, even the collapse of black exclusivism within contemporary global Rastafari, Howell's vision and his hope at the beginning of the twentieth century have had no earthly correspondence as that century closes and a new one begins. But as with many a failed prophecy, the power of Howell's vision does not reside in its fulfillment but in the force of its very proclamation. Hope has its own reality and can impart dignity, self-worth, and a vision of justice that corrects what is now being done.

When we assess this brief work, what we appear to have in *The Promised Key* is a distillation, even the substance, of Howell's street preaching. Maybe one of Howell's students wrote down one of his speeches for him. Perhaps he inscribed it himself. Rhetorical repetitions ("if you please"); bombastic statements ("shot down from off the face of God Almighty's beautiful earth"); sharp, punching images ("college hogs and dogs," "Anglo Saxon apple tree")—all blend to evoke the image of a powerful preacher delivering a searing message. If logic, clarity, accuracy, and reality are missing here, power, decisiveness, and a call to commitment are potently at work. Through the words flow the power of the man. Marcus Garvey once proclaimed, "If the white man has the idea of a white God, let him worship his God as he desires. . . . We Negroes believe in the God of Ethiopia, the everlasting God."[41] Howell took that idea and concretized it by positing his contemporary emperor of Ethiopia as "the everlasting God." By apotheosizing Haile Selassie, Howell attempted to create a symbol of immanent deity that was accessible to Blacks.

Notes

1. See, for example, M. G. Smith, Roy Augier, and Rex Nettleford, *The Rastafari Movement in Kingston, Jamaica* (Mona, Jamaica: Institute of Social and Economic Research, University College of the West Indies, 1960), 6; Barry Chevannes, *Rastafari: Roots and Ideology* (Syracuse, N.Y.: Syracuse University Press, 1994), 121; Horace Campbell, *Rasta and Resistance: From Marus Garvey to Walter Rodney* (Trenton, N.J.: Africa World Press, 1987), 71; Ernest Cashmore, *Rastaman: The Rastafarian Movement in England* (London: George Allen & Unwin, 1979), 22. According to O'Neal A. Walker, "The first who openly preached the divinity of Ras Tafari was Leonard P. Howell. . . . He spoke many African dialects and it was he who introduced the teaching that Rastafari is the 'Living God' in Jamaica" ("A Brief Study of Rastafarianism" [unpublished thesis, Jamaica Theological Seminary, Kingston, November 1975], 1–2). Robert Hill, "Leonard P. Howell and Millenarian Visions In Early Rastafari," *Jamaica Journal* 16, 1 (1983): 28, quotes Paul Earlington as naming Howell as "the first man who came to Jamaica and introduced his Imperial Majesty Emperor Haile Sellassie [*sic*] as Rastafari the creator of heaven and earth."

2. Smith, Augier, and Nettleford, *The Rastafari Movement*, 6.

3. Hill, "Leonard P. Howell," 28.

4. *Daily Gleaner,* July 31, 1941, 16, cited in Smith, Augier, and Nettleford, *The Rastafari Movement,* 8.

5. *Jamaica Times* article exposed details of Howell's life to the public on May 28, 1938, cited in Smith, Augier, and Nettleford, *The Rastafari Movement,* 7.

6. See, for example, Timothy White's acknowledgment in *Catch a Fire: The Life of Bob Marley* (New York: Henry Holt, 1983), 9ff., 459; Chevannes, *Rastafari,* 121ff., 286.

7. See Hill, "Leonard P. Howell," 27. This is an interest shared by Timothy White, who noted Howell's "plagiarism" of the *Parchment* (White, *Catch a Fire,* 10).

8. Smith, Augier, and Nettleford, *The Rastafari Movement,* 6.

9. The 1960 University of the West Indies report points out that at Pinnacle, Howell told his followers to call him "Gangungu Maraj" (ibid., 9). Edward J. Osei-Bonsu, a Ghanaian scholar in Accra, advises, "Gangungu Maragh [*sic*] is not an African word." To him it sounds "Indian, derived from these Eastern Religions" (telephone interview with the author, ca. fall 1995). Sanskrit scholar, author, and physician, Madhukar Shah agrees, pointing out that neither is "a clearly Hindi word." *Gangun* (pronounced "gung") appears to be a corruption tacked onto the front of *gu* (shortened from *guru,* "teacher of wisdom"?). *Maragh* is another "corruption," close to *marg,* "path or road," or more likely *maharaja* (with the "a" removed in corruption), a term that would mean "king of kings." To Shah, the odd spellings suggest the terms were overheard or received orally, perhaps from contact with East Indians laboring in Jamaica, and transliterated as well as Howell or his amanuensis

could render them. (Madhukar Shah, interview with the author, Beverly, Massachusetts, ca. fall 1995.) For Ajai Mansingh and Laxmi Mansingh, "Gangunju Mahraj" is "a misspelling of Gyangunji, meaning knowledgeable, virtuous" ("Hindi Influences on Rastafarianism," in Rex Nettleford, ed., *Caribbean Quarterly Monograph: Rastafari* [Kingston: Caribbean Quarterly, University of the West Indies, 1985], 109).

10. George E. Simpson, "Political Cultism in West Kingston, Jamaica," *Social and Economic Studies* 4, 2 (1955): 137.

11. Addison E. Southard, "Modern Ethiopia: Haile Selassie the First, Formerly Ras Tafari, Succeeds to the World's Oldest Continuously Sovereign Throne," *National Geographic* 59, 6 (June 1931): 683.

12. Ibid., 682.

13. Ibid., 734–36.

14. As Nathaniel Samuel Murrell noted in the Introduction, obeisance by the duke of Gloucester has since become a fixed tenet of Rasta lore. Some fascinating versions of the story abound in Rastafarian thought.

15. He said, "As Sarah was to Abraham, so was she obedient to me" (Haile Selassie I, *Selected Speeches of His Imperial Majesty Haile Selassie First, 1918 to 1967* [Addis Ababa: The Imperial Ethiopian Ministry of Information Publications and Foreign Languages Press Department, 1967], 650).

16. Queen Omega Communications, "Who Is Queen Omega?" *The Beat* 4, 6 (December 1985): 9.

17. A photograph of the touring car—though without white laborers—may be seen in Southard, "Modern Ethiopia," 680.

18. Ianthe Robinson, "Right against Might," *Plain Talk* (September 21, 1935): 7.

19. L. F. C. Mantle, "The Italo-Ethiopian Conflict: 'Things That Affects Us Here,'" *Plain Talk* (November 2, 1935): 11.

20. L. F. C. Mantle, "Diffusion of Ethiopic Knowledge Needed," *Plain Talk* (September 28, 1935): 7.

21. Barbara Makeda Lee (Blake Hannah), *Rastafari: The New Creation*, 2d ed.(Kingston: Jamaica Media Productions, 1981), 13. See Marcus Garvey's criticism of Haile Selassie in *The Blackman* 10 (1935); 7–8 (1936); 2(1939), collected in E. U. Essien-Udom and Amy Jacques Garvey, eds., *More Philosophy and Opinions of Marcus Garvey* (Totowa, N.J.: Frank Cass, 1977), 3:229–42.

22. Lee (Hannah), *Rastafari*, 35, 59, 34.

23. Ibid., 32.

24. Ibid., 30.

25. Smith, Augier, and Nettleford, *The Rastafari Movement*, 9.

26. To their Akan forebears, *obayifo* was a "sorcerer," the word for sorcery being derived from two words meaning "to snatch a child"—that is, causing a child to die through sorcery ("cannibalizing at a distance"). Some helpful articles on African sorcery are Birgit Meyer, "'If You Are a Devil, You Are a Witch and, if You Are a Witch, You Are a Devil': The Integration of 'Pagan' Ideas into the Conceptual Universe of Ewe Christians in Southeastern Ghana," *Journal of Religion in Africa* 22, 2, (1992): 98–132; Sheila S. Walker, "Witchcraft and Healing in an African Christian Church," *Journal of Religion in Africa* 10, fasc. 2 (1979), 127ff.; Joseph Martin Hopkins, "Theological Students and Witchcraft Beliefs," *Journal of Religion in Africa* 11, 1 (1980), 56–66.

27. Simpson, "Political Cultism," 147. This seems to be the spirit of Peter Tosh's references in the songs "Bush Doctor" and "Mystic Man" (both popular titles for an Obeah worker), "Crys-

tal Ball," etc. The ironic side of the issue can be seen when dub poet Mutabaruka, in his musical adaptation of Malcolm X's phrase "(We Have to Free Africa by) Any Means Necessary" (*Outcry*, Shanachie 43023, 1984), chants that the faithful might have to resort to a "little voodoo," a "little juju." Devout Rastas, as exemplified by the home photographed in Tracy Nicholas and Bill Sparrow's *Rastafari: A Way of Life* (Garden City, N.Y.: Doubleday Anchor Books, 1979), 119, post on their walls "Remember you must not have more than one woman neither you must not be a belly killer nigher a Batty Man nigher a Obeah worker."

28. Hill, "Leonard P. Howell," 30. Readers may see a photograph of a Rasta baptizing in Stephen Davis and Peter Simon's *Reggae International* (New York: Rogner and Bernhard GMBH, 1982), 66.

29. His Imperial Majesty, Haile Selassie I, "Building an Enduring Tower," Carl F. H. Henry and W. Stanley Mooneyham, eds., *One Race,* in *One Gospel, One Task,* vol. 1 of *World Congress on Evangelism, Berlin, 1966,* Official Reference Volumes: Papers and Reports (Minneapolis: World Wide Publications, 1967), 20.

30. Ibid.

31. Ibid.

32. Selassie, *Selected Speeches,* 142.

33. Perhaps Howell's disappointment in the persistence of Selassie's ineluctable inclusivism is what eventually made him abandon the real emperor and take the title for himself—Howell reforming Haile Selassie in Howell's own image.

34. Southard, "Modern Ethiopia," 737–38; Simpson, "Political Cultism," 137.

35. Despite Howell's hostility against "all the Churches," especially "the Pope of Rome who is satan the devil" ("The False Religion"), the reaction of the churches to Rastafari was surprisingly mild. After his positive comments on Rastafari in 1973 (essay in Idris Hamid, ed., *Troubling of the Waters* [San Fernando, Trinidad: Rahaman Printery, 1973], Joseph Owens, a Roman Catholic priest, published a detailed plea for understanding the Rastafarians in his volume *Dread: The Rastafarians of Jamaica* (Kingston: Sangster's Book Stores, 1976). Among Protestants, the reaction was mixed. William A. Blake called for a response "in deed, and in love" ("Beliefs of the Rastafari Cult" [unpublished thesis, Jamaica Theological Seminary, Kingston, Jamaica, Kingston: November 1961], 29), and O'Neal A. Walker called for "personal testimony and identification, rather than argumentation" ("Brief Study of Rastafarianism," 4); though Roger Ringenberg noted, "The 'Christian Church' has, to a large extent, remained silent, at least in print, regarding the movement" ("Rastafarianism: An Expanding Jamaican Cult" [unpublished Thesis, Jamaica Theological Seminary, Kingston, Jamica, January 1978], 1). That this attitude continues I noted when a student spoke up during a lecture I gave on reggae at Jamaica Theological Seminary in 1991: "Our pastor tells us just to let that pass by." Others, however, such as former moderator of the United Church of Jamaica and Grand Cayman Earl F. Thames, perceive that "one of the most serious challenges to the Christian Faith in Jamaica today, is the Rastafarian cult" ("Christianity and Rastafarianism" [essay published in aid of the St. Andrews Scots Kirk United Church Renovation Fund, Jamaica, 197?], 1). Like the Protestant leaders mentioned above, Thomas called for a refutation by argument and acts of love.

36. John Moodie, *Hath . . . the Lion Prevailed . . . ?* (Lake Worth, Fla.: Americana Label & Printing, 1992), 12.

37. Ibid., 7.

38. Ansel Cridland of the Meditations explained to me in our telephone conversations of May 21, 1993, and February 1996, "Them [Blacks] old kindlyheart." "White man sit down and or-

ganize slavery. First thing, them approach in Africa first, get to the black people now, first going for the gold, human life, for the animal, then they go for the land. They take everything back and take it all over the world."

39. Judeo-Christianity has historically resisted attempts to posit God as a gendered deity who needs a consort; see Aída Besançon Spencer, with D.F.G. Hailson, C. C. Kroeger, and W. D. Spencer, *The Goddess Revival* (Grand Rapids: Baker Book House, 1995), for a careful historical-biblical-theological discussion of the issues involved in the debate over the gender of God. Facing a similar reluctance among Christians of his day, Howell consciously calls his married god and mate new "type setters" whose revelation and "eternal appointment" will wipe away traditional ("Adam Abraham Anglo Saxon the leper") interpretations of the Bible.

40. See a discussion in Campbell, *Rasta and Resistance,* 224–26.

41. Marcus Garvey, *Philosophy and Opinions of Marcus Garvey,* ed. Amy Jacques Garvey, 2 vols. (New York: Atheneum Publishers, 1969), 1:44.

22 Rastafari's Messianic Ideology and Caribbean Theology of Liberation

NATHANIEL SAMUEL MURRELL AND
BURCHELL K. TAYLOR

In Chapter 19 of this anthology, Nathaniel Samuel Murrell and Lewin Williams raise the question of whether the Rastafarian interpretation of the Bible and its messianic ideology carry any significance for theological engagement in the region, and if they do, what bridges must be built connecting Rastafari and other Caribbean schools of thought before theological exchange becomes a reality. In this chapter, we analyze the nature of the Rastafarian messianic ideology—as derived from biblical religion and the advent of Haile Selassie—as a way of addressing social, economic, and spiritual realities in the region in the context of Caribbean theology of liberation. The analysis constitutes a reflective pause, showing a plausible structure for doing theology for liberation, particularly among the Caribbean poor. Although we offer no "made to fit" theological bridge connecting Rastafari's messianic ideology to Caribbean theology of liberation, enough of a familial resemblance exists to make borrowing appropriate.

It is our position that the messianic ideology of Rastafari can be a conduit for theological reflection and liberation in the Caribbean. At worst, one could use Rastafarian ideas to "trouble the consciousness of comfortable Jamaicans," since "even the most protected come to hear about the words they [the Rastas] preach."[1] At best, forging a link between Rasta messianic ideology and the liberation strivings in the Caribbean is perhaps the morally responsible theological thing to do at this time; it is an attempt to "do the right thing" in light of the Rastafarians' challenge to colonial hegemonic conceptions of life in the African diaspora. The emphasis that Rastas place on Caribbean political and economic transformation and development since the 1970s and their incisive criticism of colonialism and other forms of economic control of black Jamaicans may be considered indispensable in a discussion on Caribbean theology of liberation.

Rastafari's Messianic Ideology

In spite of their publication of what might be considered "official documents" (*The Promised Key, The Living Testament of Rasta-For-I, The Holy Piby, The Royal Parchment Scroll of Black Supremacy,* etc.), Rastas' theological doctrines are not formalized; many versions of their theological thought have surfaced in the literature.[2] This is one of the things that prompted Ian Boyne, a specialist writer on religion for the Jamaica *Daily Gleaner,* to call for a Rasta systematic theology. That Rastafari has no central doctrinal commission, formal or informal, that defines and determines its orthodoxy is not surprising. Its passion for freedom and liberation and its antipathy toward hegemonic control allow individual members of the movement to define personal "reasoning" and "citing-up," that is, engaging in appropriate reflection and interpretation of their experience and arriving at personal conviction and conclusion on matters of their belief. The belief system is itself also dynamic; it is responsive to changed circumstances and the emergence of new realities while making needed adjustments. Former Rasta and Columbia University–trained psychologist Leahcim Semaj (or Michael James) calls one of those change situations "the third phase" in the movement's development (the 1980s). In this phase he sees "the beginning of the articulation of a Rasta social theory" or "organized set of values" that explain what Rastas stand for, what they are going to do, and how they are going to do it. Semaj surmises, "I also see more political and economic assertion and creative experimentation on the part of Rastas resulting in a share of state power."[3] In a conversation at his Kingston office in the summer of 1994, Semaj told Nathaniel Samuel Murrell and Clinton Chisholm, "The Brethren are getting more and more secular, materialistic, commercialized, and less committed to the basic doctrines."[4]

But even given the varied nature of its beliefs and practices, a central focus that the Rastafarian movement has always managed to maintain is evident. This is possible because certain core concepts have remained consistent and are shared by most, if not all, Rastas. No representation of the belief system exists that does not include those theological views, and in substantially the same form as they present in the other representations. Chief among these is the messianic concept that gives Rastafari its distinctive character in relation to similar movements that are usually characterized as millenarian religious sects. The concept of Messiah is thoroughly biblically based; it is influenced directly by the movement's own interpretation of selected biblical material that deals with messianic promise and hope. This material comes mainly from the Hebrew Bible, especially the prophetic books and the Psalms, but the Book of Revelation in the New Testament (NT) is also a very important part of the biblical tradition on which Rastafari builds its messianic ideas.

Although Rastafari's interpretation of the Bible has been discussed at great length in Chapter 19, it is not possible to speak about the distinct character of its messianic ideology without reference to Scripture. The Rastafarian biblical perspective is served by a strong historical consciousness in which emphasis is placed on the people as the subject of their own story; they are the ones who engage in reflection on their historical experience and relate it to their own reading of the Bible. These activities are done in association with Rastas' analysis of the sociopolitical and cultural realities of their daily lives. In Rastafari, a sense of subjectivity, selfhood, and community defies the kind of objectification and depersonalization that occurs in the context of domination and oppression. The language of self-expression and self-reference, used in terms of relationship, bears this out effectively. The expression "I-an-I" is very significant in this regard; it links a vibrant hope to a clearly perceived destiny of freedom, justice, righteousness, and peace.

The thrust of the Rastafarian messianic ideology puts it in tension with the present "Babylon" order, which is undesirable and unacceptable since it represents and subsists on the denial of the human rights and freedom of Africans. As noted throughout this anthology, Babylon constitutes oppression and exploitation of the black race in general and is therefore an evil system. Rastas have a very strong expectation of a new order of existence in a radically new setting. In this new environment, current wrongs and wickedness perpetrated against Rastafarians will be corrected. Freedom, righteousness, justice, peace, and love will prevail. The advent of a specially chosen and divinely endowed Messiah will embody both the sign and the means of fulfillment of the messianic expectation. These beliefs are grounded in an appropriation of biblical messianic expectations and promises, in which Rastafarians see themselves as the true recipients of the messianic promise and hope spoken of in the Bible.

Since the Christian tradition and its Scriptures have been made tools of deception and oppression by those who justify and maintain their position of domination,[5] Rastafarians will have no part in perpetuating its legacy. Instead, they are bearers of the truth concerning who the original people of God were (the Rastafarians) and who will continue to be their true descendants in the modern world. Their Messiah has actually come in fulfillment of the messianic promise; the ascension of Haile Selassie I to the throne of Ethiopia marked the event. To most Rastas, the emperor is the incarnation of Jesus. He brings to fulfillment Christ's promised return for the full and final establishment of the messianic kingdom. Others view Selassie as the personal Jewish Messiah whose coming was foretold in the Hebrew Bible. He is the Immanuel—"God with us"—spoken of by the prophet Isaiah.

Rastafarian scholar Dennis Forsythe remarks that Rasta orthodoxy has declared Selassie to be the returned Messiah, "the King of all African kings and a descendant of David." Forsythe cites a 1968 statement of an apparent Rasta convert from Christianity, which reads "Every Rastafarian recognizes HIM. . . . Haile Selassie of Ethiopia to be the returned Messiah; the only Mediator between God and man representing Christ. . . . We base these beliefs on the interpretation of the Scriptures and can quote many passages in the Bible which endorse these beliefs and the concept of the Divinity of HIM. He is the 225th rebirth of Solomon. . . . He is the black Christ of his era."[6] For Rastas, then, belief in Haile Selassie's divinity is key to the messianic expectation. Africa (Ethiopia) is the promised land, Zion, or the new Jerusalem of biblical messianic expectation. Repatriation to the promised land is the goal of the liberation that the messianic promise and hope imply. It is not migration (escapism) but repatriation (a return to what was owned before). It is not the pilgrimage of a foreign spectator so much as a return home.

The imagery of Babylon in the Bible, particularly in the Book of Revelation, is the interpretive context for the Rastafarians' belief in the messianic liberation of black people from captivity and oppression in contemporary, global Babylon. Rastas have a strong expectation that soon they will experience the final movement toward full liberation through repatriation to Ethiopia. The nonfulfillment of this expectation and even the "disappearance" of Selassie have not altered the hopes of orthodox Rastafarians. The belief system has made adjustments and accommodations in terms of the dissonance created by Selassie's absence, but the core beliefs still hold firm.

An issue that Caribbean theology of liberation finds most appealing in the Rastafarian messianic ideology is its attempt to contextualize theology within the Caribbean community. At an ecumenical symposium on development held in Chaguaramas, Trinidad, in 1971, a Rastafarian representative, Mikael Kezehemohonenow, delivered a paper that outlined, among other things, the social and political roles of the Rastafarians in the Caribbean. He said, "The Rasta does not play a part in keeping up Babylon politics but would take part in the development of a just and true politics [a way of running the country], along that of the Holy Bible and any other equal and just way that would benefit the people of the Caribbean, Africa and the world."[7] This position is spelled out rather clearly in the *Rastafarian Manifesto, EATUP (The Ethiopian-African Theocracy Union Policy)*, which has drawn up a very ambitious social, political, and economic agenda for solving Jamaica's problems[8]—an idea that was a principal theme at the Trinidad symposium, out of which came several important papers and statements on liberation theology and Caribbean development.

The Rastafarians' view of the social and economic history of Blacks in the African diaspora is also stated unabashedly in the thirteen articles that open the Manifesto. Articles 2 and 3 of *EATUP* open:

> Whereas the presence of people of Ethiopian-African descent in Jamaica and other British colonial territories, is the direct historical consequence of the African Slave Trade; the foundation of which was laid by Elizabeth I of Tudor Queen of England with the granting of a British Royal charter . . . who initiated the trade in human cargo with the capture of 300 Africans from the coast of Guinea in 1565; & Whereas the African Slave Trade has been designated "the curse of Western Civilization" for more than 200 years. . . . (3–4)

EATUP makes it very clear that the problems and suffering in the black diaspora have been caused not by Africans themselves (whom Europeans accuse of selling their people into slavery) but by the Elizabethan colonial policies of political domination and exploitation of the African continent and the Americas. Without European "invasion" of Africa, millions of Africans would not have experienced slavery. As far as Rastas are concerned, there is no evidence that the emancipation of 1834 lifted the "curse of colonialism," namely, the slavery and economic and political exploitation of Africans. Article 4 of *EATUP* declares that

> 420 years of Racial Commercial Bondage & Western Colonial Exile . . . has since elapsed, with no current historical evidence to demonstrate that such curse to Western Civilization has ever been lifted; seeing that the British Throne and Parliament has [*sic*] been morally

negligent, in failing to grant a Repatriation Act to return descendants of emancipated Ethiopian-African peoples to their ancestral borders; on the principled decision taken to dismantle the vast British Slave Empire, with the signing of an Emancipation Act in 1834. (4–5)

Article 5 of *EATUP* notes that Jamaica has elevated "five African Patriots to the status of National Heroes, from the days of Samuel Sharpe to Marcus Mosiah Garvey who have paid the supreme sacrifice with their lives, to establish a policy for survival of the African Slave population; the revival of the Racial culture, divine fundamental human rights and national sovereignty of the Ethiopian-African peoples held in Western Colonial captivity."[9] Unfortunately, the "blood-sacrifice" of these national heroes has not yet paid its dividends to the people for whom they laid down their lives. Articles 6 through 13 make it clear that the post-emancipation colonial state, the "two-party Westminster Parliamentary Adult Suffrage" system, Jamaica's attainment of independence in 1962, and the country's entry into the International Monetary Fund (IMF) have not alleviated Jamaica's woes or freed its people from economic bondage.[10] With this revisiting of history from the point of view of Ethiopians in the African diaspora, Rastafari provides a background for developing its alternative cosmology and political and economic ethic, along with the use of biblical and other traditions.

Rastas' attempt to interpret the Bible in the social and political context of the Caribbean and to make Scripture speak to social and economic realities in Jamaica was seen, in 1971, as being in harmony with the Caribbean liberation theology project. Caribbean scholars at the Trinidad symposium emphasized that in its projection of a new society based on justice and solidarity, the gospel calls for the total liberation of human society and condemns forces that work against this project. God must be viewed as working among humans, especially the poor and oppressed, "incorporating the acts of human liberation with the larger context of the salvation of the world, offering the kingdom of God upon earth as the consummation of the human struggle for freedom from internal and external forms of oppression."[11] The liberation that the kingdom of God brings to humanity is not "a pie in the sky" that Christians will receive "in the sweet by-and-by"; it is to be experienced now, in all aspects of human life, especially in the social, political, and economic improvement of Caribbean peoples' lives.

Other Caribbean theologians who attended the symposium in Trinidad made it clear that the Caribbean liberation theology project cannot separate salvation from political and economic liberation; development is liberation that facilitates salvation. Robert Cuthbert, for example, says a world of blindness, prisons, malnutrition, infant mortality, commercial exploitation, and nation lifting up swords against nation is a world without salvation[12] and liberation. While making allowance for the experience of personal faith in God, theologians Cuthbert, the late Idris Hamid, William Watty, and Clive Abdullah view Caribbean salvation as development and liberation from domination, exploitation, oppression, and other aberrations from the colonial past. As Caribbean New Testament scholar John Holder of Codrington College, Barbados, noted recently, these Caribbean theologians found a powerful paradigm of liberation in the biblical narratives of the Exodus tradition and insisted that the God of the colonist must be replaced by the God of the Exodus and of liberation.[13] That is, the European perception of theology as divorced from human needs and suffering has only limited value in a Caribbean environment where many people are not sure where their next meal is coming from or with which relative or friend they will spend the night. The theological task demands "a new style of doing theology, with emphasis on *doing*,"[14] in the context of Caribbean development.

Clearly, the kind of theological reflection represented here engages the people's socioeconomic and political situation in the light of the witness of Scripture. This is integral to the practice of the faith to which the people of God are called in the larger Christian community. One expects that out of this theological project will emerge new possibilities of authentic self-understanding, fulfillment of human potential, and real hope for the excluded, exploited, oppressed, and impoverished Caribbean majority. No doubt exists that the chief focus of this theological reflection is liberation.

A Liberating Messianic Exegetical Link

In grounding their messianic ideology in biblical materials, Rastas display a remarkable anticipation of what has now come to be called "liberating exegesis."[15] Admittedly, Rastafarian scholar Dennis Forsythe does not think highly of the movement's excessive preoccupation with the Scriptures. As if to echo Karl Marx's view that religion acts like opium, robbing people of their senses, Forsythe speaks of Rastas as "cocained" by the Bible, which left them "partly subservient to ancient superstition that rendered them unable to deal with present realities." He adds, "That was the whole point for the introduction of the Bible to slaves in the first place."[16] This is by no means a balanced and accurate view of the role of the Bible in Rastafarian thought. The approach of Rastafari to the biblical materials, particularly in the area of messianism, is far subtler than what Forsythe suggests; it is also far more subversive of the proslavery and oppressive teachings[17] that have been passed on by traditional methods (which Forsythe says have deceived and trapped the brethren) than appears on the surface.

Rex Nettleford noted that Rastas have developed a worldview that is in line with black people's search for dignity and identity in a context that, for a long time, has been dominated by those who have understood themselves in terms of their alleged superiority to, and the corresponding inherent inferiority of, the black race. The Rasta messianic ideology constitutes a challenge to some of the basic tenets of the Christian faith that were framed according to traditional interpretation of the Bible.[18] Whether one accepts any or none of the specific conclusions that the Rastafarians have arrived at in their exegetical work, one must yet admit that, in an uncanny way, they have paved the way for the kind of liberating exegesis sought and undertaken in contexts where the theology of liberation is being done. No theological project that is relevant to the Caribbean reality can truly ignore this Rastafarian exegesis as a source and paradigm for theological engagement in the region.

The ideological critique and an associated hermeneutical suspicion, considered so important for liberating exegesis, are already at work in the interpretive approach that Rastafarians adopt to Christian tradition and to Scripture in particular. They are convinced that all interpretations coming from the traditional, or "Eurocentric," way of reading Scripture—backed by whatever learning and supported by whatever technical interpretive tools—must be treated with suspicion for ideological bias. From their perspective, prevailing hegemonic biases work in favor of people who control economic power and who exercise domination in the world over those who are victimized by the state of affairs, among whom are the Rastafarians themselves. The Rastas' interpretive messianic approach to Scripture is meant to confront what they perceive as the ideological captivity of the Bible and its interpreters and to liberate a message from the text that is relevant to them and their own situation. The appropriation of the biblical message on this basis is, in itself, a liberating exercise.

We have already seen (e.g., in Chapter 19) the direct identifications that Rastas make in the transference of symbols and the appropriation of hope in their understanding of the Scripture. What happens here is that the Bible is brought nearer to the experience of the reader. This is a reader for whom previously reading has always been done by "the other"; Blacks always had Europeans interpret the Bible for them. Prior to the advent of Rastafari, the meaning and understanding of Scripture in Jamaica were predetermined by those who applied the Bible to people's situation without due regard to those people's historical experience. Through Rastafari the biblical materials used to determined Christian morality in society and to undergird a religious piety that prepared one for the afterlife, with little interest in one's social and economic condition, are now challenged, and a new basis is established for approaching the Scripture that has definite liberating significance. Rasta exegesis affords opportunity for entry on their own self-understanding as a group in the light of Judeo-Christian Scripture, making use of their own hermeneutical privilege as a once oppressed group. That there is a place here for drawing on insights gained from this indigenous religious movement for a theological project that is contextually relevant is more than plausible, and to do so would be most appropriate.

Liberating exegesis is central to the various expressions of the theology of liberation, and a Caribbean theology of contextual relevance and sensitivity falls within this category. The Bible is seen as the chief source of a messianic message that brings the good news of liberation to the oppressed. This message is accessible to the oppressed themselves, from their own reading and reflection. According to American theologian Robert McAfee Brown Frei Betto, a Brazilian priest, portrays the contrast between the traditional Western approach to the Bible and the interactive approach of the oppressed. The Western tradition sees the Bible as a window; it enables readers to see what happened elsewhere, namely, in biblical times. The oppressed, in contrast, see the Bible as a mirror; it enables its readers and interpreters to see their own reality and to learn about themselves in the process—"the people feel as though they are seeing their own lives revealed in the accounts of the Bible."[19] With lively imagination, keen sensitivity, insight, and a sense of community of experience with the people of the Bible, the oppressed make a connection of great significance with reference to a new and liberating experience.

This represents a point of departure that opens up possibilities for self-understanding and hope on a basis completely different from what has been the norm in Christian circles but consistent with the approach to Scripture in the African American tradition.

Speaking in terms of the experience of Afro-Americans and others of the black race on this issue, African American Bible scholar Cain Hope Felder writes:

> The Black Church and others within black religious traditions give allegiance to biblical faith and witness, primarily because their own experiences seem to be depicted in the Bible. Many of the Biblical stories reflect the existential reality of the black story for the last few centuries in an environment typically hostile to the interest of Blacks attaining their full sense of human potential. Blacks have become all too familiar with being oppressed by the socio-economic forces of political powers, foreign and domestic, arrayed against them. They have found in the Bible ancient symbols of their predicament, namely the saga of the Egyptian bondage, the devastation of Assyrian invasions, the deportation into Babylonian captivity and the bedevilment by principalities and powers of the present age. Blacks have subsequently developed an experiential sympathy with much of the biblical witness which they in turn give reverent attention as quite literally the revealed Word of God.[20]

Some critics may say this is a "romanticizing" of the black presence in the Bible, which, given Rastas' deep mistrust of Scripture and the Christian tradition, presents has a rosy view of Rastafarian thought. However, our contention that the emphasis on and practice of liberation exegesis in Rastafari can speak to a Caribbean theology of liberation in this context is quite valid. In liberating exegesis, one finds a shared conversation with the Bible in a continuing story, and the sharing of experience with liberation of the oppressed as the focus. No great distance is felt between the words of the Bible and the words of the reader. Jurgen Moltmann, a voice from one of the traditional centers for doing and dispensing theological teachings and influence, shows that liberating exegesis is being noticed by some even in such places of power and domination. He writes:

> Reading the Bible with the eyes of the poor is a different thing from reading it with a full belly. If it is read in the light of the experience and hopes of the oppressed, the Bible's revolutionary themes—Promise, Exodus, Resurrection, Spirit—come alive. The way in which the history of Israel and the history of Christ blend with that of the hungry and oppressed is quite different from the way they have often been linked with the history of the mighty and the rich.[21]

Good evidence exists that the methodology which the Rastafarians employed in establishing their messianic ideology on biblical religion anticipated "liberating exegesis." This particular form of exegesis is integral to the way of doing theology that we call "liberation theology"—a project to which a Caribbean theology would quite rightly belong, albeit with distinctive characterizing marks of its own. In this way, the messianic ideology of Rastafari represents an interpretive trend that is important to liberating exegesis and theological reflection as these are of current significance in the Caribbean.

The Historical Project

The messianic ideology of Rastafari conveys the distinct impression that the liberation that is the essence of its promise and hope is essentially a historical project. The expected liberation of the oppressed people held in captivity in Babylon is a reality in history.

Both its immediate and its long-term prospects are of historical significance. This is not a viewpoint that will immediately win the agreement of many scholars; some might claim that the historical character of Rastafari is understood in a way that undercuts its contemporary relevance in modern Jamaica. Of course, the messianic vision that Rastafari espouses looks for the experience of full and final liberation beyond its immediate context of the captivity and oppression characterized as Babylon. Some critics see this expectation as providing the basis for a kind of otherworldliness or millenarianism, escapism, and separatism that does not accept the present dwelling place as home.

Scholars often view Rastafari as a millenarian religious group, which casts it, along with other chiliastic (millenarian) sects, in an unfavorable light. Such sects are usually regarded in two, contrasting ways: they are charged either with escapism, which classifies them as socially and politically irrelevant, or with fanaticism, which makes them socially and politically dangerous. The first attitude would have no interest in liberation as a historical project within its context, while the second would have the kind of interest that could only undermine the possibility of the historical-theological enterprise, despite its intention to have it. Because of its messianic ideology, Rastafari has had both charges laid against it by different critics. And some Rastafarians have expressed themselves in ways that could give credence to either charge. However, when the core concept of Rastafari's messianic ideology is examined, neither view fits the movement. As Carole Yawney puts it, "The Rastafarians are not an encapsulated religious cult, a characteristic of millennial cults! but on the contrary, they have frequent and meaningful interchanges on a daily basis with non-Rastas in the communities in which they live."[22] In addition, Barry Chevannes has issued a timely warning against any rush to categorize Rastafari as millenarian. He observes that only three times in six decades (1934, 1958, 1959) did Rastafarians exhibit any manifestations of millenarian activity. He then comments, "The growth and impact of Rastafari have not been dependent on the dream of the millennium."[23] This truly puts us on guard against generalizations concerning the movement based on stereotyping that ignores its peculiar and unique features.

Under such generalizations, the view is expressed that Rastas do not show any commitment to Jamaica or show a sense of responsibility for the country's welfare; liberation is not linked to transformation of the immediate historical context or to any participation of Rastas in society. But no one who has read the Rastafarian Manifesto *EATUP* and other Rasta literature or who has listened to the Rastas' message in song (especially reggae) could arrive at such a conclusion. As much as two-thirds of the *EATUP* document is dedicated to the total transformation of the Jamaican political, economic, legal, and social systems.[24] In addition, Rastafarian writers and reggae lyricists constantly echo the themes of societal transformation and liberation.[25] Since the 1970s, Rastas have been calling for socioeconomic and political revitalization of Jamaica and other Caribbean countries. After the leadership of the Rastafarian group the Twelve Tribes of Israel returned from their visit to Ethiopia, for example, they decided not to repatriate but to invest more time and resources in developing Jamaica's economy and culture. Hence the messianic ideology of Rastafari reveals that the liberation expected is a this-worldly historical reality or social-political transformation. This must be of interest to a Caribbean theological project that has liberation as its emphasis.

By its very nature, the messianic ideology of Rastafari requires a critical distancing from the elements of oppression within the dominant culture. This is shown in the protest and resistance that the movement expresses in its values, distinctive lifestyle, and goals of identity and human dignity, perceived and shared with society—inspired and influenced by the hope and vision of life to be experienced in the promised land. The vision shows a way of practicing an alternative lifestyle that is considered the authentic one of the chosen people, which at the same time challenges the dominant culture and shows up its unworthiness. Inspired by the messianic vision and hope, the practice of the alternative lifestyle is meant to influence things as they exist in the immediate context. The absence of activism or corresponding political rhetoric in some sectors of the Rastafarian movement does not necessarily mean the lack of effective impact or influence on the social and political process.

One sees here indications that the messianic ideology is significant in the immediate historical context, even though it looks beyond it for fulfillment. Prompted by the hope and vision of liberation, Rastafari's particular forms of self-awareness, self-discipline, self-reliance, and self-expression show that liberation has already begun for Rastas in Babylon; they are beginning, while in captivity, to taste the liberation expected in repatriation. Rastas' commitment to issues that emphasize true identity, full human dignity and equality, the value of community, and corporate solidarity support this conclusion. This is borne out also in terms of the practice of the faith and the consciousness that goes hand in hand with it. The liberation already in process is not "aspectual" but integral; that is, it is not dominated by a single issue or aspect of life but embraces the cultural, racial, social, economic, political, psychological, and spiritual. Liberation is therefore not removed from daily life but embraces the whole range of one's experience.

The ongoing "reasoning," an essential part of the Rastafarian movement's ethos, is itself a form of what liberation theologian and educator Paulo Freire calls "conscientization"[26]—arousing a people's consciousness and sense of self-redemption from the bottom up, with liberating significance. The meaning, purpose, and hope of the messianic ideology are the subject of ongoing deliberations and reflection on a community-wide basis, which at the same time afford individuals an opportunity for participation. In this liberation project, the forces of oppression, their identity, nature, and character, are exposed. The individual and collective potential of the members of the group are identified, and openness toward fulfillment is encouraged—though this will be fully realized only in repatriation to the promised land. This gives the poor a self-assurance and confidence in the present that the culture assigns only to the wealthy, the privileged, and the powerful. The liberating significance of this is most noteworthy. Although the promised land of the messianic hope, Ethiopia, is beyond the bounds of Jamaica, for Rastas it is an actual historical location; it is the home of the Messiah-king, who is both divine and human. No dichotomy exists between the historical and the eschatological, the earthly and the heavenly, the natural and the supernatural, the present age and the future age, to make these mutually exclusive. At the same time, there is no denial that the fulfillment of the promise is God's doing. Consequently, the Babylon-exile repatriation imagery is receiving greater emphasis in Rastafari than the Egypt-exodus pilgrimage imagery; among other things, the former is considered a more accurate historical representation of both the captivity Rastas experience and the liberation they expect.

This way of representing the messianic ideology, setting forth the promise and the expectation associated with it as a historical project, is another point of interest to Caribbean theology of liberation. It functions within the oppressed people's situation of deprivation. The individualistic, pietistic, exclusively otherworldly, and futuristic view of the promised liberation by God through Jesus the Messiah, predominant in traditional Western theological thought, is challenged by this theology that sees liberation as embracing an essential historical dimension. The inspiration for this linkage of coming messianic deliverance and immediate liberation imperatives is nearer at hand than is usually imagined. Theological emphasis that creates a divide between the material and the spiritual, the sacred and the secular, by claims that faith has no interest in culture, that hope bears no immediate significance or relevance to the political and economic order, that the future cannot be anticipated in the present, and that what is beyond cannot be manifested now in our midst is also seriously challenged. The messianic ideology of Rastafari stands as a reference point for any theological reflection that focuses on liberation, as an authentic Caribbean theology should.

The messianic ideology of Rastafari conceives God as being on the side of the oppressed. This is both an explicit and an implicit fact of the ideology, called, in liberation theology, the "hermeneutical privilege of the poor." Essentially, the concern is to set the oppressed at liberty. The Rastafarian view that black people are the reincarnation of Israel and subject to the promises made to Israel, including the messianic promises, supports this. Rastas' understanding of themselves now as being in a captivity imposed on them by Babylon is in line with such a hermaneutical agenda. Speaking about the African Babylonian captivity in the Americas, Rastafari author Tennyson Smyth (Ras-J-Tesfa) writes; "The assimilation of JAH's children by the poli-tricks of confusion, into the world of the Babylonians, brought them the Nigger Status, reprobated by the God of their captors, and institutionalized racial discrimination by their paler human counterparts."[27] Smyth believes that Christians who enslaved and continue to oppress their African brothers and sisters forget that humankind was created to "forever be together, with none dominating, but rather accommodating each other."[28] Rastas' experience of persecution intensifies the sense of their oppressed condition, but at the same time, it strengthens their belief in the faithfulness of "Jah," who will liberate them. They look forward to their liberation in the promised land of Ethiopia and put Jah firmly on their side. The evidence of this is the advent and enthronement of Haile Selassie I, which is viewed as God establishing his presence in their midst for the fulfillment of his promise of the liberation of his oppressed people.

No doubt exists, therefore, that one of the things that sustains hope and inspires endurance in Rastas is the view that they are the direct concern of God, who became incarnate in Haile Selassie. Joseph Owens records the following Rasta conviction about Selassie:

The God-king still concerns himself in most providential fashion with the needs and desires of the poor lonely Rastas in exile here in the West. Not a cry goes forth from the wretched slums of western Kingston but is heard by the Emperor in his compassion. Every Rastafarian knows that he can take his own personal plea to the king and receive a just hearing. The same power that rules the world and raises the dead is directed to the Rasta's own needs and they are dissolved.[29]

The concept of solidarity goes hand in hand with the view that God, in the person of Haile Selassie, is the God of the oppressed and the one concerned about their welfare. To Rastas, "Selassie shows his solidarity with the poor worker by laboring daily himself, Selassie is not a despot who sits back and lives off the labours of his people." Indeed, "his governance takes the form of working side by side with them."[30] Although many Ethiopians saw their emperor as an oppressor, to Rastafari, Selassie is a friend of the poor and the oppressed; he does not leave them friendless and hopeless. He knows their cause and will vindicate them in full. This is what his presence and solidarity assured Rastafarians of while the emperor lived. Now the Selassie reality is construed differently among various Rasta groups. Up to the mid-1970s, Selassie was a material presence in the world, but only some Rastas believe he is alive today. Regardless of whether Selassie is dead or alive, however, the liberating messianic ideology has not lost its force.

The view that puts God firmly on the side of the oppressed and victimized, as an essential aspect of the belief system and theological reasoning of Rastafari, should be seen as providing fruitful resource for theological development within the Caribbean region. Here is a strong sense that a Caribbean theology must bear a thematic emphasis of preferential option for the poor—if it is to be truly meaningful in the light of the Caribbean reality—and that it should be grounded on the fact that God is the God of the oppressed. As a way of doing theology that would give expression to this theme, the Rastafarian messianic ideology can be instructive. Theologies that have originated from the traditional centers of learning in North America and Europe have often indicated otherwise. Such theologies basically ignore the fundamental condition of the poor and disfranchised. They defend the status quo and encourage acceptance and conformity of a kind that will promise no real transformation of the lot of the poor and oppressed. Tacitly, Western theology presents God as biased toward the strong, the powerful, the wealthy, and the privileged, rather than privileging the poor and oppressed.

Areas of Difference and Commonality

That Rastafarian thought and Caribbean theology of liberation have important ideological and theological differences is not in dispute. The question is: Can the two collaborate on a theological project for liberation? Methodologically, Caribbean theology of liberation must be selective in its use of Rastafarian concepts that support its project but do not negate any aspect of it. For example, Caribbean theology of liberation parts with the Rastafari brethren on the issue of the dignity, respect, and liberation of women. Caribbean theology must respect women and work for the liberation of both sexes, using theological ideas to address the social and political issues facing Caribbean peoples. Therefore, the strong patriarchalism evident in Leonard Howell's view of women in *The Promised Key* and in Rastafari in general—which was exacerbated by the "rudeboy culture" of the 1970s and 1980—is inimical to a Caribbean theology project that has liberation, justice, equality, inclusion, and community as its watchwords.

Instead of demonizing women as the "evil cause" of "original sin," as Howell did to Eve in his commentary on the Genesis narrative in *The Promised Key,* Caribbean theology of liberation embraces the new antihegemonic consciousness that Rasta "sistren" Maureen Rowe, Imani Tafari-Ama, Carole Yawney (self-styled follower), Barbara Makeda Lee (Blake Hannah), Sister Ikeda, and many others bring to the conversation on theology, liberation and economic development in the region.[31] Although these sistren do not pretend that they all speak with the same voice—as is clear from the literature on Rasta women[32]—they all have nonetheless articulated clearly the need to make the liberation of women from male dominance an essential part of the call for liberation and equality. Maureen Rowe underscored in Chapter 4 the fact that for Caribbean women in general, inequality, unemployment, underemployment, and other social and economic problems are much more pressing on women's consciousness than patriarchy. At the same time, Rowe, Yawney, Tafari-Ama, and other sistren have issued a call to remove stereotypical male ways of thinking and acting, both within and outside the Rastafarian movement.

Caribbean theology of liberation hears this call loud and clear and demonstrates to Rastafari that there can be no true liberation of the oppressed male, messianic or otherwise, until the program for liberation involves and benefits female and male alike. As a Jamaican sistren from Half Way Tree Road, Kingston, said to Nathaniel Samuel Murrell so profoundly in 1994, "The male oppress the female but him nuh realize that the liberation of the male is tied up with the freedom and liberation of the female." Carole Yawney expresses the same idea in more academic language: "Male dominance is built into the basic nature of Rastafari in such a way as to constitute its central contradiction." But "if Rastafari shares with the social system to which it is so oppressed a fundamental oppression of women, how can it represent in the final analysis a genuine alternative social form"[33]—and in this case, messianic liberation? Indeed, the God who favors the poor and oppressed Caribbean Rastaman is also the God of the woman—of both the mother of Jesus and the mother of Selassie—who made possible messianic theology and true liberation.

Caribbean theology of liberation also finds elements of early Rastafari's view on race unproductive. We applaud Rastafari's determined effort to deconstruct race and class prejudice in the society at large as an ongoing project. We also affirm categorically that God favors the poor and the oppressed, and that Christ, as a Palestinian, assumes ethnic characteristics (as does Selassie, the Ethiopian) and identifies with the oppressed "sufferers." However, since the Caribbean poor, as a group, are not defined by color, this affirmation is not a statement *against* a specific ethnic group and must not be seen as a justification for reverse racism or bigotry against people of European descent. While Rastas' criticism of white prejudice is a welcome critique of Eurocentrism, Howell went beyond the bounds of rationality when he portrayed Europeans as "evil white leprous Anglo-Saxons," people who are cursed with the Whiteness of leprosy and directly associated with descendants of Bible characters, such as the patriarchs and Eve, whom Howell calls "evil lepers."[34]

This anti-white rhetoric, explicit in early Rastafarian thought, is understandable in an earlier Jamaican context but is too divisive for a Caribbean theology project in the late twentieth century that sees God as favoring the multiethnic poor of Caribbean society. The Caribbean population is made up of people from many different ethnic groups (Africans, Indians, Portuguese, Hispanics, etc.) and with varied socioeconomic backgrounds, and the majority of those people are poor and needy—much poorer than the Rastas who have entered the Jamaican middle class since the Michael Manley era. Caribbean theology of liberation sees God as favoring not soley the African continent or the black diaspora—although Blacks comprise a high percentage of the world's poor—but poor, oppressed peoples in general and the Caribbean poor in particular.

Even the affirmation that Christ is black (used literally or symbolically), when understood in context and in the positive light in which Garvey and most African American theologians[35] used it, does not require, de facto, a discriminatory approach to messianic theology and liberation. As much as the Divine is not white and racist, God is also not a black racist. In black theology, Christ's Blackness is inseparably tied to the suffering and pain that result from oppression and exploitation of the people of God. According to America's most renowned liberation theologian, James Cone, "Jesus is black because he is a Jew" who has suffered and who continues to suffer with his people. That is, "the affirmation of the Black Christ can be understood when the significance of his past Jewishness is related dialectically to the significance of his present blackness." Cone explains further, "The Jewishness of Jesus located him in the context of the Exodus," a context of pain and suffering, "thereby connecting his appearance in Palestine with God's liberation of oppressed Israelites from Egypt"[36]—and in our case, with liberation from Caribbean oppression. Indeed, the Blackness of the Messiah as a symbol of identification with all oppressed and suffering peoples of the world, and with Caribbean peoples in particular, is a powerful tool of liberation and empowerment.

Belief in the divinity of Selassie could be another source of tension between the Rastafarian messianic ideology and Caribbean theology of liberation. Students often magnify the theological differences between Rastafari and Caribbean theology in a way that puts them in dialectic tension with each other. An American student at the University of North Carolina who saw the Contents for this anthology asked Murrell pointedly, "How do you reconcile the non-Christian elements in Rastafarian doctrines with your Caribbean liberation theology, which is, as I understand it, by and large a Judeo-Christian project, without doing violence to the essential character of either of them?" As Joseph Owens noted, Rastafari and Christianity are similarly juxtaposed in a "Christian versus non-Christian" dichotomy, as if the two were mutually exclusive.[37] Some Christians regard as heresy (if not blasphemy) the view that Selassie shares divinity and equality with God. They reserve the title *King of Kings, Lord of Lords* (attributed to Selassie) for Christ and regard the Christ event as a sacred and nonnegotiable theological tenet for Christian faith. As a Jamaican woman exclaimed at a 1978 "Youth for Christ" rally in Spanish Town, Jamaica, in Murrell's presence, "Jesus is fee me lord and king, not the Hemperor of Hetiopia."

In our attempt to establish a workable link between Caribbean theology of liberation and the Rastafarian messianic ideology, we regard the question of the divinity of Haile Selassie I as neither methodologically insurmountable nor theologically necessary. This position, of course, is not unprecedented. On several occasions, Selassie himself denied that he was divine, and during his historic official visit to Jamaica, he made it abundantly clear that he did not consider himself God. While he was visibly moved by the warm reception he received from Jamaicans in Kingston and was aware of the Rastafarians' view of him, no evidence exists that the emperor attempted to live out the "divine persona" ascribed to him.[38] Rather, he sought to prove the reverse—that he was a follower of Christ.[39] Although Selassie's divinity is still the most fundamental teaching in Rastafari and comes as an important part of Rastafari's messianic ideology, we do not consider belief in a divine Selassie an absolute necessity for accepting the emperor as a black Messiah or for the messianic ideology of Rastafari to powerfully inform Caribbean theology of liberation. As Hannah notes, the Divine could have manifested in and worked through Selassie as God did through Martin Luther King, Mahatma Gandhi, Malcolm X,[40] and many other modern prophets (if not black messiahs).

In spite of their theological differences, Rastafari and Caribbean theology of liberation share many things. Both movements originated from a British Caribbean Judeo-Christian culture, which allows them to engage in fruitful dialogue and borrowing of ideas. Rasta theology is laced with Judeo-Christian ideas, albeit nuanced for liberation from Eurocentrism, and is refreshingly appealing and effective as a tool in the fight against injustice and oppression. Most Caribbean Rastas grew up in Christian homes or were exposed to Christian ideas, which they often use to express their most fundamental doctrines. In both movements the Bible is cherished and used for theological teaching, defining religious concepts and the practice of faith, forming social and economic theories, and outlining ethical principles by which to order human relations and society.

One cannot develop an authentic Caribbean theology without biblical warrant any more than one can define Rastafarian beliefs void of all reference to Scripture. In their approach to theology, both movements employ an equally scathing critique of Eurocentric prejudices against Blacks and the exploitation of African countries, resources, and cultures; the issue of liberation from all forms of domination is a central concern. Rastafari and Caribbean theology of liberation also share an Afrocentric consciousness that affirms the worth, dignity, and pride of the black race in general and the Caribbean poor and oppressed in particular. Part of that affirmation involves appreciation for and the promotion of African culture and traditions as important experiences of the peoples about whom we write or speak, and to whom we address the ideology of liberation and messianism.

In an effort to highlight similarities in beliefs and practices between Christianity and Rastafari, some scholars have attempted to Christianize Rastas; and as Nathaniel Samuel Murrell, Joseph Owens, Barry Chevannes, and others have noted in this an-

thology and elsewhere, some Rastas and former Rastas have tried to portray the movement as a form of black Christianity or reform movement,[41] even referring to themselves
as Christians. But as much as the movement has built its essential doctrines and ideology on Christian ideas and Scriptures and shares common concerns with Christians and
Caribbean theology of liberation, Rastafarians as a group are not Christians, and no attempt is made in this chapter to portray them as embracing Christian faith. Rastas have
consistently voiced their vendetta against Christianity, especially the Vatican, for what
they regard as the Roman Catholic Church's role in Italy's invasion of Ethiopia and the
enslavement of Africans. Howell said of Christians that they are "the false teachers under the supervision of the Pope of Rome who is satan the devil. The agents of his speaking lies, in the churches, and let the people walk in darkness."[42] Why, then, use the ideas
of a non-Christian (or anti-Christian) tradition to do liberation theology? Caribbean
theology of liberation draws on the powerful imagery of Rastafari's messianic ideology
in the same way that liberation theologians in Latin America find useful concepts in
Marxist and communist ideologies—avowedly anti-Christian philosophies—which
they use to critique and expound Christian thought and action.

As it searches for appropriate methodologies, practices, and insights to guide its task,
this theological project incorporates local or contextual antecedents, paradigms, and
sources. In this context, Rastafari becomes an important source of reference for de-
signing a Caribbean theology of liberation, particularly Rastas' messianic ideology and
the social, political, and economic context that it addresses. Whereas our approach is
not a wholesale endorsement of Rastafarian beliefs in all of their facets, it recognizes
that this is a religious movement with strong Judeo-Christian influences that, by its
unique reflective and meditative processes and vision of liberation, has exhibited features significant for any serious theology project in the Caribbean. The view described
here represents a departure from the negative bias against Rastafari generally displayed
within Christian circles in the region.

The Rastafarian messianic ideology is rooted in the cultural traditions of the
Caribbean and Africa. As a result, Afro-Caribbean songs, stories, religions, folklore,
language, and other cultural traditions (except Anancyism and Obeah, which Rastas de-
test) have enhanced the legitimacy of Rastafari's thought and messianic ideology. In the
same way, African Americans have grounded their black theology of liberation and
African American hermeneutics in the spirituals, slave narratives, poems, songs, folkloric traditions, and culture of the marginalized and much-maligned antebellum and
postbellum black church. It stands to reason, therefore, that Caribbean theology of liberation, which shares much in common with Rastafari and black theology, should enhance its theological content and appeal with Rastafari's messianic ideology and other
cultural traditions of the region—Jamaica talk evident in "Jamaica's First Lady of Comedy" Louise Bennett's folkloric repertoire and Caribbean people's stories, myths, and
songs. Native traditions that have already crossed the frontiers of a reflective process
that offers insight to understandings of God in the region should not be ignored, especially when those traditions insist that theology must be interpreted contextually and
analyzed hand in hand with economic development and national transformation.

Caribbean Liberation and Self-Criticism

An important challenge to Caribbean theology of liberation is the need to be self-critical of its own shifting vantage point of "dominance." The fact is, the Christian tradition out of which the call for Caribbean liberation theology comes constitutes an important part of the Caribbean Babylon,[43] and occasionally, the church has spoken on religious issues and "the Caribbean reality" from a position of dominance and power somewhat similar to that of the European model it assails. As Ashley Smith, former president of United Theological College of the University of the West Indies (UTC,WI), has noted, up to the 1960s, that dominance was exercised in Jamaica by expatriate missionaries; but between the 1960s and the 1980s, mainline Christian churches incorporated with Babylon in the spirit of independence, under the motto "Out of Many One Nation." Several prominent leaders from the "established church" have also been active in politics and peacemaking in Jamaica. Since the 1980s, however, "politicians have been known not only to favor the new 'evangelical' churches, with their ultra-conservative theology, but also to be openly critical of the church leaders who have dared to articulate the need for the contextualization of God-talk and popular lifestyle."[44] Caribbean liberation theology is, therefore, in the unenviable position of being a part of Babylon while having to distance itself from the Babylon ideology in order to join forces with the Rastafarians to reform Babylon and challenge it to work for liberation of the poor.

Caribbean theology of liberation also has not yet decided whether it will allow Caribbean religions generally despised by the Caribbean church but which have drawn on biblical themes and Christian traditions—Santeria, Voodoo, Myalism, Pocomania, convince cult, Orisha, and others to contribute to its theological conversation. Many of these syncretistic religious traditions have already been absorbed into elements of Caribbean Christianity. A colloquial myth even has it that most Haitians are 100 percent Catholic and 95 percent Voodoo. The numerical hyperbole in the myth is obvious, but one wonders whether the African-Catholic cross-fertilization in Trinidad Orisha, Haitian Voodoo, and Santeria in Cuba—religions of people who have known oppression for most of their lives—may not provide an excellent context and relevant data for theological conversation. The same question is raised with regard to Eastern religions in the Caribbean. As former UTC,WI academic dean George Mulrain noted, "Christians in the Caribbean have never really learned to respect other faiths. By contrast, a Christian from Asia is not as scathing in his or her remarks about the faiths of Hinduism, Sikhism and Islam."[45] How, then, can we engage in theological dialogue with them? Can Caribbean theology of liberation learn from and inspire the theologies of these major world religions in the region? Since the 1970s, the *Caribbean Journal of Religious Studies* and other journals have published the essays of several Caribbean theologians who are calling for a broadening of the circle of inclusion in the theological conversation with Rastafari and other Caribbean religious traditions.[46]

By any criterion, it is questionable whether we can have a true Caribbean theology of liberation for all peoples of the region and at the same time exclude from the project also the so-called obnoxious and conservative Christian groups. According to Ashley Smith, these form, "by and large, the new Christianity of black people; which, in some measure, is refuting the claim of those who speak for traditional European Christianity that divinity can only be perceived through the eye of the people of Europe."[47] Even when some religious groups show "no sign of readiness to tackle sin as a corporate reality" and are "prepared to deal with salvation [only] at its most personal and individual level,"[48] oblivious of Caribbean social, political, and economic problems, Rastafari's antihegemonic messianic ideology requires that these people who enrich the Caribbean religious plurality be given a voice (if they wish to speak) in the struggle for liberation. As theologian Dale Bisnauth, now a senior member in the Guyana Parliament said, "A relevant theology is an urgent necessity to help the Church—in its pluriformity—to understand and make clear the dynamics of the ideology" of liberation that is "behind this pluriformity, which can, and does create the kinds of crises in our ranks that polarize our relationships and dissipate and fracture our visions and challenges to governments and peoples regarding development. Our own active engagement in development awaits the emergence of that theology."[49]

Bisnauth argues forcefully that "doing" and ecumenical "cooperation" are essential elements of a Caribbean theology of liberation supported by Christian traditions, whether those traditions are operating under a capitalist model, socialist concept, or military dictatorship. "But," Bisnauth admits, "the way is fraught with difficulties. Traditionally, Hindus, Muslims, Vodunists, Rastafarians, and what have you, have been marginalised to the fringes of society. It was primarily from among their ranks that converts have been recruited for the Christian churches. From the standpoint of the 'greater tradition,' non-Christians have been regarded as socially inferior. From the standpoint of Christian orthodoxy, their beliefs (which have been hardly understood) have been regarded as inferior, if not demonic." So Bisnauth asks, "On what terms can Christians of the present time engage with non-Christians" in the Caribbean "in joint developmental [and theological] enterprises without undermining their integrity or ours?"[50]

The use of the Rasta messianic ideology in Caribbean theology of liberation must be an inclusive project that allows many voices to contribute to the theological conversation, even when those voices produce a discordant sound to the untrained or unsympathetic ear. With seeds already sown in the messianic ideology of Rastafari, the ground is prepared for a Caribbean theological project to rediscover the strong prophetic witness that God is biased toward neither the powerful nor the neutral. Rather, God is biased toward the poor and oppressed and commits the people of God to a practice of their faith that will reflect this. Instead of closing the circle or narrowing the framework, this opens up the possibility of liberation to an amazing extent.

Appropriate questions to raise at the end of this chapter are: Might Rastafari's messianic theology become dated? Might it be subsumed under Jamaicanism or Christian orthodoxy? And should that happen, what will become of a Caribbean theology of liberation that is informed by or closely aligned with the messianism of Rastafari? For example, the theology that aligned itself closely with Marxism in this century has since outlived its usefulness. Even before the collapse of communism and the death of Marxism in Grenada in the 1980s, the prophecy of a dialectic theology converting the poor masses into a petite bourgeoisie in a classless society was seen as an illusion. Will the Rastafarian messianic hope suffer a similar fate?

Leachim Semaj contends that the Rasta social theory is being subsumed under the Jamaican society, which has itself undergone a social evolution. "This process is being articulated and motivated by Afro-centric Jamaicans who, though inspired by Rasta, do not necessarily share the Rasta religion." Semaj continued, "Ten years ago I concluded that if a Rasta intelligentsia did not emerge and take hold of the transformation process, 'then Rastafari would move from being the most powerful ideological force in Jamaica to take its place beside, if not behind, the other systems of escape, ignorance or solace that influence the lives of our people.'" The former Rastafarian concludes, "It is quite possible that Rastafari has fulfilled its promise and is now a spent force, one that can only be further utilized by Afro-centric individuals who are able and willing to go beyond the dictates and limitations of religion."[51]

But the possibility for future change, positive and negative, in Rastafarian theology must always be an open question. As Yawney has accurately noted, "With remarkable lucidity they [Rastafarians] have sensed the contradictions of capitalism and colonialism and they have adopted a policy of peaceful resistance and noncooperation with any established authority. The principal tenets of the movement are peace and love, truth, and justice."[52] It is clear that the Rastafari promise based on peace, love, truth, and justice has not been fulfilled; Babylon is "still in business" and needs to hear the prophetic voice and critique of Rastafari. We think that as long as prejudice toward African peoples and their culture exists, as long as impoverishment exists in the face of wealth controlled by a small minority, as long as greed and selfishness drive our communities, as long as political corruption mars the functioning of good government, there will be the need to hear the voice of Rastafari and its messianic theology.

Notes

1. Joseph Owens, "The Rastafarians of Jamaica," in Idris Hamid, ed., *Troubling of the Waters* (San Fernando, Trinidad: Rahaman Printery, 1973), 165.

2. Ibid., 165–70; Michael N. Jagessar, "JPIC and Rastafarians: A Call for Dialogue," *One World* (February 1991): 15–17.

3. Leahcim Semaj [formerly Michael James], "Inside Rasta: The Future of a Religious Movement," *Caribbean Review* 14, 1 (1985): 38. In the new phase, some Rastas have moved away from what Semaj describes as "I man don't wear shoes no more, I man don't drive in car" to sporting shining leather and driving BMWs, Mercedes Benzes, and Volvos.

4. Semaj himself has moved from his doctrinal "center," which he espoused in the 1960s, and is now operating a very successful practice and radio program in Kingston.

5. Joseph Owens, *Dread: The Rastafarians of Jamaica* (Kingston: Sangster's Book Stores, 1976), 32. See also Chapter 19 by Nathaniel Samuel Murrell and Lewin Williams.

6. Dennis Forsythe, "West Indian Culture through the Prism of Rastafarianism," in Rex Nettleford, ed., *Caribbean Quarterly Monograph: Rastafari* (Kingston: Caribbean Quarterly, University of the West Indies, 1985), 77.

7. Haile Mikael Yenge Flagot Kezehemohonenow, "The Role of Rastafarianism in the Caribbean" (paper delivered to the Ecumenical Symposium of the Caribbean Council of Churches, Chaguaramas, Trinidad, November 1971), 3.

8. Issembly of Elders, *The Ethiopian-African Theocracy Union Policy: EATUP, True Genuine Authentic Fundamental Indigenous Original Comprehensive Alternative Policy: FIOCAP* (Kingston: Jahrastafari Royal Ethiopian Judah-Coptic Church, n.d.).

9. Ibid., 3–5.

10. Ibid. See also Chapter 8 by Rupert Lewis in this anthology.

11. Robert Cuthbert, ed. *Called to Be: Report on the Caribbean Ecumenical Consultation for Development* (Bridgetown, Barbados: Caribbean Conferences of Churches, 1972), 24. Cited also in John Holder, "Is This the Word of the Lord? In Search of Caribbean Biblical Theology and Hermeneutics" (paper delivered at the annual meeting of the Society of Biblical Literature, Philadelphia, November 1995), 1.

12. Robert Cuthbert, "Development and the Caribbean Christian," in Idris Hamid, ed., *With Eyes Wide Open* (Bridgetown, Barbados: Caribbean Development Ecumenical Council, 1973), 112. See also the essays by William Watty, Clive Abdullah, Patrick Gomes, Geoffrey Williams, and Harold Sitahal in Hamid, ed., *Troubling of the Waters;* and Idris Hamid, *Out of the Depths* (San Fernando, Trinidad: St. Andrews Press, 1977).

13. Holder, "Is This the Word?" 8. See Idris Hamid, "Theology and Caribbean Development," in Hamid, ed., *With Eyes Wide Open,* 126; and Robert Cuthbert, "Development and the Caribbean Christian"; Clive Abdullah, "Any Word from the Lord"; and William Watty, "De-Colonization of Theology," all in Hamid, ed., *Troubling of the Waters.*

14. Dale A. Bisnauth, "Religious Pluralism and Development in the Caribbean: Questions," *Caribbean Journal of Religious Studies* 4, 2 (1982): 28.

15. See Christopher Rowland and Mark Corner, *Liberating Exegesis: The Challenge of Liberation Theology to Biblical Studies* (Louisville, Ky.: Westminster John Knox Press, 1990).

16. Forsythe, "West Indian Culture," 75.

17. This was true in the case of Episcopal bishop William H. Coleridge's sermon, preached in Barbados in 1827 to the newly "confirmed," in which he admonished them to be contented with their station in life, whether bound or free, and to be good Christian servants to their masters; see William Coleridge, *Charges Delivered to the Clergy of the Diocese of Barbados and the Leeward Islands* (London: J. G. & F. Rivington, 1835), 263–64. Cited in Holder, "Is This the Word?" 2.

18. Rex M. Nettleford, *Inward Stretch, Outward Reach: A Voice from the Caribbean* (London: Macmillan Publishers, 1993), 86.

19. Robert McAfee Brown, *Liberation Theology* (Louisville, Ky.: Westminster/John Knox Press, 1993), 81.

20. Cain Hope Felder, "The Bible Re-Contextualization and the Black Religious Experience," in Gayraud S. Wilmore, ed., *African American Religious Studies: An Interdisciplinary Anthology* (Durham, N.C.: Duke University Press, 1989), 156–57.

21. Jurgen Moltmann, *The Church in the Power of the Spirit* (London: SCM Press, 1978), 17.

22. Carole D. Yawney, "Remnants of All Nations: Rastafarian Attitudes to Race and Nationality," in Frances Henry, ed., *Ethnicity in the Americas* (Chicago: Mouton Publishers, 1976), 231–62.

23. Barry Chevannes, "Healing the Nation: Rastafari Exorcism of the Ideology of Racism in Jamaica," *Caribbean Quarterly* 36, 1–2 (1994): 69.

24. See Issembly of Elders, *EATUP.*

25. See, among others, Chapters 1, 11, 16, 17, and 20 in this anthology.

26. Paulo Freire, *The Pedagogy of the Oppressed,* trans. Myra B. Ramos (New York: Herder & Herder, 1970).

27. Tennyson Smyth [Ras-J-Tesfa], *The Living Testament of Rasta-For-I* (Kingston: Ras-J-Tesfa, 1980), book 1, 5.

28. Ibid., book 1, 3.

29. Owens, *Dread,* 100.

30. Ibid., 101.

31. For Leonard Howell's commentary in *The Promised Key.* See Chapter 21. For the growing contributions and consciousness of Rasta sistren, see Hazel G. Byfield, "Women in the Struggle for True Community: A Caribbean Perspective," *Mid-Stream* 25, 1 (January 1986): 49–56; Carole D. Yawney, "Moving with the Dawtas of Rastafari: From Myth to Reality," in Ulrich Fleischmann and Ineke Phaf, eds., *El Caribe y America Latina* (The Caribbean and Latin America) (Berlin: Verlag Klau Dieter Vervuert, 1987), 193–99. See also Chapters 4 (Maureen Rowe) and 5 (Imani Tafari-Ama) in this anthology.

32. Barbara Blake Hannah, "No More Rasta for-I," *Gleaner Sunday Magazine,* September 11, 1983, 2–4; Sister Ilaloo, "Rastawoman as Equal," *Yard Roots* 1 (1981): 5–7; Barbara Makeda Lee, "What Is a Rastaman?" *Caribbean Times* 25 (1982): 15; Maureen Rowe, "The Woman in Rastafari," *Caribbean Quarterly* 26, 24 (1980): 13–21; Makeda Silvera, "An Open Letter to Rastafarian Sistren," *Fireweed* (spring 1983): 115–20; Carole D. Yawney, "To Grow a Daughter," in A. Miles and G. Finn, eds., *Feminism in Canada* (Toronto: Black Rose Books), 119–44.

33. Yawney, "Moving with the Dawtas," 194.

34. See the section in *The Promised Key* titled "Eve the Mother of Evil," in Chapter 21 of this anthology.

35. James H. Cone, *God of the Oppressed* (New York: Seabury Press, 1975), 133–36; idem, *Black Theology and Black Power* (New York: Seabury Press, 1969). See also Albert B. Cleage, Jr., *The Black Messiah* (New York and London: Sheed & Ward, 1968); William James, *Is God a White Racist?* (Garden City, N.Y.: Doubleday & Co., 1973).

36. Cone, *God of the Oppressed,* 134.

37. Owens, *Dread,* 103–4.

38. Selassie commissioned Archimandrite Laike M. Mandefro to Jamaica to establish the Ethiopian Orthodox Church there mainly as a goodwill gesture to Jamaican Rastas.

39. At the World Congress on Evangelism in Berlin, November 1966, organized by the Billy Graham Evangelistic Association, the emperor opened the congress with a clear statement concerning his Christian commitment and intention to work for the promotion of forgiveness, tolerance, justice, and love in the world. See His Imperial Majesty, Haile Selassie I, "Building an Enduring Tower," Carl F. H. Henry and W. Stanley Mooneyham, eds., *One Race, One Gospel, One Task,* vol. 1 of *World Congress on Evangelism, Berlin, 1966,* Official Reference Volumes: Papers and Reports (Minneapolis: World Wide Publications, 1967), 20. In the summer of 1994, Zenas Gerig directed Samuel Murrell to a copy of Selassie's Berlin speech at the Zenas Gerig Library Jamaica Theological Seminary, Kingston.

40. Barbara Blake Hannah, personal conversation with William Spencer, Kingston, Jamaica, summer 1989.

41. See Owens, "Rastafarians of Jamaica," 165–66; William Spencer's commentary on *The Promised Key,* Chapter 21 in this anthology; Barry Chevannes, *Rastafari: Roots and Ideology*

(Syracuse, N.Y.: Syracuse University Press, 1994); Barbara Makeda Lee (Blake Hannah), *Rastafari: The New Creation* (Kingston: Jamaica Media Productions, 1981), 35. See also the Introduction to this anthology, by Nathaniel Samuel Murrell.

42. G.G. Maragh [Leonard Howell], *The Promised Key,* ed. Nnamdi Azikine (Accra, Ghana: The African Morning Post, Head Office, n.d.), 3. Howell said the church is a "false organization, it is a hypocritical religious system that has three elements, first commercial political and ecclesiastical, to keep the people in ignorance of their wicked course" ("False Religion," in *The Promised Key,* 2).

43. For example, we in that tradition are active in the political process, and our members include, among others, prominent public officials—politicians, legislators, law-enforcement officials, doctors, nurses, professors, and other teachers. Often Caribbean governments also respect the church, which politicians use to special advantage during elections and in times of national and domestic crises.

44. Ashley Smith, "Mainline Churches in the Caribbean: Their Relationship to the Cultural and Political Process," *Caribbean Journal of Religious Studies* (CJRS) 9, 2 (1989): 38.

45. George M. Mulrain, "Christian Faith and Other Faiths," *CJRS* 10, 1 (April 1989): 8–10. See also Ajai Mansigh and Lamini Mansingh, "The Impact of East Indians on Jamaican Religious Thoughts and Expressions," *CJRS* 10, 1 (April 1989): 36–52.

46. See the brief review essay by J. Emmett Weir, "Towards a Caribbean Liberation Theology," *CJRS* 12, 1 (April 1991): 41–53; Burchell Taylor, "Caribbean Theology," *CJRS* 3, 2 (September 1980): 18–32. See also the essays by William Watty, Idris Hamid, Clive Abdullah, Robert Cuthbert, et al., in Hamid, ed., *Troubling of the Waters;* Hamid, *Out of the Depths;* and Cuthbert, *With Eyes Wide Open,* referenced at nn. 11 and 12, above.

47. Smith, "Mainline Churches in the Caribbean," 32–33.

48. Lewin Williams, "What, Why and Wherefore of Caribbean Theology," *CJRS* 12, 1 (April 1991): 31.

49. Bisnauth, "Religious Pluralism," 26.

50. Ibid., 17–33.

51. Leahcim T. Semaj, "Rastafari Today: Promise Fulfilled, Force Spent" (unpublished manuscript shared with Nathaniel Samuel Murrell and Clinton Chisholm at Leachim Semaj & Co., 6 Ivy Green Crescent, Kingston, Jamaica, 1994), 5.

52. Yawney, "Remnants of All Nations."

Appendixes

Appendix A

Emissaries of Rastafari: An Interview with Professor Leonard Barrett

INDIGO BETHEA, MICHAEL BRUNY, AND
ADRIAN ANTHONY MCFARLANE

The cultural reach of Rastafari transcends the hitherto ethnocentric ideology of its nascence in favor of a "soulful" depth of personal, communal, and natural ecology. Rastas have always invoked the words of the psalmist with conviction: "The earth is [Jah's] and the fullness thereof; the world and they that dwell therein" (Psalm 24:1 KJV). This psalm constitutes the expression of Jah's (God's) sovereignty over nature and persons, as well as intimates a sense of community or concord among the active agents of Jah's will. As such, the Rastafarians see themselves as the "new" or "real" Israel, Jah's chosen vessels for social and mental reconstruction. But Rastas do not regard themselves as the exclusive instruments of Jah's transvaluation of "Babylon" thinking and practices. They acknowledge that "none but ourselves can free our minds" (Bob Marley), and they are unrelenting in their service as voices of protest in the wilderness of confused identity and as battering rams against the walls of colonial mental prisons. The responses to the Rastafarian voice of protest range from indifference to curiosity and even a life of transformation and advocacy that seeks to "chant down Babylon," once and for all.

An important group of agents who, in their response, have succeeded in spreading abroad the emerging ideas of the Rastafarian movement are scholars. Since Roy Augier, Rex Nettleford, and M. G. Smith, under the aegis of the then University College of the

We are deeply indebted to Mrs. Theodora Barrett, who, along with Dr. Barrett, welcomed us into their home and fed us sumptuously, physically and intellectually. Correspondingly, we thank the Reverend Nancy Schluter and State Senator William Schluter for welcoming us into their home as we journeyed to and from Philadelphia—a ten-hour trip! Finally, special recognition and thanks to Indigo Bethea for transcribing (and assisting with the editing of) the interview, as well as to Mrs. Connie Mravlja, for the patience she showed in retyping the five revisions we did.

West Indies (UCWI), undertook the first scholarly study (published in 1960) of the Rasta phenomenon, many students and trained research scholars have sensitively and carefully disseminated the Rastafarian ideas of cultural "detoxification," Afro-focal reeducation, identity reconstruction, sartorial and linguistic liberation, indigenous artistic expression, and self-reliance. By introducing Rastafarian ideas to the "hallowed halls" of the academy, scholars have symbolically reenacted the original cleansing of the proverbial temple of ignorance on matters related to the Rastafarian phenomenon.

The serious scholarship on the movement in Europe, Canada, the United States, Africa, and the Caribbean has made the study of Rastafari international and transcultural in a way that introduces for consideration Jah's word of "peace and love"—the original message of the movement. Among the most prolific scholars in Rastafarian research and other areas of the study of the African experience in the diaspora is Leonard Barrett, now professor emeritus at Temple University in Philadelphia. While doing extensive field research on Rastafari, often risking his reputation and life in the process, Barrett unearthed invaluable information on the movement's ethos and ideology that, for the past thirty years, has been widely received in the academy. Barrett's writings, along with his public and university lectures, have functioned as a reliable source for the intelligent understanding of Rastafari, particularly in the United States and Canada, where Rastas were vilified on the basis of their nonconforming ideology and appearance.

Given Barrett's depth of scholarship and long-standing association with Rastafari, Adrian Anthony McFarlane and two of his students elected to have an informal conversation with him in an effort to obtain a Janus view of Rastafari. The excerpts below are part of a two-hour recorded conversation that we believe are worth sharing in honor of Barrett, who has pioneered research on Rastafarian and other cultural phenomena in the African diaspora with unflinching devotion and academic integrity. The conversation is allowed to stand on its own in this anthology, without interpretation and commentary, to allow our readers to view the depth of Barrett's knowledge of Rastafari even in the evening of his years.

ADRIAN ANTHONY MCFARLANE

One-on-One with Professor Barrett
(Tuesday, September 23, 1996)

ADRIAN ANTHONY MCFARLANE: We are very happy to be with you today. I have with me two of my most able students from Hartwick College: Indigo Bethea, whom both you and Mrs. Barrett have met, and Michael Bruny. Both of them are students who are interested in diasporic studies, particularly as those studies relate to the Americas; and since you have written extensively about the connections between Africa and the Americas, we thought it wise to come and speak with you, particularly about the Rastafarians. I would like to begin with a question and then give you a sense of where we propose to go. In an unpublished paper, which you have so kindly shared with us, you made a statement with which some might demur; the statement is "The greatest singer of reggae was the honorable Robert Nesta Marley who died in 1981." From your perspective, was Marley really the greatest singer of reggae, or was he one of the most popular reggae singers internationally?

LEONARD BARRETT: Popular internationally isn't correct. Marley was not a great singer by traditional European standards; his talent transcends those old categories.

MCFARLANE: I'm going to back up a little bit, and of course, Indigo and Michael can come in at any point. The thrust of my question, however, was not whether or not Marley had a Westernized voice that was considered to be beautiful, the question was whether or not Marley was perceived in Jamaica as the most outstanding reggae singer, or was Marley mostly a product of [Chris] Blackwell, Island Records, England, the United States, and Germany, repackaged and sent back to us in Jamaica?

BARRETT: I would say that Marley was repackaged and sent to us from Island Records as a great singer. But the average Jamaican, in evaluating "a good voice," would probably say that Marley did not have a good voice. But in my thinking, Marley had a good voice. Haven't you heard that man sing "No Woman No Cry" or "Me Belly Full but Me Hungry"? He had a voice for the folklore of Jamaica. He was singing because he loved those songs—"No Woman No Cry" [which Marley said was the best song in his repertoire]—and sang them with an unparalled depth of feeling. When you look at him, he was completely taken up with what he was doing. He did not talk about his voice or beauty. He talked about singing, and singing in that style as a medium of expression and social transformation.

MCFARLANE: Is it not part of the mode of operation of Rastafari that they strove then, and now, to express themselves in their unique way without emulating foreign aesthetic values?

BARRETT: Very much so. I'm not sure if I wrote in the paper you currently have, or in another chapter, but ska, for example, came to the World Fair in New York, sponsored by [Edward] Seaga, who was present. He thought it would take the whole world. But it never did. The reason why is because he took the spice out of Jamaican songs, the unique things that made it Jamaican were repackaged for an American audience. If you want to sell America something unique, don't try to make that item seem American.

MCFARLANE: But that is the paradox I'm finding, because I was in Jamaica in the seventies, and although Marley was popular, from my perspective he was not as popular as the Mighty Diamonds, Burning Spear, or some other "roots" group, Burning Spear, of course, being the most "rootsy." Marley, at that time, was making it internationally, which was good for tourism, Jamaica's image abroad, etc. However, his music became more cerebral and less visceral during that period. Consequently, his music wasn't very popular in the dance halls, in comparison to the many other performers.

BARRETT: No. Perfectly so. Marley's music wasn't dance music. In other words, he was against colonialism and all of its false images of comfort, which distract the mind from the process outside. At one time in Jamaica local songs could not be played on the Jamaican radio station. The music had to be R&B and ballads from U.S.A. or some other imported musical genre.

MCFARLANE: Sam Cooke, Jerry Butler, Fats Domino, and so on, even Elvis Presley.

BARRETT: And believe it or not, they could not touch the Jamaican sound. But the Jamaicans were sometimes overly suggestive in some of the lyrics they sang.

MCFARLANE: I am pleased with your explanation and interpretation, because I was concerned about the self-validation of our own value system, rather than allowing our indigenous values to be sent abroad and certified in order to be reembraced. So when I saw the word *greatest singer,* I wondered whether there might not be some need to unpack that to say that Bob was the most popular by international standards, but by Jamaican standards he was one of many great singers who have left a legacy for us in terms of lyrics, style, etc. That was what concerned me, because someone reading those words might think otherwise. Most people who go to Jamaica assume that reggae and Bob Marley are synonymous. In fact, Bob Marley seems to function as an icon of reggae and Rastafari for most visitors—a veritable form of cultural idolatry.

BARRETT: However, a little cultural idolatry is necessary now and then. Now, there is a reason for that; take, for instance, Don Drummond, one of the finest trombonists the world ever saw, nobody has ever said anything about the man. I have used some superlative words to idolize the men who try to do something in the island, not because they got validation from abroad but because they did well there. Again, there is a Jamaican woman who, having read my book on the Rastafarians, decided to do a Ph.D. in cultural studies, and so she came to talk with me. I told her to go and study just two miles up the road from where she lived. There is a woman who lives next door named Maude, one of the finest healers the island ever saw. Not a word has been written about her. Since this woman wants to research Pocomania, I told her she would probably be the first, I think; no, Seaga was the first. But I said, "Go on and hit it, hit the road." And I hope she will do it, because we need to write about the people of the island, although very few people from the outside world recognize them as great.

INDIGO BETHEA: You have spoken about Pocomania, can you clarify for us what that is?

BARRETT: The word *poco* means "small," *mania* means "mad" or "crazed." Collectively, *Pocomania* means "little crazy" or "little madness." Now the little madness that Pocomania brought was first evidenced in slavery, and the English tolerated it as harmless when practiced now and then. But it has remained the island's native religion. In Jamaica, I lived next door to a Pocomanian woman who brought some of the influential men in the area to seek her counsel. One man in particular, Poppy Scott, used to ride a donkey some distance to confer with those who required his service. He's remembered and pictured today on a donkey portraying Christ. He was super! Anyone who saw him just took their hat off to him. Now, why can't we write and make a little noise about men such as that? Although they're not a part of the recognized denominations such as Moravians, Presbyterians, etc., they are, nevertheless, outstanding Pocomanians who ought to be celebrated. For the island's sake, we have some good men and women who need to be recognized and celebrated! Although they did not possess degrees, they were great in their time. Presbyterian parson, help me.

[To McFarlane.] What do you think? Would you recognize men like those? I will not marginalize them.

MCFARLANE: I was just thinking that in every serious community those who have little, and do much with it, ought to be applauded over against those who have much and do only little. But, beyond that, I wondered whether the root of the word *Pocomania* is not traceable to the Spanish colonists?

BARRETT: Yes, to be truthful, I think it's the Spanish that used that word and called it that name. *Pocomania* is a word that is endemic to the islands; everyone knows about it.

BETHEA: Was the term *Pocomania* used pejoratively at first?

BARRETT: Yes, most certainly. Honestly, my aunt was a Pocomanian. I used to visit her up in the hill and every now and then I would hear her with a throaty, guttural voice. I began to recognize that she was using that sound when an obstacle comes her way, then she would shout it out. I used to observe Pocomanians with a sense of awe. I always watch my aunt working and every now and then she would make that guttural, throaty sound. I could write endlessly about those little, seeming "nonsensical" activities. And the same thing happened with Mother Rita that I wrote about in my book *The Sun and the Drum*. She always used those sounds. And the interesting thing is, if you're sick and go to her for a healing, she turns you around. Now this "turning around" means you have gotten rid of the badness, or evil, and she can now see your situation clearly, and prepare you to understand what she is going to say. She has a way of saying things and making expressions that are not easily made by the average person. People of those type have mystic qualities about them that need to be pondered and respected. A Pocomanian can stand for hours staring straight ahead. You'll laugh at them, but they were serious mystics and they could perceive such things. For example, I myself had fever when I was a youngster, to the point of blackwater fever. When you have blackwater fever, you are close to the end of your life. I went to her, and she gave me "a turn." Then looked straight ahead, went into her house, and took out a bottle of boiled medicine, which she gave to my mother, prescribing that I take it three times a day, starting at that moment. To get there, I had to ride on my uncle's back. When I left, they had to run to catch me. I've never had fever to this day! That's Jamaican life . . .

MICHAEL BRUNY: In other words, if you believe in the abilities of Mother Rita, you can be healed? I have a similar situation. My parents are from Haiti, and I definitely believe in the mystic powers as illustrated by Mother Rita.

BARRETT: A colleague of mine, his name just slipped me, went to Haiti and, if you ask, he'll say, "I believe in Obeah, I believe in witchcraft." He said, "If you live in Haiti, you'll believe in it!" That is a statement I'll never overstate. If you live in Haiti, it's all around you—so much that you're led to believe in it.

BETHEA: I believe that to be true also in the black communities in the U.S.

BARRETT: If you go to Haiti, for a while, you will be "up and up," but after a while, the beliefs are likely to get in your brain. To be truthful, the same thing happens in Jamaica. And I could see the people who became Pocomanian; this was the thing that came over them. First they become subdued, and then they accept the beliefs.

BETHEA: Well, Dr. Barrett, you have answered my question, but what I'm curious about now are the religious practices of the Pocomanians.

BARRETT: Dr. McFarlane, maybe you can correct me, but I think healing is their primary religious practice—they are a curative people. They insist on curing or insist in dividing evil from good. And I think Pocomania does resemble Voodoo or Voodun. The doctrine is mostly Christian in origin. But they are more known for their healing qualities. They learn of the weeds of the land, are able to use herbs of all sorts to effect recovery and maintain health.

BRUNY: Yeah, that's the way my father does it.

BARRETT: They can pick fifteen weeds, which you would consider to be a bush, and they take them and start working on you.

MCFARLANE: So, Pocomania is an African Christian syncretism?

BARRETT: Yes, the remembrance of Africa is close to those people. For example, we call them "psychics" here, a group of people who are not like the ones in the Caribbean. The Caribbean ones are religious psychics. The difference between them and here is the psychics you see in the United States will drive Mercedes Benz. Those in the Caribbean are poor people, but they are very able. For example, once I was behind a curtain [when Mother Rita allowed him to sit in on a session], and a woman came to her and said, "Mother, I'm sick. I have not slept for days." Then Mother takes over: "You have this bile, this, that, this, that, etc." Mother Rita told the woman what she had. The woman didn't say anything, and Mother got close to her and started telling her how she got those things. The woman didn't want to hear anymore, so she just got up and left. She's such a convinced psychic that she can tell you what you ate yesterday or whether or not you slept last night. That's the kind of woman she was. And I said to her, "Mother, tell me something, I heard you diagnose a few minutes ago. Can you tell me how you got those things?" Well, beside her is a chair that is only sat on by the people who come to visit with her. It was her mother's chair. She said, "Please, Doctor, come and sit in this chair. I can tell you, but I have to have some illustration. I don't speak the King's English, I speak Jamaican." She said, "In this leg, you had an accident that messes up this leg. Every now and then you have a charlie horse" (the first I had learned of such a term). I was in the mountain, and we were playing baseball and I thought we were playing cricket, so I hit the ball over the boundary and was running with the bat. So the boy said, "Fling away the bat." So I flung the bat, but it caught me at my leg and it was swollen for weeks; I was on crutches. And she said, "You had fallen." Tell me how she knows? She has never seen me before. She said, "You have a son who is in trouble." Lenny was in trouble . . . And believe it or not, Lenny was in trouble. He sings. He gazed off in the clouds, and before long he was out of that trouble. Now tell me, how this woman got all of those things so accurately?

MCFARLANE: I think you're right on target, because I know several people in Jamaica who go to a Mother Shepherd who's head of the Pocomania group. Usually women are head of these groups. I know of a number of persons who have gone to a Mother

Shepherd to get information on their lover, to find out if that's the person they should really settle down with. And the Mother Shepherd can usually tell them about the person, without having met the person, as well as whether the person has a good history and is a good prospect for their future together.

BARRETT: Hold on. Dr. "G.W.," at whose home I stay when I go to Jamaica, is a very close friend. All of a sudden, the children called me saying, "Please come see my dad, he is sick." So I went and saw that he had diabetes, and his retina dropped; all of a sudden he couldn't see. He asked me to go to Mother Rita to find out whether his sickness was due to natural causes or if someone had Obeahed him. I went to Mother Rita and told her what happened to "G.W." She knows him well. She said, "Oh my God, such a lovely boy, his friend did him that, his friend messed him up." When I told "G.W.," who is a physician, having studied in Scotland, he responded positively to what Mother Rita had to say. The burden just left him, and all of a sudden he was at peace with himself to know the things that he was thinking were true.

BRUNY: About the Rastafarians, do they believe in the mystic healing of the Pocomanians?

BARRETT: Here's a problem: Ras Brown, who has a car, takes people to these healers, but Ras Brown denies that there is such a thing as Pocomania healing. And I don't know if this is true for all Rastas, but the ones I've studied are against the Pocomanians. But the question is: Do they engage in healing? There's a part of me that says yes, but I cannot document it. But the Rastas are Jamaicans, and Jamaicans of that type do have this other world outlook, and I believe they do. Dr. McFarlane, can you tell me?

MCFARLANE: They are involved in herbal medicine, and one of the reasons why is because many of them have come out of Pocomanian backgrounds. Those who do bring with them some of the African elements of Pocomania, but they reject some of the Christian elements of Pocomania and place instead of Jesus, Selassie. So they think that Pocomanians are at best unwitting instruments of Jah's healing and transforming power.

BARRETT: I've told you that the Rastas use herbal medicine, but deny any of the religious qualities. I don't know that all deny it. As was said, they are from Christianity. But they use the African aspects. If you test them long enough, you may find that they do believe in it.

MCFARLANE: Right! What my brother says is that Jah reveals to different persons (those who are willing to listen) the secrets of nature, such that one can use herbs in a way that can be healing. So the mystical quality is not in the herb itself. The mystical quality is in the revelation that Jah brings to the consciousness of the person such that you know what herbs together and in what quantity, etc.

BARRETT: You are right; [Dennis] Forsythe writes in that way in his book *The Healing of the Nation*. It is an interesting thing. In that paper, is there anything else that buzzes your mind?

MCFARLANE: Let's take a break and resume after lunch.

Post-Lunch Conversation on Rastafari

MCFARLANE: Well, for the time remaining, we can be somewhat concise. We would like to get a Janus view of Rastafari from your perspective, not in terms of its total development, but your involvement in its early work, and your view as to where Rastafari might go.

BARRETT: This is a very important subject for someone who arrived on the scene before the emergence of Rastafari. I had gone to school up to twelve years old, and for the first time, we saw these "crazy men" then in Kingston. They were just chased out of Pinnacle, the property that was founded by Leonard Howell, the founder of the movement.

BETHEA: One of the founders, because there were four.

BARRETT: That's right. I'll come to that. He [Howell] was arrested by the Jamaican police. So, of course, in those days the British superintendent and commissioner gave the order to round up dissidents in the areas where Rastafarians frequented. And the police went in there, beat them, and arrested the founder, and took him to the asylum. So the Rastas were scattered here and there; some were in Montego Bay, and others in the northern parishes. In those days, they were like birds of passage. They were in every little cubbyhole you could find, and most interestingly, they slept in the woods, trees, caves; only a few slept in homes. And of course they were like stalking mad people. They would stand outside screaming, "Babylon is falling down!" That was when the word *Babylon* came into popular use. To Rastafarians, Babylon means everything that is in disorder, and for them, the island was in disorder.

BRUNY: Where does that word come from?

BARRETT: As a matter of fact, the word was common even in [Martin] Luther's day! Some Reformers called the Catholic Church "Babylon."

MCFARLANE: Babylon is the name for an old Persian empire in biblical times.

BARRETT: It has come through the vine straight to the Rastafari? I'm not sure how it came into being, have you any word on that?

MCFARLANE: The Rastafarians read the Hebrew Scriptures and interpret their religious experiences on the basis of biblical texts where certain words occur. In fact, they do the same thing with Selassie, whom they see as a direct descendant of David, through Solomon and the queen of Sheba, and so they see Selassie as the real Messiah. So in Selassie is the fulfillment of all of the prophecies and the teachings of the Hebrew Bible. They see themselves as the real Israelites, and so they aspire to attain the promise of Zion, but not in the same way as the present-day Jews do. Zion is always in opposition to Babylon and Rome. They didn't like the Catholics either, because the Catholics helped the Italians to colonize Ethiopia and frustrate Ras Tafari and his people.

BARRETT: Getting back to Babylon, the Rastas were having meetings here and there, mostly near Dungle. They had a convention at which it is alleged that they wanted a policeman's head as a sacrifice. They were nice for a time, and then they got a little excited and decided to kill a policeman to offer as sacrifice. Whether such early tales are true or not, we do not know, but it is said that they gave the government a lot of trouble. They moved from the convention site to the park [in Kingston] and decided to take it in the name of Haile Selassie. The police had to stop them, and in the process beat a lot of them. This action represented the Babylonian system to the Rastas.

BRUNY: How did Haile Selassie feel about this?

BARRETT: Most interesting subject. Selassie came to Jamaica in 1966, and that was the first time he became truly aware of his being adored by the Rastafarians in such a way. You heard of the commotion at the airport?

MCFARLANE: Yes, I was in Jamaica at the time.

BARRETT: The people hung around the airplane. It was raining, as it is now, and the people said, "As soon as our God comes, the rain will cease." And the plane hovered over the airport, then the sun came out. They set up a red carpet for the emperor to walk on. The Rastas kicked that thing out of the way and got under the plane smoking their marijuana, even though oil was spilling from the plane—that thing could have been set on fire.

MCFARLANE: It was reported that they actually moved the plane.

BARRETT: Now, Mortimo Planno, an important Rastafarian who went to Ethiopia, escorted the emperor out, and the brethren went home, after paying homage to Selassie. I am sorry I wasn't there to record that event. I was in a different part of the island, visiting the Rasta camps at Wareika Hill, and never was able to make it to the airport. But that event brought a great deal of attention to Jamaica. The emperor did not know he was so honored, and when he found out, he never uttered a word of denial, he was humbled. Somehow or the other, I believe that the emperor had a mixed feeling. The mixed feeling was expressed by the Abuna of Ethiopia, who is the head of the Ethiopian Orthodox Church. They went and declared to the Abuna that Selassie was God. The Abuna said no, he worships here in our church. They said, regardless of what he does, he is God. The men were so strong in their beliefs that the Abuna could not dissuade them.

BRUNY: How did Selassie view the Rastas?

BARRETT: That's a good question because to this day people have grappled with that issue. The emperor did not say anything. Nor did the average person know if this was a lift for the emperor or a setback. He went on normally, but the men who were there, Ras Amos, and others, made this statement: "He lifted us from the dust of the earth and let us sit between princes and kings." The average person is not usually invited to the King's House, the official residence of the governor general. But invitations were extended to Rastafarians to join in the high-level reception for the emperor. Therefore, the Rastafarians say Selassie lifted them to sit with princes and kings. And from there on, Rastafari gained new status, because the emperor was so polite to them. He received all kinds of carved works of art, mostly made from mahogany. For the first time, the Rastas had something to boast about, and they did boast about it. Well, from there on the movement grew more rapidly. Soon after the emperor had arrived, migration increased and Rastas began to go everywhere. Some went to England, some went to Ethiopia—to this day I believe some people are still in Ethiopia.

The movement attracted a lot of people among whom was a group of male composers, including the great trombonist Don Drummond, as well as sympathizers like
the saxophonist Roland Alponso and band leader Carlos Malcolm.

BRUNY: What about women?

BARRETT: Oh no, no. One thing about Rastafarians, at that time, was that a woman
in the Rasta movement was a "Rasta woman."

BETHEA: In the possessive sense? She belonged to a man?

BARRETT: Yes. She was the wife of a Rasta, or a friend of the Rasta. However, lately
the women have begun to move. They are no more Rasta women. They are Rastas
who are converted, and they have begun to trouble the waters of Rasta patriarchy.

MCFARLANE: That's said positively of course! [Laughter.]

BARRETT: I don't know if you would find a Rasta leader in Jamaica who is a woman.

MCFARLANE: I am told that at least three of the leading radio personalities in Jamaica
have embraced Rastafari.

BRUNY: So there are several influential supporters of and converts to Rastafari in Jamaica, then?

BARRETT: Indeed! And you can't say too many stupid things about the Rasta, because
you're going to hurt some big people. Right now, the Rastas feel themselves a part of
Jamaica. Right now they have established themselves between rich and poor. One of
"G.W.'s" daughters read my paper and decided to become a Rasta. It knocked his
wife so hard that she died suddenly. So they create a lot of challenges to the old order. Rasta has conquered Jamaica, let us say, would you agree?

MCFARLANE: Perhaps it would be safer to say that they have done so culturally.

BARRETT: Their presence is like a lion. If a lion comes in your midst, you know it is
there. And when a Rasta comes to any meeting or gathering, you know that he is
there. His presence alone makes for problems. The natty dread, the long hair, the
speech. A Rasta can talk you to nothing. It may seem like he's talking nonsense, but
in the long run, he can humble you with his speech. In the beginning of the movement, they were against any person who was non-Black [of course, they were against
oppressors of all colors]. They were quick to verbally assault anyone who was white.

BETHEA: So they were racist?

BARRETT: Yes.

MCFARLANE: But they never really beat up white people, they merely harass them?

BARRETT: Let us say they harassed verbally, but I know of a man who got beaten up.
They've ceased those actions. Now the Rastas are free to go anywhere with anybody.
They can marry anybody, regardless of their color. They have a presence. They make
things very different in Jamaica, they actually changed the average Jamaican. The average Jamaican never knew what he was. Am I an Englishman, am I Jamaican? But
the Rastas said, "Listen, we are Jamaicans, we are black, we have natty dreads, we
are all right." So they created a difference in Jamaican society. One of the things I noticed about the movement was their insistence on leaving the island. Repatriation was
their highlight. But now, it is a little difficult to interpret. They believed that the Black
Star Line was going to take them to Ethiopia. That was out of the question; the Black

Star Line was then finished. They believed that the Ethiopian emperor was sending ships to Jamaica. I was in the island when I saw several people running around on bicycles, buzzing the people about the arrival of the Haitian ambassador to Ethiopia, who came to talk to the people and government of Jamaica. And that gave them an excited feeling that the king was sending to take the people home now. They were very disappointed when it did not turn out to be so. Now there is a question whether this repatriation is dominant, or is silent. And what would you say?

MCFARLANE: They have reinterpreted repatriation, that Africa is not so much a place for them to go to as it is a state of mind for them to inhabit.

BARRETT: Which was Garvey's notion in the beginning.

BRUNY: Africa for Africans.

BARRETT: I was at a convention recently, where the repatriation issue came as a stock idea. Some believed it, some didn't. Let's say it is a doctrine. The question is: How do they get their doctrine so widely transmitted so that the average man can learn the Rasta belief? Because somehow or the other, they only have to put out the word and it will spread until the masses know of it. The question that we face is whether the Rastas need a central idea to gather all of these beliefs and practices together in a book. I talked to a theological head of a seminary in the West Indies who said to me, "Doc, there is a Rastalogy in the island." This is the first time I had heard of the word. He said, "Yes, there is a doctrine that is intellectually sound." You can interpret it only if you have a voice to carry it. On the other hand, the Twelve Tribes of Israel didn't do anything. They had the wherewithal to be effective but they did more dancing, socializing, etc., rather than theologizing. Now, where we are now is a very difficult period. To give a brief Janus view: the movement came out of nothing, it gathered mass in the middle [1960s to 1970s] like a big snowball. At the moment, we are not sure what the movement is going to do. As Jamaica sees the movement, since 1975 until the present, the momentum seems to be reduced in intensity as it grows in number. There are sections of the movement which are totally religious. Prince Emmanuel, and a few others, have a church, and a developed doctrine. The other side is the political one which fights the dirty fight for the movement. Then the sect side is the Twelve Tribes of Israel, which is sensible and had some very important men like Bob Marley; but what they are doing in terms of pressing forward, I do not know.

MCFARLANE: I have one final question, which has to do with the inclusiveness of Rastafari over the last fifteen or so years! Does not the racial inclusiveness of Rastafari compromise its Afro-focal principles?

BARRETT: Yes, that is what I mean. There is a slippage. If you go to the Twelve Tribes headquarters, you'll find a multiethnic gathering inclusive of white women who are the wives of the men of Twelve Tribes. Some Rastas carried a lot of economic weight in the island. They had the biggest cars and the women loved them because of their "lion appearance," and when they walked about, one usually exclaims, "My God, what kind of Lions are these? Many Rasta look-alikes are not humble folks, they're big shots. They sell the weed, which brings in a lot of money. (I'm going to get in trouble for saying this, but the weed is probably sold by people who resemble Rastas but are not Rastas, just like the singing groups you see.) But, of course, many of them are not Rastas, but they wear the hairstyle, *but the locks do not the Rasta make.* Now, with regard to the future of the movement, I just said it a while ago: development of a Rastalogy, and claiming of sections where they can build their own temples or something of that type. Or, if they don't, the movement may end up like the Garvey movement, although, perhaps, it might not end up like the Garvey movement—since Garvey had established lots of institutions like Liberty Halls and economic and literary assemblies. But the Rastas can do it. However, they don't seem to have the spokespersons who possess enough credibility to meet everybody. I could be wrong because there are lawyers who are Rastas, there are pilots who are Rastas, there are musicians, artists, and doctors and so on. I met some of the best Rastas, and they could be the help to the movement as such. But somehow or the other, they don't see it. What is your view on where the Rasta movement is going?

MCFARLANE: My personal opinion is that the strategy of integration could either work for or against the movement. It could be the slippage that you speak about in that it is watered down so much, or rather so adulterated that it loses its orthodoxy and its distinctiveness, thereby allowing all kinds of criminals to hide behind the locks and so forth. On the other hand, it can bring to the consciousness of many people the importance of what I call the Rastafarian "demurrals" or objections to Babylonian-type practices, power plays, etc., in society. If Rasta ideas are widely circulated, they would be a force to be reckoned with, and eventually Rastas may even enter politics to establish a new order.

BARRETT: I do agree! There are Rastas who use the movement only as a lifestyle. And there are Rastas who only believe in the movement as a religion. If you should put out a sign tomorrow that you wanted to see all of the world's Rastas in Jamaica, Jamaica wouldn't have a place to hold them. Now, the movement has become so strong that it can do almost anything. But God knows, I don't think they have as yet identified the person who can achieve that now. The movement, though, is there to stay. It has enough people and enough diversity to stay until it either decays or grows further. With the singing, for example, as in the reggae singing, which has been popularized and reenergized by the Rastas and is so strong a movement, a beat and a chant, that it will last them for years to come. Until someone, I could not say the man Prince Emmanuel, he is old. However, someone may come along, much like what happened in the sixties, who will offer a leadership role. If we could find a man like [Claudius] Henry [in the 1960s], who had a heavy swing and was arrested several times; if we could get a few of those men to keep on making strides, in the long run, a person may emerge who sees the possibilities of the movement, and responds to the call for continued leadership.

MCFARLANE: The way in which I perceive it is that it could be either a man or a woman. However, I'm not so sure that Rastas believe in a one-man or one-woman leadership of the movement, since that is too autocratic and seems too much like the Western style. Many of the Rastas in Jamaica, now, took their cue from what happened to Michael Manley in the seventies with socialism, even though they were not in favor of socialism, yet some of it rubbed off on them. Some of them see leadership more in terms of a spontaneous democratic type of expression in which persons may interpret how Jah speaks to them, and then live out that kind of experience in a heartical way with their brothers and sisters. Correspondingly, there are large communities of Rastas in England, Amsterdam, Canada, and Japan, and so I do not see Rastafarians dying out. I think the movement is going to garner more and more force. But what needs to happen is that Jamaica needs to continue acting as the Mecca for Rastafarians so that they can go back there and be renewed, irrespective of where they come from. Thus the cutting edge has to be fashioned in Jamaica, but other interesting things can be done elsewhere so that Jamaica can also learn from these places.

BETHEA: My final question is: Would you please clarify the concept of Rastalogy?

BARRETT: Like theology, all the ideas and beliefs are interpreted so that it fills up a chapter on something like the idea of repatriation: what is it, when is it, etc. They have a whole lot of ideas that can form a book, so they need to put their ideas down and not get it messed up by every other person.

BETHEA: So, instead of having people write on them, they should write for themselves?

BARRETT: The Rastas can write for themselves, many of them have written. What I'm referring to is a body of beliefs and practices which function as guiding principles.

MCFARLANE: Is it a systematic expression of their ideas of which you speak?

BARRETT: Exactly, the word *Israelites,* that worried me, and for a time I did not know what it meant. They claim to be the original Israelites. So all people who claim to be present-day Jews are not. From 1934, a man by the name of David Harris and his wife went to Ethiopia as missionaries. They came back to Jamaica after five years and founded the Israelite movement just the time when Rastafari began. And for such a long time, the name lingered in Jamaica and was taken by the Rastafarians. So they're claiming to be the original Israelites. Even amongst the slaves in Jamaica the word *Israelite* was used. [Edward] Braithwaite found the document in an office in London [dated from the time of slavery] which read "We Israelites." So the name is a very important one and has been in Jamaica from slavery days. As a matter of fact, there are several black Jews who are West Indians.

BRUNY: Do you mean by their descendance from Jewish families, by adoption, or by assuming a Jewish identity? I've heard that there are many people of African and Jewish descent in Jamaica.

BARRETT: I do agree with you, but, even before those people, there are certain rabbis who were in Harlem from the West Indies who are Jews, and they know enough Hebrew to talk to the Jews themselves. So this was a very endemic name during the time of slavery as well as postslavery. The name, in other words, is a name that the Rastas knew from way back, and they claim it. "No Jews are Jews, we are the Jews." So, I repeat, the Rastas will be here for many, many years. They are going to grow or die, but I prefer to say they will grow, rather than die. So you can laugh at them, but in the long run, they will be parliamentarians, so treat them well.

BETHEA: One of the psalms that the Rastafarians were familiar with and used a lot was the 137th Psalm, "By the rivers of Babylon, where we sat down, and where we wept when we remembered Zion." That has been the theme for a number of Rastafarians. How do they sing the songs of Zion or "I-thiopia" in a strange land?

MCFARLANE: Of course, I believe they are now beginning to sing the songs of I-thiopia in that land because the land is being transformed so that I-thiopia isn't so much a place as it is a state of mind where the people of Jah are. But more important, *they are singing Jah's songs as a triumphant chant against the arrogance of Babylon.* At least, my reading has led me to this conclusion.

BARRETT: There is a great market for researching the Rastafarians. Honestly, if I were young, I'd be out there now! The beautiful thing about it is the movement is always filled with new ideas, and what you need to do is go out there and do research, and before you know it will you have a book! And if you have a good book on the Rastas, you can make money! [Laughter.] The movement has new things every day. Again, thanks to you, Indigo, Michael, and my friend, and your professor, Dr. McFarlane, for giving me this opportunity to share my reflections. Remember now: Go out and research, write and publish, but make sure to get to know as many Rastafarians as you can, and include them as active participants in your work.

Appendix B

Who Is Who in the Rasta Academy: A Literature Review in Honor of Leonard Barrett

NATHANIEL SAMUEL MURRELL

Rasta Research Pathfinders

The first academic interest in the Rastafarian culture actually predated Leonard Barrett's work by fourteen years; it began when Fernando Henriquez's *Family and Color in Jamaica* (1952) raised questions related to the role of Rastafari and the family in Jamaican culture. The next year, Oberlin College professor George Eaton Simpson conducted the first field study of four Rastafarian groups in Jamaica. Because of his interest in Caribbean religions, Simpson focused primarily on the belief system, teachings, street meetings, and cultus (religious exercise) of Rastafari and saw the movement as a derivative of the millenarian revivalist tradition. In 1955, Simpson published his findings in two essays[1] that formed the basis for his volume *The Ras Tafarian Movement in Jamaica: A Study of Race and Class Conflicts*. Even though this work was an introduction to the social and cultural Jamaican context of the movement, as a groundbreaking project, it remained the only published book on the subject and the main source of reference for the next five years. But it was Simpson's later study in the history of religions, *Black Religion in the New World* (1978), that established him as a clear authority on Caribbean religions in general.

The University of the West Indies (UWI)–sponsored study by Michael G. Smith, Roy Augier, and Rex Nettleford, published as *The Rastafari Movement in Kingston Jamaica* (1960), set the tone for serious investigation of Rastafari as an urban phenomenon in Kingston. The three-week-long "public policy" study provided a brief history of the movement and its development in the 1950s, spelt out in some detail its doctrinal beliefs and practices, looked at its diverse organizational structure, and highlighted the pressing needs and social conditions of Rastas in Kingston. Although the UWI study left the in-depth analysis of the social, economic, and political context of the Rastafari in Jamaica to later researchers, it nonetheless provided some helpful insights into the movement's composition. Its revelation that not all Rastas were addicted to ganja, that only a few of them were criminals, and that Rastafari was very popular among the youths caused many Jamaican students to change their view of the movement.

William A. Blake's *Beliefs of the Rastafari Cult* (1961) and Mosley O. Leonard's *Haile Selassie: The Conquering Lion* (1964) were virtually unknown and had little impact on the academic community. However, Orlando H. Patterson's novel *The Children of Sisyphus* (1964; 1971) and his essay "Ras Tafari: The Cult of the Outcast" (1968) exposed the movement to a broader literary audience in the mid-1960s. But the Eurocentric Jamaican theorist Patterson construed Rastafari as an "escapist cult," rather than a creative anti-hegemonic attempt by the underclass to reform its country's institutions and traditions as a solution to their acute economic problems. Patterson contended that the Rastas' attempt to improve their position in Jamaica in order to find acceptance in the wider society was displaced to a medium of group fantasy and apocalyptic escapist doctrines.[2] Although a highly rated classic, much of *The Children of Sisyphus* is a dolorous tale about the Rastafarian brethren, at the end of which Patterson had the despondent "Brother Solomon," one of his Rasta characters, commit suicide (chapter 21)–an image of Rastas that fed into anti-Rasta stereotypes among "highbrow" Jamaicans in the 1960s.

Horace Campbell's *Rasta and Resistance: From Marcus Garvey to Walter Rodney* (1966; 1985) finally gave the international reading audience a sense of the social and political upheavals and struggles out of which Rastafari was born. The book presented a scattered topical (rather than systematic) treatment of the basic political, social, religious, and cultural characteristics of the movement, as well as of its ideological and historical ties to Ethiopia, qua Africa. But Campbell correctly portrayed Rastafari as a twentieth-century black resistance socioreligious and political movement in the region, with international reach. He was the first to view it as being rooted in the traditions of the seventeenth- and eighteenth-century Maroons, the popular uprisings in nineteenth-century Jamaica, Marcus Garvey's Pan-Africanist movement, Black Nationalists of Harlem, the anti-imperialist spirit in Africa and the Caribbean, and the Black Consciousness movement internationally. In the important volume *The Groundings with My Brothers* (1969), written at a time when public perception of Rastas was changing, pro-Rastafari Walter Rodney validated Campbell's analysis of the social and political context and ethos of the movement.

The Barrett-Nettleford-Owens Contribution

A year after Campbell's 1966 publication, Leonard Barrett completed his doctoral thesis at Temple University: "The Rastafarians: Messianic Cultism in Jamaica West Indies," a work that would form the basis for many of his later writings on Caribbean culture. Barrett's dissertation was first published in the Caribbean Monograph series by the Institute of Caribbean Studies at the University of Puerto Rico in 1968 and became an instant reference on Rastafari's cultural ethos. Since 1969, Barrett has published more than a dozen articles[3] and five books on the Rastafarian movement. In fact, throughout the 1970s and 1980s, Barrett's scholarly lectures and publications dominated the discussion on Rastafari in American classrooms, conferences, and the academy. In a chapter of his book *Soul Force* (1974, 1st ed.), Barrett portrayed Rastafari as an African "soul asserting itself" through a black revolutionary cult movement in the traditions of Marcus Garvey, the Black Muslims, the Black Panthers, and the Black Power movement, from the postemancipation period on. Barrett provided valuable information on "the cult's origin," its development, its beliefs, its ritual practices, its function, and the Ethiopian connection, within the Jamaican context of the 1930s through the 1960s.

Barrett's second book, *The Sun and the Drum: African Roots in Jamaican Folk Tradition* (1975), further established him as an anthropologist in the fields of comparative religion and the history of religions. One year after Vera Rubin and Lambros Comitas published the intriguing *Ganja in Jamaica* (1976), Barrett produced his third book, *The Rastafarians: The Dreadlocks of Jamaica* (1977), reissued the same year as *The Rastafarians: Sounds of Cultural Dissonance* and considered his definitive work on Rastafari. This book expands on previous publications, adding three valuable chapters, and discusses the important question of what happens when prophecy fails and repatriation is not realized. According to Barrett, the movement diversified, with several splinter groups holding different versions of Selassie's divinity and the importance of repatriation. Hence, rather than dying a natural death after the demise (disappearance) of Selassie, Rastafari spread internationally. After two decades, Barrett's book (revised and published as *The Rastafarians* in 1988) continues to command respect in Rastafarian scholarship and is referenced constantly by younger scholars.

Rex Nettleford's book *Identity, Race and Protest in Jamaica* (1972), recognized as a standard work on Rastafarian scholarship and required reading in the field of Caribbean Studies, offers several clarifications and rebuttals to criticisms of the UWI report and provides readers with an insightful analysis of the interaction between the Rastafarians and the wider Jamaican society. Essentially, Nettleford raised the question of the role, on the one hand, of the Rastafarian ideology in the multiracial community of Jamaica during its move toward independence and nationalism in the late 1950s and early 1960s and, on the other hand, of the Rasta doctrine of redemption, repatriation, and separation. According to Nettleford's *Caribbean Cultural Identity: The Case of Jamaica* (1978), Rastas describe Jamaica as "a labor camp with a transient work force waiting to flee to better opportunities" and "as a state of 'Babylonian captivity' whose victims are waiting to be delivered into some Promised Land." Nettleford showed that this anti-Jamaican sentiment among Rastas and their reinterpretation of traditional Christian theology put them at odds with the wider Jamaican society. The Rastas remained staunchly opposed to the view that Jamaica must rehabilitate the "dirty Rasta dem," refused to give up the idea of repatriation, and continued to chant down Babylon with anti-Jamaican separatist rhetoric while holding allegiance to a foreign sovereign, Haile Selassie, and a foreign country, Ethiopia (58–78). Nonetheless, since 1960, the wider society has assimilated the dynamic and revolutionary views of the Rastafari at critical points. Nettleford's social, religious, and cultural expositions on Rastafari have inspired several works since 1976.[4]

Joseph Owens is recognized as the first nonblack scholar to pursue ethnographic research among the Rastas of Jamaica by joining their ranks and living among them for a substantial period of time. Building on his own 1975 essay "Literature on the Rastafari, 1955–1974," Owens published the results of his intriguing study under the title *Dread* (1976). This book has become a standard work on Rastafarian doctrines and contains several important features of the dread experience. Owens, as a white foreigner, offers a corrective to the most widely misunderstood aspect of Rastafarian teaching on the question of race; while he admits that a pronounced race consciousness exists among the Rastas, he refutes the argument that Rastas are anti-White or supporters of the aberrations of prejudice so characteristic of U.S. culture. *Dread* views Rastafari as a Bible-based yet creative Afrocentric religious expression that seeks both to escape and to transform Babylonian Jamaica. Owens's book joined Barrett's and Nettleford's to make up the major reference works on Rastafari prior to 1992. The non-Christian nature of the Rastafarian movement was later articulated in Ivor Morrish's *Obeah, Christ, and Rastaman* (1982), a work whose history-of-religions approach to Rastafari casts it in the mold of other Caribbean religious expressions that are often at variance with Christian doctrines.

European Rastafari Scholarship

Ken Post's often-cited *Arise Ye Starvelings: The Jamaican Labour Rebellion of 1938 and Its Aftermath* (1978), a Marxist critique of Rastafari, and Tracy Nicholas's *Rastafari: A Way of Life* (1979) were packaged for European and U.S. audiences, respectively. Like Barrett, Post provides an excellent analysis of the political, social, and economic environment in which Rastafari was bred and of the potential of its message for social change. By the time Post's monograph appeared in print, the development of European Rastafarian scholarship was well underway in Britain. In 1978, Adrian Booth and Michael Thomas published *Jamaica: Babylon on a Thin Wire* and John Plummer wrote *Movement of Jah People: The Growth of the Rastafarians*. Len Garrison expanded his 1969 UWI thesis and his essays "Rastafarians: Protest Movement in Jamaica" (1975) and "The Rastafarians: Journey out of Exile" (1976) into a timely book, *Black Youth, Rastafarianism and the Identity Crisis in Britain* (1979). Garrison spelt out the racial and cultural tensions that Rastas faced in metropolitan England in the 1970s and their clashes with law-enforcement authorities.

In 1980, Peter Michaels published *Rastafari*, and K. M. Williams's *The Rastafari,* a small book of about sixty pages, appeared in Hong Kong for an English-speaking audience in 1981. The latter book gives a skeletal outline of the Jamaican setting of the Rastafarians; their beliefs, rituals, and practices; and the role prophet Bob Marley played in bringing the two opposing Jamaican political leaders Michael Manley and Edward Seaga together, albeit symbolically, after years of bitter umbrage. This book offers nuggets of information on such personalities as Leonard Howell, Marcus Garvey, Haile Selassie, and Ras Sam Brown, as well as on black survival, Rastafarian parents and children, and music in Britain.

Ernest Cashmore's *The Rastafarian Movement in England* (1983) is another important study of the Rastafarians in Britain between 1970 and 1978. Cashmore argues that the British Rastafarian movement owes its origin to a branch of the Black Power movement that, as Barrett argued, was influenced by Ethiopianism. According to Cashmore, British Rastas differ from Jamaican Rastas in that the latter viewed "complete political emancipation as a solution" to the black problem while Rastas in Britain sought "redemption." (See also Cashmore's "The Rastafarians," *Minority Rights Group Report*, no. 64, [London, 1984]). Although Cashmore's book is referenced in many essays in this and other books, as Barrett noted in a reprint edition of *Soul Force*, it has received its full share of criticism in the academy on technical and factual questions. Like Cashmore's work, Simon Jones's *Black Culture, White Youth: The Reggae Tradition from JA to UK* (1987) showed the impact of Rasta-reggae culture on the British people. This is an easy-to-read and informative book for the fans of Bob Marley and the Rastafari.

Peter Clarke's one-hundred-page *Black Paradise: The Rastafarian Movement* (1986) belies its importance. The book deals with the origin of Rastafari in Jamaica and with Rasta rituals, beliefs, practices, lifestyle, and self-consciousness and gives important insights into the changing perception of and interaction between the movement and the wider British society. Unlike other scholars, Clarke places the rise of the movement in Britain in the context of the West Indian Pentecostal religious movements of 1952, which served to cushion many West Indians against the harsh realities of life in Britain: "alienation, discrimination and racialism that they experienced in everyday life" (53, 57). But unlike the Pentecostal groups, which accepted the status quo of white society's "values and definition of black people," the Rastafarians demonstrated an aggressive political ideology that was misread and colored by already established British prejudice against a group that brought disfavor in the eyes of the government. Clarke explains that after the riots in Brixton and Handsworth, the churches in Britain slowly began "to build bridges with the young Rastafarians in an effort to diffuse some of the bitterness that existed between them—by, for example, offering the local church hall for their services" (57). Under popular pressure, the Home Office also made two major concessions to Rastafari in 1981 by regarding it as a legitimate religion and by respecting the locks of its adherents (i.e., not cutting their hair when they were in prison), although their marijuana ritual was still prohibited.

Derek Bishton's *Black Heart Man: A Journey into Rasta* (1986) is another interesting book that locates the Rastafarian phenomenon within the tradition of Jamaican freedom fighters: the Maroons, Sam Sharpe, Paul Bogle, Alexander Bedward, and Marcus Garvey. Bishton, however, offers no detailed doctrinal analysis, and (in the same way that Ajai Mansingh, and Vera Rubin and Lambros Comitas exaggerated East Indian influence on Rastas' use of ganja, he makes too much of the Jewish perspective on Ethiopia and the role of the *Kebra Nagast* in the Rastafari tradition. As Maureen Rowe commented, Bishton's analysis of the Jamaican Rastafari phenomenon is also a journey into his own self-discovery as a European; "he interprets history for himself and his readers as he journeys." Although "neither the facts nor the interpretations are new," Bishton has presented them "to cohere with the history of Rastafari"[5]—but not without controversy.

Also in Britain, Obadiah Goynor and Petra Goynor (husband and wife) wrote an intriguing book for children, *I Am a Rastafari* (1986), and Billy Bergman published *Reggae and Latin Pop: Hot Sauce* (1985).

In the last two decades the following foreign-language publications on Rastafari have appeared in Europe, some of which, like Post's book, have been translated into English. For example, Peter M. Michaels published *Rastafari* in Munich (1980), and Karl Erich Wiss surveyed the development of Rastafari in his essay "Die Rastafari-bewegung auf Jamaica: Entwicklungsphasen und Ausdrucksformen einer Gegenkultur" (1981). Wolfgang Bender expanded his essay "Liberation from Babylon: Rasta Painters in Jamaica" (1983) in the publication *Rastafari-Kunst aus Jamaika* (Bremen, 1983). Peter E. J. Buiks's *Surinaamse jongeren op de Kruiskade: Overleven in een etnische randgrope* (Deventer, 1983) and Hans Vermeulen's *Etnische groepen en grenzen: Surinamers, Chinezen en Turken* (Weesp, 1984) discuss several aspects of the intriguing Rastafari phenomenon in Amsterdam and its Suriname (South America) connection. Frank Jan van Dijk's *Jahmaica: Rastafari en de Jamaicaanse Samenleving, 1930–1990* (1993), discussed below, is the most substantive and scholarly publication on the Rastafari movement up to 1993.

Male-Female Rastafari Scholarship

In spite of the patriarchal nature of the movement, quite clearly, Rastafarian research is not a male-dominated enterprise. For example, Margaret Ebanks researched Rasta cooking in *The Rastafari Cookbook: Ital Recipes* (1981); Barbara (Makeda Lee) Blake Hannah wrote the insightful *Rastafari: the New Creation* (1981); Anno Wilms published a book of photographs *Rastafari* (1982), and Sister M. Lee Whitney produced *Bob Marley: Reggae King of the World* (1982). Jette Steensen gave the academy the thought-provoking *Racism, Reggae and Rastafari* in 1984; Virginia Jacobs published *Roots of Rastafari* in 1985; Anita M. Waters's *Race, Class and Political Symbol* appeared the same year; and Rasta sistren Margarett E. Groves published *Lamentations* (1989).

Rasta sistren have written dozens of theses, essays, commentaries, book reviews, and conference papers on the movement. For example, Rastafarian Maureen Rowe, former director of the Center for African Culture in Jamaica and a contributor to this book, has written several essays and reviews on Rastafari sistren (e.g., "The Woman in Rastafari," 1980) and is a well-known and often-referenced scholar in this field. Makeda Lee ("What Is a Rastaman?" 1982), Makeda Silvera ("An Open Letter to Rastafarian Sistren," 1983), Imani M. Tafari-Ama ("An Historical Analysis of Grassroots Resistance in Jamaica: A Case Study of Participatory Research on Gender Relations in Rastafari," 1989), and self-styled Rasta Euro-Canadian academic Carole D. Yawney ("Moving with the Dawtas of Rastafari: From Myth to Reality," 1987) are but a few of the female Rasta voices on women's issues in the discourse.

Other female essayists, such as Seretha Rycenssa ("The Rastafarian Legacy: A Rich Cultural Gift," 1978), Terisa Turner ("Rastafari and the New Society: Caribbean and East African Feminist Roots of a Popular Movement to Reclaim the Early Commons," 1994), Maureen Warner-Lewis ("African Continuities in the Rastafari Belief System," 1993), Claudia Rogers ("What's A Rasta?" 1978), and Sheila Kitzinger ("Protest and Myalism: The Rastafarian Cult of Jamaica," 1969, and "The Rastafarian Brethren of Jamaica," 1971), make invaluable contributions to the conversation. So also do Monica Schuler ("Myalism and the African Religious Tradition in Jamaica," 1980); Karlene Faith ("One Love—One Heart—One Destiny: A Report on the Rastafari Movement," 1990); and Marian A. L. Miller ("The Rastafarian in Jamaican Political Culture: The Marginalization of a Change Agent," 1993). Their voices, along with those of the Rasta Sistren, appear frequently in the chapters in this anthology.

Because of the unorthodox language that Rastas use and the skepticism about the movement prevalent among many publishers, some Rasta authors in Britain and the Caribbean have had to publish their own works. In a classic but very controversial work, Leonard Howell adapted much of Robert Athyli Rogers's *The Holy Piby* (1924) and published *The Promised Key* (1935). Ras I. Dizzy published *Run Wide Run Deep* (1979) and Ras Jah Bones (Jamaican-born Gladstone Warburton), after searching for a publisher for three years, was forced to publish his own *One Love Rastafari: History, Doctrine and Livity* (1985). Jah Bones's book attempts to articulate Rastafari beliefs under four very important questions: "What is Rasta? How and when do Rastas worship? Who is the Rasta leader or Messiah? And what do Rastas hope for, or want to achieve?" The Rastafarian scholar and British-schooled social theorist Dennis Forsythe published his provocative *Ras Tafari for the Healing of the Nation* (1983), in which he gives a substantive introduction to the ideology, beliefs, and practices of Rastafari, as well as its role in and impact on Jamaican society. (See also Forsythe's often-cited "West Indian Culture through the Prism of Rastafarianism," in Rex Nettleford, ed., *Caribbean Quarterly Monograph: Rastafari*, 1985). *The Living Testament of Rasta-For-I* (1980), published by Ras-J-Tesfa (Tennyson Smyth), is an important source of information on the study of Rastafarian theology from within; so also is the *Rastafari Manifesto, The Ethiopian-African Theocracy Union Policy (EATUP)*, which includes a draft constitution proposal and a very ambitious agenda for reforming all aspects of the government of Jamaica.

William Curtis Ahkell's *Rasta: Emperor Haile Selassie and the Rastafarians* appeared in 1982, and Brother Miguel (Michael Anthony Lorne) published his modest *Rastaman Chant* in 1983. E.S.P. McPherson's *Rastafari and Politics—Sixty Years of a Developing Cultural Ideology: A Sociology of Development Perspective* (1991) offers a very informative interpretation of the emerging cultural ideology of Rastafari—with its roots in Ethiopianism, Garveyism, and anticolonialism—and its impact on Jamaican thought between 1930 and 1990. The Rastafarian Mcpherson follows Afrocentric scholars such as Ivan Van Sertima (*They Came before Columbus: The African Presence in Ancient America*, 1977) and Maulana Marenga (*Introduction to Black Studies*, 1993) in arguing that Africans were in the Americas before the Europeans, but he provides no substantiating evidence for his claim. Millard (Mihlawhdla) Faristzaddi's book *Itations of*

Jamaica and I Rastafari (1987; 1991) gives a view of Rastafari from the inside. Prince Michael's (John Moodie's) *Hath . . . the Lion Prevailed . . . ?* (1992) is another insider's portrait of Emperor Haile Selassie "the first of Ethiopia" as "Jesus Christ returned, as promised, in His kingly and conquering form." The artistic pictorial, portraying Bible characters and Selassie and his family, has an interesting elementary school appeal to it.

In May 1994, I was browsing through Ras Tekla Mekfet's ninety-three-page book *Christopher Columbus and Rastafari: Ironies of History* (1993) in a bookstore in Kingston. Just then, the author, who teaches at the Wesley campus of Browns Town Community College in St. Ann's Bay, came over and introduced himself with a warm handshake and a very courteous greeting: "One Father, one love me brethren." I was thrilled! After I got him to autograph my copy of his book, a very interesting conversation ensued over its content and some of Mekfet's own beliefs and practices. The book includes a number of artistic pieces, features on reggae artists and political leaders, and gives brief commentaries on the visits of Nelson Mandela and Haile Selassie to Jamaica. As one would expect, Mekfet critiques the role of Columbus and the pope in the "Babylonian captivity" of Africans in the West and the negating of the African reality and achievements.

Rastafarian males have also written a large number of essays and brief commentaries on the movement. For example, in addition to Dennis Forsythe and other Rastas mentioned above, former Rasta Leahcim Tufani Semaj has written several articles, referenced in this volume, on race relations, family, ritual practices, history, and the future of the movement (e.g., "Rastafari: From Religion to Social Theory," 1980; "Race and Identity and the Children of the African Diaspora," 1980; and "Inside Rasta: The Future of a Religious Movement," 1986). E.S.P. Mcpherson has written "Rasta Chronology" (1985). Ras Stafford Ashani ("Rasta Now," 1991), Ras Dizzy ("The Rasta Speaks," 1967), Hale M.Y.F. Kezehemohonenow ("The Role of Rastafarianism in the Caribbean," 1978), I. Jabulani Tafari ("The Rastafari—Successors of Marcus Garvey," 1985), and Garth White ("Rudie O Rudie," 1967) are a few of the many Rastafarians who have written multiple articles or commentaries on the movement.

A 1986 issue of *Caribbean Review* (15, 2) published the article "Rasta Crime: A Confidential Report by the N.Y.C. P.D.," which documents stereotypes of Rastafari among the police of New York City. This article now generates further research on the movement among scholars in Jamaica and the United States.

Recent Academic Emissaries

Among the most recent works published by non-Rastas, many of which have been inspired by Barrett, William F. Lewis's monograph *Soul Rebels: The Rastafari* (1993) provides a concise, topical, nontechnical introduction to the Rastafari. It is ideal for college students who have little or no knowledge of the movement and need a quick grasp of its characteristic features. After tracing briefly the historical setting of the black struggle that gave birth to the Rastafari, Lewis revisits the origin and fundamental beliefs of the movement in order to expose its complex inner workings and structure. This white Catholic priest supplies interesting ethnographic material on specific Rasta communities, which he garnered from urban Jamaica and the United States, and he discusses Rastas' confrontation with the law, conflicts between Rasta culture and Jamaican middle-class values, Rasta family relations, conflicting images and self-perception of Rastas, and the problem of repatriation. In spite of its brevity, this is a must-read book for anyone studying Rastafari.

Since 1971, Barry Chevannes has been studying Caribbean religious "revivalist" movements with a passion. He has contributed more than a dozen essays and book chapters to the research on Rastafari and other Afro-Caribbean religious groups.[6] Chevannes first book, *Rastafari: Roots and Ideology* (1994), and his latest edited work, *Rastafari and Other Afro-Caribbean Worldviews* (1995), show the imprint of a social anthropologist whose work is rooted in historical and field research. (Readers are directed to Rex Nettleford's "Discourse on Rastafarian Reality," Chapter 18, for an accurate review of *Rastafari: Roots and Ideology*.) Worth mentioning here is the fact that, like Barrett and Campbell, Chevannes places the Rastafarian movement within the context of two dominant social and cultural genres: the spirit of black resistance, characteristic of Africans enslaved in the diaspora and manifesting itself in many different forms, and the revivalist movement, which has strong ties to African and Caribbean religions and cultures. But issues such as Ethiopianism, apocalyptic Zionism, the "Back to Africa" movement, and repatriation, which other scholars regard as part of Rastafarian African identity, Chevannes calls the "idealization" of Africa. He also exposes seven Garvey myths that impacted on the beginning of Rastafari and gives social, political, and religious analyses of the revivalist elements in the preaching of early Rasta leaders (Leonard Howell, Joseph Hibbert, Archibald Dunkley, Robert Hinds) and their organizations. Chevannes has written the most provocative and substantive social treatment of the Bobo Dreads in print.

Dutch anthropologist Frank Jan van Dijk's *Jahmaica: Rastafari and Jamaican Society 1930–1990* (1993) is a thorough, scholarly work on a black movement, researched and written by a white European. Since the 1980s, van Dijk has also published several essays on the specific beliefs and practices of the Rastafari internationally (e.g., "The Twelve Tribes of Israel: Rasta and the Middle Class," 1988). To my knowledge, no other scholar has produced a work of such size and scope on the movement. Van Dijk says he attempted to tell *a* story, rather than *the* story, about the Rastafari in Jamaican society—"a story written from a diachronic perspective and based on certain types of sources, mainly newspaper accounts, along with pamphlets, government correspondence, interviews and . . . the literature on Rastafari" (*Jahmaica*, 21). Following Barrett, the book details the evolution of a people's rising spirit of resistance to total economic and political domination under colonialism, their dream of salvation in Zion (Ethiopia or Africa), and their search for respect and dignity in Babylon (Jamaica and the West). Essentially, *Jahmaica* is a book about the historical evolution of Rastafari and the Rastafarians' resolve to let the world hear the voices of the despised sons and daughters of Africa in a new way. Anyone who is engaged in serious Rastafarian research will find a wealth of information on van Dijk's "obnoxious minority" in England, the Caribbean, the United States, Canada, Africa, Europe, and New Zealand, as well as on a variety of events, such as the death and state funeral of Bob Marley, Rasta culture among the middle class, and Rasta involvement in the Ethiopian Orthodox Church.

These publications, most in book form, tell only a part of the fascinating story of Rastafarian research and literature. There are dozens of invaluable essays and book chapters among the hundreds of publications on this intriguing phenomenon. Robert A. Hill, a well-known Marcus Garvey scholar, has researched and published several essays and sections of books on the history and practices of the Rastafarians. His essays "Dread History: Leonard P. Howell and Millenarian Visions in Early Rastafari Religions in Jamaica" (1981) and "Leonard P. Howell and Millenarian Visions in Early Rastafari" (1983) have been invaluable sources of information on the early Rastafarian prophet. Hill has also published several essays in popular journals such as *The Beat* (e.g., "From Marcus to Marley: Prophecy and Reggae Music," *The Beat* [August 1985]: 15–18) that are important interpretations of Rastafarian culture. Kenneth M. Bilby's essays "Black Thoughts from the Caribbean: I-deology at Home and Abroad" (1983; "The Holy Herb: Notes on the Background of Cannabis" (1985); and his coauthored (with Elliot Leib) "Kumina, the Howellite Church and the Emergence of Rastafarian Traditional Music in Jamaica" (1986) are now well known in Rastafarian scholarship. Most academic discussions on Rastafarian ethos relative to the ritualization of cannabis and Nyabinghi take their cue from Bilby and Leib's 1986 essay. In 1991, W. J. Payne of Howard University published a brief but important reference essay, "Rastafarianism," in the *Dictionary of African American Religions*. The late Robert E. Hood's book *Must God Remain Greek?* (1990) written about African peoples in the diaspora, has a substantive chapter on Rastafari.

Verena Reckord's essays "Rastafarian Music: An Introductory Study" (1977) and "Reggae, Rastafarianism and Cultural Identity" (1982); Sebastian Clark's *Jah Music: The Evolution of Popular Jamaican Song* (1980); Timothy White's *Catch a Five: The Life of Bob Marley* (1983); Stephen Davis's *Bob Marley* (1985) and *Reggae Bloodliness: In Search of the Music and Culture of Jamaica* (1979); as well as Stephen Davis and Peter Simon's *Reggae International* (1982) are samples of the ever-growing library on the development of reggae music that popularizes Rastafarian culture internationally in print. The 1990s yielded a plethora of books, a few of which are worth mentioning here: Errol Miller, *Men at Risk* (1991); Graem Evans, *Africa-O-Ye: A Celebration of Music* (1991); Ian McCann, *Bob Marley in His Own Words* (1993); and Peter Manuel, *Caribbean Currents: Caribbean Music from Rasta to Reggae* (1995). Brian John and Tom Weber's *Reggae Island: Jamaican Music in the Digital Age* (1992), an accessible pictorial-narrative text on reggae musicians and their work, is also in that literary tradition. Roger Steffens has recently published one of the most intriguing biographies of Bob Marley, the "King of Reggae."[7] Carolyn Cooper's "Chanting Down Babylon: Bob Marley's Song as Literary Text," in *Noises in the Blood* (1995), is part of a much larger collection of essays on reggae music in dozens of journals, tabloids, magazines, books, and other media too numerous to mention here.

As of 1995, Jack A. Johnson-Hill's *I-Sight, the World of Rastafari: An Interpretative Sociological Account of Rastafarian Ethics* (1995) represented the best example of the maturing of dissertation research on Rastafari that results in a full-size book publication focused on the sociological and ethical aspects of Rastafarian beliefs and livity. The very scholarly four hundred-page textbook defines the movement, traces its development within the social and cultural context of early twentieth-century Jamaica, and gives a scholarly review of the literature on the movement. A huge section (parts 2 and 3) of the book is devoted to Rastafari's self-concept, lifestyle in the world of Babylon, and the Ethiopian vision of "Ipatriation" (repatriation) to Africa. The final section of the book (part 4) explores the implications of Rastafarian ethics for the world from a sociological and ethical perspective. Much more problematic for the student, however, is Aakhun George W. Singleton's difficult 1997 *Esoteric Atannuology, Egyptology and Rastafariology* (Volume 1). Singleton reads Rastafarian thought back into Egyptology, "the study of the beginning of western civilization," by summoning a wealth of Egyptian material to posit Egypt as the source of Rastafari's beginnings. An anachronistic approach and unsubstantiated claims limit the value of this publication.

Mention must be made here, however, of a significant number of young scholars who have published substantive essays, book chapters, and dissertations on the Rastafarian movement. Carole Yawney was in Trench Town, Jamaica, doing field research on Rastafari during the time that Joseph Owens was pursuing his important study of the movement and has reported that she wrote the first, unedited introduction to *Dread*. As a product of her extensive ethnographic research on the movement and her close relationship with many leading Rastas, such as Mortimo Planno, Yawney has done a Ph.D. dissertation and published many often referenced essays on Rastafari.[8] John Paul Homiak of the Smithsonian Institution in Washington, D.C., also researched his Ph.D. dissertation on Rastafari (as have Randal Hepner, John Pullis, and dozens of others) and has published on different aspects of the movement in Jamaica and the United States.[9] Trinidad-born Ansley Hamid completed his controversial Ph.D. dissertation "A Pre-Capitalist Mode of Production: Ganja and the Rastafarians in San Fernando, Trinidad," in 1981. New Zealander William G. Hawkeswood did an M.A. thesis called "I'N'I Ras Tafari: Identity and the Rasta Movement in Auckland" at the University of Auckland, New Zealand, in 1983.

UWI professors Carolyn Cooper's and Velma Pollard's essays and book chapters on Rasta culture and language in the Caribbean are well known and often cited in the literature. (See Velma Pollard, "Dread Talk," 1980, and "Word Sounds: The Language of Rastafari in Barbados and St. Lucia," 1984). Klaus de Albuquerque's "The Future of the Rastafarian Movement" (1979) and Linden F. Lewis's "Living in the Heart of Babylon: Rastafari in the U.S." (1989) raise important questions on the movement's direction. But Ajai Mansingh and Laxmi Mansingh's "Hindu Influences on Rastafarianism" (1985) exaggerates the influence of Hindu tradition on aspects of Rastafarian rituals, and Patrick Taylor's "Rastafari, the Other, and Exodus Politics: EATUP" overemphasizes the millenarian characteristic of the movement.

Forty-one years after he began research on Rastafari in Jamaica, George Eaton Simpson published yet another essay, "Some Reflections on the Rastafari Movement in Jamaica West Kingston in the Early 1950s" (1994). It has been reissued in its entirety in this anthology. (See Chapter 13, "Personal Reflections on Rastafari in West Kingston in the Early 1950s.")

Neil Savishinsky's essays "The Baye Faal of Senegambia: Muslim Rastas in the Promised Land?" *Africa: Journal of International African Institute* 2 (June 1994); "Transnational Popular Culture and the Global Spread of the Jamaican Rastafarian Movement," *New West Indian Guide* 68, 3–4 (1994); and "Rastafari in the Promised Land: The Spread of a Jamaican Socioreligious Movement among the Youth of West Africa," *African Studies Review* 37 (December 1994) are the most substantive treatments of the Rastafari in West Africa to date. "Rastafari in the Promised Land" is an exposition on the diffusion of Rasta culture in Africa (reggae music, ganja use, and fashions). Savishinsky places West African Rastafari "within the basic pattern or scheme of the growing number of syncretistic, independent Christian-based churches and religious movements that have flourished on the continent since the turn of the century" (35). This reflects the "dramatic break with various elements of traditional religions . . . moral reform as a major theme and the subsequent prohibition of corrupting influences like alcohol and tobacco, . . . the evolution of new forms of social organization . . . and a deep concern for personal and corporate spiritual renewal" (36).

Although they do not carry the name of Rastafari, reggae, or Bob Marley, the following works are nonetheless important in the discussion on the Rastafari movement: *Selected Speeches of His Imperial Majesty: Haile Selassie First 1918–1967* (1967); Ivy Baxter, *The Arts of an Island: The Development of Cultures and Other Folk Creolize Art in Jamaica 1944–1962, Independence* (1970); Sylvia L. Thurpp, ed., *Millennial Dreams in Action: Studies in Revolutionary Religious Movements,* (1970); Archbishop Yesehaq, *The Ethiopian Tewahedo Church: An Integrally African Church* (1989). This strong body of literature demonstrates the maturing of Rastafarian scholarship, to which Barrett made a leading contribution.

Notes

1. George Eaton Simpson, "The Rastafari Movement in Jamaica: A Study of Race and Class Conflict," *Social Forces* 34, 2 (December 1955): 167–71; "The Ras Tafari Movement in Jamaica in Its Millennial Aspect," in Sylvia L. Thrupp, ed., *Millennial Dreams in Action: Studies in Revolutionary Religious Movements* (New York: Schocken Books, 1970), 160–65. These essays were published also as "Jamaican Revivalist Cults," *Social and Economic Studies* 5, 4 (1956); *Religious Cults in the Caribbean: Trinidad, Jamaica and Haiti* (Rio Piedras: Institute of Caribbean Studies, University of Puerto Rico, 1970); and under a variety of other titles.

2. See Orlando Patterson, "Ras Tafari: The Cult of the Outcast" (unpublished essay; University of the West Indies Collection, University of the West Indies, Mona, Jamaica, 1968); idem, *The Children of Sisyphus* (New York and London: Longmans, Green & Co., 1964), 6.

3. See, for example, Leonard Barrett, "The Rastafari Movement," in Keith Crim, ed., *Abingdon Dictionary of Living Religions* (Nashville: Abingdon Press, 1979); idem, "Rastafarianism as a Life Style," in Vincent D'Oyley, ed., *Black Presence in Multi-Ethnic Canada* (Vancouver: Center for the Study of Curriculum and Instruction, Faculty of Education, University of British Columbia, 1978); idem, "African Roots in Jamaican Indigenous Religion," *Journal of Religious Thought* 35, 1 (spring–summer 1978): 7–26; idem, "African Religions in the Americas: The Is-

land in Between," in C. Eric Lincoln, ed., *The Black Experience Religion: A Book of Readings* (New York: Doubleday, 1974).

4. For example, in 1976, Garry W. Trompf edited the book *Cargo Cults and Millenarian Movements,* in which Karlene Faith wrote an often-cited chapter, "One Love—One Faith."

5. Derek Bishton, *Black Heart Man: A Journey into Rasta* (London: Chatto & Windus, 1986), reviewed by Maureen Rowe (Sister P Rastafari), *Caribbean Quarterly,* 34, 3–4 (September– December 1988): 95–96.

6. See, for example, Barry Chevannes, "Jamaican Lower Class Religion: Struggles against Oppression" (M.A. thesis, University of the West Indies, Kingston, 1971): idem, "The Impact of the Ethiopian Revolution on the Rastafari Movement," *Socialism: Theoretical Origin of the Workers Liberation League* 2, 3 (1975); idem, "The Repairer of the Breach: Reverend Claudius Henry and Jamaican Society," in Frances Henry, ed., *Ethnicity in the Americas* (The Hague: Mouton Publishers, 1976), 263–89; idem, "The Literature of Rastafari," *Social and Economic Studies* 26, 2 (1977): 239–90; idem, "Social Origins of the Rastafarian Movement" (thesis, University of the West Indies, Kingston, 1978); idem, "Rastafarianism and the Class Struggle: The Search for a Methodology," University of the West Indies (UWI) Symposium Paper (Kingston: UWI Library, 1978): 240–52; idem, "The Rastafari and the Urban Youth," in Carl Stone and Aggrey Brown, eds., *Perspectives on Jamaica in the Seventies* (Kingston: Jamaica Publishing House, 1981), 392–422; idem, "Some Notes on African Religious Survivals in the Caribbean," *Caribbean Journal of Religious Studies* 5, 2 (September 1983): 18–28; idem, "Rastafari: Towards a New Approach," *New West Indian Guide* 64, 3–4 (1990): 127–48; idem, "Healing the Nation: Rastafari Exorcism of the Ideology of Racism in Jamaica," *Caribbean Quarterly* 36, 1–2 (June 1990): 59–84; idem, "The Rastafarians of Jamaica," in T. Milton, ed., *When Prophets Die* (Albany: State University of New York Press, 1994), 135–47.

7. See Roger Steffens, "Bob Marley: Spirit Dancer," in Bruce W. Talamon, ed., *Bob Marley: Spirit Dancer* (New York: W.W. Norton & Co., 1995), 15–31.

8. See, for example, Carole D. Yawney, "Remnants of All Nations: Rastafarian Attitudes to Race and Nationality," in Henry, ed., *Ethnicity in the Americas,* 231–62; idem, "Dread Wasteland: Rastafarian Ritual in West Kingston, Jamaica," in N. Ross Crumrie, ed., *Ritual Symbolism and Ceremonialism in the Americas: Studies in Symbolic Anthropology* (Occasional Publications in Anthropology, Ethnology Studies 33; Greeley: Museum of Anthropology, University of Northern Colorado, 1978); idem, "Lions in Babylon: The Rastafarians of Jamaica as a Visionary Movement" (Ph.D. diss., McGill University, 1978); idem, "Rasta Mek a Trod: Symbolic Ambiguity in a Globalizing Religion," in Thomas Bremer and Ulrich Fleischman, eds., *Alternative Cultures in the Caribbean* (Frankfurt: Vervuert Verlag, 1988), 161–68; idem, *The Herb and the Chalice: The Symbolic Life of the Children of Slaves in Jamaica* (Toronto: Addiction Research Foundation Substudy 522, 1972).

9. John Paul Homiak, "The 'Ancient of Days' Seated Black: Eldership, Oral Tradition and Ritual in Rastafari Culture" (Ph.D. diss., Brandeis University, 1985); idem, "The Mystic Revelation of Rasta For-Eye: Visionary Communication in a Prophetic Movement," in Barbara Tedlock, ed., *Dreaming: Anthropological and Psychological Approaches* (Cambridge: Cambridge University Press, 1985), 220–45.

Glossary

ABUNA (ABUN): The official title of the head of the local Ethiopian Orthodox Church. When the official is named, the title is Abuna (e.g., Abuna Blackheart of the Royal Ethiopian Judah Coptic Church); when the person is not named, the title is Abun.

ACEPHALOUS: Having no organizational head or leader; used to describe Rastafari.

AFRICANISMS: Those elements of African culture or heritage that survived and are manifested in black cultures outside Africa.

AFROCENTRIC: Beliefs, practices, and ideas that privilege African peoples; used in a black consciousness context with reference to African aesthetic, spirituality, and cultural identity.

AKETE: A form of drum and drumming that evolved from Burru drum and dance; Burru drums became known as *akete* drums, and the Burru dance was swallowed up in the Rastafari Nyabinghi celebration.

AMORPHOUS: Lacking a definite or discernable character with reference to organizational structure or form; used of Rastafari as a movement.

ANACHRONISTIC JUDEO-CHRISTIAN HERESY: The historical misplacement of ideas that renders Christianity inconsistent and goes against established explanations.

ANANCYISM: The Jamaican practice whereby one appears weak, innocent, and nonthreatening but uses trickery, con artistry, or deception to get one's way in society. Anancy is the smart spiderman in Jamaican folktales.

ANDROCENTRIC: Refers to any idea, way of thinking and acting, organization, or society that is conceived as favoring males.

ANGLOPHONE CARIBBEAN: English-speaking peoples of the Caribbean.

APOCALYPTIC MOVEMENT: A group that is preoccupied with a prophetic disclosure or revelation of a dramatic collapse or ending of the natural order, probably by supernatural means.

ARCHIMANDRITE: Title of the bishop of the Ethiopian Orthodox Church; often used as a synonym of *Abun (Abuna)*.

ARGOT (OF RASTAFARI): A tailored vocabulary or set of idiomatic expressions that Rastas use to communicate in everyday speech.

ATTITUDINAL REMNANT OF THE COLONIAL PAST: Certain colonial ideas and ways of acting and doing things in modern Jamaica and the broader Caribbean.

AUTOCHTHONOUS: Homegrown, aboriginal, or native to a particular culture; a good example is the calypso and steel-band music phenomenon in Trinidad and Tobago.

BABYLON: Describes what Rastas perceive as the oppressive social, political, economic, and cultural realities of Jamaica and the Western world.

BADMAN: A macho, brave, fearless, and courageous Rasta; sometimes may mean violent or showing unsavory behavior.

BALDHEADS: Non-Rasta members of one's family.

BEDWARDISM: The ideas and practices of Alexander Bedward, a charismatic Jamaican preacher in the 1890s and early twentieth century who believed in the apocalyptic destruction of oppressive colonial governments and the divine redemption of oppressed Blacks.

BEEF: A politically incorrect label for "woman"; used in rudeboy culture to describe one's female sexual partner or any desirable woman.

BINGI: Rastafari's sacred assembly or celebration of noteworthy events; an abbreviated form of *Nyabinghi.*

BLACKHEART MAN: A Jamaican who is conscious of African roots or takes pride in African culture, on the continent and in the African diaspora.

BLUE BEAT: One of the musical art forms that predated reggae; it has its origin in the "Great Black Migration" from the Southern United States.

BONGO: An African Jamaican cultural tradition that survived in Kumina culture. Bongo, often a synonym for *kongo, bkongo,* and *bungo,* is the name of an African tribe in the Congo region, as well as a religious cult appearing among the Maroons of early Jamaica.

BONGO NATTY (BONGO NYAH): A alternate term for *Rastaman.*

BONGO WATTO (CONGO WATTO): A well-known Rasta named Watson, one of the early Dreadlocks, who is credited with founding the important Rastafarian group the Youth Black Faith in 1949.

BREDREN (BRETHREN): A term that denotes brotherhood and a sense of unity among Rastas, as well as with friendly non-Rastas; the word may be singular or plural, depending on the context.

BRITISH BULLDOG: A person, frequently one of the police, acting on Britain's behalf by intimidating and oppressing the colonized African peoples.

BUCKRA BABY: A child of European parentage or a baby of very light pigmentation born of an African mother and European father; Jamaican patois for a mulatto child.

BUNGO: Used in Jamaica to characterize persons as stupid; Jamaican patois.

BURRU: A rich African cultural tradition identifiable in the rhythmic beating of three special drums and a lively dance; the three most important drums in reggae music were taken from the drums of the Burru people in the 1940s.

CALYPSO MUSIC: A popular Afro-Caribbean musical style played on a variety of percussive instruments, especially in a steel band, and combining musical rhythm with poetry, dance, rhetoric, artistry, and social and political commentary on society, in pulsating, staccato beats designed to stir both emotions and critical thought. Autochthonous to colonial Trinidad and Tobago, calypso, steel band, and carnival form the *locus classicus* of modern Trinidadian culture.

CAMP (RASTA CAMP): A local Rasta community made up of several Rastafarians with a leader.

CANNABIS RITUAL: The Rasta ritual of ganja (marijuana) smoking during Rasta reasoning sessions; *cannabis* is the biological name for marijuana, or the ganja plant.

CHALICE: The Rastafarian ritual name for the two pipes used in the ceremonial smoking of ganja; it originated from the traditional meaning of a cup or goblet that holds the wine of the Christian Eucharist.

CHILLUM PIPE: A conical or cylindrical pipe, believed to be of East Indian origin; one of the two types of pipes used by Rastafari brethren in the ritual smoking of ganja. (The other type is called "kochi" or "cutchie" and is African in origin.)

CHRISTIAN APOLOGETICS: The rational defense of Christian beliefs, with a view to changing people's negative attitude to the faith, or defending a Christian doctrine.

CHURCHICAL: The identifying characteristics of Rasta groups that emphasize the development of Rastafari's religiousness and the cultivation of African consciousness and lifestyle (e.g., Prince Edward's Ethiopian National Congress and the Twelve Tribes of Israel); churchical Rastas contrast with the politically minded ("statical") Rastas.

CITING UP: A way of arguing or reasoning in which Rastas summon biblical, historical, and other materials to support reflective discourse.

COLONIALIST MENTALITY: The mind-set that acquiesces to, advocates, or defends colonial ideas and practices, without question or challenge; often despises things African or Afro-Caribbean.

COLLY: Another name for *ganja.*

COMBSOME: A term used by Rastas to describe persons who comb their hair.

COMMUNE, RASTA: A Rasta camp or community made up of several Rastas and often having an identifiable leader.

CONJUGAL LIVING: A euphemism for common-law marriages or unions. It denotes the intimacy of a couple who share themselves with each other, often living in the same home.

CONSCIENTIZING: The act of becoming oneself or making another aware of the sociopolitical and psychological dimensions of oppression and the possibility of liberation and self-empowerment.

CONVINCE CULT: An African Jamaican religious tradition in which the spirits of the ancestors guide the devotee; like Kumina and Pocomania (Pukumina), spirit possession, religious enthusiasm, and revivalism are distinguishing characteristics of convince.

CREOLE-SPEAKING: Pertaining to any of the various vernaculars that have developed in the Americas. "Creolization" in Jamaica is also the Jamaicanizing of European ideas and attitudes.

CULTUS: Used of any religious practice or tradition; in the academy of religion, this German-Latin term does not carry the negative connotation of "cult" or "cultic" that is common in popular usage.

DANCEHALL: A popular dance musical genre fashioned after the religious dance rhythm of Pocomania (Pukumina) and the revivalist African Christianized Kumina. Secularized dancehall has an almost frenetic hybrid and waltzing flavor, with three beats inside (the bar) and an alternating, syncopating "straight" or pulsating kick on the fourth beat.

DAWTA (THE DAWTAS DEM): An affectionate term for woman (and women) in Rasta lingo; replaces the politically incorrect *ting* and *beef* in rudeboy culture; patois for *daughter.*

DECOLONIZATION PHILOSOPHY: A philosophy, common in the African diaspora, that advocates the end of colonialism and the removal of its ugly legacy or aftereffects. It has many facets and has received the attention of political scientists, economists, sociologists, theologians, psychologists, and reform movements such as Rastafari and Pan-Africanism.

DEIFICATION OF HAILE SELASSIE: The divinization, or making divine, of Haile Selassie as Messiah and God.

DENUDED HOUSEHOLD: A household where sisters choose a family life shared by different women in the home; also used for a home with a woman as head of household, where the father visits only occasionally.

DIASPORA, AFRICAN: People of African descent living outside the continent, mainly as a result of colonialism and slavery.

DISFRANCHISED MASSES: People deprived of the right to vote, own property, obtain civil services, or participate in governing themselves, locally or nationally.

DISSONANCE, RASTA: Rasta rejection of and disengagement from the dominant life or social reality of Jamaican culture as a protest against the "politricks" and oppression in Babylon.

DOWNPRESSION: A Rasta term for "oppression." Rastas believe that the meaning of the word is in its sound and symbol; hence, *down*pression reflects more correctly the meaning of *op*pression.

(THE) DREADS: A group and movement within Rastafari characterized by a fierce-looking persona, long natty hair, and unkempt clothes. The Dreadlocks arose in the late 1940s as an Afrocentric lifestyle and reform movement to purge Rastafari of revivalist elements like Pocomania (Pukumina), convince cult, and Obeah.

DREAD TALK: The fascination with certain words and expressions that places intrinsic value on word-sounds. Influenced by the Youth Black Faith, the Dreads transformed Rasta language into a subdialect, most identifiable in the prefix "I," as in "I-an-I."

DUB: The scaled-down reggae pulse rhythm that kicks on the second and fourth beats, emphasizing drum and bass, with high hats (cymbals) punctuating the "ends," one and *two* and three and *four;* often used as a setting for poetry. Often the melody is taken from the music, leaving only the percussion to carry the rhythm and accompany the lyrics.

DUNGLE, DUNGHILL: A Rasta commune located in the slum or a depressed area of the inner city.

DUPPIES: Ghostlike creatures who, in Caribbean folklore, could harm or overpower you; they are reputed to live in scary places and dark alleys.

EARTHFORCE: The conception of a mystical power of Jah, immanent in the universe, that Rastas can tap into for oneness and strength through their "earthy-looking" locks.

EARTICAL: Refers to emotions, feelings, and spiritual upliftment (not necessarily religious) as an attachment to the Rasta culture; a synonym of *heartical.*

ELIZABETHAN CODES: Certain colonial stereotypes, unwritten codes, and social expectations that survive in the modern anglophone Caribbean; comparable to Jim Crow culture in pre-1963 America.

EMASCULATED MALES: Men robbed of the feeling of "maleness," especially in reference to male domination in Jamaica without the income or economic power to undergird it.

EPISTEMOLOGICAL: Relating to a branch of philosophy that deals with the study and ground of knowledge, especially with reference to limits, truth, or validity.

ESCAPIST MOVEMENT: A movement characterized by disengagement from the official social establishment; sometimes used of Rastafari, with its hope for repatriation to Africa.

ESCHATOLOGICAL MOVEMENT: A movement obsessed with events related to the end of the world; eschatology, in Christian dogmatics, is the study of the last things or ultimate human destiny, and ideas about God's plan for the world.

ETHIOPIANISM: The advocacy or idealization of Ethiopia as "the motherland" and the hope, held by a group of Jamaicans, to be repatriated there; also symbolizes a system of belief in the positive cultural consciousness of African roots that first surfaced in the Americas.

ETHOS OF RASTAFARI: The distinguishing characteristics or spirit of the Rastafarian movement.

ETU: An African-influenced folk tradition in Jamaica that originated from an African tribe; shows some characteristics of Kumina and jonkunnu.

EUROCENTRIC: A view of reality that privileges Europe and Europeans above other places and peoples, particularly above Africa and Africans.

EXEGESIS: Critical interpretation of a text or portion of Scripture to derive meaning; a tool of hermeneutics that involves study of the language, context, and genre of biblical texts.

EXORCISE THE DEMONS: To get rid of false ideas or experiences, as in the ceremonial removal of demons from one's consciousness.

EXPOSITION: The interpretation, enlargement on, and application of a text, scriptural passage, or idea to life's concerns.

FALASHAS: Ethiopian or black Jews, believed to be descendants of one of the lost tribes of Israel; some Rastas regard Falashas as the true Israelites and the ancestors of Rastas.

FISSIPAROUS: Having factional tendencies; used of a movement that grows through divisions or splits.

FRANCOPHONE: French-speaking countries or territories in Africa and the Americas, especially in the Caribbean.

FUNDEH: A relatively long, narrow drum with a nine-inch-wide head made of goatskin and played as the lead drum in reggae music; like the repeater and the bass, fundeh was taken over from Burru.

GANJA: The term most frequently used for marijuana (cannabis) in Jamaica, believed to be of Indian origin. Not all Rastas smoke ganja casually, and some do not smoke at all.

GENITORS: A term used of persons, especially male, in common-law unions.

GROUNDATION, GROUNDINGS (GROUNDATION DAY): A Rasta assembly to "reason," celebrate, and build community spirit through the ritual smoking of ganja and open-ended discussion on any issue from a Rastafarian perspective. Designed to contrast with the uncertainty in the wider Jamaican society, "Groundation Day" marks the visit of Haile Selassie I to Jamaica in 1966 and offers hope and certainty to the Rasta brethren.

GOMBAY: A traditional folk cultural and musical form that surfaced in colonial Jamaica, much like jonkunnu, Burru, and Etu.

HAIL THE MAN: A form of greeting or salutation among the early Rastafarians, sometimes carrying allusions to Haile Selassie.

HEARTICAL: Refers to emotions or feelings as an attachment to the Rasta culture, especially expressed in the "ridim" drums; used synonymously with *eartical.*

HERMENEUTICS: The attempt to interpret a text, oral or written, and the art of such interpretation; the use of certain historical methods in the academy to interpret texts, especially Scripture.

HISTORICALITY OF GOD'S WORKING: The historical nature of God's involvement in human experience.

(THE) HOLY PIBY: A book written in 1924 by Athlyi Rogers to spread Ethiopianism; *The Holy Piby* and Fritz Pettersburgh's *Royal Parchment Scroll of Black Supremacy* (published in Jamaica in 1926) provided the material for Leonard Howell's plagiarized book *The Promised Key* (1934). *The Holy Piby* is regarded as the "black man's Bible."

I-AN-I, I-N-I: A Rastafarian argot expression that usually replaces the first-person singular or plural in everyday speech. "I-an-I" is an expression of consciousness of Rastas' divine essence that captures the harmony between the inner and outer person, among Rastas.

IDEATION: Supporting, emulating, or advocating a pervasive idea or practice that defines cultural values and norms (e.g., the ideation of race and class in Jamaica).

I-DREN: Often refers to a Rastaman's own children, the "I" as a possessive, used in place of "my," and the "dren" as an abbreviation of "children."

IMPART: Making a worthwile contribution to one's family financial support; Jamaican patois for contribution.

INDENTURED LABOR: Laborers who hired themselves out (especially on plantations) on contracts for wages or service to repay debts; generally, they were not regarded as slaves.

IRATION: Positive stimulation derived from the philosophical reasonings, musical rhythm, and livity of Rastafari; a synonym for *creation* or *production.*

I-SSEMBLY, ISSEMBLY: A meeting or assembly of Rastas for reasoning and groundation; the I-Ssembly of Elders is a group of Rastafarian "leaders" or highly respected devotees.

ITAL LIVING: Rastas' "natural living," demonstrated in the use of organic, locally grown foods (from the ground) and certain dietary restrictions and practices that reflect a consciousness of and care for the environment and one's personal health.

ITATIONS: Meditations, reflections, citations, and iconographic representations of Rastafari on life in modern society, especially Jamaica.

IYARIC: Dread talk and linguistic style that preferences the use of "I," which originated in the late 1940s with the coming of the Dreads.

JAH: The Rastafarian name for God. It often refers to Haile Selassie and, more often than not, to the Creator whose power (earthforce) pervades the universe.

JAH RASTAFARI: Refers specifically to Emperor Haile Selassie I as the Deity; used occasionally as an honorific title given to Rastas.

JONKUNNU (DANCE): An African cultural tradition that survived in Jamaican folkloric dance and dates back to slavery.

KABALLAH: A syncretistic African Trinidadian religious phenomenon that mixes Hindu, Jewish, Muslim, and Orisha practices with Christian rituals and ceremonies.

KATTA: Punctuated or staccato "ridims" (rhythms) of sticks played on the open end of one of the Rasta drums.

KBANDU: A large drum used in Kumina musical rhythms.

KETE (DRUM): A large, single-headed drum played with the hands and heels in Rasta "ridims"; in early Rastafari, its sound symbolized the ideology "death to deckman" (death to whites).

KINGMAN: A Rastawoman's honorific title for her man.

KOCHI: The ritual name for one of the two pipes used in the smoking of ganja; a kind of water pipe that originated in Africa and has a bowl-shaped container at the top to hold the ganja.

KOFI: A Jamaican stereotypical "day name" for males born on Friday, believed to characterize idiocy or stupidity. "Him kofi, him born pon Friday" means the person is an idiot.

KUMINA: An African Jamaican religious retention that emphasizes personal creativity in music and spiritual experiences or renewal. A derivation of the Akan *akom-ana,* which means "to be possessed by an ancestral spirit," Kumina is concentrated mostly in the eastern part of Jamaica.

LIFELINE RIDIM: The very distinct, audible, and steady rhythm that drives Rasta music, played either on the first and third beats of the bar or on the second and fourth.

LIVITY: The strict Rastafarian lifestyle based on an adherence to certain dietary practices aimed at healthy living and the preservation of the environment; also entails ritualistic, ceremonial practices and doctrinal teachings.

LOCUTION, I-AN-I: A form of expression or way of thinking that, when used by Rastas, makes a cultural, political, and philosophical statement about their reality in Babylon.

LUB: Patois meaning "love." "Him lub a buckra baby" means "He loves white or light-skinned children."

MANSIONS, RASTA: Divisions, houses, communities, or camps; occasionally used as a synonym for *yard,* the home or dwelling of a family or group.

MAROON: A member of a community founded by runaway slaves; also the practice of running away and forming communities independent of the plantation system in the Americas. In the eastern Caribbean, a maroon is also a large gang of workmen who voluntarily join forces, mainly on Saturdays, to plow one another's garden plots during the planting seasons.

MASSA: Patois for a "slave master," black or white, or for someone who demonstrates such a mentality by dominating persons of his or her own race, especially black people.

MATRIFOCAL: Relating to a familial organization or family structure in which the woman or mother is dominant or central in the functioning of the social unit.

MBAQANGA: A South African cultural tradition made popular in the lyrics of the song "I Am in Love with a Rastaman."

MBIRA: A thumb piano used in an ethnic group in Zimbabwe. The music of Shona.

MENTO: A Jamaican creole folk-song genre played on a variety of instruments, especially the banjo, in a four-beat-to-the-measure rhythm with an upbeat feel. The guitar carries the rhythm with an upbeat stroke on the "ands"—one *and* two *and* three *and* four *and*—while kettle floor drum and hand drum underscore and enhance the beat. Burru, mento, ska, and rock steady are the precursors of reggae.

MERCANTILIST PILL: A postfeudalist trade practice that Europeans enforced in their colonization of foreign territories; the metropole (colonizing European country) instituted several restrictions on their colonies as a way of monopolizing all aspects of trade and commerce.

MESSIANIC MILLENNIAL CULT: Used of Rastafari because its beliefs are fueled by the hope of a period of joy, peace, justice, truth, and righteousness for its members when the Messiah appears.

METAPHYSICS: Branch of philosophy dealing with the questions What is there? What is real? Do things exist in reality or only in the mind? Is perception a reliable guide to knowledge?

METROPOLE: European countries that controlled Caribbean colonies during the colonial era and often up to the eve of independence.

MISSION, JAMAICA: A mission that Haile Selassie I authorized, after his 1966 visit, under the leadership of Abba Laike Mandefro, to evangelize the Rastas with Ethiopian Orthodox Christianity. The 1970 mission encountered steep opposition from staunch supporters of the belief that Haile Selassie is divine.

NAZIRITE: A religious person who takes a vow of chastity and to abstain from certain dietary, social, sexual, and cultural habits; the practice originated in ancient Israel and biblical traditions.

NEBER: Patois for "never!" "absolutely not."

NYABINGHI I-SSEMBLY: A concept borrowed from East Africa and revised as the most sacred, exclusive, and important annual I-ssembly of Rastafari. The Nyabinghi slogan that originally meant "Death to the white oppressor," or "Death to the deckman," was used by Prince Edward Emmanuel to call the first general synod in 1958.

OBEAHISM: A form of sorcery practiced in the Caribbean and West Africa, the practioners of which are reputed to be able to cast spells or unleash spiritual powers against their victims or enemies.

ONES: A special term used by Rastas to describe persons who belong to Rastafari.

ONOINTING: Describes Rastas feeling a sense of inspiration or sacredness, the equivalent of *anointing*—catching the Spirit or being inspired—in some Christian traditions; originates from Rastas' love for wordplay (the emphasis is on *on*).

ONTOLOGICAL: Relating to a theory of being, of the basic "stuff" or foundation of reality.

ORISHA: A syncretistic African Caribbean religious phenomenon that emphasizes spirit possession, animal sacrifice and "spirit-controlled ritual." Like Voodoo, Orisha (the name it carries in Trinidad and Tobago; Oricha in Cuba) is practiced secretly by some Christians and other religious devotees.

OVERSTANDING: A Rastafari-inverted expression for "*under*standing." True to their conviction that the meaning of a word is related to its sound, Rastas find the "under" in understanding to be a negative sound and hence replace it with "over," which is a more positive sound connected to the act of comprehending.

PARLANCE: A particular local manner of speaking; language, style, expressions, and idioms whose shades of meaning are context-bound or localized.

PATRIARCHY: The rule of a group by men; a system of social organization in which descent and precession are traced through the male line; also an attitude of adherence to male-dominated structures or systems.

PATRO-CLIENTELISM: Nepotism; pandering political favors to one's supporters.

PERICOPE: A small, isolatable literary piece of a larger text that warrants careful examination.

PERMANENT SCREW: The lasting negative effects of colonialism on Jamaica; the "screw face" is a scarey dread look.

PERSONALITY CULT: A group of persons who are believed to be driven by strong personalities, either their own or that of a charismatic figure.

PETA: The repeater drum, one of the three drums in Rasta "eartical" celebration and reggae music; adopted from Burru drum culture that grew out of a plantation society.

PINNACLE HILL: A rural village where Rastafari founder Leonard Howell established his Rasta commune on an old, abandoned plantation. Pinnacle Hill was self-supporting and produced a large assortment of short crops for sale to the prisons, hospitals, and other government institutions in Jamaica.

PLANTACLASS: Argot for "planter class" or plantation owners and other persons who supported, protected, and benefited from the plantation system and its cultural trimmings.

PLANTOCRACY: The economic, social, and political system developed and controlled by the plantation elites in the Americas. Rule by the planter class often involved a divide-and-conquer practice.

PLAYING CAST: A special kind of drum, used in Kumina, that has a distinct role in supporting the rhythm of the music.

POCOMANIA (PUKUMINA): An African traditional religious retention (sect) from slavery that is practiced by many Jamaicans, often simultaneously with, and almost indistinguishable from, "established" Christian worship. Pocomania is also known as "revivalism" and emerged as "Revival Zion" in the early 1860s during the "Great Revival."

POLITRICKS OF BABYLON: The oppressive political and economic system that is fueled by guile, greed, deception, nepotism (patro-clientelism), pandering political favors only to one's supporters and family members.

POLLUTED, POLLUTANT: A Rasta taboo regarding women as unclean, especially during menstruation.

POLYCEPHALOUS: Many-headed; used of Rasta groups exhibiting a multiplicity of leaders, with no clear demarcation of a hierarchy among the various camps.

POLYGAMOUS HOUSEHOLD: Multiple consensual unions sharing the same compound or "yard."

POLYRIDMIC: Originally referred to the rhythmic sounds produced by the three Rasta drums, *peta*, bass, and *fundeh*; now describes musical nuances in reggae.

POSSESSION CULT: A religious phenomenon that emphasizes spirit possession and the use of dreams and visions in rituals; Voodoo, Santeria, and Orisha are good examples.

PROLETARIAT: The masses or the working class; a term barrowed from Marxist social-political theory.

PROOF-TEXTING: The indiscriminate, uncritical, and often unhermeneutical use of biblical materials to support an argument or defend a religious belief

PROVOCATEUR: A trickster or humorist; one who makes provocative statements to challenge or verbally prod others in a humorous way.

QUASHIE CHARACTERISTICS: A Jamaican characterization describing one who is compliant, self-effacing, and docile, sometimes to the point of being foolish or a "dummy." Quashie is a stereotypical Twi day name for males born on Sunday and regarded as deceitful.

QUASI-ORGANIZED: Having limited organization or only a semblance of organization.

QUIXOTIC: Far-fetched, unrealistic, untrue, or unattainable.

RAGAMUFFIN: The unkempt or poorly clad style of non-Rastas, often of unsavory character, who imitate and sport the Rastafari persona for personal gain.

RASCALS AND IMPOSTORS: Self-proclaimed Rastas who do not follow the doctrines of Rastafari; also used of Rasta pretenders who live as wolves in sheep clothing, that is, "posse" who hide behind the Rasta persona to commit crimes or break the law.

RASSES: A name used by some followers of Rastafari

RASTA CHIC: The celebration of violence in some Rasta circles.

RAS TAFARI: The Amharic (Ethiopian language) title meaning "head ruler" or "emperor" of Ethiopia; one of the titles that Ras Makonnen of Harar, who became Haile Selassie I, assumed upon his coronation in 1930, and used by Rastas to deify the emperor.

RASTAFARIAN: Pertaining to Rastas; also, persons who identify with or adhere to the tenets of the Rastafari movement.

RASTAFARIANITY: A term used by African music artist Majek Fashek to describe the mixing of African, Rastafarian, and Christian culture.

(THE) RASTAFARI MANIFESTO: A written document outlining a series of basic principles and social and economic policies on which Rastas hope to establish their proposed theocratic government, under the rule of Jah Rastafari, when the corrupt Babylon "shitstem" collapses.

RASTOLOGY: The body of basic beliefs in Rastafari, common to all Rastas, and the Rasta expression of them in the livity.

REGGAE: The distinctly Jamaican musical style that blends lyrics with drumming, guitar, and percussive instruments. Popularized worldwide by music superstar Nesta Robert Marley, reggae has the opposite of a rhythm-and-blues or rock beat; the "kick" is on the second and fourth beats, and the "clap" is on the first and third.

REIFICATION OF THE ROLE OF WOMAN AS EMPRESS: The resurgence of the concept of women as being part of the complex of royalty and authority in Rastafari.

REPATRIATION: The doctrine that Blacks should migrate voluntarily to the promised land, Africa, to reconnect with their roots. The idea began with the early "Back to Africa" movement, became popular during the Pan-Africanist era, and is still defended in various forms by Rastas. Repatriation may be experienced as literal or physical, symbolic or cultural.

RETICULATE: Consisting of a network or having a weblike structure.

REVIVALISM: The spirit of or movement toward religious reform and renewal through subjective internal experience; may be characterized by prophetic utterances, unintelligible linguistic expression, shouting, spirit possession, or ideological and mental renewal.

RHYGING: A Jamaican slang for *raging,* derived from six weeks of terror when a lone gunman/desperado in Kingston went on a crime spree of armed robbery, larceny, and murder. After escaping from prison, he was finally shot by police in early fall of 1948.

RIDIMS: Refers to the drum and percussion patterns and tempo in which the melody might be taken out leaving only the percussion; most popular in reggae, *ridims* is also Jamaican patois for *rhythms*.

(THE) RISING OF THE IRIX: Setting the right tempo and beat in Rasta rhythms to capture the spirit of the music and the moment.

ROOTS, ROOTS MAN: The African heritage of black people or the grassroots culture of the black diaspora. In Jamaican argot, a "roots man" is one who is conscious of himself as an unapologetically independent African Jamaican.

RUDEBOY PHENOMENON: A militant, antiestablishment cultural phenomenon of Jamaica during the 1960s and 1970s, in which young men from the inner city (mostly Kingston) challenged the status quo and practiced violence in a culture of threatening nonconformity and dissonance. They were also characterized as "macho gangsters," some of whom sexually harassed women. The rudeboy phenomenon was an answer to police brutality toward Rastas and ghetto youths.

RUMBA, RHUMBA: An African Cuban music and dance genre that has spread throughout Latin America, the Caribbean, the United States, and Europe as a Spanish ballroom dance. The rumba box is used in Rasta music for rhythm effect.

SACRAMENTALITY OF NATURE: Rastafari's view of the sacredness of nature and the human responsibility to care for and preserve the environment on behalf of Jah; the view that everything in nature is sacred and must be protected from pollution and destruction.

SANKEY: A moving Christian musical style that inherited the name of U.S. songwriter Ira David Sankey (1840–1908), an activist in the Dwight L. Moody evangelistic campaigns.

SAXA: A homemade musical instrument in which Saran Wrap or cellophane is stretched over the mouth of a bottle and musical notes are produced with the human vocal chords.

SCREW FACE: A contorted facial expression, ritualized aggression, or antagonistic discourse employed by Rastas as a defense mechanism against opponents.

SEH: Jamaican patois for "think" or "say." "Wah im ah seh?" often translates, "What in the world is he or she saying?" or that one does not know what another is talking about.

SENEGAMBIA: A name derived from the colonial practice of Europeans "naming and claiming" African countries; Senegal and Gambia held as one under colonial rule.

SERIAL POLYGYNY: Morally despised consensual or common-law unions that some Jamaicans entered during their first fifteen years of cohabitation, resulting in offspring locked into a complex system of half brothers and half sisters. *Polygyny* is Jamaican patois for polygamous relations where marriage is not a major factor.

SHAKKA: A homemade Rasta musical instrument used to give percussive rhythm, similar to the Spanish maraca.

SHITSTEM, BABYLON: Describes the politically and socially corrupt system of government that facilitates the rich and powerful and further impoverishes the poor. Reggae artist Peter Tosh probably first used the term with reference to Jamaica.

SHONA: A major ethnic group and cultural tradition in Zimbabwe.

SIGHTING UP: Acquiring Rastafari consciousness or joining the Rasta commune.

SISTREN: Rastafari women; a term always used in the singular or collective singular, meaning either one woman or many.

SKA: A pre-reggae Jamaican music and dance genre and era that merges mento and North American rhythm and blues (R&B); it has the "kick" on the second and fourth beats, with the guitar emphasizing the "up" of the second, third, and fourth beats.

SOULJAHS: The "army" of persons committed to protect and enlarge the African birthright of the colonized against the colonizers.

SPEECHIFY: To expound the Rasta doctrine and ideology and interpret historical and cultural events with relevant application for "overstanding" (understanding) in the "house."

STATICAL: Characterizes groups of Rastas who put political and social aspirations above the heartical, passionate feelings derived from Rasta rhythms and Nyabinghi celebration.

STRATIFICATION: The division of a social order into layers or hierarchical levels of importance.

(THE) SUFFERERS: The poor, especially Rastas, who are attuned to the rhythms of nature, reggae, and the community; they contrast with the powerful in the Babylon shitstem.

SUPERORDINATION: Exceeding the expected limit of one's responsibilities.

TING: A politically incorrect term for woman or dawta. Ting is also the refreshing Jamaican national beverage made from grapefruit; it won several international awards.

TROD: To follow the way of Rastafari or to join the Rastas, as in the phrase "Rasta mek a trod."

TWELVE TRIBES OF ISRAEL: A progressive Rastafari group founded by Vernon Carrington, the "Prophet of Gad" (Hebrew), in 1968 that has revised (or modernized) many Rasta doctrines and is open to women participating in the Nyabinghi and reasonings. The largest and most influential of the Rastafari sects, it holds that Selassie is Jesus Christ returned.

TWI: The language of an ethnic group in Ghana; a Twi day name is an Afro-Jamaican pejorative term for someone who Jamaicans believe was born the "wrong day" of the week and thus is not as sensible as he or she should be.

VERSION(S): Expressions or permutations of a reggae piece; could take the form of "ridim" without melody, a new melody, or a speaking voice over a set rhythm.

VOODOO, VOUDOU: A complex African traditional religion, syncretized with elements of Christianity, that emphasizes the need to appease and be on good terms with the gods and spirits (*lwas*) in the universe. Voodoo is practiced in Africa, the Caribbean, and New Orleans and uses possession, trance, and animal sacrifice as essential to its rituals and ceremonies.

WISDOMWEED: The ritual smoking of ganja, believed to give wisdom and enlightenment.

YORUBA: An African traditional religion that was widespread in the Caribbean during colonial times; it survives in the names of gods, spirits, and religious practices in Voodoo, Santeria, Orisha, and other non-European religions.

(THE) YOUTH BLACK FAITH: A reform movement that arose in 1949 to purge Rastafari of revivalism, Obeah, Pocomania (Pukumina), and convince. It was made up chiefly of young men who migrated to the city, converted to Rastafari, and passionately preached the Rasta doctrines and livity; part of the Dreadlocks movement.

(THE) ZION COPTIC CHURCH: A Garveyite version of "Orthodox" Christianity based in New York City and Jamaica, revived in the 1960s by Blacks and Whites of the hippie generation; the church had foreign leadership but strong Afro-Jamaican support.

Prepared and complied by Nathaniel Samuel Murrell, Indigo K. Bethea, Ennis B. Edmonds, and Adrian Anthony McFarlane.

About the Contributors

KEVIN J. AYLMER, schoolteacher, archivist, and a student of folk music, is an authority on Marcus Garvey's Harlem years (1916–1925). He combines field research in Caribbean culture with radio broadcasting in his forthcoming book *Word, Sound and Power: Reggae Music and the Return of Marcus Garvey*. He has contributed numerous articles to publications such as the *Boston Globe, Yankee, Reggae and African Beat, Reggae Report, Rhythm Music,* and *American History Illustrated*.

BARRY CHEVANNES is a leading Caribbean social anthropologist and head of the Department of Sociology and Social Work, as well as dean of the Faculty of Social Sciences, at the University of the West Indies, Mona, Jamaica. An authority on Afro-Caribbean religions and culture, Chevannes has done extensive research among the Rastafarians over the last three decades. He is the author of *Rastafari: Roots and Ideology* (1994), editor of *Rastafari and Other African-Caribbean Worldviews* (1995), and has written numerous articles on Rastafari.

REV. CLINTON CHISHOLM, consulting editor for this *Reader* and Jamaica's well-known modern Christian apologist, has studied and debated on Rastafari for more than twenty years. From his many tapes, radio and television talks and interviews, and newspaper columns, Chisholm has authored two volumes, *A Matter of Principle* and *For the Record* (1997–1998). He is a Human Resource Development and Training consultant and lecturer at the Caribbean Graduate School of Theology.

ENNIS B. EDMONDS is the director of Afro-American Studies at Barnard College of Columbia University. He teaches Caribbean Religions at Barnard and has done a dissertation on Rastafari and the Caribbean class struggle. He has published essays on Caribbean studies and is coauthoring an *Introduction to Caribbean Religions* (forthcoming) with Nathaniel Samuel Murrell.

RANDAL L. HEPNER did his Ph.D. in sociology at the New School for Social Research and taught sociology and religion at New York University. His Ph.D. dissertation, "Movement of Jah People: Race, Class, and Religion among the Rastafari of Jamaica and New York City," is the first substantive historical and ethnographic study of the Rastafari movement in North America.

CLINTON HUTTON, Jamaican political scientist, artist, and painter, teaches in the Department of Government at the University of the West Indies. He has published several works on social-political movements in nineteenth-century Jamaica and has a forthcoming book, *Race, Philosophy, Social Psychology and Identity in the Caribbean* (1998). Hutton's painting hobby covers multicultural themes, peoples, and the environment; he did the Rastafari painting on the cover of this *Reader*.

RUPERT LEWIS, political scientist and Marcus Garvey scholar, heads the Department of Government as well as African and African-Diaspora Studies in the Faculty of Social Sciences at the

University of the West Indies. He has authored and coauthored five books on Marcus Garvey and Caribbean politics. His *Walter Rodney: An Intellectual and Political Study* is scheduled for release in 1998.

ADRIAN ANTHONY MCFARLANE is professor of philosophy and chair of the Department of Philosophy and Religious Studies at Hartwick College in Oneonta, New York. The Jamaican-born Princeton-Oneonta resident teaches a winter study-abroad course on Marcus Garvey and Rastafari every year in Jamaica, where his Hartwick students get to meet and hear his brother and other leading Rastafarians. He has also taught at Rider University, New Jersey, and was a visiting scholar at Oxford University. He is the author of *A Grammar of Fear and Evil: A Husserlian-Wittgensteinian Hermeneutic* and has contributed several essays to academic journals.

NATHANIEL SAMUEL MURRELL is assistant professor of Philosophy and Religion at the University of North Carolina at Wilmington. He has taught at the College of Wooster in Ohio, as well as at the Caribbean Graduate School of Theology in Kingston, Jamaica, which he cofounded in the mid-1980s. Through awards from the American Academy of Religion and the College of Wooster, he conducted research on Rastafari in Jamaica in the early 1990s and has contributed to books and encyclopedias on multicultural issues and African American and Caribbean studies. He is coauthoring an *Introduction to Caribbean Religions*.

REX NETTLEFORD, internationally known Caribbean scholar, trade union educator, social and cultural historian, and political analyst, is deputy vice-chancellor of the University of the West Indies. The founder, artistic director, and choreographer of the internationally acclaimed National Dance Theatre Company of Jamaica, he was also adviser to the government of Jamaica, the CAO, OAS, UNESCO, and other international organizations. Nettleford is also editor of the *Caribbean Quarterly*, a pioneer in Rastafarian research in Jamaica, and author of more than a dozen books and numerous articles on Caribbean culture.

VERENA RECKORD, journalist and folklorist, is a specialist in Caribbean art and culture, working with radio, newspaper and other Jamaican media. From her research on Jamaican culture prior to the 1980s, she published two of the most important essays in print on Rastafarian music; her 1977 and 1983 publications are recast in this volume.

MAUREEN ROWE, or "Sister P," is the former director of the African-Caribbean Institute of Jamaica and the executive director of the National Environmental Societies Trust of Jamaica. As a practicing Rastafarian who has witnessed firsthand significant shifts in the movement, she is one of the most authentic Rastafarian voices in the literature and the leading authority on women in Rastafari. She writes and lectures on RastafarI when her full-time employment in the Babylon shitstem makes it possible for her to do so.

NEIL J. SAVISHINSKY teaches anthropology at Columbia University, New York. He has won several fellowships that have allowed him to do extensive research on Rastafari in Africa, South Asia, Western Europe, and the Caribbean. Savishinsky is the author of several essays on the global spread of Rastafari and is a leading authority on the movement in West Africa.

GEORGE EATON SIMPSON, professor emeritus of sociology and anthropology at Oberlin College, Ohio, is the pioneer in the field of Caribbean religions. He was among the first scholar to do field research on revivalism and the first to undertake a scholarly investigation of Rastafari in Jamaica (in 1953). Simpson has published several often-cited works on Rastafari and religions in the African diaspora and is a seasoned authority on Rastafari.

WILLIAM DAVID SPENCER has been an adjunct professor of theology for over two decades, first for New York Theological Seminary and currently for Gordon-Conwell Theological Seminary's Center for Urban Ministerial Education in Boston. He also teaches periodically at the Caribbean Graduate School of Theology in Kingston, Jamaica, and he has done research on Rastafari since 1976. He has authored, coauthored, and edited several books, among them *The Prayer Life of Jesus, Mysterium and Mystery: The Clerical Crime Novel, God Through the Looking Glass, Joy through the Night, Second Corinthians: Bible Study Commentary, The Goddess Revival, The Global God,* and the forthcoming *Dread Jesus.* He has an impressive collection of reggae music and primary sources on Rastafari.

ROGER STEFFENS, actor, lecturer, and archivist, is the founding editor of *The Beat* magazine and creative director, writer, and narrator of *Soul Almighty,* the first Bob Marley CD-ROM (1996). He is the chairman of the Reggae Grammy Committee and has lectured widely on the life of Bob Marley. Steffens is coauthor of *Bob Marley: Spirit Dancer* (1994) and two forthcoming volumes: *Old Fire Sticks: The Autobiography of Bunny Wailer* and *Bob Marley and the Wailers: The Definitive Discography.*

IMANI M. TAFARI-AMA, Rastafarian sistren, media journalist, and researcher of Jamaican popular culture, has done extensive research on Rastafari Boo Boo Camps in Jamaica and was part of an entourage to Jamaica of the grandson of Haile Selassie. She is also an activist in the Caribbean women's movement and a courageous critical voice in patriarchal Rastafari.

BURCHELL K. TAYLOR, the most beloved Baptist pastor and sought-after pulpiteer in Jamaica (pastor of Bethel Baptist Church in Kingston), did his doctoral dissertation for the University of Leeds on "Caribbean Theology of Liberation and the Book of Revelation." The former president of the Jamaica Baptist Union taught ethics and theology at the Jamaica Theological Seminary and United Theological College of the University of the West Indies. His published essays are a constant reference source on Caribbean theology of liberation.

FRANK JAN VAN DIJK, Dutch cultural anthropologist and managing director of Utrecht University's Department of Developmental Psychology, has done extensive research on Rastafari over the last two decades under the auspices of the Netherlands Foundation for Scientific Research and the Center for Latin American and Caribbean Studies. In addition to his impressive doctoral dissertation, *Jahmaica: Rastafari and Jamaican Society, 1930–1990,* published in 1993, van Dijk has published several essays on the global spread of Rastafari.

ELEANOR WINT is a senior lecturer in the Department of Sociology and Social Work, University of the West Indies, Mona Campus. She has presented numerous papers on the role of women in Rastafari and is featured in the film *Rastafari Woman,* produced by CEDDO films, Britain. She is also the author of two books for children titled *Marcus Garvey Teaches Us* and *The Life of Marcus Garvey.*

THE STUDENTS: Indigo Bethea and Michael Bruny are seniors at Hartwick College, Oneonta, New York, who have their roots in the United States and the Caribbean. They conducted a very interesting interview with Professor Leonard Barrett, and Indigo who has a book-length manuscript of poems about the challenges of growing up in an urban setting, *Calling Out of Nubia,* was a great resource for completing the Glossary in this volume.

Index